Instructor's Annotated Edition

D0882358

Stepping Stones

A Guided Approach to Writing Sentences and Paragraphs

Instructor's Annotated Edition

Stepping Stones

A Guided Approach to Writing Sentences and Paragraphs

Chris Juzwiak

Glendale Community College

Bedford/St. Martin's

Boston ◆ New York

For Bedford/St. Martin's

Executive Editor: Carrie Brandon
Developmental Editors: Beth Castrodale and Caroline Thompson
Senior Production Editor: Rosemary Jaffe
Senior Production Supervisor: Nancy Myers
Marketing Manager: Casey Carroll
Production Assistant: David Ayers
Copyeditors: Steven Patterson and Jacqueline Rebisz
Text Design: Claire Seng-Niemoeller
Photo Research: Linda Finigan
Indexer: Mary White
Cover Art and Design: Sara Gates
Composition: Pre-Press PMG
Printing and Binding: RR Donnelley and Sons

President: Joan E. Feinberg
Editorial Director: Denise B. Wydra
Editor in Chief: Karen S. Henry
Director of Marketing: Karen R. Soeltz
Director of Editing, Design, and Production: Marcia Cohen
Assistant Director of Editing, Design, and Production: Elise S. Kaiser
Managing Editor: Elizabeth M. Schaaf

Library of Congress Control Number: 2008923924

Copyright © 2009 by Bedford/St. Martin's

All rights reserved. No part of this book may be reproduced, stored in a retrieval system, or transmitted in any form or by any means, electronic, mechanical, photocopying, recording, or otherwise, except as may be expressly permitted by the applicable copyright statutes or in writing by the Publisher.

Manufactured in the United States of America.

4 3 2 1 0 9
f e d c b a

For information, write: Bedford/St. Martin's, 75 Arlington Street, Boston, MA 02116 (617-399-4000)

ISBN-10: 0-312-46657-9 ISBN-13: 978-0-312-46657-2 (Student Edition)
0-312-48606-5 978-0-312-48606-8 (Instructor's Annotated Edition)

Acknowledgments

Sarah Adams. "Be Cool to the Pizza Dude." Copyright © 2005 by Sarah Adams. From the book *This I Believe*, edited by Jay Allison and Dan Gediman. Copyright © 2005 by Sarah Adams. Copyright © 2006 by This I Believe, Inc. Reprinted by arrangement with Henry Holt and Company, LLC.

Angela Adkins. "Dr. Dana." Originally appeared in the University of Akron Wayne College's Student Writing Awards publication. Used with permission.

Sherman Alexie. "The Joy of Reading and Writing: Superman and Me." Originally published in *The Most Wonderful Books*, edited by Michael Doris and Emilie Buchwald, Milkweed Editions, 1997. Copyright © 1997 by Sherman Alexie. Reprinted by permission of Nancy Stauffer Associates.

Lynda Barry. "The Sanctuary of School." From the *New York Times* Education Section, January 5, 1992, issue, p. 58. Copyright © 1992 the *New York Times*. Reprinted by permission. All rights reserved. Used by permission and protected by the Copyright Laws of the United States. The printing, copying, redistribution, or retransmission of the Material without express written permission is prohibited.

Acknowledgments and copyrights are continued at the back of the book on page K-25, which constitutes an extension of the copyright page. It is a violation of the law to reproduce these selections by any means whatsoever without the written permission of the copyright holder.

Preface for Instructors

If your teaching experiences are like mine, many of the students entering your classroom have encountered repeated failure in the past. As children or young adults, they may have had negative experiences learning writing and grammar, considering these pursuits boring or confusing. They may even enter your course expecting to fail. Their prospects for success are not improved by textbooks that assume that students can make great strides in their writing skills based on minimal examples and activities. For example, how many students can truly learn to generate good ideas based on a few examples of clustering, listing, and freewriting and a few activities? And will they really be able to organize their ideas effectively based on only one or two examples of outlining? Often, when students are asked to make big leaps from their current skill levels to the skill levels required for college success, they become frustrated — and many of them give up.

Stepping Stones addresses these challenges head-on. The book is based on the premise that if students are taken through a thorough and seamless sequence of engaging instruction and activities, they will master writing and grammar skills with enthusiasm. More advanced students will proceed quickly through the activities, gaining confidence, while less skilled students will get all the "stepping stones" they need to reach mastery. All along, students learn by doing, not by being told how to write. Also, I have designed the tasks and practices to grow incrementally more challenging to build skills and confidence gradually while leaving no student behind.

BACKGROUND ON THE PEDAGOGY

The pedagogical innovations in this text reflect my ten years of experience teaching basic writing; my personal drive to provide engaging, effective materials for students; and, more recently, sponsored research into how students write and learn. Over my years of teaching, I became dissatisfied with the available textbooks, finding that they either presented material in a manner that did not interest students or oversimplified instruction, making it difficult for students to truly learn writing and grammar concepts and transfer them to their own writing. Therefore, I spent nights and weekends writing my own writing and grammar materials, developing carefully sequenced instruction and exercises. The response from my students was immediate and enthusiastic. When I sought to avoid boredom and confusion with clear, inventive, and fun materials, I saw a transformation in students' attitude and behavior: They became readily self-motivated, demanding more high-quality, high-interest learning activities and tools.

More recently, I directed a three-year Carnegie Foundation SPECC grant (Strengthening Pre-Collegiate Education in Community Colleges) in which my colleagues and I were able to test more thoroughly the materials that I developed and to study students' writing and learning processes. We spent countless hours observing students as they wrote and completed exercises, and we studied hours of videotape of students' work at computer monitors, noting how they started and stopped compositions; cut, added, and moved text; and generally worked through their individual composing processes. We also interviewed students in detail about their writing processes and responses to various learning materials. Like my own students, the students in the study responded enthusiastically to the instruction and exercises that I had developed, and their skills improved markedly. Through this research, my colleagues and I became convinced that developmental learners flourish when their critical thinking and imagination are challenged with fresh, precisely honed sequences of instruction and activities.

The positive responses to the materials that I developed prompted me to write *Stepping Stones*. As I worked on the book, I further refined the instruction and exercises, benefiting all along from the insights of an expert team of reviewers from around the country. With this text in hand—in your hands and the hands of your students—we trust that your classroom will come alive with unparalleled intellectual energy and excitement.

Stepping Stones recognizes that *all* students have the potential to become better writers and just need the right tools to succeed.

FEATURES

Helps Students Tap Rich Sources of Ideas—and Then Organize Those Ideas

Recognizing that two of the most serious challenges that developmental writers face are, first, generating solid ideas and, second, organizing those ideas, I wanted *Stepping Stones* to give more help with these tasks than any other text of its kind.

After getting advice on analyzing and responding to writing assignments, students learn fun, innovative ways of **generating ideas** for a topic (such as playing the roles of a detective, an investigative reporter, and so on), with scores of examples and activities.

Next, an extensive, dedicated chapter gives students **unusually thorough guidance in organizing their ideas.** For example, in preparation for in-depth instruction in outlining, students first

Detective: At the Scene of the Crime

Sometimes, you may be asked to write about *an important event or place in your life*. Suppose that you have selected for your topic *my high school graduation*.

Now, imagine that you are a detective: you must recreate the scene. Close your eyes, drift back in time, and walk through your entire high school graduation. Look carefully at everybody and everything. You are searching for clues about what made the graduation an important event. Once you have allowed your imagination to recreate the event, you can begin to respond to the five *Ws*:

Who? Name all the people involved in the graduation.
Where? Describe all the details of the place of the graduation.
When? Describe the date, time of day, season, or period of the graduation.
What? Describe every important thing that happened during the graduation.
Why? Give reasons why things happened or why people might have acted as they did.

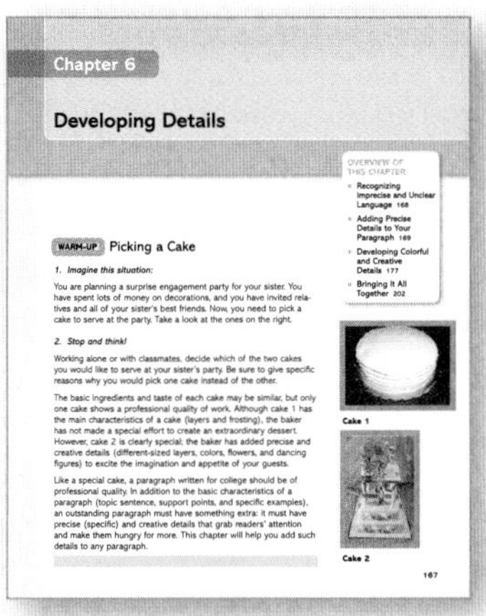

Chapter 6

Developing Details

OVERVIEW OF THIS CHAPTER

- Recognizing Imprecise and Unclear Language 168
- Adding Precise Details to Your Paragraph 169
- Developing Colorful and Creative Details 177
- Bringing It All Together 202

WARM-UP Picking a Cake

1. Imagine this situation:

You are planning a surprise engagement party for your sister. You have spent lots of money on decorations, and you have invited relatives and all of your sister's best friends. Now, you need to pick a cake to serve at the party. Take a look at the ones on the right.

2. Stop and think!

Working alone or with classmates, decide which of the two cakes you would like to serve at your sister's party. Be sure to give specific reasons why you would pick one cake instead of the other.

The basic ingredients and taste of each cake may be similar, but only one cake shows a professional quality of work. Although cake 1 has the main characteristics of a cake (layers and frosting), the baker has not made a special effort to create an extraordinary dessert. However, cake 2 is clearly special; the baker has added precise and creative details (different-sized layers, colors, flowers, and dancing figures) to excite the imagination and appetite of your guests.

Like a special cake, a paragraph written for college should be of professional quality. In addition to the basic characteristics of a paragraph (topic sentence, support points, and specific examples), an outstanding paragraph must have something extra: it must have precise (specific) and creative details that grab readers' attention and make them hungry for more. This chapter will help you add such details to any paragraph.

Cake 1

Cake 2

167

practice ordering single-word items, then phrases, and then sentences.

A separate chapter provides fun and innovative activities to help students develop **vivid details** to bring their ideas to life. The chapter focuses on generating concrete details, action details, emotive details, quoted details, and more.

Uses an Innovative and Proven System to Give Students a Deep Mastery of Sentence Patterns

KEY TO BUILDING BLOCKS

FOUNDATION WORDS
- NOUNS
- VERBS

DESCRIPTIVE WORDS
- ADJECTIVES
- ADVERBS

CONNECTING WORDS
- PREPOSITIONS
- CONJUNCTIONS

This system combines visual explanations, consistent labels, extensive and carefully sequenced practices, and inventive activities. In an introductory grammar chapter, students first learn the **building blocks of sentences** and their functions. These building blocks are color-coded within examples throughout the grammar chapters, showing how these words work together and imprinting the patterns of effective sentences (noun + verb; noun + verb + comma + conjunction + noun + verb; etc.).

With each successive chapter, students see how to use these building blocks to construct progressively longer and more complicated sentences.

Let's look at one chapter (Chapter 11: The Simple Sentence). Students first get a preview of the sentence patterns they will be asked to create.

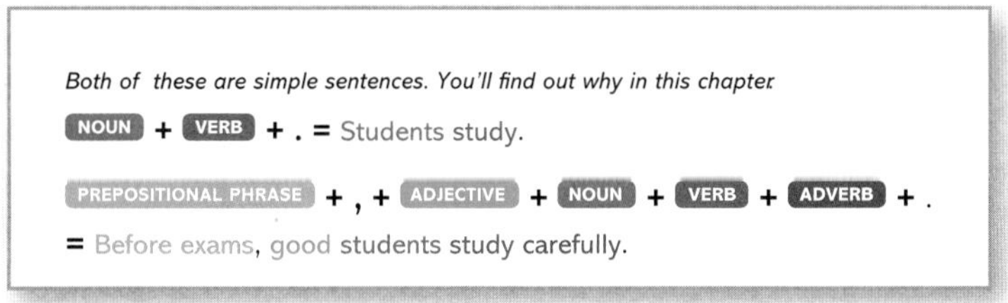

Both of these are simple sentences. You'll find out why in this chapter.

NOUN + VERB + . = Students study.

PREPOSITIONAL PHRASE + , + ADJECTIVE + NOUN + VERB + ADVERB + .

= Before exams, good students study carefully.

Then, they see how to create progressively longer sentences and recognize important elements in them. At every stage, abundant practices grow incrementally more challenging.

The process of building each sentence type is broken down into the smallest possible steps—with plenty of examples and practice—to build competency in all learners, including ESL and Generation 1.5 students.

At the end of most grammar chapters, students learn how to solve problems in the sentence type at hand.

Covers Grammar Problems in Context—Not as Isolated Errors

Instead of offering separate chapters on fragments, run-ons, comma splices, and other common errors, *Stepping Stones* addresses these problems in the context of the sentence patterns in which they are most common. This approach focuses students on their abilities as problem-solvers rather than on their identities as writers with problems. It also builds students' awareness of situations in which errors are most likely to occur, making them better editors of their own writing.

Appeals to Visual Learners with a Colorful, Innovative Design

Stepping Stones uses color and visuals to make information clearer and more appealing to visual learners and to students who in the past may have been discouraged in reading and writing. Aside from color-coding the building blocks of sentences, *Stepping Stones* uses color to identify main ideas, support, and other key writing concepts to underscore the structure of effective writing.

Additionally, color photographs and illustrations engage students and clarify important concepts.

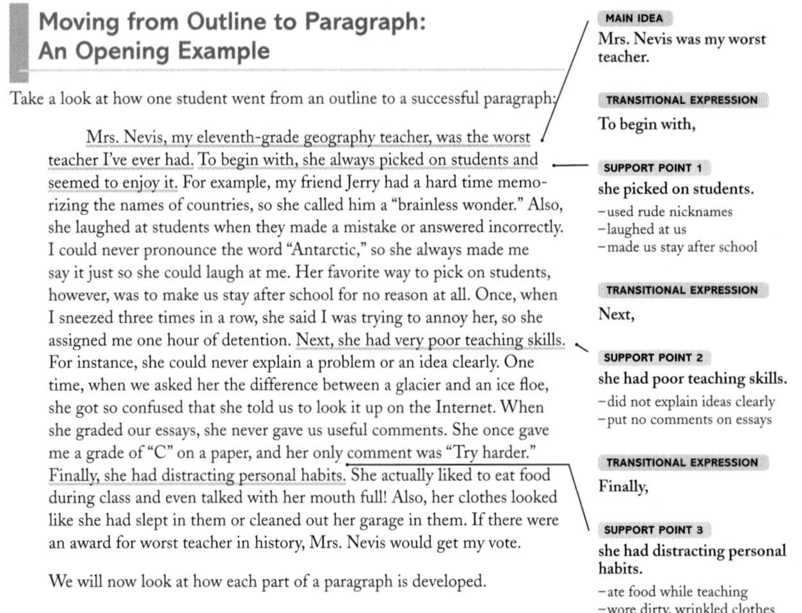

Moving from Outline to Paragraph: An Opening Example

Take a look at how one student went from an outline to a successful paragraph:

Mrs. Nevis, my eleventh-grade geography teacher, was the worst teacher I've ever had. To begin with, she always picked on students and seemed to enjoy it. For example, my friend Jerry had a hard time memorizing the names of countries, so she called him a "brainless wonder." Also, she laughed at students when they made a mistake or answered incorrectly. I could never pronounce the word "Antarctic," so she always made me say it just so she could laugh at me. Her favorite way to pick on students, however, was to make us stay after school for no reason at all. Once, when I sneezed three times in a row, she said I was trying to annoy her, so she assigned me one hour of detention. Next, she had very poor teaching skills. For instance, she could never explain a problem or an idea clearly. One time, when we asked her the difference between a glacier and an ice floe, she got so confused that she told us to look it up on the Internet. When she graded our essays, she never gave us useful comments. She once gave me a grade of "C" on a paper, and her only comment was "Try harder." Finally, she had distracting personal habits. She actually liked to eat food during class and even talked with her mouth full! Also, her clothes looked like she had slept in them or cleaned out her garage in them. If there were an award for worst teacher in history, Mrs. Nevis would get my vote.

We will now look at how each part of a paragraph is developed.

MAIN IDEA
Mrs. Nevis was my worst teacher.

TRANSITIONAL EXPRESSION
To begin with,

SUPPORT POINT 1
she picked on students.
–used rude nicknames
–laughed at us
–made us stay after school

TRANSITIONAL EXPRESSION
Next,

SUPPORT POINT 2
she had poor teaching skills.
–did not explain ideas clearly
–put no comments on essays

TRANSITIONAL EXPRESSION
Finally,

SUPPORT POINT 3
she had distracting personal habits.
–ate food while teaching
–wore dirty, wrinkled clothes

Offers a Thematic Reader with High-Interest Topics for Developmental Learners

I have found that the themes in many readers just don't connect with my students. For the reader in Part Three of *Stepping Stones,* I chose themes and selections that will resonate with students and spark writing that they will be invested in. The themes include kindness and empathy, school and learning, making mistakes, and more.

Accompanying each reading are comprehension questions, discussion questions, prompts asking students to examine the various rhetorical patterns used by writers, and writing assignments. Also, additional assignments ask students to draw on various readings and their own experiences to write about the themes addressed in the reader.

ANCILLARIES

For information on ordering the following ancillaries and to get ISBNs for packaging these resources with your students' books, see page xi.

Print Resources

Instructor's Annotated Edition by Chris Juzwiak. Provides answers to activities, teaching tips, and ideas for classroom activities—right at your fingertips. ISBN-10: 0-312-48606-5 / ISBN-13: 978-0-312-48606-8

Resources for Teaching Stepping Stones by Chris Juzwiak, with additional articles from a panel of expert instructors. Offers guidance on teaching with the book, including advice on engaging all students, no matter their skill level; teaching ESL and Generation 1.5 students and those with disabilities; facilitating collaboration; assessing writing; and more. ISBN-10: 0-312-48598-0 / ISBN-13: 978-0-312-48598-6

Tests and Exercises to Accompany Stepping Stones. Provides diagnostic pre- and post-tests and additional practices to build students' writing and grammar skills. ISBN-10: 0-312-48601-4 / ISBN-13: 978-0-312-48601-3

***Teaching Developmental Writing: Background Readings,* Third Edition.** This professional resource, edited by Susan Naomi Bernstein, former co-chair of the Conference on Basic Writing, offers essays on topics of interest to basic writing instructors, along with editorial apparatus pointing out practical applications for the classroom. ISBN-10: 0-312-43283-6 / ISBN-13: 978-0-312-43283-6

The Bedford/St. Martin's ESL Workbook. Covers grammar issues for multilingual students with varying English-language skills and cultural backgrounds. Instructional introductions are followed by illustrative examples and exercises. ISBN-10: 0-312-44503-2 / ISBN-13: 978-0-312-44503-4

The Bedford/St. Martin's Planner with Grammar Girl's Quick and Dirty Tips. Includes everything that students need to plan and use their time effectively, with advice on preparing schedules and to-do lists and blank schedules and calendars (monthly and weekly) for planning. Integrated into the planner are tips from the popular Grammar Girl podcast; quick advice on fixing common grammar errors, note-taking, and succeeding on tests; an address book; and an annotated list of useful Web sites. The planner fits easily into a backpack or purse, so students can take it anywhere. ISBN-10: 0-312-48023-7 / ISBN-13: 978-0-312-48023-3

From Practice to Mastery (study guide for the Florida Basic Skills Exit Tests in reading and writing). Gives students all the resources they need to practice for—and pass—the Florida tests in reading and writing. It includes pre- and post-tests, abundant practices, and clear instruction in all the skills covered on the exams. ISBN-10: 0-312-41908-2 / ISBN-13: 978-0-312-41908-0

New Media Resources

WritingClass. *WritingClass* is the first online learning space shaped by the needs of the developmental course. Students stay focused because assignments, grades, and writing instruction are all in one place. It's easy for you to monitor student progress and offer feedback when it counts most. *WritingClass* comes preloaded with our best media, for you to use when building your course: *Exercise Central,*

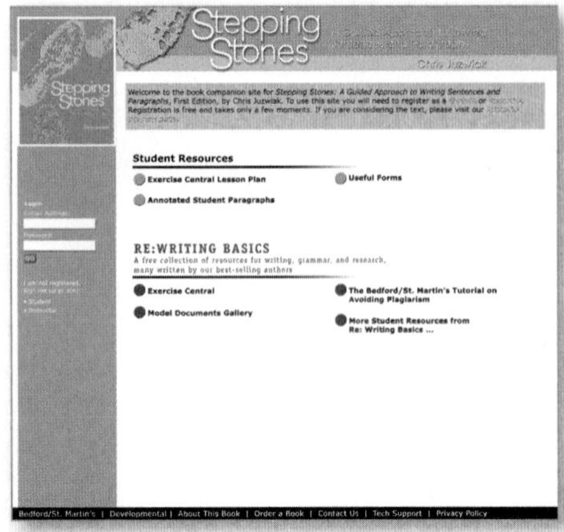

video tutorials for challenging concepts, writing guides, and more. ISBN-10: 0-312-48604-9/ISBN-13: 978-0-312-48604-4

Free book companion site, at bedfordstmartins.com/steppingstones. Offers grammar and writing exercises with immediate scoring, annotated examples of student writing, instructor PowerPoints, and more.

***Re:Writing Basics,* at bedfordstmartins.com/rewritingbasics.** Collects in one place the most popular Bedford/St. Martin's resources for developmental writing, including annotated student models, a learning style inventory, diagnostics, interactive tutorials, and more.

For access to premium resources, there's ***Re:Writing Plus,* bedfordstmartins .com/rewritingplus**. This brings together a variety of fun, innovative learning tools, such as *Make-a-Paragraph Kit* (see below), video tutorials, an online peer-review game, model documents, and more.

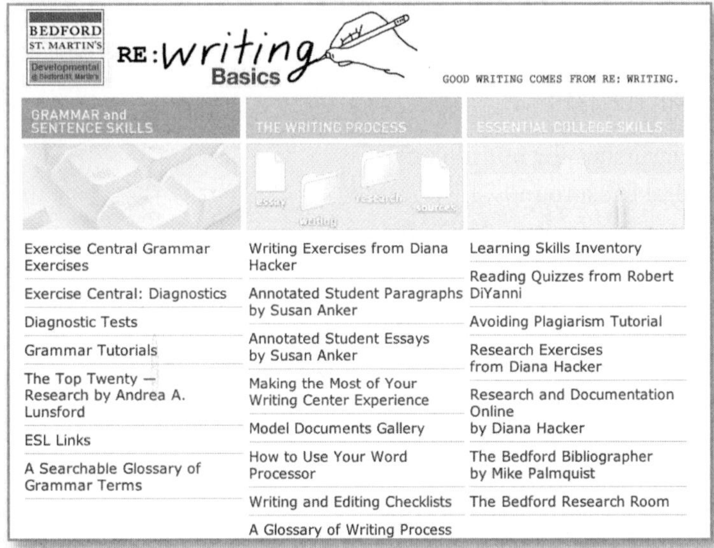

***Just-in-Time Teaching,* at bedfordstmartins.com/justintime.** Looking for last-minute course materials from a source you can trust? We've culled the best handouts, teaching tips, assignment ideas, and more from our print and online resources and put them all in one place.

Make-a-Paragraph Kit with Exercise Central to Go. This fun, interactive CD-ROM includes an "Extreme Paragraph Makeover" animation teaching students about paragraph development as well as activities that guide students through creating their own paragraphs. Additionally, it offers a set of audiovisual tutorials on fragments, run-ons and comma splices, subject-verb agreement problems, and verb problems. Grammar exercises are also included. ISBN-10: 0-312-45332-9 / ISBN-13: 978-0-312-45332-9

Exercise Central to Go: Writing and Grammar Practices for Basic Writers. This CD-ROM includes hundreds of practice items to help basic writers build their writing and editing skills and provides audio instructions and instant feedback. Drawn from the popular *Exercise Central* resource, the practices have been extensively class-tested. No Internet connection is necessary. ISBN-10: 0-312-44652-7/ ISBN-13: 978-0-312-44652-9

Testing Tool Kit: A Writing and Grammar Test Bank. This CD-ROM allows instructors to create secure, customized tests and quizzes to assess students' writing and grammar competency and gauge their progress during the course. The CD includes nearly 2,000 test items on 47 writing and grammar topics, at two levels of difficulty. Also, ten pre-built diagnostic tests are included. Scoring is instantaneous when tests and quizzes are administered online. ISBN-10: 0-312-43032-9/ ISBN-13: 978-0-312-43032-0

ORDERING INFORMATION

To order any of the ancillaries for *Stepping Stones,* please contact your Bedford/St. Martin's sales representative, e-mail sales support at **sales_support@bfwpub.com**, or visit our Web site at **bedfordstmartins.com**.

Use these ISBNs when ordering the following supplements packaged with your students' books:

Tests and Exercises to Accompany Stepping Stones
ISBN-10: 0-312-55387-0
ISBN-13: 978-0-312-55387-6

The Bedford/St. Martin's ESL Workbook
ISBN-10: 0-312-55382-X
ISBN-13: 978-0-312-55382-1

The Bedford/St. Martin's Planner
ISBN-10: 0-312-55761-2
ISBN-13: 978-0-312-55761-4

From Practice to Mastery
ISBN-10: 0-312-55383-8
ISBN-13: 978-0-312-55383-8

WritingClass
ISBN-10: 0-312-55379-X
ISBN-13: 978-0-312-55379-1

Re:Writing Plus
ISBN-10: 0-312-55384-6
ISBN-13: 978-0-312-55384-5

Make-a-Paragraph Kit
ISBN-10: 0-312-55381-1
ISBN-13: 978-0-312-55381-4

Exercise Central to Go
ISBN-10: 0-312-55380-3
ISBN-13: 978-0-312-55380-7

ACKNOWLEDGMENTS

Stepping Stones would not have been possible without the diligence, insights, and plain hard work of a large number of instructors, students, and other contributors.

Reviewers

Throughout the development of this book, a dedicated group of instructors, part of an Editorial Advisory Board, reviewed every page of the manuscript, offering helpful comments and fresh ideas, suggesting revisions large and small, and generally helping to shape the manuscript to make it more useful to students and other teachers. A few of these instructors are expert in teaching ESL and Generation 1.5 students, and their comments helped us address the needs of those students throughout the text. Following are the members of the Editorial Advisory Board:

- Barbara Craig, Del Mar College
- Kristen di Gennaro, Pace University
- Matthew Fox, Monroe Community College
- Sally Gearhart, Santa Rosa Junior College
- Susan Brown Rodriguez, Hillsborough Community College
- Valerie Russell, Valencia Community College

Additionally, many other instructors reviewed the manuscript at different points or offered comments through focus groups or workshops: Shannon Bailey, Austin Community College; Kay Blue, Owens Community College; Rhonda Carroll, Pulaski Technical College; Frank Cronin, Austin Community College; Gigi Derballa, Asheville-Buncombe Technical Community College; Connie Gulick, Central New Mexico University; Lisa Hatfield, Portland State University; Paula Ingram, Pensacola Junior College; Karen Lemke, Adams State College; Lourdes Lopez-Merino, Palm Beach Community College; Craig Machado, Norwalk Community College; Patricia McGraw, Cape Cod Community College; Caryn Newburger, Austin Community College; Viethang Pham, Cerritos College; Francie Quaas-Berryman, Cerritos College; Karen Roth, University of Texas, San Antonio; Jennifer Rusnak, Florida Community College at Jacksonville; Kimberly Samaniego, California State Long Beach; Jack Swanson, Cerritos College; Melissa Thomas, University of Texas, San Antonio; Monette Tiernan, Glendale Community College; Julie Tilton, San Bernardino Valley College; Christine Tutlewski, University of Wisconsin–Parkside; Rhonda Wallace, Cuyahoga Community College; Shelley Walters, Temple College; Ronald Weisberger, Bristol Community College; Elizabeth Whitehead, Bristol Community College; Julie Yankanich, Camden County College; and Betsy Zuegg, Quinsigamond Community College.

Students

Several student writers contributed paragraphs and essays to this book and its supplements. I am grateful for their dedication and for their willingness to share their work. These students include Angela Adkins, Jennifer Baffa, Samantha Castaneda, Francisco Fragoso, Arlene Galvez, Leanna R. Gonzales, Susan

Janoubi, Sarah Littmann, Cleva Nelson, Anallely Orozco, Adam F. Perez, Brian Rickenbrode, Maurice Rivera, Ekaterina Savchenkova, and Angela Vargas.

Other Contributors

I am also grateful to a number of other people whose hard work made this book possible. Julie Nichols of Okaloosa-Walton College carefully and energetically crafted exercises for both the book and its supplements, while Karin Paque researched and wrote elegant author headnotes for the readings in Part Three. Linda Finigan researched images and also cleared art permissions, while Warren Drabek ably cleared text permissions under the guidance of Sandy Schechter. Brian DeTagyos and Claire Seng-Niemoeller created colorful illustrations to aid students' understanding of writing and grammar points.

For their insightful contributions to *Resources for Teaching Stepping Stones,* I would like to thank Matthew Fox of Monroe Community College, Sally Gearhart of Santa Rosa Junior College, Erin M. O'Brien of University of Massachusetts Boston, and Susan Brown Rodriguez of Hillsborough Community College.

At Glendale Community College, my colleague Denise Ezell deserves a lion's share of gratitude for her generous support when my morale and imagination were running low. At these junctures, she rescued me by co-writing various activities and sample paragraphs for the book. Invariably, with her pedagogical common sense and wit, she got the project back on track, infusing it with fresh clarity and charm.

Also at Glendale Community College, several colleagues inspired me to think outside the pedagogical box. For their guidance, I am grateful to Ida Ferdman, Linda Griffith, Darren Leaver, Mark Maier, Alice Mecom, Brett Miketta, and Monette Tiernan.

Bedford/St. Martin's and Beyond

At Bedford/St. Martin's, a large number of people were part of bringing *Stepping Stones* into being. Early on, Stacy Luce, my Bedford/St. Martin's sales representative, and Rachel Falk, former marketing manager for developmental English, helped to connect me and Bedford/St. Martin's. As the book headed toward signing, former editor David Mogolov helped me to shape my ideas and offered many valuable suggestions based on his own market experience and extensive reviews. Carrie Brandon, who succeeded David, has continued to share market knowledge and other insights, and she's helped us shape a strong message for the book.

Throughout the book's development, President Joan E. Feinberg, Editorial Director Denise B. Wydra, and Editor in Chief Karen S. Henry have generously contributed many wise ideas and thoughtful suggestions for *Stepping Stones* based on years of experience listening to, and responding to the needs of, writing instructors. Throughout the development process, Stephanie Naudin assisted with countless tasks large and small, from helping to find engaging readings to running numerous review programs and managing a multitude of administrative details. Later in the process, Anne Leung stepped in to help with the ancillaries, and she insightfully edited *Resources for Teaching Stepping Stones.*

Making *Stepping Stones* colorful and engaging while ensuring its ease of use was a design challenge ably met by Art Director Anna Palchik and Designer Claire Seng-Niemoeller. Their creativity, energy, and problem-solving skills resulted in a design as attractive as it is practical. Elise Kaiser also contributed many useful suggestions for the design. Additionally, Elise and Elizabeth M. Schaaf oversaw many details regarding the production of the book. Production Editor Rosemary Jaffe skillfully guided the book through the production process, offering many practical suggestions and helping to solve a range of problems with patience, intelligence, and good humor. Rosemary brought on Jacqueline Rebisz and Steven Patterson as the copyeditors and Linda McLatchie and Andrea Martin as the proofreaders, and they deserve praise for their thoroughness and careful eye for details.

Also contributing to the look of the book was Sara Gates, who designed the appealing cover with the aid of Billy Boardman and Donna Dennison. Additionally, Martha Friedman helped with the art program in the early stages.

In New Media, several talented people helped to shape and produce the electronic ancillaries for *Stepping Stones*. Daniel Cole helped with the early stages of developing *WritingClass with Stepping Stones e-Book;* Kamali Thornell and Rebecca Merrill produced an attractive and robust companion Web site; Kim Hampton advised on the creation and formatting of online exercises; and John Amburg ably oversaw the copyediting of the online materials. Nick Carbone continues to travel the country, gathering information on how to develop the best online resources for *Stepping Stones* and Bedford/St. Martin's other texts and responding to instructor needs for workshops and other support for online instruction. I am also grateful for the new-media expertise and endless creativity of Alanya Harter, Katie Schooling, and Harriet Wald.

In marketing, sincere thanks go to Karen R. Soeltz, Jane Helms, and Casey Carroll for their creative ideas in getting out the word on *Stepping Stones*. Casey Carroll, as marketing manager, helped to shape the book's message and coordinate a number of sales efforts for it. Also, Karita dos Santos assisted with market development, offering many innovative ideas.

Additionally, I would like to thank those who developed and produced promotional materials for the book: Kim Cevoli, who designed an attractive brochure with the guidance of Shelby Disario, and Jessamyn Jones McEnoy, who oversaw the production of catalog materials.

My enduring gratitude goes to Beth Castrodale, who as editor of this book and professional mentor, sustained and elevated me through the composition process with her insightful criticism, intellectual rigor, and collaborative generosity. I couldn't imagine a more auspicious or edifying introduction to the work of textbook writing than my partnership with Beth. *Merci beaucoup, mon amie.*

I also want to thank my family members and friends, whose unflagging enthusiasm and patience were as crucial to this work as any other component: Doug Mann, Lael Mann, Estella Martinez, Ruth Owens, Sandra and Ernie Gomez, Catherine Leh, James Geyer, Shelley Aronoff, Michael Ritterbrown, Christine Menardus, George Gharibian, Ildy Lee, and Marilyn Selznick.

—*Chris Juzwiak*

Brief Contents

Contents

Readings by Patterns of Development

This table of contents organizes the readings in Part Three of *Stepping Stones* ("A Writer's Reader," page 523) according to the patterns of development they use. (Within each category, readings are listed in order of appearance. Each reading may appear in more than one category.) For more information on the patterns of development, see Chapter 1, pages 26–30, and Appendix A.

Description

Exemplification

Narration

Process

Definition

Cause and Effect

Comparison and Contrast

Argumentation

Introduction for Students

Can a single class make a difference in your life? We definitely believe it can. If you commit to regularly attending and participating in this class, and to doing all of the assigned work, your writing will certainly improve. And better writing skills increase your likelihood of achieving success not just in this class but in all of your college courses and in the workplace, where clear, correct communication is essential.

Stepping Stones will help you get the most out of your class by giving you plenty of examples, activities, and other support to improve your writing and grammar skills. It is written *for students,* and we hope it will become an essential learning tool for you, motivating you to explore the chapters and learn on your own. To help you work through the book on your own, we have

- kept the explanations clear and direct so that you can get to work on the activities as quickly as possible
- arranged the activities from easy to difficult so that you can build mastery gradually and confidently
- made the activities creative and fun to challenge your thinking and spark your imagination

The following sections explain how you can get the most out of *Stepping Stones.*

FINDING WHAT YOU NEED IN *STEPPING STONES*

Here, we review several important features that can help you find just what you need in this text.

Index. In any book, the index (an alphabetical list of topics covered, with page numbers) is often the quickest way to find a topic of interest. For the index in *Stepping Stones,* turn to page I-1 at the back of the book. Say you are looking for all of the relevant information on topic sentences. You would turn to *T* in the index and then scan down until you find "topic sentence." Next to this entry, you will find all the pages on which this subject is discussed.

Detailed list of contents. This resource, on pages xvii–xxvii, lists all the chapters in the book and tells you what topics are covered in each one. Page numbers are provided for each chapter and its subtopics so you can find information. Your instructor may refer you to certain chapters and chapter subsections, so be sure that you are comfortable with using the table of contents.

Additionally, each chapter begins with a brief list of contents to give you a preview of the topics covered.

Readings by "patterns of development." This list, on pages xxix–xxx, organizes the readings in Part Three according to the various patterns of development discussed in Chapter 1 and in Appendix A, providing page numbers. You can turn to this list whenever you want to see additional models of different types of writing (description, exemplification, narration, and so on).

Page headers. As you page through the book, you will find headings at the top of the left- and right-hand pages. Take a look:

36 Chapter 2 • Understanding and Working with Writing Assignments

Understanding the Parts of Writing Assignments 37

The left header shows the number and the title of the chapter that you are in. The right header shows the major section that you are in.

List of helpful lists, charts, and visuals. This resource, at the back of the book, directs you to important writing and grammar aids that you may want to turn to regularly.

List of correction symbols. When your instructor marks writing or grammar issues in your papers, he or she may use various correction symbols. These symbols and their meanings are presented at the back of the book to help you translate your instructor's markings.

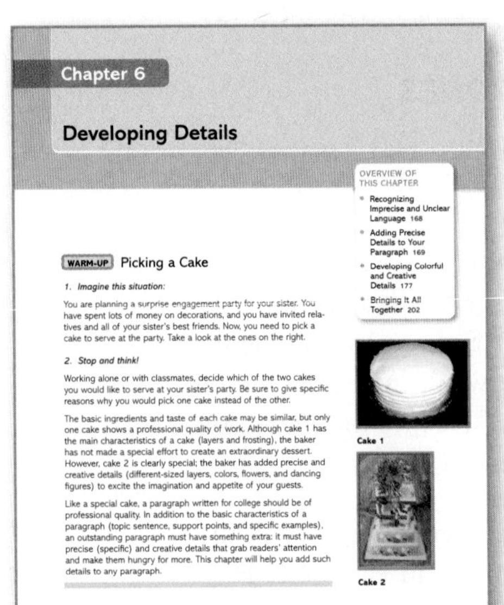

Chapter 6

Developing Details

OVERVIEW OF THIS CHAPTER

- Recognizing Imprecise and Unclear Language 168
- Adding Precise Details to Your Paragraph 169
- Developing Colorful and Creative Details 177
- Bringing It All Together 202

WARM-UP Picking a Cake

1. Imagine this situation:

You are planning a surprise engagement party for your sister. You have spent lots of money on decorations, and you have invited relatives and all of your sister's best friends. Now, you need to pick a cake to serve at the party. Take a look at the ones on the right.

2. Stop and think!

Working alone or with classmates, decide which of the two cakes you would like to serve at your sister's party. Be sure to give specific reasons why you would pick one cake instead of the other.

The basic ingredients and taste of each cake may be similar, but only one cake shows a professional quality of work. Although cake 1 has the main characteristics of a cake (layers and frosting), the baker has not made a special effort to create an extraordinary dessert. However, cake 2 is clearly special; the baker has added precise and creative details (different-sized layers, colors, flowers, and dancing figures) to excite the imagination and appetite of your guests.

Like a special cake, a paragraph written for college should be of professional quality. In addition to the basic characteristics of a paragraph (topic sentence, support points, and specific examples), an outstanding paragraph must have something extra: it must have precise (specific) and creative details that grab readers' attention and make them hungry for more. This chapter will help you add such details to any paragraph.

Cake 1

Cake 2

167

USING SPECIAL FEATURES TO IMPROVE YOUR WRITING

Stepping Stones has a number of special features to help make you a better writer. Let's look at a few of them.

"Warm-ups" for the writing chapters. Each chapter in Part One ("The Academic Paragraph") introduces the writing topic that you are about to study by comparing it to a situation that you probably are already familiar with. Activities in these "warm-ups" get you thinking about the topic before you work with it in greater detail.

Abundant activities. The following experience might be familiar to you: You are given instruction in something several times, but it doesn't "sink in" until you actually perform the task yourself. *Stepping Stones* is based on the "learning by doing" philosophy, giving you lots of activities that help writing and grammar lessons stick in your mind.

Again, assignments grow more and more challenging as you progress through chapters. You may find that you go through earlier practices quickly but need more time to complete later ones. This is natural and expected. You may want to attempt more challenging exercises more than one time.

Color-coding of sentence parts and patterns in the grammar chapters. Chapter 10, the second chapter in Part Two ("Grammar for Academic Writing") describes the various "building blocks" of language that we use to create sentences. So that you can see how these building blocks work together, they are color-coded within examples throughout the grammar chapters.

At the beginning of each grammar chapter, you get a preview of how the building blocks are used to create the sentence type discussed in the chapter:

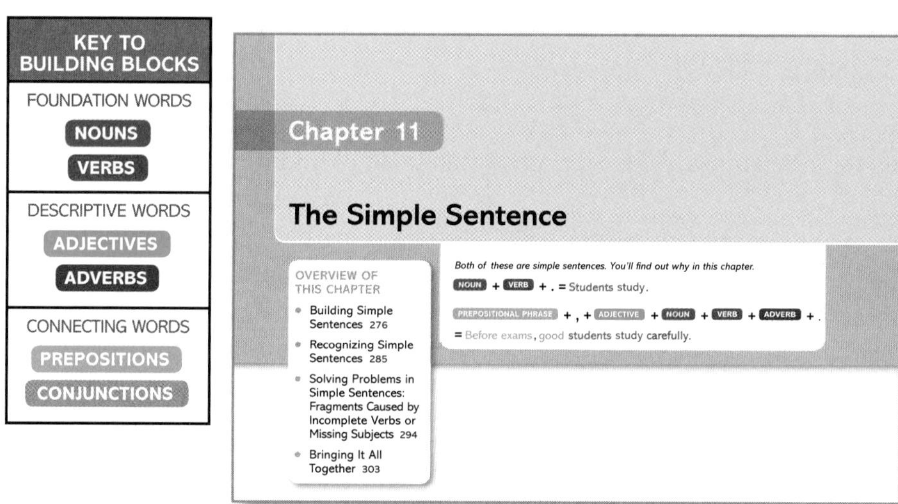

Helpful tips in the margins. These tips provide extra advice, explain writing and grammar terms, and refer you to additional exercises on *Stepping Stones'* companion Web site.

For online practice with building simple sentences, visit this book's Web site at **bedfordstmartins .com/steppingstones**.

Power Tip
Information that seems to be missing from an assignment, including the due date, may actually be specified in the course syllabus. Read the syllabus carefully at the beginning of any course and refer back to it for details about particular assignments as you start them.

Terminology Tip
In English grammar, the verb that follows a helping verb is often called the *main verb*. Often, the main verb is an action verb.

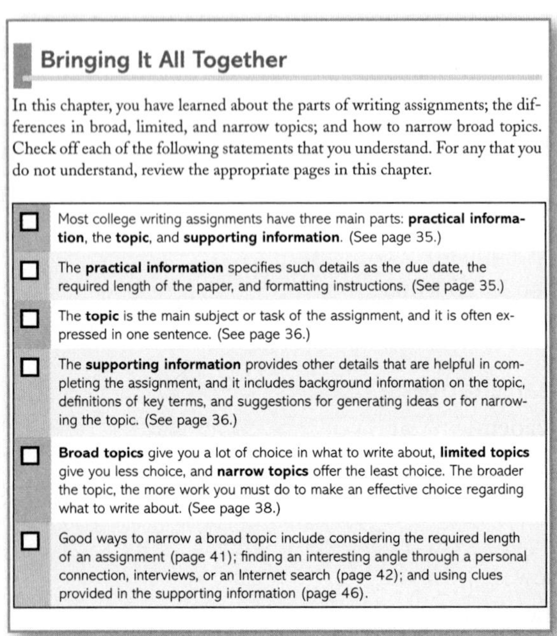

Bringing It All Together

In this chapter, you have learned about the parts of writing assignments; the differences in broad, limited, and narrow topics; and how to narrow broad topics. Check off each of the following statements that you understand. For any that you do not understand, review the appropriate pages in this chapter.

- ☐ Most college writing assignments have three main parts: **practical information**, the **topic**, and **supporting information**. (See page 35.)
- ☐ The **practical information** specifies such details as the due date, the required length of the paper, and formatting instructions. (See page 35.)
- ☐ The **topic** is the main subject or task of the assignment, and it is often expressed in one sentence. (See page 36.)
- ☐ The **supporting information** provides other details that are helpful in completing the assignment, and it includes background information on the topic, definitions of key terms, and suggestions for generating ideas or for narrowing the topic. (See page 36.)
- ☐ **Broad topics** give you a lot of choice in what to write about, **limited topics** give you less choice, and **narrow topics** offer the least choice. The broader the topic, the more work you must do to make an effective choice regarding what to write about. (See page 38.)
- ☐ Good ways to narrow a broad topic include considering the required length of an assignment (page 41); finding an interesting angle through a personal connection, interviews, or an Internet search (page 42); and using clues provided in the supporting information (page 46).

Chapter-ending checklists. These checklists, appearing under the title "Bringing It All Together," summarize important information and refer you back to specific sections that you might want to review.

A thematic reader. This resource, in Part Three ("A Writer's Reader"), offers not only good models of professional writing but also a source of ideas for your own writing. Each reading is accompanied by writing assignments and by questions that help you study and understand strategies used by experienced writers.

Answers to odd-numbered activities. We have provided answers to odd-numbered activities (see page K-1) so that you can check your work as you move through the writing and grammar instruction.

GETTING EXTRA HELP

Stepping Stones comes with an easy-to-use companion Web site: **bedfordstmartins.com/steppingstones**. This site offers hundreds of additional practices, annotated examples of student writing, and other resources to help you improve your writing and grammar skills. Registration is free and easy; just follow the "Sign me up" link on the left side of the page.

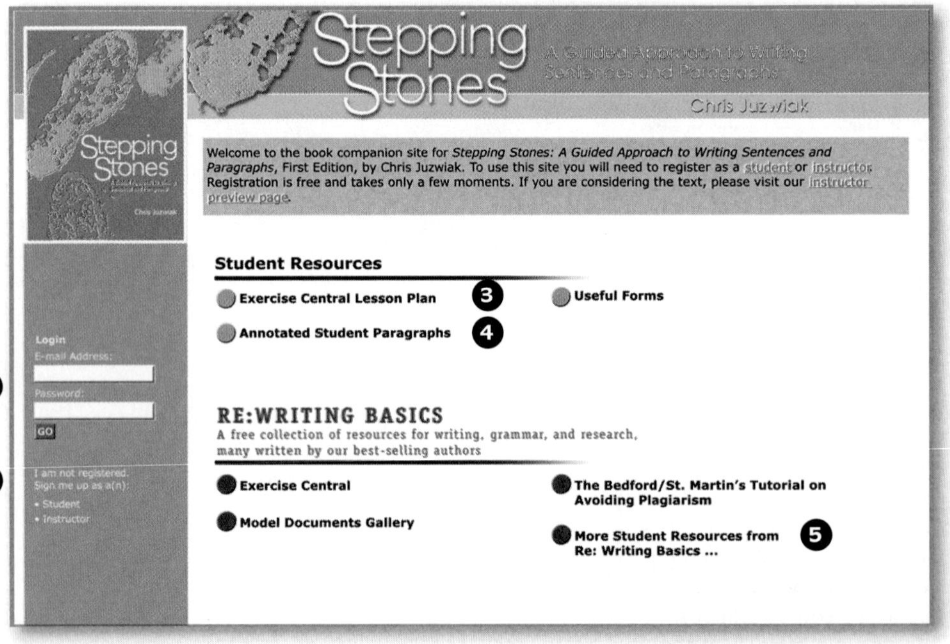

1. Register here.
2. After registration, log in here.
3. Complete more writing and grammar activities here.
4. View more writing models here.
5. Explore other resources.

Aside from offering exercises written specifically for *Stepping Stones,* the Web site provides access to thousands more practices on *Exercise Central* and to *Re:Writing Basics,* offering model documents, advice on avoiding plagiarism, and more.

Print versions of the *Stepping Stones* Web exercises, as well as diagnostic and mastery tests, are published in *Tests and Exercises to Accompany Stepping Stones.*

Instructor's Annotated Edition

Stepping Stones

A Guided Approach to Writing Sentences and Paragraphs

PART ONE

The Academic Paragraph

Chapter 1

Seeing the Big Picture

OVERVIEW OF THIS CHAPTER

WARM-UP Making a Movie

1. *Imagine this situation:*

You are a movie director, and in this role, you are responsible for the **big picture** of a film. That means you'll have to be able to answer questions like the following:

- What **kind** of film will this be? (a drama, a comedy, a documentary, an animated feature, or something else?)
- What is the **purpose** for making the film? (to entertain, to inform, to inspire, to change people's opinions, or something else?)
- Who is the **audience** for the film? (men, women, adults, teenagers, children, Americans, Australians, or others?)
- What **strategies** (in terms of set design, lighting, special effects, acting styles, and so on) will be used in making the film?

2. *Stop and think!*

Working alone or with classmates, pick a popular film and try to identify the **big picture** that the director had for the film. Then, try to answer each of the four previous questions in relation to the film.

Like a film director, you should have a big picture in mind for each writing assignment. Specifically, you will need to know

- what you will write (the **type of paragraph**)
- why you will write (your **purpose**)
- for whom you will write (your **audience**)
- how you will write (your **rhetoric**)

Understanding Paragraphs

Let's begin with an obvious question: What is a paragraph? Many people will be able to provide only a general or unclear definition. Related questions include

- What should an ideal paragraph look like?
- How long should it be?
- Are there rules for constructing a paragraph?
- Why do so many paragraphs look so different from one another?

Knowing the answers to these questions will give you a more confident vision for your writing projects.

Teaching Tip

If your students do not have their own dictionaries for completing Activity 1, you may need to copy a definition of *paragraph* onto the board or show it on an overhead projector. The definition should be shown after students have come up with their own answers.

ACTIVITY 1: Teamwork

Form a group with two or three other classmates and follow these steps:

- Each of you should write your own definition of the word *paragraph* without looking in a dictionary.
- Compare your definitions and write a group definition of the word.
- Look the word up in a dictionary. Discuss how the group definition is similar to or different from the dictionary one. After reading all the definitions, do you have a clearer understanding of what a paragraph is? Do the definitions answer any of the questions raised above: What should an ideal paragraph look like? How long should it be? Are there rules for constructing a paragraph?

The definitions that you discussed in Activity 1 probably did not do much to improve your understanding of what a paragraph is. Most dictionary definitions of the word *paragraph* say something very general, like "a distinct section or portion of a piece of writing, usually indented." This sort of definition certainly does not provide any clear guidelines or rules for writing paragraphs.

If you want to build your understanding of what a "good" paragraph is, the best way is to look at some examples, noting that *different types of writing use different types of paragraphs.* In this chapter, we will discuss five types of writing that college students encounter most frequently:

- journalism
- business writing
- popular fiction and nonfiction
- personal writing
- academic writing

Ultimately, your goal in college will be to write effective academic paragraphs. However, to have a good understanding of academic paragraphs, you must first see how they differ from paragraphs in other types of writing. Remember: if you confuse the academic paragraph with other types of paragraphs, your writing might not be as successful as possible.

PARAGRAPHS IN JOURNALISM

Journalism is writing for newspapers, magazines, or news-related Web sites. It typically covers recent events and current topics of interest. The following activity will help you become more familiar with the features of paragraphs in journalism.

ACTIVITY 2

First, notice that the following newspaper selection is separated into distinct paragraphs. Each paragraph is indented (set in from the left margin by a few spaces) to show where it begins. Place a check mark at the beginning of each new paragraph.

Next, to understand the basic features of paragraphs in journalism, answer the following questions about both the newspaper article and the newsmagazine excerpt that follows it. Answers may vary.

1. Count the number of sentences in each paragraph. Are all the paragraphs similar in length?
2. In your opinion, are the paragraphs long or short?
3. How many major ideas are expressed in each paragraph? Try to identify these ideas.

A Newspaper Article (from *USA Today*, October 30, 2007)

Calif. fire crews brace for return of Santa Anas

By Alan Gomez
USA TODAY

As most firefighters continued beating down the wildfires still burning through Southern California on Monday, some were repositioning for a possible return of the seasonal Santa Ana winds later this week.

About 420 firefighters, 25 fire engines and 14 bulldozers were pulled off the remaining active fires to prepare for the expected return Friday of the Santa Anas – dry, hot winds that blow westward from the Mojave Desert. The winds fueled the wildfires, which have burned more than 517,000 acres, destroyed more than 2,000 homes and killed seven people.

Those fires are now largely under control. Crews achieved full containment of two more fires Monday, leaving only five of the original 23 fires still active.

Jerry Rohnert of the U.S. Forest Service in San Bernardino said that even if a fire is declared 100% contained, that doesn't mean the fire is out. It simply means crews have established sufficient fire lines around flames to stop them from advancing further.

So a return of the Santa Ana winds could mean a resurgence of some of those blazes.

"That's going to really test the fire lines," Rohnert said. "If they hold, everything is going to be fine. If not ... it could be that we're starting all over again."

Tom Moore, a meteorologist with The Weather Channel, said the winds expected Friday and Saturday may be only half as strong as the gale-force winds that fanned the original blazes.

"Even that can be problematic," he said.

Mary Ann Aldrich of the California Governor's Office of Emergency Services hopes that won't be the case, though, as her office predicted having all the remaining fires fully contained by the end of the week.

thinking outside the book

Look at a newspaper or magazine article and compare the paragraphs you see there with the ones shown here. Although not all the paragraphs will be exactly alike, most of them will have the basic features of a journalism paragraph: they will be *short* (usually one to three sentences), and each will express one or two key ideas.

PARAGRAPHS IN BUSINESS WRITING

Business writing consists of all written communication in the workplace: between individuals or groups within companies, between businesses and their customers, and between institutions (such as hospitals and county courthouses) and the people they serve. The following activity will help you become more familiar with the features of paragraphs in business writing.

ACTIVITY 3

First, notice that the following example of business writing is separated into distinct paragraphs. Place a check mark at the beginning of each new paragraph.

Next, to understand the basic features of business paragraphs, respond to the following questions. *Answers may vary.*

1. Count the number of sentences in each paragraph.
2. In your opinion, are the paragraphs long or short?
3. How many major ideas are expressed in each paragraph? Try to identify them.
4. Are these paragraphs similar to or different from the journalism paragraphs? Explain your opinion.

Teaching Tip
In response to question 4, students might notice that the journalism paragraphs include quotations, while the business example does not. Ask them why journalists might include quotations in their writing.

A Response to a Complaint Made to a Business

On October 17, 2007, Ace Appliance received your phone call that a stove delivered to your home that morning arrived in damaged condition—specifically, the front panel of the broiler was dented. We apologize for any inconvenience or frustration that you experienced as a result and want to assure you that we will resolve the situation to your satisfaction.

According to our call logs, you reported that the delivery staff handled the stove roughly while carrying it up the three flights of stairs to your apartment. As a result, you declined to sign the form indicating that the appliance had arrived in good condition. On removing the packaging from the stove and discovering the damage, you phoned in the complaint.

Please call 800-555-7650 at your earliest convenience so that we can arrange a time to replace the stove at no additional charge to you. Also, please let us know if our description of your complaint is inaccurate in any way, because we are trying to keep complete and accurate records of complaints in an ongoing effort to improve our customer service. Finally, please accept the enclosed Food World gift certificate as a token of our appreciation for your business. We value you as a customer, and again, we apologize for any difficulties that we have caused.

thinking outside the book

Look at a document that you received from a company, your employer, or your college. Compare the paragraphs you see there with the one shown here. Although not all the paragraphs will be exactly alike, most of them will have the basic features of a business paragraph: they will be of *medium length* (usually two to five sentences), and each paragraph may express a few key ideas. However, some may express only one or two.

PARAGRAPHS IN POPULAR FICTION AND NONFICTION

Fiction is writing from the imagination, with invented characters, plots, dialogue, and so on. **Popular fiction** refers to novels and short stories (usually collected) of the kind that you will find in most major bookstores, like Barnes & Noble. Nonfiction is based on fact and reality, and **popular nonfiction** includes biographies, autobiographies, and informational books (such as the popular ____ *for Dummies* and "self-help" books) that you will find in most major bookstores. Although nonfiction, technically, can include journalism, business writing, personal writing, and academic writing, we are referring in this section to the nonfiction that is typically published in book form and that is aimed at a wide audience.

The following activity will help you become more familiar with the features of paragraphs in popular fiction and nonfiction.

ACTIVITY 4

First, notice that the following examples of popular fiction and nonfiction are separated into distinct paragraphs. Next, to understand the basic features of paragraphs in these types of writing, respond to the following questions. Answers may vary.

1. Count the number of sentences in each paragraph. Are the paragraphs in both selections similar in length?
2. In your opinion, are the paragraphs long or short?
3. How many major ideas are expressed in each paragraph? Try to identify them.
4. Are these paragraphs similar to or different from the journalism and business paragraphs? Explain your opinion.

Excerpt from Popular Fiction (Book)

These paragraphs come from British author Zoë Heller's 2003 novel *Notes on a Scandal,* which was made into a 2006 movie of the same name. The novel describes the consequences of an affair between a schoolteacher (Sheba Hart) and

CONTINUED >

one of her students (Connolly). The following scene takes place at the school, before the affair has begun.

> One Friday afternoon, not long before the Christmas holidays, Connolly appeared at a Homework Club that Sheba was minding. The two had not encountered each other in a public setting since they had become friends, and Sheba felt somewhat uneasy. Connolly arrived late, in the company of a skinny, grinning boy called Jackie Kilbane. According to the notes that they handed in, they had been caught earlier in the week sharing a cigarette together in the school's crumbling outdoor lavatories. They were now serving a fortnight's worth of hour-long detentions. Sheba detected something sly and furtive in Connolly's manner as he stood before her desk. When she smiled at him, he would not meet her eye.
>
> As soon as he and the Kilbane boy had been registered, they retreated to the back of the room, where they began tipping back on their chairs and whispering. Sheba could not make out what they were saying, but she had an uncomfortable sense that it was obscene in nature and connected, in some way, to herself. The suspicion grew when Kilbane got up and approached her desk to ask for more paper. Kilbane is an unpleasant boy with an ugly, yellow face and an insolent, insinuating attitude. A thin line of fur skulks on his upper lip, like a baby caterpillar. He gave Sheba the creeps. As she burrowed in the desk drawer for paper, he seemed to be standing uncomfortably close to her chair, but only when she sat up did it dawn on her that he was attempting to look down her shirt. She handed him a sheet of paper and sharply ordered him back to his desk. "All right, all right," he said mockingly, as he strolled away. "Don't get your knickers in a twist." Sheba glanced at Connolly. He had been watching this exchange intently. As he met her eye, there was a hard, unfriendly look on his face.

fortnight: two weeks

furtive: secretive

insolent: disrespectful

insinuating: hinting or suggesting

knickers: British term for *underwear.* To get one's "knickers in a twist" is to become upset or agitated.

Excerpt from Popular Nonfiction (Book)

These paragraphs come from writer and political activist Elie Wiesel's 1958 book *Night,* in which he tells of his experiences in the German death camps of Auschwitz-Birkenau and Buchenwald during World War II. Approximately 6 million European Jews, including members of Wiesel's family, were killed during the war, many of them in death camps. This mass murder has come to be known as the Holocaust.

These paragraphs describe events that occurred after the arrival of Wiesel's family at Auschwitz-Birkenau. The "SS" to whom Wiesel refers is a camp officer. Tzipora is Wiesel's youngest sister.

> THE BELOVED OBJECTS that we had carried with us from place to place were now left behind in the wagon and, with them, finally, our illusions.
>
> Every few yards, there stood an SS man, his machine gun trained on us. Hand in hand we followed the throng.
>
> An SS came toward us wielding a club. He commanded:
>
> "Men to the left! Women to the right!"
>
> Eight words spoken quietly, indifferently, without emotion. Eight simple, short words. Yet that was the moment when I left my mother. There was no time to think, and I already felt my father's hand press against mine: we were alone. In a fraction of a second I could see my mother, my sisters, move to the right. Tzipora was holding Mother's hand. I saw them walking farther and farther away; Mother was stroking my sister's blond hair, as if to protect her. And I walked on with my father, with the men. I didn't know that this was the moment in time and the place where I was leaving my mother and Tzipora forever. I kept walking, my father holding my hand.

throng: group or crowd

wielding: carrying

Teaching Tip

If you are teaching grammar in conjunction with Part One's chapters on writing, you might point out that the fifth paragraph of Wiesel's writing begins with two fragments. Explain that these are examples of poetic license, often taken by experienced writers to create special effects. For more on poetic license, see page 261.

thinking outside the book

Visit a popular bookstore, such as Barnes & Noble, and look at several books that interest you. Compare the paragraphs you see in those books with the ones shown here. Although authors of popular fiction and nonfiction often write short to medium-length paragraphs (one to five sentences), *there are no rules for fiction and nonfiction paragraphs.* As a result, you may find a lot of variation in the length of these paragraphs and the number of ideas they include.

PARAGRAPHS IN PERSONAL WRITING

Personal writing includes written communication among friends and family members. It also includes private writing, such as that done in personal journals or diaries. The following activity will help you become more familiar with the features of paragraphs in personal writing.

ACTIVITY 5

First, notice that the following example of personal writing is separated into distinct paragraphs. Next, to understand the basic features of paragraphs in personal writing, respond to the following questions: Answers may vary.

1. Count the number of sentences in each paragraph. In your opinion, are the paragraphs long or short?
2. Compare this example with the fiction and nonfiction examples on pages 7–9. Then, explain how the paragraphs from the personal writing are similar to or different from the fiction and nonfiction paragraphs.

Wedding Day Speech from a Father to His Daughter

I remember the first time I held you in my arms. When I looked into your tiny face, I knew that my life would never be the same.

I remember the first time you said "Daddy." I had never heard a sound so beautiful in all of the world. Even today when you say "Dad," it sounds like music to my heart.

I remember the first time you walked. I was holding your hand. I knew that I would always be one step behind you wherever you went in the world.

I remember the first time you hurt yourself. Your pain was the worst pain I had ever felt in my life. I knew then that life would be full of risks.

And I will always remember today, the day you were married. As I walked you down the aisle, I remembered your tiny face, your first steps, the music of your voice, the hurt, and the risks. And I knew again that my life would never be the same.

thinking outside the book

Find a letter or e-mail that you received from a friend, or if you keep a journal, open it up to any page. Compare the paragraphs you see in those writings with the one shown here. Although most people write short to medium-length paragraphs (one to five sentences) in their personal writing, *there are no rules for personal paragraphs.* As a result, you may find a lot of variation in the length of these paragraphs and the number of ideas they include.

PARAGRAPHS IN ACADEMIC WRITING

Academic writing is typically used in (and often produced at) colleges and universities; it includes student essays, textbooks, and scholarly books and articles by professors and other academics. Because you will be writing academic paragraphs for this class and most of your college classes, you will benefit from looking at several examples.

The following activity will help you become more familiar with the features of paragraphs in academic writing.

ACTIVITY 6

Below are three examples of academic paragraphs. Notice that each example is made up of *one* paragraph only. Next, to understand the basic features of academic paragraphs, respond to the following questions: Answers may vary.

1. Count the number of sentences in each paragraph. Are all the paragraphs similar in length?
2. In your opinion, are the paragraphs short or long?
3. Of the five types of paragraphs, which type is the most distinct from the other four? Why?

Teaching Tip

Even if there isn't enough time for students to do all the activities in this chapter, it's worthwhile to have them complete Activity 6. If students can answer question 3 correctly (indicating that academic paragraphs are the most distinct because they tend to be significantly longer than other types of paragraphs), they will have come to an important understanding about the nature of academic paragraphs.

Excerpt from a Textbook (*Psychology*, Eighth Edition, by David G. Myers)

Although mindful that preserving weight loss is a constant challenge, Stanley Schachter (1982) was less pessimistic than most of today's obesity researchers about the dieter's chances of success. He recognized the overwhelming rate of failure among those in structured weight-loss programs, but he also noted that these people are a special group who probably have been unable to help themselves. Moreover, the failure rates recorded for these programs are based on single attempts at weight loss. Perhaps when people try repeatedly to lose weight, more of them do eventually succeed. When Schachter interviewed people, he found that one-fourth had at one time been significantly overweight and had tried to slim down. Of these, 6 out of 10 had *succeeded*: They weighed at least 10 percent less than their maximum prediet weight (an average loss of 35 pounds) and were no longer obese. A 1993 survey of 90,000 *Consumer Reports* readers found 25 percent of dieters claiming an enduring weight loss. Aided by media publicity, the National Weight Control Registry has identified more than 4000 people who have maintained significant weight loss for at least one year and are being studied over time. On average, these people have lost 60 pounds and kept it off for five years, virtually always with continued diet and exercise.

Excerpt from a Professional Journal (*Teaching English in the Two-Year College*)

Power Tip

As these examples show, academic writing often includes information from outside sources. For more on various sources of ideas, see Chapter 3.

This paragraph is from an article titled "Writing Back," in which scholar Sharon J. Mitchler discusses instructor responses to student writing and what students want in instructor comments.

[. . . What] should instructor's comments look like? There is no consensus. In fact, a look at recent discussion reveals a different answer from each researcher. Tracey Baker, associate professor of English at the University of Alabama at Birmingham, focused on conflict in her study of student reaction to teacher comments (179). Using student questionnaires distributed at the beginning and then again at the end of her courses, Baker identified areas where conflict is a part of the learning process (180). She discovered that conflict results when students "set themselves up for failure [. . .] think effort is enough [. . . when] expectations of the course, the

CONTINUED >

instructor and their writing are contradicted [. . .] misunderstand instructor's comments [. . .] set inappropriate goals [. . .] set unrealistic goals [and . . .] don't want to revise" (181–88). This means that comments need to reflect an awareness of these conflicts (190). Expectations need to be clearly communicated by the instructor (190). Importantly, talking with students in conferences, as well as "before, during, and after class" will help the instructor check to be [. . .] sure there has been no miscommunication (190). Comments need to connect with experiences in other courses in order to decrease student concerns, and, during each assignment, the criteria need to be "emphasized, taught and retaught" so students can succeed and feel "in control of their work" (190). For Baker, written comments are not isolated components of the course but are instead one part of a dynamic series of exchanges between instructor and student.

Paragraph Written for an English Course

Hip-hop music speaks to me like no other music. First of all, I just love the sound of it. Great rappers like Mos Def and Nelly have an energetic vocal style that gets me to my feet, and they get a solid rhythm down even if there's no drumming or other music in the background. When there is music, whether from instruments or sampling, the sound can be even richer. Drum tracks, guitar riffs, and even horns add to the energy and style. Second, I love the poetry and storytelling of hip-hop music. The poetry comes partly from rhyming, but it's more than that; the words of these artists (like Kanye West talking about giving "salty looks") can create vivid pictures in the listeners' minds. Also, whether they are singing about their own lives or things that are going on in the streets or in the larger world, talented rappers know how to "tell it like it is"; they tell stories that their listeners can relate to. Finally, I love the tradition of inventiveness in hip-hop music. For example, artists sample tracks of other musicians to create new songs. Also, hip-hop has inspired invention in the worlds of fashion and dance. Artists are always coming up with new clothing styles and dance moves that fans want to imitate. For all these reasons, I love hip-hop, and it will always be in my heart.

thinking outside the book

Find a textbook for another course, or get an academic journal from the college library. Compare the paragraphs you see in those examples with the ones shown here. Although not all the paragraphs will be exactly alike, most of them will be *long* (usually more than five sentences and sometimes up to ten or fifteen), and often the sentences will be longer than in other types of writing. Also, academic paragraphs often express one main idea (typically at the beginning of the paragraph), which is thoroughly supported by examples or other details. Can you find the main ideas and support in the previous academic paragraphs and in the examples you found on your own? (You will learn more about main ideas and support in Chapters 4 and 5.)

REVIEW

Let's review the basic features of the different types of paragraphs:

Features of Different Types of Paragraphs

Journalism **Business writing**	Paragraphs are of short or medium length (usually one to five sentences), expressing one or a few ideas.
Popular fiction and nonfiction **Personal writing**	Paragraphs may be of any length, although short to medium-length paragraphs are common.
Academic writing	Paragraphs are long (usually more than five sentences, and sometimes up to ten or fifteen), often expressing a main idea that is thoroughly supported.

Most colleges offer courses in journalism, business writing, and English composition; these courses usually offer specific guidelines for the length, content, and structure of paragraphs. In courses teaching fiction and nonfiction writing, the guidelines will be more flexible, and greater originality will be encouraged.

In your English composition course (and in the course for which you are using this book), you will practice the skills necessary for writing academic paragraphs in particular. You will not be writing short or medium-length paragraphs; rather, you will be writing well-developed paragraphs, usually of more than five sentences, with a main idea and a series of supporting points. Keep in mind, however, that the skills you will learn for academic writing—organization, development, and grammar—will help you write more effectively in any other course or situation.

Teaching Tip
If you have specific requirements for the length of paragraphs that students will write for this course, now is a good time to share your expectations with students.

ACTIVITY 7: Teamwork

With your classmates, discuss the basic features of each of the following excerpts. Then, identify which type of writing each excerpt belongs to. As a reminder, the types are

- journalism
- business writing
- popular fiction
- popular nonfiction
- personal writing
- academic writing

EXAMPLE:

Tolls on state turnpikes will be raised by as much as fifty cents by early 2010 if a state legislative committee's plan is approved.

"We can't maintain our roadways at the current level of funding," said state senator Rick Bartley, chair of the State Transportation Committee and a chief architect of the plan. "Unless we raise tolls—or take funds from other projects—desperately needed road and bridge repairs will not be possible."

CONTINUED >

In response, Rita Mendos, Ways and Means Committee chair, commented, "That's a lot of nonsense. We shouldn't be looking at fifty-cent toll hikes until we have exhausted all other possibilities."

Type of writing: journalism

1. Being a good listener is more than sitting quietly while another person speaks and occasionally making acknowledging sounds like "um-hum" and "yeah." Good listeners listen *actively,* meaning that they really take in others' words and monitor whether they *understand* what is being said and what they *think* about it. For example, if a friend is describing a conflict in a relationship, the listener might ask herself questions like, "Do I really understand what the conflict is? What chain of events led to the conflict? Do I agree with the speaker's assessment of the situation?"

   As odd as it might sound, good listeners feel comfortable occasionally interrupting the speaker to ask clarifying questions. Speakers generally appreciate the opportunity to make their points clear, and listeners will be able to converse with greater engagement when it is their turn to speak.

   In this chapter, we'll take a closer look at these and other strategies for effective listening.

   Type of writing: popular nonfiction

2. Binge drinking, consuming a large volume of alcohol in a brief period, is a common and serious problem at many colleges (Comer, 2007). Disturbing findings from several studies have led some experts to call binge drinking "the No. 1 public health hazard" for full-time college students (Wechsler et al., 1995). Researchers have found that 43.4 percent of college students binge drink at least once annually, with around 50 percent of students engaging in this behavior six or more times a month (Sharma, 2005; Wechsler et al., 2004, 2000, 1997, 1994). Disturbingly, alcohol is a factor in nearly 40 percent of academic problems and in 28 percent of all drop-out cases (Anderson, 1994). Additionally, binge drinking has been linked to car accidents, bodily injury, date rape and other aggressive behavior, and psychological problems (Wechsler & Wuethrich, 2002). As a result, the problem affects not only the drinker but also his or her friends and acquaintances, and even strangers. Even students who are well-behaved and nonaggressive when sober can act out in disturbing, even violent, ways when they have had too much to drink. In the mid-1990s, a survey of U.S. college students found that those most likely to binge drink tended to center their social lives on parties, to engage in other high-risk behaviors, and to live in fraternity or sorority houses (Wechsler et al., 1995). Many universities are targeting these at-risk populations by offering counseling and alternatives to drinking-centered social activities, among other responses. Additionally, some universities are declaring certain dorms "substance-free."

   Type of writing: academic writing

3. Dear Uncle Paul,

I want to thank you for your generous graduation gift, but more than that, I want to thank you for being there for me at all times.

You know it hasn't been easy for me and Mom, and I haven't always been the best son to her or nephew to you. But you've always understood the situation and haven't judged me or Mom. Instead, you've helped us with kind words and acts of support.

Also, you've been like a father to me in so many ways. You've done the fun stuff, like taking me to baseball games and movies, but you've also had the courage to do the tough things, like telling me to stay in school and act like an adult, even though other kids might make fun of me. I got angry when you said these things, but I know now that you said them out of love for me, and I appreciate it.

I just want to thank you again for everything, Uncle Paul. I couldn't have made it through high school without your support.

Love always,
Anthony

Type of writing: personal writing

4. A Middleton teen is in critical condition after crashing her sport utility vehicle into the Myers Road overpass on Route 87 Tuesday evening, state police reported.

Seventeen-year-old Lexie Peters, a senior at Catholic Memorial High School, was taken to Mercy Hospital in Rogersville after the crash. Witnesses reported that her vehicle, which was traveling south on Route 87 at around 11 p.m., swerved a few times before the crash. No other vehicles were involved.

Police are investigating the cause of the accident.

Type of writing: journalism

5. Detective Banes could tell by the way Phillips walked into the interrogation room that he had something to hide. Phillips shuffled in, pale and slouched, and he was wearing sunglasses, of all things, on this dark and rainy day.

"Take those things off," Banes said, pointing to the glasses, "and sit down."

Phillips hesitated, then removed his glasses, revealing bloodshot eyes. Without the glasses he looked more like the kid he was than the murderer he might be. Phillips sat down and leaned so far back in the chair his head rested on the back.

"Let's talk about what you were doing on the night of the thirteenth," Banes began.

"That's easy," Phillips laughed. "I had Chinese takeout and went to bed at ten."

"All right," Banes replied, smiling in spite of himself. "But let's talk about what happened between the fortune cookie and lights out."

Type of writing: popular fiction

CONTINUED >

6. I am pleased to report on the excellent performance of shipping manager Dave Nuñez for the year ending December 31, 2007. Dave is hard-working, highly competent, and admired by his employees.

Dave is one of our most skilled workers. In 2007, he took steps to improve his performance even more, including attending educational seminars and the special managers' course. Also, he created and implemented our new shipping efficiency program this year, and this program has increased the productivity of our shipping operation by 25% since it began in March.

Additionally, Dave is one of the best trainers at our company. His shipping crew is the most efficient in the company's history, and this year he introduced a bonus program to reward top employees in the shipping department. This incentive program has increased productivity even further. Dave is known for encouraging teamwork and collegiality among his employees, and as a result, the working environment in the shipping area is as pleasant as it is professional. Dave's employees appreciate his efforts and take pride in their work.

Type of writing: business writing

ACTIVITY 8

Identify the type of paragraph that is appropriate for each of the following writing projects. The types are

- journalism
- business writing
- popular fiction
- popular nonfiction
- personal writing
- academic writing

EXAMPLE: a textbook chapter on causes of the Vietnam war

Type of paragraph: academic writing

1. an article in *People* magazine
   Type of paragraph: journalism
2. a short story about aliens
   Type of paragraph: popular fiction
3. a letter of apology to your girlfriend
   Type of paragraph: personal writing
4. a book that helps you analyze your dreams
   Type of paragraph: popular nonfiction
5. an essay for your American history class
   Type of paragraph: academic writing
6. a description of policy changes from your health maintenance organization (HMO)
   Type of paragraph: business writing

Understanding Your Purpose: Why You Will Write

Now, let us turn to the issue of *why* you write. Every time you write, you write for a reason, or **purpose**. It is hard to imagine anyone deciding to write something without a reason for doing so. To illustrate this simple point about purpose, complete the following activity.

ACTIVITY 9: Teamwork

Discuss with your classmates the reason, or purpose, for each of the following writing projects. Then, fill in the blank with the author's likely purpose. Answers may vary.

EXAMPLE: a computer buyer's complaint about poor service

Her purpose: to have her concerns heard and addressed

1. a supervisor's one-year review of your job performance

   Her purpose: to let you know what you are doing well and what you need to improve on; also, possibly, to show that you do or do not deserve a raise

2. an e-mail in which you give a friend directions to your apartment

   Your purpose: to make sure your friend gets to your apartment

3. a movie critic's review of a new action film

   His purpose: to give others an opinion of the movie to help them decide whether or not they want to see it

4. a scary new novel from Stephen King

   His purpose: to entertain (scare) readers; also, possibly, to sell books

5. a medical researcher's article about the discovery of a new AIDS drug

   His purpose: to inform readers about the discovery

From these examples, it is clear that we always write for some purpose or reason. But why is it necessary for a writer to understand his or her purpose? Why is purpose an important part of the big picture?

To answer this question, we need to look more closely at the idea of purpose itself. In truth, a writer may have *more than one* purpose for a writing project. Identifying all the purposes for a particular writing project will help you make important decisions about what type of paragraph to write, what information to include, and what information to leave out. Having a strong sense of purpose will also motivate you to write with clarity and power.

For any writing that you do, you should be aware of three levels of purpose:

- general purpose
- specific purpose
- personal purpose

KNOW YOUR GENERAL PURPOSE

In the broadest sense, the purpose of all writing is to communicate information or ideas. Beyond this, we can identify the following general purposes for most of the writing that we do:

- **to inform:** to provide information about a specific issue or topic. For example, a visitors' center at a state park might offer a brochure informing hikers about the causes and prevention of forest fires.
- **to educate:** to broaden someone's knowledge or expertise, often for academic or professional purposes. For example, a textbook for a human development course might offer an in-depth discussion of the stages of emotional development in children.
- **to entertain:** to provide fun or amusement. For instance, a celebrity magazine might share gossip about a star's wedding.
- **to inspire:** to positively influence or motivate others. For example, an essay about the challenges and rewards of running a marathon might inspire others to admire the effort, if not to run a marathon themselves.
- **to persuade:** to argue that a certain action should be taken. For instance, a well-written letter might persuade city officials that a parking fine that you received was excessive and should be lowered.

Power Tip
Common purposes of academic writing are to inform, to educate, and to persuade.

Knowing the general purpose of your writing project will help you make effective choices about the information to include and how to present this information. If you are trying to inform readers, you will need to include the relevant facts and present them clearly and directly. If your purpose is to educate readers, you may need to present more complex information, but it will need to be stated as clearly as possible. If your aim is to entertain readers, you will need to present fun or interesting details, as creatively and originally as possible. If your aim is to inspire readers, you will need to include facts and details that will appeal to the readers' emotions or otherwise motivate them. And if you hope to persuade readers, you will need to provide good evidence for a proposed course of action.

To sum up, a general purpose answers this question: *What is the main goal of my writing project?* Do I want to inform, educate, entertain, inspire, or persuade my audience?

ACTIVITY 10

Identify the general purpose for each of the following writing projects: to inform, to educate, to entertain, to inspire, or to persuade.

EXAMPLE: a humorist writing a column on the different types of baseball fans

General purpose: to entertain

1. a nurse writing a memo to a doctor about a patient's condition

   General purpose: to inform

2. a student writing an e-mail to a friend explaining why she should go to college

   General purpose: to persuade

3. a cancer survivor writing a story about surviving the illness to give other patients hope

   General purpose: to inspire

4. a blogger describing a humorous experience he had

   General purpose: to entertain

5. a scholar explaining the causes of the "black death" that killed millions in the Middle Ages

   General purpose: to educate

In college, the purpose of many writing assignments will be to demonstrate to an instructor that you understand concepts from readings, lectures, or other material. Often, this purpose will not be directly stated in an assignment, but you will need to fulfill it to get a good grade. Consider this assignment from a psychology course:

> **Explain what *biofeedback training* is and how it is used to treat physical disorders.**

The unstated purpose of this assignment is for students to demonstrate that they understand a lecture or textbook material on the practice of biofeedback training. For more information on understanding and responding to writing assignments, see Chapter 2.

Teaching Tip
You might point out to students that the *form* of writing is often tied to its purpose. For example, journalistic pieces are often written in short paragraphs because the purpose usually is to present the facts as clearly and briefly as possible.

KNOW YOUR SPECIFIC PURPOSE

Once you have identified the general purpose for your writing project, you will need to select the specific information or ideas you want to communicate to your audience. For example, suppose that you are asked to write an essay on soccer for your physical education class. There is a lot of information that you could provide about the sport of soccer, so you will have to narrow your options and select one specific purpose. You could

- explain the rules of soccer
- give a brief history of soccer
- explain the organization of soccer leagues
- give a report on this year's World Cup

For a short writing assignment, one of these specific purposes should be sufficient. Identifying your specific purpose will help you include only the information that is necessary to achieve your purpose. In Chapter 2, you will get more advice on how to make writing assignments more specific (narrow) so that you can address them effectively.

To sum up, a specific purpose answers the question: *What specific information or ideas do I want to communicate to my audience?*

ACTIVITY 11: Teamwork

With your classmates, discuss the different information you could give about each of the following paragraph topics. Then, write down the specific purpose you would choose if you were writing on the topic. Answers will vary.

EXAMPLE: marriage

Specific purpose: to give reasons for not marrying

1. college

   Specific purpose: ______________________

2. spending money

   Specific purpose: ______________________

3. your ideal job

   Specific purpose: ______________________

4. religion

   Specific purpose: ______________________

5. the opposite sex

   Specific purpose: ______________________

IDENTIFY A PERSONAL PURPOSE

As a student or an employee, much of the writing you do will be **required writing**. This is writing that you must complete in order to pass a class or keep your job. Sometimes, it is difficult to feel motivated to do required writing because you may have little personal interest in the topic. To stay motivated when doing required writing, it is a good idea to identify a personal purpose that may or may not be related to the topic you are writing about.

A personal purpose answers this question: *Why is this writing project important for me, the writer? How can I benefit from doing this assignment?* If the topic is of personal interest to you, you may be motivated to learn more about the topic. If the topic is not of personal interest to you, you may have to find a personal purpose that is not related to the topic.

Power Tip
Whenever possible, choose a writing topic that is of personal interest to you so that you will stay motivated during the writing process.

For example, if you are writing about communication skills for your psychology class, you may decide that your personal purpose is to learn more about these skills so that you can communicate better with your family.

However, you will sometimes be assigned a topic for which you cannot find an angle of interest. In this case, you may have to find a personal purpose that is not related to the topic. Here are some examples of personal purpose statements that are not related to a specific topic:

- I will write the best essay I have ever written.
- I will be excited about learning something new and becoming a more knowledgeable person.
- I will keep an open mind and try to learn something new about myself.

- I will take pride in my work.
- I will think of myself as the person responsible for my success; I am in charge.
- I will show my teacher how much I have improved.

For more advice on finding a personal purpose for any writing assignment, see Chapter 2, page 42.

Power Tip
If you are writing on a topic that is not of personal interest to you, always try to formulate a personal purpose statement that will help you stay motivated.

ACTIVITY 12

Consider whether each of the following paragraph topics would be of personal interest to you as a writer. If the topic *is* of personal interest to you, explain why you would like to write about it (your personal purpose). If the topic is *not* of personal interest to you, write a personal purpose statement that is not related to the topic. Answers will vary.

EXAMPLES: a life lesson you learned of personal interest

Personal purpose: to understand myself better

biodiesel as an alternative to gas not of personal interest

Personal purpose: I will learn more about a way to help the environment.

1. the most beautiful person you have ever seen ______

   Personal purpose: ______
2. an algebraic principle that you learned in your math class ______

   Personal purpose: ______
3. the life of Martin Luther King ______

   Personal purpose: ______
4. identity theft ______

   Personal purpose: ______
5. electronic voting equipment ______

   Personal purpose: ______

Understanding Your Audience: For Whom You Will Write

Whenever you write, you always write *for someone*. If you are writing in a diary or journal, you will probably be writing *for yourself*. However, with most writing projects, you will be writing *for someone else*—your **audience**, or readers. This audience could be your instructor, your employer, your family or friends, or some other individual or group of people. To write effectively for any audience, you should

- identify who your audience will be
- understand the needs and expectations of your audience

- use language that is appropriate for your audience
- include information that is appropriate for your audience

IDENTIFY YOUR AUDIENCE

To identify the audience for any writing project, simply answer this question: *Who is the main person or persons who will read my work?*

For example, if you are writing an article for your college newspaper, your audience will be the students, faculty, and staff of the college. If you are writing a blog, your audience might consist of people with similar interests who found your blog during a Web search or through a link from another site. For most of your college writing, your audience will be your instructor and perhaps your classmates.

ACTIVITY 13: Teamwork

With your classmates, identify the main person or persons who would be reading each of the following writing projects. *Answers may vary.*

EXAMPLE: **a letter to the editor of your local newspaper about vandalism in your neighborhood**

Audience: ***readers of the newspaper***

1. an essay on inflation for your economics class

   Audience: *your instructor (and maybe other students)*

2. a personal statement for a college application

   Audience: *college admission officials*

3. a letter to the sheriff's department about reckless drivers in your neighborhood

   Audience: *department officers who are in a position to address the problem*

4. an e-mail to iTunes customer service about a refund that iTunes didn't send you

   Audience: *customer service representatives*

5. a speech that you will give at a Parent Teacher Association (PTA) meeting at your child's elementary school

   Audience: *parents, teachers, and others attending the meeting*

UNDERSTAND THE NEEDS AND EXPECTATIONS OF YOUR AUDIENCE

Different audiences have different needs and expectations. For example, if you were writing about your job as a firefighter for your daughter's third-grade class, you would need to express your ideas in simple language so that the children (your audience) would understand. Also, as young readers, the third graders would probably appreciate colorful and imaginative details. On the other hand, if you were writing a report for the fire chief on how your crew put out a blaze in a factory, the chief (your audience) would expect an honest and detailed explanation of the actions taken to put out the fire. Because the chief is an expert, you could use technical terms in your report, but you would still want your writing to be as clear as possible.

To understand the needs and expectations of your audience, try developing an **audience profile** by asking some of the following questions:

- What is your audience's general age range?
- What is your audience's educational background?
- What are your audience's language skills?
- Does your audience consist of experts or nonexperts?
- What is your relationship to the audience? (Do you know them well or not so well? Are you friendly with them, or is the relationship more formal?)
- How much time does the audience have to read?
- What are your audience's interests?

Your answers do not need to be exact. Often, you will have only a general sense of your audience's needs and expectations.

Teaching Tip
Ask students how they would describe the audiences of various television shows—for example, reality-TV shows, science programs, news shows, and crime dramas. How do the audiences differ in terms of age, interests, and other characteristics?

ACTIVITY 14

Create an audience profile for each of the following writing projects. To develop a profile, answer three or four of the questions preceding this activity. In some cases, you will need to make your best guess about the characteristics of a particular audience; use your imagination. *Answers will vary.*

EXAMPLE: a memo to your boss about new equipment purchases

Audience profile: My boss is very educated and has good language skills. She knows a little about the new equipment but would probably appreciate more information. She is busy and so doesn't have much time to read.

1. a letter to your state representative on school funding in your district

   Audience profile: ____________________

2. an article for your college newspaper on student loan policies

   Audience profile: ____________________

CONTINUED >

3. a presentation to seventh graders on sex education

   Audience profile: ______________________________

4. an essay for your literature professor on a Shakespeare play

   Audience profile: ______________________________

5. an e-mail to *Newsweek* magazine about an article it published

   Audience profile: ______________________________

USE LANGUAGE THAT IS APPROPRIATE FOR YOUR AUDIENCE

slang: informal language often used between friends or within other social groups. *Dis* for *disrespect* is an example of slang.

If you are writing an e-mail or text message to a friend, you can use abbreviations (like *CU* for *see you* or *UR* for *you are*) that make your writing fast and fun. You will probably use some slang, and you may break grammar rules. On the other hand, if you are writing a letter to your apartment manager, you will want to avoid abbreviations, slang, and any profanity that could offend your manager. Although you will want your writing to be clear and easy to understand, your grammar will probably be "relaxed"—correct enough for clear communication but not perfect.

Finally, if you are writing an essay on cloning for your biology class, your instructor will expect you to use more formal language and grammar. Also, you may need to use some technical language related to the topic of cloning; because your audience (the instructor) will be knowledgeable about the topic, such language will be acceptable, even expected. You will also need to follow grammar rules carefully and to write complete, correct sentences.

The following chart summarizes the expectations of a few common audiences for whom you will write.

Teaching Tip
You might ask students to write an e-mail to a friend that complains about a campus problem. Then, ask them to rewrite the e-mail to address an administrator who is in a position to correct the problem. They should describe the problem, indicate why it is a serious issue, and, if possible, identify some ways to address it. After the students have finished the activity, ask some of them to read their e-mails aloud to the class. Finally, as a class, discuss the differences between the e-mails and how the language changed (or should have changed) to address the two different audiences. You might point out that even though the medium of the two messages is the same (e-mail), the language is different because of the different audiences.

Different Audiences' Expectations for Writing

Audience	Level of Formality Expected	Level of Vocabulary Expected	Acceptance of Grammar Errors
Friends	informal; slang acceptable	simple vocabulary (usually)	accepted
Instructors	formal; slang not acceptable	moderate to difficult vocabulary (technical terms may be used)	not accepted
Work supervisors or employees	formal; slang not acceptable	moderate to difficult vocabulary (technical terms may be used)	not accepted

ACTIVITY 15: Teamwork

With your classmates, discuss what type of language would be appropriate for each of the following pieces of writing. Then, describe the language, referring to the three features shown in the previous chart. Answers may vary.

EXAMPLE: a memo to employees about changes to health benefits

Appropriate language: formal language; moderate to difficult vocabulary; correct grammar

1. a paper on exploration of the American West for a history class

   Appropriate language: formal language; moderate to difficult vocabulary; correct grammar

2. a letter to the principal of your child's elementary school

   Appropriate language: formal language; moderate vocabulary; correct grammar

3. an online party invitation (to friends)

   Appropriate language: informal language; simple vocabulary; relaxed grammar

4. an in-class essay exam for your literature class

   Appropriate language: formal language; moderate to difficult vocabulary; correct grammar

5. an e-mail to your supervisor asking for a meeting about a project you are working on

   Appropriate language: formal language; moderate to difficult vocabulary; correct grammar

INCLUDE INFORMATION THAT IS APPROPRIATE FOR YOUR AUDIENCE

If your audience has little knowledge about or experience with your topic, you will need to include the most basic information possible. For example, if you are giving car maintenance advice to someone who knows little about cars, you will need to provide very basic advice, such as the need to change the oil regularly.

If your audience has a lot of knowledge or experience, you may skip very basic information and move directly to more advanced information. A car expert would already know about the need for regular oil changes but might want to hear about the latest technology for increasing engine efficiency.

If your audience is somewhere in between, be careful to balance the amount and difficulty of the information you provide. If the information you provide is too simple for your audience, you may lose their interest; if the information is too advanced for your audience, they may not understand your writing.

Power Tip
Consider the amount of time your audience has, too. If you are writing to a busy boss or co-worker, for example, it's best to make your writing as brief and to the point as possible. E-mails, especially, should be as brief as possible.

To decide what kind of information is appropriate for your audience, always answer this question: *How much experience or knowledge does my audience have regarding the topic?*

Note: Even though your college instructors will usually have a lot of knowledge about the topics on which they ask you to write, they might want your writing to include even basic information about a topic so that they know that you understand the topic fully. Whenever you are in doubt about the type of information that is appropriate for a college paper, ask your instructor.

ACTIVITY 16

Write down the type of information (basic, intermediate, or advanced) that would be appropriate for the following audiences. Answers may vary.

EXAMPLE: a description of the making of stained-glass windows for second graders

Appropriate information: basic

1. an essay on jazz for your modern dance instructor

   Appropriate information: advanced, but verify with your instructor that basic information should not be included

2. a paragraph on campfire safety for first-year Girl Scouts

   Appropriate information: basic

3. a description of how wine is made for a group of wine drinkers

   Appropriate information: intermediate

4. an explanation of how to use PowerPoint for your mother or father

   Appropriate information: basic

5. a list of safety reminders for hikers climbing Mount Everest for the second time

   Appropriate information: intermediate

Understanding Your Rhetoric: How You Will Write

In this section, you will be introduced to the idea of **rhetoric**. Rhetoric is *the art of using language effectively*. When you use language that is appropriate for your audience and your purpose, your writing projects will be more successful.

In our everyday communication, we use a number of **rhetorical strategies**, or **patterns of development**, to express our ideas clearly and effectively. Let's look at the five most common patterns:

- We can describe something (**description**).
- We can give examples of something (**exemplification**).

- We can tell a story (**narration**).
- We can explain how something happens or how to do something (**process**).
- We can explain what something means (**definition**).

If your art professor talks about the brush technique in a painting, she will probably use description. If you tell your family about your successes in college, you will probably use exemplification. If you tell your friend what happened in last night's episode of *Cold Case*, you will probably use narration. If you explain to your mother how to download music to her iPod, you will probably use process. If you ask the cashier at Starbucks what a "triple grande frappuccino wet latte decaf" is, he will probably respond with a definition, telling you the drink's ingredients.

When we write, we use these same patterns of development to communicate our ideas. Good writers are especially aware of when and how they use these patterns. (You will learn more about these and other development strategies in Appendix A.)

ACTIVITY 17

In each of the following paragraphs, the author uses one major pattern of development to communicate the information. First, read the paragraph. Then, identify the pattern and answer the question connected to it.

- Description (What is described?)
- Exemplification (What idea or concept are the examples intended to show?)
- Narration (What story does it tell?)
- Process (What steps or instructions are explained?)
- Definition (What idea or term is being defined?) Answers may vary.

EXAMPLE:

The best recipe for apple crisp is also quite simple. First, preheat the oven to 350 degrees. Then, line a 9-by-12-inch baking dish with six cored, peeled, and sliced baking apples (preferably, tart ones). Pour one-half cup of apple juice over the apples, followed by one-fourth cup of honey. Mix well. In a separate bowl, combine one and a half cups of oatmeal, one-half cup of whole-wheat flour, one-half teaspoon of salt, and one teaspoon of cinnamon. Then, using two knives, cut into this mixture one stick of slightly softened butter, until the butter is evenly distributed through the dry ingredients. Spread this mixture evenly over the apples, and place the dish in the oven. Bake for 45 minutes and serve warm, adding vanilla ice cream if you'd like.

Pattern used/answer to question about pattern: process.
The paragraph explains the steps of making apple crisp.

CONTINUED >

1. My daughter, who just got engaged, asked me what it means to have a good marriage. I had to think about her question for a bit, but then I came up with an answer that satisfies me, and I hope it satisfied her. To me, a good marriage is being with someone you look forward to seeing at the end of the day, even after years of togetherness. The two of you will have your disagreements, but you will always come back to wanting to share the stories, fun times, and difficulties of your lives. A good marriage is one in which you find balance, not only in responsibilities but also between together time and alone time; you give each other space and room to grow. Perhaps most important, a good marriage is one in which each person truly respects the other, for when respect isn't there, nothing positive can happen. Last, but certainly not least, a good marriage requires laughter. I'm not kidding when I tell people that I married my husband because he makes me laugh more than anyone else. Then, I realized that he was smart and good-looking, too!

Pattern used/answer to question about pattern: definition. The paragraph defines "a good marriage."

2. My uncle's farm is one of the most beautiful places that I have ever seen. Set in a valley between two high ridges, it is a patchwork of well-tended fields that are deep green in the summer and golden in the fall. A brook runs along the southern end of the property, and willow trees bend toward the clear water, where there are darting little fish. Between the brook and the main barn is my uncle's flower and vegetable garden, which at the peak of summer is crowded with fragrant bushes of yellow and pink roses, thick vines of tomatoes, and towering sunflowers. The farmhouse itself is a gem—a 150-year-old wooden structure that is as plain and white as a country church yet striking in its simple beauty. The rocker-lined front porch seems to welcome anyone who might drive up the lane.

Pattern used/answer to question about pattern: description. The paragraph describes the uncle's farm.

3. The longer you study, the greater your chances of scoring well on a test, right? That's not necessarily true. It's not uncommon for students who score poorly on an exam to protest, "But I studied for hours!" However, they might not have learned to study *effectively*, making the best use of their time. To study effectively, successful students follow several key steps. First, before an exam, these students respectfully ask their instructor for study guidelines. (Instead of saying, "So tell us what's on the test," they might ask, "Can you give us some general guidelines about what topics will be covered or how we should prepare?") This information provides a *purpose* for studying. Next, when it is time to study, successful students find a place where they will remain awake and undistracted: a desk in a library is preferable to a bed near a television. Then, with their purpose in mind, they reread lectures, textbook sections, and other materials, underlining material that is especially relevant to the purpose and marking questions next to points that they do not understand. When they have finished this review, they go back to these questions and try to answer them, using any chapter summaries or other review materials that are available. Finally, if the instructor has provided sample test questions—or if review questions are available in the textbook—the students may try to answer these as a final check of their readiness for the exam.

Pattern used/answer to question about pattern: process. The paragraph explains the steps of studying for an exam.

4. Small expressions of gratitude take little effort yet go a long way toward letting people know that others care. For example, thank-you notes take minutes to write but make givers of gifts or favors feel appreciated. (In contrast, not receiving a thank-you can have the opposite effect: making the giver feel that the gift was not important or worth acknowledging.) As another example, acknowledging the hard work of an employee or co-worker can take seconds, but it shows that the person's efforts are noticed and appreciated, and it may motivate him or her further. It is especially thoughtful and productive to share such positive information with supervisors or others who are in a position to give the employee a promotion or a raise. It is even worthwhile to extend the small courtesy of saying "thank you" to someone who holds a door open for you. Such gratitude rewards and encourages kindness, and it just makes people feel good. Think of how nice it is to hear "thank you," no matter what your good deed.

Pattern used/answer to question about pattern: exemplification. The paragraph gives examples that show how small expressions of gratitude are beneficial.

5. The most difficult time of my life was when my wife and I learned that our son, Aidan, was autistic. When he was a baby, he didn't smile and react to others the way his older sister, Lara, did. He cried a lot, and he didn't like to be held. As he grew older, he didn't learn to speak as early or as well as Lara and the other children around him did, and he didn't play well with other kids. When he was five, my wife and I received the official diagnosis of autism for Aidan, and we were crushed. We knew that he would have a much tougher time succeeding in life than kids without this problem, and we were worried that we wouldn't know what to do to help him. However, we have received great counseling, and Aidan is now thriving at a school that has teachers who are experts in working with autistic children. Aidan is speaking more, doing well in school, and even playing more with other children. The future will be challenging, but Aidan is a bright and wonderful kid, and my wife and I are hopeful.

Pattern used/answer to question about pattern: narration. The paragraph tells the story of an autism diagnosis and its outcome.

ACTIVITY 18: Teamwork

For each of the following writing projects, discuss with classmates which pattern of development would communicate the information most effectively. Then, write your chosen pattern in the space provided. You do not have to agree with your classmates in your final choice.

As a reminder, patterns of development are

- description
- exemplification
- narration
- process
- definition Answers may vary.

EXAMPLE: **Purpose:** to explain to your roommate why the two of you should move from your current apartment

Pattern of development: exemplification

1. **Purpose:** to teach someone to perform mouth-to-mouth resuscitation

   Pattern of development: process

2. **Purpose:** to tell someone about the final dramatic minutes of a championship soccer match

   Pattern of development: narration

3. **Purpose:** to help someone understand the different ranks in the U.S. Army

   Pattern of development: definition

4. **Purpose:** to explain why you are the most dedicated employee at work

   Pattern of development: exemplification

5. **Purpose:** to tell someone about the most beautiful sunset you have ever seen

   Pattern of development: description

Identifying Different Features of Paragraphs

The following activity will give you more practice in identifying the different features of the types of paragraphs discussed previously.

Teaching Tip
For additional practice, students might identify the type of paragraph, general purpose, and so on for paragraphs in the readings in Part Three of this book.

ACTIVITY 19

For each of the following paragraphs, identify the type of paragraph, the general and specific purposes, the audience, and the pattern(s) of development used. (You may not be able to identify the exact audience. Do your best to suggest a likely audience for each paragraph.) Answers may vary.

Here is a reminder of the types of paragraphs, general purposes, and patterns of development. For a discussion of specific purposes, see page 19.

TYPES OF PARAGRAPHS	GENERAL PURPOSES	PATTERNS OF DEVELOPMENT
• journalism • business writing • popular fiction or nonfiction • personal writing • academic writing	• to inform • to educate • to entertain • to inspire • to persuade	• exemplification • description • narration • process • definition

EXAMPLE:

What overpublicized teen queen was caught sharing an intimate dinner with her "Reform School Musical" co-star over Labor Day weekend? Yes, Destiny Dearwood and her new man, Fate James, were seen dining over candlelight at the Ritz Club. Spies reported that the pretty pair sat so close together that you couldn't have slipped a cocktail napkin between them, and Destiny was running her fingers through Fate's thick, dark curls. Destiny wore a champagne-colored Versace minidress and matching Christian Louboutin heels, while Fate was pure elegance in a light blue Prada suit.

Type of paragraph: journalism

General purpose: to entertain (could also be to inform)

Specific purpose: to describe the intimate dinner date of two stars

Audience: readers of a celebrity publication

Pattern of development (one): description

1. Hey Jameel,

   I'm on break, so I wanted to e-mail you about why I think you should consider Hampton Beach for your kids' vacation week. First, there's an inexpensive motel, the Seaside Lodge, right on the beach. It's clean and comfortable, and it costs $500 a week for a room with two double beds—not bad for a whole week. Also, Hampton Beach has lots of fun things to do. The kids can swim and play in the sand, and there's a business that rents bodyboards and rafts for $10 a day. Also, the beach has an arcade and a little amusement park. The games in the arcade are fun but not violent. Finally, there are lots of good places to eat, including delicious seafood restaurants and fast-food stands in case your kids don't eat fish. I hope this helps!—Cassandra

   Type of paragraph: personal

   General purpose: to persuade

   Specific purpose: to explain why Hampton Beach is a good place for a family vacation

   Audience: Jameel (a friend)

   Pattern of development (one): exemplification

CONTINUED >

2. To: All Blumax Software employees
Fr: The management

It is time to nominate the employee of the year, so I would like to inform you about the type of person to whom we hope to give the award and about how to nominate a candidate. The employee of the year should be someone who has made a positive difference in the performance of the company by implementing a new policy or procedure, by working especially hard or creatively, by motivating others, or by taking any other action that has significantly improved our operations. To nominate a candidate, please write his or her name on the attached form and your reason for selecting this person. (Please be as specific as possible.) Then, put your completed form in the "Employee of the Year" box outside of Rebecca Liu's office on the third floor. Thank you for your cooperation.

Type of paragraph: business writing

General purpose: to inform

Specific purpose: to explain the characteristics of the employee of the year and how to nominate someone for the award

Audience: Blumax Software employees

Patterns of development (two): definition, process (Exemplification is also a possibility.)

unsanitary: unclean or unhealthy

punctuality: being on time or on schedule

3. In *Down and Out in Paris and London,* the famous social critic George Orwell wrote of the unsanitary conditions in a hotel kitchen, where he washed dishes practically around the clock. He commented: "[W]e had no orders to be genuinely clean, and in any case we had no time for it. We were simply carrying out our duties; and our first duty was punctuality, we saved time by being dirty." In a two-week investigation of three campus restaurants, two other students and I discovered much the same sacrifice of cleanliness to punctuality. For example, at the first restaurant, we discovered employees who did not wash their hands after handling raw meat and those who served food after it had been dropped on the floor. At the second restaurant, gobs of old, smelly grease were dripping from the stove fans, and piles of food-speckled dirt had been swept into the corners but not removed. At the third restaurant, we made rounds with a city health inspector, who found rodent droppings in a food storage area and behind the stove. He also noticed that vegetables were being cut on a surface that had recently held raw beef. Our conclusion, developed in the remainder of this article, is that public health officials need to monitor local restaurants more carefully and be more aggressive in fining establishments that do not comply with health regulations. Those that have received three fines without taking action to address health concerns should be closed. This is in line with the "three strikes" policy recently adopted in other cities in our state.

Type of paragraph: academic writing (Journalism is also a possibility.)

General purposes (two): to inform, to persuade

Specific purpose: to describe unsanitary conditions at local restaurants and explain why stricter health measures are needed

Audience: readers of a student academic journal or other serious publication

Patterns of development (two): exemplification, description

Bringing It All Together

In this chapter, you have learned what a paragraph is, the differences between various types of paragraphs, the importance of knowing your purpose and audience, and various patterns for developing paragraphs. Check off each of the following statements that you understand. For any that you do not understand, review the appropriate pages in this chapter.

☐ Different types of writing use different types of paragraphs. College students encounter the following types of writing most frequently:

____ **journalism**, writing for newspapers, magazines, or news-related Web sites (See page 5.)

____ **business writing**, consisting of all written communication in the workplace (See page 6.)

____ **popular fiction**, novels and stories, and **popular nonfiction**, including biographies, autobiographies, and informational books (See page 7.)

____ **personal writing**, including written communication among friends and family members, as well as private writing, such as that done in personal journals or diaries (See page 9.)

____ **academic writing**, typically used at (and often produced at) colleges and universities, and including student essays, textbooks, and scholarly books and articles by professors and other academics (See page 10.)

☐ Paragraphs in journalism and business writing are of short to medium length (usually one to five sentences), expressing one or a few ideas. In popular fiction and nonfiction, as well as in personal writing, paragraphs may be of any length, although short to medium-length paragraphs are common. Academic paragraphs are long (usually more than five sentences), often expressing a main idea that is thoroughly supported. (See page 12.)

☐ Your purpose is why you write. There are three levels of purpose:

____ your **general purpose**: to inform, to educate, to entertain, to inspire, or to persuade (See page 18.)

____ your **specific purpose**: the specific information or ideas you want to communicate to your audience about a topic (See page 19.)

____ your **personal purpose**: something to motivate you to write; this purpose may or may not be related to the topic you are writing about (See page 20.)

☐ Your **audience** is the person or people you write for. To write effectively, you should identify who your audience will be, understand the needs and expectations of your audience, use language that is appropriate for your audience, and include information that is appropriate for your audience. (See page 21.)

☐ We use a number of **rhetorical strategies**, or **patterns of development**, to express our ideas clearly: we can describe something (*description*), give examples of something (*exemplification*), tell a story (*narration*), explain how something happens or how to do something (*process*), or explain what something means (*definition*). (See page 26.)

Chapter 2

Understanding and Working with Writing Assignments

OVERVIEW OF THIS CHAPTER

WARM-UP Playing to Win

1. *Imagine these situations:*

- You're an expert video game player who has been invited to compete in a national championship. As a special challenge, you and the others will be required to use a new and unfamiliar game, *Death Star Showdown.* Fortunately, you have all received the game's description and rulebook in advance.
- You are applying for a job that you really want. In addition to submitting a résumé with your qualifications, you must answer the following question on the application: "Describe a challenging work situation that you handled well. Be sure to tell us exactly what you did to resolve the situation."

2. *Stop and think!*

Pick one of the situations and, working alone or with classmates, consider what you would do to prepare for the video game championship or to answer the question on the job application.

In these situations, it's important for the game player and the job applicant to understand exactly what's expected of them. For example, the player would need to know that the "death star" is red, not blue or green—or he might blast the wrong star and be eliminated. He'd want to review the rulebook carefully, perhaps highlighting key instructions.

The job applicant will need to be very specific in describing the work situation she handled well. If she says only, "I won back a disappointed customer," it won't be clear why the customer was disappointed and what the applicant did to satisfy the customer. The potential employer might judge the applicant as having poor attention to detail.

Similarly, you need to understand—and specifically meet—the expectations of writing assignments to succeed in your college courses. This chapter will help you do just that.

Understanding the Parts of Writing Assignments

In Chapter 1 you learned about the features of different types of paragraphs. You also learned the importance of keeping a clear purpose and audience in mind, no matter what type of writing you are doing. In college, you will typically write *academic* paragraphs in response to specific assignments. Although these assignments may look quite different, most of them will have three main parts:

- Practical information
- The topic
- Supporting information

Here is a short writing assignment that has all three parts:

> **Week 3 Paragraph Assignment: Due January 19th**
>
> All of us have had to make hard decisions—from what expenses to eliminate from a tight budget to whether or not to start or end a romantic relationship. In a paragraph of at least two hundred words, describe a hard decision you had to make and discuss what the consequences have been (good, bad, or both). Be sure to include a topic sentence, specific examples, and a concluding sentence. Proofread your paragraph for grammar and spelling before you turn it in.

If an assignment is carefully formulated, you should be able to identify each of these parts quite easily. However, in some cases, you may not be able to distinguish one part from another. Or one or more of the parts may be missing from the assignment. In these cases, you should feel confident about asking your instructor for clarification or additional information.

Now, let's look more closely at each part of the writing assignment.

Teaching Tip
For models of various documents, with information about how papers in various disciplines should be formatted, refer students to **bedfordstmartins.com/modeldocs**.

PRACTICAL INFORMATION

Practical information may specify some or all of the following:

- Whether the writing is a take-home or in-class assignment.
- How much time you have to complete the assignment.
- Required number of words, paragraphs, or pages.
- Formatting instructions (how pages should be labeled and spaced, what size margins are required, what fonts are allowed, and so on).

Power Tip
Information that seems to be missing from an assignment, including the due date, may actually be specified in the course syllabus. Read the syllabus carefully at the beginning of any course and refer back to it for details about particular assignments as you start them.

- Required or recommended sources for gathering your ideas (textbook, class discussions, articles, Web sites, and so on).
- Requirements for citing and documenting (providing publication information for) any outside sources used.
- Rules about seeking help from a tutor, from friends, and from others.
- Information on grading, for example, how much value the assignment has and how it will be factored into your larger grade.
- Specifics about features your paper should include, such as an introduction, topic sentences, examples, details, and a conclusion.
- Recommendations for drafting, revising, and proofreading.

For more on developing topic sentences and drafting, see Chapter 5. For more on generating examples and details, see Chapters 3 and 6. For more on revising and proofreading, see Chapter 7.

THE TOPIC

The topic is the main subject or task of your writing assignment. A good writing assignment will make the topic very clear. When looking for the topic, keep in mind the following:

- The topic is often expressed in one sentence (as one main idea).
- The topic may be expressed as a single question or as a series of questions.
- You may have a choice of topics.

SUPPORTING INFORMATION

Supporting information provides other details that are helpful in completing the assignment. It may include some or all of the following:

- Background information on the topic.
- Definitions of key terms in the topic.
- A series of questions to help you explore the topic.
- Suggestions for generating ideas or for narrowing the topic.
- Recommendations about information to include or avoid.
- Information about the general purpose of the assignment (to inform, to entertain, to persuade, and so on). For more details, see page 16.
- Suggestions about the audience for the assignment. For more on writing for a specific audience, see page 21.

Not all assignments will include supporting information. For more detailed advice on working with supporting information, see page 46.

Power Tip
Pay attention to oral as well as written instructions for an assignment, because some important information might be spoken but not written down. Be sure to *take notes* while your instructor is describing an assignment.

ACTIVITY 1

Label the practical information, the topic, and the supporting information in the assignments below.

EXAMPLE: Human Development 101

Jean Piaget defines intelligence as the ability to adapt what one has learned in one situation to a new situation. Others define intelligence in terms of an ability to absorb and retrieve facts and other information. In a paper of no more than 500 words, write your own definition of intelligence. You can work with one other classmate to discuss possible definitions and generate ideas, but each of you should write a separate paper. This assignment is due at the start of class on Monday, December 3rd.

Supporting information
Practical information
Topic
Practical information

1. English 201: American Literature

   Philip Roth's novel *Everyman* describes the decline and death of an unnamed "everyman" with whom any of us might identify or sympathize. At different points in the novel, from youth to old age, he is hospitalized for various conditions. In a paper of 750–1,000 words, discuss the everyman's attitude toward the hospitalizations at the time they occur and what they say about mortality and the fragility of the human body. How, if at all, do the everyman's attitudes toward these hospitalizations—and his own body—change over time? Be sure to proofread your paper carefully before handing it in. Due date: Monday, November 19th

   Supporting information
   Practical information
   Topic
   Supporting information, or continuation of topic
   Practical information
   Practical information

2. Sociology 101: Take-Home Exam

   Practical information

   John N. Edwards has defined a "social exchange theory" of marriage in which each partner contributes something of value to the relationship. However, as your textbook notes, "the equity that is sought is not an exchange but rather shared contributions of a similar kind": both husbands and wives are now expected to do chores that were once done primarily by one gender (for example, child rearing for women and wage earning for men).

   Supporting information

   Write a brief paper in which you do **one** of the following:

   One assignment; two separate topics

   - Revise or expand the definition of "social exchange theory" to reflect the current realities of marriage. To support your definition, provide examples from marriages that you have observed or that have been described in the text or other course materials.
   - Argue for or against the contention in the text that what matters most in marriage is the "perception of fairness, not absolute equality." To support your position, provide examples from marriages that you have observed or that have been described in the text or other course materials.

   Format your paper according to the guidelines in the course syllabus. This exam is worth 20 points. No late papers will be accepted.

   Practical information

ACTIVITY 2: Teamwork

Working with a classmate, come up with at least two questions that you have about the assignments in Activity 1. You might want to look back at the bulleted lists on pages 35–36 to see typical features of practical information, topics, and supporting information. You should ask these types of questions about any writing topic that is not completely clear to you. Answers will vary.

EXAMPLE: See the example for Activity 1 on page 37.

Questions: Where should the information from the paper come from? (A textbook? Class notes? Observations?)
How much value/weight does the assignment have?

1. **Questions:** What parts/features should the paper include?
How much value/weight does the assignment have?

2. **Questions:** When is the paper due?
What is meant by "brief"? How many words or pages?

Understanding Broad, Limited, and Narrow Topics

Some topics are very *broad* or general, offering a lot of choice in what to write about. Other topics are more carefully defined, offering a *limited* choice in what to write about. In some cases, a topic may be very *narrow*, offering little or no choice in what to write about.

To work effectively with a topic, you should know how much choice you have and how much further narrowing, if any, you will have to do.

Let's review the three types of topic:

- **A broad topic:** You have a lot of choice in what you will write about, but you must do a significant amount of work to make an effective choice.
- **A limited topic:** You have some choice in what you will write about, and you must do less work to make an effective choice.
- **A narrow topic:** You have little or no choice in what you will write about, so you have little or no work to do to make an effective choice.

Whether you like or dislike having a lot of choice in what you will write about, you should be able to work effectively with any type of topic.

Now, let's look at some writing assignments for a geography class. The instructor might formulate the writing assignment as broad, limited, or narrow:

BROAD **Write an essay on contemporary China.**

For online practice with working with writing assignments, visit this book's Web site at **bedfordstmartins .com/steppingstones**.

For this assignment, you would have a great deal of choice in what to write about. For example, you could write about Chinese politics, economy, education, art, or other aspects of contemporary China. However, if you select one of these broad categories, you would probably need to narrow it even further. For instance, if you want to write about the Chinese economy, you might decide to focus on international trade relations.

Now, let's look at a more limited topic:

LIMITED **Discuss China's population challenges.**

For this assignment, you would have a limited choice in what to write about because the topic has already been narrowed to "China's population challenges." For example, you might write about the growth rate of the population, the economic impact of population growth, and so on.

Now, let's look at an even more limited topic:

NARROW **Discuss whether China's one-child policy is an effective solution to the country's population growth.**

For this assignment, you have little or no choice in what to write about because the instructor has narrowed the topic for you. Here, you know that you must take a position on whether China's one-child policy is effective. The only choice you have is in deciding whether or not you believe this policy to be effective.

Teaching Tip

If you have access to assignments from other instructors and other disciplines, bring copies to class or display them on a projector. Ask students to identify the parts of these assignments and to classify them as broad, limited, or narrow. What questions would students have for the instructor?

ACTIVITY 3

Examine each of the following groups of topics. Then, for each group, decide which topic offers the most choice in what to write about, which one offers a limited choice, and which one offers little or no choice. Label each topic *broad, limited,* or *narrow*.

EXAMPLE: Write about a hero from 9/11. limited

Write about heroism. broad

Write about Todd Beamer's heroic actions on 9/11. narrow

1. Write about one type of pride that many people feel. limited

   Write about something that you are especially proud of. narrow

   Write about pride. broad

2. Write about whether mistakes can be valuable in life. broad

   Write about some common mistakes that college students make. limited

   Write about a mistake that changed your life. narrow

ACTIVITY 4: Teamwork

Each of the following topics was assigned by an actual college instructor. With your classmates, discuss what decisions you would have to make for each topic. Then, identify the topic as *broad, limited,* or *narrow.* Answers may vary.

EXAMPLE: **Topic:** Discuss a quality that makes someone an American.

Decisions/topic identification: The writer would have to decide what it means to be American and choose a quality that fits with this definition. This is a limited topic.

1. **Topic:** For your political science class, explain one amendment to the U.S. Constitution and how it is important in your life.

   Decisions/topic identification: The writer would have to decide which amendment to explore and think about how it is important in his/her life. This is a limited topic.

2. **Topic:** For your music appreciation class, explain the difference between a soprano and a tenor.

   Decisions/topic identification: The writer doesn't have much choice as to what to say. He or she would have to be able to state the difference between a soprano and a tenor. This is a narrow topic.

3. **Topic:** For your health class, write about sexually transmitted diseases.

   Decisions/topic identification: The writer would have to choose which sexually transmitted diseases to write about and what to say about these diseases—for example, how they are transmitted, how they can be prevented, or what health policies are concerned with them. This is a broad topic.

Narrowing a Broad Topic

If you are assigned a broad topic, you will need to narrow it to a more specific topic. To do this effectively, you should consider three things:

1. the required length of the assignment
2. what interests you most about the topic
3. clues provided in the supporting information

CONSIDERING THE REQUIRED LENGTH OF AN ASSIGNMENT

Your instructor will usually require a certain length for your writing assignment. Here are some common lengths for college writing assignments (typed and double-spaced):

- one paragraph
- one to two pages (short essay)
- three to five pages (standard essay)
- more than five pages (long essay or research paper)

Suppose that you have been assigned the following topic:

Discuss your college experiences.

Clearly, this topic is too broad for a paragraph or an essay. There are so many experiences that you could discuss that you could never complete the assignment successfully in the space of a paragraph or essay. Here is how the topic could be narrowed for a standard essay and for a short essay or paragraph.

NARROWED FOR A STANDARD ESSAY (THREE TO FIVE PAGES) **Discuss my struggles in college.**

In a standard essay, you could effectively describe a number of struggles that you've had in college, such as keeping up with homework, communicating with instructors, and paying for tuition and books. You would have plenty of room to provide specific examples and details to illustrate each of these struggles.

For a paragraph or short essay, you will need to narrow the topic more tightly.

NARROWED FOR A SHORT ESSAY (ONE TO TWO PAGES) OR PARAGRAPH **Discuss a difficult class I've had.**

In the space of a short essay or paragraph, you will be able to provide a few good examples to illustrate just the difficulties that you had in *one* class.

ACTIVITY 5

For each of the following broad topics, first narrow the topic for a standard essay (three to five pages). Then, narrow the topic further for a short essay (one to two pages) or paragraph. *Answers will vary.*

EXAMPLE: **Broad topic:** Write about neighborhoods.

Narrowed for a standard essay: The people who live in my neighborhood

Narrowed for a short essay or paragraph: Ina Sanchez, my great neighbor

CONTINUED >

1. **Broad topic:** Write about boredom.

   Narrowed for a standard essay: Several ways to overcome boredom

   Narrowed for a short essay or paragraph: One or two strategies to overcome boredom

Power Tip
When narrowing a topic for a writing assignment, it is always a good idea to have your instructor check your narrowed topic. If you have trouble narrowing a broad topic, do not hesitate to ask your instructor for help.

2. **Broad topic:** Write about responsibility.

   Narrowed for a standard essay: What it means to be a responsible parent

   Narrowed for a short essay or paragraph: An incident or event that showed me what it means to be a responsible parent

CONSIDERING WHAT INTERESTS YOU (FINDING YOUR PERSONAL PURPOSE)

The second thing to consider when narrowing a topic is what interests you most about it. Sometimes, a topic might seem to be of no interest to you, but it is your job to find an angle that excites you. Remember, with a broad topic, you have plenty of choice about what you will write; you should see this choice as an opportunity to make the topic work for you.

When you are assigned a broad topic, you can use a number of strategies to discover what might interest you:

- Explore your personal connection to the topic.
- Interview family, friends, or other people you know about the topic.
- Do a quick Internet search to find more information about the topic.

Strategy 1: Finding a Personal Connection

The best way to get interested in a broad topic is to *relate it as honestly as possible to your own life*. Look at this example:

TOPIC **Write about friendship.**

Although friendship is important for most people, you should think about your own experiences with friendship. Write down the two or three most important things you can say about friendship in your life. For example:

My best friends know absolutely everything about me.
In tenth grade, my best friend was killed in a car accident.
My friends are more important than my family.

Each of these statements is very personal and very powerful. Any one of them should keep you interested in writing about friendship. From here, you can select one of these ideas and narrow it further if necessary. For example:

My friends know absolutely everything about me.

This topic seems appropriate for a standard essay (three to five pages). It will probably take several pages to discuss "absolutely everything" that your friends know about you. However, for a short essay (one to two pages) or paragraph, you could narrow the topic further:

My friends know all my moods.

This topic is still very personal and very powerful. However, it is much narrower. You should be able to discuss your friends' familiarity with your moods in a well-developed short essay or paragraph.

Teaching Tip

Write a few broad topics on the board, such as *campus problems, career goals,* and *marriage.* Then, ask students to suggest narrower versions of these topics, based on their personal interests and experiences. Write down their responses. Finally, ask them which narrowed topics they find to be most compelling.

ACTIVITY 6: Teamwork

With your classmates, discuss some of your personal experiences with each of the following topics. Then, write down the two or three most important things you can say about your personal connection to each topic. Answers will vary.

EXAMPLE: **Topic:** Write about the Internet.

I have made friends from all over the world using the Internet.

I feel like I am addicted to shopping on the Internet.

The Internet has been useful for my college assignments.

1. **Topic:** Write about surprises.

2. **Topic:** Write about sickness or death.

3. **Topic:** Write about pets (yours or other people's).

Strategy 2: Interviewing

Sometimes, you may not be able to find any personal connection to a topic. In this case, it is a good idea to interview your family, friends, co-workers, classmates, or other people about the topic. Their thoughts on the topic may spark your interest. For example:

TOPIC **Write about the neighborhood you live in.**

Teaching Tip

At first, interviewing may be difficult for some students. As a warm-up, you might pair up students and have them do in-class interviews on a sample topic (such as *an important person in my life*). They can take turns presenting the results of their interviews to the class.

Suppose that you have never thought much about your neighborhood; to you, it's just the place where you live, and you don't have any strong personal feelings about it. In this case, you can get ideas by interviewing your family, friends, and neighbors to find out what they think about your neighborhood. Listen *very carefully* and write down any interesting ideas they share. For example:

Anna, friend: "What I like about this neighborhood is that someone is always watching your back."
Elderly neighbor: "I've lived in this neighborhood for sixty years and seen a lot of changes. Today, our neighborhood is nothing like it was sixty years ago."
Your mother: "I did not want to raise you in this neighborhood. I was afraid that you would go down the wrong path."

Each of these statements offers an interesting idea for writing about your neighborhood:

- You could explain why you agree or disagree with Anna's point that "someone is always watching your back" in your neighborhood.
- You could ask your elderly neighbor for more information about how the neighborhood has changed. Then, in your paper, you could describe the important changes that have taken place.
- You could write about the negative influences in your neighborhood that might have taken you down the "wrong path." You might demonstrate that your mother's worries were either realistic or exaggerated.

Power Tip
More strategies for generating ideas about a topic are presented in Chapter 3. Whenever you have difficulty coming up with ideas for a topic, try some of the ideas presented here and in Chapter 3.

ACTIVITY 7

Pretend that you have no personal interest in any of the following topics. Interview two or three classmates, family members, friends, co-workers, or other people about their ideas on the topics. For each topic, write down at least two interesting ideas you heard. Answers will vary.

EXAMPLE:

Topic: Discuss writing timed essays in college.

Lucy, friend: I always do my best writing under pressure.
Ernesto, classmate: I always fall apart writing timed essays. They are unfair to students like me.
Mrs. Lutz, instructor: Timed essays prepare students for working in the "real" world.

1. **Topic:** Write about picking a career that's right for you.

____

____

____

2. **Topic:** Write about managing your money.

3. **Topic:** Write about the importance of forgiving people who have hurt you.

ACTIVITY 8: Teamwork

With one or two classmates, share the results of your interviews for each of the topics in the previous activity. Discuss which ideas you like best and which ones might help you become more interested in the topic.

Strategy 3: Searching the Internet

Sometimes, you may have no personal interest in a topic because you don't know enough about it. In these cases, a simple Internet search can give you quick access to information on a topic and help you develop a greater interest in it. For example:

TOPIC Discuss whether you are a responsible citizen.

Suppose that this topic seems boring to you. You do not have a clear sense of what it means to be a "responsible citizen," so you don't really care. Still, you must complete this assignment, and you probably care about receiving a passing grade. To get ideas, you might type the words "responsible citizen" into an Internet search engine, such as Google. When you do this, you might learn the following things:

Power Tip
For most search engines, including Google.com, place quotation marks around groups of words that you are treating as one term—for example, "*responsible citizen.*" If you typed in the two words without quotation marks, you would get all the entries that include just the word *responsible* and all the entries that include just the word *citizen*—far more results than you would want or need.

From the U.S. Department of Education's Web site: Responsible citizens "are honest and fair, display self-discipline in setting and meeting goals, make good judgments, show respect to others, show courage in standing up for beliefs, have a strong sense of responsibility, are good citizens who are concerned for their community, and maintain self-respect."

From Central Michigan University's Web site: Responsible citizens "speak up in potentially risky situations, take action to stop negative behaviors from continuing, perfect communication skills in order to feel comfortable speaking out among peers, effectively work with diverse groups of people."

From Project Appleseed's Web site: Being a responsible citizen includes "fulfilling responsibilities, such as voluntary service to the community, participating in the political system, acquiring knowledge about civic life, and demonstrating a public commitment to the values of constitutional democracy (for example, liberty, justice, and the rule of law)."

In your writing assignment, you may choose to argue that you are or are not a responsible citizen according to these definitions.

The Internet information might also prompt you to come up with your own definition of "responsible citizen." Then, you can discuss whether that definition applies to you.

Power Tip
Be aware that plagiarism—using the words or ideas of another person without giving proper credit—is a serious academic offense. To avoid plagiarism, never use any information from a Web site or another source without naming the source, even if you put the ideas in your own words. For example, you might say *According to the Partnership for Safe Driving, cell phones . . .* If you quote from a source, put quotation marks around the source's exact words. Ask your instructor for more specific directions on citing sources. For a tutorial on avoiding plagiarism, visit **bedfordstmartins.com/rewritingbasics**.

Teaching Tip
This is a good time to explain your expectations for citing and documenting sources. For example, if you want students to formally document sources in MLA style, refer them to explanations and models like those in *Research and Documentation Online*, at **dianahacker.com/resdoc**. Also, Quick Reference cards for MLA and APA style are available with this book.

ACTIVITY 9

For each of the following broad topics, type the underlined words into an Internet search engine, such as Google. Write down two or three things that you learned about the topic. Answers will vary.

EXAMPLE: **Topic:** Write about the risks of using a cell phone.

1. From the Sun Sentinel Web site: Three European research groups in separate studies have found an increased risk of brain tumors in people who have used the phones for ten years or more.
2. From the Partnership for Safe Driving: A yearlong government study videotaped drivers to determine what behaviors cause crashes. Cell phones came out as the number-one distraction.

1. **Topic:** For your health class, write about the safety of female condoms.

2. **Topic:** For your political science class, write about women serving in the Iraq war.

3. **Topic:** For your literature class, write about the U.S. poet laureate.

WORKING WITH THE SUPPORTING INFORMATION

Often, the best way to narrow the topic and discover what interests you about it is to use the **supporting information**. This is especially true for in-class essays, when time restrictions mean that you cannot search the Internet or conduct interviews to gather ideas.

The supporting information can "jump-start" your work on the topic by

- providing important background information or key definitions
- focusing your attention on important details or parts of the topic
- offering clues to help you narrow the topic or get ideas about it
- generating enthusiasm for the assignment

In this section, you will learn how to recognize the important assistance given to you in the supporting information.

Following is a writing assignment with supporting information that does all four things to jump-start your work.

Art History 101, Essay Question

You are giving an elaborate and formal dinner party. You have been lucky enough to use a time machine to bring some famous guests from the past. Joining you for your party will be

Gives background information

- Akhenaton and Nefertiti (rulers in Ancient Egypt)
- Menkaure (a ruler and pyramid builder in Ancient Egypt) and his queen
- Paris and Helen of Troy (characters in Greek mythology, involved in the start of the Trojan War)
- Polyclitus (a famous Greek sculptor)

The guests' conversation about cultural beliefs and art is amazing, and you are absolutely fascinated! Therefore, you want to record this event for history. Make a detailed record of their conversation. You may do this in essay form or as a script.

Builds enthusiasm

Sample script:

Me: So how are you this evening, Helen?

Helen: I'm a little bit tired from the time machine, but how do I look?

Me: ______________________________

Offers clues for generating ideas

To get started, think of a conversation between just two of the guests. Then, add one guest at a time to the conversation.

This essay should be at least, but not more than, three typed, double-spaced pages. Be sure to proofread carefully and send it through spell check. A good tip is to have someone else read your paper before you turn it in. He or she may catch errors you have overlooked. Remember that this assignment is designed to give you practice in writing; therefore, spelling, punctuation, and paragraphing all count! You may get help on the mechanics of writing, but not on the content of your script.

This is a creative and synthetic essay, not a research assignment. I do not want to read what the book or the Internet has to say about these people, their art, and their culture. Imagine what they might say to each other if they were in the same room.

Suggests a focus

Some students read the supporting information quickly or only once; then, when they try to begin the assignment, they get stuck. On the other hand, successful college writers know that the supporting information contains important clues, so they look at it closely before beginning to write.

Below and on the next page are three writing assignments on money. (The practical information has been omitted.) The first topic is very broad, giving you a lot of choice. The second topic is limited, giving you some choice. The last topic is narrow, giving you little choice. In each case, the supporting information should help you make an effective choice regarding what to write about.

BROAD TOPIC

> Money seems to be an important part of everyone's life. We need money to survive, to pay the bills, and to buy groceries. We also need money to enjoy many of life's pleasures. When we don't have enough money, this can be a source of pain and conflict. For some people, money is the most important thing in the world, and they spend all their time thinking about how to get it. The desire for money can even get people in trouble. On the other hand, some people don't care that much about money and try to live simply without overspending. Finally, some people claim that money is the "root of all evil," while others argue that money is the solution to many problems in the world.
>
> In a well-developed paragraph, discuss money. Be sure to narrow your topic for a paragraph. Give three supporting points for your main idea. Remember to provide specific examples and details to illustrate your points.

For this topic, you have a great deal of choice: there are many different things that you could write about money. Refer to the supporting information for clues about how you might narrow this broad topic. In searching for these clues, it is a good idea to use a highlighter, pen, or pencil. Below, we have italicized clues contained in the supporting information.

> Money seems to be an important part of everyone's life. We *need money to survive*, to pay the bills, and to buy groceries. We also *need money to enjoy many of life's pleasures*. When we don't have enough money, this can be *a source of pain and conflict*. For some people, *money is the most important thing in the world*, and they *spend all their time thinking about how to get it*. The desire for money *can even get people in trouble*. On the other hand, *some people don't care that much about money* and *try to live simply without overspending*. Finally, some people claim that *money is the "root of all evil,"* while others argue that *money is the solution to many problems in the world*.

Each of these clues could help you narrow the topic. For example:

Clue in the Supporting Information →	**Possible Topic for Your Paragraph**
need money to survive	As a single mom, I have to be careful with my money.
need money to enjoy life's pleasures	I enjoy spending money.
a source of pain and conflict	Money has caused problems in my family.
money is the most important thing in the world	My best friend promises to marry only a rich person.
spend all their time thinking about how to get it	My cousin thinks only about making money.
can even get people in trouble	Stealing money was the worst mistake I ever made.
some don't care that much about money	My uncle is poor but the happiest person I know.
try to live simply without overspending	My mother set a good example for handling money.
money is the "root of all evil"	I've seen money ruin people's lives.
money is the solution to many problems in the world	I try to donate money to important causes.

LIMITED TOPIC

For many people, money has the power to create positive or negative emotions. Most of us remember some good and bad experiences we've had with money. Perhaps when you were a child, you found a $10 bill on the ground, and you felt lucky and rich. Maybe you saved your allowance and gift money to buy something important, and you were happy with your accomplishment. Perhaps when you received your first paycheck, you felt strong and independent. On the other hand, perhaps you once stole some money from your parents, and you lived with guilt until you returned it. Or maybe your father lost his job, and the whole family had to pull together to save money. Maybe you went to a casino and lost all your rent money, so you felt embarrassed when you had to ask your friend for a loan.

In a well-developed paragraph, discuss a good or bad experience you've had with money. Give at least three reasons why this experience was good or bad. Remember to support your reasons with specific examples and details.

For this topic, you have a limited choice. You must write about *one experience* you've had with money and give at least three reasons why this experience was good or bad. Refer to the supporting information for examples to get you thinking about your own experiences with money. Below, we have italicized examples of good and bad experiences with money:

> For many people, money has the power to create positive or negative emotions. Most of us remember some good and bad experiences we've had with money. Perhaps when you were a child, you *found a $10 bill on the ground*, and you felt lucky and rich. Maybe you *saved your allowance and gift money to buy something important*, and you were happy with your accomplishment. Perhaps *when you received your first paycheck*, you felt strong and independent. On the other hand, perhaps you once *stole some money from your parents*, and you lived with guilt until you returned it. Or maybe *your father lost his job*, and the whole family had to pull together to save money. Maybe you *went to a casino and lost all your rent money*, so you felt embarrassed when you had to ask your friend for a loan.

Each of these clues could help you think of a good or bad experience you've had with money. For example:

Clue in the Supporting Information →	**Possible Topic for Your Paragraph**
found a $10 bill on the ground	I won $100 at bingo.
saved your allowance and gift money to buy something important	I worked all summer to buy my first car.
when you received your first paycheck	I was successful in getting a student loan for college.
stole some money from your parents	I borrowed money from a friend and never paid it back.
your father lost his job	My parents always fought about money.
went to a casino and lost all your money	I maxed out my credit card and couldn't pay the bill.

NARROW TOPIC

> Everybody needs money to live, but money can make you happy or miserable, depending on how you manage it. Some people are good at managing their money. They do not overspend or buy foolish things. They learn how to save a little money for monthly bills or emergencies, and they do not borrow, use credit, or go into debt. On the other hand, some people are unsuccessful when it comes to managing their money. They may spend their money foolishly without thinking about the consequences. Sometimes, they borrow money from friends or use credit cards they can't afford. In addition, they may have no sense of how to

save, so when it's time to pay the bills or handle a financial emergency, they are stuck with no cash. How well do you manage your money?

In a well-developed paragraph, discuss whether you are good at managing your money. Give at least three reasons why you believe you are good or bad at managing your money. Remember to support your reasons with specific examples and details.

This topic has been narrowed for you by the instructor. The only choice you have to make is in deciding whether you are good or bad at *managing your money,* a very specific issue. The supporting information gives you many clues to help you evaluate your own habits with money. Below, we have italicized the clues that describe good versus bad money management.

Everybody needs money to live, but money can make you happy or miserable, depending on how you manage it. Some people are good at managing their money. They *do not overspend or buy foolish things.* They learn how to *save a little money for monthly bills or emergencies,* and they *do not borrow, use credit, or go into debt.* On the other hand, some people are unsuccessful when it comes to managing their money. They may *spend their money foolishly* without thinking about the consequences. Sometimes, they *borrow money from friends or use credit cards they can't afford.* In addition, they may have *no sense of how to save,* so when it's time to pay the bills or handle a financial emergency, they are stuck with no cash. How well do you manage your money?

Each of these clues should help you decide whether you are good or bad at managing your money. For example:

Clue in the Supporting Information →	**Possible Topic for Your Paragraph**
Good: do not overspend or buy foolish things	
Bad: spend money foolishly	I am a crazy spender (bad money manager!).
Good: save a little money for monthly bills/emergencies	
Bad: no sense of how to save	I never save money (bad money manager!).
Good: do not borrow, use credit, or go into debt	
Bad: borrow money from friends or use credit cards they can't afford	I owe my aunt $200 and my roommate $40 (bad money manager!).

ACTIVITY 10

For each of the following writing assignments, read the topic and decide whether it is *broad, limited,* or *narrow*. Then, read the supporting information carefully and mark any clues that could help you narrow the topic effectively. Use a highlighter, pen, or pencil to mark the clues. For examples of how to mark an assignment, refer to pages 46–51. Answers will vary.

1. Common dictionary definitions of *happiness* include "contentment" or "the state of being full of joy." However, people tend to define this word in very individual ways, such as "having close friendships," "having a satisfying job," or "making a lot of money." In a well-developed paragraph, discuss your definition of *happiness*. Be sure to provide at least three supporting points for your main idea, and make sure to give specific examples to back up the supporting points.

   Is this topic broad, limited, or narrow? broad

2. In the last five years, one of the most popular ways of meeting people has been through Internet dating. Many people claim that the Internet is an effective way to find people with similar interests and values, even allowing searchers to view photos of potential dates before meeting them. Many people claim they found true love and even marriage through the Internet, or at least had fun and made new friends. On the other hand, some people believe that Internet dating is a poor substitute for traditional ways of meeting people. For example, Internet dating can be impersonal, and people may lie about themselves; furthermore, actual encounters might even be dangerous.

   Write a well-developed paragraph discussing whether Internet dating is a healthy and positive way to meet people. Give three reasons why you believe Internet dating is or is not a positive way to meet people. Remember to support your reasons with examples and details.

   Is this topic broad, limited, or narrow? narrow

ACTIVITY 11: Teamwork

With your classmates, discuss the supporting information in the topics in the previous activity. Compare the clues that you marked in each piece of supporting information and discuss how you could use each clue to narrow your topic. Write down your ideas for narrowing each topic.

Bringing It All Together

In this chapter, you have learned about the parts of writing assignments; the differences in broad, limited, and narrow topics; and how to narrow broad topics. Check off each of the following statements that you understand. For any that you do not understand, review the appropriate pages in this chapter.

- ☐ Most college writing assignments have three main parts: **practical information**, the **topic**, and **supporting information**. (See page 35.)
- ☐ The **practical information** specifies such details as the due date, the required length of the paper, and formatting instructions. (See page 35.)
- ☐ The **topic** is the main subject or task of the assignment, and it is often expressed in one sentence. (See page 36.)
- ☐ The **supporting information** provides other details that are helpful in completing the assignment, and it includes background information on the topic, definitions of key terms, and suggestions for generating ideas or for narrowing the topic. (See page 36.)
- ☐ **Broad topics** give you a lot of choice in what to write about, **limited topics** give you less choice, and **narrow topics** offer the least choice. The broader the topic, the more work you must do to make an effective choice regarding what to write about. (See page 38.)
- ☐ Good ways to narrow a broad topic include considering the required length of an assignment (page 41); finding an interesting angle through a personal connection, interviews, or an Internet search (page 42); and using clues provided in the supporting information (page 46).

Remember: Whenever you do not understand an assignment, ask your instructor for clarification!

Chapter 3

Gathering Support for Your Topic

OVERVIEW OF THIS CHAPTER

WARM-UP Getting the Details Down

1. Imagine this situation:

Your friend Miguel would like to be in a serious relationship. He has many great qualities, such as kindness, intelligence, honesty, and loyalty, but he's stubborn about certain things. For example, he insists on staying in on nights when his favorite sports teams are on television, and he can't stand a mess. As she was breaking up with him, his last girlfriend said, "Can you be in my house for five seconds without picking my socks up off the floor?"

At a party, you and Miguel see another friend of yours, Katie, and Katie and Miguel end up talking for hours. Miguel is clearly interested, and Katie calls you the next day to ask, "So, what's the story on Miguel?" You realize, with relief, that Katie is a sports fan.

2. Stop and think!

Working alone or with classmates, consider what kind of information you would share with Katie about Miguel to give her a realistic picture of him. You can make up stories and details if you'd like.

To give Katie an accurate picture of Miguel, you'd want to be as detailed as possible about him and his qualities. You might explain how loyal a friend he is by telling about the time when he got out of bed in the middle of the night to help you when your car broke down. You might explain how kind he is by telling how he shovels his elderly neighbors' snow in the winter. And, yes, you'll also need to tell Katie about Miguel's sports nights and his "Museum of Cleaning Supplies," as you've come to call his hall closet.

Similarly, when you write, you'll want to provide all the information readers need to understand your point. This chapter will help you develop this information, known as support, for any topic.

Understanding What Support Is

In Chapter 2, you learned how to narrow a topic. Now, you are ready to begin gathering all the ideas and information you can about the topic. These ideas and information are called **support**. The more support you gather, the more you will have to say in your paragraph or essay.

The process of gathering ideas is often called **brainstorming**. Although most students have heard this expression, many do not understand what it means or where it comes from. The expression *brainstorming* is a metaphor—an image of what should occur in your brain as you begin to gather ideas and information about your topic. Ideally, your brain should be a "storm" of creative energy and ideas. Take a look at the illustration.

Brainstorming—or gathering support—can be easy if you've selected a topic that is of personal interest to you. However, many students have difficulty "igniting" that storm of energy and ideas in their brain. It would be wonderful if we had a switch to turn it on! Since we do not have such a switch, this chapter will give you some strategies for accessing your brain's amazing reserve of ideas and energy.

Understanding the Sources of Support

In college, the support for writing topics will come from one or more of the following sources:

- your personal experience and knowledge
- assigned texts
- independent research

Power Tip
Sometimes, a writing assignment will require you to find support from a combination of the three sources discussed in this section. If you are not sure where you should look for support on a topic, always ask your instructor for clarification.

PERSONAL EXPERIENCE AND KNOWLEDGE

Many college writing assignments require you to use information and ideas from your own experience and knowledge—*what you already know*. Your brain is a wonderful resource of memories, emotions, facts, and opinions that you have accumulated through your personal and educational experiences. Also, any ideas that your instructor has discussed in class now count as part of your personal knowledge.

ACTIVITY 1: Teamwork

With classmates, take turns discussing whether you have ever been asked to use your personal experience and knowledge as support for a writing topic. If you have, explain what personal experience or knowledge you used for the assignment. What did you like about the assignment? What, if anything, was challenging? Was the assignment useful?

ASSIGNED TEXTS

In many college courses, you will be asked to consider the ideas of authors of texts that you have been assigned—stories, journal articles, textbook chapters, and so on. For example, you may be required to explain why a certain character makes an important decision in a story that you read. This assignment requires you to find supporting ideas in the text. Often, you will need to summarize or quote the ideas that you find in texts, as in the following assignment:

ASSIGNMENT: Based on your reading of Chapter 10 of *America: A Concise History,* name and define the nineteenth-century production innovation that increased manufacturing output in the shoe industry. Then, briefly state the benefits and drawbacks of this innovation as described in the text.

Terminology Tip
Summarizing is putting another's idea in your own words, in brief form. *Quoting* is using someone's exact words, enclosed in quotation marks. In both cases, you need to name the source of the information. For more information on summarizing and quoting, see **bedfordstmartins.com/researchroom/sources**.

ACTIVITY 2: Teamwork

With classmates, take turns discussing whether you have ever been asked to work with an assigned text for a writing assignment. If you have, explain what text you worked with and what ideas you had to find in it. What was useful about this assignment? Did you find it interesting?

INDEPENDENT RESEARCH

As you progress in college, some of your writing assignments will require you to do independent research to find support for your topic. Independent research means that *on your own* and *outside of the classroom,* you must find and read others' ideas on your topic. You might locate these ideas in books from the college library, in magazines and journals, in online databases (*ProQuest, Opposing Viewpoints,* and so on), and on appropriate Web sites. You might also interview others. (See Chapter 2, page 43, for more details.)

In research writing, you will be required to include the ideas of others, but instructors will often expect you to come to an original conclusion based on this information. Additionally, you will have to list all of your sources, typically in a "Works Cited" list.

Power Tip
Before beginning research for an assignment, take some time to brainstorm for any ideas or knowledge that you already have on the topic. Then, as you research, you can more effectively identify new information that fills in the gaps of your understanding or challenges your opinions. For more research advice, visit **bedfordstmartins.com/researchroom**.

Teaching Tip
If you plan to assign research writing, you might emphasize that the college library and library Web site (if one is available) are two of the best resources for finding reliable sources.

Also, if you want students to formally document sources in MLA style, refer them to explanations and models like those in *Research and Documentation Online,* at **dianahacker.com/resdoc**. Additionally, Quick Reference cards for MLA and APA style are available with this book.

ACTIVITY 3: Teamwork

With classmates, take turns discussing whether you have ever been asked to do independent research for a writing assignment. If you have, explain what sources of information you used and what you found. What was useful about doing research? Was the project interesting?

Accessing Support

For the writing assignments in this course, most of your support will come from your own experience and knowledge. Therefore, in this chapter, you will learn and practice the following strategies for accessing *what you already know:*

- the five *W*s of critical thinking
- role-playing

THE FIVE *WS* OF CRITICAL THINKING

Critical thinking is deep thinking, going beyond our first impressions and looking at a topic from different viewpoints. Often, our best ideas lie just below the surface of our conscious thoughts. Taking the time to find these ideas can be a rich and exciting process of discovery.

Many professionals rely on critical thinking skills to evaluate complicated issues. For example, in re-creating a crime scene, a detective must look below the surface and examine the scene from different viewpoints to find important clues. In exploring an ancient burial site, an archaeologist must look below the surface and from different viewpoints to piece together the past.

archaeologist: one who studies the remains of past civilizations

What do these professionals—and many others—have in common? They all use the five *W*s of critical thinking: ***Who? Where? When? What? Why?*** As a college writer, you can use these questions to get below the surface of a topic and look at it from different viewpoints. Here is a list of questions that can be formed with the five *W*s. Following each one is an example of how one writer applied the question to a significant event: a car accident in which she was involved.

> ***Who*** are the important people involved in my topic? (Identify these people and their role in the topic.) **EXAMPLE:** My sister and I were in one car, and a speeding teenager was in the other car—the one that caused the accident. I was driving, and my sister was the passenger.
>
> ***Where*** did events connected to my topic take place? (Identify these places and any important details about them.) **EXAMPLE:** The accident happened at the intersection of Main and Elm streets. The streets were slick with rain.
>
> ***When*** did the experiences in my topic happen? (Identify the date, time, season, duration, and/or concurrent events that provide a time frame for your experiences.) **EXAMPLE:** The accident occurred on a late spring night as we were driving home from a movie. It was over in seconds.
>
> ***What*** important things happened in relation to my topic? (Identify any important events, experiences, activities, results, and so on.) **EXAMPLE:** When the light turned green, we pulled into the intersection. Just then, a car in the cross street ran a red light and skidded into the front of our car. Our airbags opened, and no one was injured, but we were shaken up!
>
> ***Why*** did these things happen, and ***why*** did people act the way they did? (Identify the reasons for these events and behaviors.) **EXAMPLE:** The accident resulted from the other driver's haste and inexperience: he was late for work; also, he had just gotten his license and wasn't used to sudden stops.

As you begin to use the five *W*s to gather your support, keep the following points in mind:

- Not all the *W*s work for every topic. Generally, you should be able to use three or four of the *W*s for a given topic. If one *W* does not make sense for your topic, move on to the next *W*.

For online practice with the five *W*s, visit this book's Web site at **bedfordstmartins .com/steppingstones**.

Teaching Tip
Students often think that they have to use every idea that they generate for an assignment. Explain that they will probably use just a small number of these ideas in their final papers; however, the idea-generating process helps them find angles they might not have considered otherwise, and it provides a lot of choice.

- Sometimes, two *W*s will produce the same answers or ideas. *In clustering or listing, repetition is beneficial* because it can help you identify ideas that might be especially important for your topic. (Clustering and listing are two strategies for recording support that are discussed on pages 64–79.)
- The five *W*s should jump-start your brainstorming, but they should not restrict the free movement of your thinking. Once your brain warms up, you may decide to drop the *W*s and follow your thoughts in other directions.
- You may use the five *W*s in any order you like, but try to start with one that is easy for you. Many students find it easy to begin with *who, where,* or *when.*

ACTIVITY 4: Teamwork

With classmates, form *W* questions for the following topics. (It is not necessary to answer the questions.) If one *W* does not fit a topic, just write "does not fit" in the space provided. Answers will vary.

EXAMPLE: Discuss a powerful dream you've had.

Who? were the people in my dream

Where? did the events in my dream take place

When? did the events in my dream happen

What? happened in my dream

Why? did these things happen

1. Discuss a competition (sports or otherwise).

Who? ______

Where? ______

When? ______

What? ______

Why? ______

2. Write about your "fantasy" job: the job you would have if anything were possible.

Who? ______

Where? ______

When? ______

What? ______

Why? ______

ROLE-PLAYING

With role-playing, you ask the five *W*s while acting out a role that will help you investigate your topic from a fresh point of view. This section describes six roles that you can choose from when you want to come up with support for a topic:

- detective
- investigative reporter
- archaeologist
- fortune-teller
- psychologist
- judge

As we will discuss, certain roles are especially suited to certain topics, but you may find that you prefer to use just one or two roles for any topic.

Playing these roles requires you to use your *imagination,* a powerful idea-generating tool. If you do not feel confident about using your imagination, you may want to try these helpful tips:

- Put yourself in an environment where you will not be distracted by things going on around you. This will allow you to concentrate.
- Stick with the role-playing activity for at least fifteen or twenty minutes. This will allow your brain to warm up.
- Close your eyes. This will allow your imagination to take you to another place and time.
- Play your favorite role as often as you can. This will help you to become expert at the strategy.

Teaching Tip
If you want your students to do some researched writing, you might point out that both the five *W*s and role-playing can help them come up with interesting research questions to pursue and good terms to enter into search engines and search fields of online databases.

Detective: At the Scene of the Crime

Sometimes, you may be asked to write about *an important event or place in your life.* Suppose that you have selected for your topic *my high school graduation.*

Now, imagine that you are a detective: you must re-create the scene. Close your eyes, drift back in time, and walk through your entire high school graduation. Look carefully at everybody and everything. You are searching for clues about what made the graduation an important event. Once you have allowed your imagination to re-create the event, you can begin to respond to the five *W*s:

> ***Who?*** Name all the people involved in the graduation.
>
> ***Where?*** Describe all the details of the place of the graduation.
>
> ***When?*** Describe the date, time of day, season, or period of the graduation.
>
> ***What?*** Describe every important thing that happened during the graduation.
>
> ***Why?*** Give reasons why things happened or why people might have acted as they did.

ACTIVITY 5

Teaching Tip
You might have students pair up to work on the role-playing activities. They can take turns asking each other the five *Ws* and recording the responses. The interviewer should ask for clarification if any of the interviewee's responses aren't clear.

Select one of the following topics. Next, imagine that you are a detective. Close your eyes and re-create the event or place. Then, on a separate sheet of paper, respond to the five *Ws*. Answers will vary.

- **Topic 1:** Write about your high school graduation.
- **Topic 2:** Write about a time when you were especially frightened.
- **Topic 3:** Write about a happy place from your childhood.
- **Topic 4:** Write about a memorable date that you had.
- **Topic 5:** Write about your favorite place to spend time outdoors.

Investigative Reporter: On the Beat

Sometimes, you may be asked to write about *a general situation or experience*. Suppose that you have selected for your topic *problems at my workplace.*

Now, imagine that you are a reporter. To give an accurate report on problems at your workplace, you will need to hear the opinions of different people—employees, bosses, customers, and so on. Close your eyes and imagine that you are interviewing individuals at your workplace. Listen carefully to what they say and evaluate the situation fairly. Once you have allowed your imagination to start this investigation, you can begin to respond to the five *Ws*:

Who? Name all the people involved in problems at work.

Where? Describe the places where problems occur at work.

When? Describe the date, time of day, season, or period when problems occur.

What? Describe every important thing that happens at work to cause problems.

Why? Give reasons why things happen or why people might act as they do.

ACTIVITY 6

Teaching Tip
Bring in a newspaper or Web article investigating a crime or some other activity. Ask students to re-create the specific five *Ws* that the reporter might have asked to get the information that he/she did.

Select one of the following topics. Next, imagine that you are an investigative reporter. Close your eyes and start your interviews. Then, on a separate sheet of paper, respond to the five *Ws*. Answers will vary.

- **Topic 1:** Write about problems in your workplace.
- **Topic 2:** Write about students who cheat in college.
- **Topic 3:** Write about a challenge that your family has faced.
- **Topic 4:** Write about something that you and your friends all like.
- **Topic 5:** Write about someone who never gave up on you.

Archaeologist: On the Big Dig

Occasionally, you may be asked to write about *someone or something from the past.* Suppose that you have selected for your topic *my great-grandfather.* However, your great-grandfather died when you were six, and you have just a few memories of him.

Now, imagine that you are an archaeologist. You must search for clues about this person you hardly knew. Close your eyes and begin to remember everything you can about your great-grandfather: his voice, his appearance, his movements, and so on. Then, look for other clues about your great-grandfather. Do you have any photographs of him or possessions that he left behind? What stories does your family tell about him? Once you have allowed your imagination to search for clues about your great-grandfather, you can begin to respond to the five *W*s:

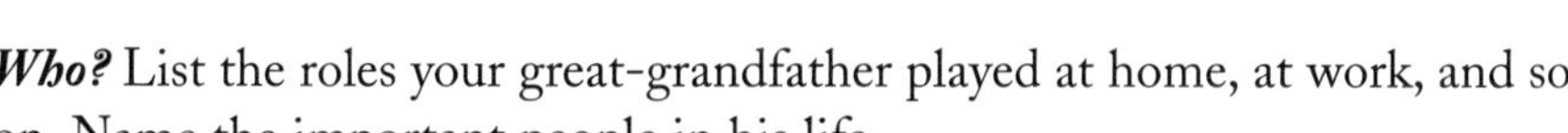

Who? List the roles your great-grandfather played at home, at work, and so on. Name the important people in his life.

Where? Describe all the details of the place where you saw your great-grandfather or where he lived.

When? Describe the date, time of day, season, or period when you spent time with him.

What? Describe every important thing that happened between your great-grandfather and you.

Why? Give reasons why you feel the way you do about your great-grandfather.

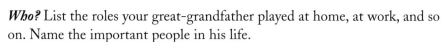

ACTIVITY 7

Select one of the following topics. Next, imagine that you are an archaeologist. Close your eyes and search for clues about the past. Then, on a separate sheet of paper, respond to the five *W*s. Answers will vary.

- **Topic 1:** Write about a relative you met a long time ago.
- **Topic 2:** Write about a vague or unclear memory.
- **Topic 3:** Write about an important historical event that happened during your childhood.
- **Topic 4:** Write about your first favorite toy.
- **Topic 5:** Write about a dream that you used to have when you were younger.

Fortune-Teller: At the Crystal Ball

Occasionally, you may be asked to write about *the future or imaginary situations.* Suppose that you have selected for your topic *what my life will be like in twenty years.*

Now, imagine that you are a fortune-teller. You will need to look deeply into your crystal ball until some images of the future appear. Close your eyes and imagine the glowing crystal sphere in front of you; you may need to rub your hands gently over the surface to bring it to life. Think hard about your hopes and dreams. Once you have allowed your imagination to open this window onto the future, you can begin to respond to the five *W*s:

Who? Name the important people who will be involved in your life twenty years from now.

Where? Describe all the details of the place where you might be living twenty years from now.

When? Describe the date, time of day, season, or period of significant events or experiences in your future, like a graduation, marriage, or job promotion.

What? Describe every significant event, experience, or achievement.

Why? Give reasons why things happened or why you made the decisions you did.

Teaching Tip
Have students briefly try out some or all of the strategies covered in this chapter (using the five *W*s, role-playing, clustering, listing, and freewriting) so that they can see which ones work best for them.

ACTIVITY 8

Select one of the following topics. Next, imagine that you are a fortune-teller. Close your eyes and look deeply into your crystal ball. Then, on a separate sheet of paper, respond to the five *W*s. Answers will vary.

- **Topic 1:** Write about what you would like your life to be like in twenty years.
- **Topic 2:** Write about the career you would choose if anything were possible.
- **Topic 3:** Write about spending a day with your favorite celebrity.
- **Topic 4:** Write about a city in the world that you would like to visit.
- **Topic 5:** Write about what you would do if you won the lottery.
- **Topic 6:** Write about who you would be if you were the opposite gender.

Psychologist: With the Patient

Sometimes, you may be asked to write about *your own personality, emotions, or beliefs.* Suppose that you have selected for your topic *It's hard for me to express my feelings.*

Now, imagine that you are both a psychologist and your own patient. You will need to ask yourself some very hard questions and answer them as honestly as you can. Close your eyes and imagine that you are sitting in a very comfortable chair. From behind you, you hear a friendly and reassuring voice. You know that you can trust this person with your innermost thoughts and feelings. Take a deep breath and relax. Once you have allowed your imagination to create this trusting relationship, you can begin to respond to the five *W*s:

Who? Name all the people to whom you have tried to express your feelings.

Where? In what important places have you had trouble expressing your feelings?

When? During what specific periods of your life have you had difficulty expressing your feelings?

What? What are some important feelings that you have not been able to express?

Why? What are some possible reasons why you have trouble expressing your feelings?

ACTIVITY 9

Select one of the following topics. Next, imagine that a trusted psychologist is asking you the five *W*s about the topic. Then, on a separate sheet of paper, respond to these questions. Answers will vary.

- **Topic 1:** Write about something that makes you angry.
- **Topic 2:** Write about something that gives you hope.
- **Topic 3:** Write about something that you regret.
- **Topic 4:** Write about something that you don't like to think about.
- **Topic 5:** Write about whether you like the way you look.

Teaching Tip
You might tell students that it's OK to "B.S." when they write. Then, explain that this means "be specific."

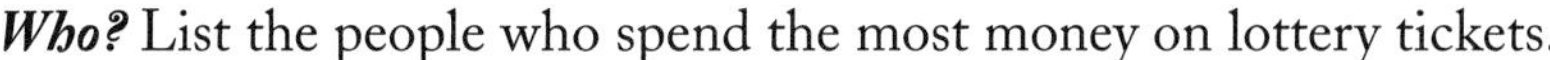

Judge: On the Bench

Sometimes, you may be asked to write your *opinions* about *a current event or social issue*. Suppose that you have selected for your topic *people who spend money on lottery tickets.*

Now, imagine that you are a judge. You will need to make a decision about whether spending money on lottery tickets is good, bad, or both good and bad. In order to form a judgment, you will need to listen carefully to witnesses who spend their money on lottery tickets. Close your eyes and picture yourself sitting on the judge's bench. Now, invite witnesses to the stand and summarize their collective responses to the five *W*s:

Who? List the people who spend the most money on lottery tickets.

Where? Describe the places where people buy lottery tickets.

When? Describe when and how often people buy lottery tickets.

What? Describe what happens when people spend their money on lottery tickets. What benefits can there be? What problems can result?

Why? Give reasons why people buy lottery tickets.

ACTIVITY 10

Select one of the following topics. Next, imagine that you are a judge. Close your eyes and begin to call witnesses to the stand. Then, on a separate sheet of paper, respond to the five *W*s. Answers will vary.

- **Topic 1:** Discuss whether people should spend money on lottery tickets.
- **Topic 2:** Discuss whether you approve or disapprove of the high salaries of celebrity athletes.
- **Topic 3:** Discuss whether rap music has too much violence.
- **Topic 4:** Discuss whether a woman would make a good president of the United States.
- **Topic 5:** Discuss whether high schools should have dress codes.

ACTIVITY 11

Power Tip
For most search engines, including Google.com, place quotation marks around groups of words that you are treating as one term—for example, *"lottery tickets."* If you typed in the two words without quotation marks, you would get all the entries that include just the word *lottery* and all the entries that include just the word *tickets*—far more results than you would want or need.

Using a topic from Activity 10, generate more ideas through independent research. Select an Internet search engine such as Google.com and type in the key words (underlined) for the topic. As you begin reading others' ideas about your topic, write down more information down response to the five *W*s.

Recording Support

Using the five *W*s and role-playing should "ignite" your brainstorm. Once the ideas start flowing, it is important to record them—*get them down on paper*. Here are three helpful methods for recording your support:

- clustering
- listing
- freewriting

Clustering and listing are especially effective when you must work quickly. Since many of your college writing assignments will be in-class, with time restrictions, we recommend that you practice at least one of these methods.

Freewriting generally requires more time; therefore, it may not be the most efficient way to record your ideas during an in-class writing assignment. However, many students prefer freewriting, especially when they have plenty of time to record their ideas.

CLUSTERING

Power Tip
Clustering may also be the best method for you if you are a *visual learner*—for example, if you'd rather look at a diagram than read instructions when assembling something.

This method involves using a series of bubbles (circles) and connecting lines to record your ideas. Clustering is especially useful for students who have trouble organizing their ideas; the bubbles and lines help group related items together. (For more on clustering, see Chapter 4. For blank clustering forms, see this book's Web site, at **bedfordstmartins.com/steppingstones**.)

Clustering with the Five Ws

If you are using the five *W*s, you can start by drawing a cluster like the following one on a blank sheet of paper. In the center bubble, write your **topic**. In outer bubbles, write the **five *W*s**.

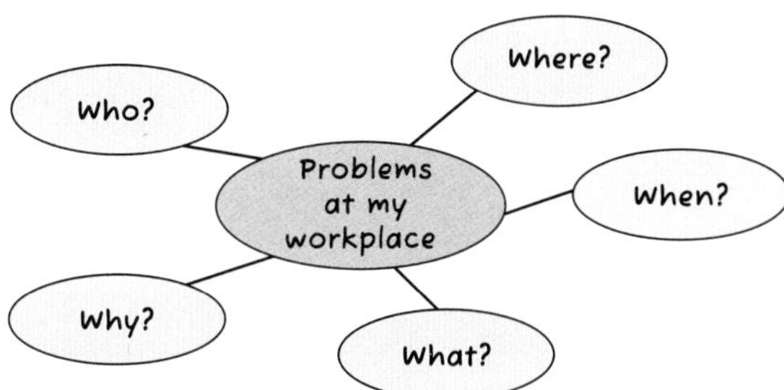

Next, focus on one *W* at a time. Give yourself at least five minutes to work with the first *W* before moving on to the second *W*. An easy place to start is with ***Who?*** Begin by adding the names of all the important people connected to your topic. In the following example (and later clusters), this first level of support is in *purple:*

Teaching Tip
Point out to students that they don't have to move through the five *W*s in the order presented here. They might start where they have the most ideas and inspiration. If they are blocked about a certain *W*, they should move on to the next one.

The next step is to add any important ideas to each name. Here, remember that the topic is ***problems** at my workplace,* so any ideas added to the names should be about problems. In the following example (and later clusters), this second level of support is in *green:*

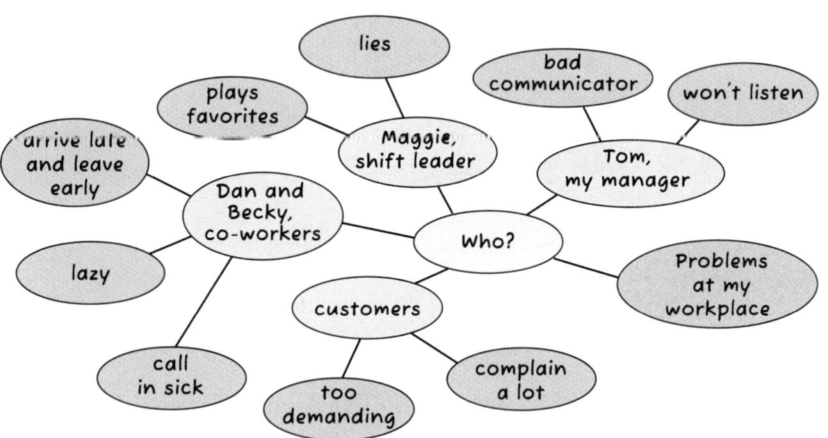

Power Tip
As your cluster expands, remember to look back at your topic (the center bubble) and make sure that all your ideas are connected to the topic.

ACTIVITY 12

Answer the following questions about the cluster immediately preceding this activity.

1. Who complains and demands too much? the customers
2. What do we know about Maggie? She plays favorites and lies.
3. Who is a bad communicator? Tom
4. What problems might Dan and Becky cause? a loss in productivity (Answers may vary.)

ACTIVITY 13

Build a cluster using *Who?* Follow these steps:

1. Begin by identifying a powerful memory.
2. Next, pick a role-playing strategy to help you explore the memory. (See page 59 for more on role-playing.)
3. Identify the important people who are part of the memory. Write their names in the purple bubbles.
4. Think about what each person does in the memory. Fill in the green bubbles to describe each person's part in the memory.

Note: You may leave some bubbles empty or add extra bubbles if necessary.
Answers will vary.

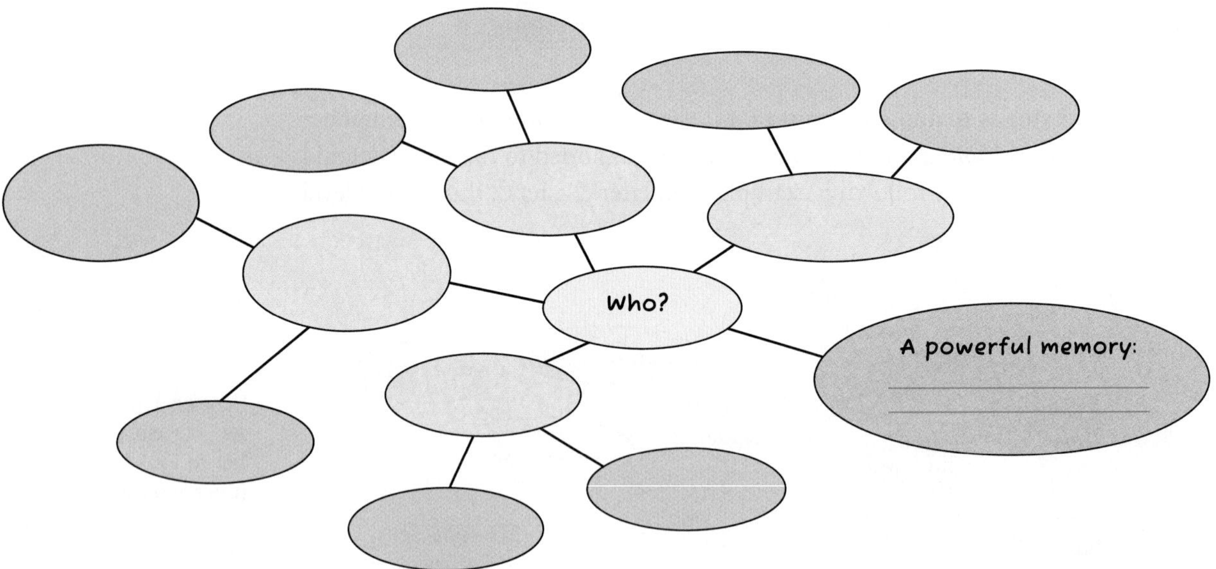

Now, move on to another *W*. Many students like to cluster around ***Where?*** because it is usually easy to use. When responding to *Where?*, begin by identifying all the important places connected to your topic. (In the following cluster, the writer is investigating *where* problems happen at work.) In some cases, you will name only one or two places, which is fine.

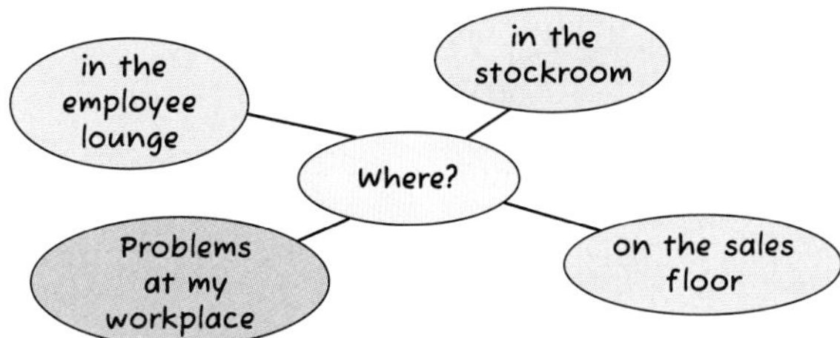

Next, add additional information or ideas to describe each place or explain what happens there. As you reach this second level of support, remember to look back at your center bubble to stay focused on the topic.

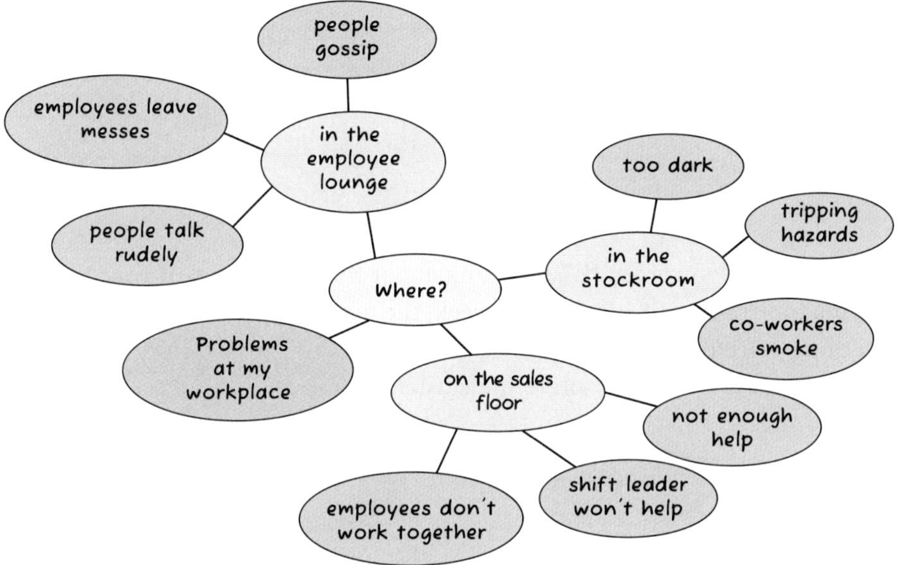

ACTIVITY 14

Answer the following questions about the cluster immediately preceding this activity.

1. Where does the shift leader not help out? on the sales floor
2. In which places do the employees cause problems? in all locations (the employee lounge, the stockroom, and the sales floor)
3. Where would you need to be careful about getting hurt at this workplace? in the stockroom

ACTIVITY 15

Build a cluster using *Where?* Follow these steps:

1. Use the same powerful memory and the role-playing strategy that you used for Activity 13 (page 66).
2. Think of the place or places where the remembered event or situation happened. Fill in the purple bubbles with the names of the place or places.
3. Fill in the green bubbles to add more information or ideas about each place.

Note: You may leave some bubbles empty or add extra bubbles if necessary.
Answers will vary.

CONTINUED >

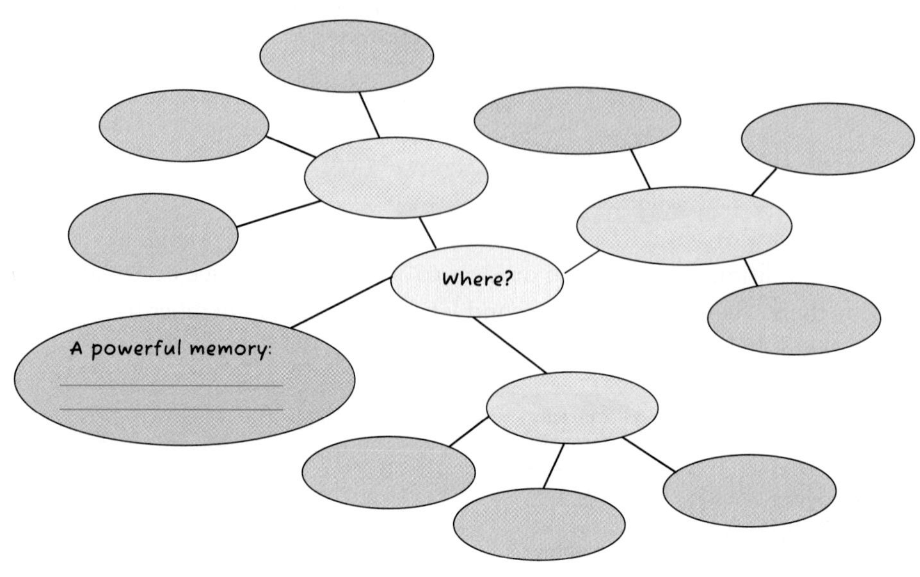

Power Tip
By the third *W*, you may see some repetition of ideas. Remember, repetition is beneficial in clustering or listing because it can help you identify important ideas. Later, you can always cross out ideas that are repetitive or that you don't want to use.

Another good *W* to ask is ***When?*** Think about the time frame of your topic: the date, the time of day, the days of the week, the month, the season, your age, when something started, when something ended, how long something lasted, and so on. Then, add this information to the cluster.

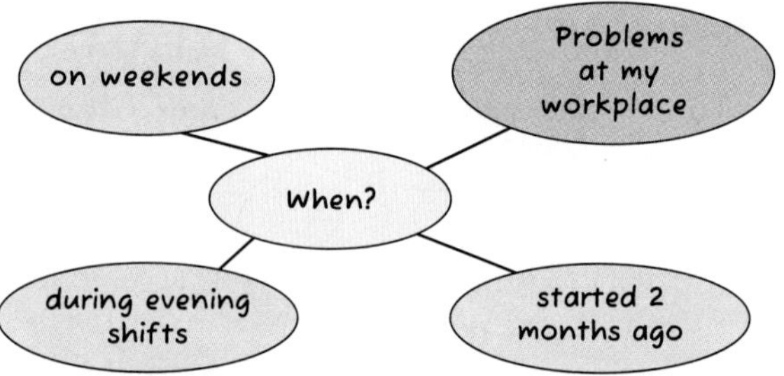

The next step is to work with one of these bubbles at a time and add any extra ideas you may have. Again, when developing this second level of support, it's important to look back at the topic (the center bubble). Any added information should be related to the topic.

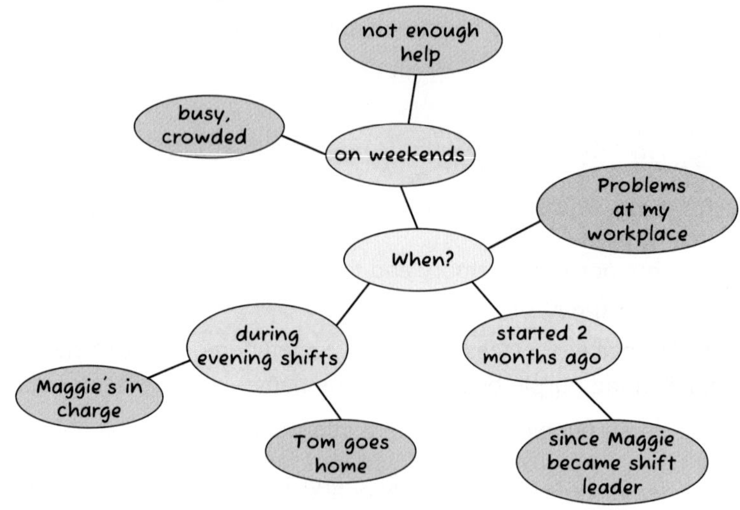

ACTIVITY 16

Answer the following questions about the cluster immediately preceding this activity.

1. When did Maggie become the shift leader? two months ago
2. What happens on the evening shift that causes problems? Answers may vary, but students should at least note that Maggie is in charge. (The problems with her and Tom are shown in the cluster on page 65.)
3. When does the store become too busy for the employees to handle? on weekends

ACTIVITY 17

Build a cluster using *When?* Follow these steps:

1. Use the same powerful memory and the role-playing strategy that you used for Activity 13 (page 66).
2. Think of the time frame of the event or situation in your memory. Fill in the purple bubbles with details about when the remembered event or situation happened, how long it lasted, and so on.
3. Fill in the green bubbles with more information or ideas about each of the time examples.

Note: You may leave some bubbles empty or add extra bubbles if necessary.
Answers will vary.

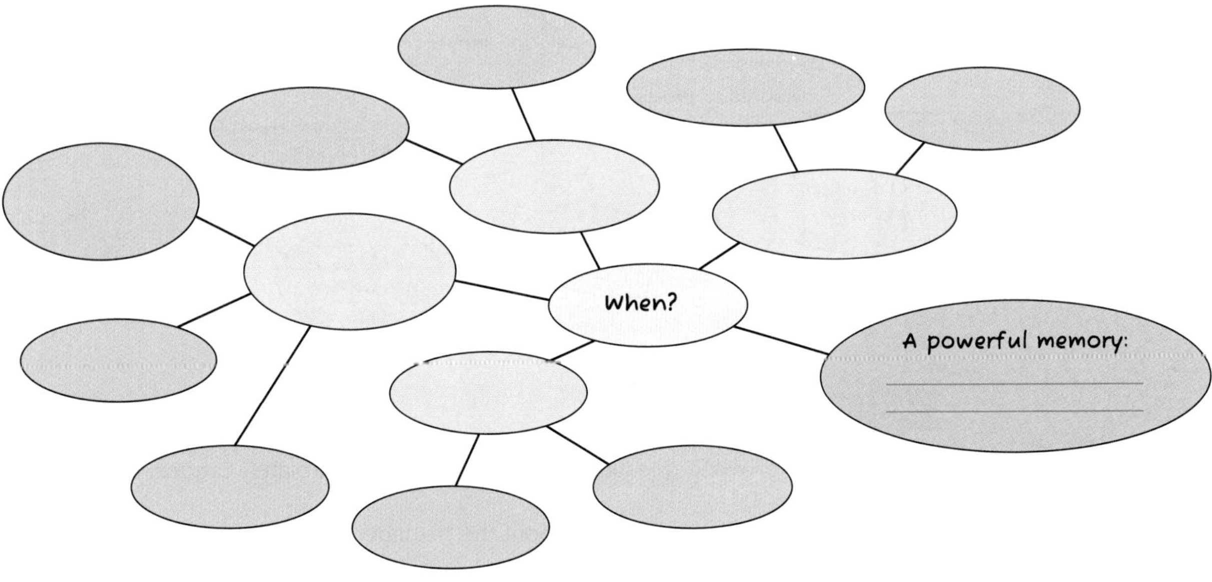

What? questions are easy to use and can produce important ideas about your topic. In the example we've been working with, the obvious question is "What are the problems at my workplace?" As the first level of support (the purple bubbles), the student has listed examples of problems at her job.

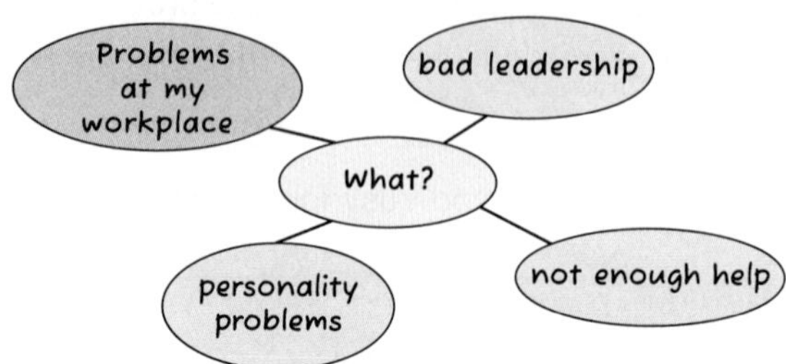

Next, add additional information or ideas to describe or explain each example. As you reach this second level of support, remember to look back at your center bubble to stay focused on the topic.

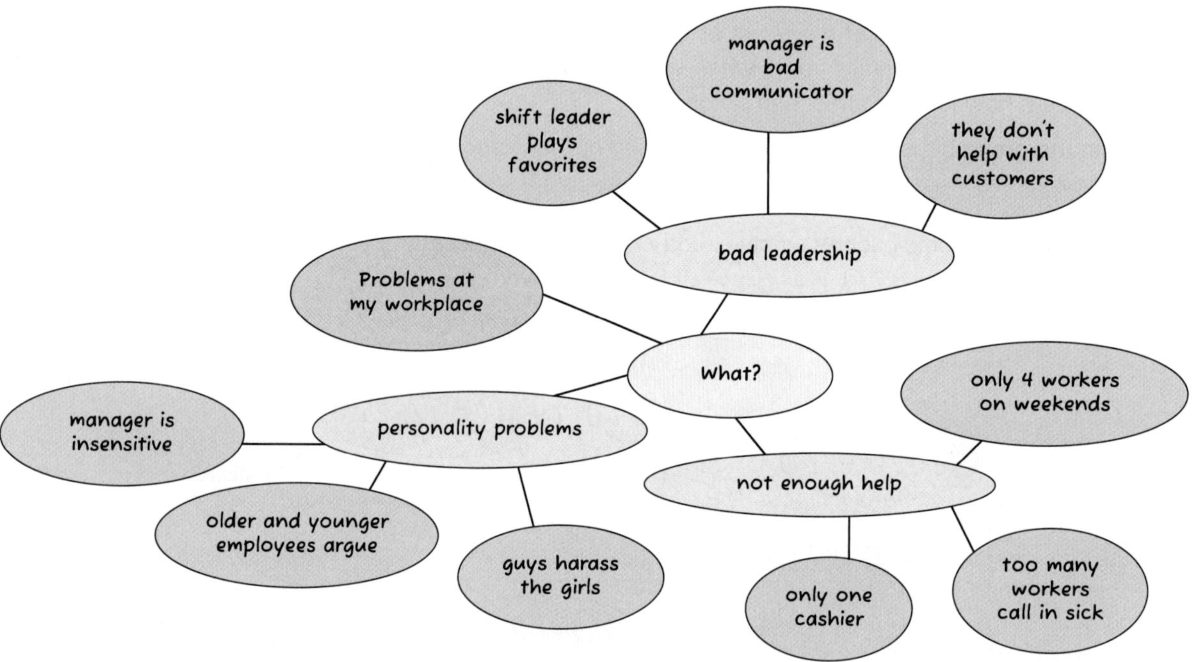

ACTIVITY 18

Answer the following questions about the cluster immediately preceding this activity.

1. What are two complaints about the manager? The manager is insensitive and a bad communicator.
2. Which groups of employees do not get along with one another? older and younger employees
3. What is one reason for staff shortages? Too many workers call in sick.

ACTIVITY 19

Build a cluster using *What?* Follow these steps:

1. Use the same powerful memory and the role-playing strategy that you used for Activity 13 (page 66).
2. Ask yourself the following question: *What happens in my memory?* Then, fill in the purple bubbles with answers or examples.
3. Fill in the green bubbles with more information or ideas about each of the examples.

Note: You may leave some bubbles empty or add extra bubbles if necessary.

Answers will vary.

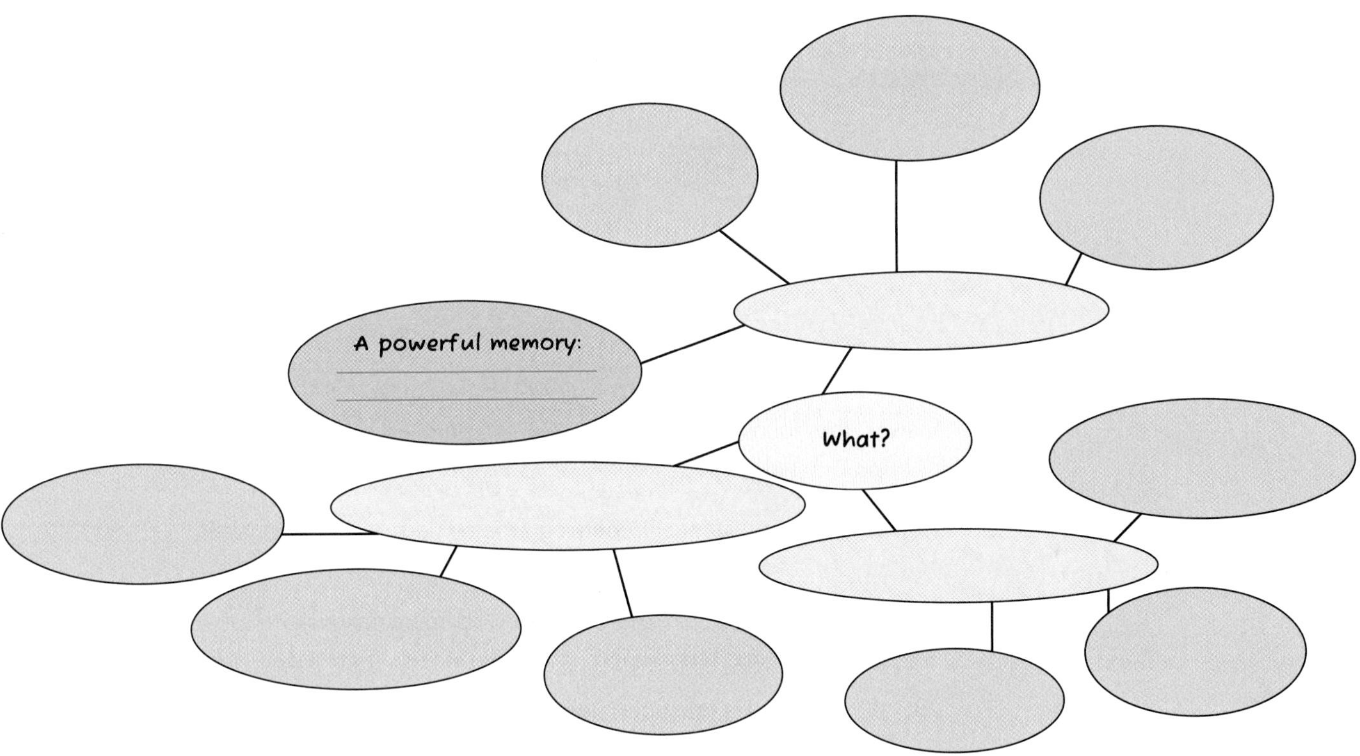

Many students like to save ***Why?*** for the last *W*. To fully understand your topic, you need to ask why things happen and why people act the way they do. These questions may be easier to answer after you have explored all the other *W* questions. In the following example, the student has asked herself, "Why do these problems continue to occur at my workplace?" Her answers are in the purple bubbles:

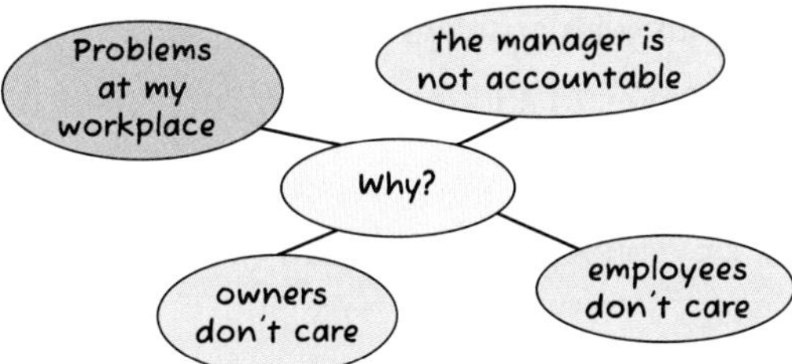

Next, the student added information to describe or explain each example. As you reach this second level of support, remember to look back at your center bubble to stay focused on the topic.

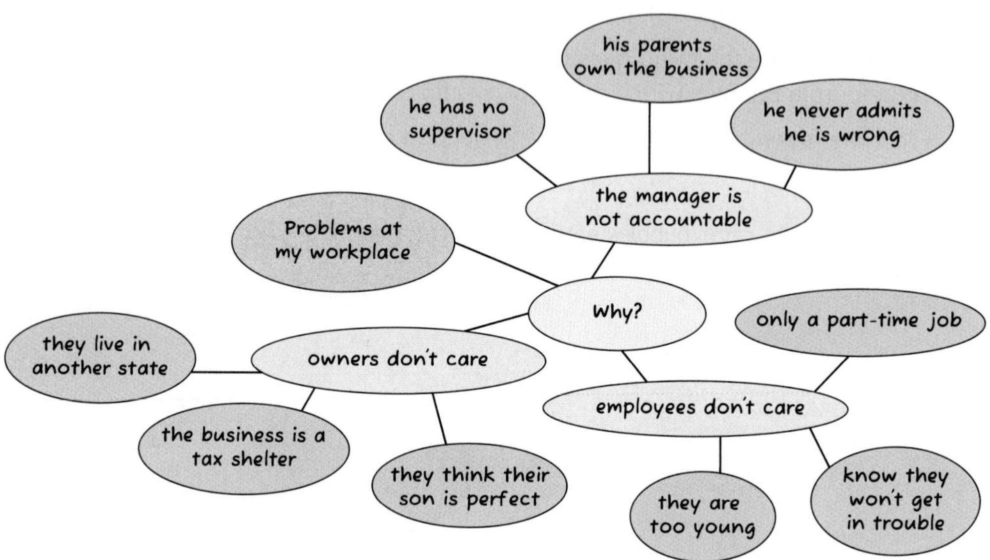

ACTIVITY 20

Answer the following questions about the cluster immediately preceding this activity.

1. What is the relationship between the owners and the manager? The owners are the manager's parents.
2. Why don't the employees take their work more seriously? It is only a part-time job, they are too young, and they know they won't get in trouble.
3. What does the manager always refuse to do? admit that he is wrong

ACTIVITY 21

Build a cluster using *Why?* Follow these steps:

1. Use the same powerful memory and the role-playing strategy that you used for Activity 13 (page 66).
2. Ask yourself the following question: *Why is this memory powerful?* Then, fill in the purple bubbles with answers or examples.
3. Fill in the green bubbles to add more information or ideas about each of the examples.

Note: You may leave some bubbles empty or add extra bubbles if necessary.
Answers will vary.

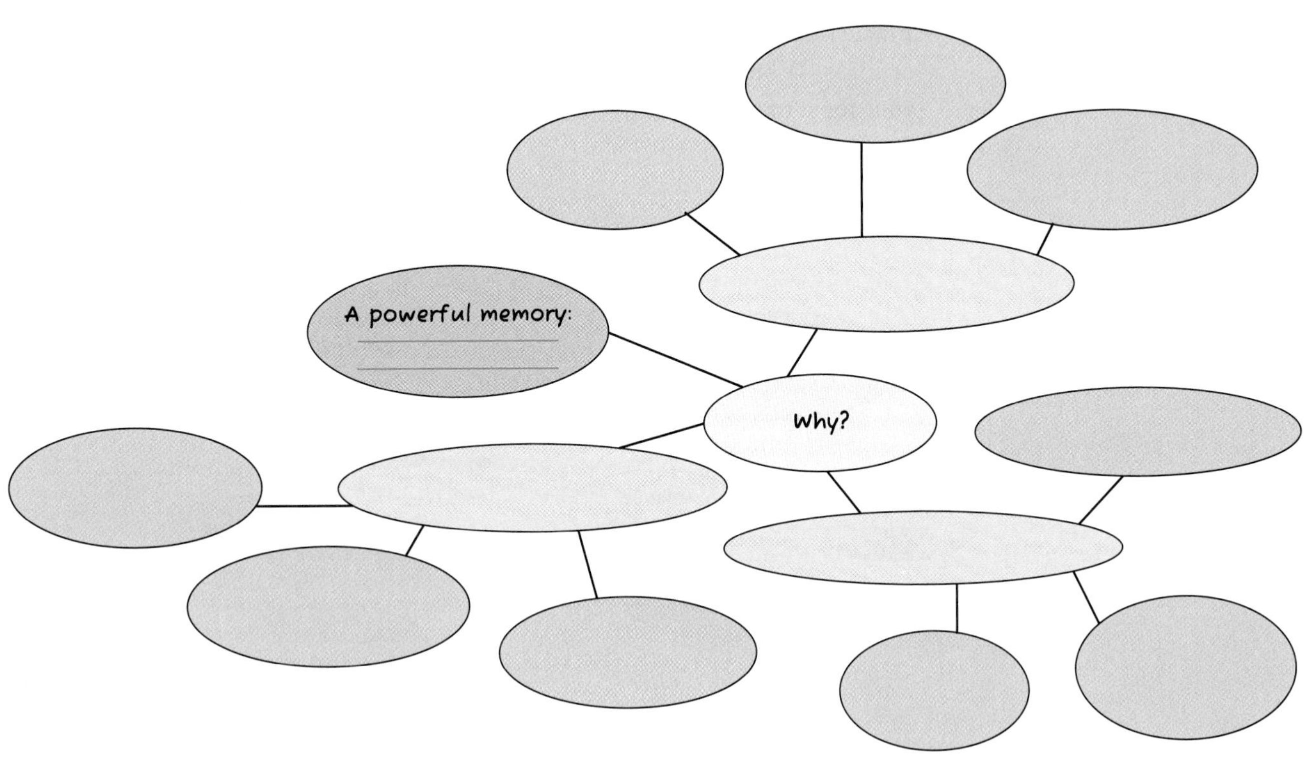

Clustering without the Five Ws

Some students prefer to skip the five *W*s and go directly to identifying major **examples**. In this case, examples would be in the first set of bubbles around the topic.

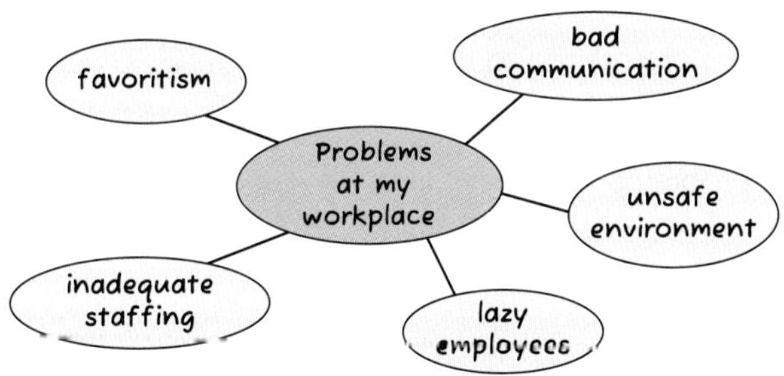

Next, focus on one problem at a time and provide specifics for each:

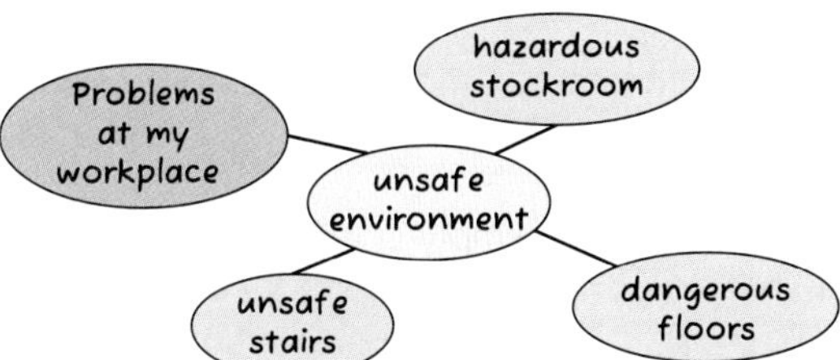

Finally, focus on one specific example at a time, adding any additional information or ideas. When you reach this final level of support, remember to look back at your topic to stay focused.

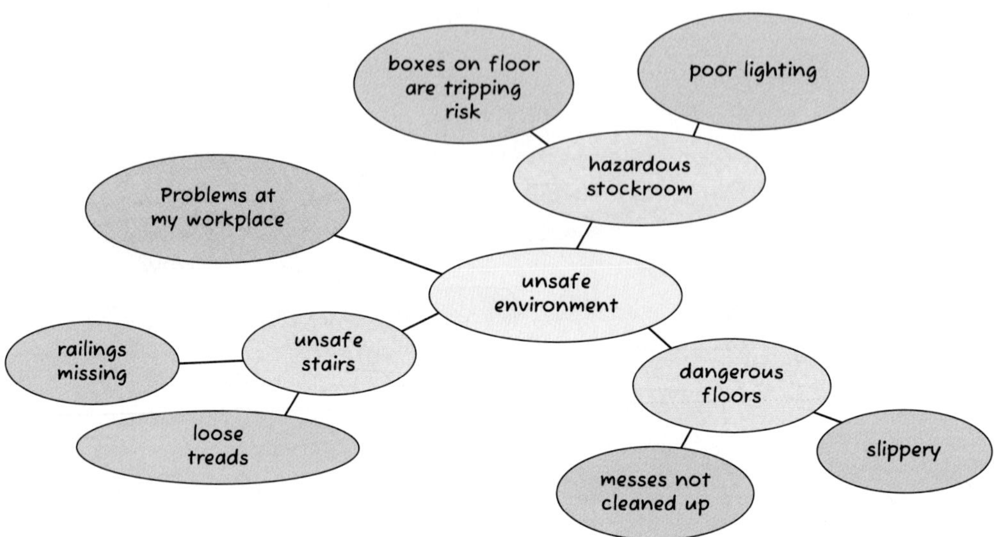

ACTIVITY 22

Answer the following questions about the cluster immediately preceding this activity.

1. What are the three major examples of an unsafe environment? the hazardous stockroom, the dangerous floors, and the unsafe stairs
2. What are causes of hazards in the stockroom? boxes on the floor and poor lighting
3. What problems are related to the floors? They are messy and slippery.
4. How many problems with the stairs are named? two

ACTIVITY 23

Complete the following cluster without using the five *W*s. Follow these steps:

1. Fill in the *green* bubbles with examples of things you like about your favorite course.
2. Fill in the *purple* bubbles to add more information or ideas about each of the examples.

Note: You may leave some bubbles empty or add extra bubbles if necessary.
Answers will vary.

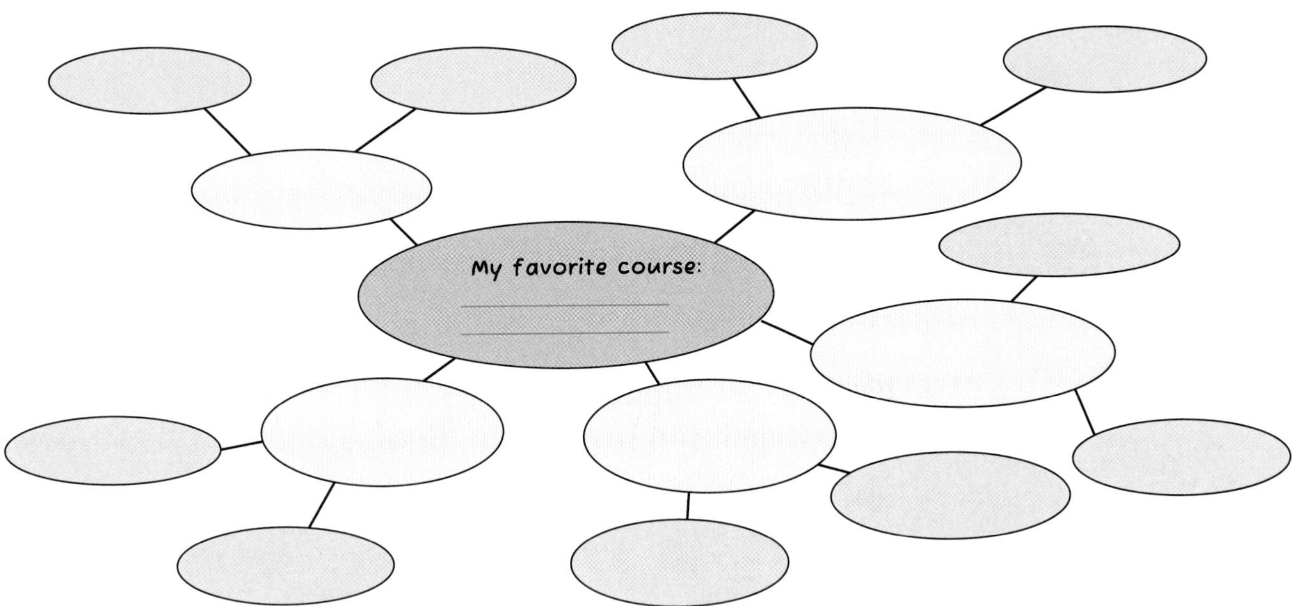

ACTIVITY 24: Teamwork

With classmates, compare what you wrote in the bubbles for Activity 23. See if your classmates found good examples that you might be able to use in your cluster as well. Then, discuss whether you could add some green bubbles (another level of support) to some of the purple bubbles. What sort of additional information, ideas, or examples could you include?

LISTING

Some students do not like using bubbles and lines to record and connect their ideas. Instead, they prefer to list ideas on paper or a computer screen. If you use this method, it is helpful to think of your list as *a series of short lists*, with headings (such as the five *W*s) setting up each short list. This will help you group related ideas together.

Listing with the Five Ws

If you are using the five *W*s, you can draw the following list on a blank sheet of paper. At the top of the page, write your topic. Remember to leave space between the five *W*s for additional information. You may want to underline these words to set them off from the additional information. If you prefer to work on a computer, open a new document and type in your topic and five *W*s. Save the file with a clear name—for example, "Idea list_workplace problems."

Problems at My Workplace

Who?

Where?

When?

What?

Why?

Next, create a short list under each *W,* answering the question with examples and other information. For example, if you begin with *Who?,* you might make a short list of names, identifying all the important people connected to your topic.

Problems at My Workplace

Who?

Maggie, shift leader
Tom, my manager
Dan and Becky, co-workers
the customers

Where?

The next step is to add any further ideas to each name. Here, remember that the topic is ***problems** at my workplace,* so any additional ideas should be about problems.

Problems at My Workplace

Who?

Maggie, shift leader—lies and plays favorites
Tom, my manager—won't listen and is a bad communicator
Dan and Becky, co-workers—lazy, call in sick, come late and leave early
the customers—too demanding, complain a lot

Where?

From this point, you can continue creating one list at a time for each *W.* Give yourself at least five minutes for each *W.*

Listing without the Five Ws

You may also create a list without using the five *W*s. In this case, try to identify major examples or ideas about your topic. Write them down as a list, leaving space between each item. Or, you may type them into a computer file.

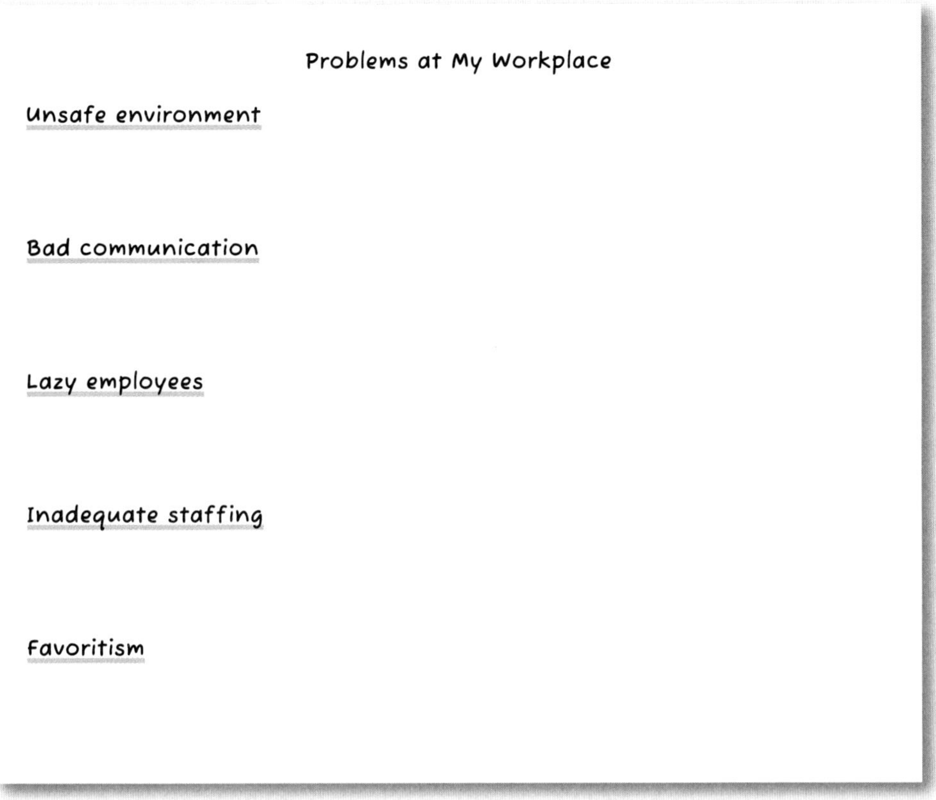

Problems at My Workplace

Unsafe environment

Bad communication

Lazy employees

Inadequate staffing

Favoritism

From this point, you can build your list by working on one major idea at a time. For each major idea, give yourself at least five minutes to list additional information or examples.

Problems at My Workplace

Unsafe environment

hazardous stockroom — boxes on floor are tripping risk, poor lighting
dangerous floors — slippery, messes not cleaned up
unsafe stairs — railings missing, loose treads

Bad communication

ACTIVITY 25

Make a five *Ws* list (see page 75) or major ideas list (see page 77) for one of the following five topics. For topics 4 and 5, you may do independent research to find additional ideas. Answers will vary.

- **Topic 1:** the kind of parent/aunt/grandparent (or role model) I'd like to be
- **Topic 2:** a story or tradition that is important to my family
- **Topic 3:** a problem I'd like to be free of
- **Topic 4:** bringing back the military draft
- **Topic 5:** keeping or getting rid of college placement tests

Clustering and listing are not always as neat as the previous examples suggest. Because you will be writing quickly, expect to have to squeeze in ideas and bubbles where you don't have enough space. Also, don't expect your cluster or list to be perfectly organized. However, if you build your cluster or list one item at a time, you may be able to keep related ideas grouped together. Here are some samples from real students:

SAMPLE OF CLUSTERING

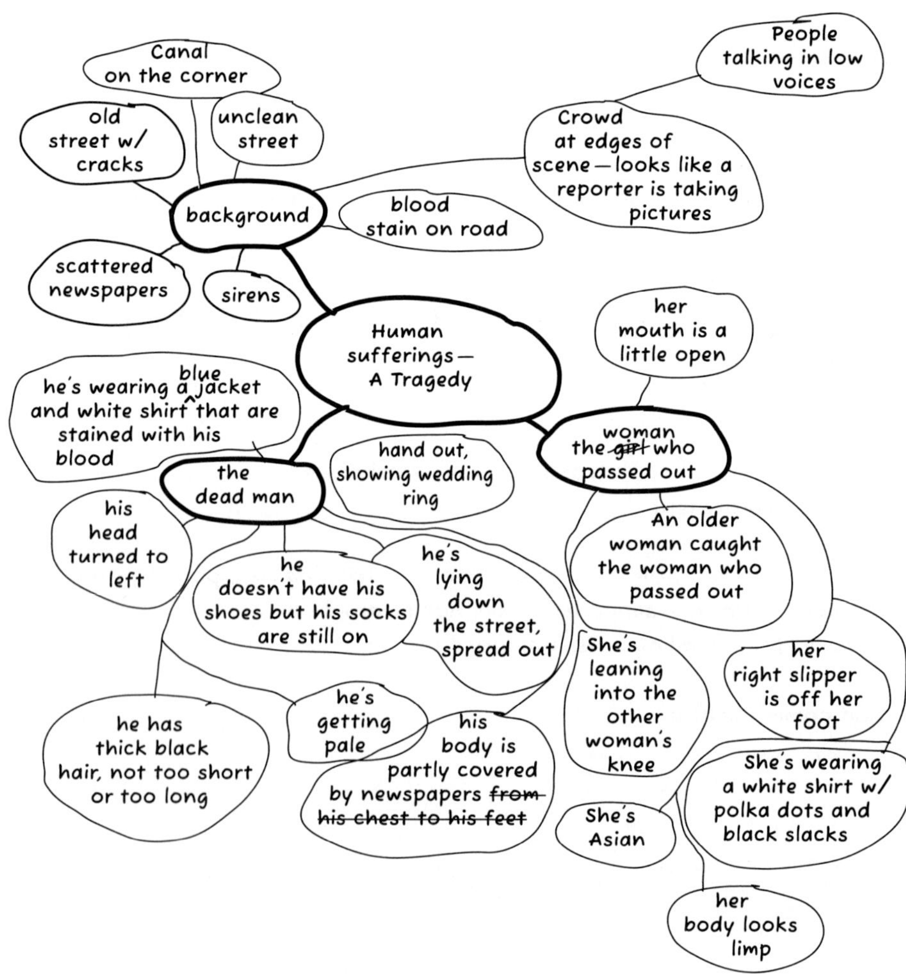

SAMPLE OF LISTING

Rock climbing photo 6

Drive
test of manhood
Strenuous vacation
China, Australia, Brazil
group of close friends
falling down
250 to 300 feet walk
money at stake
extreme sports
Fathers all ~~age~~ ages
at home dads

weather change
dark, winds, drizzling

could not believe
mid life crisis
~~they would look down~~
lucky hat
he was respected and
he was the one that was
scared to do things

Emotions
scared
fired up
nauseous
~~evil~~
focus
sweating
live or dead
upset how did I get into this

Senses
* Smell = mist fresh air
** ~~sig~~ sights = ~~th~~ friend the other end
* Sound = deer, wind, animals, music, MP3
* Taste = the last meal, vomit
touch = rope, ruff shirt wet, sweat
6th sense = visualize himself somewhere else

lesson
no limits
challenge
better confidence
Inspirational

FREEWRITING

Another method of recording your ideas is called freewriting. Generally, freewriting requires more time than clustering or listing, so it may not be ideal for in-class, timed writing assignments. If you prefer freewriting, we recommend that you also practice either clustering or listing as a back-up method for timed writing assignments.

Freewriting is like recording your thoughts in a diary. Keeping your topic in mind, put down whatever thoughts occur to you about it. Even if your ideas seem silly or disconnected at first, keep going; you are giving your mind time to warm up. Do not worry about grammar, spelling, or organization. This continuous stream of thoughts and movement helps many students relax and produce ideas that might not have occurred to them otherwise.

Before you begin freewriting, it is a good idea to decide on a time limit, usually about ten minutes for the first freewriting. (As you will learn shortly, you may do more than one freewriting session on a topic.) Then, *keep writing* until the time is up.

Here is an example of freewriting for the topic *problems at my workplace*. Notice how this sample sounds like an e-mail to a friend or an entry in a personal diary.

I can't believe how much I hate my job! On Saturday I came home from work dead tired, it was sooooooooo busy and we only had four workers on the sales floor. Of course, Maggie won't lift a finger to serve a customer because she has to "supervise" (which basically means talking on the phone to her boyfriend). At one point I slipped on some spilled liquid on the floor and twisted my ankle. And where were my wonderful co-workers? Off smoking in the stockroom which is not allowed anyway and it wasn't their break time. And Tom makes me so mad—he won't listen to anything I have to say, he never admits that he's wrong and his parents think that he's perfect. I am surprised that this business stays open but the owners (Tom's parents of course!) use it as a tax shelter or something funny like that. The whole thing is a big mess and I don't know if I can survive another weekend. . . . HELP!

tax shelter: a financial setup that reduces or eliminates taxes

The next step in freewriting is to read what you have written and circle two or three powerful ideas that you would like to explore further. Remember to select ideas that are closely connected to your topic (in this case, *problems at my workplace*). Here is what this student circled in her original freewriting:

I can't believe how much I hate my job! On Saturday I came home from work dead tired, it was sooooooooo busy and we only had four workers on the sales floor. Of course, Maggie won't lift a finger to serve a customer because she has to "supervise" (which basically means talking on the phone to her boyfriend). At one point I slipped on some spilled liquid on the floor and twisted my ankle. And where were my loyal co-workers? Off smoking in the stockroom which is not allowed anyway and it wasn't their break time. And Tom makes me so mad—he won't listen to anything I have to say, he never admits that he's wrong and his parents think that he's perfect. I am surprised that this business stays open but the owners (Tom's parents of course!) use it as a tax shelter or something funny like that. The whole thing is a big mess and I don't know if I can survive another weekend. . . . HELP!

Now, select one of these ideas and freewrite about it for five minutes. Once again, *just keep writing* until the time is up, even if your ideas go off the topic somewhat. Here is what this student wrote:

Maggie is such a pain! When Tom made her a shift leader she got a BIG ATTITUDE she also flirts with Tom and gets away with murder. Like I said, she spends more time on the phone with her boyfriend than she does helping us or assisting customers. She also lets Dan and Becky take longer breaks and come in late just because they are friends of hers. Of course, when I complained about this she told me to mind my own business which is soooooooo unprofessional—not like she cares anyway. This is just a part-time job for her and she is only 18 years old. A shift leader is hardly president of the united states, but the power goes to her head. She never ASKS me to do anything she ORDERS me. She needs a reality check. . . .

Next, read what you have written and circle one or two of the most powerful ideas. Then, select one idea from *either* your first or second freewriting and freewrite about that idea for five minutes.

Continue this process of freewriting, reading, circling, and freewriting again until you have explored all your ideas about the topic or until you run out of time.

Teaching Tip

Mention that students can use freewriting and other idea-generating strategies at any stage of the writing process—for example, they might freewrite to get ideas for fleshing out a weakly supported statement in a draft.

ACTIVITY 26

Using freewriting, discuss *someone you admire*. Follow these steps:

1. Freewrite for ten minutes on the topic.
2. Read what you wrote and circle two or three powerful ideas that you would like to develop.
3. Select ONE of those ideas and freewrite on it for five minutes.
4. Read what you wrote and circle one or two powerful ideas that you would like to develop.
5. Select ONE idea from *either* your first or second freewriting. Then, freewrite on this idea for five minutes.
6. If you wish, continue this exercise until you have fully explored your ideas on the topic.

Power Tip

When using freewriting, it is important to remember that this exercise is *not a draft* of your paragraph or essay. Before drafting your paragraph or essay, you will need to organize your ideas and develop an outline. (See Chapter 4 for more information on organizing and outlining.)

FREEWRITING WITH THE FIVE *W*S AND ROLE-PLAYING

Some students find it helpful to freewrite using the five *W*s, role-playing, or both of these strategies. You might pick the two or three *W*s that seem most promising for your topic and freewrite on each for five to ten minutes. Try to start with a *W* that is easy or interesting for you.

If you find role-playing helpful, select a role and close your eyes. As your imagination warms up and allows you to get into character, start freewriting about the first *W*. This student chose the role of investigative reporter. (See page 60 for more on this role.)

Who causes problems at my workplace? Well, Maggie is the biggest pain of all because she lets a little bit of power go to her head. Tom is the manager and since Maggie flirts with him he lets her get away with murder. Even on the weekends when we are really busy, Maggie will spend most of the day talking to her boyfriend on the phone. She never lifts a finger to help us when there are customers waiting and Tom has NEVER once asked her to get off the phone and help us. Why doesn't Tom care? Well, he doesn't have to answer to anybody basically. His parents own the business but they live in Montana so they never come to the store and Tom is not accountable to anyone. His parents use this business as a tax shelter so they don't care if it is profitable or not. So Tom just goofs off, flirts with Maggie and bosses the rest of us around. My wonderful co-workers, Becky and Dan are friends of Maggie's so they come in late, take long breaks, and sneak off to smoke in the stockroom. . . . UNBELIEVABLE! I complained about it once and Maggie told me point blank to mind my own business! On top of all that, the customers are demanding and rude. . . .

When the first five to ten minutes are up, move to a new line on your paper and begin freewriting on another *W*. If a *W* does not fit your topic, just skip it and go on to the next *W*.

ACTIVITY 27

Select one of the following topics and freewrite about it, using two to three of the five *W*s. Write for five minutes on each of the *W*s, one at a time. If one of the *W*s does not fit your topic, skip it and go on to the next *W*. (If you would like to use role-playing, select a role, close your eyes, and give yourself a few minutes to get into character.) Answers will vary.

- **Topic 1:** Discuss how people perceive you when they first meet you.
- **Topic 2:** Write about your favorite form of entertainment.
- **Topic 3:** Discuss the role of religion in your life.

Bringing It All Together

In this chapter, you have learned what support is, where it comes from, and how to generate and record support based on your own experience and knowledge. Check off each of the following statements that you understand. For any that you do not understand, review the appropriate pages in this chapter.

- ☐ **Support** consists of the ideas and information that a writer gathers for a topic. (See page 55.)
- ☐ Support can come from personal experience and knowledge, from assigned texts, and from independent research.
  - ____ Personal experience and knowledge are what you already know about a topic: memories, emotions, facts, and opinions that you have accumulated through your personal and educational experiences. (See page 55.)
  - ____ Assigned texts include readings that have been assigned for a course: stories, journal articles, textbook chapters, and so on. (See page 55.)
  - ____ Independent research is finding, on your own and outside of class, others' ideas on a topic. (See page 56.)
- ☐ **Critical thinking** is going below the surface of our first impressions and looking at a topic from different viewpoints. A good way to think critically about a topic is to ask **the five *Ws*** about it (***Who? Where? When? What?*** and ***Why?***). (See page 57.)
- ☐ A good way to investigate your topic from a fresh point of view is to ask the five *Ws* while acting out a role (detective, investigative reporter, archaeologist, fortune-teller, psychologist, or judge). (See page 59.)
- ☐ **Clustering**, **listing**, and **freewriting** are ways to record (get down on paper) ideas about a topic. (See pages 64–82.)
- ☐ **Clustering** involves using a series of bubbles and connecting lines to record and relate your ideas (see page 64). It can be done with the five *Ws* (see page 65) or with major examples instead of the five *Ws* (see page 73).
- ☐ **Listing** is making lists of ideas, without bubbles or connecting lines. It can be done with the five *Ws* (see page 75) or with major examples instead of the five *Ws* (see page 77).
- ☐ **Freewriting** is like recording your thoughts in a diary. Keeping your topic in mind, you put down whatever thoughts occur to you about it. Then, you circle two or three powerful ideas in what you have written and freewrite on them, continuing the process of circling and freewriting until you have explored all of your ideas about a topic or run out of time. (See page 79.)

A final note: Even after you have generated lots of support for your topic, there are always ways to make the support more vivid and detailed for your readers. For more advice on developing details, see Chapter 6.

Chapter 4

Organizing and Outlining

OVERVIEW OF THIS CHAPTER

WARM-UP Shopping for a Party

1. *Imagine this situation:*

You're planning a party, and you will have only thirty minutes to shop on your way home from school. You know that you will need a wide variety of supplies, from drinks to food to paper products. Your friends' food and drink preferences vary, so you know that you must buy a lot of different items. If you forget any important items, your party will not be a success. Which of the following plans will help you accomplish your shopping goals in the thirty minutes you have?

- **Plan A:** Rush to the market and pull items off the shelves as you walk down the aisle.
- **Plan B:** Take a list like the white one to the store.
- **Plan C:** Take a list like the yellow one to the store.

2. *Stop and think!*

Alone or with classmates, consider the advantages and disadvantages of each plan. Which one would allow you to shop most quickly and efficiently? Which plan would result in the most successful shopping and, as a result, the most successful party?

Making an outline—a plan for your writing—is like making a shopping list. The more organized your shopping list, the better you'll shop and the more successful your party will be. The more organized your outline, the better you'll write, and the more successful your paper will be. This chapter will help you get organized to become a better writer.

Organizing Basics

In Chapter 3, you learned how to brainstorm (generate) a lot of good ideas for any topic. Now, you'll learn how to organize ideas in preparation for developing an effective outline, a plan for your writing. Organizing involves several mental strategies, the most common of which are

- **ordering:** arranging the ideas you developed through brainstorming in a logical way
- **grouping:** putting related ideas together
- **eliminating:** removing ideas that are not related to your topic

Often, these activities are like puzzle solving, and they can be a lot of fun. The more you practice them, the more your organizing skills will improve.

Teaching Tip
Bring to class different colors and kinds of socks (children's, adults', sports, dress, and so on), as well as a couple of items that are not related, such as a scarf and tie. First, ask students how they'd group the items. For example, they might group socks by color or kind. Then, ask what items they would eliminate (the scarf and tie). This is a fun way to warm up students for this chapter.

ORDERING

The first skill to practice is **ordering**. To order your ideas effectively, you will need to be able to recognize the difference between **general ideas** and **specific examples**. General ideas usually come first in order, and they are followed by specific examples. Look at the following example:

jobs
clerk
engineer
cook

The word *jobs* expresses a general idea because there are many types of jobs. The words *clerk, engineer,* and *cook* are specific examples of jobs.

Ordering Single-Word Items

As shown in the previous example, a *single word* can express either a general idea or a specific example. Now, take a look at the following lists and decide which one is ordered correctly:

carrots	**vegetables**
broccoli	tomatoes
vegetables	carrots
tomatoes	broccoli

The second list is correct: The word *vegetables* expresses a general idea because there are many types of vegetables. The words *broccoli, tomatoes,* and *carrots* are specific examples of vegetables.

Power Tip
While working through the activities in this chapter, use a dictionary to look up the meaning of any words you do not recognize. Doing so will help you complete the activities successfully and build your vocabulary at the same time.

Teaching Tip
Have students pair up in groups of two. Each student should then write two or three scrambled lists of words (including the general idea), following the model of Activity 1. Then, students should exchange their work and try to unscramble each other's lists. Finally, they should exchange unscrambled lists to check each other's work. This can be done with other similar activities in this chapter.

ACTIVITY 1

Rewrite each of the following lists, putting the *general idea* first. If a list is correct as is, write "OK" on the first line.

EXAMPLE:

peanuts	nuts
cashews	peanuts
nuts	cashews
almonds	almonds

1. hamster	pet	**4.** wires	electrical
cat	hamster	electrical	wires
pet	cat	plug	plug
dog	dog	fuse	fuse
2. shirt	clothes	**5.** transportation	OK
clothes	shirt	bicycle	
socks	socks	helicopter	
tie	tie	automobile	
3. rain	weather	**6.** church	building
snow	rain	apartment	church
weather	snow	house	apartment
thunder	thunder	building	house

If you used clustering—putting related ideas in bubbles—to generate ideas, you will need to order your ideas in the same way. The following activity will give you practice with moving items from clusters to lists. (For more on clustering, see Chapter 3.)

Teaching Tip
If students didn't work through Chapter 3, or if they used it only minimally, you might want to refer them to the clustering instructions and examples in that chapter now.

ACTIVITY 2: Teamwork

Working with one or two classmates, study the clusters, and then draw lines from the *general idea* to the specific examples. Next, move the items from the clusters to a list, putting the general idea first.

EXAMPLE:

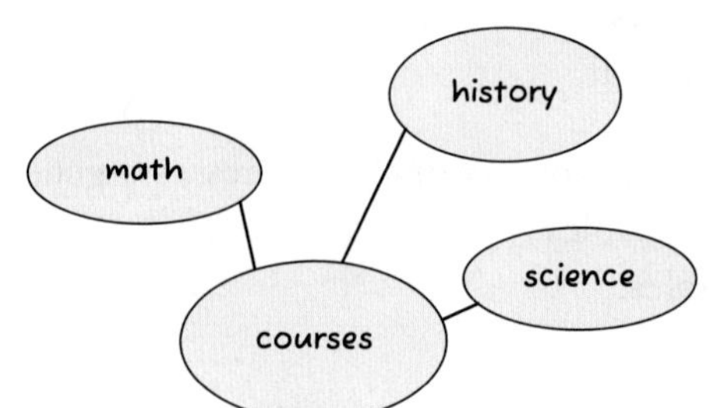

courses
math
history
science

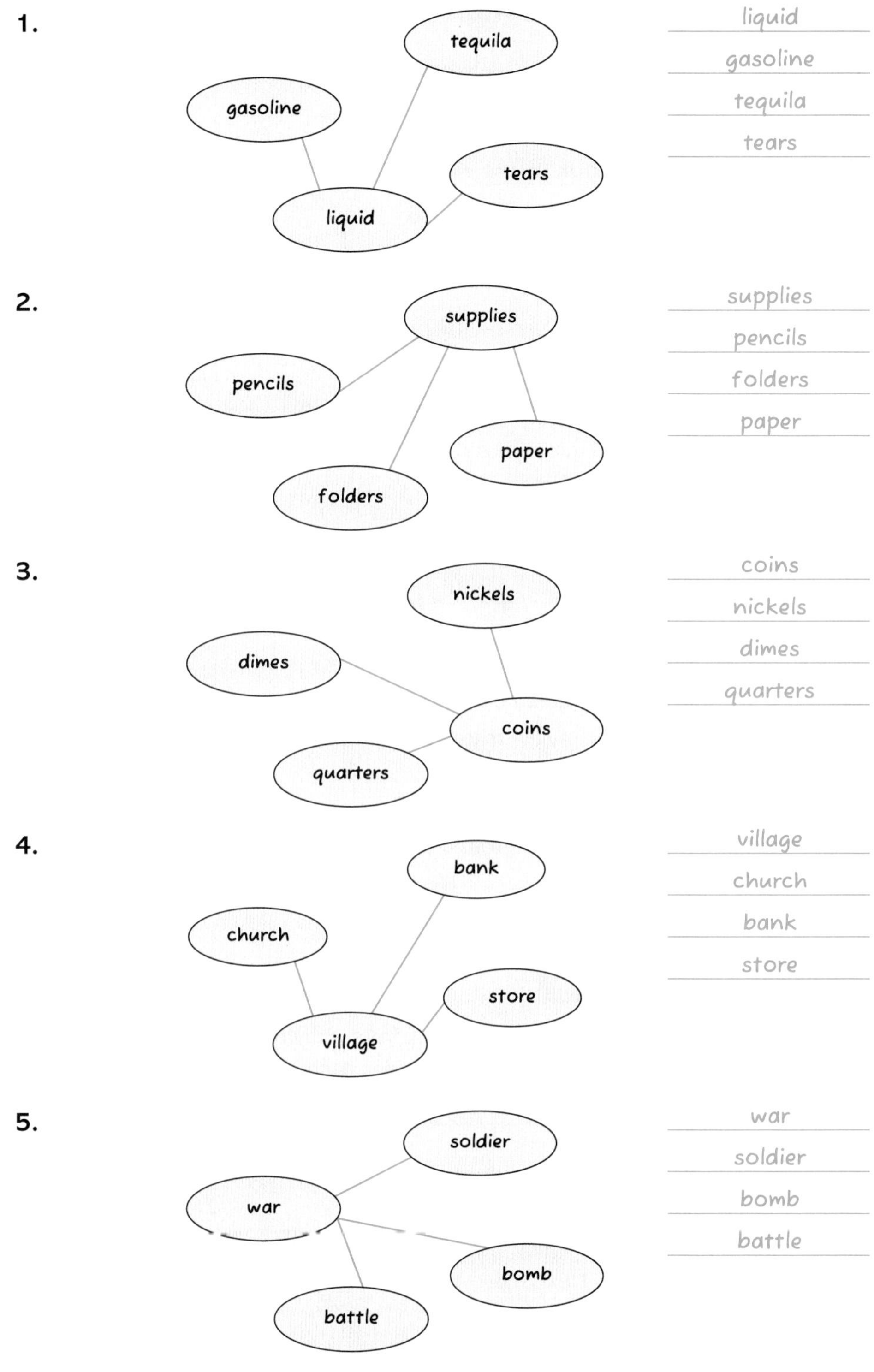

Ordering Phrases

Usually, we express our ideas with more than one word. A **phrase** is a group of words that can express either a *general idea* or a *specific example.* For example, the phrase *healthy food* expresses a general idea because there are many types of healthy food. The phrases *organic fruits and vegetables, whole-grain breads and cereals,* and *low-fat milk and cheese* are each a specific example of healthy food.

ACTIVITY 3

Rewrite each of the following lists, putting the *general idea* first. If a list is correct as is, write "OK" on the first line.

EXAMPLE:

look in the want ads	look for a job
write a résumé	look in the want ads
look for a job	write a résumé
prepare for interviews	prepare for interviews

1. | | |
   |---|---|
   | ice cream sundae | cold desserts |
   | cherry snow cone | ice cream sundae |
   | cold desserts | cherry snow cone |
   | frozen banana | frozen banana |

2. | | |
   |---|---|
   | build a sand castle | day at the beach |
   | lie in the sun | put on lotion |
   | put on lotion | lie in the sun |
   | day at the beach | build a sand castle |

3. | | |
   |---|---|
   | dust furniture | household chores |
   | vacuum carpets | dust furniture |
   | wash the floor | vacuum carpets |
   | household chores | wash the floor |

4. | | |
   |---|---|
   | my dream wedding | OK |
   | three-layer cake | |
   | lots of friends and family | |
   | great music | |

5. | | |
   |---|---|
   | learning procedures | starting a new job |
   | meeting co-workers | learning procedures |
   | starting a new job | meeting co-workers |
   | filling out forms | filling out forms |

6. | | |
   |---|---|
   | reread chapters | study for a test |
   | review material with classmates | reread chapters |
   | review notes | review material with classmates |
   | study for a test | review notes |

ACTIVITY 4: Teamwork

With one or two classmates, pick three items from Activity 3 and, as a group, think of at least four additional examples that fit under each *general idea.*

ACTIVITY 5

In clustering, we often write *phrases* in cluster bubbles. In the following exercise, study the clusters, and then draw lines from the *general idea* phrases to the specific examples. Next, move the phrases from the bubbles to a list, putting the general idea first.

EXAMPLE:

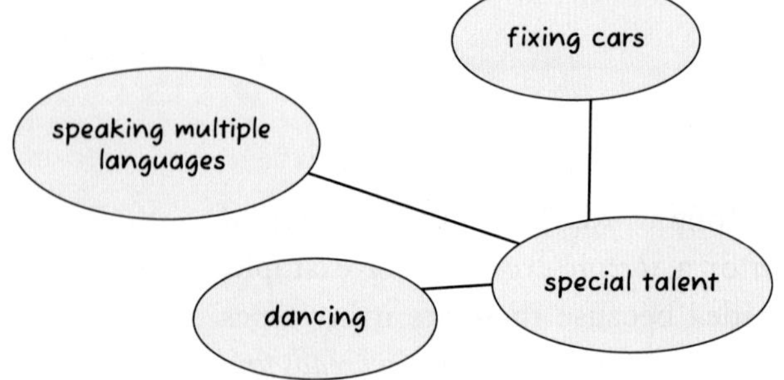

special talent
fixing cars
dancing
speaking multiple languages

extreme sport: a potentially dangerous sport that can involve high speeds, extreme heights, and other risks

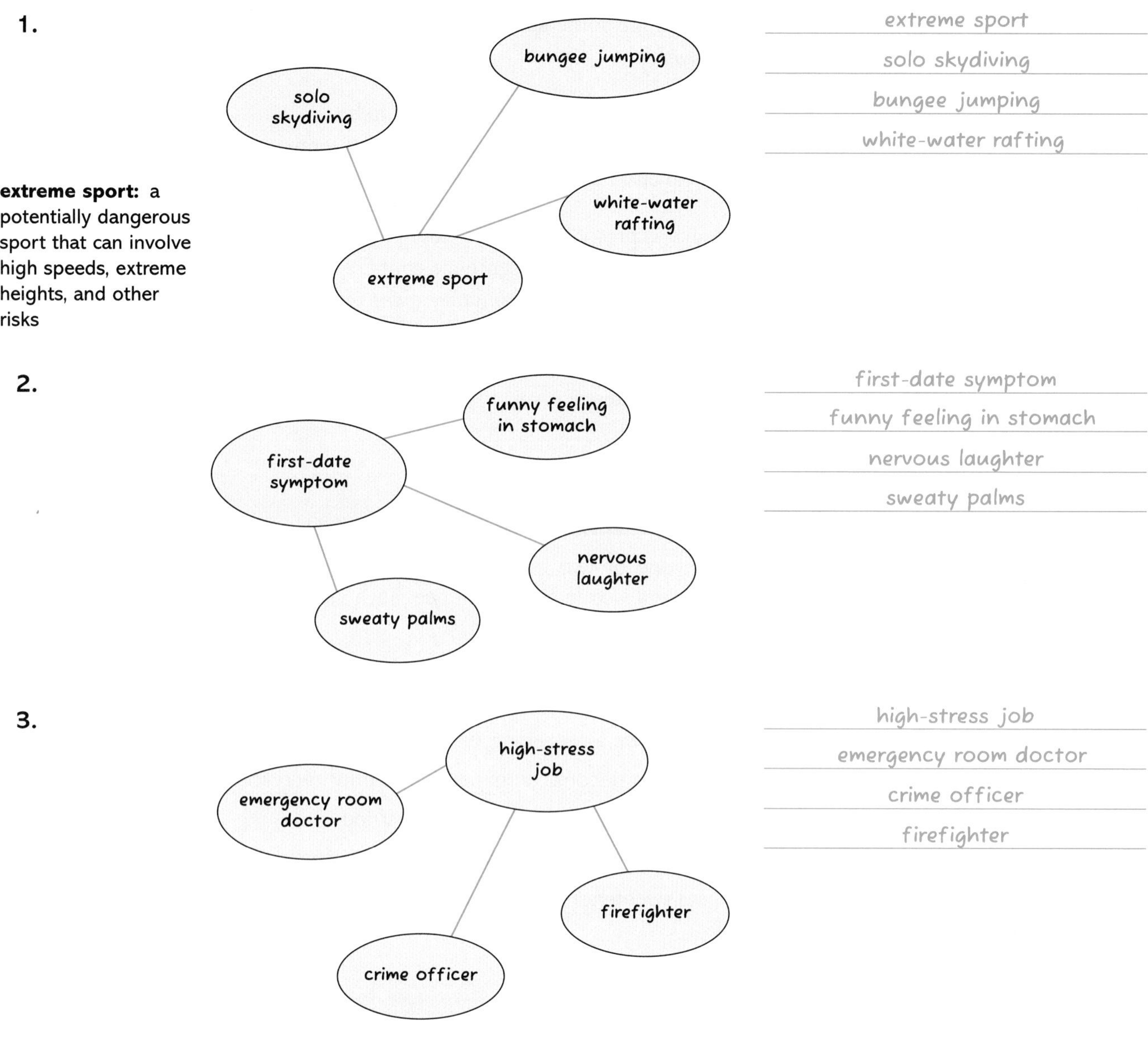

Ordering Sentences

Sometimes, when we brainstorm, we use a **complete sentence** to express our ideas. A complete sentence can express either a *general idea* or a *specific example.* Consider the following sentence:

> **Making costumes allows children to be creative.**

When we use a complete sentence to express a general idea, there will usually be *two or more key words* that define the idea. For example, in the previous sentence, the words *making, costumes, children,* and *creative* define the general idea. (The other words in the sentence are not as specific in their meaning.) Get in the habit of marking the key words in any sentence that expresses a general idea; this will help you decide what types of specific examples you can use.

Power Tip

Notice that a complete sentence begins with a capital letter and ends with a period. It also has a subject, a verb, and a complete thought. You will learn more about these important sentence parts in Chapter 11.

Now, here are some specific examples of how *making costumes* allows *children* to be *creative:*

Children can be anything they want to be.
They can use any materials they want to: scrap paper, glue, paint.
They can enter imaginary worlds while wearing their costumes.

Each sentence expresses a specific example of creativity related to making costumes. Notice also that each sentence contains *two or more key words* that define the example (such as *be anything they want to be . . . use any materials they want to . . . enter imaginary worlds*). So, whether a sentence expresses a general idea or a specific example, there will always be two or more key words that define the meaning of the sentence.

Teaching Tip
Bring in copies of articles or essays in which you have underlined the thesis statements, topic sentences, or other key sentences. Then, ask students to find the key words. You might have to model this process at first.

ACTIVITY 6: Teamwork

Working with one or two classmates, identify and underline the *key words* that define the *general idea* in each sentence. Each sentence will have at least two key words. Answers may vary.

EXAMPLE: It's possible to have a fun yet inexpensive vacation.

1. College can be a rewarding experience.
2. Camping has become an expensive form of recreation.
3. Good communication skills can be learned.
4. Learning geometry requires a lot of memorization.
5. Artificial sweeteners often have a funny taste.

ACTIVITY 7

Power Tip
If you have trouble identifying the general idea, remember to mark the *key words* in each sentence. See page 89 for more on key words.

Rewrite each of the following sets of sentences, putting the *general idea* first. The *specific examples* can be in an order of your choice. You can begin with your favorite example and end with you least favorite; or you can begin with your least favorite example and end with your favorite. If the general idea already appears first, write "OK" on the first line.

EXAMPLE:	It can save money.	Cooking is a good skill to have.
	It can help you eat nutritiously.	It can help you eat nutritiously.
	Cooking is a good skill to have.	It can save money.
	It's satisfying for yourself and others.	It's satisfying for yourself and others.

1. I was afraid my parachute would not open. — *Skydiving was a frightening experience.*

   Stepping out of the plane took my breath away. — *Stepping out of the plane took my breath away.*

   Skydiving was a frightening experience. — *I was afraid my parachute would not open.*

   Free-falling made my heart stop. — *Free-falling made my heart stop.*

2. My old job was not a good one. — *OK*

   The pay and benefits were poor. ______

   My hours changed every week. ______

   I wasn't learning many new skills. ______

3. College offers social and work connections. — *Getting a college degree is beneficial.*

   Education improves one's self-esteem. — *College offers social and work connections.*

   Degree holders earn better salaries. — *Education improves one's self-esteem.*

   Getting a college degree is beneficial. — *Degree holders earn better salaries.*

GROUPING

The second skill that is useful for organizing your ideas is **grouping**. To group ideas effectively, you will need to be able to recognize items that are *related to one another.* Often, when we brainstorm, our ideas come to us in random order. When we organize these ideas, we need to sort through them and put them in distinct groups.

Grouping Single-Word Items

Let's begin with lists of single-word items that need to be put in separate groups. Let's see how one group of items could be sorted into two groups.

Items to be grouped: piano / rock / jazz / drums / hip-hop / guitar

Group 1: musical instruments	**Group 2:** types of music
piano	rock
drums	jazz
guitar	hip-hop

Notice that as you group items, you begin to develop a sense of the *general idea* that connects the items to one another. For example, the general idea that connects the items in group 1 is *musical instruments;* the general idea that connects the items in group 2 is *types of music.*

Teaching Tip
Break students into groups of two or three and then call out the number for each item in Activity 8. The first group to correctly categorize the words under two logical general ideas wins. This game can be done with other grouping activities in this chapter, too.

ACTIVITY 8

Rearrange each of the following sets of items into separate groups, following these steps:

- At first, leave the first line after "Group 1" and "Group 2" blank.
- Fill in the other lines with the items that should go in each group, making sure to keep related items together.
- Think of a general idea that connects the items in each group and write it on the first line, following the example on page 91. General ideas may vary.

1. wine / cola / tea / beer / champagne / coffee

Group 1: non-alcoholic drinks	**Group 2:** alcoholic drinks
cola	wine
tea	beer
coffee	champagne

2. pen / notebook / diary / highlighter / crayon / calendar

Group 1: writing tools	**Group 2:** things that we write in
pen	notebook
highlighter	diary
crayon	calendar

3. brunette / redhead / eyelashes / mustache / blonde / bangs

Group 1: hair colors	**Group 2:** hair fringes
brunette	eyelashes
redhead	mustache
blonde	bangs

4. accountant / landscaper / banker / ranger / secretary / lifeguard

Group 1: indoor jobs	**Group 2:** outdoor jobs
accountant	landscaper
banker	ranger
secretary	lifeguard

5. rabbit / snake / chipmunk / lizard / frog / squirrel

Group 1: warm-blooded animals	**Group 2:** cold-blooded animals
rabbit	snake
chipmunk	lizard
squirrel	frog

ACTIVITY 9: Teamwork

Exchange your answers to Activity 8 with a classmate. Did you sort any of the items differently? How do your general ideas for each group compare? Can you find any ways to refine or improve your general idea statements?

Grouping Phrases

As you learned in Chapter 3, clustering is a brainstorming method that helps us group related ideas. The bubbles and lines are a visual reminder to keep related ideas in separate groups or *clusters.* Often, clusters express ideas in *phrases.* Here is an example of a small clustering that keeps related phrases in separate groups:

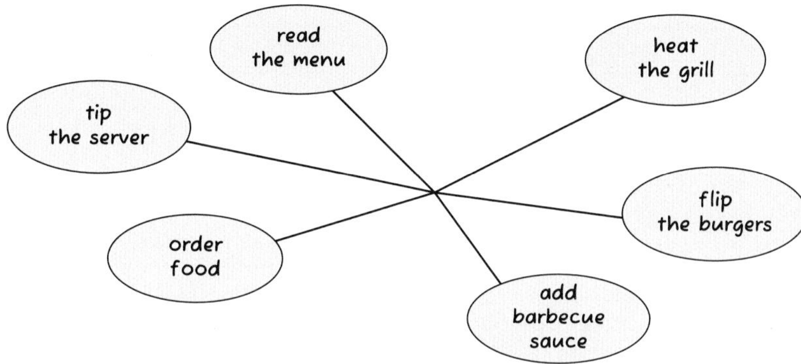

Group 1: eating in a restaurant

read the menu

order food

tip the server

Group 2: grilling burgers

heat the grill

flip the burgers

add barbecue sauce

Lists can also be used to group phrases, as shown in the example below the cluster. Notice that *general ideas* connect the items in each group.

Keep in mind that clusters are rarely this simple and neat. As we move from a cluster to a list (and to an outline), we have to be on the lookout for items that are incorrectly grouped together.

ACTIVITY 10

Move the items from each of the following clusters into separate groups, *being careful of items that are clustered incorrectly*. Follow these steps:

- At first, leave the line after "Group 1" and "Group 2" blank.
- Fill in the other lines with the items that should go in each group, making sure to keep related items together.
- Think of a *general idea* that connects the items in each group and write it on the first line.

General ideas may vary.

EXAMPLE:

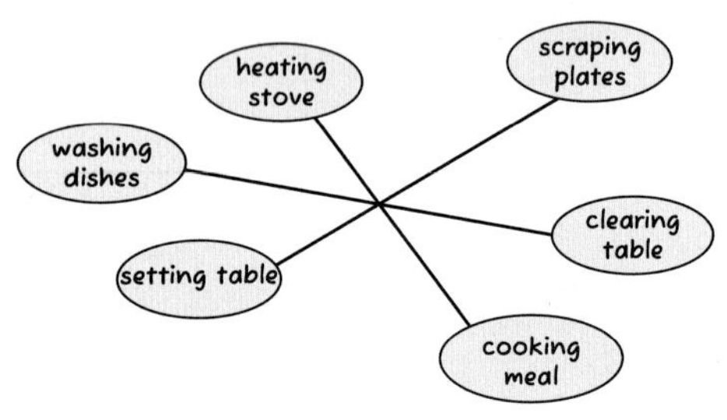

Group 1: before-dinner tasks	Group 2: after-dinner tasks
setting table	clearing table
heating stove	scraping plates
cooking meal	washing dishes

1.

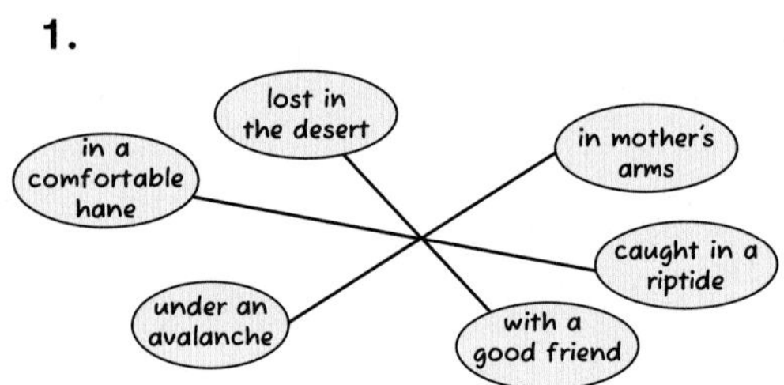

Group 1: safe/comfortable places	Group 2: unsafe/uncomfortable places
in a comfortable home	lost in the desert
in mother's arms	under an avalanche
with a good friend	caught in a riptide

2.

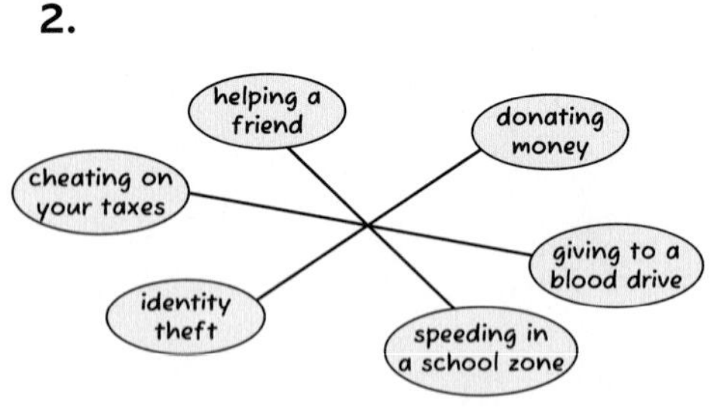

Group 1: good deeds	Group 2: bad deeds
helping a friend	cheating on your taxes
donating money	identity theft
giving to a blood drive	speeding in a school zone

avalanche: a sudden, potentially deadly falling of snow, ice, rocks, or earth

riptide: a powerful current of water near a seashore that can cause drownings

identity theft: stealing someone's Social Security number or other identifying information to make purchases or do other things under that person's name

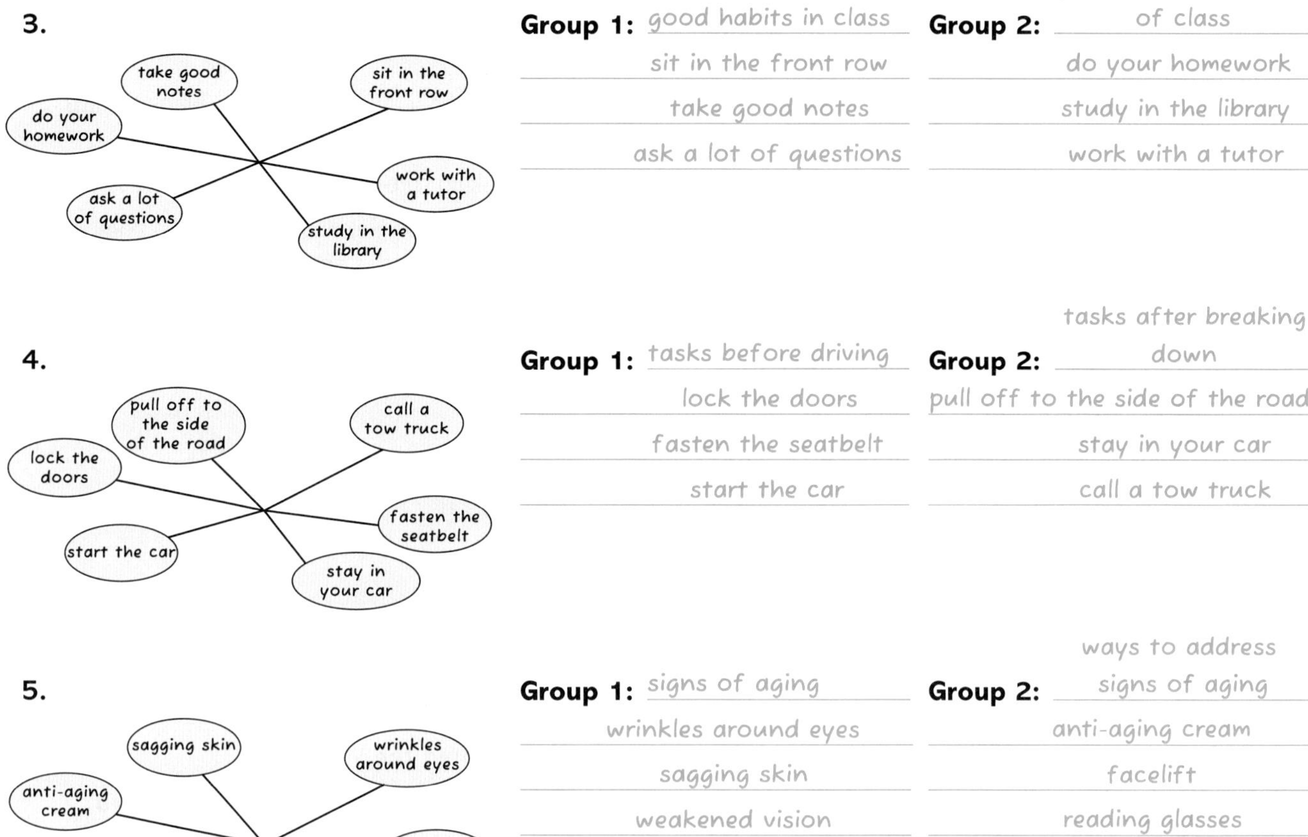

ACTIVITY 11: Teamwork

Exchange your answers to Activity 10 with a classmate. Did you sort any of the items differently? How do your general ideas for each group compare? Can you find any ways to refine or improve your general idea statements?

Grouping Sentences

Like words and phrases, sentences can also be grouped together by topic. To come up with a *general idea* to connect sentence groups, it's a good idea to circle the key words in the sentences and ask yourself how these words are related. (For more on key words, see page 95.)

ACTIVITY 12

Move the sentences from each of the following lists into separate groups, following these steps:

- At first, leave the line after "Group 1" and "Group 2" blank. (You can also leave the next line blank to give yourself more room to write.)
- Fill in the other lines with the sentences that should go in each group, making sure to keep related sentences together.
- Think of a *general idea* that connects the items in each group and write it on the first line, using a complete sentence. (To get this idea, you might want to circle key words in the sentences and ask yourself how these words are related.) General ideas may vary.

EXAMPLE: Roberta planted flowers in front of the house.

Del cleaned out the gutters.

Manuel painted the living room.

Tamsin cut the grass and swept the porch.

Pat polished the floors until they sparkled.

Doug cleaned the bathrooms and dusted.

Group 1: Everyone helped with outside chores to make the house look great.

Roberta planted flowers in front of the house.

Del cleaned out the gutters.

Tamsin cut the grass and swept the porch.

Group 2: Everyone helped with inside chores to make the house look great.

Manuel painted the living room.

Pat polished the floors until they sparkled.

Doug cleaned the bathrooms and dusted.

1. Medical professionals often work long hours with few breaks.

Nurses, medical assistants, and other health professionals are in high demand.

Medical work can be physically and emotionally tiring.

Health professionals get the satisfaction of helping others.

Health workers are held responsible for the well-being of all their patients.

Starting salaries for nurses can approach $40,000.

Group 1: Medical work can be demanding and stressful.

Medical professionals often work long hours with few breaks.

Medical work can be physically and emotionally tiring.

Health workers are held responsible for the well-being of all their patients.

Group 2: Health care can be a great field to pursue.

Nurses, medical assistants, and other health professionals are in high demand.

Health professionals get the satisfaction of helping others.

Starting salaries for nurses can approach $40,000.

2. Many parents allow their children to eat sweetened cereals.
Schools often serve items like french fries and corn dogs for lunch.
More daycare centers are serving fresh fruit for snacks.
Saturday morning commercials advertise mostly junk foods.
Media campaigns are promoting healthy food choices.
The local high school has removed the soda vending machines.

Group 1: It's no surprise that many kids have bad diets.
Many parents allow their children to eat sweetened cereals.
Schools often serve items like french fries and corn dogs for lunch.
Saturday morning commercials advertise mostly junk foods.

Group 2: People and organizations are understanding the need for healthy food choices.
More daycare centers are serving fresh fruit for snacks.
Media campaigns are promoting healthy food choices.
The local high school has removed the soda vending machines.

3. Rachel sits slumped in class.
When meeting strangers, Sarah looks them directly in the eye.
Juan usually crosses his arms when he talks to others.
Michael's posture and gestures show an interest in others.
At school, Jessica sits up straight and tall at her desk.
Robert lowers his eyes when girls approach him.

Group 1: Rachel, Juan, and Robert have negative body language.
Rachel sits slumped in class.
Juan usually crosses his arms when he talks to others.
Robert lowers his eyes when girls approach him.

Group 2: Jessica, Michael, and Sarah have positive body language.
At school, Jessica sits up straight and tall at her desk.
Michael's posture and gestures show an interest in others.
When meeting strangers, Sarah looks them directly in the eye.

ACTIVITY 13: Teamwork

Exchange your answers to Activity 12 with a classmate. Did you sort any of the items differently? How do your general ideas for each group compare? Can you find any ways to refine or improve your general idea statements?

ELIMINATING

One of the most important skills you will need for organizing your ideas is **eliminating**. When we brainstorm, we write down all the ideas that come to mind, without judging their individual value. However, as you move from brainstorming to outlining, you will need to select your best ideas (those that are most appropriate for the topic) and eliminate those that are weak (ideas that do not fit the topic especially well). Generally, you will want to look for groups of related items that clearly support the topic and eliminate isolated items that do not fit. With practice, your ability to recognize and eliminate these items will improve.

Eliminating Single-Word Items

Again, let's start with single-word items. You can see that most of the following words are related; however, one is not. Can you find the unrelated item?

compassion
understanding
impatience
humor

Compassion, understanding, and humor are all *positive* qualities, ones that most of us would like a friend or partner to have. Impatience, a *negative* quality, doesn't fit, so we could eliminate it.

ACTIVITY 14

For each group of words below, do the following:

- Cross out the item that does not fit.
- For the remaining items, think of a *general idea* that connects them and write it on the first line of the new list.
- Add the remaining items to the list, using an order of your choice.

General ideas may vary.

EXAMPLE:	comedy	categories at a video store
	action	comedy
	horror	action
	~~theaters~~	horror

1. tornado	natural disasters	2. ~~diamond~~	types of jewelry
hurricane	tornado	necklace	necklace
flood	hurricane	earring	earring
~~damage~~	flood	bracelet	bracelet

3.	teaching	careers
	firefighting	teaching
	farming	firefighting
	~~danger~~	farming
4.	organs	body parts
	~~mind~~	organs
	muscles	muscles
	bones	bones
5.	treadmill	exercise equipment
	weights	treadmill
	~~aerobics~~	weights
	bicycle	bicycle
6.	picture	wall decorations
	print	picture
	painting	print
	~~frame~~	painting

Teaching Tip
As an additional team activity, you might have students pick a paragraph that they wrote for this class or another course. Then, have students pair up and exchange their paragraphs. Next, each student should write down what he or she thinks is the general idea of the other's paragraph. Additionally, students should cross out any points that don't seem related to the general idea. Finally, they should return the paragraphs and discuss the suggestions.

ACTIVITY 15: Teamwork

Exchange your answers to Activity 14 with a classmate. Did your choices about what items to eliminate vary in any cases? If so, see if you can determine which answer is correct and why. Can you find any ways to refine or improve your general idea statements?

Eliminating Phrases

Just as you need to eliminate words from your brainstorming that do not fit your topic, you must eliminate unrelated phrases. The following activity will give you practice with this skill.

ACTIVITY 16

For each cluster, do the following:

- Cross out the item that does not fit.
- For the remaining items, think of a *general idea* that connects them and write it on the first line of the new list.
- Add the remaining items to the list, using an order of your choice. General ideas may vary.

EXAMPLE:

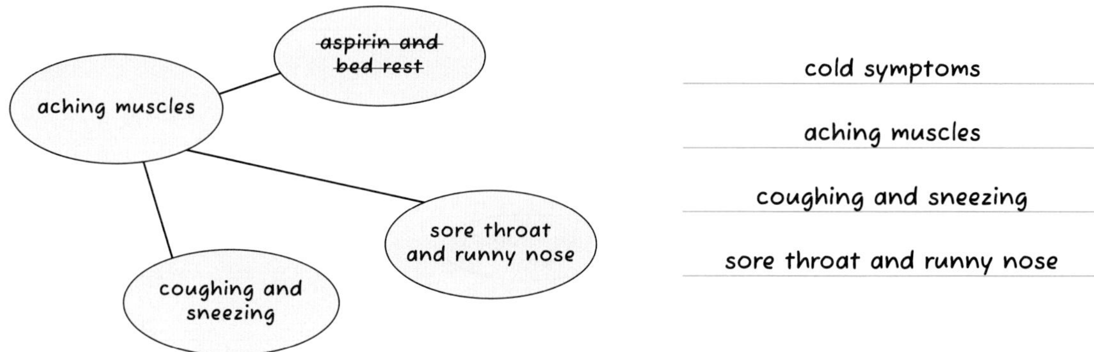

CONTINUED >

1.

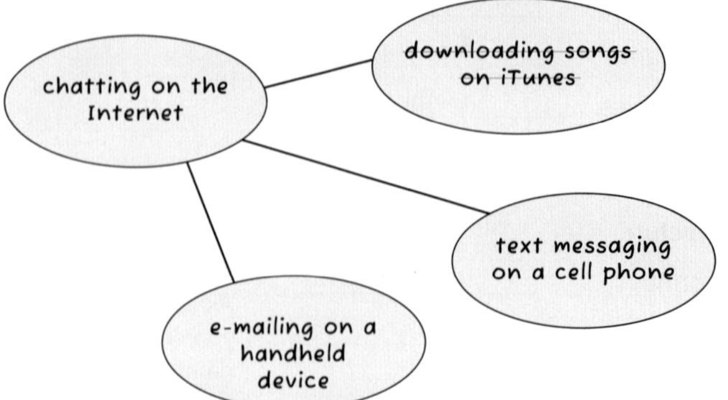

electronic communication

chatting on the Internet

e-mailing on a handheld device

text messaging on a cell phone

2.

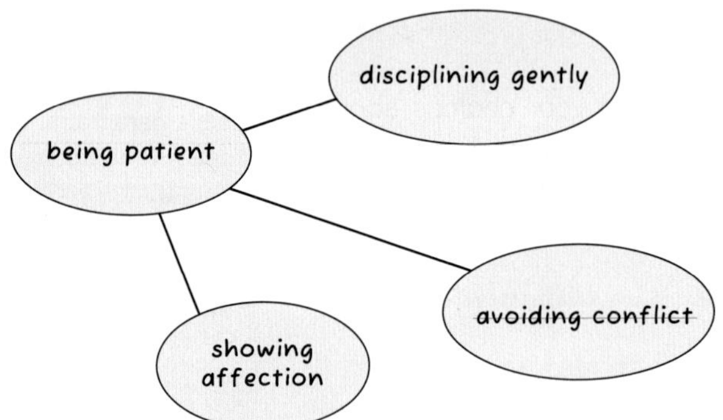

good parenting

being patient

disciplining gently

showing affection

3.

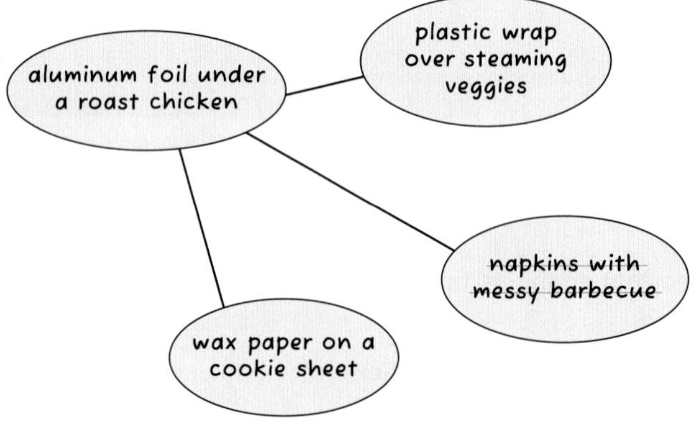

coverings used with food

aluminum foil under a roast chicken

plastic wrap over steaming veggies

wax paper on a cookie sheet

4.

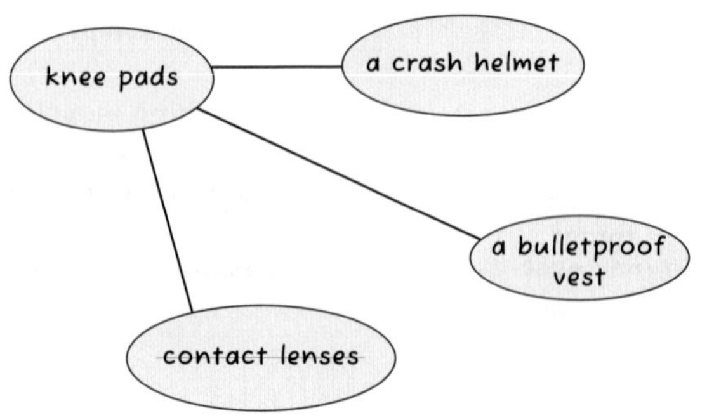

body protection

knee pads

a crash helmet

a bulletproof vest

5.

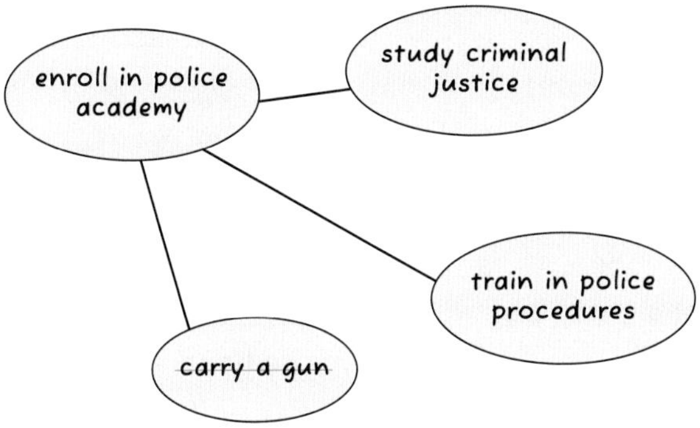

enroll in police academy — study criminal justice; train in police procedures; carry a gun

police training

enroll in police academy

study criminal justice

train in police procedures

ACTIVITY 17: Teamwork

Exchange your answers to Activity 16 with a classmate. Did your choices about what items to eliminate vary in any cases? If so, see if you can determine which answer is correct and why. Can you find any ways to refine or improve your general idea statements?

Eliminating Sentences

Like words and phrases that do not fit your topic, irrelevant sentences should also be eliminated. To come up with a *general idea* to connect the remaining sentences, it's a good idea to circle the key words in the sentences and ask yourself how these words are related. (For more on key words, see page 89.)

ACTIVITY 18

For each list, do the following:

- Cross out the sentence that does not fit.
- For the remaining sentences, think of a *general idea* that connects them and write it on the first line of the new list. Try to state this idea as a complete sentence.
- Add the remaining sentences to the list, using an order of your choice. General ideas may vary.

EXAMPLE:	Kids of every age need support.	Parenting can be challenging.
	~~Grandparents may babysit.~~	Babies are totally dependent.
	Teens test parents' limits.	Teens test parents' limits.
	Babies are totally dependent.	Kids of every age need support.

CONTINUED >

1. ~~My mom hasn't had the flu in two years.~~

   I drink gallons of water and sweat it out.

   My dad takes large doses of vitamin C.

   My sister goes straight to bed and rests.

   People treat illness in different ways.
   I drink gallons of water and sweat it out.
   My dad takes large doses of vitamin C.
   My sister goes straight to bed and rests.

interest: a charge for borrowing money that is typically a percentage of the amount borrowed

2. Ask for a lower credit-card interest rate.

   ~~Shop only during sales.~~

   Put all debt on the lowest-interest credit card.

   Make more than the minimum payment each month.

   Try these strategies to pay off credit cards.
   Put all debt on the lowest-interest credit card.
   Ask for a lower credit-card interest rate.
   Make more than the minimum payment each month.

3. Oil from roads contaminates water supplies.

   Emissions from cars and factories trap heat and harm air quality.

   Garbage landfills leak harmful chemicals.

   ~~Recycling has only limited benefits.~~

   Pollution has many bad effects.
   Oil from roads contaminates water supplies.
   Emissions from cars and factories trap heat and harm air quality.
   Garbage landfills leak harmful chemicals.

4. Open-air stadiums give concerts a free, natural feeling.

   The lighting at a concert can set a certain mood.

   ~~The ticket price of a concert is important.~~

   A good sound system involves listeners in the music.

   Setting and effects are important at a concert.
   Open-air stadiums give concerts a free, natural feeling.
   The lighting at a concert can set a certain mood.
   A good sound system involves listeners in the music.

5. Make a list of your accomplishments at work.

   Know what raise is reasonable based on your accomplishments.

   ~~Show up to work early every day.~~

   Set up a meeting to ask for the raise.

   Follow these steps to ask for a raise.
   Make a list of your accomplishments at work.
   Know what raise is reasonable based on your accomplishments.
   Set up a meeting to ask for the raise.

ACTIVITY 19: Teamwork

Exchange your answers to Activity 18 with a classmate. Did your choices about what sentences to eliminate vary in any cases? If so, see if you can determine which answer is correct and why. Can you find any ways to refine or improve your general idea statements?

COMBINING STRATEGIES

In most writing situations, we need to use all the mental strategies (ordering, grouping, and eliminating) at the same time. In the following activities, you will be required to

1. **group** the items into separate groups
2. **order** the items in each group by putting the general idea first and the rest of the ideas in an order of your choice
3. **eliminate** any items that do not fit in either group

ACTIVITY 20

For each list that follows, you will be given *one* of the general ideas. For each list, do the following:

- Determine the other general idea.
- For each group, write the general idea on the first line.
- Add the rest of the ideas under the appropriate general idea, eliminating any ideas that do not fit. General ideas may vary.

EXAMPLE: Web sites / camping / cruise / maps / resort / travel agent / vacations / binoculars

Group 1: vacations	**Group 2:** tools for planning
resort	a vacation
cruise	travel agent
camping	Web sites
	maps

Eliminate one item: binoculars

1. toothpaste / deodorant / razor / grooming tool / teeth / toothbrush / shampoo / comb

Group 1: grooming tool	**Group 2:** personal-care product
razor	toothpaste
toothbrush	deodorant
comb	shampoo

Eliminate one item: teeth

CONTINUED >

entrée: typically the main course of a meal

2. lunch / restaurant / appetizer / dessert / breakfast / dinner / courses / entrée

Group 1: courses	Group 2: meals
appetizer	breakfast
entrée	lunch
dessert	dinner

Eliminate one item: restaurant

3. rent / salary / income / gift check / food / lottery winnings / bank / utilities

Group 1: income	Group 2: expenses
salary	rent
gift check	food
lottery winnings	utilities

Eliminate one item: bank

4. blood pressure / heart attack / ambulance / stroke / pulse / medical technician / seizure / breathing rate / vital signs (signs of life) / body temperature / car accident

Group 1: vital signs (signs of life)	Group 2: medical emergencies
blood pressure	heart attack
pulse	stroke
breathing rate	seizure
body temperature	car accident

Eliminate two items: ambulance, medical technician

5. infancy / friendship / childhood / parent / life stages / family history / worker / adulthood / friend / adolescence / spouse

Group 1: life stages	Group 2: life roles
infancy	friend
childhood	spouse
adolescence	parent
adulthood	worker

Eliminate two items: friendship, family history

ACTIVITY 21: Teamwork

Each of the following items consists of two joined clusters. In each cluster, the *general idea* appears in a central (green) bubble. Work with one or two classmates to do the following:

- For each group, write the general idea on the first line.
- Add the rest of the ideas under the appropriate general idea, eliminating any ideas that do not fit.

Watch out for items that are clustered incorrectly.

EXAMPLE:

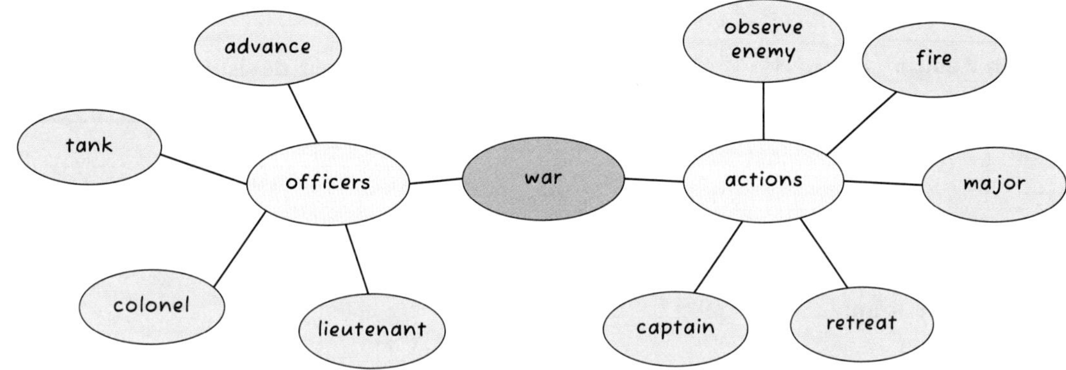

War (Group 1): officers
colonel
lieutenant
captain
major

War (Group 2): actions
observe enemy
advance
fire
retreat

Eliminate one item: tank

1.

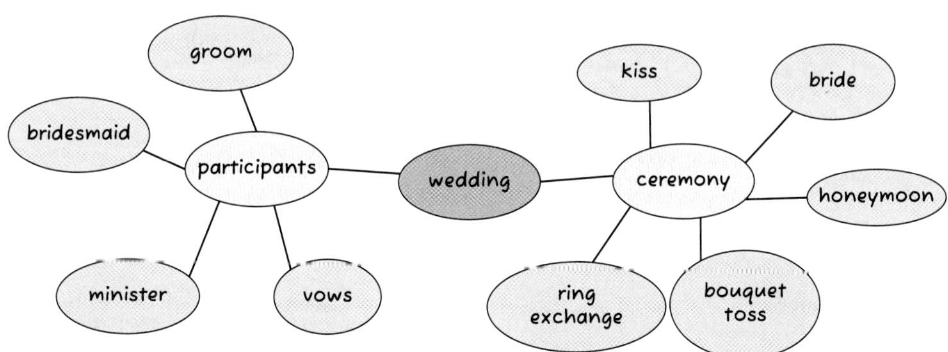

Wedding (Group 1): participants
minister
bride
groom
bridesmaid

Wedding (Group 2): ceremony
vows
ring exchange
kiss
bouquet toss

Eliminate one item: honeymoon

CONTINUED >

2.

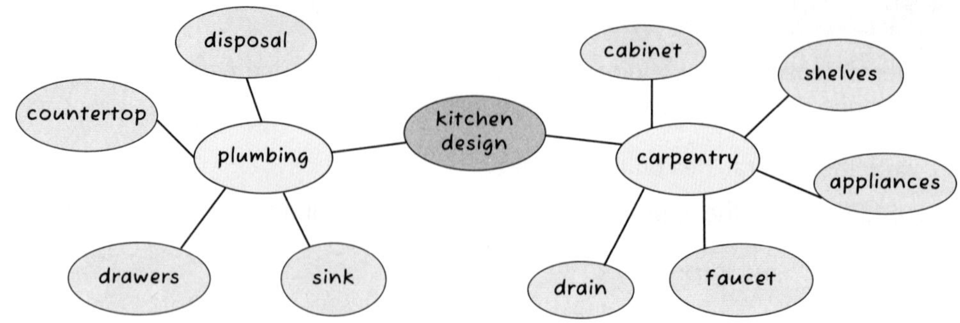

Kitchen design (Group 1): plumbing
sink
faucet
drain
disposal

Kitchen design (Group 2): carpentry
countertop
drawers
cabinet
shelves

Eliminate one item: appliances

ACTIVITY 22

Although *general ideas* should appear in central bubbles, we sometimes put them in the wrong place by accident. The following clusters are trickier because more items are incorrectly clustered, including some of the general ideas. For each item, do the following:

- For each group, write the general idea on the first line.
- Add the rest of the ideas under the appropriate general idea, eliminating any ideas that do not fit.

EXAMPLE:

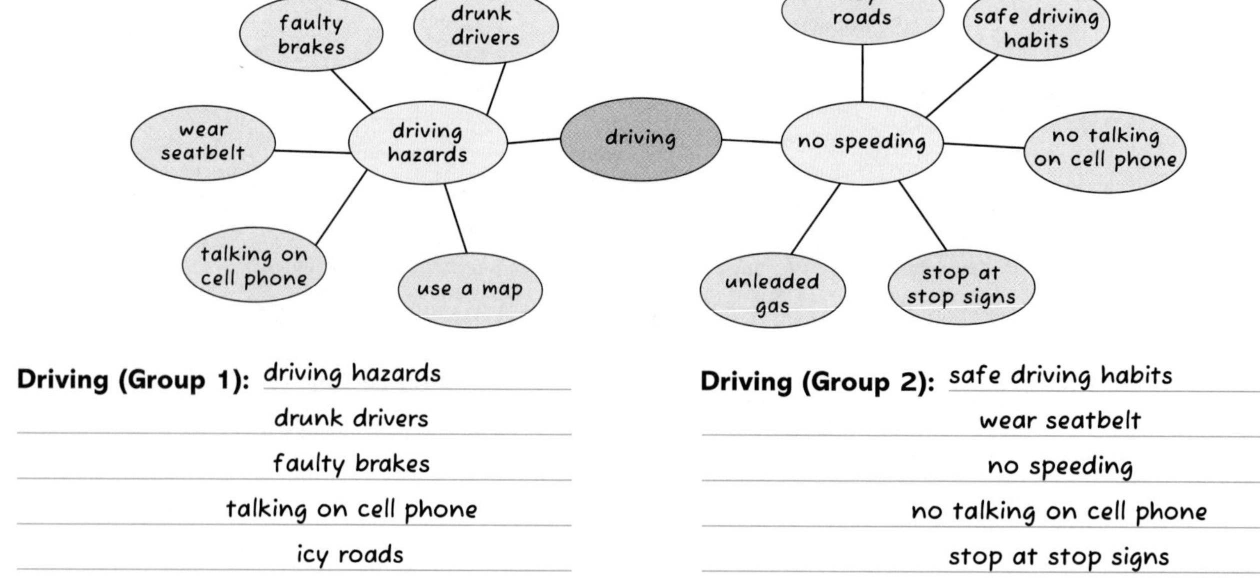

Driving (Group 1): driving hazards
drunk drivers
faulty brakes
talking on cell phone
icy roads

Driving (Group 2): safe driving habits
wear seatbelt
no speeding
no talking on cell phone
stop at stop signs

Eliminate two items: use a map, unleaded gas

1.

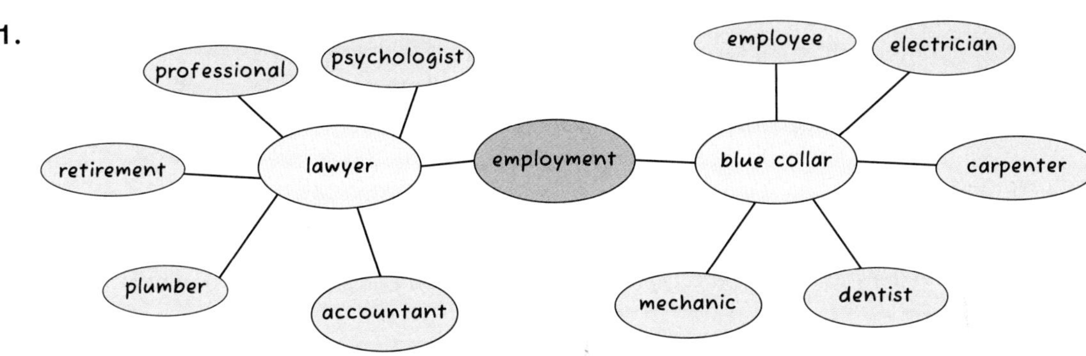

blue collar: refers to jobs that typically involve working with the hands to build, assemble, or repair something. The name comes from the blue work clothes that such employees often wear.

Employment (Group 1): professional
psychologist
lawyer
accountant
dentist

Employment (Group 2): blue collar
plumber
electrician
carpenter
mechanic

Eliminate two items: retirement, employee

2.

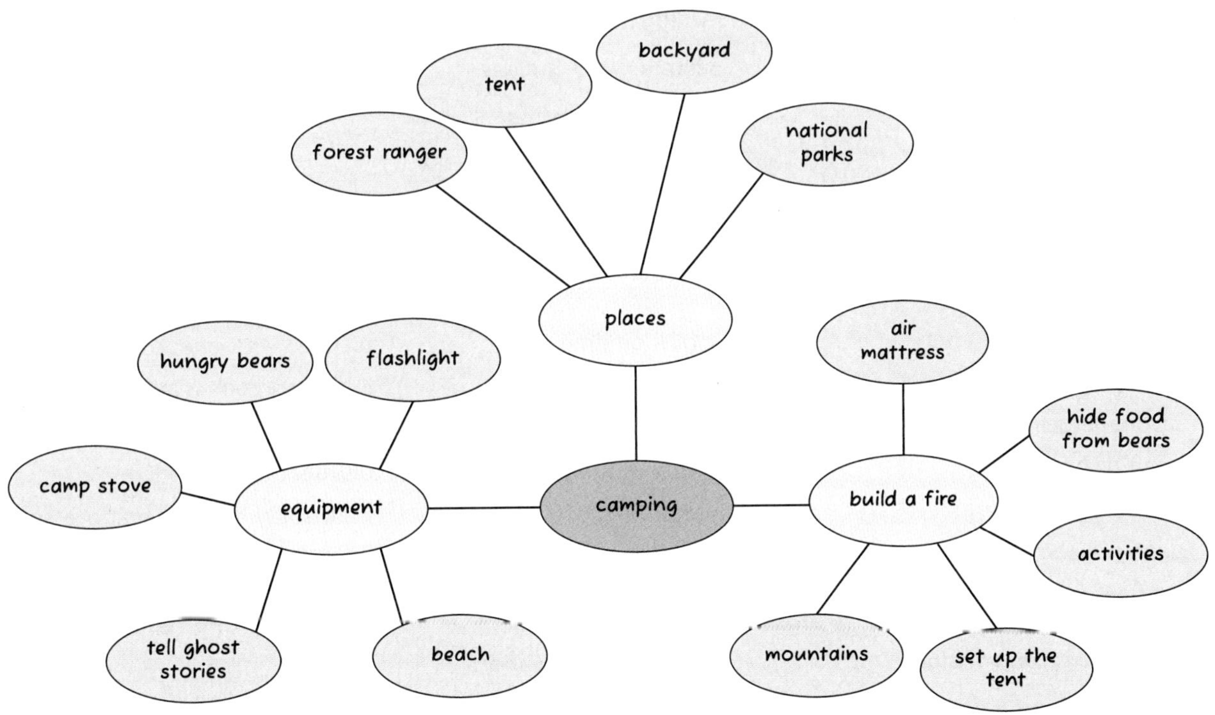

Camping (Group 1): equipment
tent
flashlight
camp stove
air mattress

Camping (Group 2): places
backyard
mountains
beach
national parks

Camping (Group 3): activities
set up the tent
hide food from bears
build a fire
tell ghost stories

Eliminate two items: hungry bears, forest ranger

ACTIVITY 23

In this activity, you will need to form three ordered lists from three scrambled lists, and each list should begin with a *general idea*. You will be given *two* of the general ideas. For each set of lists, do the following:

- Determine the third general idea.
- For each group, write the general idea on the first line.
- Add the rest of the ideas under the appropriate general ideas, eliminating any ideas that do not fit.

General ideas may vary.

EXAMPLE:

go to the movies	study for driver's test	drive with experienced person
attend job training	practice writing	read about the job
take driver's education	learning a job	learning to write better
read good writing	watch other workers	get comments on your writing
ask questions about tasks	take a writing class	
read driver's ed materials	volunteer regularly	

Learning (Group 1):	**Learning (Group 2):**	**Learning (Group 3):**
learning a job	learning to write better	learning to drive
read about the job	take a writing class	take driver's education
attend job training	practice writing	read driver's ed materials
watch other workers	get comments on your writing	study for driver's test
ask questions about tasks	read good writing	drive with experienced person

Eliminate two items: go to the movies, volunteer regularly

1.

don't be alone too often	pay your bills on time	balance your checkbook
don't play loud music	don't overspend on credit	look for a roommate
save emergency funds	respect your neighbors	end parties at decent hour
wash dishes regularly	keep up with your laundry	disinfect the bathroom
don't argue loudly	throw out spoiled food	walk softly if you live above someone
clean house responsibly		

Living Alone (Group 1):	**Living Alone (Group 2):**	**Living Alone (Group 3):**
clean house responsibly	respect your neighbors	manage money well
wash dishes regularly	don't play loud music	save emergency funds
keep up with your laundry	don't argue loudly	pay your bills on time
throw out spoiled food	end parties at a decent hour	don't overspend on credit
disinfect the bathroom	walk softly if you live above someone	balance your checkbook

Eliminate two items: don't be alone too often, look for a roommate

2. e-mail friends
visit celebrity Web sites
download songs
socializing online
e-mail your teachers
try Internet dating
improve your virus protection
find movie schedules
research your papers
exchange personal photos
register for classes
finding entertainment options online
find your grades
get free Web access
join live chat rooms
play video games

Going Online (Group 1):
socializing online
e-mail friends
try Internet dating
exchange personal photos
join live chat rooms

Going Online (Group 2):
finding entertainment options online
visit celebrity Web sites
download songs
find movie schedules
play video games

Going Online (Group 3):
doing school-related activities online
e-mail your teachers
research your papers
register for classes
find your grades

Eliminate two items: improve your virus protection, get free Web access

ACTIVITY 24

Go back to one of the clusters or lists that you generated for Chapter 3 and do the following:

- Make sure that the ideas are *grouped* in a way that makes sense. (You can write your changes on the cluster or list or transfer your work to a fresh piece of paper.)
- Make sure that there is a *general idea* that connects the items in each group.
- Especially if you are working with a list, make sure that the ideas are *ordered* in a way that makes sense.
- *Eliminate* any ideas that do not fit your topic.

Outlining Basics

In this part of the chapter, you will learn about outlining, an important process for planning papers. All outlines have the same basic functions, which are already familiar to you:

- They **order** ideas, starting with general ideas and moving to specific examples and details.
- They **group** items that are related to one another.
- They **eliminate** any items that do not fit well.

Take a look at the following outline, in which key features are noted. (It is based on a cluster from Chapter 3; see page 70.)

The main idea responds directly to a writing topic. In this case, the topic is *problems at work*.

The support points back up the main idea, and they are often based on the *general ideas* from clusters or lists.

Specific examples are grouped sensibly under each support point.

Unrelated ideas are eliminated.

MAIN IDEA Three serious problems make my workplace an unpleasant environment.

SUPPORT POINT 1 The leadership is poor.

- shift leader plays favorites
- manager is a bad communicator
- ~~staff meetings are boring~~
- shift leader and manager don't help with customers

SUPPORT POINT 2 The staffing is inadequate.

- only four workers on weekends
- ~~conditions are dangerous~~
- only one cashier
- too many workers call in sick

SUPPORT POINT 3 There are serious personality problems.

- manager is insensitive
- older and younger employees argue
- guys harass the girls

ACTIVITY 25

Move the items from question 2 of Activity 23 (*Going Online*) to the outline form that follows, using the outline above as a model. To get you started, we have filled in the main idea for you. You will need to

- turn each *general idea* from Activity 23 into a *support point.* In this case, each support point is a reason why going online can be beneficial. (The first support point has been provided for you.)
- write each reason as a completion of this sentence: *Going online can be beneficial because . . .*
- write three specific examples below each support point. These examples can be left as short phrases.

Answers will vary.

MAIN IDEA Going online can be beneficial. (BECAUSE...)

SUPPORT POINT 1 It can help you with school.

____

____

____

SUPPORT POINT 2 ________________

____

____

____

SUPPORT POINT 3 ________________

____

____

____

A note about outline formats: In your college career, you will use many different outline formats. In this book, we show a simple format, with a main idea followed by support points (usually three) and blanks for specific examples. Once you complete this course, you will be able to transition to other outline formats with confidence and efficiency.

Sometimes, you may have only two support points. At other times, you may have more than three support points. In these cases, ask your instructor for suggestions. Often, you may be allowed to leave the third point blank, or, if you have extra support points, you may be able to write them on the back of the outline.

Power Tip
You may think that making outlines is a waste of time, but organizing your ideas before you write can actually save time, especially if you are writing under a deadline.

Teaching Tip
If you require students' papers to have a specific number of support points, this is a good time to explain your expectations. Also, if you require an outline format that is different from the one shown in this chapter, you might introduce it to students at this time.

UNDERSTANDING KEY FEATURES OF OUTLINES

The following sections give more details on the three key features of outlines: the main idea, the support points, and the specific examples.

Feature 1: The Main Idea

In college, each paragraph that you write must contain a *main idea* that responds directly to a topic, the *main subject or task* of a writing assignment. (See Chapter 2 for more details on writing assignments.) Consider the following topic:

Discuss the career you would choose if anything were possible.

In writing a main idea in response to this topic, you should do all of the following:

- Identify a career of your choice.
- Use *key words* from the topic itself (*career, if anything were possible*).
- Express your idea as *a complete sentence.*

Here are three students' main ideas in response to this topic:

If anything were possible, I would be a pilot for my career.
I would like to be an elementary school teacher if any career were possible.
The career I would pick if anything were possible is president of the United States.

Teaching Tip
Point out that identifying—and responding to—key words in topics is a very helpful strategy to use in timed writings, including essay exams. If you emphasize timed writing, you might instruct students to flag or clip this section.

Notice that each main idea identifies a specific career. Also, each one uses key words from the topic (*if anything were possible, career*). Finally, each main idea is expressed as a complete sentence.

Later in college, you may do writing that is not specifically in response to an assigned topic. In most of these cases, you will still need to state a main idea. In the absence of an assigned topic, think of the main idea as the central, or controlling, idea for your writing. Often, you can arrive at this idea by completing statements like *This issue is important because of* ____________________ or *The thing that I most want to communicate about my subject is* ____________________.

Power Tip

Whenever you have trouble coming up with a main idea, look back at ideas that you've brainstormed in response to a topic. You might circle words in your brainstorming that directly respond to the topic. Then, use these words in your main idea. (See Chapter 3 for more on generating ideas.) In Chapter 5, you will learn how to turn main ideas into *topic sentences,* an important feature of effective paragraphs.

Teaching Tip

The purpose of this activity is to help students get in the habit of expressing a main idea using key words from the topic. If you would like students to write on the topics in the activity, you might refer them to the advice on narrowing a topic in Chapter 2 and on gathering support in Chapter 3. You'll want to allow them sufficient time for those tasks.

ACTIVITY 26

For each of the following topics, invent a *main idea* and write it, using *key words* from the topic. Answers will vary.

EXAMPLE: Topic: Identify an activity at which you would like to excel.

Main idea: One activity at which I would like to excel is poker.

1. Topic: Discuss whether you possess the qualities of a good friend.
   Main idea: ____________________

2. Topic: Describe something that scares you.
   Main idea: ____________________

3. Topic: Explain whether you use your time efficiently.
   Main idea: ____________________

Feature 2: The Support Points

In an outline, you'll need to include *support points* that back up your main idea. Often, these can be drawn from the *general ideas* in your clusters and lists. It's a good idea to state the support points as complete sentences.

Let's look at this slightly modified cluster from Chapter 3. The general ideas are in the green circles.

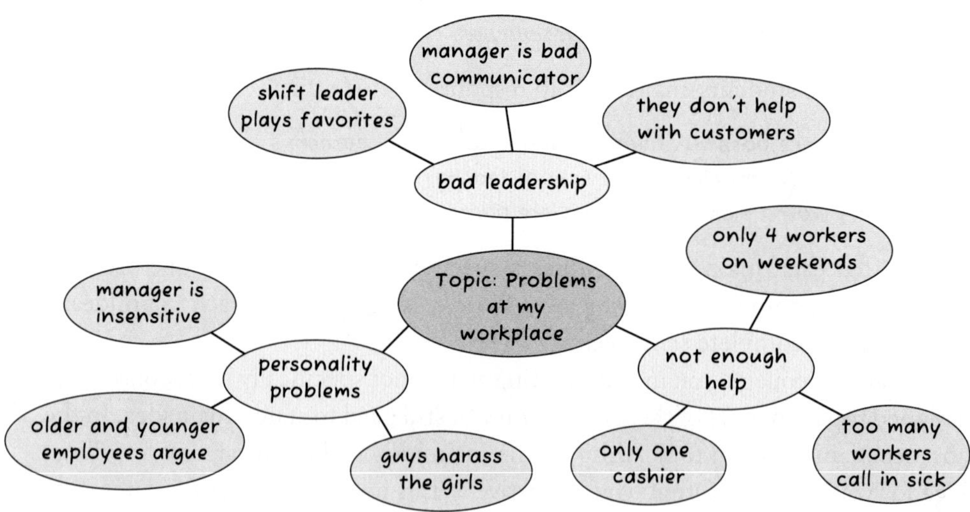

Here is the start of an outline that turns the general ideas into support points:

MAIN IDEA Three serious problems make my workplace an unpleasant environment.

SUPPORT POINT 1 The leadership is poor.

- shift leader plays favorites
- manager is a bad communicator
- shift leader and manager don't help with customers

For a full outline on this topic, see page 110.

Often, adding the word *because* to the end of your main idea will help you develop support points that make sense. For example, suppose your main idea is

Good communication between parents and teenagers is important (*because* . . .)

Now, you will have to complete this thought with a support point that makes sense. Here are several examples of how you might complete this idea:

> **It builds trust.**
> **It avoids misunderstandings.**
> **It shows care and concern.**

Notice that each support point is expressed as *a complete sentence* and connects clearly with the main idea. You should always verify that each support point makes sense by reading it in conjunction with the main idea. For example:

> **Good communication between parents and teenagers is important *because* it builds trust.**

This idea makes clear sense. However, suppose you tried to express your support point as a single word (like *trust*) or as a short phrase (like *builds trust*). When you connect a single word or short phrase to your main idea, it will not make sense:

> **Good communication between parents and teenagers is important *because* trust.**
> **Good communication between parents and teenagers is important *because* builds trust.**

In Chapter 13, you will learn more about why sentences like this don't make sense.

ACTIVITY 27

Select one of your main ideas from Activity 26, and add the word *because* to develop three *support points*. Remember to

- express each support point as a complete sentence (never as a single word or short phrase).
- read each support point together with the main idea to confirm that it makes sense. Answers will vary.

MAIN IDEA ______________________ (because...)

SUPPORT POINT 1 ______________________

SUPPORT POINT 2 ______________________

SUPPORT POINT 3 ______________________

In Chapter 5, you will learn how to develop support points more fully as you draft paragraphs.

For online practice with organizing and outlining, visit this book's Web site at **bedfordstmartins .com/steppingstones**.

Feature 3: The Specific Examples

For each support point in your outline, you will need to provide *specific examples* to illustrate your point. For example, if you say,

Good communication between parents and teenagers builds trust.

your readers will expect you to name some *specific examples* of how good communication builds trust. For example:

Teenagers know that they can go to parents with problems.
Teenagers know that they can share important experiences with parents.
Parents see that they can express fears and concerns.

In an outline, your specific examples may be expressed as *short phrases* or even as *single words.* Be sure that your specific examples fit with the point you are trying to prove. If you are not sure what kind of example fits, underline or circle the key words in the support point. For example:

Good communication between parents and teenagers avoids misunderstandings.

For this support point, you should provide specific examples of how good communication avoids misunderstandings. For example:

Parents can specify rules and expectations.
Teenagers know when they've broken the rules.
Every conversation is clearer.

Clusters, lists, and other brainstormed ideas are a great source of specific examples. For example, in the cluster on page 112, the outer circles give examples for the general ideas (support points) in the green circles. For an outline based on this cluster, see page 110.

ACTIVITY 28

Circle the key word or words in the following support points. Then, provide two or three *specific examples* for each point. If you have trouble thinking of examples, you might try some of the brainstorming strategies from Chapter 3. Examples will vary.

MAIN IDEA I like spending time with friends (because...)

SUPPORT POINT 1 I can be myself around them.

SUPPORT POINT 3 We have a lot of fun together.

SUPPORT POINT 2 They help me in different ways.

FILLING IN OUTLINES

Again, to write an outline, you must move the items from your brainstorming to an outline form. As shown in the example on page 110, outlining requires the same strategies that you practiced in the first part of this chapter: ordering, grouping, and eliminating. Moving items from your list or cluster requires careful thinking and patience.

ACTIVITY 29

For each of the topics in this activity, you are presented with scrambled ideas in both list and cluster form. For each topic, do the following:

- Print a blank outline form from this book's Web site, at **bedfordstmartins.com/steppingstones**. If listing is your preferred brainstorming method, use the list; if clustering is your preferred brainstorming method, use the cluster.
- Move the items from the list or cluster to the outline form. Start by filling in the *main idea* and the *support points,* putting the support points in an order that makes sense to you. Both the main idea and support points should be stated as complete sentences, and the main idea should include some key words from the topic.
- Go back and fill in the specific examples for each support point, eliminating items that do not fit.

For an example of an outline based on brainstorming, see page 110. Answers may vary.

Topic 1: Discuss your favorite restaurant.

Burt's BBQ Shack

there's an old tractor inside
I love the fun decorations
BBQ is my favorite food
some of my best memories are at Burt's
it's open seven nights a week
the shredded beef sandwich is piled high
the pork ribs are meaty and sweet
all the food is outstanding
football championship celebrations
you sit at old picnic tables
my sixteenth birthday party
my family goes on New Year's Day
Burt's been in business for 15 years
the coleslaw is better than my mom's
sawdust all over the floor
the prices are very reasonable

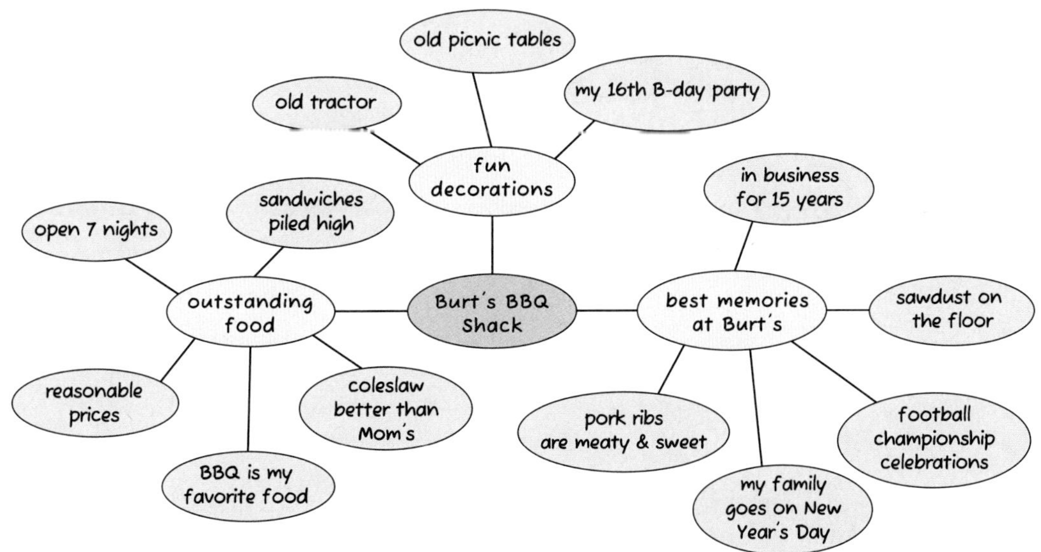

CONTINUED >

Topic 2: Discuss whether or not music has an important role in your life.

Music—not important to me

audio books in my car
country music irritates me
rap music makes me angry
bad reactions to music
jazz and hip-hop
my girlfriend loves music
live basketball broadcasts
distracts me from important activities
learning my football plays
downloading songs
prefer listening to other things
studying for school
heavy metal gives me a headache
one day I may like music
iPod and iTunes
news radio
classical music relaxes some people
staying focused at work
2Pac and Mos Def
Internet options

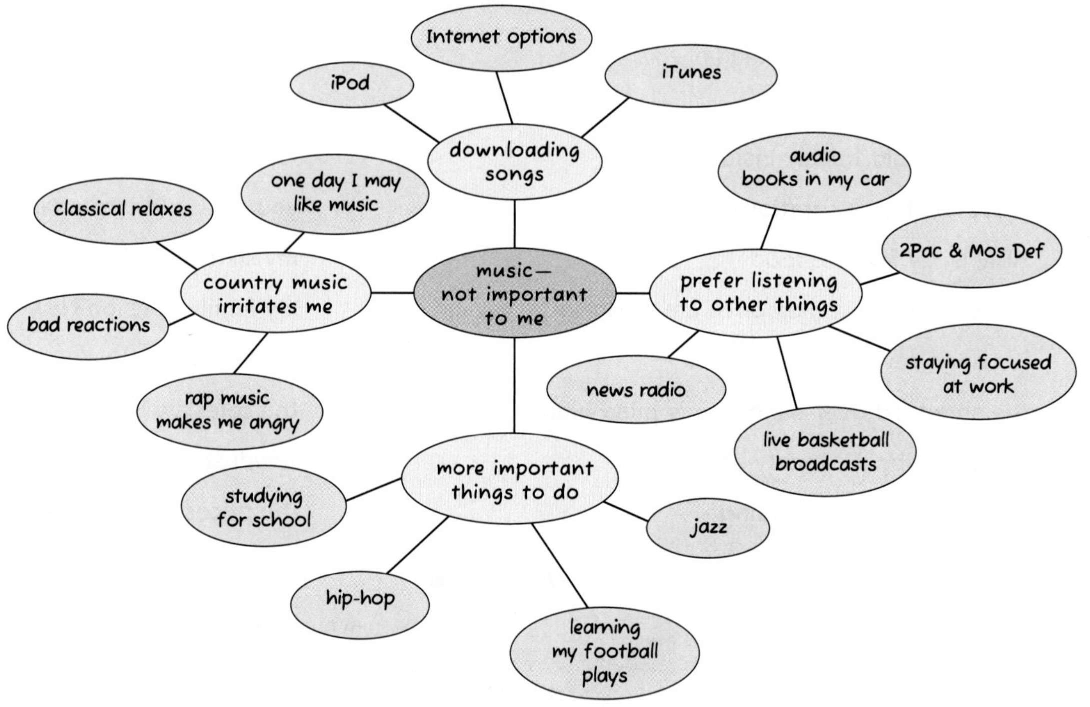

ACTIVITY 30: Teamwork

With a classmate, exchange outlines for the same topic from Activity 29. Compare how you listed the support points and examples and stated the main idea. Where were your choices the same, and where, if at all, did they differ? Did you eliminate the same points? If you find differences, does one approach seem to be better than the other? If so, why?

ACTIVITY 31

Go back to at least one of the clusters or lists that you generated in Chapter 3 and do the following:

- Print a blank outline form from this book's Web site, at **bedfordstmartins .com/steppingstones**.
- Move the items from the list or cluster to the outline form. Start by filling in the *main idea* and the *support points,* putting the support points in an order that makes sense to you. Both the main idea and support points should be stated as complete sentences. **Note:** You will have to come up with a main idea that directly addresses the topic. For advice, see page 111.
- Go back and fill in the specific examples for each support point, eliminating items that do not fit.

Because you will be asked to work with your own outlines in Chapter 5, it's a good idea to do an outline for more than one cluster or list to give yourself different options. For an example of an outline based on brainstorming, see page 110.

Teaching Tip
Because many students enjoy outline scrambles, you might make a game of them. Before class, choose a good outline from another class. Make enough copies so that groups of two or three students will be able to work with a different copy. Then, cut up the outlines so that the main ideas, support points, and examples are separated. In class, give each group a scrambled set of scraps for the outline and ask students to work together to put the parts in an order that makes sense. The first group that unscrambles the outline correctly wins.

ACTIVITY 32

On the next page, (on the left) is scrambled information for two outlines. For each one, do the following:

- Circle the topic (the most general idea) in the scrambled list.
- Identify the main idea and write it in the outline as a complete sentence.
- Identify the support points and write them in an order that makes sense to you, using complete sentences.
- Fill in the three specific examples for each support point.

For an example of a completed outline, see page 110. Answers may vary.

CONTINUED >

1. cleanings hurt my gums
I paid over $100 for a filling
he always finds more cavities
he says I'm grinding my teeth down
novocaine injections sting
something you hate doing
he said I may be developing gum disease
treatments are expensive
the dentist always gives me bad news
a crown or bridge would bankrupt me
drilling leaves my jaw sore
I hate going to the dentist
check-ups cost $85
treatments are always painful

MAIN IDEA I hate going to the dentist.

SUPPORT POINT 1 The treatments are expensive.
I paid over $100 for a filling.
Check-ups cost $85.
A crown or bridge would bankrupt me.

SUPPORT POINT 2 The treatments are always painful.
Cleanings hurt my gums.
Novocaine injections sting.
Drilling leaves my jaw sore.

SUPPORT POINT 3 The dentist always gives me bad news.
He always finds more cavities.
He says I'm grinding my teeth down.
He said I may be developing gum disease.

2. he came to my family's celebrations
he had a fun class Web site
helped us get involved in extracurricular activities
the best or worst teacher you ever had
he had a good sense of humor
he brought in interesting guest speakers
started every class with a joke
he related to us outside the classroom
we played learning games in teams
listened to our personal problems
he could laugh at himself when he made a mistake
he used creative teaching methods
Coach Hendricks was my best teacher
he appreciated the students' humor

MAIN IDEA Coach Hendricks was my best teacher.

SUPPORT POINT 1 He used creative teaching methods.
We played learning games in teams.
He had a fun class Web site.
He brought in interesting guest speakers.

SUPPORT POINT 2 He related to us outside the classroom.
He came to my family's celebrations.
He helped us get involved in extracurricular activities.
He listened to our personal problems.

SUPPORT POINT 3 He had a good sense of humor.
He started every class with a joke.
He could laugh at himself when he made a mistake.
He appreciated the students' humor.

USING TRANSITIONAL EXPRESSIONS IN OUTLINES

Your movement from one support point to another needs to be marked with a **transitional word or phrase**. These transitional cues help your reader follow the development of your thoughts.

Therefore, before you write a paragraph based on an outline, remember to do a simple but tremendously important step: *Write on your outline transitional words or phrases for each of your support points.* If the transitional expressions are not on your outline, you may forget to include them in your paragraph, making it difficult for your reader to understand the flow of your ideas.

The following example shows how you can add transitions to each part of an outline for a paragraph.

MAIN IDEA ______________________

To begin with,

SUPPORT POINT 1 ______________________

____

____

____

Second,

SUPPORT POINT 2 ______________________

____

____

____

Finally,

SUPPORT POINT 3 ______________________

____

____

____

Major Transitional Expressions

Group 1
First,
In the first place,
For starters,
To begin with,
One reason

Group 2
Second,
In the second place,
More important,
In addition,
Next,
Furthermore,
Another reason

Group 3
Third,
Finally,
Most important,
Last,
A final reason

For more on transitional expressions, see Chapter 5, page 158.

ACTIVITY 33

Go back to at least two of the earlier outlining activities (25, 27, 28, 29, or 31) and fill in transitional words or phrases in them. Then, for the remainder of this chapter, add transitional expressions to each outline that you work on.

SOLVING PROBLEMS IN OUTLINES

After completing your outline—and before you begin writing your paragraph—it is a good idea to double-check the outline to make sure that it is free of the common problems discussed in the following sections.

A Missing Item

When filling in an outline based on brainstormed ideas, you may find that you are *missing support points or examples.* Therefore, outlining is a great way to identify weaknesses in your ideas even before the paragraph-drafting stage. The result will be a much stronger, fully developed paragraph. Let's look at the following cluster:

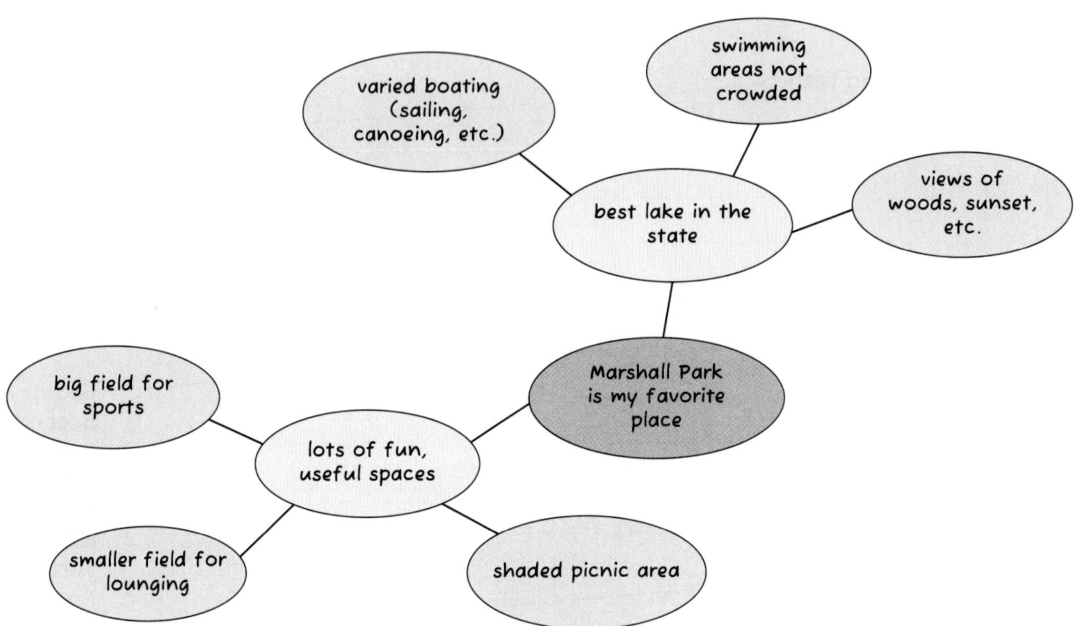

Now, let's see how a student might build an outline based on this cluster, assuming that her instructor requires three support points and three examples for each support point.

MAIN IDEA **Marshall Park is my favorite place.**

SUPPORT POINT 1 **It has the best lake in the state.**

- varied boating
- swimming areas not crowded
- views of woods, sunset

SUPPORT POINT 2 **It has lots of fun, useful spaces.**

- big field for sports
- smaller field for lounging
- shaded picnic areas

As you can see, the writer is missing a third support point with examples. Therefore, she would need to add another support point (such as *It has a huge garden with many varieties of flowers*) and examples to back it up. In some cases, you might have enough examples but be missing a support point. In other cases, you might have a support point but not enough examples.

ACTIVITY 34

Add the missing support points and examples to the following outlines. You will have to make up the missing information, but make sure that the support points are appropriate for the examples and vice versa. **Note:** This activity assumes that there should be three examples for each of three support points. Answers will vary.

1. **MAIN IDEA** I definitely want to have children.

SUPPORT POINT 1 Children can be loving.

want to cuddle with you

look up to you and admire you

SUPPORT POINT 2

make you laugh

fun to play with

never boring

SUPPORT POINT 3 Children can give you a sense of pride.

great to see them growing up smart and strong

nice to see them doing well in school

2. **MAIN IDEA** There's no way that I want to have children.

SUPPORT POINT 1 A young child would depend on me from morning to night.

During the day, I'd have to watch his/her every move.

At night, I'd have to feed the child and get him/her to bed.

SUPPORT POINT 2 I would never be as free as before.

wouldn't be able to see friends that often

wouldn't be able to relax

SUPPORT POINT 3

Kids' clothes and shoes cost a lot.

Grocery bills can be expensive.

CONTINUED >

3. **MAIN IDEA** I would never get a tattoo.

SUPPORT POINT 1 ____________

parents would be angry

minister would be offended

____

SUPPORT POINT 2 I am afraid of the pain.

____

healing process can hurt

infection could cause pain

SUPPORT POINT 3 ____________

artist might mess it up

I might not like the design after a year or two.

might look bad as my skin ages

4. **MAIN IDEA** I would get another tattoo.

SUPPORT POINT 1 Tattoos represent who I am.

zodiac symbol for my birth month

anchor for marines

____

SUPPORT POINT 2 ____________

girlfriend has a swan on her back

father has marines symbol

____

SUPPORT POINT 3 ____________

My body is pierced in six different places.

My hair is dyed purple and spiked.

I wear a spiked collar.

An Item That Does Not Fit

Another problem that can occur with your outline is *an item that does not fit.* An item does not fit when it is not clearly connected to a main idea. Take a look at this outline, in which just the first support point has been developed with examples. Can you see a problem with one of the examples?

MAIN IDEA I have excellent people skills.

SUPPORT POINT 1 My friends often turn to me for advice.

- My friend Malika asks my opinion on relationship problems.
- My friend Tari asks me for job advice.
- My best friend, Emile, has the most problems of all.

SUPPORT POINT 2 I am good at resolving conflicts in my personal life and at work.

SUPPORT POINT 3 I work well with others.

You might have noticed that the third example (*My best friend, Emile, has the most problems of all*) doesn't fit with the main idea (*I have excellent people skills*) or with the support point it's under (*My friends often turn to me for advice*). A better example would show how the writer's friends turn to him for advice. For instance, a good example might be *My best friend, Emile, asks me for parenting advice.*

When you have finished an outline, first read each support point together with the main idea to make sure the point fits the main idea. Then, check the specific examples under each support point to make sure they belong. If they do not, revise them so that they fit better.

ACTIVITY 35

In the following outlines, cross out any item that does not fit. Then, use your imagination and write in a new item that does fit. Replacement items will vary.

1. **MAIN IDEA** The Olive Grove is my favorite restaurant.

SUPPORT POINT 1 It has a romantic atmosphere.
soft music
candles on the table
intimate tables for two

SUPPORT POINT 2 The food is delicious.
chewy, cheesy pizza
~~cheap prices~~
best New York cheesecake

SUPPORT POINT 3 ~~Everyone has a favorite restaurant.~~
parking valets are fast
waitresses are attentive and helpful
~~managers yell at the staff~~

2. **MAIN IDEA** Music is important in my life.

SUPPORT POINT 1 It helps me work better.
cleaning the house
stocking the shelves at my job
~~wearing earplugs~~

SUPPORT POINT 2 It calms me down.
~~I'm nervous a lot~~
after a fight with my parents
when I'm stuck in traffic

SUPPORT POINT 3 It motivates me.
helps me get up in the morning
~~motivates my girlfriend~~
gets me going at the gym

ACTIVITY 36

In the following two outlines, some of the *specific examples* have been incorrectly listed as *support points*. As a result, the items do not fit, and the outline does not make sense. This is a common problem in academic outlines. To correct the error, switch the specific example and the support point to their correct positions.

PARTIAL EXAMPLE:

MAIN IDEA My mother is the person I admire most.

SUPPORT POINT 1 She succeeded despite difficult circumstances.
~~She raised a family without help from others.~~

She got an education while working full time.

She raised a family without help from others.
~~She succeeded despite difficult circumstances.~~

She has advanced in a difficult job.

1. **MAIN IDEA** I am an excellent student.

SUPPORT POINT 1 I have good study habits.
~~I participate in study groups.~~

I do my homework daily.

I participate in study groups.
~~I have good study habits.~~

I see a tutor when I need extra help.

SUPPORT POINT 2 I communicate well with my instructors.

I talk with instructors during office hours.

I ask questions during lectures.

I e-mail instructors with homework questions.

SUPPORT POINT 3 I have clear academic goals.
~~I want to be a biology major.~~

I want to get a 4.0 grade point average.

I want to be a biology major.
~~I have clear academic goals.~~

I plan to earn my PhD in seven years.

2. **MAIN IDEA** There are good reasons why I don't own a car.

SUPPORT POINT 1 I can walk everywhere.

I walk to school.

I walk to work.

I walk to shops and restaurants.

SUPPORT POINT 2 Having a car is too expensive.
~~Car insurance costs too much.~~

Gas prices are high.

Car insurance costs too much.
~~Having a car is too expensive.~~

I can't afford tune-ups and repairs.

SUPPORT POINT 3 There are other ways to get around.
~~My friends give me rides.~~

I borrow my parents' car.

I take the bus or subway.

My friends give me rides.
~~There are other ways to get around.~~

An Item That Repeats Another Item

Another problem that can occur with outlines is *an item that repeats another item.* Sometimes, we express the same idea more than once, but we do not recognize this repetition because we have changed the words. Take a look at this example:

MAIN IDEA	**I like buying secondhand clothing (*because* . . .)**
SUPPORT POINT 1	**it is less expensive than new clothing.**
SUPPORT POINT 2	**it doesn't cost as much as new clothes.**
SUPPORT POINT 3	**it is cheaper than new clothing.**

Even though each support point uses different words, the same idea (about used clothing being less expensive than new clothing) has been repeated. However, repetitions are not always this easy to spot, so we have to be very careful about the ideas and words that we use. Now, here is an example of three *distinct* support points:

MAIN IDEA	**I like buying secondhand clothing (*because* . . .)**
SUPPORT POINT 1	**it is less expensive than new clothing.**
SUPPORT POINT 2	**many items are in "like new" condition.**
SUPPORT POINT 3	**some older clothes are better made than new items.**

ACTIVITY 37

In the following outlines, cross out any item that repeats another item. Then, use your imagination and write in a new item that is *distinct* from the others. Replacement items will vary.

1. MAIN IDEA My dream career is nursing.

SUPPORT POINT 1 Nurses help other people.
- give patients dignity and hope
- provide a high standard of medical care
- treat patients with tenderness and concern

SUPPORT POINT 2 Nurses have good compensation and good job security.
- nurses always in high demand
- salaries are very competitive
- ~~nurses always able to find work~~

SUPPORT POINT 3 Nurses are admired.
- shown as competent and helpful in TV dramas
- seen as role models
- media show positive images of nurses

CONTINUED >

2. **MAIN IDEA** Mario's Gym is the best place to work out.

SUPPORT POINT 1 The equipment is high-quality.

state-of-the-art workout machines

~~good equipment~~

brand-new free weights

SUPPORT POINT 2 The location is convenient.

near my home, school, and work

close to a highway exit

~~close to me~~

SUPPORT POINT 3 It's a good deal.

regular monthly fee is $30

you get a discount if a friend signs up

fees rarely go up

An Item That Is Unclear

The last major problem that can occur in outlines is the use of *an item that is unclear.* Often, items are unclear because they express an idea that is not specific enough. Be especially careful about single-word items in your outline; it is common for single-word items to be overly general.

An unclear item in your outline can lead to a serious breakdown of organization and focus in your paragraph. Always try to correct any unclear items *before* you attempt to write the paragraph. In the examples below, compare the unclear words (in bold) with the specific examples in the revision. Can you see the difference?

UNCLEAR	The first-aid training was **good**. I learned a lot of **cool stuff**.
SPECIFIC	The first-aid training was practical and thorough. I learned how to clean and dress a wound, administer CPR, treat a patient for shock, and summon emergency assistance.
UNCLEAR	Tyndall College should **do more** for struggling students.
	Tyndall College should **help** struggling students.
SPECIFIC	Tyndall College should provide more tutors for struggling students.

For more unclear (imprecise) words to look out for, see Chapter 6, page 169.

ACTIVITY 38

In the following outlines, cross out and replace any unclear items. You can work with another student or on your own. *Replacement items will vary.*

1. **MAIN IDEA** Volunteering benefits both the volunteers and their communities.

SUPPORT POINT 1 Volunteer work takes many forms.

fund-raising helps charities serve more people

collecting food for pantries benefits the hungry

building a playground is ~~nice~~

SUPPORT POINT 2 Volunteer work teaches volunteers new skills.

working with others

managing money

~~other skills~~

SUPPORT POINT 3 Volunteer work makes volunteers feel connected to their communities.

volunteers can meet others during projects ~~satisfaction~~

recipients of assistance usually express gratitude

2. **MAIN IDEA** Three key qualities are essential in a president of the United States.

SUPPORT POINT 1 A president should act ethically.

not lie to American citizens or other members of government

not go around the law to carry out policies

~~be good~~

SUPPORT POINT 2 A president should work tirelessly to help Americans.

pursue affordable health care

~~help~~ military

provide greater funding for schools and teachers

SUPPORT POINT 3 A president should do ~~good stuff~~ on the world stage.

meet regularly with world leaders to avoid conflicts

promote nuclear disarmament

provide humanitarian aid to discourage terrorism

Combined Problems

Often, an outline will have more than one of the problems described on pages 128–134. The following activity will give you practice identifying and fixing multiple problems in an outline.

ACTIVITY 39

In each outline below, do the following:

- Label any item that (1) does not fit, (2) repeats another item, or (3) is unclear.
- Note where items are missing. (Assume that each main idea should have three support points and each support point three examples.)

1. **MAIN IDEA** Rita Cervino is the best manager I have worked with.

SUPPORT POINT 1 She is competent and experienced.

She has been a manager for ten years.

She accomplishes her goals, even with limited resources. *missing example*

SUPPORT POINT 2 She listens to her employees.

She holds weekly meetings to hear employee concerns.

When a worker raises a concern, she addresses it.

Stuff she does lets you know she hears you. *unclear*

SUPPORT POINT 3 She works as hard as her employees do.

If her workers stay late for a deadline, she does too.

She is fair in distributing work. *does not fit*

No employee works harder than she does. *repeats*

2. **MAIN IDEA** To prevent the spread of germs, follow this procedure for hand washing.

SUPPORT POINT 1 Use soap and water properly.

Wet your hands with warm water.

Wipe your hands thoroughly on the soap bar, or use a generous squirt of liquid soap.

Apply the soap. *repeats*

SUPPORT POINT 2 Do it right. *unclear*

Rub your hands together until suds form.

Wash all parts of your hands, including under the nails. *missing example*

SUPPORT POINT 3 Rinse properly.

Many prefer soft water. *does not fit*

Hold your hands under warm water.

Rub them together for at least ten seconds.

Bringing It All Together

In this chapter, you have learned how to organize your ideas to write an outline (or plan) for your paragraph. These ideas come from brainstorming, idea-generating strategies that you learned about in Chapter 3. Check off each of the following statements that you understand. For any that you do not understand, review the appropriate pages in this chapter.

☐ Organizing involves the mental strategies of **ordering**, **grouping**, and **eliminating**:

- ____ **Ordering** is arranging the ideas that you developed through brainstorming in a logical way. You can order single-word items, phrases, or whole sentences. (See page 85.)
- ____ **Grouping** is putting related ideas together. You can group single-word items, phrases, or whole sentences. (See page 91.)
- ____ **Eliminating** is removing ideas that are not related to your topic. You can eliminate single-word items, phrases, or whole sentences. (See page 98.)

☐ To organize ideas effectively, you need to know the difference between **general ideas** and **specific examples**. General ideas usually come first in order, and they are followed by specific examples. The word *jobs* expresses a general idea because there are many types of jobs. The words *clerk, engineer,* and *cook* are specific examples of jobs. (See page 85.)

☐ In outlining, you move the items from your brainstorming into an outline form. Outlines have three main features:

- ____ the **main idea**, which responds directly to the topic (the main subject or task) of a writing assignment. (See page 111.)
- ____ **support points**, which back up the main idea. Often, these can be drawn from the general ideas in clusters and lists. (See page 112.)
- ____ **specific examples**, which illustrate the support points. (See page 114.)

☐ It's a good idea to add to your outline **transitional words and phrases**. These mark your movement from one part of a paragraph to another and help readers follow the development of your thoughts. (See page 118.)

☐ After completing your outline—and before you begin writing your paragraph—you should double-check it to make sure that it is free of the following common problems: missing items (page 120), an item that does not fit (page 122), an item that repeats another item (page 125), and an item that is unclear (page 126).

Chapter 5

Composing the Paragraph

OVERVIEW OF THIS CHAPTER

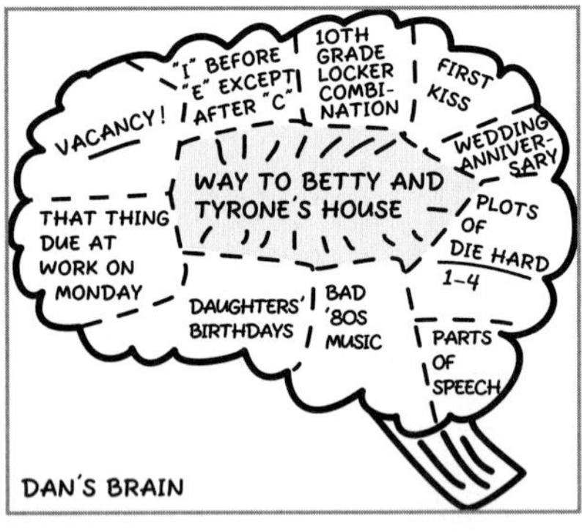

WARM-UP Reaching Your Destination

1. *Imagine this situation:*

Betty and Tyrone have invited four friends to their new home for Thanksgiving dinner. To reach their house, the friends will need to take a highway and several smaller streets. Each friend has a different plan:

- Dan will rely on his memory to find the house. He has been to the house once, and he thinks he can find his way back to it again even though it might be tricky.
- Alberto will go online to MapQuest, put in Betty and Tyrone's address, and print out a detailed map.
- Luce has a navigation system in her SUV. She will enter Betty and Tyrone's address and follow the step-by-step directions. The navigation system not only shows each step of the trip but also talks to Luce, reminding her to slow down and prepare to turn.
- Veronica wrote down some directions when she talked to Betty on the phone. Betty could not remember the names of all the streets, but she told Veronica the approximate distance between streets and described some landmarks.

— I-20 to 408N
— Off Mt. Creek Rd—2 mi ?
— Right by Target—1 mi ?
— Left across from ballpark

2. *Stop and think!*

Working alone or with classmates, decide which friend is most likely to find Betty and Tyrone's house with the least difficulty. Then, decide which friend is most likely to get lost trying to find the house.

In Chapter 4, you learned how to develop a detailed outline for your paragraph. This outline is your map—or navigation system—to writing a successful paragraph. However, to reach your destination, you must pay close attention to the outline and follow it step by step. If you skip any item on the outline, you may get lost while writing the paragraph; moreover, your reader may get lost while *reading* the paragraph.

In this chapter, you will learn how to follow your outline step by step in order to write a clearly organized and well-developed paragraph.

Moving from Outline to Paragraph: An Opening Example

Take a look at how one student went from an outline to a successful paragraph:

Mrs. Nevis, my eleventh-grade geography teacher, was the worst teacher I've ever had. To begin with, she always picked on students and seemed to enjoy it. For example, my friend Jerry had a hard time memorizing the names of countries, so she called him a "brainless wonder." Also, she laughed at students when they made a mistake or answered incorrectly. I could never pronounce the word "Antarctic," so she always made me say it just so she could laugh at me. Her favorite way to pick on students, however, was to make us stay after school for no reason at all. Once, when I sneezed three times in a row, she said I was trying to annoy her, so she assigned me one hour of detention. Next, she had very poor teaching skills. For instance, she could never explain a problem or an idea clearly. One time, when we asked her the difference between a glacier and an ice floe, she got so confused that she told us to look it up on the Internet. When she graded our essays, she never gave us useful comments. She once gave me a grade of "C" on a paper, and her only comment was "Try harder." Finally, she had distracting personal habits. She actually liked to eat food during class and even talked with her mouth full! Also, her clothes looked like she had slept in them or cleaned out her garage in them. If there were an award for worst teacher in history, Mrs. Nevis would get my vote.

We will now look at how each part of a paragraph is developed.

MAIN IDEA

Mrs. Nevis was my worst teacher.

TRANSITIONAL EXPRESSION

To begin with,

SUPPORT POINT 1

she picked on students.

–used rude nicknames
–laughed at us
–made us stay after school

TRANSITIONAL EXPRESSION

Next,

SUPPORT POINT 2

she had poor teaching skills.

–did not explain ideas clearly
–put no comments on essays

TRANSITIONAL EXPRESSION

Finally,

SUPPORT POINT 3

she had distracting personal habits.

–ate food while teaching
–wore dirty, wrinkled clothes

Writing an Effective Topic Sentence

The **topic sentence** expresses the main idea, or topic, of a paragraph; typically, it is the first sentence of a paragraph. To write the topic sentence, simply take the main idea from your outline and make sure that it is a complete sentence, with a subject, a verb, and a complete thought. In some cases, as in the following example, you might also add other words to flesh out the main idea; however, these words should not change the meaning of the main idea. (For more on main ideas in outlines, see Chapter 4, page 111. For more on complete sentences, see Chapter 11, page 293.)

MAIN IDEA	**Mrs. Nevis was my worst teacher.**
TOPIC SENTENCE	**Mrs. Nevis, my eleventh-grade geography teacher, was the worst teacher I've ever had.**

As you will see, there are several ways to form a topic sentence, from very basic to more complex and creative. However, the most important function of a topic sentence is to *express the main idea clearly*. If you like writing more complex or creative topic sentences, be very careful not to lose the clarity of the main idea.

Power Tip

A subject is the *main actor* in a sentence, or *who or what* the sentence is about. A verb expresses an *action* or a *state of being*. You will learn more about these important sentence parts in Part Two of this book.

SIX WAYS TO FORM A TOPIC SENTENCE

Six kinds of topic sentences are commonly used by experienced writers. They aren't the only kinds, but if you learn how to write them, you'll be able to express the main idea of almost any paragraph.

1. A Basic Topic Sentence

A basic topic sentence is the quickest and simplest way to begin your paragraph. Just copy the main idea from your outline, making sure that the sentence has a subject and verb and expresses a complete thought. Make sure, too, that the sentence begins with a capital letter and ends in a period. When you write a basic topic sentence, do not change any key words or add any new words that might change the meaning of your main idea. Here are three examples:

Power Tip
Key words are those essential to the meaning of the main idea. For more on key words, see Chapter 4.

MAIN IDEA	**Tango is my favorite restaurant.**
TOPIC SENTENCE	**Tango is my favorite restaurant.**
MAIN IDEA	**Music is important in my life.**
TOPIC SENTENCE	**Music is important in my life.**
MAIN IDEA	**I could not live without my car.**
TOPIC SENTENCE	**I could not live without my car.**

Basic topic sentences are clear and direct, and they get you writing quickly. You might want to use a basic topic sentence in the following situations:

- if you are being timed and must write quickly
- if you get stuck when you try to begin writing
- if a topic is difficult for you

When you begin your paragraph with a basic topic sentence, you can always go back and revise it later if you have time.

ACTIVITY 1

For this activity and others in this chapter, you will need to work with the outlines that you developed in Chapter 4. (You might want to complete Activity 31, page 117, in Chapter 4 if you haven't already.)

Refer back to these outlines. Then, for each main idea in the outlines, write a basic topic sentence.

2. A Topic Sentence That Adds a Description

A topic sentence that adds a description is similar to a basic topic sentence but requires just a little more work. Copy the main idea from your outline and add a brief descriptive phrase to clarify the subject of the paragraph. Here are three examples with the descriptive phrase underlined:

MAIN IDEA **Tango is my favorite restaurant.**

TOPIC SENTENCE **Tango, <u>an Argentinean restaurant in my neighborhood</u>, is my favorite place to eat.**

MAIN IDEA **Music is important in my life.**

TOPIC SENTENCE **<u>Hip-hop and classical</u> music are important in my life.**

MAIN IDEA **I could not live without my car.**

TOPIC SENTENCE **I could not live without my car, <u>a beat-up 1992 Honda Civic</u>.**

A topic sentence that adds a description is more precise and colorful than a basic topic sentence. With practice, you will be able to add a brief descriptive phrase to your topic sentences with little effort or loss of time. However, in order to keep your main idea clear, remember these suggestions:

- Use only *brief* descriptive phrases.
- Do not change any key words or add any new words that might change the meaning of your main idea.
- If a descriptive phrase does not fit smoothly into your main idea, do not force it. Some main ideas do not work well with an added description.

Power Tip
Later in this chapter, you will learn about situations in which you can change key words to words with a similar meaning; this strategy can make your writing more lively and creative. However, as you learn the steps of building different types of topic sentences, it's a good idea to retain the key words from your main idea.

ACTIVITY 2

Using your completed outlines from Chapter 4, write each main idea as a topic sentence that adds a description. (You may not be able to add a descriptive phrase to every main idea.) Then, exchange your topic sentences with a classmate. Check each other's work and share any ideas that you may have for revising the sentences.

3. A Topic Sentence That Creates a Contrast

A contrast is another effective way to start your paragraph. To form this type of topic sentence, you will need to write a complex sentence beginning with *although, even though,* or *while.* Here are three examples:

Teaching Tip
As students become more experienced writers, they may form contrasts in ways other than the three patterns shown here. However, starting with these three patterns will give them valuable practice and confidence before they move on to other patterns.

MAIN IDEA **Tango is my favorite restaurant.**

TOPIC SENTENCE **Although I have eaten at many good restaurants, Tango stands out as my favorite.**

Power Tip
Make sure to join the two parts of a sentence that sets up a contrast.
Incorrect: Even though I don't get to listen to music as often as I would like. It is very important in my life. (The first word group doesn't express a complete thought; it is an error known as a *fragment*.)
Correct: Even though I don't get to listen to music as often as I would like, it is very important in my life. (The two word groups are joined to form a complete thought.)
For more on avoiding fragments in complex sentences, see Chapter 13.

MAIN IDEA — **Music is important in my life.**

TOPIC SENTENCE — **Even though I don't get to listen to music as often as I would like, it is very important in my life.**

MAIN IDEA — **I could not live without my car.**

TOPIC SENTENCE — **While I could survive without many of my possessions, I could not live without my car.**

A topic sentence that creates a contrast shows that you have a deep understanding of your main idea. However, since this type of topic sentence tends to be longer than a basic topic sentence, you must be careful that your main idea stays clear. Keep these suggestions in mind:

- Make sure that the *first word* of your sentence is *although, even though,* or *while.*
- Be sure that your main idea is in the *second half* of the sentence.
- When writing the main idea, do not change any key words or add any new words that might change its meaning.

ACTIVITY 3

Using your completed outlines from Chapter 4, write each main idea as a topic sentence that creates a contrast. Then, exchange your topic sentences with a classmate. Check each other's work and share any ideas that you may have for revising the sentences.

4. A Topic Sentence That Identifies Your Support Points

Identifying your support points is another popular and effective way to begin your paragraph. This type of topic sentence includes the main idea and briefly identifies the support points that you will develop in your paragraph. These support points may be introduced by the word *because,* as shown in the following examples. Keep your list as brief as possible so that it flows smoothly.

MAIN IDEA	TOPIC SENTENCE
Tango is my favorite restaurant.	**Tango is my favorite restaurant because of the delicious food, romantic atmosphere, and reasonable prices.**
SUPPORT POINT 1 **The food is delicious.**	
SUPPORT POINT 2 **The atmosphere is romantic.**	
SUPPORT POINT 3 **The prices are reasonable.**	

A topic sentence that identifies the support points gives the reader a "snapshot" of your paragraph, and it demonstrates that you have a firm grasp on the organization. However, since this type of topic sentence tends to be longer than a basic topic sentence, you must be careful that your main idea stays clear. Keep these suggestions in mind:

- Be sure that your main idea is in the *first half* of the sentence.
- When writing the main idea, do not change any key words or add any new words that might change its meaning.
- When copying the support points from your outline, you may shorten them so that they flow smoothly; however, do not omit any of them or change their meaning.
- If you use the word *because* before the support points, it should come *in the middle* of your topic sentence.

Power Tip

When you list support points, make sure that each item is parallel, that is, in the same form.
Not parallel: My favorite sports are swimming, skiing, and to skateboard. ("Swimming" and "skiing" are *ing* verbs, but "to skateboard" is the word "to" plus a verb.)
Parallel: My favorite sports are swimming, skiing, and skateboarding. ("Swimming," "skiing," and "skateboarding" are all *ing* verbs.)

ACTIVITY 4

Using your completed outlines from Chapter 4, write each main idea as a topic sentence that identifies the support points. Then, exchange your topic sentences with a classmate. Check each other's work and share any ideas that you may have for revising the sentences.

5. *A Topic Sentence That Creates a Contrast* and *Identifies the Support Points*

This type of topic sentence shows your deep understanding of the main idea and your firm grasp on the organization of the paragraph. To form this type of topic sentence, do the following:

- Make sure that the *first word* of your sentence is *although, even though,* or *while,* and complete the contrast statement.
- Follow the contrast statement with the main idea. In other words, the main idea will be *in the middle* of the sentence.
- When writing the main idea, do not change any key words or add any new words that might change its meaning.
- Copy the support points from your outline. You may shorten them so that they flow smoothly; however, do not omit any of them or change their meaning. Also, you can precede the support points with *because* if that makes sense for your topic sentence.

MAIN IDEA	TOPIC SENTENCE
Tango is my favorite restaurant.	Although I have eaten at many good restaurants, Tango is my favorite because of the delicious food, romantic atmosphere, and reasonable prices.
SUPPORT POINT 1 The food is delicious.	
SUPPORT POINT 2 The atmosphere is romantic.	
SUPPORT POINT 3 The prices are reasonable.	

MAIN IDEA	TOPIC SENTENCE
Music is important in my life.	Even though I don't get to listen to music as often as I would like, it is important in my life because it helps me relax, work, and party.
SUPPORT POINT 1 It helps me relax.	
SUPPORT POINT 2 It helps me work.	
SUPPORT POINT 3 It helps me party.	

ACTIVITY 5

Using your completed outlines from Chapter 4, write each main idea as a topic sentence that creates a contrast *and* identifies the support points. Then, exchange your topic sentences with a classmate. Check each other's work and share any ideas that you may have for revising the sentences.

6. A Topic Sentence That Uses Creative Language

To form this type of topic sentence, use any of the other methods, but think about ways to grab the reader's attention. You might look for vocabulary and ideas that are playful, inspirational, or interesting in some other way. Try the following strategies:

- Ask yourself: Would I want to read this paragraph based only on the main idea? If not, think about what excites you most about the topic. What words might express your enthusiasm more clearly?
- Try to use strong, active verbs (action words) and vivid descriptions. For more on verbs and descriptive words, see Chapter 10.
- Use a portable or online thesaurus to search for fresh, new words to express your ideas. (A thesaurus is a dictionary that, for each word, gives words with similar meanings.)

Here are some examples of topic sentences that use creative language:

MAIN IDEA	TOPIC SENTENCE
Music is important in my life.	To me, music is an essential life companion, from the moment hip-hop gets me out of bed to the time I fall asleep to my favorite jazz station.
SUPPORT POINT 1 It helps me work.	
SUPPORT POINT 2 It helps me party.	
SUPPORT POINT 3 It helps me relax.	

MAIN IDEA	TOPIC SENTENCE
I could not live without my car.	Like Cinderella's pumpkin that turned into a golden carriage, my beat-up 1992 Honda Civic is a magical vehicle that I couldn't live without.
SUPPORT POINT 1 I need it for work.	
SUPPORT POINT 2 I need it to help my family.	
SUPPORT POINT 3 I need it to escape.	

Power Tip
The comparison between the Honda Civic and fairy-tale character Cinderella's magical pumpkin/carriage is known as a metaphor. You will learn more about metaphors and how to use them in your writing in Chapter 6.

A topic sentence that uses creative language can grab the reader's attention with its originality. However, when you search for more creative ways of expressing your ideas, you run a higher risk of losing the clarity of your main idea. With sufficient practice, you should be able to use creative language *and* keep your main idea clear. Keep the following suggestions in mind:

- As you add new vocabulary and ideas, be sure to keep two or three of the key words from your main idea (as they appear on your outline).
- If you use a thesaurus, be careful in choosing words. Not all the words listed will have exactly the same meaning, and a poor choice may change or obscure your main idea. When possible, select a word that you are somewhat familiar with, or ask your instructor for advice. You might also want to check your word choices in a dictionary.
- Try building on one of the five types of topic sentences discussed earlier (basic, one that adds a contrast, one that identifies the support points, and so on).

Teaching Tip
You might bring a thesaurus to class and explain its functions. Then, ask students to call out possible words to fill in the following blank: *I am a ______ person.* Choose one of the words and look it up in the thesaurus. Then, read some of the synonyms to the class. Ask students which synonyms fill the blank effectively. Which ones just sound "wrong"? This is a good way to introduce students to the benefits and limitations of thesauruses and to the subtle differences in meaning among words listed there.

ACTIVITY 6

Look at the topic sentences that you have written for the previous activities in this chapter. Select one or two of them and rewrite them, using more creative language. Then, exchange your topic sentences with a classmate. Check each other's work and share any ideas that you may have for revising the sentences.

ACTIVITY 7

Following is an outline and topic sentences based on the outline. For each topic sentence, indicate the type (basic topic sentence, one that adds a description, one that creates a contrast, one that identifies the support points, one that creates a contrast and identifies the support points, and one that uses creative language).

MAIN IDEA	I hate shopping at Ruby Gate Mall.
SUPPORT POINT 1	The crowds are annoying.
SUPPORT POINT 2	The stores are geared to teenagers.
SUPPORT POINT 3	The prices are too high.

EXAMPLE: **Topic sentence:** I hate shopping at Ruby Gate Mall.

Type: basic topic sentence

1. **Topic sentence:** Although I enjoy shopping in general, I hate going to Ruby Gate Mall because the crowds are annoying, the stores are geared to teenagers, and the prices are too high.

   Type: creates a contrast/identifies support points

2. **Topic sentence:** Although I enjoy shopping in general, I hate going to Ruby Gate Mall.

   Type: creates a contrast

3. **Topic sentence:** After shopping at Ruby Gate Mall, I feel as if I need a vacation and then a second job to pay the bills.

   Type: uses creative language

4. **Topic sentence:** I hate shopping at Ruby Gate Mall because the crowds are annoying, the stores are geared to teenagers, and the prices are too high.

   Type: identifies the support points

5. **Topic sentence:** I hate shopping at Ruby Gate Mall, the only mall in Danville City.

   Type: adds a description

PROBLEMS WITH TOPIC SENTENCES

After you have taken the time to develop an outline, the worst mistake you can make is to leave it at home, in your notebook, or anywhere out of sight. Remember: a carefully crafted outline is your navigation system—you should refer to it closely throughout the writing process. If you ignore any important information in your outline, you may get lost while writing the paragraph.

In writing a topic sentence based on your outline, you must not change the meaning of the main idea in any significant way. If you do this, your topic sentence may not make sense or fit the paragraph. Generally, students accidentally change the main idea by

- leaving out a key word from the main idea
- changing a key word in the main idea
- adding inappropriate new ideas to the main idea

Let's look at these problems one at a time.

Problem 1: Leaving Out a Key Word from the Main Idea

Usually, a main idea has two or more key words. Each of these may be essential to the meaning of your main idea, so if you omit one, your topic sentence may not be accurate. For example, the following main idea has four key words:

	KEY WORD 1		KEY WORD 2	KEY WORD 3	KEY WORD 4
MAIN IDEA	Tango	is	my	favorite	restaurant.

Each key word is essential to the main idea. If you omit one or more of them, your topic sentence will not be complete. Now, imagine that you wrote the following topic sentence based on this main idea:

I have a favorite restaurant.

Here, the name of the restaurant is missing. In your mind, it may be clear that Tango is meant; however, it won't be clear to readers, who might be frustrated by the missing information. Imagine that someone described a terrific movie to you but then forgot to tell you the name of the movie! Let's look at another example:

Tango is a favorite restaurant.

This sentence leaves out the word *my,* which tells whose favorite restaurant is described in the paragraph. Readers may be left wondering whether Tango is a favorite restaurant of students, local residents, food critics, or some other person or group of people. Here's another example.

Tango is my favorite.

In this case, it may not be clear to readers that Tango is a restaurant. This may be obvious to you, but readers who have never heard of Tango might think that you are talking about a favorite dance. Finally, let's look at this example:

Tango is a restaurant.

Here, two key words have been omitted: *my* and *favorite.* Readers will have a very unclear sense of the purpose of the paragraph. The simple fact that Tango is a restaurant fails to communicate the most interesting aspect of the paragraph—that this restaurant is your personal favorite.

Power Tip
Remember also to check that your topic sentence has a subject and a verb and that it expresses a complete thought. Otherwise, it will be considered a fragment, a serious error.

As you can see from these examples, paying close attention to your outline is essential for the success of your paragraph. Some students omit important key words from their main idea when they are distracted or glance too quickly at the outline. Also, as you begin to form more complex and creative topic sentences, the chances of misstating your main ideas become greater.

ACTIVITY 8: Teamwork

With two or three classmates, read each main idea and its related topic sentences and do the following:

- Identify which key words from the main idea have been left out of the topic sentences.
- Explain how the missing key words change the meaning of the topic sentences. Explanations may vary.

EXAMPLE: **Main idea:** I am a responsible student.

Topic sentence: I am responsible.

Key word(s) left out: student. Without this word, readers will think the writer is responsible in general, but she is referring to herself as a responsible student.

Topic sentence: I am a student.

Key word(s) left out: responsible. Without this word, readers will learn just that the writer is a student—not that she is responsible.

Topic sentence: A student is responsible.

Key word(s) left out: I. Without this word, readers will not know that a specific responsible student is meant.

1. **Main idea:** Pets are good for their owners' health.

   Topic sentence: They're good for their owners' health.

   Key word(s) left out: pets. Without this word, readers won't know what's good for owners' health.

   Topic sentence: In addition to being loyal companions, pets are good for their owners.

   Key word(s) left out: health. Without this word, readers won't know the exact benefit of pet ownership.

   Topic sentence: Without a doubt, pets are good for health.

   Key word(s) left out: their owners'. Without these words, it won't be clear exactly who benefits from pet ownership.

2. **Main idea:** My parents are happily married.

   Topic sentence: Despite many difficulties, my parents are happy.

   Key word(s) left out: married. Without this word, readers won't see that a happy marriage (not just general happiness) is meant.

   Topic sentence: After years of togetherness, my parents are still married.

   Key word(s) left out: happily. Without this word, readers won't know that the parents are content with their marriage; they might be miserable.

   Topic sentence: After twenty-two years, they are still happily married.

   Key word(s) left out: my parents. Without these words, readers won't know who is happily married.

Problem 2: Changing a Key Word in the Main Idea

When writing your topic sentence, you should keep one or more of the key words from your main idea. If you search for more creative language to replace any of the key words, be sure not to change the meaning of your main idea by accident. The following main idea has four key words.

	KEY WORD 1		KEY WORD 2		KEY WORD 3	KEY WORD 4
MAIN IDEA	Music	is	important	in	my	life.

Which of these key words could be replaced without changing the meaning of the main idea? To see, let's change three of them, one at a time. Imagine that you have written the following topic sentence based on this main idea:

> **Entertainment is important in my life.**

Here, the word *music* has been changed to *entertainment.* Since music is a form of entertainment, this idea makes sense generally. However, readers will expect the paragraph to discuss several forms of entertainment, and they may be confused when your examples relate only to music. Now, let's see another possibility:

> **My iPod is important in my life.**

Here, the word *music* has been changed to *my iPod.* Because you may listen to music all the time on an iPod, this idea makes sense to you. However, readers will expect you to discuss several uses of the iPod (for photos, podcasts, music, and so on), and they may be confused when the examples relate only to music. Here's another possibility:

> **Hip-hop is important in my life.**

Here, the word *music* has been changed to *hip-hop.* Since hip-hop may be your favorite type of music, this idea makes sense to you. However, readers will expect you to discuss *only* hip-hop. If you discuss any other types of music, this topic sentence will not fit the paragraph. On the other hand, if all your examples relate to hip-hop, this topic sentence will work for the paragraph. Here's one more possibility:

Songs are important in my life.

Here, readers will expect you to discuss only *songs* in the paragraph. If all your examples relate to songs, this topic sentence will work for the paragraph. On the other hand, if you discuss any other forms of music (such as symphonies), this topic sentence will not fit the paragraph.

From the examples we have just discussed, you can see that changing the key word *music* is risky. Now, let's change a different key word (*important*) in the main idea:

Music is necessary for my life.

Here, the word *important* has been replaced with *necessary*. This substitution does not change the meaning of the main idea in a significant way. In fact, you could replace the word *important* with many different words (*essential, vital, crucial,* and so on) without changing the meaning of the main idea. The same is true of this substitution of *survival* for *life:*

Teaching Tip
Write on the board two or three additional main idea statements, such as *Children need to feel secure to be happy* or *Exercise and occasional breaks from work can reduce stress.* First, ask students to identify the key words. Then, ask them which of these words could be replaced. Can they identify possible substitutions?

Music is important for my survival.

Here, the word *survival* suggests surviving *life,* so this replacement does not significantly change the meaning of the main idea. In fact, you could substitute several words here (*existence, lifestyle,* and so on) and not obscure the meaning of the main idea.

ACTIVITY 9: Teamwork

With two or three classmates, read each main idea and its related topic sentences and do the following:

- Underline the key word or words from the main idea that have been replaced in each topic sentence.
- Indicate whether or how the new words change or obscure the meaning of the main idea.
- If the new words *do not* change or obscure the meaning of the main idea, explain why. Answers may vary.

EXAMPLE: **Main idea:** Failing my history class taught me some important lessons.

Topic sentence: Repeating my history class taught me some important lessons. Meaning changed: "repeating" is not the same thing as "failing."

Topic sentence: Failing my history exam taught me some important lessons. Meaning changed: "exam" is not the same thing as "class."

Topic sentence: Failing my history class taught me some useful lessons. Meaning the same: "useful" and "important" both suggest the benefits/importance of the lessons.

1. **Main idea:** My parents used several strategies to teach me responsibility.

   Topic sentence: Using several creative strategies, my parents helped me become a mature person. Meaning changed: "helped me become" is roughly similar to "teach" but being "mature" is different from being "responsible."

   Topic sentence: My mother and father always demanded that I be responsible. Meaning changed: "mother and father" is a clear rewording of "parents," but "demanding" is not the same thing as "teaching."

   Topic sentence: I learned responsibility thanks to my parents' effective parenting methods. Meaning the same: "learned" indicates that the writer was taught, and "parenting methods" has a similar meaning to "strategies."

2. **Main idea:** My procrastination causes problems in my life.

   Topic sentence: My habit of waiting to the last minute is a source of difficulty in my life. Meaning the same: "habit of waiting to the last minute" is the same as "procrastination"; "source of difficulty" has a similar meaning to "problems."

   Topic sentence: My procrastination gets me into trouble with my boss. Meaning changed: "trouble with my boss" is a type of problem, but it is more specific than the general problems referred to in the main idea.

   Topic sentence: My procrastination is something I've lived with all my life. Meaning changed: The underlined words have a completely different meaning from "causes problems."

Problem 3: Adding Inappropriate New Information to the Main Idea

While writing a topic sentence based on a main idea, some students add new information that changes the focus of the main idea; this can confuse readers about what the writer intends to discuss in the paragraph. Consider the following outline:

MAIN IDEA	I could not live without my car.
SUPPORT POINT 1	I need it for work.
SUPPORT POINT 2	I need it to help my family.
SUPPORT POINT 3	I need it to escape.

Say you wrote the following topic sentence for this main idea:

> **My family and I could not live without my car.**

Here, you have added new information (*my family*) to the topic sentence. According to this statement, the paragraph will focus on both you and your family. However, if you look at the outline, you will see that your family will probably not be discussed in support points 1 and 3. Therefore, adding *my family* to the topic sentence is inappropriate and confusing. Let's consider another example:

I could not live without my car for work.

Here, new information (*for work*) has been added to the topic sentence. According to this statement, the entire paragraph will focus on how you use your car for work. However, if you look at the outline, you will see that your job will probably not be discussed in support points 2 and 3. Therefore, adding *for work* to the topic sentence is inappropriate and confusing. Let's consider one more example:

I could not live without the enjoyment my car brings me.

According to this topic sentence, the entire paragraph should discuss how you use your car to enjoy life. However, looking at the outline, you will see that enjoying life will probably be discussed only in support point 3. As a result, adding *enjoyment* to the topic sentence is inappropriate and confusing.

As you begin to write more complex and creative topic sentences, you should be careful not to add any inappropriate new ideas that might significantly change or obscure the meaning of the main idea.

ACTIVITY 10: Teamwork

With two or three classmates, read each main idea and its related topic sentences and do the following:

- Underline any new information added to the topic sentence.
- Indicate whether or how the new information changes or confuses the meaning of the main idea.
- If added information *does not* change or confuse the meaning of the main idea, explain why. Answers may vary.

EXAMPLE: **Main idea:** The salaries of professional athletes are too large.

Topic sentence: The salaries <u>and expense accounts</u> of professional athletes are too large. The underlined information changes the meaning because the main idea refers only to salaries, not to salaries and expense accounts.

Topic sentence: The salaries of professional athletes are too large <u>compared with those of other professionals.</u> The underlined information is not in the main idea, but it might be fine to include it if such a comparison is made in the support points of the outline.

Topic sentence: The salaries of <u>celebrity</u> professional athletes are too large. The underlined information changes the meaning because the main idea refers to the salaries of professional athletes in general, not to those of celebrity professional athletes.

1. **Main idea:** My cousin's community service was a life-changing experience.

   Topic sentence: My cousin's probation and community service changed his life. *The underlined information changes the meaning because the main idea refers only to community service, not to community service and probation.*

   Topic sentence: Doing community service and enrolling in the police academy changed my cousin's life. *The underlined information changes the meaning because the main idea refers only to community service, not to community service and enrolling in the police academy.*

   Topic sentence: My cousin's community service changed his life, especially his attitude toward women. *The underlined information is not in the main idea, but it might be fine to include it if the support points of the outline focus on changes in the cousin's attitude toward women.*

2. **Main idea:** Spending four hours in an emergency room taught me a lot about human suffering.

   Topic sentence: Being near death in a four-hour emergency room ordeal taught me a lot about human suffering. *The underlined information changes the meaning because the main idea does not concern the writer's near-death experience in an emergency room.*

   Topic sentence: Spending four hours in an emergency room taught me a lot about human suffering and medical incompetence. *The underlined information changes the meaning because the main idea refers only to human suffering, not to human suffering and medical incompetence.*

   Topic sentence: Spending four long hours in an emergency room taught me a lot about human suffering. *The underlined information adds a description but does not change the meaning of the main idea.*

A final note: If, despite the previous advice, it just "feels right" to add new information to your main idea, this could be a sign that this information is indeed important and should be included—or emphasized more—in your outline and paragraph. If it just "feels right" to leave out or change a key word from a main idea, this could be a sign that your outline includes information that is inappropriate or irrelevant to your topic. Try these steps:

1. Put your outline and topic sentence side by side, and reread both of them.
2. Ask whether you need to add, drop, or change any information in your outline based on your topic sentence or second thoughts about your topic. Make any changes that are necessary.
3. Ask whether you need to refine your topic sentence based on your revised outline. Make any changes that are necessary.

You'll have more opportunities to revise your work, as we'll discuss in Chapter 7. Activity 11 combines all the problems with topic sentences that you've just learned.

Teaching Tip
For helpful articles on teaching basic writers, see *Teaching Developmental Writing: Background Readings,* available with this text.

ACTIVITY 11: Teamwork

With two or three classmates, do the following:

- Look at each topic sentence and decide whether it changes the main idea before it. If it does, write "Changed" next to the topic sentence. If it doesn't, write "OK." (Do not mark as "Changed" topic sentences that are different from the main idea but have the same basic meaning.)
- If you write "Changed" by a topic sentence, explain the problem: key word(s) left out, key word(s) changed, and/or inappropriate new information added. Answers may vary.

EXAMPLE: **Main idea:** Most nutritionists now share the belief that the fats in olive oil, cold-water fish, and nuts are good for the heart.

Topic sentence: Most nutritionists now share the belief that the fats in olive oil and cold-water fish are good for the heart. Changed. Key words left out.

Topic sentence: Most nutritionists now agree that the fats in olive oil, cold-water fish, and nuts are good for the heart. OK

Topic sentence: All doctors now share the belief that the fats in olive oil, cold-water fish, and nuts are good for the heart and blood vessels. Changed. Key words changed and inappropriate new information added.

1. **Main idea:** As long as I am in college, living at home with my parents makes good sense.

   Topic sentence: Living at home with my parents is the best situation for me. Changed. Key words left out and changed.

   Topic sentence: As a college student, living at home with my parents is the only option. Changed. Key words changed.

   Topic sentence: As long as I am in college or until I get married, living at home with my parents is a sensible choice. Changed. Inappropriate new information added.

Teaching Tip
Another common problem is topic sentences that are too broad or too narrow. If students have worked through the preceding chapters of this book, their topic sentences should avoid this problem. However, if they are still struggling with this issue, you might refer them to Chapter 2, page 38, in particular.

2. **Main idea:** The police in my community work hard to have good communication with the residents.

   Topic sentence: The police in my community have good communication with the residents. Changed. Key words left out.

   Topic sentence: Although it is hard work, the police in my community are dedicated to having good communication with the residents. OK

   Topic sentence: The police in my neighborhood have good communication and complete trust with the residents. Changed. Key words left out and inappropriate new information added.

Writing the First Support Point

After you have written the topic sentence, it is time to move on to developing your first support point. Follow these steps:

- Copy the transitional expression that introduces your first support point from your outline. If your outline doesn't include a transitional expression, add one. Put a comma after this expression. (For more on transitional expressions, see Chapter 4, page 118, and page 149 of this chapter.)
- Follow the transitional expression with the first support point from your outline, making sure that it is a complete sentence with a subject and a verb. Take a look:

MAIN IDEA Mrs. Nevis was my worst teacher. **TRANSITIONAL EXPRESSION** To begin with, **SUPPORT POINT 1** she picked on students.	Mrs. Nevis, my eleventh-grade geography teacher, was the worst teacher I've ever had. To begin with, she picked on students frequently and unfairly.

As with the topic sentence, you may use creative language to express your support point; however, be careful not to change or obscure the meaning of the support point as you move from your outline to drafting your paragraph. Follow the same guidelines that you learned for the topic sentence:

- Do not leave out any important key words from the support point.
- Do not change any essential key words from the support point. (However, you may use words with similar meanings in some cases.)
- Do not add inappropriate new information to the support point. (However, as in the previous example, you may add descriptive language and other information that won't change the essential meaning of the support point.)

If you are unsure about changing key words or adding new information, ask your instructor for advice. Also, if you are writing under time pressure or can't seem to get started, you may want to keep the support point simple, taking it directly from your outline. Here is an example:

MAIN IDEA Tango is my favorite restaurant. **TRANSITIONAL EXPRESSION** To begin with, **SUPPORT POINT 1** the food is delicious.	Although I have eaten at many good restaurants, Tango stands out as my favorite. To begin with, the food is delicious.

For online practice with the five Ws, visit this book's Web site at **bedfordstmartins.com/steppingstones**.

To express this support point more creatively, you might want to search for more original and descriptive language that does not change the basic meaning. Here are some examples:

To begin with, all the dishes are fresh and tasty.
To begin with, the flavors are distinctive yet harmonious, from the appetizers to the desserts.
To begin with, the food at Tango makes my taste buds stand up and shout.

Now, let's look at some examples that change or confuse the meaning of the support point in a significant way. Suppose that you wrote the following:

To begin with, I always eat a lot when I go to Tango.

You know that you always eat a lot at Tango because the food is delicious. However, readers will not necessarily make this connection. They may assume that you eat a lot because the food is cheap or the portions are large.

To begin with, Tango has a reputation for its food.

Here, the important idea *delicious* has been left out. Readers might assume that the reputation is for cheap food, healthy food, bad food, or something else.

To begin with, the desserts at Tango are out of this world.

Here, you focus on just the desserts, so readers may assume that the paragraph will discuss desserts only.

ACTIVITY 12: Teamwork

Following are main ideas from different outlines, followed by the first support point and three versions of a sentence based on this support point. Working with two or three classmates, do the following for each sentence:

- If a sentence changes or confuses the meaning of the support point, underline the parts of the sentence that cause the problem.
- Explain how the sentence changes or confuses the meaning of the support point.
- If a sentence does not significantly change the meaning of the support point, write "OK" next to it. Answers may vary.

EXAMPLE: **Main idea:** Babbo's Pizza is my favorite restaurant.

Support point: To begin with, the service is excellent.

Sentence: To begin with, the staff makes you feel welcome.
A welcoming staff is only one part of good service.

Sentence: To begin with, I can count on professional service.
OK

Sentence: To begin with, the whole experience is excellent.
The "whole experience" is broader than just the service.

1. **Main idea:** My cousin's community service was a life-changing experience.

   Support point: In the first place, he learned that other people's problems are worse than his own.

   Sentence: In the first place, he learned that everyone has problems. "Everyone has problems" is a broader statement than "other people's problems are worse than his own."

   Sentence: In the first place, he learned that his own problems are not so bad. His problems may in fact be bad, even if others' problems are worse.

   Sentence: In the first place, he realized that his own problems are not as bad as other people's problems. OK

2. **Main idea:** My habit of waiting until the last minute is a source of difficulty in my life.

   Support point: First, I never get projects done on time.

   Sentence: First, I never turn papers in on time. The support point refers to all projects, not just papers.

   Sentence: First, I never get projects done on time, and I'm always late for work. The support point doesn't refer to being late for work.

   Sentence: First, I'm always late in turning in projects. OK

When students first learn to write support points, three main problems may occur:

1. forgetting transitional expressions
2. writing support points as fragments
3. combining the first specific example with a support point

These problems usually occur when students are working quickly and do not follow their outline carefully. Remember, the outline is your navigation system: you should refer to it closely throughout the writing process. If you ignore any important information in your outline, you may get lost while writing the paragraph or cause your reader to become lost.

REMEMBER TRANSITIONAL EXPRESSIONS

As you learned in Chapter 4, transitional expressions are essential for good academic writing; they help the reader follow your ideas, especially in a long paragraph, more efficiently. If you forget transitional expressions, your reader may have difficulty following your thoughts. If you are worried about forgetting the transitional expressions, *use a bright highlighter* to mark them on your outline.

This visual aid should help you remember to write the transitional expressions in your paragraph. Take a look:

MAIN IDEA	I could not live without my car.
	First,
SUPPORT POINT 1	I need it for work.
	Second,
SUPPORT POINT 2	I need it to help my family.
	Last,
SUPPORT POINT 3	I need it to escape.

Teaching Tip
At this point, you might ask students to take out their outlines and highlight the transitions in them. If their outlines are missing transitions, students should add them now. They might exchange outlines with peers and mark possible transitions in each other's outlines, referring back to Chapter 4 if necessary.

For more on transitional expressions, see Chapter 4, page 118, and page 158 of this chapter.

DO NOT WRITE SUPPORT POINTS AS FRAGMENTS

When students begin a sentence with a transitional expression, they sometimes forget to include both a subject and a verb in the sentence. (Again, the subject is the *main actor* in a sentence, or *who or what* the sentence is about. A verb expresses an *action* or a *state of being*.) Consider the following examples:

MAIN IDEA Tango is my favorite restaurant. TRANSITIONAL EXPRESSION To begin with, SUPPORT POINT 1 the food is delicious.	Although I have eaten at many good restaurants, Tango stands out as my favorite. To begin with, delicious food.

MAIN IDEA Music is important in my life. TRANSITIONAL EXPRESSION First, SUPPORT POINT 1 it helps me relax.	Even though I don't get to listen to music as often as I would like, it is important in my life because it helps me relax, work, and party. First, helping me relax.

MAIN IDEA I could not live without my car. TRANSITIONAL EXPRESSION In the first place, SUPPORT POINT 1 I need it for work.	I could not live without my car because I need it for work, to help my family, and to escape. In the first place, work.

Now, let's look at these three support sentences from the previous examples:

To begin with, delicious food.
First, helping me relax.
In the first place, work.

When you begin a sentence with a transitional expression, remember that what *follows the comma* must be a complete sentence with a subject and a verb. Do not let the presence of the transitional expression confuse you. Now, let's revise the examples to make them complete, correct sentences:

SUBJECT VERB

To begin with, the food is delicious.

SUBJECT VERB

First, music helps me relax.

SUBJECT VERB

In the first place, I need my car for work.

If it is helpful, cover up the transitional expression with a finger and look at the word group that follows. If the word group is a fragment, revise it. (For more on avoiding fragments, see Chapters 11 and 13.)

Teaching Tip
At this point, you might refer students to the chapters that cover fragments (11 and 13) and have them do a few exercises to improve their skills in finding and correcting this grammar problem.

AVOID COMBINING THE FIRST SPECIFIC EXAMPLE WITH A SUPPORT POINT

Combining the first specific example with a support point is a very serious and frequent problem among students who are new to academic writing and paragraph organization. Paying close attention to your outline can help you avoid this problem in your writing.

<table>
<tr>
<td>MAIN IDEA
Tango is my favorite restaurant.
TRANSITIONAL EXPRESSION
To begin with,
SUPPORT POINT 1
the food is delicious.
– spicy appetizers
– tender, juicy beef
– luscious desserts</td>
<td>Although I have eaten at many good restaurants, Tango stands out as my favorite. To begin with, the spicy appetizers are delicious.</td>
</tr>
</table>

Here, the writer has combined the first specific example (*spicy appetizers*) with the first support point (*the food is delicious*). This error will cause significant confusion for readers because they will assume that the point here is all about the appetizers instead of the food in general.

MAIN IDEA Music is important in my life. **TRANSITIONAL EXPRESSION** First, **SUPPORT POINT 1** it helps me relax. – before a big test – getting to sleep – after a fight with my girlfriend	Even though I don't get to listen to music as often as I would like, it is important in my life because it helps me relax, work, and party. First, music helps me relax before a big test.

Here, the writer has combined the first specific example (*before a big test*) with the first support point (*music helps me relax*). This error will cause significant confusion for readers because they will assume that the point here is all about using music to relax before a test instead of using music to relax in a variety of ways.

MAIN IDEA I could not live without my car. **TRANSITIONAL EXPRESSION** In the first place, **SUPPORT POINT 1** I need it for work. – to make deliveries – to drive clients – for business travel	I could not live without my car because I need it for work, to help my family, and to escape. In the first place, I need it to make deliveries for my job.

Here, the writer has combined the first specific example (*to make deliveries*) with the first support point (*I need it for work*). This error will cause significant confusion for readers because they will assume that the point here is all about the deliveries the writer makes instead of ways that she uses her car for work in general.

ACTIVITY 13: Teamwork

With two or three classmates, read each main idea, its first support point, and the examples for the support point. Then, read the sentences that come after them and do the following:

- If the first specific example has been combined with the support point, underline the words in the sentence that show the presence of the first specific example. Then, write "Combined" next to the sentence.
- If the sentence is fine as is, write "OK" next to it. Answers may vary.

EXAMPLE: **Main idea:** Kaleidoscopes are my passion.

Support point: First, I love the images.

—the bright colors

—the fluid movement

—the endless arrangements

Sentence: First, I get excited by the beautiful images. OK

Sentence: First, the images delight my imagination. OK

Sentence: First, I love the images with their rainbow colors.

Combined

1. **Main idea:** The police in my community work hard to have good communication with the residents.

   Support point: In the first place, they ride bikes so they can stop and chat with people.

   —people who have questions

   —children

   —business owners

   Sentence: In the first place, they ride bikes so they can stop and answer people's questions. Combined

   Sentence: In the first place, they ride bikes because it's easier to slow down and talk to people. OK

   Sentence: In the first place, they ride bikes because it's easier to provide information to people who need it. Combined

2. **Main idea:** As long as I am in college, living at home with my parents makes good sense.

   Support point: To begin with, I don't have to struggle financially.

   —paying rent

   —paying for food

   —paying for books and tuition

   Sentence: To begin with, as long as I am living at home with my parents, I won't have financial struggles, like paying my own rent. Combined

   Sentence: To begin with, I don't have to pay for my own apartment and struggle with money. Combined

   Sentence: Living at home with my parents means that I am more financially secure. OK

Teaching Tip
For an animated cartoon on paragraph development and guided writing practices, refer students to the *Make-a-Paragraph Kit* CD available with this text.

ACTIVITY 14

Continue working with your outlines from Chapter 4 that you used earlier in this chapter. For each of the topic sentences that you have already written for these outlines, add the first sentence of support. Remember to begin this sentence with a transitional expression, and make sure the sentence has a subject and a verb. You may keep the sentence simple and direct or search for more creative language to express your ideas. After you have finished, exchange papers with a classmate and check each other's support sentences.

Writing the Specific Examples

After writing the first support point, it is time to develop your specific examples. Follow these guidelines:

- Discuss the examples *one at a time.*
- Write at least one complete sentence for each example.
- Add some colorful details to the examples.
- Use *minor* transitional expressions to introduce examples, to move from one example to another, and to introduce details.

Now, let's discuss each guideline for writing the specific examples.

DISCUSS THE SPECIFIC EXAMPLES ONE AT A TIME

As you already know, each item on your outline is like a separate direction on a car navigation screen. If you miss one direction—like turning down a small street, for example—you may get lost. Good writers know that each specific example is important for the success of the paragraph, so they pay close attention to the outline and discuss the examples carefully, one at a time.

Here is a case where specific examples have been combined in a confusing manner:

<table>
<tr>
<td>MAIN IDEA
Tango is my favorite restaurant.

TRANSITIONAL EXPRESSION
To begin with,

SUPPORT POINT 1
the food is delicious.
– spicy appetizers
– tender, juicy beef
– luscious desserts</td>
<td>Although I have eaten at many good restaurants, Tango stands out as my favorite. To begin with, the food is delicious. You can enjoy the best desserts in town if you have any room left over after eating a juicy 16-ounce steak. The mud pie is so perfect that it is on my mind from the minute I sit down and order an appetizer. The beef for the steak is flown in from Argentina and has an unbeatable flavor.</td>
</tr>
</table>

In the examples on page 154, notice that the writer starts by talking about the desserts; this isn't very logical because dessert is usually the last item in a meal. (This is probably why the student listed it last on the outline.) Next, the student jumps back and forth between the desserts and the steaks. Not only is this confusing for the reader, but the writer forgets to present and develop his example(s) of the spicy appetizers.

Now, let's look at these same examples discussed one at a time, in an order that makes sense.

MAIN IDEA Tango is my favorite restaurant. TRANSITIONAL EXPRESSION To begin with, SUPPORT POINT 1 the food is delicious. – spicy appetizers – tender, juicy beef – luscious desserts	Although I have eaten at many good restaurants, Tango stands out as my favorite. To begin with, the food is delicious. I always start with a spicy appetizer to set my taste buds on fire. One of my favorites, the lamb empanadas, is made with special chilis from Argentina that complement the meat. I try not to eat too many, however, because I know what's coming next: piles of grass-fed Argentinean beef seasoned with plenty of garlic and rosemary. The beef is so tender and buttery that it melts in my mouth. If I have any room left, I order one of the luscious desserts, like the fried banana, which is a heavenly combination of butter, cinnamon, rum, and banana.

Here, the writer is careful to follow the outline step by step, discussing the specific examples one at a time. Each example comes in order and is thoughtfully developed. This approach is clearer and more informative for the reader.

WRITE AT LEAST ONE COMPLETE SENTENCE FOR EACH SPECIFIC EXAMPLE

As you learned in Chapter 1, academic paragraphs typically contain more than five sentences, and sometimes they have as many as ten or fifteen sentences. To achieve this level of development in your paragraph, you will need to write at least one complete sentence for each specific example. If you rush and combine all your examples into only one or two sentences, you will not meet the minimum requirement for the paragraph. More important, your paragraph may appear poorly developed and superficial.

Power Tip
Be aware that some graders of standardized tests and exit tests will actually assign a lower score to even well-written paragraphs if they are very brief.

Here is an example of specific examples that have been squeezed into one sentence:

MAIN IDEA Music is important in my life. TRANSITIONAL EXPRESSION First, SUPPORT POINT 1 it helps me relax. – before a big test – getting to sleep – after a fight with my girlfriend	Even though I don't get to listen to music as often as I would like, it is important in my life because it helps me relax, work, and party. First, nothing calms me down and relaxes me like music. For instance, it settles my nerves when I have a big test coming up, when I can't get to sleep, and after I've had an argument with my girlfriend. I argue with my girlfriend a lot.

In this example, the writer has merged all the examples into one sentence. As a result, the paragraph feels rushed, and the last sentence (*I argue with my girlfriend a lot.*) seems like a weak afterthought instead of a careful development of the examples. Students who find themselves in this situation often feel stuck and do not know how to move ahead. To avoid this problem, discuss the examples one at a time, giving each its own sentence.

Now, let's see a revision of the previous paragraph, with each example discussed in a separate, complete sentence:

MAIN IDEA Music is important in my life. TRANSITIONAL EXPRESSION First, SUPPORT POINT 1 it helps me relax. – before a big test – getting to sleep – after a fight with my girlfriend	Even though I don't get to listen to music as often as I would like, it is important in my life because it helps me relax, work, and party. First, nothing calms me down and relaxes me like music. For instance, I tend to get nervous before a big test, so I listen to soft music on my iPod to calm down. If I have trouble getting to sleep, gentle classical music works better for me than a sleeping pill. Also, fighting with my girlfriend is a high-anxiety event for me; fortunately, I can relax and remember how much I love her by listening to our favorite singer, Norah Jones.

Here, the student has written one complete, thoughtful sentence for each specific example. Not only does this method allow him to illustrate each example more effectively, it also ensures that he will have a fully developed paragraph. Of course, it is also perfectly acceptable to write *more than one* sentence for each specific example.

ADD SOME COLORFUL DETAILS TO THE SPECIFIC EXAMPLES

In your outline, you generally write specific examples as short phrases. However, as you present these examples in your paragraph, try to develop them with colorful details that *bring the examples to life* and *give them personality.*

Here is an example in which the writer has *not* added colorful details to the specific examples:

MAIN IDEA I could not live without my car. TRANSITIONAL EXPRESSION In the first place, SUPPORT POINT 1 I need it for work. – to make deliveries – to drive clients – for business travel	I could not live without my car because I need it for work, to help my family, and to escape. In the first place, my car is essential for my job. For example, I use it to make deliveries. Sometimes, I drive clients in my car. I also use it for business travel.

Here, the writer has discussed the specific examples one at a time and written a separate, complete sentence for each example. However, the writer has not added any colorful details to bring the examples to life. As a result, the examples seem bland and unconvincing. It feels like the writer doesn't really care about the ideas in the paragraph.

Now, consider this example in which the writer has added colorful details to the specific examples:

MAIN IDEA I could not live without my car. TRANSITIONAL EXPRESSION In the first place, SUPPORT POINT 1 I need it for work. – to make deliveries – to drive clients – for business travel	I could not live without my car because I need it for work, to help my family, and to escape. In the first place, my car is essential for my job. Because I work for an interior designer, I am on the road five days a week delivering fabric and wallpaper samples, catalogs, and small decorative pieces, such as lamps and vases. Often, my boss wants clients to visit showrooms and design centers. Rather than ask the clients to drive their own cars, my boss depends on me to take them in my car. At least once a month, I am expected to attend a regional design conference to learn my trade. Without my car, I would have to struggle with buses, trains, and taxis to get to these events.

Power Tip
You do not necessarily have to develop details for *every* example, especially if you are writing under time pressure. However, it's always a good idea to look back at all of your examples and ask which ones could be made more vivid through added details.

Teaching Tip
Ask students to look for newspaper, magazine, or Web articles that include effective examples and details. They should bring these to class. If you have a projector that can show print materials, share the students' articles with the rest of the class and discuss how the details and examples add to the writing.

Here, we get a vivid and convincing picture of why the writer needs a car for her job. The colorful details bring the examples to life and give the writing personality. In Chapter 6, you will learn some fun and effective strategies for developing details in your writing.

USE TRANSITIONAL EXPRESSIONS TO INTRODUCE EXAMPLES, TO MOVE FROM ONE EXAMPLE TO ANOTHER, AND TO INTRODUCE DETAILS

Writing a paragraph is a process of constant movement, or *transition,* from one idea to another:

1. from a main idea (topic sentence) to a support point
2. from a support point to an example of the support point
3. from one example to another
4. from an example to detail that illustrates the example
5. from one detail to another
6. to a new support point, and so on

Some transitions tend to indicate a major shift in your ideas (types 1 and 6 above), while others indicate minor shifts (types 2–5 above). For example, when you introduce a new support point, this is considered a major shift in the paragraph; when you introduce an example or move from one example to another or from one detail to another, these are considered minor shifts.

Below, notice how three transitional expressions (underscored in yellow) help the writer introduce an example, move smoothly from one example to another, and move from example to detail:

MAIN IDEA Mrs. Nevis was my worst teacher. **TRANSITIONAL EXPRESSION** To begin with, **SUPPORT POINT 1** she picked on students. – used rude nicknames – laughed at students – made us stay after school	Mrs. Nevis, my eleventh-grade geography teacher, was the worst teacher I've ever had. To begin with, she always picked on students and seemed to enjoy it. For example, my friend Jerry had a hard time memorizing the names of countries, so she called him a "brainless wonder." Also, she laughed at students when they made a mistake or answered incorrectly. I could never pronounce the word "Antarctic," so she always made me say it just so she could laugh at me. Her favorite way to pick on students, however, was to make us stay after school for no reason at all. Once, when I sneezed three times in a row, she said I was trying to annoy her, so she assigned me one hour of detention.

In Chapter 4, you were introduced to a list of transitional expressions commonly used to indicate major shifts within a paragraph; these are the expressions you marked on your outlines to introduce support points. However, some transitional expressions are more appropriate for indicating minor shifts in your writing.

The following charts show a range of transitional expressions: those used most commonly for major and minor shifts. Notice that some expressions (in bold) are frequently used for both major and minor shifts. However, as a beginning writer, you should not mix these expressions within a single paragraph. For example, if you use "Next" to introduce one of your support points (a major shift), do not use "Next" to introduce one of your examples (a minor shift). Mixing these expressions within a single paragraph can make your organization confusing for the reader.

Teaching Tip
You might suggest that students flag or clip this chart of transitional expressions so that they can refer to it easily as they draft their paragraphs.

Common Transitional Expressions

FOR MAJOR SHIFTS		
First,	Second,	Third,
In the first place,	In the second place,	Finally,
For starters,	More important,	Most important,
To begin with,	**In addition,**	Last,
	Next,	
	Furthermore,	
One reason	Another reason	A final reason

FOR MINOR SHIFTS	
For example,	For instance,
As an example,	Then,
Another example,	In fact,
In particular,	Once
Specifically,	One time,
To illustrate,	Another time,
Another illustration	Sometimes,
In addition,	Also,
Next,	Plus,
Furthermore,	Moreover,

ACTIVITY 15

Continue working with your outlines from Chapter 4 that you used earlier in this chapter. For each of the first support points that you have already written, add specific examples. Remember the guidelines for writing specific examples:

- Discuss the examples *one at a time*.
- Write at least one complete sentence for each example.
- Add some colorful details to the examples. (See Chapter 6 for suggestions.)
- Use *minor* transitional expressions to introduce examples, to move from one example to another, and to introduce details.

ACTIVITY 16

The following paragraphs have topic sentences, support points, and concluding sentences, but they are missing specific examples and details. For each paragraph, do the following:

- Add examples and details, being as creative as you can.
- Be sure to use minor transitional expressions to introduce examples and details. Refer to the chart on page 159 if you need to. Answers will vary.

EXAMPLE:

All kinds of pets can improve our lives in many ways. First, dogs can comfort us by being excellent companions and guardians. For example, Labradors and English sheepdogs are great playmates for children, but they are happy to be around just about anyone. They are gentle yet fun-loving and have a lot of patience. Other dogs, like German shepherds and collies, are excellent guard dogs. Their piercing barks warn owners about possible intruders, yet they can also be gentle friends to humans. In addition, cats, though not always as friendly as dogs, can also be excellent companions. For instance, many cats like to curl up on their owners' laps and purr happily, reducing stress for both human and animal. Also, cats love to play with string, rubber balls, and other toys, and it's fun for owners to both watch and participate. Finally, even cold-blooded creatures like fish and lizards can make enjoyable pets. For example, the graceful movements of fish are relaxing, and their various colors can be both soothing and stimulating. Lizards also can be fascinating to watch. For instance, some species change colors to match their surroundings. Whether warm and furry or cool and scaly, pets truly can bring joy into our day-to-day lives.

1. Spending time by any body of water can be fun, restful, and good for the soul. First, ponds and lakes have calm water that you can swim or boat in or just admire from the shore. ______________________________

Second, whether fast and churning or slow and lazy, rivers are fun to watch and, of course, to fish in. ______________________________

Last, but perhaps most impressive, are oceans, which blend the qualities of ponds, lakes, and rivers. ______________________________

Just about any body of water has the power to soothe, entertain, and enrich us.

2. Although the most obvious reason to get a college education is to get a job, some other benefits can be just as important. One reason to go to college is to learn about different fields and to find out what we like and don't like. ______________________________

Another reason to get a college education is to meet people who can offer emotional, educational, and career support. ______________________________

A final reason to go to college is to become exposed to exciting new ideas, even those not directly related to getting a job. ______________________________

For all these reasons, a college education can be so much more than a gateway to the job market.

Teaching Tip
Ask students their reasons for attending college. What other support points might they add to the second paragraph in Activity 16? What support points might they drop or change?

Completing the Paragraph

Now, you have only three things to do to complete your paragraph:

- Write the second support point with the specific examples.
- Write the third support point with the specific examples.
- Write the concluding sentence.

WRITE THE SECOND AND THIRD SUPPORT POINTS WITH THE SPECIFIC EXAMPLES

Once you have written your first support point with its specific examples (and any details about the examples), you will probably be warmed up and writing a bit faster. While you have this momentum and focus, make good use of it by moving immediately to your second support point. If you take a break now and come back to your paragraph later, you may lose valuable ground and time.

First, introduce the second support point with a major transitional expression. Then, write the second support point and its examples, using the same instructions that you used for the first support point. Look at this example, in which transitional expressions have been underscored in yellow:

MAIN IDEA Mrs. Nevis was my worst teacher. **TRANSITIONAL EXPRESSION** To begin with, **SUPPORT POINT 1** she picked on students. – used rude nicknames – laughed at students – made us stay after school **TRANSITIONAL EXPRESSION** Next, **SUPPORT POINT 2** she had poor teaching skills. – did not explain ideas clearly – put no comments on essays	Mrs. Nevis, my eleventh-grade geography teacher, was the worst teacher I've ever had. To begin with, she always picked on students and seemed to enjoy it. For example, my friend Jerry had a hard time memorizing the names of countries, so she called him a "brainless wonder." Also, she laughed at students when they made a mistake or answered incorrectly. I could never pronounce the word "Antarctic," so she always made me say it just so she could laugh at me. Her favorite way to pick on students, however, was to make us stay after school for no reason at all. Once, when I sneezed three times in a row, she said I was trying to annoy her, so she assigned me one hour of detention. Next, she had very poor teaching skills. For instance, she could never explain a problem or an idea clearly. One time, when we asked her the difference between a glacier and an ice floe, she got so confused that she told us to look it up on the Internet. When she graded our essays, she never gave us useful comments. She once gave me a grade of "C" on a paper, and her only comment was "Try harder."

When you have finished writing your second support point and the examples that go with it, write your third support point and its examples, following the process that you used earlier.

ACTIVITY 17

Continue working with your outlines from Chapter 4 that you used earlier in this chapter. Add your second and third support points and specific examples for each of them. Remember to introduce your support points with *major* transitional expressions. Use these guidelines for adding examples:

- Discuss the examples *one at a time.*
- Write at least one complete sentence for each example.
- Add some colorful details to the examples.
- Use *minor* transitional expressions to introduce your examples, to move from one example to another, and to introduce details.

WRITE THE CONCLUDING SENTENCE

The last sentence of a paragraph should restate or summarize your main idea in a fresh, thoughtful manner. An unimaginative or missing concluding sentence can indicate your lack of commitment and may leave the reader unsatisfied or confused. Instead, restate your main idea in a way that expresses your sincerity, enthusiasm, or conviction about the ideas discussed in the paragraph.

Follow these guidelines for writing the concluding sentence:

- Do not repeat your topic sentence in an overly simple or mechanical manner.
- Find creative, persuasive ways to restate the main idea. (See the examples below.)
- Never omit the concluding sentence, even if your paragraph has met any length requirement provided by your instructor.

Power Tip
Some writers begin concluding sentences with expressions like "For these reasons," "In conclusion," or "To sum up." Although these are acceptable transitions, make sure that what follows them is not a mechanical restatement of your main idea; try to think of creative ways to end your paragraphs.

Now, let's take a look at the beginnings of some of the paragraphs that you saw earlier. Read the paragraph excerpts and then possible concluding sentences (both ineffective and revised) for each of them. Can you see the differences?

PARAGRAPH BEGINNING

Although I have eaten at many good restaurants, Tango stands out as my favorite. To begin with, the food is delicious. I always start with a spicy appetizer to set my taste buds on fire. One of my favorites, the lamb empanadas, is made with special chilis from Argentina that complement the meat. I try not to eat too many, however, because I know what's coming next: piles of grass-fed Argentinean beef seasoned with plenty of garlic and rosemary. The beef is so tender and buttery that it melts in my mouth. If I have any room left, I order one of the luscious desserts, like the fried banana, which is a heavenly combination of butter, cinnamon, rum, and banana. . . .

OVERSIMPLIFIED AND MECHANICAL CONCLUSIONS

In conclusion, Tango is my favorite restaurant. For these reasons, I really like to eat at Tango.

Teaching Tip
Ask students if they can come up with another creative and persuasive conclusion for each paragraph excerpt.

CREATIVE AND PERSUASIVE CONCLUSIONS

While other restaurants may tempt me from time to time, my heart belongs to Tango. Whenever I crave a treat or want to celebrate a special occasion, Tango never disappoints.

PARAGRAPH BEGINNING

Even though I don't get to listen to music as often as I would like, it is important in my life because it helps me relax, work, and party. First, nothing calms me down and relaxes me like music. For instance, I tend to get nervous before a big test, so I listen to soft music on my iPod to calm down. If I have trouble getting to sleep, gentle classical music works better for me than a sleeping pill. Also, fighting with my girlfriend is a high-anxiety event for me; fortunately, I can relax and remember how much I love her by listening to our favorite singer, Norah Jones. . . .

OVERSIMPLIFIED AND MECHANICAL CONCLUSIONS

For these reasons, music is important in my life. In conclusion, I listen to music for many reasons.

CREATIVE AND PERSUASIVE CONCLUSIONS

Reflecting on the role of music in my life, I've come to understand that it is a powerful medicine for me. Without music, I'm afraid that I could not face the daily challenges that my life brings.

PARAGRAPH BEGINNING

I could not live without my car because I need it for work, to help my family, and to escape. In the first place, my car is essential for my job. Since I work for an interior designer, I am on the road five days a week delivering fabric and wallpaper samples, catalogs, and small decorative pieces, such as lamps and vases. Often, my boss wants clients to visit showrooms and design centers. Rather than ask the clients to drive their own car, my boss depends on me to take them in my car. At least once a month, I am expected to attend a regional design conference to learn my trade. Without my car, I would have to struggle with buses, trains, and taxis to get to these events. . . .

OVERSIMPLIFIED AND MECHANICAL CONCLUSIONS

To sum up, I could not live without my car. For these reasons, my car is really important to me.

CREATIVE AND PERSUASIVE CONCLUSIONS

If I had to live without my car, I think my life would come to a screeching halt. Although my life is very busy, I like to believe that I am on the road to success, and it is my car that keeps me going.

ACTIVITY 18: Teamwork

Following are several topic sentences followed by ineffective concluding sentences. With two or three classmates, discuss the problems with the concluding sentences. Then, rewrite the sentences to make them more creative and persuasive. Answers will vary.

EXAMPLE: **Topic sentence:** Barden Hall, the oldest building on our campus, is falling apart to the point of becoming dangerous.

Concluding sentence: To sum up, Barden Hall is a mess.

Rewrite: Given the dangers that I have described, Barden Hall needs to be renovated soon, or someone could be seriously injured.

1. **Topic sentence:** Because nurses are in high demand, command good salaries, and get the satisfaction of helping others, nursing can be a great career.

   Concluding sentence: Nursing is an excellent career to pursue.

   Rewrite: ______

2. **Topic sentence:** A lot of people look down on television, but even "silly" shows can teach us about human behavior, the workings of institutions, and more.

   Concluding sentence: To restate my point, television has a lot to teach us.

   Rewrite: ______

3. **Topic sentence:** It's been hard to return to college after twenty years, but age brings with it wisdom, patience, and a strong desire to make the most of my educational experience.

   Concluding sentence: In conclusion, going back to college has been hard but worthwhile.

   Rewrite: ______

Power Tip
Notice that the rewritten concluding sentence for the Activity 18 example makes a recommendation. This is another way to end on a strong note; however, make sure that any recommendation is closely related to the main idea and support points that you have provided.

Teaching Tip
Now that students have completed draft paragraphs, you might have them write a brief reflection on what they have learned from the writing process and what they are struggling with. Collect the reflections and drafts, and consider setting up individual conferences to discuss students' progress and concerns.

ACTIVITY 19

Write a concluding sentence for one or two of the paragraphs you have been writing throughout this chapter.

A final word: After you complete your paragraph, you'll want to reread it to make sure that you have provided all of the support that you need to and that every support point and example is relevant to the main idea expressed in the topic sentence. Chapter 7 will give you specific strategies for revising your paragraph.

Bringing It All Together

In this chapter, you have learned how to carefully refer to your outline (see Chapter 4) to develop a paragraph with a clear main idea, effective support and examples, and a strong conclusion. Check off each of the following statements that you understand. For any that you do not understand, review the appropriate pages in this chapter.

☐	The **topic sentence** expresses the main idea, or "topic," of a paragraph; typically, it is the first sentence of a paragraph. (See page 131.)
☐	Six common types of topic sentences are basic topic sentences, which simply restate the main idea from the outline (page 132); topic sentences that add a description (page 133); topic sentences that create a contrast (page 133); topic sentences that identify your support points (page 134); topic sentences that create a contrast *and* identify the support points (page 135); and topic sentences that use creative language (page 136).
☐	Most problems with topic sentences occur when students do not pay close attention to their outline. Three common problems are leaving out a key word from the main idea (page 139), changing a key word in the main idea (page 141), and adding inappropriate new information to the main idea (page 143).
☐	After you have written the topic sentence, it is time to develop your first **support point**. Begin by copying the transitional expression that introduces your first support point from your outline. Follow this transitional expression with the first support point from your outline. You may use creative language to express your support point, but be careful not to change or obscure the meaning of the support point as you move from your outline to drafting your paragraph. (See page 147.)
☐	When students first learn to write support points, three main problems may occur: forgetting transitional expressions (page 149), writing support points as fragments (page 150), and combining the first specific example with a support point (page 151).
☐	After writing the first support point, it is time to develop your **specific examples**. It is important to discuss the examples *one at a time* (page 154); to write at least one complete sentence for each example (page 155); to add some colorful details to the examples (page 157); and to use *minor* transitional expressions to introduce examples, to move from one example to another, and to introduce details (page 158).
☐	To complete the paragraph, write the second and third support points with the specific examples (page 162), and then draft a **concluding sentence** (page 163). Try to find creative and persuasive ways to conclude your paragraph.

Chapter 6

Developing Details

OVERVIEW OF THIS CHAPTER

WARM-UP Picking a Cake

1. Imagine this situation:

You are planning a surprise engagement party for your sister. You have spent lots of money on decorations, and you have invited relatives and all of your sister's best friends. Now, you need to pick a cake to serve at the party. Take a look at the ones on the right.

2. Stop and think!

Working alone or with classmates, decide which of the two cakes you would like to serve at your sister's party. Be sure to give specific reasons why you would pick one cake instead of the other.

The basic ingredients and taste of each cake may be similar, but only one cake shows a professional quality of work. Although cake 1 has the main characteristics of a cake (layers and frosting), the baker has not made a special effort to create an extraordinary dessert. However, cake 2 is clearly special; the baker has added precise and creative details (different-sized layers, colors, flowers, and dancing figures) to excite the imagination and appetite of your guests.

Like a special cake, a paragraph written for college should be of professional quality. In addition to the basic characteristics of a paragraph (topic sentence, support points, and specific examples), an outstanding paragraph must have something extra: it must have precise (specific) and creative details that grab readers' attention and make them hungry for more. This chapter will help you add such details to any paragraph.

Cake 1

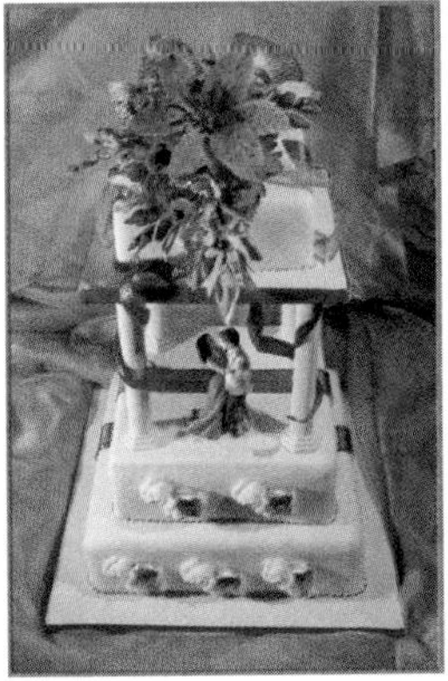

Cake 2

Recognizing Imprecise and Unclear Language

In everyday conversation, we use many imprecise expressions to communicate our thoughts. These expressions are so familiar to us that we do not recognize how unclear they may be. Here are some examples:

> **The teacher gives a lot of homework. (How much, exactly?)**
> **The test was really hard. (How hard, specifically?)**
> **My son rarely brushes his teeth. (How many times does he brush them, precisely?)**
> **I asked someone to take notes for me. (Who specifically?)**
> **We've got stuff to do. (What, exactly?)**

Notice that each underlined expression is imprecise, leaving an unanswered question. When we use such expressions, we assume that the listener will understand or agree with our general meaning. However, this is not always the case. Take a look at this dialogue.

> **Jason: My history teacher gives a lot of homework.**
> **Kayla: How much?**
> **Jason: Five pages of reading a day.**
> **Kayla: You call that a lot? My art teacher gives twenty pages plus study questions!**

We can see that the expression *a lot* has a different meaning for each speaker. For Jason, five pages of reading is a lot of homework; for Kayla, it is not.

Fortunately, in a conversation, one speaker can ask the other for clarification of an idea. When you write, however, your reader may not be able to ask for clarification; therefore, you must use precise and clear language to communicate your ideas completely and effectively.

As a college writer, you should understand that imprecise expressions may weaken your writing. The following chart contains some of the most common examples. Keep in mind that you cannot avoid these words absolutely, but be aware of when you use them and think about whether you can find more precise words.

Imprecise Expressions

IMPRECISE QUANTITIES/ DEGREES	IMPRECISE OBJECTS	IMPRECISE LOCATIONS	IMPRECISE PERSONS
a couple	anything	anywhere	anybody
a few	everything	here / there	anyone
a little less	it	nowhere	no one
a little more	something	places	nobody
a lot of	stuff	someplace	people
a ton of	things	somewhere	somebody
about	**IMPRECISE FREQUENCY**	**IMPRECISE QUALITIES**	**IMPRECISE SLANG**
almost	always	bad	all that
around	at times	beautiful	awesome
fairly	frequently	big	cool
generally	infrequently	good	hot
kind of	occasionally	happy	sweet
loads of	often	nice	totally
many	rarely	okay	way
nearly		pretty	
plenty of		sad	
really		short	
roughly		small	
some		tall	
sort of		ugly	

slang: informal language often used between friends or within other social groups. *Dis* for *disrespect* is an example of slang.

To personalize this chart and make it more useful for you, use a highlighter to mark some of the expressions that you use most often in your speaking and writing. Also, you might add other expressions to the list.

Adding Precise Details to Your Paragraph

In Chapter 5, you learned that a well-developed paragraph should include details about the examples presented for each support point. In reality, three situations are common:

1. Some college writers add insufficient details; as a result, they end up with short, poorly developed paragraphs.
2. Other writers add imprecise or unclear details that can confuse the reader and leave many questions unanswered.
3. The best writers work hard to include precise and colorful details.

On the following pages, you will see examples of all three of these possibilities. Let's begin by looking at an outline for a paragraph. It shows where details should be added when the paragraph is written.

MAIN IDEA — This semester, I improved my study skills.

TRANSITIONAL EXPRESSION — First,

SUPPORT POINT 1 — I was better prepared for class.

- did more homework
- studied for tests
- joined study groups

ADD DETAILS

TRANSITIONAL EXPRESSION — Next,

SUPPORT POINT 2 — I took a more active role in class.

- did not fall asleep
- took more notes
- asked questions

ADD DETAILS

TRANSITIONAL EXPRESSION — Last,

SUPPORT POINT 3 — I got help outside of class.

- a tutor
- the librarian
- my instructors

ADD DETAILS

Now, let's consider three paragraphs based on this outline. The specific examples for each support point from the outline are highlighted in yellow. As you can see, these examples show varying levels of detail.

A Paragraph with Insufficient Details

This semester, I improved my study skills in college. First, I prepared more carefully for class. For instance, I did more homework than before. I started studying for tests. Also, I joined study groups. Next, I participated more actively in class. I made sure that I did not fall asleep in class. Since I was awake, I was able to take more notes. Also, I asked questions. Last, I got help from people outside of class. For example, I started working with a tutor. The librarian helped me. I also visited my instructors to get assistance. With determination and practice, I changed my study habits and became a better student in just one semester. (114 words)

Compare the examples in this paragraph to the examples in the outline above. You will see that the writer has not added any details. As a result, the paragraph lacks precise information and *personality;* we do not get a sense of a strong, individual voice behind this writing. We get the impression that the writer doesn't really care about the ideas in the paragraph.

Teaching Tip
Encourage students to highlight the details in their own writing. This strategy will help them to focus on the details and identify places where they are imprecise or insufficient.

A Paragraph with Imprecise and Unclear Details

This semester, I improved my study skills in college. First, I prepared more carefully for class. Most of the time, I tried to finish my homework assignments. I spent a lot of time studying for tests, especially the important ones. Also, I joined study groups for some of my classes.

Next, I participated more actively in class. In order to do this, I had to stay awake, so I learned a few tricks that kept me from falling asleep. Then, I took better notes, writing down a lot of useful stuff. When I didn't understand something, I would ask someone a question. Last, I got help from people outside of class. I started working with a good tutor in one of the campus labs. When I needed help on a big project, I talked to a librarian. I also visited a couple of instructors during their office hours. After midterm, I visited them nearly once a week. With determination and practice, I changed my study habits and became a better student in just one semester. (175 words)

In this paragraph, the writer has added details, but the language is imprecise and unclear. As a result, many of the details leave an unanswered question:

most of the time (How much time, exactly?)
tried to finish (How much was done, specifically?)
a lot of time (How much time, precisely?)
important ones (Which ones, specifically?)
some of my classes (Which ones, exactly?)
a few tricks (What tricks, exactly?)
better notes (How were they better, exactly?)
stuff (What, specifically?)
something (What, precisely?)
someone (Who, specifically?)
good tutor (How was he or she good, exactly?)
one of the campus labs (Which one, specifically?)
big project (What project, precisely?)
a couple of instructors (Which instructors, exactly?)
nearly once a week (How often, specifically?)

A Paragraph with Precise Details

This semester, I improved my study skills in college. First, I prepared more carefully for class. I completed 80% of my homework in English, math, and geography to maintain a B average. I spent two or three hours studying for each midterm test and twice that for each final exam. To improve my math scores, I joined a study group that met twice a week. For my English class, I joined a group to practice proofreading. Next, I participated more in class. In order to stay awake, I slept eight hours on school nights and drank strong coffee before my classes. I learned to take accurate notes, writing down key examples, facts, and terms. Once, I wrote four pages of notes for my geography class! Mrs. Bosch, my English professor, taught me to raise my hand whenever I didn't understand the material, so I started asking questions in all my classes. Last, I got help from people outside of class. I met with my math tutor, Sandra, twice a week in the math lab. When I needed help finding a book on U.S. presidents, I asked the librarian for assistance. I also learned how to visit my instructors during their office hours. Mr. Vega, my math instructor, encouraged me to stop by once a week, and I did. With determination and practice, I changed my study habits and became a better student in just one semester. (236 words)

In this last paragraph, the writer has taken the time to add clear and precise details. As a result, the information is powerful, and the paragraph has *personality:* we get a sense of a strong, individual voice behind the writing. Notice that each new detail is specific or exact:

80% of my homework (an exact number)
in English, math, and geography (specific subjects)
to maintain a B average (a precise grade)
two or three hours (exact number)
each midterm / each final exam (specific tests)
to improve my math scores (a precise goal)
twice a week (an exact number)
to practice proofreading (a specific activity)
slept eight hours (a precise strategy)
drank strong coffee (a precise strategy)
accurate notes (a precise description)
four pages of notes (an exact amount)
Mrs. Bosch (a specific person)
raise my hand (a precise strategy)
my math tutor, Sandra (a specific person)
twice a week (a specific time frame)
the math lab (a precise place)
finding a book on U.S. presidents (a specific project)
the librarian (a specific person)
Mr. Vega (a specific person)
once a week (an exact number)

Teaching Tip
For some assignments (such as descriptive writing), the following advice is helpful for students: Include enough details so that another person could draw a picture of the person, place, or situation that you are writing about.

ACTIVITY 1

For each sentence pair below, do the following:

- Read the sentences carefully.
- Decide which sentence contains an unclear detail or details. Write "unclear" in the space after the sentence and circle the unclear word(s) or phrase(s).
- Decide which sentence contains precise details. Write "precise" in the space after the sentence and circle the precise word(s) or phrase(s).

EXAMPLE: When Juan woke up, he felt kind of weird. **unclear**

When Juan woke up, his head throbbed and he felt dizzy. **precise**

1. a. My fresh-squeezed orange juice had pulp fibers floating in it. precise
   b. My fresh-squeezed orange juice had something strange floating in it. unclear
2. a. Bernadette squeaks through her nostrils when she laughs. precise
   b. Bernadette makes a funny noise when she laughs. unclear
3. a. On the desert mission, the troops covered a greater distance than they had planned on. unclear
   b. On the desert mission, the troops covered fifty kilometers more than they had planned on. precise

4. a. By the time the paramedics arrived, a diabetic man in the crowd had fainted. precise

b. By the time the paramedics arrived, someone in the crowd had fainted. unclear

5. a. By Edgar's worried expression, I can tell he is nervous about his blind date. precise

b. By the way Edgar looks, I can tell something is wrong. unclear

ACTIVITY 2

For each pair of paragraphs below, do the following:

- Read the paragraphs carefully.
- Decide which one contains unclear details. Write "unclear" next to the paragraph and underline all the unclear details.
- Decide which paragraph contains precise details. Write "precise" next to the paragraph and underline all the precise details. Answers may vary.

1. **Paragraph A:** precise

Carol frowned and narrowed her eyes when her husband, Leon, came home from his manager's job at McDonald's. He had promised that he would be home at 6 P.M., but it was almost 9. Carol had been slicing, dicing, chopping, and sautéing since 10 that morning. Now, the braised beef was cold and dry, the colorful vegetable medley looked faded, and the ice cream cake was a puddle on the cake plate.

Paragraph B: unclear

Carol looked pretty angry when her husband, Leon, came home from his job. He promised that he would be home at the usual hour, but he was a few hours late again. Carol had spent so long preparing a nice dinner, and now it was ruined.

2. **Paragraph A:** unclear

We trained a long time to prepare for the famous event. We got up early on the special day and ate some healthy food. Then we went to the place where the race starts. Other people were doing all sorts of things to get ready for the race. I did a special exercise that someone taught me a while ago. By the time the race started, I was feeling good.

Paragraph B: precise

My brother and I trained for five months to prepare for the New York City Marathon. We got up at 6 A.M. on race day and ate scrambled eggs and buckwheat pancakes. Then we went to Staten Island near the approach to the Verrazano-Narrows Bridge, where the race starts. A group of runners from Ethiopia was doing yoga to prepare mentally for the race. I did lunges that my trainer, Joe, taught me last summer. When the race started at 9 A.M., I felt strong and relaxed.

For online practice with choosing precise language, visit this book's Web site at **bedfordstmartins .com/steppingstones**.

Teaching Tip
Several of the activities in this chapter ask students to read out loud. Students may not be aware that reading aloud can let them hear problems with writing that they might not detect through silent reading alone.

ACTIVITY 3: Teamwork

The following paragraph contains a mix of precise and unclear details. With two or three classmates, do the following:

- Have one member of your group read the paragraph out loud, slowly.
- Each time you get to an underlined section, see who can be first to call out "precise" or "unclear." At this point, stop and discuss whether all of you agree with this label. Once you reach an agreement, write "precise" or "unclear" on the corresponding line beneath the paragraph.
- Next, for any unclear details, decide on a more precise and colorful detail and add this to the corresponding line beneath the paragraph.
- Continue with this process until you have completed the paragraph.

The first blank has been filled in for you. Answers will vary.

Unfortunately, road rage is all too common, and it can occur where you'd least expect it. Everyone has heard of road rage on busy streets and highways during rush hour. Drivers (1) do crazy stuff when someone cuts them off or (2) doesn't react quickly enough when a stoplight turns green. I've even seen drivers (3) step out of their cars during traffic jams to yell at each other. However, I've noticed that some drivers react angrily even on quiet side streets. Once, while picking me up in front of my house, a taxi blocked the way of a truck for (4) a short time. The truck driver blasted his horn and started screaming. (5) His face was bright red, and I thought he was going to have a heart attack. The taxi driver and I laughed nervously, but the truck driver's actions upset us. Perhaps most disturbing, I've witnessed road rage among pedestrians and bikers. On weekends, a forest trail by my house draws (6) a lot of (7) different people. You would think that people would be more civil without a car body around them, but that's not necessarily the case. Just last week, I saw a biker and a jogger get into a fist fight because (8) the jogger didn't get out of the way when the biker zoomed up behind him yelling "On your left!" (9) Some other pedestrians and I ran up to them to break up the fight. We could hardly believe that two adults would behave this way. However, the depressing truth is that road rage can flare up any time that more than one person is trying to get somewhere by the same route.

1. unclear. Possible revision: honk and scream angrily
2. precise
3. precise
4. unclear. Possible revision: less than a minute
5. precise
6. unclear. Possible revision: hundreds of
7. unclear. Possible revision: bikers, walkers, joggers, and skaters
8. precise
9. unclear. Possible revision: two

ACTIVITY 4

Referring to the outline and paragraphs below, do the following:

- First, read the outline carefully.
- Next, read each of the three paragraphs.
- Decide which paragraph has insufficient details. On the line provided, write "insufficient details."
- Decide which paragraph has unclear details. On the line provided, write "unclear details." Then, underline or highlight all of the weak details in the paragraph.
- Last, decide which paragraph has precise details. On the line provided, write "precise details." Then, underline or highlight all the precise details in the paragraph. Answers may vary.

MAIN IDEA Online chat rooms are an excellent way to meet people.

TRANSITIONAL EXPRESSION To begin with,

SUPPORT POINT 1 people don't judge you.
- your age
- your race
- your looks

TRANSITIONAL EXPRESSION Second,

SUPPORT POINT 2 you can meet people with different viewpoints.
- people from other parts of the world
- people from different economic backgrounds
- people in trouble

TRANSITIONAL EXPRESSION Best of all,

SUPPORT POINT 3 it's convenient and inexpensive.
- any time of day or night
- don't have to go out
- cheap

1. In my experience, online chat rooms are an excellent way to meet people. To begin with, people can't see you, so they are less likely to judge you. For example, I am young, but when I chat online, nobody judges me for my age. In "real" life, people sometimes discriminate against me because of my race, but nobody notices my race in a chat room. When I go online, I also appreciate that people don't judge me for my looks. Second, chat rooms are a great way to meet people with different viewpoints. I like to talk to people from faraway countries because they have such unique opinions about the world. I have had conversations with rich people and poor people. Sometimes, I chat with individuals who are in abusive situations. Finally, meeting people in chat rooms is convenient and inexpensive. When I need to talk to someone at an unusual time, I know that I can always find a friendly person online. It's also convenient because I don't have to leave the comfort of my own place to go out and meet someone. Best of all, meeting people online is cheaper for many reasons. For all these reasons, I'm grateful for online chats and the ways in which they have broadened and enriched my world.

unclear details

globalization: the increasing connection among the world's peoples politically, economically, socially, and culturally as a result of advances in transport, communication technology, and so on

2. In my experience, online chat rooms are an excellent way to meet people. To begin with, people can't see you, so they are less likely to judge you. For example, I am eighteen but I look about fifteen, so adults often treat me like a child. Online, I chat with others who take my opinions very seriously because they don't know my age. As an Asian-American, I am sensitive to the stares that I get from people who discriminate, but in a chat room my race is invisible. I also appreciate the fact that men can't judge my worth based on a glance at my figure and face. Second, chat rooms are a great way to meet people with different viewpoints. Last week, I discussed the war in Iraq with people from China, France, and India, and they helped me understand how the world views America's presence in Iraq. I chatted about globalization with a super-rich Wall Street stockbroker and a super-poor Vietnamese farmer who uses the Internet café in his village. For several months, I stayed in touch with a woman whose husband beat her, and I learned how hard it can be for a woman to escape domestic violence. Finally, meeting people in a chat room is convenient and inexpensive. Often, I wake up around 4 A.M. and can't get back to sleep. I wouldn't call my friends and wake them up, but I can go online and chat with a person who lives in England or South Africa, where it is afternoon. I don't have to get dressed or leave my house to meet people in a chat room; I love to sit in my bed with my pajamas on and chat. Best of all, I don't have to spend four dollars on a cappuccino to meet people at Starbucks; the Internet doesn't cost me a penny because my parents pay for the connection. For all these reasons, I'm grateful for online chats and the ways in which they have broadened and enriched my world.

precise details

3. In my experience, online chat rooms are an excellent way to meet people. To begin with, people can't see you, so they are less likely to judge you. For example, nobody will know your age. Also, nobody notices your race. In addition, it never matters how you look. Second, chat rooms are a great way to meet people with different viewpoints. You can hear the experiences of people from other parts of the world. You can meet people from different economic backgrounds. Sometimes, you can learn about people who are in trouble. Best of all, meeting people in chat rooms is convenient and inexpensive. You can connect with people any time of the day or night. You don't have to go out to meet them. Since you don't have to go out, it's cheap. For all these reasons, I'm grateful for online chats and the ways in which they have broadened and enriched my world.

insufficient details

ACTIVITY 5: Teamwork

With two or three classmates, discuss the three paragraphs from Activity 4 one at a time.

- Why did each of you label the paragraphs as you did? Point to specific details in explaining your choices.
- If any of your choices differ, discuss why this might be the case.
- Consider other details that even the precise paragraph might have included.

An important note: Another common problem is details that do not relate to the main idea (topic sentence) of a paragraph. You will be learning more about this problem in Chapter 7 (see page 207).

Developing Colorful and Creative Details

As a college writer, you should first aim for details that are precise and clear. Then, make sure that your details are as colorful and creative as possible.

Although there are many strategies for developing colorful and creative details, we will focus on seven in this chapter. Notice that each type of detail has a specific purpose:

1. **Concrete details:** identifying persons, places, and things
2. **Action details:** energizing your verbs
3. **Sensory details:** describing what you see, hear, smell, taste, and touch
4. **Quoted details:** recording what people say
5. **Emotive details:** exploring emotions
6. **Humorous details:** making readers smile or laugh
7. **Comparative details:** using metaphors and similes

USING CONCRETE DETAILS

Looking at the chart on page 169, you will see that most of the words do not name *specific* persons, places, or things. (Notice especially the words under *Imprecise persons, Imprecise locations,* and *Imprecise objects.*) These words are called *abstract.* When you use abstract words in your writing, you may end up with details that are imprecise and unclear. Take a look at the underlined words in this sentence:

Terminology Tip
Words that name people, places, or things are known as *nouns.* For more details, see Chapter 10, page 268.

I want to go <u>somewhere special</u> for my birthday.

In this sentence, the phrase *somewhere special* is abstract because it does not identify a specific place; for the reader, it is unclear what this special place might be. However, we can replace this abstract phrase with a more precise detail:

I want to go to <u>an amusement park</u> for my birthday.

Terminology Tip
Six Flags Over Georgia is known as a *proper noun* because it names a specific (brand-name) amusement park. Proper nouns begin with capital letters. For more on proper nouns, see Chapter 10, page 268.

Teaching Tip
Call out "person" and ask students to name as many specific people as they can think of. Do the same thing with "place" and "thing."

The phrase *amusement park* identifies a specific place. Any detail that names a specific person, place, or thing is called a *concrete* detail. Now, the reader has a clear idea about where the writer would like to go. However, the writer can make this detail even clearer by naming an actual amusement park:

> **I want to go to Six Flags Over Georgia for my birthday.**

Six Flags Over Georgia tells the reader *exactly* where the writer would like to go.

Basic Guidelines for Using Concrete Details

- Avoid the abstract words in the chart on page 169.
- Identify specific persons, places, and things.
- Whenever possible, use a proper noun to name specific persons, places, and things.

ACTIVITY 6

For each sentence below, do the following:

- Underline the imprecise or abstract word(s) or phrase(s).
- Rewrite the sentence, adding precise and colorful concrete details. When possible, use a proper noun to name a specific person, place, or thing. (You may find words other than nouns that can be made more specific.)

Underlining and rewrites will vary.

EXAMPLE: After the all-night party, Jeremy found something in his ear canal.

After the all-night party, Jeremy found a pinto bean in his ear canal.

1. Compared to that guy who is six feet four, Ben is fairly short.

2. Although I avoid eating sugary things, I occasionally have a hot fudge sundae.

3. My book club is reading a new novel that is just OK.

4. Everyone is invited to the band's New Year's Eve party.

5. My old job at the factory was pretty cool, but my new job in construction is awesome.

ACTIVITY 7: Teamwork

With two or three classmates, do the following:

- Choose a person to read the first passage below out loud.
- Underline, circle, or highlight all the concrete details that you can find.
- Discuss why these details make the writing powerful.
- Repeat this process with the second passage. Answers will vary.

1. **Student Writer**

Being on a tight budget isn't easy, especially when your kids want (and sometimes need) expensive gadgets. Now that the holidays are approaching, Myla, my oldest, has been asking me for a MacBook computer. Myla is planning to study design in college next year, and since Macs are supposed to be the best computers for design projects, I think this investment will be wise. She will be able to practice design skills on the computer and use it in college. I feel less sure about the request of my middle child, Tarik. He already has an iPod and a cell phone, but now he wants an iPhone. I can see from all the advertising that this phone has a lot of fancy features, like Internet browsing, but does a fifteen-year-old really need all of them? When Tarik is a successful executive, he can buy a phone that communicates with Mars, but until then, I think I'll just keep paying for his guitar lessons. My youngest, Daniel, wants a Wii video game, which lets you play sports like tennis, baseball, and bowling indoors. This gadget isn't cheap, but Daniel can get hyper when he's penned up, which happens often during the cold winter months here. Therefore, the Wii might actually be a gift for Mom, if you know what I mean. As much as I can, I want to make my kids' holiday dreams come true, but I also want to be practical, because that's in *all* of our best interests.

2. **Professional Writer** (This passage is about a single mother raising her son, Jason.)

The plan for Jason, of course, is private school, at a cost of close to $20,000 a year. But then I owe it to him to balance that with a hefty dose of African-American culture—the culture he will surely miss out on at an elite boarding or country day school. Added to the mix is the fact that I am a Generation-X child of hip-hop who embraces rap music and identifies with the likes of Allen Iverson. How do I balance all that? I imagine conversations that will go something like, "OK, Jason, *general* bling-bling is fine and has its place if you work hard for it . . . but not watching videos of booty-shaking objectified women!"

He comes from an athletic background, so naturally everybody is attempting to put a basketball or football in his hands and get him signed to Reebok tomorrow, but I shun the pressure, until I realize that I have put my own pressures on him, too. I could read at the age of 2, and called his pediatrician when he couldn't (she laughed at me). I skipped grades and breezed through school, and want him to do the same. All he wants right now, the summer before pre-K, is Thomas the Tank Engine.

Generation X: people born in the 1960s and 1970s

Allen Iverson: star player for the Denver Nuggets basketball team

bling-bling: jewelry or other personal decoration

objectified: treated as an object rather than as a person

Power Tip

To see how this writer uses other concrete details, read the complete essay on pages 611–612.

ACTIVITY 8: Teamwork

With two or three classmates, do the following:

- Read the paragraph below, underlining all the imprecise and unclear details.
- Working as a team, rewrite the paragraph, making persons, places, and things more concrete and adding other precise and colorful details.
- Have one person write the new paragraph on a separate sheet of paper.
- When all the teams in the class have finished writing, have someone from your team read the paragraph out loud to the class. Underlining and rewrites will vary.

The other night, a few of us went to a place around the corner to have some fun. When we got there, somebody had fallen several feet from a high place and was hurt really bad. One of us is in the medical field, so he volunteered to do something. A little while later, the person who fell was sitting up and feeling pretty good. We stayed way late and had an awesome time.

ACTIVITY 9

- First, look carefully at the photograph.
- Next, on a separate sheet of paper, freewrite a brief description of the photograph. Use as many concrete details as possible. (For more advice on freewriting, see Chapter 3, page 79.)
- When you have finished writing, try to get together with a few of your classmates and read your descriptions out loud to one another. Decide who uses the most precise and colorful details. Freewriting will vary.

ACTIVITY 10

Write a paragraph. Using as many concrete details as possible (specific persons, places, and things), discuss or describe one of the following:

- your favorite Web site
- a college class that you hated going to
- the best vacation you ever took
- your bedroom or another room where you spend a lot of time
- your favorite television commercial Answers will vary.

Teaching Tip
You might have students turn some of the freewriting that they do in this chapter into fully developed paragraphs following the advice throughout Part One.

USING ACTION DETAILS

Good writing has *energy*. One of the best ways to energize your details is to use precise and colorful *verbs*. Inexperienced writers often rely on common and inexpressive verbs rather than searching for more original and powerful verbs. Take a look at the underlined verb:

Terminology Tip
A *verb* expresses an *action* or a *state of being*. You will learn more about verbs in Chapters 10 and 16.

After the batter struck out, he walked toward the umpire.

The verb *walked* does not paint a strong picture of the batter's movement, and it tells us nothing about the batter's purpose for approaching the umpire. However, we can replace this verb with a more precise and colorful action:

After the batter struck out, he stomped toward the umpire.

Here, the verb *stomped* creates a stronger image of the batter's movement; it also suggests why the batter is approaching the umpire: he's probably angry. If the writer of this sentence is especially creative, she may experiment with other powerful verbs. For example,

After the batter struck out, he stormed toward the umpire.

Here, the verb *stormed* paints a powerful picture of the batter's movement. It also suggests the aggressive intention of the batter toward the umpire.

Basic Guidelines for Using Action Details

- When describing an action, close your eyes and try to imagine the specific image that you want to create in readers' minds.
- Use a portable or online thesaurus to help you find more precise and original verbs. (A thesaurus is a dictionary that, for each word, gives words with similar meanings. Remember to check with your instructor or other students if you are unsure about whether to use an unfamiliar word.)
- In a notebook, keep a list of new verbs that you would like to incorporate into your vocabulary.
- When possible, try to replace state-of-being verbs (*am, is, are, was, were*) with action verbs (like *stomped* or *stormed*). A good time to make these changes is when you are proofreading and editing your writing. (For more advice on proofreading, see Chapter 7.)

Teaching Tip
To help students think of good action verbs, tell them to pretend they are a director who has to tell actors on a movie set what to do.

ACTIVITY 11

For each sentence below, do the following:

- Underline the inexpressive verb or verbs.
- Rewrite the sentence, adding precise and colorful action verbs. Underlining and rewrites will vary.

EXAMPLE: My boyfriend touches my hair.
My boyfriend caresses my hair.

1. The red Corvette went around the corner.

2. When she won the $4 million lottery, Alisa smiled.

3. When my male pit bull sees another male pit bull, he always goes toward him.

CONTINUED >

4. The student who sits next to me in my geography course is overeager; every time he knows an answer, he raises his hand.

5. The nervous bank robbers told us to get on the floor.

ACTIVITY 12: Teamwork

With two or three classmates, do the following:

- Choose a person to read the passage below out loud.
- Underline, circle, or highlight all the action verbs that you can find.
- Discuss why these verbs make the writing powerful. Answers will vary.

Student Writer (This writer enters a dangerous race with a prized car, but he escapes the worst consequences—just barely.)

Monday arrived and I raced to work. As I accelerated up a hill, I approached two vehicles traveling much too slowly for me. Common traffic laws were for the weak and inexperienced; I was a man and made my own rules. I darted up the left lane; the initial vehicle posed no challenge, and I passed it with ease, the first of many victories, or so I thought. My car raced beside the second vehicle. A kid no older than sixteen looked at me with pride and contempt as he sped up. I pushed the gas pedal harder; I was flying, going almost 90 mph. The other car kept pace, and I could not catch him.

Then I saw it, cresting the top of the hill: a semi truck headed straight toward me. I panicked. I looked over to my right, and there was no room to fit between the two cars I attempted to pass. Seconds flew by; I had to react as the truck barreled closer. He approached too quickly and would crush me if I tried to brake. I jerked the steering wheel to the right, not knowing what would happen. My cherished possession squeezed between the two cars—surely the sign of an expert driver. Then momentum carried me on. I veered off the road, and a telephone pole did what my brakes could not: brought me to a dead halt.

Power Tip
To see how this writer uses other action details, read the complete essay on pages 585–586.

ACTIVITY 13: Teamwork

With two or three classmates, do the following:

- Read the paragraph below, underlining all the inexpressive verbs.
- Working as a team, rewrite the paragraph, making verbs more vivid and adding other precise and colorful details.
- Have one person write the new paragraph on a separate sheet of paper.
- When all the teams in the class have finished writing, have someone from your team read the paragraph out loud to the class. Underlining and rewrites will vary.

After the concert, the crowd moved onto the stage and took the musicians' instruments. The musicians tried to exit the stage, but the crowd stopped them. At this point, someone hit one of the musicians, and the performer made a noise and fell onto the stage. Suddenly, a police officer asked everyone to get down. The crowd became quiet and stepped off the stage.

ACTIVITY 14

- First, look carefully at the photograph.
- Next, on a separate sheet of paper, freewrite a brief description of the photograph. Use as many precise and colorful action verbs as possible. (For advice on freewriting, see Chapter 3, page 79.)
- When you have finished writing, try to get together with a few of your classmates and read your descriptions out loud to one another. Decide who uses the most precise and colorful verbs. *Freewriting will vary.*

ACTIVITY 15

Write a paragraph. Using as many action details as possible, discuss or describe one of the following:

- a favorite, high-action video game
- your job, if lots of action is involved
- an exciting play from a sporting event or your favorite Olympic event
- an action-packed scene from a movie or television show
- a situation or event you were involved in where there was a lot of action *Answers will vary.*

USING SENSORY DETAILS

We use our five senses (sight, hearing, smell, taste, touch) to connect with the world around us. When we read, we look for details that help our senses connect with the writer's world. These details are called **sensory** because they describe the way things look, sound, smell, taste, and feel. Unfortunately, many writers use imprecise adjectives. Look at the underlined adjective in this example:

Terminology Tip
Adjectives describe nouns (persons, places, or things). For instance, in the phrase *happy child*, *happy* is an adjective that describes the noun *child*. For more on adjectives, see Chapter 10, page 271.

By the end of her shift, the nurse's uniform was dirty.

In this sentence, the adjective *dirty* gives an unclear picture of the nurse's uniform. The person reading this sentence will have to guess what the uniform really looked like. However, we can replace the imprecise adjective with more specific and original details:

By the end of her shift, the nurse's uniform had yellow and brown stains on it.

Now, the reader has a clearer picture of how the nurse's uniform actually looked. However, an especially creative writer might search for even more powerful images:

> **By the end of her shift, the nurse's uniform was covered with dried blood, coffee stains, and a large blue spot where a pen had leaked in her pocket.**

In this example, we can clearly see how the addition of precise and colorful details gives the writing more *power* and *personality*. We have not only a vivid picture of the nurse's uniform, but also a snapshot of her whole workday.

Basic Guidelines for Using Sensory Details

- Close your eyes and try to imagine the sights, sounds, smells, tastes, and feelings of a situation or scene. Think of descriptions that will re-create the situation or scene in readers' minds.
- Use a portable or online thesaurus to help you find more precise and original descriptions. (Remember to check with your instructor or other students if you are unsure about whether to use an unfamiliar word.)

ACTIVITY 16

For each sentence below, do the following:

- Underline the imprecise adjective.
- Rewrite the sentence, adding precise and colorful sensory details.

Underlining and rewrites will vary.

EXAMPLE: Harold heard a strange noise outside his bedroom window.
Howard heard a high-pitched screeching and a feathery flapping outside his window, followed by a low growl.

1. My grandmother's house is full of weird smells.
2. My mother uses a sponge to wet her postage stamps because she can't tolerate the strange taste of the stamp glue.
3. The campers saw an odd ball of light in the night sky.
4. The mechanic heard a suspicious noise when he pumped the brake.
5. The dermatologist felt something unusual on my back.

ACTIVITY 17: Teamwork

With two or three classmates, do the following:

- Choose a person to read the paragraph below out loud.
- Underline, circle, or highlight all the sensory details that you can find.
- Discuss why these details make the writing powerful. Answers will vary.

Student Writer

Last year, I went to a Japanese tea ceremony with my grandmother, and it was a great honor and delight. All the guests wore simple kimonos of colorful silk. My grandmother had given me a blue kimono decorated with large white flowers, and I wore it with pride, loving the feeling of the soft fabric on my skin. After we had cleansed our hands and mouths in a basin outside of the tearoom, the hostess invited us inside. We took off our shoes and entered a small, simple room with woven straw mats on the floor. Long banners with graceful Japanese writing hung from the walls, and tall ceramic vases held branches of orange blossoms. The sweet scent of the flowers perfumed the air. The room was quiet except for the low whispers of the guests admiring the decorations. As the ceremony began, we sat on the mats, feeling the cool stone of the floor beneath them. Then, we watched the hostess go through the traditional ritual of placing green tea powder in a ceramic bowl and mixing in hot water with a special whisk. When she whisked the tea, its sharp, leafy aroma filled the air. Then, carefully, the hostess passed the bowl to the first guest. The two exchanged bows, and then the guest drank from the bowl, wiped the rim, and rotated the bowl before passing it to the next guest. When it was my turn, I was a little nervous, but my grandmother had explained each step of the ritual to me. I bowed, drank the rich, bitter tea, wiped the bowl's rim, and passed the bowl to the next guest with a gentle smile. At that moment, I felt the simple beauty of the ceremony connecting me to all those present and to all of my ancestors.

kimono: traditional Japanese robe

When you want to describe something vividly, work through the five senses one at a time and think of details that appeal to each. Here are details that one writer came up with to describe a state fair:

SENSE	DETAILS
Sight	spinning rides; red-and-white tents; crowds of people in shorts, T-shirts, and swimsuit tops; tractors in muddy tractor-pull ring; cows, hogs, and sheep in pens for judging
Hearing	laughing and shouting children; rumbling rides; blaring announcements from loudspeakers; mooing and squealing from animal pens
Smell	fried dough and hot dogs; suntan lotion; diesel from tractor engines
Taste	sweet ice cream and fried dough; salty hot dogs and buttery popcorn
Touch	soft fur of animals in petting zoo; vibrations of old rides

ACTIVITY 18: Teamwork

With two or three classmates, select one of the following scenes and describe it with details based on each of the five senses. Work together on one sense at a time and generate the most colorful and precise details you can. (You may not have direct experience with these particular scenes, but use your imagination.) If you'd like, use the chart before this exercise as a guide. Answers will vary.

- Describe a busy emergency room.
- Describe being on the beach at an expensive tropical resort.
- Describe a crew of firefighters battling a raging forest fire.
- Describe being inside a packed subway or city bus at rush hour.
- Describe the cages of an overcrowded animal shelter.

Teaching Tip
Emphasize to students that it's always a good idea to go through one sense at a time when adding sensory details. Students often use sight-based descriptions only, missing an opportunity to add richer details to their writing.

Sight: ____________________

Hearing: ____________________

Smell: ____________________

Taste: ____________________

Touch: ____________________

ACTIVITY 19: Teamwork

With two or three classmates, do the following:

- Read the paragraph below, underlining all the imprecise and unclear details.
- Working as a team, rewrite the paragraph, adding the most vivid sensory details you can think of, as well as any other details to bring the paragraph to life.
- Have one person write the new paragraph on a separate sheet of paper.
- When all the teams in the class have finished writing, have someone from your team read the paragraph out loud to the class. Underlining and rewrites will vary.

When Mildred started her car, she heard an unusual sound coming from the engine. She waited a minute, and then she smelled a very offensive odor coming through the air conditioning. The smell was so intense that it left a strange taste in her mouth. She decided to look under the hood of the car. When she did, she saw a very surprising sight.

ACTIVITY 20

- First, look carefully at the photograph.
- Next, on a separate sheet of paper, freewrite a brief description of the photograph. Use as many precise and colorful sensory details as possible. (For more advice on freewriting, see Chapter 3, page 79.)
- When you have finished writing, try to get together with a few of your classmates and read your descriptions out loud to one another. Decide who uses the most precise and colorful details. *Freewriting will vary.*

ACTIVITY 21

Write a paragraph. Using as many sensory details as possible (taste, sight, sound, smell, touch), discuss or describe one of the following:

- an important holiday meal in your family
- a crowded food court in a shopping mall
- a beautiful natural setting that you enjoy
- the team locker room after a victorious sporting event
- a preschool filled with energetic children *Answers will vary.*

Teaching Tip
Encourage students to bring in and share articles, essays, and photographs that include strong examples of the different types of details covered in this chapter. Ask students to discuss why they made the choices they did.

USING QUOTED DETAILS

Many writing assignments require you to discuss people—friends, family members, co-workers, historical figures, or people in the news. If the person you are writing about said something interesting or important, you might want to record that person's words in your paragraph. The more precise you are in recording a person's words, the more powerful your writing will be. Take a look at the underlined phrase in this example:

> **In breaking up with me, my girlfriend said something that surprised me.**

The underlined phrase is imprecise and unclear. The reader will have to guess about what the girlfriend actually said. However, we can replace this phrase with a more precise detail:

> **In breaking up with me, my girlfriend said that I am selfish.**

In this sentence, the reader has a much clearer understanding of what the girlfriend said. However, the absence of quotation marks tells us that these may not be her *actual* words. If you remember a person's actual statement—and if this statement is especially memorable—record it precisely and put it in quotation marks:

> **In breaking up with me, my girlfriend said, "You are the most self-centered and vain man I have ever dated."**

The underlined section is called a **direct quotation** because it records a person's exact words. Clearly, this quotation presents powerful details that are missing in the other sentences. What the girlfriend *actually* said is much more interesting than the writer's general idea of what she said.

If you do not use a person's actual words (perhaps because you do not remember the words *exactly*), try to record as precisely as possible what he or she said. Take a look:

> **In breaking up with me, my girlfriend said that I was the most self-centered and vain man she had ever dated.**

Because you are not *directly* reporting a person's *exact* words, the underlined words in this example are known as an **indirect quotation**. For an indirect quotation, you need to change some of the speaker's original words to make the ideas fit smoothly and grammatically into your sentence. (For example, *You are* has changed to *that I was* and *I have* has changed to *she had.*) Also, with indirect quotations, quotation marks are not used.

Basic Guidelines for Using Direct Quotations

- Put quotation marks at the beginning and end of the quotation.
- If the quotation is a complete sentence, capitalize the first word of it. For example: *Bill's father said, "Don't forget to take your lunch."*
- If the quotation is not a complete sentence, you do not need to capitalize it. For example: *All of us were told about the "mysterious green glow" that shone in Petrie Forest at night.*
- Use a comma to separate the quotation from the identification of the speaker—for example, *Tom said, "Go away."* or *"Go away," Tom said.* Notice that in both examples, the closing quotation mark is *after the period or comma.*

Basic Guidelines for Using Indirect Quotations

- Do not use quotation marks.
- Usually, you will use the word *that* to introduce the speaker's statement: *John said that . . .*
- Change any words that need to be changed to make the speaker's ideas fit smoothly and grammatically into your sentence.

Teaching Tip
You might bring in newspaper and magazine articles and other texts to illustrate different uses of direct and indirect quotations.

ACTIVITY 22

For each sentence below, do the following:

- Underline the imprecise or unclear detail.
- In the first space, rewrite the sentence, adding a precise and colorful *direct* quotation, with quotation marks.
- In the second space, rewrite your sentence as an *indirect* quotation, dropping the quotation marks and rewording the quotation so that it fits smoothly into the sentence. Underlining and rewrites will vary.

EXAMPLE: Hugo said something insulting to me.
Hugo said, "You make money through dishonesty."
Hugo said that I made money through dishonesty.

1. After the patrol officer checked Bill's license, she asked him to do something.

2. At the preseason training, the coach reminded the team of an important point.

3. The palm reader whispered her gloomy prediction.

4. The professor gave a warning to students.

5. When the nurse gave the patient the wrong medicine, the doctor said something critical.

ACTIVITY 23: Teamwork

With two or three classmates, do the following:

- Choose a person to read the first passage below out loud.
- Underline, circle, or highlight all the quoted details (direct and indirect) that you can find.
- Discuss why these details make the writing powerful.
- Repeat this process with the second passage. *Answers will vary.*

1. **Student Writer**

"I need to end this," I said one evening to Randall, who had been my boyfriend for three years. They were the hardest words for me to express, but I'm glad I was able to get them out. In many ways, Randall is a good person, and I know he loved me. However, he always was suspicious and negative about anything that might mean that I'd spend less time with him. Whenever I made new friends, he'd say something like, "I'm not sure she sounds good enough for you." When I got a promotion at my job, he complained that I'd be working late more and wouldn't be able to make dinner for both of us. The incident that finally convinced me to end the relationship was Randall's complaining about my decision to reenter college after a break of five years. He said, "Why do you need college when you have a good job and you have me?" I tried to explain that it would be hard to advance in my profession without a degree. Also, I wanted to expand my mind and, yes, meet new people. Randall shook his head and didn't even seem to listen, and so I told him that I needed to break things off. "In time," I explained, "you might understand why I had to do it." In his next relationship, I hope Randall will learn to be more independent and less controlling. If not, he might be alone for a long time.

CONTINUED >

2. **Professional Writer** (This passage describes the immediate reactions to a drug overdose at a college party.)

"It's an epileptic fit, put something in his mouth!"

"Roll him over on his stomach!"

"Call an ambulance; God, somebody breathe into his mouth."

A girl kneeling next to him began to sob his name, and he seemed to moan.

"Wait, he's semicoherent." Four people grabbed for the telephone, to find no dial tone, and ran to use a neighbor's. One slammed the dead phone against the wall in frustration—and miraculously produced a dial tone.

But the body was now motionless on the kitchen floor. "He has a pulse, he has a pulse."

"But he's not breathing!"

"Well, get away—give him some f---ing air!" The three or four guests gathered around his body unbuttoned his shirt.

"Wait—is he OK? Should I call the damn ambulance?"

A chorus of frightened voices shouted, "Yes, yes!"

"Come on, come on, breathe again. Breathe!"

Power Tip
As this example shows, in dialogue, each speaker's words are often broken into separate paragraphs. This is also a common feature of fiction writing, discussed in Chapter 1, page 7.

Power Tip
To see how this writer uses other quoted details, read the complete essay on pages 569–570.

ACTIVITY 24: Teamwork

With two or three classmates, do the following:

- Read the paragraph below, underlining all the imprecise and unclear details.
- Working as a team, rewrite the paragraph, adding the most precise and colorful quoted details you can think of. You may want to add other details, too.
- Have one person write the new paragraph on a separate sheet of paper.
- When all the teams in the class have finished writing, have someone from your team read the paragraph out loud to the class. *Underlining and rewrites will vary.*

This morning, my husband, Leo, said nice things to me. I asked him whether he was feeling guilty about something. He insisted that he was thinking good things about me and that I should appreciate him. I told him that it was wrong of me to be so suspicious, since he was being so nice.

ACTIVITY 25

- First, look carefully at the photograph.
- Next, on a separate sheet of paper, freewrite a brief description of the photograph. Use as many precise and colorful quoted details as possible. (For more advice on freewriting, see Chapter 3, page 79.)
- When you have finished writing, try to get together with a few of your classmates and read your descriptions out loud to one another. Decide who uses the most precise and colorful quoted details. *Freewriting will vary.*

ACTIVITY 26

Write a paragraph. Using as many emotive details as possible, discuss or describe one of the following:

- the time in your life when you were most frightened
- the person you love or hate the most
- the time in your life when you cried the hardest
- a time in your life when you felt lonely or abandoned
- the time in your life when you felt the happiest *Answers will vary.*

USING EMOTIVE DETAILS

In college, you will sometimes be asked to write on topics that bring up strong emotions for you. Good writers take the time to explore such feelings and find precise details to describe them; these details are called **emotive**. Strong emotive details capture your emotions in a powerful way that allows the reader to connect deeply with your experiences.

Once again, start by recognizing imprecise expressions that may weaken your writing. Notice the underlined words in the following example:

> **As the first member of my family to graduate from college, I felt very happy.**

In this sentence, the phrase *very happy* gives an unclear picture of the writer's feelings. The person reading this sentence will have to guess about the writer's exact emotions. However, we can replace the imprecise expression with more specific emotive details:

> **As the first member of my family to graduate from college, I felt a deep sense of pride and achievement.**

In this sentence, the underlined expression gives a much clearer sense of the writer's feelings. However, the writer might explore even deeper levels of the emotional experience:

> **As the first member of my family to graduate from college, I felt the hope and pride of my ancestors well up in me.**

The underlined phrase contains powerful emotive details that help the reader connect with the writer's deepest feelings.

Basic Guidelines for Using Emotive Details

- Avoid the abstract words from the chart on page 169.
- Close your eyes and recall the important memory or experience in as much detail as possible.

ACTIVITY 27

For each sentence below, do the following:

- Underline the imprecise or unclear detail.
- Rewrite the sentence, adding precise and colorful emotive details.
  Underlining and rewrites will vary.

EXAMPLE: After her date, Margie was upset.
After her date, Margie ran into her house, flung herself facedown on the couch, screamed, and beat the cushions with her fists.

1. When the television executive was sentenced to thirty years in jail, he wasn't happy.

2. The paramedic felt bad when he could not revive the drowned child.

3. After dreaming of going to her state university for ten years, Julie was glad when she received her acceptance letter.

4. When the star witness disappeared before the trial, the lawyer was disappointed.

5. The pilot sounded normal when he announced the emergency landing.

ACTIVITY 28: Teamwork

With two or three classmates, do the following:

- Choose a person to read the first paragraph below out loud.
- Underline, circle, or highlight all the emotive details that you can find.
- Discuss why these details make the writing powerful.
- Repeat this process with the second paragraph. *Answers will vary.*

1. **Student Writer**

It happens too often in my neighborhood. You hear screaming and sirens, or maybe you don't, and later on, there's some kind of shrine on the street: prayer candles, red roses from the 7-Eleven, and teddy bears hugging stuffed hearts. Usually, there's a picture of the kid who got shot and taped-up signs from parents, brothers, sisters, and other kids: "We will always love you," "We miss you," "With Jesus." I've walked by shrines like these maybe four times, and each time I've felt a cold stone in my chest. The faces in the pictures are unfamiliar, and I can't make myself feel all the hurt I could feel. My attitude changed last week when I walked by a new shrine at Garden and Adams. My first thought when I saw the kid's picture was simply *I know that face.* It was like when you're on the bus and nod at someone you've seen around but don't know that well. Then, I realized it was Bo Robbins, a kid I went to grade school with. When I put this fact together with all the other things—the candles, the notes, and the flowers—it felt like someone kicked me in the stomach. I think I actually fell back a little. I had lost touch with Bo after we went on to separate schools, but I remembered him well. He got in trouble a lot for talking in class, but he was funny and made everyone laugh—even the teachers. You couldn't stay angry with him. In the picture at the shrine, he looked like he was getting ready to laugh. That's what got me. I felt the stone again, but this time it was in my throat; I couldn't swallow it down. I walked away from there fast, blinking and wiping my eyes.

2. **Professional Writer** (This paragraph is from an essay in which the writer recalls his father's alcoholism and its effects on the writer and the other members of his family.)

I am moved to write these pages now because my own son, at the age of ten, is taking on himself the griefs of the world, and in particular the griefs of his father. He tells me that when I am gripped by sadness he feels responsible; he feels there must be something he can do to spring me from depression, to fix my life. And that crushing sense of responsibility is exactly what I felt at the age of ten in the face of my father's drinking. My son wonders if I, too, am possessed. I write, therefore, to drag into the light what eats me—the fear, the guilt, the shame—so that my own children may be spared.

Power Tip
To see how this writer uses other emotive details, read the complete essay on pages 573–574.

ACTIVITY 29: Teamwork

With two or three classmates, do the following:

- Read the paragraph below, underlining all the imprecise and unclear details.
- Working as a team, rewrite the paragraph, adding the most precise and colorful emotive details you can think of. You may want to add other details, too.
- Have one person write the new paragraph on a separate sheet of paper.
- When all the teams in the class have finished writing, have someone from your team read the paragraph out loud to the class. *Underlining and rewrites will vary.*

In front of an international television audience, Christina Montero from Brazil was crowned Miss Universe. When the judge announced her name, she was surprised. The other contestants began to gather around her, which helped her feel OK. When the former Miss Universe placed the crown on her head, Christina felt special. Finally, as she walked down the runway, she felt the strongest emotion of her life.

ACTIVITY 30

- First, look carefully at the photograph.
- Next, on a separate sheet of paper, freewrite a brief description of the photograph. Use as many precise and colorful emotive details as possible. (For more advice on freewriting, see Chapter 3, page 79.)
- When you have finished writing, try to get together with a few of your classmates and read your descriptions out loud to one another. Decide who uses the most precise and colorful details. *Freewriting will vary.*

ACTIVITY 31

Write a paragraph. Using as many quoted details as possible (direct or indirect quotations), discuss or describe one of the following:

- an intense argument that you had
- an interesting cell phone conversation that you had
- your favorite dialogue from a movie or television show
- a time when you tried to convince or persuade someone
- a meaningful discussion you had with a parent, coach, professor, minister, or therapist *Answers will vary.*

USING HUMOROUS DETAILS

Humor is an essential ingredient of human life, and the ability to make people smile or laugh is a powerful gift. Many of the world's most popular writers and entertainers—from Shakespeare to Woody Allen and Chris Rock—have used humor to entertain and inform their audiences.

You may describe a funny situation or experience in what is known as an **anecdote** (a brief story). Or, you may use **critical humor** to criticize people and situations. For example, many comedians use critical humor to challenge or question the actions of politicians. Consider, for instance, this statement about the Iraq war from comedian Jay Leno: "CNN said that after the war, there is a plan to divide Iraq into three parts: regular, premium, and unleaded." Leno was suggesting that motives behind the war had more to do with protecting oil supplies than defending democracy.

Often, the most effective way to make your reader smile or laugh is through humorous details. If you have a good sense of humor and enjoy being creative, you might try one or more of the following strategies to develop humorous details in your writing:

Including a Surprising or Unexpected Image or Idea

Take a look at the underlined words in the following example:

> **Lined up for judging at last year's Centerburg Dog Show were a sleek Doberman, two fluffy collies, three carefully groomed poodles, and one proud-looking orange tabby cat. Yes, my cat Lassie thinks he's a dog, and no one can convince him otherwise. I wonder why.**

This short passage contains two humorous details: First, the image of a proud cat lined up beside show dogs is unexpected and comical. Second, the fact that the cat is called *Lassie* (the name of a famous dog from old movies and television shows) is surprising and funny.

Using a Pun

A **pun** is a play on words. Look at the underlined words in this example:

> **Some attendees of the Millersville Fair were given a "pop quiz" on Friday when a local beverage company conducted a taste test of five new sodas.**

Teaching Tip
You might describe a *pun* as having *fun* with words.

In this sentence, the word *pop* has two meanings: (1) "sudden," as in *pop quiz*, and (2) "soda." The writer is being playful with these two meanings of the word.

Exaggerating

Exaggerating is overstating something. Look at the underlined words in this example:

> **My kids' room is so messy that I need to wear a hazardous materials suit to clean it.**

Clearly, the writer is exaggerating; he doesn't need to wear such a suit to clean the room, but the expression creates a funny picture in readers' minds.

Using Playful Sarcasm

Sarcasm is saying one thing and meaning another. For example, at the end of a paragraph in which you describe a horrible work experience, you might say something like this (notice the underlined words):

> **No one should be allowed to have that much fun at a job; I certainly hope I never do again.**

Here, your comment about having so much fun is clearly sarcastic: you really mean *the exact opposite*. This is a playful way to conclude the paragraph.

Humor can be a powerful tool for communicating ideas, but inexperienced writers often use humor that is inappropriate. As a college writer, you should not be afraid to use humor, but you should recognize when it might offend the reader or interfere with the larger purpose of your writing. As a general rule for academic writing, you should avoid humor that

- uses offensive language
- makes fun of people based on their race, gender, ethnicity, or sexual orientation, or that makes fun of disabilities
- is unoriginal (for instance, humor based on popular jokes)

Teaching Tip
If you have Internet access and screen projection capability in your classroom, you might show brief clips from comedians like Jon Stewart, Stephen Colbert, and Chris Rock. (You'll probably want to screen the clips beforehand so that you can avoid offensive material.) Have students identify particular lines or ideas that they think are especially funny. What makes them funny? If students don't find the material to be funny, ask them why.

Basic Guidelines for Using Humorous Details

- Do not use humor if you are not comfortable with it.
- Do not overuse or force humor. In particular, use puns and sarcasm in moderation so that they do not annoy the reader.
- If you are unsure about the appropriateness of humor in an assignment, ask your instructor.

ACTIVITY 32

For each sentence below, do the following:

- Underline the imprecise or unclear detail.
- Rewrite the sentence, adding a precise humorous detail. *Underlining and rewrites will vary.*

EXAMPLE: The chili was so hot that I cried.

The chili was so hot that my breath nearly set the curtains on fire.

1. When my husband's lower back went out again last week, I gave him a funny suggestion about how to take care of it.

2. Joe is so easily angered that he always has an unusual experience at airport security.

3. To explain why he spent $400 on a haircut, the senator gave an unusual explanation.

4. After working with a jackhammer for five hours, something odd happened to the construction worker.

5. The bride's wedding train was so long that it caused a funny problem for her.

ACTIVITY 33: Teamwork

With two or three classmates, do the following:

- Choose a person to read the first passage below out loud.
- Underline, circle, or highlight all the humorous details that you can find.
- Discuss why these details make the writing powerful.
- Repeat this process with the second passage. *Answers will vary.*

1. **Student Writer**

One of the most memorable people in my life was my Aunt Alva, who lived in a pink house set into a steep hill in the Pennsylvania coal country. I'll never forget that house, which practically glowed on overcast days. Nor will I forget my disappointment on learning that it was pink because she and my Uncle Antonio (Tony) got a discount on the paint. I liked to think of the color as an extension of Aunt Alva's personality—fun, distinctive, and a little disruptive. As soon as my parents, my sister, and I entered her house, she offered us snacks, including my favorite: sweet-and-salty peanuts. When I think back on it, sweet and salty matched her personality perfectly. One minute, she was hugging and kissing us and saying how handsome my sister's boyfriend was. The next minute, she would snap at Uncle Tony: "Step on up and show some love, old man. They're not getting any younger." Later, Aunt Alva and I would watch reruns of *Cagney and Lacey* on her 1970 Magnavox television, which had a bright green picture. She'd put on sunglasses to cut the glare. One time, when she left the room to make lunch in the kitchen, my dad adjusted the colors so that the actors' skin looked a little less Martian-like. As soon as Aunt Alva came back, she made a face at the TV and said, "Who messed with the picture?" Then, she adjusted the knob to make the actors green again and put her sunglasses back on. I started wearing Uncle Tony's sunglasses to watch TV with her, and Dad took a picture of us slouched back in our shades. That picture has been on my refrigerator for years, and I look at it whenever I need to smile.

2. **Professional Writer** (This passage is from an essay about the writer's father, a Catholic who worked as a custodian in a Jewish synagogue and taught his Mexican-American family respect for all religions.)

As children we were made aware of the differences and joys of Hanukkah, Christmas and Navidad. We were taught to respect each celebration, even if they conflicted. For example, the Christmas carols taught in school. We learned the song about the twelve days of Christmas, though I never understood what the hell a partridge was doing in a pear tree in the middle of December.

We also learned a German song about a boy named Tom and a bomb—*O Tannenbaum*. We even learned a song in the obscure language of Latin, called "Adeste Fideles," which reminded me of *Ahh! d'este fideo*, a Mexican pasta soup. Though 75% of our class was Mexican-American, we never sang a Christmas song in *Español*. Spanish was forbidden.

Hanukkah: eight-day Jewish holiday that often falls around the time of Christmas

Navidad: Spanish-speaking cultures' celebration of the Christmas holiday

Power Tip

To see how this writer uses other humorous details (and other details), read the complete essay on pages 592–593.

ACTIVITY 34: Teamwork

With two or three classmates, do the following:

- Read the paragraph below, underlining all the details that could be funny.
- Working as a team, rewrite the paragraph, adding the most humorous details you can think of. You may want to add other details, too.
- Have one person write the new paragraph on a separate sheet of paper.
- When all the teams in the class have finished writing, have someone from your team read the paragraph out loud to the class. *Underlining and rewrites will vary.*

When Veronica came home from work, she discovered the babysitter snoring loudly on the couch. Meanwhile, Veronica's twins had gotten into crayons, paint, and spaghetti sauce in the kitchen and decorated the walls, the floors, and themselves in a way that made Veronica laugh in spite of the mess. One of the twins looked especially funny because she had poured the sauce over her head. The twins looked happier than she'd ever seen them.

ACTIVITY 35

- Think of a person, situation, or experience that really made you laugh.
- On the lines provided, write three or four sentences in which you describe this person, situation, or experience.
- Try to include humorous details—words that will surprise your readers and make them smile or laugh. *Answers will vary.*

ACTIVITY 36

- First, look carefully at the photograph.
- Next, on a separate sheet of paper, freewrite a brief description of the photograph. Use as many humorous details as possible. (For more advice on freewriting, see Chapter 3, page 79.)
- When you have finished writing, try to get together with a few of your classmates and read your descriptions out loud to one another. Decide whose description is the funniest. *Freewriting will vary.*

ACTIVITY 37

Write a paragraph. Using as many humorous details as possible (a pun, exaggeration, playful sarcasm, or a surprising image), discuss or describe one of the following:

- a silly video that you saw on YouTube
- a person who did something embarrassing on Facebook or MySpace
- a time when you could not control your laughter
- a ridiculous story that got too much media attention
- the funniest person you know *Answers will vary.*

USING COMPARATIVE DETAILS: METAPHORS AND SIMILES

Metaphors are a common feature of language, and most people use them without knowing it. The best way to understand metaphors is to look at some examples.

Let's begin with a sentence that would benefit from the addition of a metaphor:

> **My six-year-old daughter is an excellent swimmer.**

While this sentence makes a clear statement, the phrase *an excellent swimmer* does not give the reader a colorful image of the little girl as a swimmer. However, the writer might use a more creative description. Notice the underlined words:

My six-year-old daughter is a dolphin in the water.

In this sentence, the phrase *a dolphin in the water* is a metaphor that gives the reader an immediate and powerful image of the little girl gliding gracefully through the water. A **metaphor** is a creative comparison of two items with similar characteristics. Sometimes, creative comparisons (comparative details) use the words *like* or *as:*

My six-year-old daughter is like a dolphin in the water.
My six-year-old daughter swims as gracefully as a dolphin.

Comparisons that use *like* or *as* are known as **similes**.

Basic Guidelines for Using Creative Comparisons (Comparative Details)

- Do not overload your writing with these comparisons. One or two distinctive comparisons in a paragraph are usually sufficient.
- Try to avoid overused comparisons like those in the following list. (These are known as *clichés,* expressions that used to sound original and creative but have lost their spark because of overuse.)

Some Overused Comparisons (Clichés)

avoid ____ like the plague
blind as a bat
cool as a cucumber
dead as a doornail
dull as dishwater
like a bull in a china shop
rich as a king
sick as a dog
sleep like a log

ACTIVITY 38

For each of the following sentences, fill in the blank with a comparative detail.

Answers will vary.

EXAMPLE: In her brown dress covered with cowboy hats and fringes, Noreen looked like a lampshade in a ten-year-old's bedroom.

1. My sister spends every free moment reading; she says that books are like ________ to her.
2. The boxer's face had been smashed so many times that it looked like ________.
3. After three final exams in twenty-four hours, Max's brain was as jammed with facts as ________.

CONTINUED >

4. The professor's vocabulary was so difficult that listening to his lecture was like ________________.

5. After he was arrested for buying cocaine, the politician's thirty-year career ended as quickly as ________________.

ACTIVITY 39: Teamwork

With two or three classmates, do the following:

- Choose a person to read the first paragraph below out loud.
- Underline, circle, or highlight the main comparative detail(s).
- Discuss why the comparative detail(s) make the writing powerful. Can you think of other comparisons that might have been made?
- Repeat this process with the second paragraph. *Answers will vary.*

1. **Student Writer**

When my car broke down in the fast lane of the freeway, it was like being caught in the eye of a tornado. Other vehicles flew by at seventy miles per hour, causing my car to shake like a tin can; I felt as though my little Toyota would be picked up violently and slammed against a nearby overpass. I gripped the steering wheel and heard myself screaming as if I were in an echo chamber. The sound of my screaming was pierced by car horns that screeched fiercely, like giant prehistoric birds attacking their prey. A giant big-rig roared by like a meteorite. I was sure that my death had come, that I would be ripped apart in a collision of metal and concrete. I passed out. The next thing I knew, a police officer was knocking on my window, looking like an angel of mercy.

2. **Professional Writer** (This paragraph is from an essay setting out principles of why it's important to "be cool to the pizza delivery dude.")

Principle 2: Coolness to the pizza delivery dude is a practice in empathy. Let's face it: We've all taken jobs just to have a job because some money is better than none. I've held an assortment of these jobs and was grateful for the paycheck that meant I didn't have to share my Cheerios with my cats. In the big pizza wheel of life, sometimes you're the hot bubbly cheese and sometimes you're the burnt crust. It's good to remember the fickle spinning of that wheel.

empathy: identifying with or feeling the emotions of others

Power Tip
To see how this writer uses other details, read the complete essay on pages 528–529.

fickle: changeable

ACTIVITY 40: Teamwork

With two or three classmates, do the following:

- Read the paragraph below, underlining all the imprecise details and descriptions.
- Working as a team, rewrite the paragraph, adding the most creative comparative details that you can think of. You may want to add other details, too.
- Have one person write the new paragraph on a separate sheet of paper.
- When all the teams in the class have finished writing, have someone from your team read the paragraph out loud to the class. *Underlining and rewrites will vary.*

My boss has bad breath. It's so terrible that I feel sick when I smell it. The other morning, he came to work with a BIG hangover. He hadn't showered or shaved, so he looked really awful. And worst of all, his breath was a powerful force. I was standing at least six feet away from him when he spoke to me, but the blast was deadly.

ACTIVITY 41

- First, look carefully at the photograph.
- Next, on a separate sheet of paper, write a creative comparison using the image in the photograph. Begin with the following sentence: "____________ is like a rattlesnake ready to strike." Then, freewrite briefly about why ____________ is like a rattlesnake that is ready to strike. (For more advice on freewriting, see Chapter 3, page 79.)
- When you have finished writing, try to get together with a few of your classmates and read what you have written out loud to one another. Decide who uses the most precise and vivid details. *Responses will vary.*

ACTIVITY 42

Write a paragraph. Using as many comparative details as possible (metaphors or similes), discuss or describe one of the following:

- getting my driver's license was like . . .
- falling out of love is like . . .
- getting a promotion at my job was like . . .
- having my first child was like . . .
- seeing ____________ die was like . . . *Answers will vary.*

ACTIVITY 43

Look back on one or two of the paragraphs that you developed in Chapter 5 (for example, see Activity 17, page 163). Reread the paragraphs and underline or highlight any imprecise or unclear details. Then, using the strategies discussed in this chapter, rewrite the details to make them more precise and colorful. As a reminder, you might use one or more of the following:

- **Concrete details:** identifying persons, places, and things
- **Action details:** energizing your verbs
- **Sensory details:** describing what you see, hear, smell, taste, and touch
- **Quoted details:** recording what people say
- **Emotive details:** exploring emotions
- **Humorous details:** making readers smile or laugh
- **Comparative details:** using metaphors and similes

Bringing It All Together

In this chapter, you have learned how to add precise and creative details to your writing. Check off each of the following statements that you understand. For any that you do not understand, review the appropriate pages in this chapter.

☐ Imprecise expressions can weaken your writing. It's helpful to be aware of common imprecise expressions. (See page 168.) Another problem to avoid is insufficient details. (See page 169.)

☐ Although there are many strategies for developing colorful and creative details, we have focused on seven in this chapter.

___ **Concrete details** identify specific persons, places, and things. (See page 177.)

___ **Action details** use energetic, expressive verbs to describe actions. (See page 180.)

___ **Sensory details** describe the way things look, sound, smell, taste, and feel. (See page 183.)

___ **Quoted details** record what people say. (See page 187.)

___ **Emotive details** describe emotions. (See page 191.)

___ **Humorous details** make readers smile or laugh. Some techniques for adding humor to writing are (1) including a surprising or unexpected image or idea, (2) using a pun, (3) exaggerating, and (4) using playful sarcasm. (See page 194.)

___ **Comparative details** include *metaphors,* which directly compare one thing to another thing (*My six-year-old daughter is a dolphin in the water*) and *similes,* which use *like* or *as* to make comparisons (*My six-year-old daughter is like a dolphin in the water*). (See page 198.)

Chapter 7

Revising

OVERVIEW OF THIS CHAPTER

WARM-UP Taking a Closer Look

1. Imagine this situation:

Scientists have found a way to implant a magnifying lens in the human eye. Now, with just a blink, you can turn your eye into a magnifying glass, seeing objects at three to five times their normal size. With another blink, you can return your eye to its normal sight.

2. Stop and think!

Working alone or with classmates, consider how you might use this new function of the human eye. How could you use it to be more successful in your daily activities? In what situations would this function be especially helpful? Would you use it for work as well as for play? How often would you be likely to use it?

One way you could use this new function is to improve your college writing. If you could examine your papers magnified to three times their normal size, you would probably notice every comma, every missing letter or word, and so on. You would have to move slowly across the page as well, taking in each detail as it passed before the powerful lens of your eye. With this ability, you might *really see* your writing like never before.

In this chapter, you will learn to *magnify your awareness* about your work as you proceed through the final step in the writing process: revision.

Understanding the Revision Process: An Overview

The chapters preceding this one showed you how to organize and compose an academic paragraph.

> **Chapter 4** helped you to develop a careful outline for your paragraph.
>
> **Chapter 5** showed you how to follow this outline step-by-step to compose your paragraph.
>
> **Chapter 6** helped you generate precise and colorful details for your paragraph.

When you have gained some mastery over these parts of the writing process, you will be able to produce **unified** paragraphs: paragraphs that stay on track and include only information that supports the main idea as expressed in the topic sentence. However, the act of writing is not always orderly and predictable, and even experienced writers can get off track. Sometimes, you may become so closely involved with your ideas that you skip a key piece of your outline or get lost in your creative details. Also, you might make grammar mistakes and other errors. For this reason, dedicated writers recognize that the final step of the writing process—**revision**—is just as important as the earlier steps.

Revision ("re" + "vision") means looking over your paragraphs with a fresh eye to identify and fix any problems with unity. You will also want to check carefully for problems with grammar, mechanics (spelling, punctuation, formatting), and word choice.

The best way to make sure that you've fixed these problems is to perform your revision as carefully as you have performed the other steps in the writing process. Many students rush their revision or skip it altogether, which can seriously harm the quality of their writing.

Teaching Tip
As you begin this chapter, ask students what revision means to them. Have they ever attempted it before? If not, why not?

Revising for Unity

Again, **unity** means that a paragraph stays on track and includes only information that supports the main idea as expressed in the topic sentence. Because unity is so important to effective writing, it's a good idea to check for it before you look for errors in individual words and sentences.

FOUR MAJOR PROBLEMS WITH UNITY

As you learned in Chapters 4 and 5, there are several ways that you can get off track when outlining and writing a paragraph. These include

- changing your main idea when you write the topic sentence
- changing a support point, combining it with an example, or forgetting it altogether
- forgetting a transitional expression
- including information that does not fit

To see each of these problems in action, let's look at one college student's work. We'll begin by looking at the student's outline, which is complete and problem-free.

MAIN IDEA	**SeaWorld is a place where I feel especially happy.**
TRANSITIONAL EXPRESSION	**In the first place,**
SUPPORT POINT 1	**it has a relaxing atmosphere.** – coastal location – people don't rush – relieves my headaches
TRANSITIONAL EXPRESSION	**In the second place,**
SUPPORT POINT 2	**it has my favorite sea animals.** – killer whales – penguins – manatees
TRANSITIONAL EXPRESSION	**Finally,**
SUPPORT POINT 3	**it is not crowded like other theme parks.** – no long lines – uncrowded walkways – no waiting for tables

Teaching Tip
Point out to students that comparing a draft with the outline is always a good first step in revision. They can mark places in the draft that differ from the outline and make notes about what changes might help.

After writing her paragraph, the student compared it very carefully with her outline. In this revision activity, she identified four problems with her unity. The problems are numbered and underlined below, and they are discussed in more detail in the following sections.

SeaWorld in San Diego has the best entertainment of any California theme park. (1) In the first place, I like to immerse myself in its relaxing atmosphere. Located on a seacoast, SeaWorld is full of warm sunlight and is surrounded by sparkling water. I just dive into this world of happiness, and my smile doesn't leave my face the whole day. I like its pace because people there don't rush anywhere. Life is so calm at SeaWorld that any problem seems too small to be troublesome. The magic of this place is so strong that even the headaches that I sometimes get disappear without a trace as soon as I step out of my car and breathe in the ocean air. In the second place, SeaWorld has an incredible killer-whale show. (2) These whales are huge and potentially dangerous, but you would never guess it because in the arena they behave like house pets, listening and doing whatever their instructors tell them. And what always amazes me is how these gigantic creatures can swim as fast as a rocket. Also, I like observing penguins in an open aquarium. They have such a funny tread when they walk slowly to the water. In addition, I like to watch how huge manatees (sea cows) consume their salad leaves from the surface of their pool. I appreciate that SeaWorld is (3)

> not as crowded as other amusement parks, such as Disneyland. I have never had to wait forty minutes in a long line to see a show that lasts only five minutes. Because there are four great show stadiums, there is always plenty of space for everyone. Also, the park is constructed in a smart way. All the attractions are within easy walking distance from the main entrance. You never bump into someone traveling in the opposite direction because all the walkways are wide and spacious. It is equally important that the park has several convenient cafeterias where I can relax and enjoy a peaceful meal.
> 4 SeaWorld has the best hamburgers of any theme park, and the prices won't bankrupt you. One time at Knott's Berry Farm, I spent $68 for hamburgers, fries, and sodas for my husband, myself, and our two boys. Paying this amount of money for fast food ruined my whole day. When I want to enjoy a blissful experience, I just follow the tide to SeaWorld.

Problem 1: A Flawed Topic Sentence

When the student began composing her paragraph, she was excited and confident about her ideas. As a result, she wrote a bold topic sentence, praising SeaWorld:

> **SeaWorld in San Diego has the best entertainment of any California theme park.**

While this is a powerful claim, it misrepresents the main idea for her paragraph. According to this topic sentence, the entire paragraph should focus on the *entertainment* provided by SeaWorld. In fact, the paragraph discusses *all* the reasons why the writer has positive feelings about the park, including the relaxing atmosphere and lack of crowds. With this topic sentence, the reader will be confused by examples that are not connected to the entertainment at SeaWorld. The flawed topic sentence disrupts the unity of the entire paragraph.

Remember, the topic sentence is an especially important feature of your paragraph. If you misstate your main idea in the topic sentence, the rest of the paragraph may not make sense to your reader. Always double-check your topic sentence during the revision process.

Fix this problem by rewriting the topic sentence so that it clearly expresses your main idea for the paragraph. (For a detailed review of problems with topic sentences and how to fix them, see Chapter 5, page 138.)

Problem 2: An Unstated or Unclear Support Point

In rereading her paragraph on SeaWorld, the student noticed that something was missing: she forgot to state her second support point, skipping directly to her first example:

> **In the second place, SeaWorld has an incredible killer-whale show.**

This error will be quite confusing for readers, who will expect that all the examples following this sentence will relate to the killer-whale show. However, when the writer discusses the penguins and manatees, the unity will be disrupted.

Remember, each support point is a major feature of your paragraph. If you forget or misstate a support point, it can damage the unity of your writing. Always double-check your support points during the revision process.

Fix this problem by rewriting the support point so that it clearly expresses your idea and accurately sets up the examples that follow it. Often, you will need to separate the support point from the first example and rewrite them as separate sentences. (For more information on common problems with support points, see Chapter 5, page 149.)

Teaching Tip
For an animated overview of the process of writing and revising a paragraph, see the *Make-a-Paragraph Kit* CD available with this book. This CD also includes guided writing assignments with revision advice.

Problem 3: A Missing Transitional Expression

The author of the SeaWorld paragraph noticed that at one point in her writing, the ideas seemed jumbled; they did not flow as smoothly as she wanted. Then, she realized that she had forgotten her third major transitional expression (introducing the third support point):

> **I appreciate that SeaWorld is not as crowded as other amusement parks, such as Disneyland.**

For the reader, the missing transitional expression is a large gap in the unity: the abrupt shift from the description of the manatees to the third support point (that SeaWorld is not as crowded as other parks) will be confusing.

Remember, the reader cannot anticipate when you will shift to a new support point or to a new example. You must include transitional expressions to make this shift smooth and logical for your reader. Always double-check your transitional expressions during the revision process.

Fix this problem by adding the missing transitional expression. (For more information on adding transitional expressions, see Chapter 5, page 158.)

Problem 4: Digressive Details

As the writer was describing the convenient (uncrowded) cafeterias at SeaWorld, she included a digressive (unrelated) detail about the excellent hamburgers. This detail caused her to remember a time at Knott's Berry Farm when she paid too much for food:

> **SeaWorld has the best hamburgers of any theme park, and the prices won't bankrupt you. One time at Knott's Berry Farm, I spent $68 for hamburgers, fries, and sodas for my husband, myself, and our two boys. Paying this amount of money for fast food ruined my whole day.**

This is such a powerful memory for the student that it takes control of her writing. These details about the high price of food at Knott's Berry Farm do not fit with her support point, that SeaWorld is *not as crowded* as other theme parks.

Remember, digressive details can be especially confusing for your reader. When composing your paragraph, keep a close eye on your outline and don't let unrelated details get you off track. Always double-check for digressive details during the revision process.

Fix this problem by eliminating the digressive details. If taking out this information leaves your paragraph underdeveloped, add new details that fit your support point. (For a discussion of digressions that can occur in the outlining stage, see Chapter 4, page 122.)

The Revised Paragraph

In her revision, the writer corrected each of the problems with unity. Take a look:

Topic sentence rewritten

Missing support point (with major transition) added

Transitional expression added

Detail rewritten to focus on the availability of tables in the cafeteria

The place where I forget about all my problems and feel happiest is SeaWorld in San Diego. In the first place, I like to immerse myself in its relaxing atmosphere. Located on a seacoast, SeaWorld is full of warm sunlight and is surrounded by sparkling water. I just dive into this world of happiness, and my smile doesn't leave my face the whole day. I like its pace because people there don't rush anywhere. Life is so calm at SeaWorld that any problem looks too small to be troublesome. The magic of this place is so strong that even the headaches that I sometimes get disappear without a trace as soon as I step out of my car and breathe in the ocean air. In the second place, SeaWorld showcases some of my favorite sea animals. For example, it has an incredible killer-whale show. Killer whales are huge and potentially dangerous, but you would never guess it because in the arena they behave like house pets, listening and doing whatever their instructors tell them. And what always amazes me is how these gigantic creatures can swim as fast as a rocket. Also, I like observing penguins in the open aquarium. They have such a funny tread when they walk slowly to the water. In addition, I like to watch how huge manatees (sea cows) consume their salad leaves from the surface of their pool. Finally, I appreciate that SeaWorld is not as crowded as other amusement parks, such as Disneyland. I have never had to wait forty minutes in a long line to see a show that lasts only five minutes. Because there are four great show stadiums, there is always plenty of space for everyone. Also, the park is constructed in a smart way. All the attractions are within easy walking distance from the main entrance. You never bump into someone traveling in the opposite direction because all the walkways are wide and spacious. It is equally important that the park has several convenient cafeterias where I can relax and enjoy a peaceful meal. I've never had to scramble for a free table or eat elbow-to-elbow with a hungry mob. When I want to enjoy a blissful experience, I just follow the tide to SeaWorld.

Caution! A paragraph without unity can be a hazardous reading experience: the large gaps, abrupt shifts, and unexpected digressions can cause your reader to stumble and fall. To protect your reader from such hazards, always take the revision stage of the writing process seriously.

Caution: Unrevised Paragraph

ACTIVITY 1

Below is an outline-paragraph pairing. Do the following:

- Review the outline.
- Read the paragraph, comparing it carefully with the outline.
- Underline or highlight any problems with unity.
- In the spaces between the lines or in the margins, write in a revision to correct each problem.

The paragraph has four problems with unity. Revisions will vary.

MAIN IDEA	I try to be the best parent that I can be.
TRANSITIONAL EXPRESSION	For starters,
SUPPORT POINT 1	I try to be a good provider. – work two jobs – spend money on my kids rather than on myself – set up college fund
TRANSITIONAL EXPRESSION	Second,
SUPPORT POINT 2	I spend a lot of time with my children. – dinnertime – study and fun time after dinner – weekends
TRANSITIONAL EXPRESSION	Third,
SUPPORT POINT 3	I try to listen to and help my children. – tell them they can talk to me (and they do) – sometimes give advice – make sure they know they can count on me

Because I want the best for my children, I try to be the best parent I can be. For starters, I try to provide for my children as well as I can.

~~It's tough being a good parent. For starters, I work two jobs.~~ I have jobs both as a full-time administrative assistant and as a part-time salesclerk at a gift store in our town. The hours are long, especially now that I'm in school; however, the jobs allow me to meet my expenses and

CONTINUED >

For online practice with unity and other topics covered in this chapter, visit this book's Web site at **bedfordstmartins .com/steppingstones**.

those of my children, with some money to spare every month. Also, I try not to spend too much money on myself; I put my children's needs for clothing, school supplies, and occasional gifts over my own needs. Additionally, I am putting my savings into college funds for my daughter and son. I have only recently been able to afford college myself, and I don't want my kids to have to struggle for their education the same way I did. Second, I spend a lot of time with my children. Even though we all have busy schedules, I insist that we try to have dinner together every night so that we can talk about our days over a healthy meal. After dinner, I help my kids with their homework while I'm doing my own, and sometimes we'll watch a movie or a TV show together before bed. Our favorite shows are comedies, and we like to laugh together. ~~Some shows are really annoying, though; I hope the reality-TV show trend dies soon!~~ On weekends, my kids usually want to spend time with their friends, but we try to do something special together at least once a month, like going to the zoo or a museum. ^Third, I try to listen to my children and help them with their problems as much as I can. I have told my kids that they can talk to me whenever they want, and they often come into my room before bedtime to discuss things that are bothering them, like disagreements with friends. I give advice when my kids seem to want it, but I try not to be a know-it-all; I think it means the most to them when I just listen. Also, I make sure they know that they can always count on me, as long as I'm alive. I know I haven't always been an ideal parent, but my kids deserve the best, and I try to give that to them every day.

ACTIVITY 2

Reread one or more of the paragraphs that you developed in Chapters 5 and 6, marking any places where the unity has been disrupted. Then, fix the problems with unity, using the strategies discussed so far in this chapter.

SOME HELPFUL REVISION STRATEGIES

The following strategies are especially helpful early in the revision process, when you'll typically want to check for unity.

Revise with Fresh Eyes

If you try to revise your paragraph immediately after writing it, you may be too close to the ideas or too tired to see any problems. To see your work with fresh eyes, take a break before revising it. During this break, do something to relax your mind and take it off your writing: have a meal, get some exercise, take a nap, do some chores. If possible, wait until the next day to do your revision. Having fresh eyes will make it much easier for you to spot any mistakes in your paragraph.

During a timed, in-class writing assignment, you probably won't be able to take a break before revising your work. You can, however, pause to stretch, close your eyes, and breathe deeply for a minute or two. This brief moment of relaxation can clear your mind and boost your mental energy for the revision.

Use Your Outline

Suppose you are driving to an unfamiliar location and are relying mostly on a global positioning system to get there. If you turn off the navigation system several miles before reaching your destination, what will happen? You might remember some of the directions, but you will probably have to guess the rest. Chances are, you will get lost.

Many students put aside their outline after composing the paragraph. This is like turning off the navigation system before reaching your final destination. In academic writing, you have not reached your final destination until you have completed the revision, using the outline to achieve unity in your paragraph.

Keep your outline beside your paragraph to check for unity during the revision process. Cross-check each part of the paragraph with the corresponding items in the outline. Watch out for any missing, misplaced, or accidentally changed features.

Get Peer Review

One of the best strategies for revising your paragraph is to exchange papers with a **peer**, a classmate or fellow student who is at the same level of English as you, to comment on each other's work. This process is known as *peer review.* Sometimes, your instructor may pair you with another student during class for peer review. If you are not given this opportunity, you can arrange to meet with another student outside of class and conduct your own peer review.

Start by inviting a fellow student who is mature and dedicated to the work. Meet in a quiet place, like the library or an empty classroom. Plan to spend at least half an hour for the peer review. You should bring your paragraph, your outline, and the peer review form on the next page. Then, follow this process:

1. Exchange paragraphs, outlines, and peer review forms with your peer.
2. Carefully examine each other's paragraphs and outlines, completing the review form as you go.
3. Exchange and discuss the review forms and the paragraphs.

A word about attitude and intellectual honesty: Remember that many people are sensitive to criticism, so try to be polite and constructive in your comments about any paper. For example, it's better to say "I think there may be a problem here" than "You messed up." Also, specific remarks are always more helpful than general ones; for example:

GENERAL	**I'm confused.**
SPECIFIC	**I don't understand what you mean by "important object." Can you provide more of a description?**

However, remember that your job is to provide *suggestions;* it is the writer's job to make decisions and corrections. Do not try to force your opinion or act like a know-it-all. On the other hand, don't be shy or lazy about identifying potential problems. If you are overly concerned about hurting the other person's feelings, or if you aren't serious about the work, your peer review may be ineffective.

When it's your turn to get comments on your work, pay attention to what the reviewer says and try not to be defensive. If you don't understand something, ask questions. Remember, the review process is a great opportunity to improve your work, so take full advantage of it.

Peer Review Form

1. Identify the topic sentence. How well does it express the main idea of this paragraph? If the topic sentence does not clearly express the main idea, what specific problems do you see?

2. Where might transitional expressions be added to the paragraph? Should any existing transitions be revised? If so, how?

3. List the support points. Is each one clearly stated in its own sentence? If not, describe the problem(s).

4. How well do the support points back up the main idea (topic sentence)? Does any support seem to be missing? If so, what type of additional support might be helpful?

5. Does the paragraph have any digressive details (details that do not fit)? If it does, identify them.

6. Did you find anything confusing? If so, what specifically?

7. What do you like best about this paragraph?

8. Do you have other recommendations for improving this paragraph?

Power Tip
For a list of transitional expressions, see page 159.

Power Tip
Inadequate development of ideas is a common problem in writing. If a peer believes that your main idea is inadequately supported, you might try some of the strategies discussed in Chapters 3 and 6 to generate more ideas and details for your topic.

Power Tip
Feel free to add your own questions to the peer review form, especially if you have concerns that are specific to a certain piece of writing (for example, "Did you laugh or groan at my description of my uncle's suit?").

ACTIVITY 3: Teamwork

Choose a paragraph that you wrote recently, perhaps in response to one of the activities in this book. (It should be a paragraph that you haven't yet shown to an instructor.) Then, follow these steps:

- Pair up with another student who has also chosen a paragraph.
- Trade papers and evaluate each other's writing, using the peer review form on page 213.
- Next, return the evaluations and paragraphs and ask each other any questions about the evaluations. (For example, if something isn't clear, you might say, "I'm not sure what you mean by __________. Could you please explain or give me an example?")
- Revise your paragraphs, based on the feedback.

Teaching Tip
PeerFactor, an online, interactive peer review game with other resources, is available with this text.

This peer review form is also available on this text's Web site at **bedfordstmartins.com/steppingstones**.

Proofreading for Grammar, Mechanics, and Word Choice

You may recognize this scenario: An hour before class, you begin to write a paper in response to an assignment. Surprisingly, you find the topic interesting and hammer out some original ideas. With seconds left on the clock, you print your work and dash off to class. A week later, when it's time to get your paper back from your instructor, you are hopeful that the grade will reflect your original thinking. Imagine your shock when you see the paper covered in red ink, with a *C+* at the top. The instructor's comment says it all: "Great ideas, but too many errors."

What went wrong? The answer is simple: you did not proofread, that is, read your writing slowly and carefully (word by word), as if with an imaginary magnifying glass, to identify mistakes. If you had reserved ten or fifteen minutes to review your composition for errors, your grade might have been significantly better.

This experience is all too common in college. Because we are busy or because we see proofreading as optional, we may skip this important final step of the revision process. However, not taking the time for this step is often the number one cause of grammar, mechanical, and wording errors in student writing. Proofreading is not difficult; with even a modest effort, most writers can identify and fix many errors in their writing. More difficult is the task of training ourselves to proofread *every time we write.*

PROOFREADING FOR GRAMMAR AND MECHANICS

Grammar problems are discussed in detail in Part Two of this book, so we will not address them in depth here. However, the chart on the next page previews important errors to be aware of.

When proofreading for grammar, look at the words between periods to make sure that they are, in fact, complete, correct sentences. Also, pay close attention to verbs to make sure that they are in the correct tense and properly formed.

Mechanics issues include spelling, punctuation, and formatting (such as using double-spacing when required). Spelling is discussed on page 222. For a review of punctuation, see Appendix B.

PROBLEM (and where it is covered in this book)	DEFINITION	EXAMPLE
Fragments (Chapter 11, page 294; Chapter 13, page 374; and Chapter 14, page 406)	a word group that is missing a subject or a verb or that does not express a complete thought	The fastest runner. [*The fastest runner* could be the subject of a sentence, but there is no verb expressing an action.] **Corrected:** The fastest runner won.
Run-ons (Chapter 12, page 335)	joining sentences together with no punctuation or joining words	The movie ended we left. **Corrected:** The movie ended. We left. OR The movie ended, and we left.
Comma splices (Chapter 12, page 335)	joining sentences together with just a comma	The movie ended, we left. **Corrected:** The movie ended. We left. OR The movie ended, and we left.
Mistakes in verb usage (Chapter 16)	These include a wide variety of errors, such as using the wrong tense (time) of a verb; the wrong form of a verb; or a verb that does not agree with (match) a subject in number	Yesterday, I go to the movies. [The sentence is in the past tense, but *go* is a present tense verb.] **Corrected:** Yesterday, I went to the movies.

PROOFREADING FOR WORD CHOICE (AND MISSING WORDS)

When proofreading for word choice, look at every word in your writing to make sure that it exactly expresses the meaning that you intended. (When you are unsure of a word's meaning, check the definition in a dictionary.) As discussed in previous chapters, you should also make sure that your words are

- appropriate for your audience (See Chapter 1, page 25.)
- as precise as possible (See Chapter 6.)
- as original as possible; in other words, avoid overused expressions, or clichés (See Chapter 6, page 199.)

Also, look out for words that are often confused because they sound alike. The following chart lists words that are commonly confused. Pay special attention to these words in your writing, and check their definitions and uses against the chart on pages 216–217.

Commonly Confused Words

WORDS/COMMON DEFINITIONS	EXAMPLES
accept: to take; to agree to **except:** excluding	I accept responsibility for the accident. Mara likes all vegetables except broccoli.
advice: a recommendation; words intended to be helpful **advise:** to give advice	We took your financial advice. You advise us to save more money.
affect: to have an impact on **effect:** an outcome or result	The storm did not affect our travel plans. The drugs had little effect on the patient.
brake: to stop or slow; a device used for this purpose **break:** to smash or cause something to stop working; a period of rest or an interruption in an activity	I brake my car before sharp turns. Be careful not to break the crystal vase. The factory workers took a break.
breath: air inhaled (taken in) and exhaled (pushed out) **breathe:** the act of inhaling and exhaling	I am always out of breath after the 5K race. It was hard to breathe in the hot, crowded room.
buy: to purchase **by:** next to	We buy a gallon of milk every week. Martino always sits by the door.
hear: to detect with the ears **here:** present; at this location	I hear our neighbor's car stereo every morning. Is Jeremy here, or did he already leave for work?
its: a possessive (showing ownership) form of *it* **it's:** a combination (contraction) of *it is* or *it has*	The company lost its lawsuit against the town. It's clear that couples therapy has improved my marriage; it's helped my husband and me express our emotions more freely.
knew: past tense of *know* (see below) **new:** recently introduced or created	Even as a child, I knew my parents were not perfect. The new convertible gleamed in the sunlight.
know: to understand or comprehend; to be acquainted with **no:** a negative expression (the opposite of *yes*)	I know how to swim. You know Jim. No, I can't go to the game with you.
lie: to recline **lay:** to put something down	Don't lie in the sun too long. Lay the clothes on the bed, not on the floor.
loose: not tight; not fully attached **lose:** to misplace; to be defeated	I wore loose-fitting clothes after gaining twenty pounds. The loose shingle flapped in the wind. I lose a cell phone every year. The Cavaliers cannot afford to lose this game.
mind: the part of a person that thinks and perceives **mine:** belonging to *me*	I couldn't get my mind around those math formulas. Those gloves on the chair are mine.
passed: went by (past tense of *pass*) **past:** the time before now	We passed the house twice before we realized it was Josie's. In the past, I drove to work every day.
peace: lack of conflict or war; a state of calm **piece:** a part of something	We must work for peace in a violent world. Have a piece of this delicious pie.

WORDS/COMMON DEFINITIONS	EXAMPLES
principal: the leader of a school or other organization; main or major	The principal addressed the school assembly. Our principal complaint is that we waited two hours for service.
principle: a law or standard	Professor Bates lectured on economic principles.
quiet: soundless or low in sound **quite:** very; fully **quit:** to stop	The room was quiet because the children were sleeping. We are quite happy with the decision. We are not quite there yet. Joe quit smoking a year ago.
right: correct; opposite of *left*	Margo is right that our seats are on the right side of the concert hall.
write: to put words down in a form that can be read (on paper or on a computer screen)	The soldier's daughter promised to write him an e-mail every day.
set: to put something somewhere **sit:** to be seated	I set the glasses on the counter. Please sit down.
than: a word used in comparisons **then:** at another time (not now); next	Doug is funnier than Kyle. They were not as wealthy then. Peel the apples. Then, cut them into thin slices.
their: belonging to them **there:** at a certain location; not here **they're:** a combination (contraction) of *they are*	Their car broke down twice this month. Please sit there. They're still in shock about winning the lottery.
threw: past tense of *throw* **through:** finished; going in one side and out the other	Shontelle threw the ball to Dave. We are through with exams. The Cartullos drove through the snowstorm.
to: in the direction of; toward **too:** also **two:** the number between one and three	Christina ran to the lake and back. My daughter wants to go to the movies too. Two swans glided on the pond.
use: to put into service or employ **used:** past tense of *use;* accustomed	I use a rubber glove to open jars that are stuck. Bill used butter in his cooking before his cholesterol got too high. Kent is used to getting up early.
weather: climate (pertaining to the absence or presence of sun, wind, rain, and so on)	The weather was beautiful during our vacation.
whether: a word used to present alternatives	I can't decide whether or not to go to the party.
whose: the possessive form of *who* **who's:** a combination (contraction) of *who is* or *who has*	I don't know whose car is parked in front of our house. Who's the actor who's just divorced his fifth wife?
your: belonging to you **you're:** a combination (contraction) of *you are*	Your phone is ringing. You're my best friend.

ACTIVITY 4

For each sentence, decide which words in parentheses are correct. Then, circle your choices.

EXAMPLE: **(Weather / Whether) or not tomorrow's (weather / whether) is nice, we will go on the picnic.**

1. You will (loose / lose) the bracelet if the clasp on it is (loose / lose).
2. In the (passed / past), I (passed / past) by your house on my daily walks.
3. If (your / you're) car isn't repaired by the weekend, (your / you're) welcome to use mine on Saturday.
4. A summer-long drought will (affect / effect) the community in many ways; the worst (affect / effect) will be limits on water usage.
5. I can't (accept / except) that every child in the neighborhood (accept / except) Martina has been invited to the party.
6. (Its / It's) likely that the citizen group will present (its / it's) petition to the city council on Wednesday.
7. After the children (quiet / quite / quit) yelling, the playground was (quiet / quite / quit) (quiet / quite / quit).
8. (Whose / Who's) the man (whose / who's) voice booms "In a world . . ." at the start of every movie preview?
9. Take my (advice / advise) and let Dan (advice / advise) you about your home renovation.
10. (Lie / Lay) your coat over the chair and (lie / lay) down for a while.

Another common writing problem is **wordiness**: using more words than necessary to communicate an idea. If you can eliminate unnecessary words, you'll get your ideas across to your reader by the most direct route. Be aware of the following common wordy expressions, and try to avoid them in your writing. Also, ask about every sentence that you write: "Could I say this in fewer words?"

Common Wordy Expressions

WORDY EXPRESSION	POSSIBLE REVISION
at that time	then
at the present time/at this point in time	now
avail yourself of	get/use
by means of	by
due to the fact of	because
for the reason that	because
in excess of	more than
in order to	to
in spite of the fact that	although
in the event that	if
regardless of the fact that	although

ACTIVITY 5

Edit this paragraph to eliminate wordiness. Edits may vary.

Because ~~Due to the fact that~~ many employees were out sick for more than ~~in excess of~~ ten days last winter, the company strongly urges that you get ~~avail yourself of~~ a flu shot this fall. To ~~In order to~~ get a shot, simply sign up for a time slot on the sheet in Marcus Trebu's office. Please try to show up promptly for the time slot ~~that you booked in advance~~. If you realize that you will not be able to show up then ~~at that time~~, please inform Marcus ~~of that fact~~ as soon as possible. If ~~In the event that~~ you have any questions, please ~~pick up the phone and~~ call Human Resources at extension 603. Thank you.

A final note: It is very common for writers to leave out words, especially when they are working quickly. After you have checked all of your word choices in a paragraph, read through your writing to make sure that no words are missing.

The author of the following paragraph found a number of errors through proofreading and peer review. Grammar errors are underlined, word choice or spelling problems are in bold, and places where words are missing are highlighted in yellow.

Power Tip
So that you do not overlook errors, consider proofreading for only one issue at a time. For example, you might proofread for grammar first, then for mechanics, then for word choice, then for missing words.

With **it's** signs of rebirth and renewal and all **it's** festivities, spring is my favorite season of the year. For one thing, spring is about celebration. My birthday is in spring. Birthdays special to me because my family and friends treat me a queen. They take me to my favorite restaurant, Café Sole, and buy me elegant like **earings** or lingerie. On the first day of May, I look forward to the party at my daughter's school. All the kids dress up like fairies and dance around the May pole. <u>Coming from a Persian family.</u> I also celebrate the Persian New Year. We welcome the summer solstice—the longest day of the year—on June 20th with a big family barbecue. Equally important, spring is time for spring cleaning. I get rid of my old clothes and household items that I no longer use. Sometimes, I have a yard sale with my next-door neighbor, which makes me even more motivated to purge my closets of unwanted junk. <u>Spring is the time to dig out the weeds and plant new flowers I love getting my hands in the soil and clearing the ground for my new flowerbed.</u> I also like to change my eating habits in the spring, knowing that bathing **suite** season is just around the corner. I clean out the refrigerator and the cabinets, getting rid of chips, candy, and old Pop-Tarts. Most important of all, I get physically active in the spring. I start doing things that I had put aside because of the rain and cold **whether**. For example, I renew my monthly gym membership and take spinning classes. If I cannot make it to the gym, I go for a fast-paced with my husband when

CONTINUED >

> he gets home from work. With all this exercising, my energy level goes up and feel good about myself. As a result, my husband and I get more romantic and physical. It seems that Mother Nature designed spring to be a mating season. It's no surprise that both of my children were **concieved** in the month of May and born January. And if that doesn't convince you that spring is my favorite season, probably nothing will.

Through proofreading, the writer quickly discovered the two grammar errors: a fragment (the first underlined error) and a run-on (the second underlined error). She fixed these problems and was ready to hand in her work. At the last minute, she asked a peer to read her paragraph. Fortunately, her classmate spotted several places where words seemed to be missing, and she thought that a few words might be misspelled or misused. The writer decided to take action, using special strategies to strengthen her proofreading:

- She used her computer's spell checker and grammar checker to help identify errors.
- She printed her paragraph and proofread it on paper.
- She proofread her paragraph backwards.
- She used a grammar guide.
- She reviewed her spelling log to identify words that she had misspelled in the past.

As a result, the writer identified six missing words and six word choice and spelling errors!

Why did she have so much trouble seeing these twelve errors? First, missing words are often difficult to spot because we *hear* the words in our head as we read silently, even if they aren't on the page. Just as this student did, you may need to adopt special proofreading strategies to detect missing words in your writing. Also, misspelled words can be hard to identify because we get in the habit of misspelling the same words over and over again. For this reason, dedicated writers keep a spelling log in which they record these words and their correct spellings.

SOME HELPFUL PROOFREADING STRATEGIES

Next, we'll take a closer look at the proofreading strategies just discussed (and a few others). These strategies have helped thousands of students to produce better writing.

Identify Your Style of Proofreading

To a certain degree, the way you proofread is a matter of personal style and choice. Some writers proofread *as they write:* sentence by sentence, they check their grammar, spelling, punctuation, and so on. As a result, their final, overall proofreading requires less time. Other writers prefer to get their ideas down quickly, *without stopping* to proofread each sentence. For these writers, the final, overall proofreading will be a more demanding job, and they must reserve extra time for it.

Identifying your style of proofreading can help you focus your energy and manage your time during the writing process. Whatever your preference, remember that a final, overall proofreading is essential for a polished composition.

Use Spelling and Grammar Checkers—but Cautiously

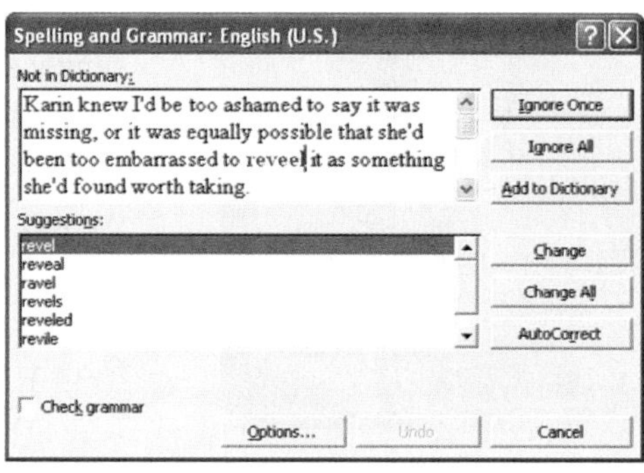

Many students who compose on a computer rely on spelling and grammar checkers to eliminate errors. However, it is important not to become overly dependent on these tools or use them without caution. For example, spell checkers may not always make the right choice, as in the example on the right, in which the correct replacement should be *reveal,* not *revel.*

Do not automatically select the first word on the replacement list; instead, take a moment to examine each word on the list until you have found the best match. If you are still unsure about the right choice, ask your instructor or a peer for advice, or check a dictionary.

Also, spell checkers will not identify words that are spelled correctly but misused, as often happens with the commonly confused words listed on pages 216–217.

Grammar checkers highlight possible grammar errors in your writing—for instance, with a green line. Often, this highlighting indicates major grammar errors, such as fragments, run-ons or comma splices, or subject-verb agreement problems. The checker also may prompt you with suggestions for fixing these errors. Once again, you should develop the habit of examining each proposed correction method. Not only will this help you make the right choice, it will build your grammar skills for those times when you do not have access to a grammar checker.

Finally, keep in mind that grammar checkers are not 100 percent accurate; they sometimes underline a sentence that is perfectly correct. Do not automatically assume that the grammar checker is right and your sentence is flawed. As your grammar awareness grows, you should begin to rely on your own judgment as much as you rely on the electronic correction tools.

Power Tip
Dictionaries are great tools for improving your spelling and for checking the definitions and proper usages of words. Invest in a portable dictionary or refer to online tools like **dictionary.com**. With **dictionary.com**, if you know the first few letters of a word but are unsure of the rest of the spelling, enter an asterisk (*) after the letters (for example, *acc** for *accidentally*). You'll get a list of words that begin with these letters, and their spellings.

Proofread in Two Views

Whenever possible, proofread your writing in *two views:* on the computer monitor and on the printed page. Each of these visual media will help you notice different details in your writing. If you proofread only on the screen, your eyes may miss quite a few errors.

After writing your composition and reading it on-screen, always print a draft and proofread *on the page.* It's a good idea to double-space your writing before you print it so that it's easier to read. Then, use a combination of pen, pencil, and/or highlighter to mark your errors. For example, you might highlight words whose spelling you need to look up in the dictionary, put a colored star by items you want to ask your instructor about, and use pencil to add missing words or make other edits. Next, go back to the computer and make any necessary corrections, consulting your instructor or other resources as needed.

Power Tip

As you practice proofreading backwards, try reading your sentences *out loud*. Pronouncing each word will force you to read more slowly and carefully, helping you to spot errors with greater ease.

Proofread Backwards

Most people would not think of riding a bicycle backwards down the street. Doing so would feel unnatural and perhaps confusing at first. However, it would certainly raise your awareness about your own body, the parts of the bicycle, and your surroundings. To advance safely and successfully, you would need to go slowly and pay careful attention to every part of the experience.

Similarly, most students would not think of proofreading their writing backwards. This too would feel unnatural and perhaps confusing at first. However, writers who use this strategy find that it raises their awareness about their grammar, word choice and word order, spelling, and punctuation. Proofreading one sentence at a time—starting with the *last* sentence of your composition—will force you to go slowly and pay careful attention to each sentence.

When we proofread a composition in the customary way—from top to bottom—we get caught up in the flow of our ideas. This momentum—just like the momentum of riding a bicycle forward—makes it difficult for us to slow down and pay careful attention to the fine points of our writing. When we proofread backwards, we interrupt the flow of our ideas, allowing us to focus more effectively on our sentence construction.

Teaching Tip

If your students are using a particular handbook, spend some class time pointing out important features, such as the index or page tabs, that will help them find what they need.

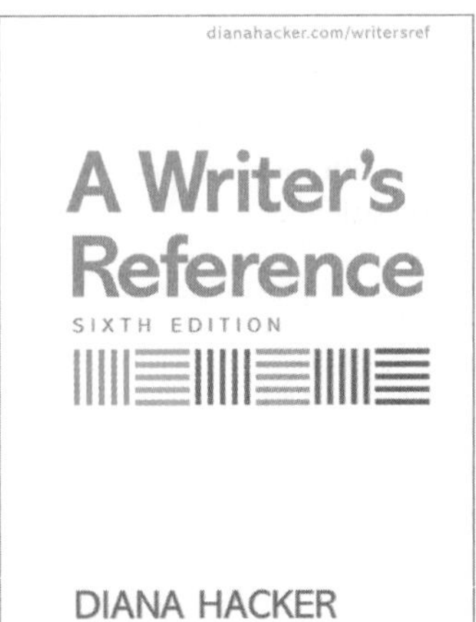

Use a Grammar Guide

In proofreading your writing, have you ever *suspected* a grammar error but could not be sure? If so, you are not alone. Many college students lack confidence in identifying their grammar mistakes. For this reason, it is helpful to keep a grammar guide beside you when proofreading. This guide can be a brief list of reminders, like the one on page 215. It can also be a separate grammar handbook. If you use a handbook, you should flag or paper-clip pages that cover how to recognize and fix common and serious errors, such as fragments, run-ons and comma splices, and verb errors. Refer to these same pages every time you proofread.

Keep Logs for Spelling, Grammar, and Vocabulary

If you frequently misspell words, keeping a spelling log is a quick and easy strategy to improve your writing. Here's how to do it: when you discover that you have misspelled a word (perhaps because of an instructor's or peer's comments), take a few seconds to write down *both* your incorrect spelling and the correct spelling in your log, which might be set up like the one on the next page.

Log of Spelling Errors			
Student ______		Course ______	
Paper Title ______ Date ______		Paper Title ______ Date ______	
Incorrect Spelling	Correct Spelling	Incorrect Spelling	Correct Spelling
1.		1.	
2.		2.	
3.		3.	
4.		4.	
5.		5.	
6.		6.	
7.		7.	
8.		8.	
9.		9.	
10.		10.	

You should also *re-log* a word each time you misspell it; this repetition will help you master the correct spelling more quickly.

You might also keep a log of your grammar errors. Each time your instructor marks a grammar error in your writing, copy the entire incorrect sentence in the log. Then, rewrite the sentence, correcting the error. If you like, you can organize your log according to types of errors (fragments, run-ons, verb errors, and so on).

Additionally, to help build your vocabulary—an important strategy for college success—consider keeping a vocabulary log. Each time you read an unfamiliar word, look up its meaning in the dictionary. Then, write the word and its definition in your vocabulary log. You might also want to write down the sentence in which you first discovered the word.

If you've never kept a log before, start with just one, selecting the issue (spelling, grammar, or vocabulary) that is the most important for your writing.

Teaching Tip
Have students write journal entries or brief reflective papers on what they would like to improve in their papers and what they have learned about the revision process by trying some of the strategies in this chapter. This exercise encourages critical thinking and greater engagement with the revision process.

Teaching Tip
If you are concerned that students will not be able to identify grammar errors until they have worked with Part Two of this book, you might have them start or revisit this activity after they have worked through some of the grammar chapters.

ACTIVITY 6

For each paragraph below, do the following:

- Proofread backwards, starting with the last sentence and examining one sentence at a time. Edit errors that you find. (You might want to consult the brief grammar chart on page 215 or some other grammar guide.)
- Start a spelling, grammar, or vocabulary log and record the errors there.

In this paragraph, look for one fragment, one run-on, one comma splice, two verb errors, three missing words, and five misspelled or misused words.

1. Although I do not make a lot of money, I have developed habits that will ensure my financial security. First of all, I carefully ~~monetor~~ monitor how much I spend. I have figured out how much extra money I have every month after ~~necesary~~ necessary expenses (rent, food, utilities, and so on), and I never spend more than that~~, in~~. In fact, I make sure that I have a "cushion" of extra money in my bank account in case an emergency expense, like a car repair bill, arises. Second, I avoid~~s~~ luxuries unless it is a special occasion. For example, I do not eat out unless it is my birthday, a friend's birthday, or some other special event. Also, I rented movies instead of going to the theater and spending a lot on tickets, popcorn, and soda. In addition, I do not ~~by~~ buy expensive cosmetics and face creams. [Added period] I make my own moisturizers with natural ingredients~~. Like~~ like olive oil and beeswax. Most important, I contribute regularly to my savings. I have joined my company's 401(k) plan, and money for this comes directly out of my pay so that I am not tempted to spend it. Also, I try to contribute money to my savings account whenever I can. I may never be rich, but because I have ~~excepted~~ accepted personal responsibility for my finances, I am ~~confedent~~ confident that I will never have to worry about money.

In this paragraph, look for two fragments, two comma splices, one run-on, three verb errors, two missing words, and three misspelled or misused words.

2. My grandfather influenced me more than anyone else in my life. In the first place, he was the role model for my life. My father ~~die~~ died when

For online practice with finding and fixing spelling errors, visit this book's Web site at **bedfordstmartins .com/steppingstones**.

I was four, before I could really get to know him, but my grandfather stepped ~~write~~ right into the role of father~~. Teaching~~, teaching me Italian (my grandfather's native language), piano, and soccer~~, in~~. In fact, he so influenced me musically that I work as a musician today, giving piano lessons and performing with traveling jazz and rock musicians who come into town. In the second place, Grandpa taught me what it means to be a gentleman~~, he~~. He had fine manners, always ~~listning~~ listening politely to others and asking them questions about themselves. Also, he held doors open for ladies, gave up his seat on the bus for expecting mothers, and ~~helping~~ helped elderly neighbors in his apartment building carry groceries upstairs—even when he was ~~quiet~~ quite old himself! To grandfather, dressing well was also a form of good manners, and he never went to any public place, even the grocery store, without wearing a suit and fedora hat. Because of him, I always ~~tries~~ try to be polite to others and to dress my best~~. Whenever~~ whenever I am performing or going to any important place. Finally, Grandpa taught me the value of humor. ~~he~~ He was a quiet and dignified man, but if he thought that anyone was acting prejudiced or "like a big shot," he would wink at me and say to the person, "You'll have to excuse me, but I'm hard of hearing." Of course, his hearing was perfect. My grandfather influenced me in many other ways, too, but it would take me a book to describe all of them. Although he passed away last year at ninety-two, I will always love and treasure him, and I hope that I am half as good a role model to my children as he was to me.

ACTIVITY 7

Refer to the paragraph(s) you worked on for Activity 2 or to any paragraph that you developed in Chapters 5 and 6. Then, proofread your writing backwards, fixing any errors that you find. Consider recording errors in a spelling, grammar, or vocabulary log.

Bringing It All Together

In this chapter, you have learned about revising and proofreading strategies that will help you improve any paper. Check off each of the following statements that you understand. For any that you do not understand, review the appropriate pages in this chapter.

☐	**Unified** paragraphs stay on track and include only information that supports the main idea as expressed in the topic sentence. (See page 204.)
☐	**Revision** ("re" + "vision") means looking over your paragraphs with a fresh eye to identify and fix any problems with unity. (See page 204.)
☐	**Unity** can be disrupted when there is a flawed topic sentence, an unstated or unclear support point, a missing transitional expression, or digressive (unrelated) details. (See page 204.)
☐	Helpful revision strategies include revising with fresh eyes, using your outline to check for unity, and getting comments from a **peer**. (See page 211.)
☐	It is important to proofread for grammar, mechanics, and word choice to avoid careless errors that can lower your grade. **Proofreading** is reading your writing slowly and carefully (word by word), as if with an imaginary magnifying glass, to identify mistakes. (See page 214.)
☐	Helpful proofreading strategies include identifying your style of proofreading, using spelling and grammar checkers (but cautiously), proofreading backwards, using a grammar guide, and keeping logs for spelling, grammar, and vocabulary. (See page 221.)

Chapter 8

Moving from Paragraphs to Essays

OVERVIEW OF THIS CHAPTER

WARM-UP Planning a Toast

1. Imagine this situation:

Your Great Aunt Betty and her husband, Uncle Bart, are celebrating their fiftieth wedding anniversary, and their daughter Mae has been planning a party for them for months. On the evening before the event, Mae calls to tell you that she has come down with pneumonia and that she needs you to organize the toast for Betty and Bart. Fortunately, Mae's other brothers and sisters will help with the other details of the party.

The complicated part is that fifteen of Betty and Bart's friends are flying in from all over the country, and most of them want to make toasts. Some of them are old school friends of the couple, some know Betty and Bart from the assembly plant where they both worked, and another group lived in their old neighborhood. You will need to meet with the toasters at the start of the party and organize them in some way.

2. Stop and think!

Working alone or with classmates, think of how you might organize the speakers. One clear way of organizing the speakers is by how they know Betty and Bart. You could divide them into three groups this way and invite the groups to come up to the front of the hall separately when it's their time to speak. You might even say a few words to introduce each group to the audience.

Similarly, when a piece of writing includes a lot of ideas that can be grouped into categories, you might want to break it into separate paragraphs of related ideas. Doing so organizes your ideas clearly for your readers. Multiple-paragraph writings are known as *essays*. This chapter will help you understand the differences between paragraphs and essays, how to develop paragraphs within essays, and what features to include in any essay.

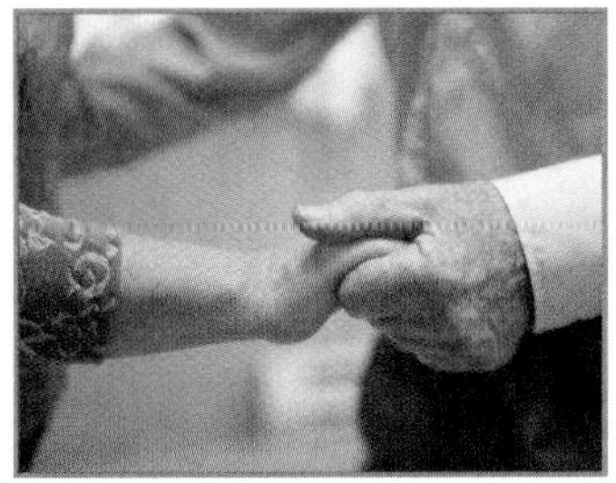

Understanding the Difference between Paragraphs and Essays

So far, you have learned the basic features of an academic *paragraph:*

- It is well developed, usually more than five *sentences.*
- It is carefully organized, with a main idea and a series of support points.
- It is grammatically correct.

Notice now that the academic *essay* (a freshman-level college essay) has similar features:

- It is well developed, usually three or more *pages.*
- It is carefully organized, with a main idea and a series of support points.
- It is grammatically correct.

In addition, most instructors will require a standard college essay to include the following:

- **an introduction:** an opening paragraph that includes the main idea, known as the **thesis statement**
- **two or more "body" paragraphs:** fully developed academic paragraphs that develop the support points
- **a conclusion:** a paragraph that may restate the main idea or make some other observation

Because you have already mastered the basics of the academic paragraph, you have an important head start in mastering the academic essay.

COMPARING THE STRUCTURES OF PARAGRAPHS AND ESSAYS

In the following example, notice how the same outline serves as the basis for *both* a paragraph and an essay. However, the amount of ideas, examples, and details is much greater in the essay. (In both the paragraph and the essay, the main ideas are highlighted in orange, and the support points are highlighted in purple.)

The Outline

MAIN IDEA	I am a responsible family member.
TRANSITIONAL EXPRESSION	First,
SUPPORT POINT 1	I help out financially. – rent – extras – emergencies
TRANSITIONAL EXPRESSION	Second,
SUPPORT POINT 2	I am a good role model for my siblings. – study habits – advice on love – unselfish acts
TRANSITIONAL EXPRESSION	Last,
SUPPORT POINT 3	I respect my parents. – no arguing – obey their rules – honor their beliefs

The Paragraph

Although I am not a perfect son or brother, I believe I am a responsible member of my family. First, I help out financially whenever I can. For example, from the pay for my part-time job, I give my parents $100 each month to help with the rent. Also, on the weekends, I pay for movie rentals and take-out pizza because I know that my parents can't afford extras. In an emergency, my family can always count on me. Last year, when my father's car got impounded, I took all the money from my savings account so he could get it back and drive to work. Second, I am a good role model for my younger siblings. For instance, I sit with them every night and do my college homework while they do their homework. In addition, my brother needs lots of advice about women, and since I am an expert, I always tell him how to treat the ladies with respect. I also change my schedule when possible to drive my sister to school and soccer practice so she doesn't have to take the bus. Last, I respect my parents. I try never to argue with them about things like yard work or girlfriends. I obey their rules, like the midnight curfew on weekends, because I know that the rules are for my benefit. Plus, I honor their religious beliefs even though I don't worship with them anymore. I know that my parents and siblings love me and appreciate my contributions to our family.

The Essay

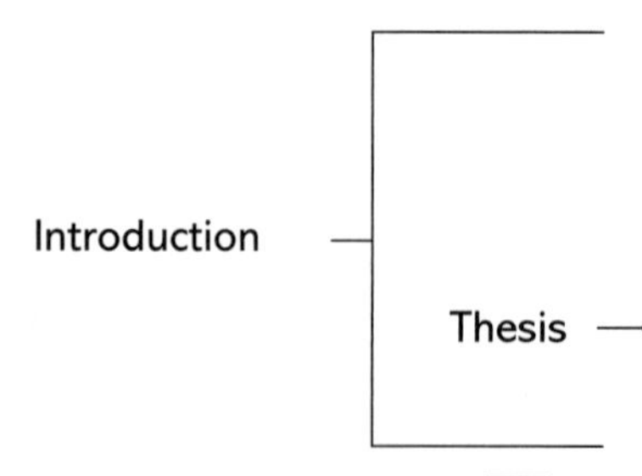

What if you woke up one day and you had no family? How would your life change if all of the love and support that you receive from your family members were suddenly gone? I never forget for a second that my family is the greatest treasure I have in life, and I honor this privilege through my actions. By giving financial support, being a role model for my siblings, and respecting my parents, I demonstrate that I am a responsible family member.

Power Tip

Notice that you start a new paragraph by indenting, that is, adding space before the first sentence. This space shows readers that you are beginning a new block of related ideas.

Teaching Tip

The thin blue underlining constitutes the answers to the questions in Activity 2 on page 232.

Body paragraphs

Although I work only part-time at Office Depot, I try to help my family financially whenever I can. To begin with, I contribute to the rent. When I got my first paycheck three years ago, I was very proud to give half of it to my mother for the rent. She was surprised and tried to refuse, but I told her that I wanted to make things easier for her and my dad. One year ago, we had to move to a new apartment, and the rent was almost double our old rent. That was when I increased my monthly contribution to $100. I also helped pay the security deposit, which was two months' rent. Also, I like to buy some "extras" that I know my parents can't afford. For instance, every Friday night I go to Blockbuster and rent two movies; then, I stop and get take-out pizza on the way home. At Christmas, I make sure that there are a lot of small presents under the tree. These gifts aren't expensive, but they always make my family happy. When my brother or sister needs to buy school supplies or soccer uniforms, I tell them to ask me for the money so my parents won't feel added pressure. In addition, I always support my family in a financial emergency if I can. Last year, I had saved $700 to buy a laptop for school. When my father's car got impounded, I didn't hesitate to take out all my savings and help him get back his car, which he needed for work. When my grandmother in Guatemala needed emergency back surgery, I contributed $200 to pay for the operation. Also, my mother was suffering once with a horrible toothache. She didn't want to spend the money to see the dentist, but I drove her there anyway and paid the bill myself. Spending money on my family is always the right thing to do.

Another way I am responsible in my family is by being a good role model for my younger siblings. To begin with, since I am the first person in our family to attend college, I try to demonstrate good study habits to my brother and sister. Every night after dinner, I sit down with Alfred and Hilaria, and we do our homework together. I show them my techniques of reviewing the assignments, organizing my materials, and planning my time. They watch my patience and concentration and try to adapt this behavior in their own work. I also enjoy tutoring Alfred when he needs help with his algebra homework. Next, I give advice to my siblings in matters of love. Because Alfred is fifteen, he needs lots of advice about women, and since I am somewhat of an expert, I always tell him how to treat the ladies with respect but not to get pushed around either. I tell him to be honest with them and to be a good listener. My sister Hilaria always asks me what boys are thinking, which is a tough question. Finally, I try to set a good example of unselfishness for my brother and sister. For example, if I'm on the computer surfing the Web, I will always ask them if they need to use the computer for schoolwork. I get them to help me pick up around the house so my parents don't have to come home to a messy environment. Also, I change my schedule when I can to drive my sister to school and soccer practice so she doesn't have to take the bus. I enjoy being a role model for my siblings because I can see them maturing into thoughtful and considerate people.

Respecting my parents is a third way I am a responsible family member. In the first place, I have a record of not arguing with my parents, no matter what. For example, my dad can be very picky about the way I do the yard work. If he's tired when he gets home, he sometimes complains that our yard doesn't look as nice as our neighbors' yards. I could argue that my priorities are school and work, but I just keep a positive attitude and tell him I'll try to do better. Since my mother wants me to marry a Latina woman, she came up with this crazy rule that the only girls I can invite to the house are Latinas. I could argue and say that her attitude is racist, but I just smile and say that *Cupido* will decide whom I marry. In the second place, I obey the rules that my parents set. I do not, for instance, invite any girls to the house who are not Latina, even though I disagree with this policy. I stay enrolled as a full-time student and keep my work hours to twenty or fewer per week because my parents ask me to. On weekends, I am always home before the midnight curfew. Last, I honor my parents' beliefs as much as possible. The belief that is most important to them is their faith in God. I no longer worship with them, but I show respect for their religious practices. They also believe that our Guatemalan heritage is important to preserve. Even though I'm a typical American teenager, I've taken ethnic studies classes on Latin America, and I keep up with news about Guatemala on the Internet to support my parents' views. One value that I have no trouble embracing is my parents' work ethic. They know, and I know, that the only way for us to attain the American dream is through hard work and determination.

Body paragraphs

I always consider it a privilege to be a responsible family member, not a burden. If it were not for my family, I would not be the happy and successful person I am today. Writing this essay only reminds me of how precious my family is to me, and it renews my conviction to always do more for them.

Conclusion

ACTIVITY 1

Compare the previous paragraph to the essay by answering the following questions.

1. What support point becomes paragraph 2 of the essay?
   the first support point
2. What support point becomes paragraph 3 of the essay?
   the second support point
3. What support point becomes paragraph 4 of the essay?
   the third support point

ACTIVITY 2

Continue your comparison from Activity 1 by answering the following questions.

1. Look at support point 1 in the outline and notice how it is developed in the individual paragraph on page 229 and in paragraph 2 of the essay on page 230. What new examples and details have been added to the essay paragraph? Underline them.
2. Look at support point 2 in the outline and notice how it is developed in the individual paragraph on page 229 and in paragraph 3 of the essay on page 230. What new examples and details have been added to the essay paragraph? Underline them.
3. Look at support point 3 in the outline and notice how it is developed in the individual paragraph on page 229 and in paragraph 4 of the essay on page 231. What new examples and details have been added to the essay paragraph? Underline them.

Teaching Tip
Visual metaphors may help students understand the differences between paragraphs and essays. For example, students might think of a paragraph as a studio apartment, in which the kitchen area, living area, and sleeping area are in one space. An essay can be compared to a house, where each area gets its own room, with more furniture and other objects in each room.

NAMING THE PARTS OF PARAGRAPHS AND ESSAYS

Although the organization of an essay mirrors the organization of a paragraph, we use different names to identify the features of a paragraph and the features of an essay. Although the names are different, the basic purpose of each feature remains the same.

FEATURE	. . . IN A PARAGRAPH	. . . IN AN ESSAY
Main idea →	Topic sentence →	Thesis statement
Support point 1 →	Support point 1 →	Topic sentence 1
Support point 2 →	Support point 2 →	Topic sentence 2
Support point 3 →	Support point 3 →	Topic sentence 3
Conclusion →	Concluding sentence →	Concluding paragraph

Teaching Tip
As additional practice, you might ask students to write outlines of other essays, such as the ones in the reader at the end of this book.

ACTIVITY 3

Read the following essay. Then, underline or highlight the thesis statement and the three topic sentences. Next, underline or highlight the support points in each body paragraph. Finally, fill in the outline for the essay based on the key features that you underlined or highlighted.

Last week, I had one of the most stressful work days that I can remember. After handling hours of customer phone calls, tedious paperwork, and a conflict with a difficult co-worker, I had a pounding headache and was in a terrible mood. Then, during the last hour of my shift, one of my favorite songs from my teen years came on the radio in my work space, and I was transported back to a sunny summer day on the beach with my friends. Before I knew it, my headache was gone, and I felt renewed. At that moment, I was reminded of how essential music is to my life.

Music is said to have healing qualities, and I know from my own experience that that is true. In the first place, when I have a headache or sinus pain, I use classical music to relieve my discomfort. In particular, I love piano composer Frédéric Chopin's *Nocturnes;* the gentle melodies caress every nerve and cell in my body, and the delicate piano strokes ease my pain more effectively than ibuprofen or Tylenol. Also, Beethoven's soothing "Für Elise" is my favorite remedy for a migraine. Furthermore, I sometimes suffer from anxiety and depression. In these instances, I listen to soulful songs, like "Bridge over Troubled Water" by Simon and Garfunkel or "Imagine" by John Lennon. The lyrics in these songs talk about hardship and hope, and they are filled with a wonderful humanity that helps me put my own difficulties in a more realistic perspective. It's as though the singer's voice reaches out to me across space and time, giving me strength to go on with my life. In addition, music helps relax me when I am overwhelmed by school or work. Instead of stressing out about an exam or a meeting with my boss, I turn on my iPod and listen to meditation music. The sounds of wind chimes or Native American flutes calm me and refocus my energy on the task at hand. Usually, taking a few minutes to meditate along with the music means I will perform better on an exam or communicate more successfully at work.

Music can also make memories as vivid as the present. For starters, country tunes remind me of growing up in Texas. When I hear a song by Loretta Lynn or Hank Williams, I can taste chicken-fried steak or cold root beer in the summer. Also, the rhythms of bluegrass take me back to Saturday night dances. Furthermore, opera music makes me recall my Grandpa Sid. Sid loved to sing along with the great arias, like "Nessun Dorma" and "Una Furtiva Lagrima." I used to swing on the front porch and listen to him croon those songs while he worked around our family farm. Sometimes, he would pretend he was a lady opera singer and imitate a dramatic aria. My cousins and I always fell on the floor laughing. Finally, nature's music reminds me of the farm. The sounds of the wind sifting through the fields, of birds singing, and of crickets chirping bring the peace of the farm back to me whenever I think of them.

arias: songs, often emotional or inspiring, that are part of operas

Best of all, music takes me out of my own small world and inspires me. To begin, when I have time for a long bath or shower, I play a CD with sounds of nature. The gentle trickling of a waterfall and the calls of tropical birds and monkeys transport me to exotic jungles. Furthermore, when I have to write an essay for school, I listen to upbeat or inspirational music to get energy and ideas. For instance, the B-52's' "Roam" always gets me excited and ready to work.

CONTINUED >

Also, songs about social problems and other issues give me ideas for writing. For example, after listening to John Gorka's "Houses in the Fields," about suburban sprawl, I was inspired to write about this topic for a sociology course. Last, when I listen to music from other countries, it takes me to other places and cultures that I might not get to otherwise, and I get new perspectives. For example, when I listen to African musician Salif Keita's songs, I can't understand the words, but I feel connected to the emotions, and I have been inspired to learn more about his home country of Mali.

Whenever I feel mentally or physically stressed, I know that I can count on music to restore me and give me hope. It truly is the best medicine for me.

Thesis: At that moment, I was reminded of how essential music is to my life.

Topic sentence 1: Music is said to have healing qualities, and I know from my own experience that that is true.

- Classical music: eases headaches or sinus pain
- Soulful songs: help with anxiety and depression
- Meditation music: calms stress

Topic sentence 2: Music can also make memories as vivid as the present.

- Loretta Lynn and Hank Williams: food memories
- bluegrass: Saturday dances
- opera: Grandpa Sid
- nature's music: family farm

Topic sentence 3: Best of all, music takes me out of my own small world and inspires me.

- sounds of nature: transport writer to exotic jungles
- upbeat or inspirational music: gives energy and ideas
- music from other countries: gives perspectives on other places and cultures

ACTIVITY 4

Working backwards, write a single paragraph based on the essay in Activity 3. You will have to eliminate some examples and details to reduce the essay to a paragraph. Try to keep the examples and details that seem most important for illustrating the support points. **Note:** Because this is an exercise rather than a writing assignment calling for original ideas, you may copy the wording from the essay if you wish.

Knowing When to Write an Essay

How do you know when to write an essay instead of an individual paragraph? The advice on the following pages will help guide you.

BY DESIGN

Most college essays are written "by design." In other words, your instructor specifically asks you to write an essay, and you must plan accordingly. Your main idea and support points should be developed with a complete essay in mind.

To better understand your task, imagine that you are an architect, and your client has asked you to design a dream home. In your design, you must plan for *all the parts* of a desirable house: living and dining rooms, kitchen, bedrooms, bathrooms, garage, and so on. Similarly, when your instructor asks you to write an essay, you must plan for a complete essay with all its necessary parts—the introduction, thesis, body paragraphs, and a conclusion. If you leave out one or more of these parts, you will not succeed with your assignment.

Teaching Tip
Have students write about their dream home for a paragraph or an essay.

We will begin by discussing how to find an appropriate main idea (thesis) for an essay and how to develop the support for the main idea. Later in this chapter, you will learn how to write an introduction containing the thesis, as well as body paragraphs and the conclusion (page 247).

Finding the Main Idea

As you learned in Chapter 2, selecting an appropriate main idea for an assignment is a crucial step in the writing process. When planning an essay, select a main idea and support points that will give you enough to write about in three to five pages. If your main idea is too narrow, you may not be able to develop enough ideas, examples, and details for a complete essay. Here's a brief example:

> **Topic (assignment):** Write about a parent or guardian.
>
> **Narrowed topic:** my mother
>
> **Main idea for a paragraph:** My mother is an excellent cook.

My mother is an excellent cook seems like an appropriate main idea for an academic paragraph. For your support points, you might discuss your mother's knowledge of recipes, her use of quality ingredients, and her inventiveness in creating new dishes. In a well-developed paragraph, you should be able to include enough examples and details to illustrate these points convincingly.

Power Tip
If your mother is a very accomplished cook, perhaps even a professional cook or a chef, you might write a complete essay based on this main idea. The best way to determine whether a main idea is appropriate for a paragraph or an essay is to begin generating ideas; the quantity and quality of your ideas should help you make a wise decision. For more on generating ideas, see Chapter 3.

> **Main idea for an essay:** My mother has been a positive influence in my life.

My mother has been a positive influence in my life seems like an appropriate main idea for a complete essay. For example, you might write separate paragraphs on how she has influenced your sense of style and taste, how she has guided you in your romantic relationships, and how she has taught you to be a strong, independent person.

Teaching Tip
If you teach in a classroom with Internet access, students might do quick research on some of the topics in Activities 5 and 6.

ACTIVITY 5: Teamwork

With your classmates, discuss which main ideas seem more appropriate for a paragraph or an essay. It is OK to disagree. Then, decide for yourself whether you would feel more comfortable writing a paragraph or an essay on each topic and write "paragraph" or "essay" in the space provided. *Answers will vary.*

1. **Topic:** U.S. cities

   Narrowed topic: Las Vegas

   Main idea for a ______________________: If I want to have fun, I go to Vegas.

   Main idea for a ______________________: Las Vegas has changed greatly in the last twenty years.

   Main idea for a ______________________: Las Vegas is entertaining, even if you don't like gambling.

2. **Topic:** being an American

   Narrowed topic: civil rights

   Main idea for a ______________________: Freedom of speech is a civil right that I exercise every day.

   Main idea for a ______________________: Civil rights in America are more protected than civil rights in other countries.

   Main idea for a ______________________: The 1960s marked an important turning point in the history of U.S. civil rights.

ACTIVITY 6: Teamwork

With your classmates, try to develop two main ideas for each topic: one that is appropriate for a paragraph and one that is appropriate for an essay. It is OK to disagree about whether a particular main idea is best suited to a paragraph or an essay. *Answers will vary.*

1. **Topic:** gender roles

   Narrowed topic: stay-at-home husbands

   Main idea for a paragraph: ______________________

   Main idea for an essay: ______________________

2. **Topic:** managing your finances

   Narrowed topic: credit cards

   Main idea for a paragraph: ______________________

   Main idea for an essay: ______________________

Generating Support

Once you have identified your main idea, you can use clustering, listing, or freewriting to generate ideas. (You might want to review these strategies, which are discussed in Chapter 3.) Remember that you will need to generate more ideas for an essay than for a paragraph; therefore, you will probably have to devote more time to this step.

For online practice with suitable topics for paragraphs versus essays, visit this book's Web site at **bedfordstmartins.com/steppingstones.**

ACTIVITY 7

From Activities 5 and 6, select *one* main idea *for an essay.* Then, on a separate sheet of paper, spend at least twenty minutes generating ideas for your choice.

Writing an Advanced Outline

As you have already seen, the same outline can be the basis of a paragraph or an essay (see page 229). However, some students prefer to prepare a more detailed (advanced) outline for their essays. The transition from a basic to an advanced outline is very logical. Each support point in the basic outline becomes a main idea (topic sentence) for a separate paragraph; the examples become the new support points. Finally, new examples must be added to the advanced outline. Look at the following outlines, which are based on the paragraph and essay on pages 229–231:

Basic Outline (Paragraph)

MAIN IDEA I am a responsible family member.

TRANSITIONAL EXPRESSION First,

SUPPORT POINT 1 I help out financially.
- rent
- extras
- emergencies

TRANSITIONAL EXPRESSION Second,

SUPPORT POINT 2 I am a good role model for my siblings.
- study habits
- advice on love
- unselfish acts

TRANSITIONAL EXPRESSION Last,

SUPPORT POINT 3 I respect my parents.
- no arguing
- obey their rules
- honor their beliefs

Advanced Outline (Essay)

THESIS I am a responsible family member.

TOPIC SENTENCE 1 I help out financially.

SUPPORT POINT 1 I contribute to the rent.
- gave half of first paycheck for rent
- increased rent contribution to $100
- helped with security deposit

SUPPORT POINT 2 I pay for "extras."
- movies and pizza
- Christmas gifts
- school supplies/uniforms

SUPPORT POINT 3 I help out in emergencies.
- father's car impounded
- grandmother's surgery
- mother's dental work

TOPIC SENTENCE 2 I am a good role model for my siblings.

SUPPORT POINT 1 I teach them good study habits.
- study together
- organization, time planning
- tutor my brother

SUPPORT POINT 2 I give them advice on love.
- respect women
- be honest/a good listener
- tell sister about boys

SUPPORT POINT 3 I try to act unselfishly.
- share computer
- pick up the house
- drive sister places

CONTINUED >

Advanced Outline (continued)

TOPIC SENTENCE 3	I respect my parents.
SUPPORT POINT 1	I don't argue with them. – about yard work – about the girls I date
SUPPORT POINT 2	I obey their rules. – girls I invite home – school and work – curfew
SUPPORT POINT 3	I honor their beliefs. – religion – Guatemalan culture – work ethic

If you write an advanced outline, it's a good idea to try to state main ideas (both the thesis statement and topic sentences) and support points as complete sentences. Doing so will help you to focus your ideas and express them precisely as you draft your essay. Examples do not have to be stated as complete sentences.

ACTIVITY 8

Comparing the two previous outlines, answer the following questions:

1. What is one "extra" that the writer pays for in his family? Answers could include movies and pizza, Christmas gifts, or school supplies and uniforms.
2. What happens to the phrase "no arguing" in the essay outline? It becomes a complete sentence.
3. Does support point 2 in the paragraph outline change when it becomes a topic sentence in the essay outline? No

   Explain why this item does or does not change. It is already stated as a complete main idea.
4. What are two examples of the author's unselfish behavior? Answers could include his sharing of the computer, picking up the house with his brother and sister, and driving his sister places.

ACTIVITY 9

Using the ideas that you generated for Activity 7, complete an advanced outline for the essay. You may write your outline on a separate sheet of paper or print an outline form from this book's Web site, at **bedfordstmartins.com/steppingstones**. Your instructor may provide additional guidelines for writing the essay.

ACTIVITY 10

Review the academic paragraphs that you have written for this class. Select one that you would like to expand into a complete essay. On a separate sheet of paper, generate some new examples and details that you can add. Then, complete an advanced outline for the essay. Your instructor may provide additional guidelines for writing the essay.

Teaching Tip
If you haven't already introduced any other specific requirements for essays, this is a good time to do so. For instance, you might want students to include particular information at the top of the first page or as labels on subsequent pages.

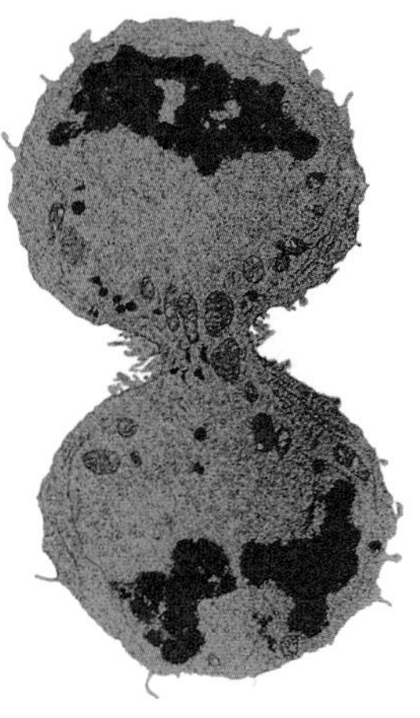

BY DIVISION

Sometimes, you may plan to write a paragraph, but the paragraph grows too large and must be divided into two or more separate paragraphs. This process is similar to cell division, which you may have learned about in a biology class.

As you can see in the photo, the original cell grows too large and begins to stretch, losing its form. Finally, the cell splits and becomes two separate cells, each with its own nucleus (the central part of a cell that controls its operations). Eventually, these new cells grow into fully developed cells.

If a paragraph grows too large and loses its form, you should split the paragraph into two separate paragraphs, each with its own topic sentence. You may add new examples and details to each new paragraph to develop it further.

Dividing a paragraph into two or more separate paragraphs is a natural part of the composition process, especially when you are writing longer essays. Experienced writers know when to divide a paragraph because they pay attention to two things: *what* they have to say and *how much* they have to say. As you develop greater awareness of these two aspects of your writing, you will feel more confident about splitting your own paragraphs.

Power Tip
This splitting usually occurs when you are writing multiple paragraphs for a longer assignment, such as an essay. However, if your instructor asks you to write a single paragraph, you should avoid splitting the paragraph. If your paragraph grows too large or loses its form, you will need to trim some examples and details, looking especially for any details that do not fit. For advice on eliminating digressive details, see Chapter 7, page 207.

What You Have to Say

Although you begin a paragraph with one main idea in mind, you may discover a new main idea emerging. When this happens, what you have to say may dictate that you need to divide the original paragraph into separate paragraphs.

Look at the following example, in which the writer discovered a new main idea emerging as she completed the development of her second support point. (The outline for the paragraph appears in the margin.)

> Working with other students in small groups can be an effective way to learn. To begin with, each student brings his or her special strengths to the group. For instance, I am good with organization, so I can usually show my classmates where their outlines need improvement. My best friend, Herve, has excellent critical reading skills, so he can point out key ideas in the stories we read. In addition, there is usually at least one student in any group who can help the rest of us find and learn how to correct our grammar errors. Equally important, college students benefit from the variety of viewpoints expressed in small groups. I especially like collaborating with older students because of their greater life experience; their opinions often bring a more mature perspective to our discussions.

CONTINUED >

MAIN IDEA
Small-group work is a good way to learn.

SUPPORT POINT 1
Each student has special abilities.
- organization
- critical reading
- grammar

SUPPORT POINT 2
Each student has different perspectives.
- age-related perspectives
- gender perspectives
- ethnic perspectives

It's also amazing how differently women and men talk about issues. Listening to men's opinions about the best parenting strategies, for example, really helped me form my own opinions more clearly. Also, if students from different ethnic backgrounds are part of a group, they can contribute remarkably different perspectives. However, sometimes differences among students can cause tension in a group, and the results can be disastrous. Too many shy students in a group can also make a discussion challenging. Nevertheless, all these problems can be managed effectively, and it's usually worth the effort.

SUPPORT POINT 3

Groups can be more comfortable and sociable.

- the whole class isn't listening
- there's no teacher in the discussion
- you can make friends while learning

In the last three (highlighted) sentences, the writer has introduced new information that does not fit with the main idea of the paragraph; in other words, this information breaks the *unity* of the paragraph. (For more on unity and how it is achieved, see Chapter 7, page 204.) As a result, the highlighted information must be deleted, or the paragraph must be split. The writer has to decide whether the new information is important enough to become the main idea for a separate paragraph. (On page 243, we will work more closely with this paragraph to see how it can be broken into two separate and complete paragraphs.)

ACTIVITY 11: Teamwork

Read the following paragraph, underlining or highlighting the section where *what* the writer says may indicate a need to divide the paragraph. Once you have identified this section, discuss with your classmates whether this information should be eliminated or developed in a separate paragraph. (The outline for the paragraph appears in the margin.)

MAIN IDEA

The police in my town have improved their relationship with the community.

SUPPORT POINT 1

They became more involved in community outreach.

- school visits
- Little League coaching
- police station "open house"

SUPPORT POINT 2

They get out of the cop cars and closer to the public.

- pedestrian patrols
- bicycle cops
- officers on horseback

The police in my town used to be perceived as unfriendly and untrustworthy; however, in the last three years, they have taken measures to improve their reputation and their relationship with the community. First, they became more involved in neighborhood outreach. Officers now visit the local elementary and high schools on a regular basis to talk to students about police work. They let students sit in the squad car and examine all the instruments, such as tracking devices, night vision gear, and sirens and speakers. Modern technology has made police operations more efficient and effective. Officers can access records databases, track suspects with global positioning systems, and use state-of-the-art forensics tools. The police also started coaching Little League baseball teams, which helps them develop trust with the local kids. Also, there is a monthly "open house" at the police station, where residents can come to socialize with the officers and their families. Next, our local police have found creative ways to get out of the cop cars and get closer to the public. For example, in the crowded shopping districts, we have pedestrian patrols; walking the beat allows the officers a chance to stop and chat with people. In our suburban neighborhoods, we now see police on bicycles, even wearing shorts in the warm weather. Bike cops definitely look more friendly and less intimidating! The latest novelty is police on horseback, like the Canadian Mounties. I've only seen a few of them at parades and in the parks, but everyone loves them. Finally, the police are doing their part to improve race relations in our town. For instance, they have hired more Hispanic, African American, and Asian officers so that the force is truly multiracial. Also, all recruits must have race-sensitivity training. In July, officers participate in a World Heritage Festival, representing their racial or ethnic communities as part of the celebration. Thanks to all these efforts, police–community relations have never been better, and I hope that the situation will continue to improve.

SUPPORT POINT 3

They have helped race relations.

- hiring more minority officers
- race-sensitivity training
- World Heritage Festival

How Much You Have to Say

In the process of writing a paragraph, you may also discover that you have a lot to say about one of your support points—much more than you had planned. Sometimes, a support point may start to dominate the whole paragraph, leaving little room for the development of the remaining support points. In this case, *how much* you have to say may dictate that you need to divide the original paragraph into separate paragraphs.

Look at the following example, in which the writer discovered that a support point was beginning to dominate the paragraph. (The outline for the paragraph appears in the margin.)

Most of my friends love their cell phones, BlackBerrys, and MP3 players, but I think these devices are harmful to good communication. For starters, instead of turning off their cell phones, people allow them to interrupt important conversations. One thing that irritates me is that my study partners answer their cell phones even if we're reviewing for an exam. Furthermore, I recently quit dating a woman because every time we were getting comfortable, she would answer her cell phone, as if any call were more important than our relationship. My sales job is tougher too because of electronic communication devices. Clients don't hesitate to answer their phones during my sales pitch; sometimes, they even use a call as an excuse to walk away and not come back. Furthermore, handheld electronic devices make it more difficult to meet people. At the bus stop, I used to talk to strangers while waiting for the bus; I actually met my roommate this way. But nowadays, it's like a law that everyone at the bus stop must be talking on a cell phone or listening to an MP3 player. The same is true for the school cafeteria. Just a few years ago, strangers would share a table and strike up a conversation. Now, you can look like a loser if you sit at a table by yourself without having a cell phone at your ear. It's even common for several people to share a table while each one has a conversation on his or her cell phone. I remember when the gym was a great place to meet other people interested in health and fitness. We would trade tips and stories on the workout floor. Now, it seems like earbuds and MP3 players have become mandatory equipment; the sharing of training tips has been replaced by people singing to themselves. Meeting people to date is also a challenge because of these devices. One time, on the train to San Diego, I was having a conversation with a woman I'd just met. When her cell phone rang, she started talking and kept talking until her stop. She could have been the woman of my dreams, but I'll never know. The most notorious

MAIN IDEA

Electronic communication and entertainment devices are bad for communication.

SUPPORT POINT 1

They interrupt important conversations.

- study conversations
- personal conversations
- business conversations

SUPPORT POINT 2

They make it more difficult to meet people.

- strangers
- people with similar interests
- people to date

CONTINUED >

SUPPORT POINT 3

They trivialize communication.

- juvenile text messages
- shallow conversation
- earbud sharing

place for a cell phone to interrupt a potential romance, of course, is the clubs. It seems to make some women feel important when they answer a cell phone and interrupt a new encounter; I guess phone calls mean they are in high demand. Last, I believe that these devices trivialize communication. The juvenile text messages that my friends send to one another are a good example. Another example is the nonstop, shallow conversations people have—talking just to be talking. Also, two friends sharing earbuds has become a common sight; it's like the music does the communicating for them. It's clear that electronic communication and entertainment devices are here to stay, but we should not abuse them or allow them to completely replace good old-fashioned face-to-face conversations.

Here, the second support point dominates the paragraph. (The development of this point is highlighted in yellow.) As a result, some of these details must be deleted, or the paragraph must be split. The writer has to decide whether the support point is important enough to become the main idea for a separate paragraph. (On page 245, we will work more closely with this paragraph to see how it can be broken into two separate and complete paragraphs.)

ACTIVITY 12: Teamwork

Read the following paragraph, underlining or highlighting the section where *how much* the writer says may indicate a need to divide the paragraph. Once you have identified this section, discuss with your classmates whether this information should be eliminated or developed in a separate paragraph. (The outline for the paragraph appears in the margin.)

MAIN IDEA

Computers have improved my quality of life.

SUPPORT POINT 1

They offer great forms of entertainment.

- video games
- DVD viewing
- music

SUPPORT POINT 2

They help me save money.

- discount shopping
- eBay
- Skype

SUPPORT POINT 3

They help me save time.

- online banking and bill pay
- finding and renewing books
- renting DVDs

I earnestly believe that computers have improved the quality of my life. For starters, my favorite forms of entertainment are on the computer. I am a video game junkie, so I play *Unreal Tournament* and *SimCity* for hours. Also, I use my laptop to watch DVDs because I can take it wherever I go and stop it and start it whenever I want. With iTunes, I've downloaded my entire CD collection onto my computer, and I create specialized playlists for my different moods and activities. Next, the computer helps me find great deals and save money. I love discount shoe sites because I can find Teva sandals and other good brands at close-out prices. There is so much competition for business online that many shopping sites offer free shipping as well. Now, everybody knows that eBay is the biggest revolution in shopping. I bought a $900 Prada handbag in excellent condition for $240 on eBay. In addition, with Skype, I can talk to my friends and family in Singapore for free, saving me hundreds of dollars annually on my phone bills. Last, computers save me a lot of time. Instead of driving to the bank, parking, and waiting in line for a teller, I can access my checking and savings accounts online. Also, I don't waste time writing and mailing payment checks for my credit cards; instead, I keep all my accounts current with online autopay. There are plenty of other bills that I no longer pay by check, such as the cable, telephone, water, and power bills. With one click of a button, I can make instant online payments, and I don't even lose time balancing my checkbook because my online account calculates the deductions and deposits automatically. Renewing library books used to be a burden on my time. Now, with online renewals, I don't have to drive to the library when the books are due. I also receive an automatic e-mail reminder from the library before the due date, which means I don't have to waste time trying to remember when the books are due. Even finding books and other reading materials is more efficient with the computer. At my college library's Web site, I can access hundreds of electronic books and thousands of journal articles. Best of all, renting DVDs online is fast and efficient; I can browse title lists in seconds, and the DVDs are mailed directly to my home. I don't squander my time drifting through the aisles at the video store or standing in impossibly long lines while people argue with the clerks about their overdue accounts. Again, there's no doubt that computers have contributed to the quality and efficiency of my life, and I don't know what I would do without them.

Forming Complete Body Paragraphs

As your writing skills progress, you should feel more comfortable dividing paragraphs; however, some extra work may be required to make each of the new paragraphs independent and complete. Each separate paragraph must have its own main idea (topic sentence), support points, examples, and details.

Let's return to two previous examples and see how the writer forms complete paragraphs when the original paragraph is divided.

Example 1

Look back at the paragraph on page 239 about group work. When we remove the highlighted section (beginning with *However, sometimes differences among students can cause tension in a group*), we need to add the third support point from the outline and sufficient examples to finish the paragraph. Take a look at the revised paragraph, paying special attention to the final highlighted section:

Working with other students in small groups can be an effective way to learn. To begin with, each student brings his or her special strengths to the group. For instance, I am good with organization, so I can usually show my classmates where their outlines need improvement. My best friend, Herve, has excellent critical reading skills, so he can point out key ideas in the stories we read. In addition, there is usually at least one student in any group who can help the rest of us find and learn how to correct our grammar errors. Equally important, college students benefit from the variety of viewpoints expressed in small groups. I especially like collaborating with older students because of their greater life experience; their opinions often bring a more mature perspective to our discussions. It's also amazing how differently men and women talk about issues. Listening to men's opinions about the best parenting strategies, for example, really helped me form my own opinions more clearly. Also, if students from different ethnic backgrounds are part of a group, they can contribute remarkably different perspectives. Finally, working in a small group can be more comfortable and sociable than having to share

CONTINUED >

information with the entire class. Students working in groups don't have to express their ideas in front of the entire class, only their group members; as a result, these students may be more relaxed. In one course, for example, my friend Diane always knew the answers to questions but was too shy to speak in front of the class. However, in a group of four students, Diane became more relaxed and spoke a lot more. It's also easier without the pressure of the teacher listening, so students might be more likely to speak up about a topic. For instance, if the class is discussing a sensitive topic, I may not want to say anything in front of the teacher, but I will say something in a group. Best of all, because students are working more closely with each other, they might make friends with one or more students in the group.

Our next task is to create a new and separate paragraph based on the section that was removed from the original paragraph. In the following paragraph and outline, notice that the removed section is the basis for the main idea of the new paragraph. Appropriate support points and examples have been added.

MAIN IDEA

Working in groups can cause tension among students; nevertheless, most of these problems can be managed effectively.

SUPPORT POINT 1

Students can work out their group problems themselves and learn how to accept—and work with—disagreement.

- find and defend right answers on their own
- discuss different opinions
- get good practice for the real world

SUPPORT POINT 2

Instructors can intervene with problems and nonparticipating students.

- help get the facts straight
- prod quiet students
- offer advice on how to solve a disagreement

SUPPORT POINT 3

Students can help and encourage each other.

- coaching
- praising good behavior

Working in groups can cause tension among students; nevertheless, most of these problems can be managed effectively, producing worthwhile collaboration. For one thing, students can work out their group problems themselves and learn how to accept—and work with—disagreement. For example, one time while I was doing a practice grammar test in a group, two students thought a sentence was a run-on, but the rest of the group thought it was a correct sentence. The students who thought it was a run-on found an example in the book and showed the rest of us why the sentence was incorrect. We all learned more about grammar, and the students who thought they were right learned the value of sticking to their point. It's also healthy for students to discuss their opposing opinions with others. Once, I was in a group discussing religion, and two people began to argue about what happens after death. At first it was tense, but we knew no one would change his or her opinion, so we just showed respect for each person's views and continued working together. These collaborative challenges are also good practice for the real world because in jobs, politics, and relationships, we will frequently meet people who don't agree with us. In the real world, we'll have to fight our own battles or learn to live with the differences. Another way to solve group problems is to ask the teacher for help. One time in a small group in health class, two students had written down opposing "facts" in their notes, so our teacher stepped in to set the record straight. Also, if some students never participate, the teacher can ask a meaningful question to get them talking. If students are having a hard time because of different opinions, the teacher can ease tensions by reframing the discussion or showing students how to avoid personal attacks. Finally, students can help and encourage each other. Some students are natural "coaches" in a group setting, encouraging shy students to share their ideas and calming disputes among dominant students. It's also a great strategy for students to praise each other for successful collaborative behavior; for example, "Elise and Anthony, you did a terrific job discussing that point!" As all these examples show, there are several ways to make sure that groups run smoothly while accommodating different opinions.

ACTIVITY 13: Teamwork

With a small group of classmates, look back at Activity 11. Identify the section in the paragraph that you marked. Then, do the following:

- Out loud, brainstorm ideas and examples that you could add to the section to form a new paragraph. Keep a list of all the useful ideas.
- Fill in an outline for the new paragraph. (Use a separate sheet or an outline form from **bedfordstmartins.com/steppingstones**.) Try to complete as much of the outline as possible, but don't worry if it's not finished.
- Have a representative from your group write the group's outline on the board, making the words as large as possible so everyone can see.
- As a class, create a "master" outline, using the best ideas from all the outlines.

Teaching Tip
If you have students do Activity 13 or 14, you will probably want to mediate the creation of the master outline, recording the final decisions. As an additional step, students might write a paragraph for the master outline that they have created.

Example 2

Look back at the paragraph on page 241 about electronic communication and entertainment devices. When we remove the second support point (*Furthermore, handheld electronic devices make it more difficult to meet people*) and the highlighted section that follows it, we need to replace this support point and provide examples for it to finish the paragraph. Take a look:

Most of my friends love their cell phones, BlackBerrys, and MP3 players, but I think these devices are harmful to good communication. For starters, instead of turning off their cell phones, people allow them to interrupt important conversations. One thing that irritates me is that my study partners answer their cell phones even if we're reviewing for an exam. Furthermore, I recently quit dating a woman because every time we were getting comfortable, she would answer her cell phone, as if any call were more important than our relationship. My sales job is tougher too because of electronic communication devices. Clients don't hesitate to answer their phones during my sales pitch; sometimes, they even use a call as an excuse to walk away and not come back. In addition, electronic communication can mislead or confuse people. For example, more than once I have sent an e-mail or a text message to a friend in a joking tone, but the text didn't carry the humor I intended, so my friend thought I was weird or rude. Plus, when you deliver some news over a cell phone and hear only silence on the other end, you don't know whether the other person is shocked, angry, or something else. In other words, there is no "body language" with electronic communication, potentially causing confusion. Also, a person walking around with a cell phone or listening to an iPod might be the friendliest guy in the world, but because he is glued to a device, he can appear unfriendly or rude. Last, I believe that these devices trivialize communication. The juvenile text messages that my friends send to one another are a good example. Another example is the nonstop, shallow conversations people have—talking just to be talking. Also, two friends sharing earbuds has become a common sight; it's like the music does the communicating for them. It's clear that electronic communication and entertainment devices are here to stay, but we should not abuse them or allow them to completely replace good old-fashioned face-to-face conversations.

MAIN IDEA
Electronic communication and entertainment devices are bad for communication.

SUPPORT POINT 1
They interrupt important conversations.
- study conversations
- personal conversations
- business conversations

~~SUPPORT POINT 2~~
~~**They make it more difficult to meet people.**~~
- ~~strangers~~
- ~~people with similar interests~~
- ~~people to date~~

SUPPORT POINT 2
They can mislead or confuse people.
- tone not conveyed in e-mail and text messages
- can't see other person's reactions/body language
- people using e-devices can seem aloof

SUPPORT POINT 3
They trivialize communication.
- juvenile text messages
- shallow conversation
- earbud sharing

Our next task is to create a new and separate paragraph based on the section that was removed from the original paragraph (on how handheld electronic devices make it more difficult to meet people). In the following example, appropriate support points and examples have been added to complete the paragraph.

MAIN IDEA

Handheld electronic devices make it more difficult to meet people.

SUPPORT POINT 1

It's harder to meet people in public places.

– the bus stop
– the school cafeteria

SUPPORT POINT 2

It's harder to meet people with similar interests.

– at the gym: health and fitness
– at the video arcade: games

SUPPORT POINT 3

It's harder to meet people to date.

– on the train to San Diego
– at the clubs

Handheld electronic devices make it more difficult to meet people. For one thing, it's harder to meet people in public places. For example, at the bus stop, I used to talk to strangers while waiting for the bus; I actually met my roommate this way. But nowadays, it's like a law that everyone at the bus stop must be talking on a cell phone or listening to an MP3 player. The same is true for the school cafeteria. Just a few years ago, strangers would share a table and strike up a conversation. Now, you can look like a loser if you sit at a table by yourself without having a cell phone at your ear. It's even common for several people to share a table while each one has a conversation on his or her cell phone. Furthermore, electronic devices have made it harder for people with similar interests to meet. For instance, I remember when the gym was a great place to meet other people interested in health and fitness. We would trade tips and stories on the workout floor. Now, it seems like earbuds and MP3 players have become mandatory equipment; the sharing of training tips has been replaced by people singing to themselves. Also, at the video arcade, kids used to talk a lot about the games, but now they're all hooked up to some personal electronic equipment. Finally, electronic devices can make it challenging to meet people to date. One time, on the train to San Diego, I was having a conversation with a woman I'd just met. When her cell phone rang, she started talking and kept talking until her stop. She could have been the woman of my dreams, but I'll never know. The most notorious place for a cell phone to interrupt a potential romance, of course, is the clubs. It seems to make some women feel important when they answer a cell phone and interrupt a new encounter; I guess phone calls mean they are in high demand. However, they don't know what they're missing out on either!

ACTIVITY 14: Teamwork

With a small group of classmates, look back at Activity 12. Identify the section in the paragraph that you marked. Then, do the following:

- Out loud, brainstorm ideas and examples that you could add to the section to form a new paragraph. Keep a list of all the useful ideas.
- Fill in an outline for the new paragraph. (Use a separate sheet of paper or print an outline form from this book's Web site, at **bedfordstmartins.com/steppingstones**.) Try to complete as much of the outline as possible, but do not worry if the outline is not finished.
- Have a representative from your group write the group's outline on the board, making the words as large as possible so everyone can see.
- As a class, create a "master" outline, using the best ideas from all the outlines.
- Last, look again at the original paragraph in Activity 12. Then, think of an additional support point and examples that might be added to replace the marked section that was removed.

ACTIVITY 15

If you did Activity 9 or 10, write body paragraphs for one of these advanced outlines. Then, look for places that you might need to give a chunk of ideas its own well-developed paragraph.

Adding an Introduction and Thesis

If your instructor asks you to write an essay with two or more body paragraphs, you will need to add an introduction and a conclusion to make that essay complete. Also, if you start out writing a single paragraph but decide to divide that paragraph into two or more separate body paragraphs, you will need to add an introduction and a conclusion.

The introduction (opening paragraph) for an academic essay has two basic purposes:

1. to "hook" your reader
2. to "pop" (present) your thesis

HOOKING THE READER

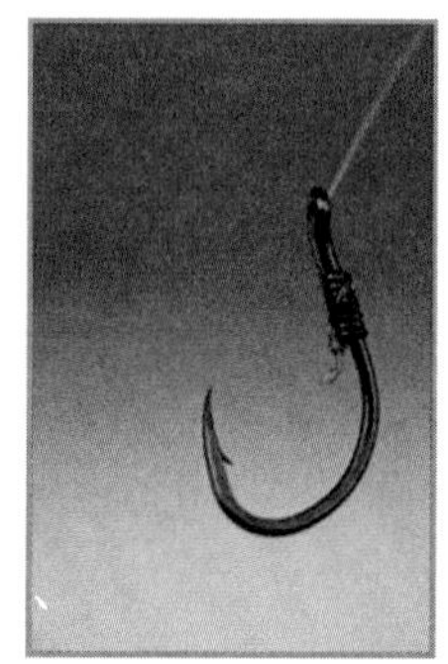

When you "hook" your reader, you get him or her interested in your topic by opening with a clever idea. You can usually develop this hook in a few carefully crafted sentences; you do not want the hook to get out of control and become a distraction for the reader.

Here are five strategies that are especially effective in hooking readers:

- starting with a series of questions
- starting with a story
- starting with a comparison
- starting with an imaginary scenario
- starting with a quotation

To see how these strategies can be used, let's return to an essay that we began building earlier in this chapter:

> Working with other students in small groups can be an effective way to learn. To begin with, each student brings his or her special strengths to the group. For instance, I am good with organization, so I can usually show my classmates where their outlines need improvement. My best friend, Herve, has excellent critical reading skills, so he can point out key ideas in the stories we read. In addition, there is usually at least one student in any group who can help the rest of us find and learn how to correct our grammar errors. Equally important, college students benefit from the variety of viewpoints expressed in small groups. I especially like collaborating with older students because of their greater life experience; their opinions often bring a more mature perspective to our discussions. It's also amazing how differently men and women talk about issues. Listening to men's ideas about the best parenting strategies, for example, really helped

CONTINUED >

me form my own opinions more clearly. Also, if students from different ethnic backgrounds are part of a group, they can contribute remarkably different perspectives. Finally, working in a small group can be more comfortable and sociable than having to share information with the entire class. Students working in groups don't have to express their ideas in front of the entire class, only their group members; as a result, these students may be more relaxed. In one course, my friend Diane always knew the answers to questions but was too shy to speak in front of the class. However, in a group of four students, Diane became more relaxed and spoke a lot more. It's also easier without the pressure of the teacher listening, so students might be more likely to speak up about a topic. For instance, if the class is discussing a sensitive topic, I may not want to say anything in front of the teacher, but I will say something in a group. Best of all, because students are working more closely with each other, they might make friends with one or more students in the group.

Working in groups can cause tension among students; nevertheless, most of these problems can be managed effectively, producing worthwhile collaboration. For one thing, students can work out their group problems themselves and learn how to accept—and work with—disagreement. For example, one time while I was doing a practice grammar test in a group, two students thought a sentence was a run-on, but the rest of the group thought it was a correct sentence. The students who thought it was a run-on found an example in the book and showed the rest of us why the sentence was incorrect. We all learned more about grammar, and the students who thought they were right learned the value of sticking to their point. It's also healthy for students to learn to discuss their opposing opinions with others. Once, I was in a group discussing religion, and two people began to argue about what happens after death. At first it was tense, but we knew no one would change his or her opinion, so we just showed respect for each person's views and continued working together. These collaborative challenges are also good practice for the real world because in jobs, politics, and relationships, we will frequently meet people who don't agree with us. In the real world, we'll have to fight our own battles or learn to live with the differences. Another way to solve group problems is to ask the teacher for help. One time in a small group in health class, two students had written down opposing "facts" in their notes, so our teacher stepped in to set the record straight. Also, if some students never participate, the teacher can ask a meaningful question to get them talking. If students are having a hard time because of different opinions, the teacher can ease tensions by reframing the discussion or showing students how to avoid personal attacks. Finally, students can help and encourage each other. Some students are natural "coaches" in a group setting, encouraging shy students to share their ideas and calming disputes among dominant students. It's also a great strategy for students to praise each other for successful collaborative behavior; for example, "Elise and Anthony, you did a terrific job discussing that point!" As all these examples show, there are several ways to make sure that groups run smoothly while accommodating different opinions.

Because the general topic of this essay is studying in small groups, we need to get the reader "hooked" on this idea. Here are five sample introductions showing how this might be done. (In the next section of this chapter, you will learn how to "pop" the thesis.)

Example: Starting with a Series of Questions

> Are two heads better than one? What about three or four heads, or more? If everyone has an opinion, isn't it more trouble than it's worth to work together? Isn't it just easier to work alone? *Pop the thesis here. . . .*

Example: Starting with a Story (about yourself or someone else)

> Mark was a bright student who planned to transfer to UCLA after two more semesters at his community college. So far, he had a 4.0 average. He worked hard studying, meeting with his instructors, and staying up late writing papers to keep his high average. But when his history instructor put the class into groups, some of the students seemed lazy, and some disagreed with his plans for how to carry out group projects. Suddenly, he worried that the group might hurt his chances of keeping straight A's. *Pop the thesis here. . . .*

Example: Starting with a Comparison (x is like y)

> Working with other students in a group is like a team sport. In baseball, for example, if the left outfielder and the first baseman are both goofing off, there is a good chance that the other team can hit some fly balls or grounders and score some runs. Similarly, in a geography class, if two members of a discussion group are talking about the parties they went to on Saturday night instead of analyzing the features of a glacier, they may cause the group to "drop the ball" in the learning opportunity. When the instructor asks the group to share its ideas with the whole class, the group may strike out. *Pop the thesis here. . . .*

Example: Starting with an Imaginary Scenario (What if . . . , Imagine if . . .)

> Imagine that you're sitting in class and the instructor says, "Get into groups of three or four students to discuss the impact that television has had on education." You're excited because you have so many ideas on that subject. However, when you join your group, things don't go so well: one person thinks the topic is dumb, one doesn't say a word, one disagrees with your ideas, and another agrees with your ideas but for different reasons than you had in mind. Suddenly, group work has become group clash. *Pop the thesis here. . . .*

Power Tip
If you start with a quotation, remember that the quotation cannot stand alone. You must explain how the quotation relates to your introduction. Also, note that you can consult special reference books and Web sites for quotations. For instance, you might type the term *popular quotations* into a search engine.

Example: Starting with a Quotation

There's a saying that goes, "Too many cooks spoil the broth," meaning that people sometimes work better alone or in small numbers than with a lot of people. Anyone who has tried to cook a pot of spaghetti with three or more people knows that arguments can arise about how much salt to add or how long to boil the pasta. If you and several classmates are working together to form an answer to a question (and you will all receive the same grade for that answer!), you can imagine the disagreements that might arise. ***Pop the thesis here. . . .***

POPPING THE THESIS

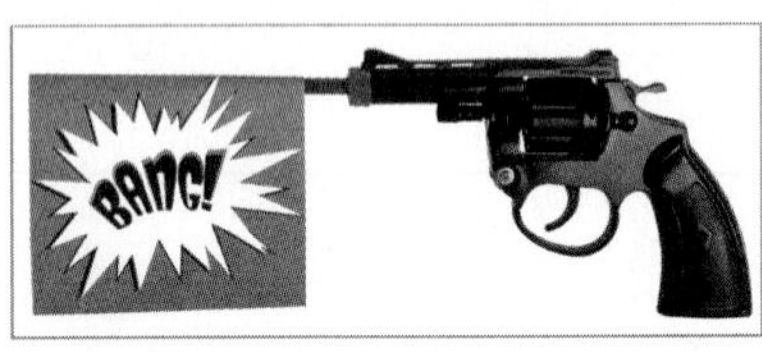

Once you have hooked your reader, it's time to "pop" your thesis, stating *loudly* and *clearly* the main point or purpose of your essay. As a beginning college writer, it is a good strategy to write your thesis in one complete sentence; this will help you focus your ideas and express them precisely. Also, it is a good habit for beginning writers to make the thesis statement the last sentence of the introduction. This way, it will be easy to verify that you have a thesis every time you write an essay.

Some students report special difficulty forming a thesis. They see the thesis as a vague or complicated part of the essay. In fact, writing the thesis is one of the easiest tasks to master in academic writing. If you created an advanced outline for your essay (see page 237), you might have developed a thesis statement already. Otherwise, you might use the following formula:

Topic sentence 1
\+ Topic sentence 2
[+ Topic sentence 3 (if the essay has this)]
= Thesis

As an example, let's look again at the essay on group work that we've been working on. Here are the topic sentences from the two body paragraphs:

Working with other students in small groups can be an effective way to learn.
+ Working in groups can cause tension among students; nevertheless, most of these problems can be managed effectively, producing worthwhile collaboration.
= Working with other students in small groups is an effective way to learn, and most problems that arise can be managed effectively.

By combining the key ideas from the two topic sentences, the thesis states *loudly* and *clearly* the main point of the essay.

If you want your thesis statement to sound less repetitive of your topic sentences, you can change some of the words from the topic sentences. However, keep in mind that some repetition of key words is helpful for your reader. Finally,

Power Tip
If you are writing an essay in response to an assigned topic, it is important that your thesis (and the entire essay) respond directly to the topic. For example, you might use key words from the assignment. For more information, see Chapter 2 and Chapter 4, page 89.

if you do change any of the key words, be careful not to sacrifice the clarity and focus of your thesis.

For example, here are two versions of the previously stated thesis. What do you notice about the second version?

Version 1

Working in small groups with other students has many benefits, and the obstacles that sometimes arise can be handled successfully.

Version 2

College students need to learn how to get along and work together or they won't be prepared for the real world.

The first version states the thesis loudly and clearly. However, the second version "misfires" because it reflects only part of the essay (group work as a preparation for real-world situations); the main point of the essay is no longer loud and clear. (For more on the importance of not leaving out or changing important information in a main idea, see Chapter 5, page 139.)

As you become a more experienced writer, you might use other strategies for developing thesis statements—for example, you might try some of the techniques described for topic sentences in Chapter 5 (page 132).

Finally, for a foolproof introduction, remember that it's a good idea to make the thesis *the last sentence* of the opening paragraph. Here's an example based on the introduction shown on page 249:

> **Are two heads better than one? What about three or four heads, or more? If everyone has an opinion, isn't it more trouble than it's worth to work together? Isn't it just easier to work alone? Although collaborating with others may seem difficult at first, small-group work has many benefits, and the obstacles that sometimes arise can be handled successfully.**

Notice that the writer changed the first part of the thesis to provide a transition from the questions to the thesis.

Teaching Tip
Consider showing your class thesis statements from a variety of student papers. For model papers in the humanities and other disciplines, visit **bedfordstmartins.com/rewriting**.

ACTIVITY 16

Review the body paragraphs on pages 252–253. Then, do the following:

- On a separate sheet of paper, write *three different* introductions for the essay, using your three favorite strategies for "hooking" the reader. (These strategies are discussed on page 247.)
- Formulate a thesis statement by combining the ideas from the two topic sentences.
- Add the thesis as the last sentence of your introductions.
- Exchange introductions with a few classmates. Discuss which of the introductions would be most likely to hook the reader and which thesis statements pop loudly and clearly.

CONTINUED >

Most of my friends love their cell phones, BlackBerrys, and MP3 players, but I think these devices are harmful to good communication. For starters, instead of turning off their cell phones, people allow them to interrupt important conversations. One thing that irritates me is that my study partners answer their cell phone even if we're reviewing for an exam. Furthermore, I recently quit dating a woman because every time we were getting comfortable, she would answer her cell phone, as if any call were more important than our relationship. My sales job is tougher too because of electronic communication devices. Clients don't hesitate to answer their phones during my sales pitch; sometimes, they even use a call as an excuse to walk away and not come back. In addition, electronic communication can mislead or confuse people. For example, more than once I have sent an e-mail or a text message to a friend in a joking tone, but the text didn't carry the humor I intended, so my friend thought I was weird or rude. Plus, when you deliver some news over a cell phone and hear only silence on the other end, you don't know whether the other person is shocked, angry, or something else. In other words, there is no "body language" with electronic communication, potentially causing confusion. Also, a person walking around with a cell phone or listening to an iPod might be the friendliest guy in the world, but because he is glued to a device, he can appear unfriendly or rude. Last, I believe that these devices trivialize communication. The juvenile text messages that my friends send to one another are a good example. Another example is the nonstop, shallow conversations people have—talking just to be talking. Also, two friends sharing earbuds has become a common sight; it's like the music does the communicating for them. It's clear that electronic communication and entertainment devices are here to stay, but we should not abuse them or allow them to replace good old-fashioned face-to-face conversations.

Handheld electronic devices make it more difficult to meet people. For one thing, it's harder to meet people in public places. For example, at the bus stop, I used to talk to strangers while waiting for the bus; I actually met my roommate this way. But nowadays, it's like a law that everyone at the bus stop must be talking on a cell phone or listening to an MP3 player. The same is true for the school cafeteria. Just a few years ago, strangers would share a table and strike up a conversation. Now, you can look like a loser if you sit at a table by yourself without having a cell phone at your ear. It's even common for several people to share a table while each one has a conversation on his or her cell phone. Furthermore, electronic devices have made it harder for people with similar interests to meet. For instance, I remember when the gym was a great place to meet other people interested in health and fitness. We would trade tips and stories on the workout floor. Now, it seems like earbuds and MP3 players have become mandatory equipment; the sharing of training tips has been replaced by people singing to themselves. Also, at the video arcade, kids used to talk a lot about the games, but now they're all hooked up to some personal electronic equipment. Finally, electronic devices can make it challenging to meet people to date. One time, on the train to San Diego, I was having a conversation with a woman I'd just met. When her cell phone rang, she started talking and kept talking until her stop. She could have been the woman of my dreams, but I'll never know. The most notorious place for a cell phone to interrupt a potential romance, of course, is the clubs. It seems to make some women feel important when they answer a cell phone and interrupt a new encounter; I guess the phone calls mean they are in high demand. However, they don't know what they're missing out on either!

ACTIVITY 17

If you did Activity 15, write an introduction (with a thesis) for the body paragraphs that you created. Try one of the strategies for hooking readers shown on page 247.

Adding a Conclusion

After you have written two or more body paragraphs and an introduction, you will need to complete your essay with a conclusion. If you do not add a conclusion, your last body paragraph will leave readers hanging; they will not have the sense of a satisfying finish.

The conclusion for an academic essay can be short or long, depending on the specific requirements of the assignment. Many instructors are satisfied with a brief restating of your main idea; other instructors expect the conclusion to be a well-developed paragraph in which you consolidate and explore the best ideas from the essay. Some instructors prefer that your conclusion include one fresh idea that leaves your reader thinking about the topic after reading the essay. (This is called the *opening a new window* strategy.) Because instructors have different expectations for the conclusion, be sure to request clarification if you are uncertain about what to include.

If your instructor requires only a brief conclusion, you might try the *opening a new window* strategy. Here are five windows that you can open:

- give advice to the reader
- make a prediction
- end with some thought-provoking questions
- make a personal growth statement
- finish the story that you used in your introduction (if you began with a story)

Following are example conclusions for each "window." The conclusions are for the previously developed essay on group work.

Teaching Tip
If your expectations for conclusions differ from those presented here, this is a good time to clarify your requirements.

Example: Giving Advice to the Reader

If you are a student, remember that group work can be one of the most powerful learning opportunities available to you. Defending your ideas, listening to others, and in some cases teaching others all provide a mental workout that your brain won't get if you are snoozing through a lecture. If you are an instructor, remember that group work is effective only if students are given clear objectives and an occasional helping hand when the discussion gets off track or overheated.

Example: Making a Prediction

I predict that by the year 2050, most colleges and universities will have a "group learning" requirement and general-education courses such as "Group Learning 101." The reason for this is the growing recognition among educators, employers, and civic leaders that collaborative skills are essential for personal, professional, and political success. In the United States, we live in a democracy whose future depends on the ability of its citizens to work together effectively. As such, developing collaborative learning skills seems at least as important as understanding the Pythagorean theorem or the process of photosynthesis.

Example: Ending with Some Thought-Provoking Questions

What if college professors were no longer allowed to lecture in class? What if every minute of class time had to be spent in small-group work with other students? Do you think college students would rise to the challenge and take more responsibility for their intellectual growth and education? Or would they just goof off and cheat themselves and their peers of a meaningful learning opportunity? What would *you* do?

Example: Making a Personal Growth Statement

Before writing this essay, I generally had a bad attitude about working in groups with other students. In my experience, college students aren't responsible enough to engage in independent intellectual discussion, and college professors aren't dedicated enough to ensuring productivity within the groups. However, because group work is clearly here to stay, I've decided to be a model participant and leader, guiding my peers to meaningful collaboration. Even if they don't reciprocate, I'll be sharpening my negotiation skills for my future career in international business.

Example: Finishing the Story That You Used in Your Introduction

(For the first part of this story, see page 249.)

Remember Mark and his fears about small-group work in history class? Well, his group experience turned out to be a near disaster. Two students disappeared from the class without doing their share of the work. Another student worked hard but produced mediocre results. Therefore, the bulk of the work fell on Mark and Dana, who resented having to do the work of five people but were determined to get an A. The professor refused to give any special allowances to the group for the troubles they were having. In the end, the group received a B for the project. Fortunately, Mark's other grades in the class brought his average up to an A. Although the experience was difficult for Mark, he learned a valuable lesson about the challenges of working with others—a lesson that he believes will benefit him later in college and beyond.

ACTIVITY 18

Review the introductions that you wrote for Activity 16. Then, do the following:

- Write *three different* conclusions for the essay, using your favorite three strategies for *opening a new window.*
- Exchange your conclusions with a few classmates. Discuss which of the conclusions would be most effective in leaving the reader thinking about the topic.

ACTIVITY 19

If you did Activity 17, write a conclusion for the essay that you drafted. Try one of the strategies for *opening a new window.*

Teaching Tip
As an additional activity, you might give students more sets of body paragraphs without introductions or conclusions. (These paragraphs can come from published essays or other student essays.) Ask them to write an introduction with a thesis, as well as a conclusion. Afterward, share some especially strong examples with the class. Additionally, you might show the original author's introduction and conclusion so that students can compare.

Revising and Proofreading

To revise and proofread your essay, use the strategies presented in Chapter 7 of this book. Keep in mind that the revising and proofreading process will take longer for an essay than for a paragraph, and plan accordingly.

ACTIVITY 20

If you did Activity 19, revise and proofread your draft essay. Try to get peer review before beginning your revision. For more on peer review, see Chapter 7, page 212.

Bringing It All Together

In this chapter, you have learned about the differences between paragraphs and essays and have seen how to develop the various parts of an essay. Check off each of the following statements that you understand. For any that you do not understand, review the appropriate pages in this chapter.

- [ ] An academic essay is well developed (usually three or more pages); carefully organized, with a main idea and a series of support points; and grammatically correct. In addition, most instructors will require an essay to include an **introduction** (an opening paragraph that includes the main idea, known as the **thesis statement**); two or more **body paragraphs**; and a **conclusion** (a paragraph that may restate the main idea or make some other observation). (See page 228.)
- [ ] Most college essays are written "by design." In other words, your instructor specifically asks you to write an essay. (See page 235.) Sometimes, however, you may plan to write a paragraph, but the paragraph grows too large and must be divided. How and when to divide a paragraph depends on *what* you have to say and on *how much* you have to say. (See page 239.)
- [ ] As your writing skills progress, you should feel more comfortable dividing paragraphs; however, some extra work may be required to make each of the new paragraphs independent and complete. Each separate paragraph must have its own main idea (topic sentence), support points, examples, and details. (See page 243.)
- [ ] It is standard to begin an essay with an **introduction**. The introduction should "hook" the reader; for example, the writer might start with a series of questions, a story, a comparison, an imaginary scenario, or a quotation. (See page 247.)
- [ ] Typically, the introduction includes the **thesis statement**. It is a good strategy to write your thesis as *one complete sentence* and to make it *the last sentence* of the introduction. Also, a good way to form a thesis is to combine key ideas from the topic sentences. (See page 250.)
- [ ] After you have written your body paragraphs and an introduction, you will need to complete your essay with a **conclusion**. Many instructors are satisfied with a brief restating of your main idea. However, another good strategy is to *open a window* to a fresh idea. For example, you might give advice to the reader, make a prediction, end with some thought-provoking questions, make a personal growth statement, or finish the story that you used in your introduction (if you began with a story). (See page 253.)
- [ ] As a final step, be sure to **revise** and **proofread** your essay. (Revising and proofreading strategies are discussed in-depth in Chapter 7.)

PART TWO

Grammar for Academic Writing

Chapter 9

Grammar for Academic Writing: An Introduction

Katharine Hepburn, actress, "If you obey all the rules, you miss all the fun."

Mark Twain, author, "It's a good idea to obey all the rules when you're young, just so you'll have the strength to break them when you're old."

OVERVIEW OF THIS CHAPTER

Grammar: Using the Rules to Your Advantage

The *American Heritage Dictionary* defines *grammar* as "the study of how words and their component parts combine to form sentences." And according to the *Oxford English Dictionary,* grammar is "speech or writing judged as good or bad according to as it conforms to or violates the rules of grammar."

This second definition seems to echo many people's worst ideas about grammar: It is a set of rules used to judge our speaking and writing. Now, most of us do not like to be judged, and as the quotations from Katharine Hepburn and Mark Twain suggest, most people would rather break rules than follow them.

However, everywhere you look, rules are a part of life: rules for driving, rules for paying taxes, rules for sports, rules for classroom behavior—the list goes on and on. Breaking rules may be convenient and fun in the short term, but it's people who learn to master rules to their advantage who are often most successful in life.

Teaching Tip
As students begin this chapter, ask them what definitions, words, or associations come to mind when they hear the word *grammar.* If the word seems to provoke a lot of anxiety, try to discover where students' fears are coming from: bad experiences with grammar in the past? fear of being judged? Emphasize to students that their work with grammar in this class should allay some of their fears and build their confidence.

Robert Graves, poet, "Every English poet should master the rules of grammar before he attempts to bend or break them."

Phil Knight, businessman, "Play by the rules, but be ferocious."

Take a look at the advice of two individuals who adopted a different approach to rules. In the photographs on the left, you can see poet Robert Graves laboring over the draft of a famous poem and Nike founder Phil Knight enjoying the fruits of his labor. Both men understood that success depends on mastering rules: After mastering the rules of grammar, Graves went on to write some of the most original poetry in the English language; after mastering the rules of business, Knight went on to manage one of the most innovative companies in the modern world.

Likewise, mastering grammar rules is an important step toward academic success: It will help your writing meet the expectations of college instructors. It will also help you make a good impression in the workplace. No matter what your past experiences with grammar, this book can help you adopt a new and positive attitude toward mastering the rules. It was designed with your academic success in mind, and any student who works through the following chapters with care and dedication will see an improvement in his or her writing.

As you begin this journey to success, you should build an awareness of three important ideas:

- grammattitude
- poetic license
- English in electronic communication

Grammar + Attitude = Grammattitude!

Many students have had negative experiences with grammar: boring textbooks, confusing terminology, seemingly pointless activities, failing grades, a sense of helplessness, and so on. As a new or returning college student, you should not let such past experiences get in the way of meeting your academic goals.

Adopting and maintaining a positive attitude about your ability to master grammar is essential for your success. You can begin by making a number of **affirmations**—positive statements that reflect your commitment to learning grammar. Below, check the box beside each affirmation that applies to you:

☐	I would like to leave my negative experiences with grammar in the past and adopt a new, positive attitude toward learning grammar.
☐	I believe that mastering the basic rules of grammar will help me succeed in college and beyond.
☐	I believe in my ability to learn the basic rules of grammar.
☐	I am willing to work through the following chapters with care and dedication.
☐	I would like to experience the confidence and sense of accomplishment that come with mastering the basic rules of grammar.

If you checked any of the above boxes, you have already taken the first step to developing **grammattitude**, a positive and proactive attitude toward mastering grammar. As you work through the following chapters, remember to wear your new attitude with pride.

proactive: acting in advance of or in preparation for a challenge

Bad Attitude **Grammattitude**

Poetic License: Breaking the Rules of Grammar

As you begin to master the basic rules of grammar in your academic writing, you may start to notice some grammar errors in newspapers, books, and magazines. At first, these errors may confuse you, causing you to question your own knowledge. However, be aware that professional writers sometimes intentionally bend or break grammar rules to achieve a specific, often dramatic, effect. When they do so, this is called **poetic license**. Let's take a look at some examples of poetic license in professional writing.

In *People* magazine, sentence fragments (incomplete sentences) may give readers a sense that they are getting "insider information" in a conversational way. The following excerpt from *People* is about a boy with a rare gastrointestinal disorder. In it, the fragment is highlighted.

> A second-grader at Uwchlan Hills Elementary School in Downington, Pa., Adam dispatches his homework, makes friends, and commands playground football games with ease. The one thing he can't do: eat.

The next excerpt is from a short story, "The Garden-Party," by Katherine Mansfield. Here, the fragments (all highlighted) call attention to particular details from the beautiful day of the party.

> If you stopped to notice, was the air always like this? Little faint winds were playing chase, in at the tops of the windows, out at the doors. And there were two tiny spots of sun, one on the inkpot, one on a silver photograph frame, playing too. Darling little spots. Especially the one on the inkpot lid. It was quite warm. A warm little silver star. She could have kissed it.

Power Tip
See Chapter 11, page 294, to learn why the highlighted examples from *People* and the Katherine Mansfield story are fragments.

The following excerpt is from Ernest Hemingway's short story "Up in Michigan." In it, the highlighted comma splices ramble like the character's thoughts. (Comma splices are two sentences joined only by a comma.)

> All the time Jim was gone on the deer hunting trip. Liz thought about him. It was awful while he was gone. She couldn't sleep well from thinking

> about him but she discovered it was fun to think about him too. If she let herself go it was better. The night before they were to come back she didn't sleep at all, that is she didn't think she slept because it was all mixed up in a dream about not sleeping and really not sleeping. (…) Liz hadn't known just what would happen when Jim got back but she was sure it would be something. Nothing had happened. The men were just home, that was all.

Power Tip
See Chapter 12, page 335, to learn why the highlighted parts of the Hemingway excerpt are comma splices.

Sometimes, a writer will *bend* the rules of grammar without actually breaking them. Take a look at the following two sentences from the novel *Look Homeward, Angel* by Thomas Wolfe. Here, Wolfe pushes the rules of grammar by using extremely long, wandering sentences, giving the writing a dreamlike, almost fevered quality.

As the excerpt begins, one of the characters, Oliver Gant, remembers how Southern (Rebel) soldiers marched past his family's Pennsylvania farm on their way to fighting Northern soldiers at the 1863 battle of Gettysburg. (This battle was part of the conflict between the North and the South known as the Civil War, fought between 1861 and 1865.) Notice how Gant, who becomes a stonecutter, is attracted to images of carved stone.

> How this boy stood by the roadside near his mother's farm, and saw the dusty Rebels march past on their way to Gettysburg, how his cold eyes darkened when he heard the great name of Virginia, and how the year the war had ended, when he was still fifteen, he had walked along a street in Baltimore, and seen within a little shop smooth granite slabs of death, carved lambs and cherubim, and an angel poised upon cold phthisic feet, with a smile of soft stone idiocy—this is a longer tale.

> And of all the years of waste and loss—the riotous years in Baltimore, of work and savage drunkenness, and the theatre of Booth and Salvini, which had a disastrous effect upon the stonecutter, who memorized each accent of the noble rant, and strode muttering through the streets, with rapid gestures of the enormous talking hands—these are blind steps and gropings of our exile, the painting of our hunger as, remembering speechlessly, we seek the great forgotten language, the lost lane-end into heaven, a stone, a leaf, a door.

cherubim: angels
phthisic: diseased (in particular, this term refers to lung disease)

Booth and Salvini: actors who appeared in the Shakespeare play *Othello* in the 1800s

Teaching Tip
Ask students how Wolfe's writing would have a different feeling if he had used very short sentences.

As the previous examples show, poetic license is fairly common in celebrity and lifestyle journalism and in fiction. It is also common in popular nonfiction and personal writing. It is used less frequently in formal journalism and business writing, and it is generally not accepted in academic writing. (For more information on these various forms of writing, see Chapter 1.)

At this point, you may wonder why it is important to follow the rules of grammar when so many professional writers choose to bend or break them. You may also ask why professional writers are granted poetic license, while students generally are not. One reason is that, unlike students, not all professional writers are addressing an academic audience, where formality is expected. For example, a gossip columnist who knows that her readers will appreciate a chatty, conversational tone may bend or even break the rules of grammar.

Also, college instructors want to make sure that you understand how to use correct grammar. Therefore, even if you are using a fragment as poetic license, they may mark your writing down for it. In addition, following the rules of grammar will help you maintain precision and clarity in your academic and professional writing. When an inexperienced writer bends or breaks the rules of grammar, the result may be unintentional confusion instead of dramatic effect.

As you advance in your college career, there may be instances when you would like to use poetic license in your academic writing. Be sure to discuss your ideas with your instructor before proceeding.

ACTIVITY 1: Teamwork

Following are two versions of the same paragraph from a work of horror fiction. Both contain errors, which are in bold. However, in the first paragraph the errors are intentional (part of poetic license), and in the second paragraph they are not.

With classmates, compare and discuss the paragraphs. How do the errors in the first paragraph contribute to the writing, and how do the errors in the second paragraph potentially harm the writing? If you think that the errors should be corrected in both versions, discuss why.

Paragraph 1: Intentional Errors (Poetic License)

Nora awoke suddenly at midnight, as if prodded. Her heart was beating in alarm, but why? **There was no sound, there were no shouts of distress in the quiet house.** The room was cold, as if a window had been opened to the winter night, but the windows and heavy curtains were closed tightly. By the door, a gauzy light wavered as if wind were blowing through it, and then the light grew and took shape before Nora's eyes. **A head, a small body, arms, legs.** The lighted form gave the impression of a child. Though the presence had no eyes, there was no doubt that it was watching Nora, and she stared back at it, frozen. It was then that Nora remembered that this had been a child's room. **A child who had died years before.**

Paragraph 2: Unintentional Errors

Nora awoke suddenly at midnight. **As if prodded.** Her heart was beating in alarm, but why? There was no sound. **There were no shouts of distress in the quiet house, the room was cold, as if a window had been opened to the winter night, but the windows and heavy curtains were closed tightly.** By the door, a gauzy light wavered as if wind were blowing through it, and then the light **growed** and took shape before Nora's eyes. The light had a head, a small body, arms, and legs. The lighted form gave the impression of a child. **Though the presence had no eyes, there was no doubt that it was watching Nora, and she stared back at it, frozen, it was then that Nora remembered that this had been a child's room.** The child had died years before.

English in Electronic Communication

The Internet may be the greatest revolution in human communication since the invention of the printing press in 1436. It has been called *the people's press* because it allows anyone with access to "publish" his or her thoughts, sharing them with people around the world. Cell phones have further contributed to the revolution, making it possible for people to call or send text messages from just about anywhere. Whether through text messaging, e-mail, chat rooms, blogs, or Web sites like MySpace and Facebook, people now have access to many new forums for personal expression.

Part of what makes these types of electronic communication revolutionary is that there seem to be few, if any, rules about how we express ourselves with them. Certainly, no one is patrolling our grammar—or lack of grammar—online. In fact, many people enjoy the opportunity to ignore grammar conventions and invent new forms of expression. Users of e-mail and text messaging have introduced a host of abbreviations to make communication more efficient. Here are just some examples:

Teaching Tip
Ask for volunteers to write on the board some text-messaging abbreviations that are not on this list. Then, have other students translate the abbreviations. Students might then discuss how often they use these abbreviations. Do they ever use them in academic papers?

- **BBL:** be back later
- **BCNU:** be seeing you
- **B4N:** bye for now
- **BRB:** be right back
- **BTW:** by the way
- **F2F:** face to face
- **GR8:** great
- **L8R:** later
- **LOL:** laughing out loud

For students who are learning the conventions of academic writing, English on the Internet or in text messaging can represent a special challenge: The more we break the rules of grammar in our personal electronic communication (and see those rules broken), the more likely we are to reproduce these errors in our academic writing. For example, more and more students are accidentally writing *u* in place of *you* in their college essays.

Now, let's take a look at some examples of English from the Internet and cell phone communications. In these examples, grammar errors, abbreviations, and other uses of nonstandard English are highlighted.

Blog on "nontoxic housekeeping"

> Every year, Americans spend millions of dollars on cleaning products that clog landfills with used packaging and introduce toxic chemicals into the water and air. For those people, I have just two words: vinegar and baking soda. These are the only two products you need to clean your house—I promise! When purchased in large (preferably, recyclable) containers, they reduce the use of packaging. And they are totally harmless to the environment, beyond that, they truly are effective. To unclog a blocked drain, pour a half cup of baking soda into the drain, add a cup of white vinegar, wait five minutes, and add boiling water. The drain will clear right out! Also, scrubbing with baking soda leave sinks and tubs spotless, and a mixture of hot water and vinegar is a great way to clean floors and other surfaces.

Text message

Can u meet at 5:30 4 movie at 6? I'll be in front of the theatR. B4N, Jo

MySpace profile

My name is Alberto Fuerizo, and I live in Pasadena, CA, USA.

What I like: playin guitarz, singing, hanging with friends. Love to listen to B-Real, Tego Calderon, A-Train.

I'd like to meet B-Real, Barack Obama, and any cool women who are into the same music as me. RU out there?

Personal e-mail

Whassup, man? Cant believe you made that joke in front of Brewer. UR crazy. Nothing 2 do here at work so just checking N. RU going to the gym later today?

Mike

As an academic writer, you should be especially aware of how exposure to these new forms of English might affect your formal writing in college. When you are writing quick messages to friends, it's fine to be more casual about grammar and usage. However, make sure that text message abbreviations, casual speech, and grammar errors do not creep into your communications with instructors and work colleagues; make sure that all school and work communications are correct in grammar and usage.

Power Tip
For more information on using language that is appropriate for academic writing, see Chapter 1, page 10.

ACTIVITY 2

Choose one of the previous examples of electronic communication and try to rewrite it in correct English, using a separate sheet of paper. Don't worry if you can't fix all the errors; you will be learning more about how to correct grammar problems in later chapters.

Bringing It All Together

In this chapter, you have learned about the importance of following grammar rules, even when those rules are sometimes broken by professional writers and in electronic communication. Check off each of the following statements that you understand. For any that you do not understand, review the appropriate pages in this chapter.

☐	Mastering grammar rules is an important step toward academic success: It will help your writing meet the expectations of college instructors. It will also help you make a good impression in the workplace. (See page 260.)
☐	Adopting and maintaining a positive attitude about your ability to master grammar (in other words, having **grammattitude**) is essential for your success. (See page 260.)
☐	Professional writers sometimes intentionally bend or break grammar rules to achieve a specific, often dramatic, effect. When they do so, this is called **poetic license**. Generally, it's a good idea to avoid taking poetic license in the writing that you do for college. (See page 261.)
☐	Electronic communication has the potential to affect your academic writing. When you are writing quick messages to friends, it's fine to be more casual about grammar and usage. However, make sure that text message abbreviations, casual speech, and grammar errors do not creep into your communications with instructors and work colleagues. (See page 264.)

The following chapters will give you plenty of advice and practice to help you master grammar and avoid the most common errors that students make. Remember: If you keep a positive attitude about grammar and make a commitment to learn more about it, your writing will definitely improve!

Chapter 10

The Building Blocks of Language

In this chapter you will learn about these important sentence parts:

FOUNDATION WORDS	DESCRIPTIVE WORDS	CONNECTING WORDS
NOUNS	ADJECTIVES	PREPOSITIONS
VERBS	ADVERBS	CONJUNCTIONS

OVERVIEW OF THIS CHAPTER

How We Construct Language

From infancy into childhood, we learn language in stages. Each stage gives us new building blocks with which to express our ideas, eventually in complete sentences.

The first stage generally takes place between the ages of one and two. In this stage, infants use single words to identify *things* (**nouns**) and *actions* (**verbs**). We call these **foundation words** because they are the foundation of all verbal communication.

With just nouns and verbs, infants begin to build simple "sentences." Take a look:

NOUN	VERB
baby	sit
doggie	run

VERBS
NOUNS

In the next stage of language building, children find words to *describe* things and actions (**adjectives** and **adverbs**). Take a look:

The **adjective** *good* describes *baby.*

good baby sit

The **adverb** *fast* describes *run.*

doggie run fast

ADVERBS
ADJECTIVES
VERBS
NOUNS

We call these **descriptive words**, and we use them to add onto the foundation of nouns and verbs. (Notice that ***ad****jective* and ***ad****verb* both begin with the prefix *ad,* showing that they are an *added* layer.)

Power Tip
Although these examples of baby talk contain a noun and a verb and are quite understandable, they are not complete, correct sentences. **Corrected:** *The baby sits. The doggie runs.* In upcoming chapters, you will learn more about why these sentences are incorrect.

In the third stage, children discover words that connect all the other words (**prepositions** and **conjunctions**). Take a look:

The **preposition** connects *sit* to *chair.*

good baby sit in chair

The **conjunction** connects *doggie* and *kitty.*

doggie and kitty run fast

At this point, a child possesses the main building blocks of language. As you will see in the next chapter, every sentence that we speak or write is a combination of these six building blocks:

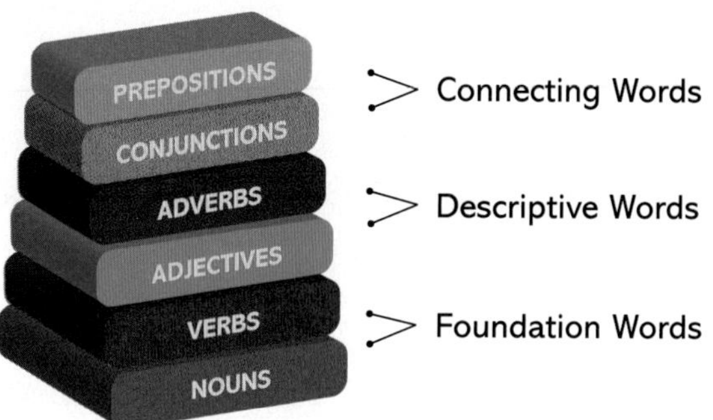

Teaching Tip
Many students, especially visual learners, will benefit from the color-coding system that is introduced in this chapter and carried into the later chapters. You might suggest that students spend some time highlighting nouns, verbs, adjectives, and so on in different colors in newspapers, magazines, and other publications. This practice will help build their awareness of grammar usage.

Next, we'll discuss each of these building blocks in more detail.

Foundation Words: NOUNS

A **noun** is a word that identifies a person, place, or thing. There are three types of nouns (concrete, proper, and abstract) and a noun substitute (**pronoun**). Children generally use concrete and proper nouns first; later, they learn abstract nouns and pronouns.

Concrete nouns. Infants' first words usually identify things in their immediate environment: *banana, cat, bottle, book,* and so on. These words are called *concrete* nouns because they identify things that can be seen or touched.

Proper nouns. At the same time, children hear and learn the names of *specific* people, places, and things in their environment: Mommy, Dadda, Max (a dog's name), Booboo (a teddy bear's name), Target, and so on. These names are called *proper* nouns, and they always begin with a capital letter when we write them. (Note that proper nouns are also concrete.)

Abstract nouns. Later, children learn words to identify emotions or physical feelings (*love, fear, sadness, hunger,* and so on) and ideas (*fun, trouble, unfairness,* and so on). Because emotions, feelings, and ideas must be sensed or understood—they cannot simply be touched or seen—they are more difficult for children to identify with words. These words are called *abstract* nouns. (As you learned in Chapter 6, abstract nouns can also refer to imprecise people, objects, locations, and other concepts: *someone, something, anywhere,* and so on.)

Pronouns. At a later stage, children learn a group of small words (*I, you, he, she, it, they, we*) to substitute for nouns: *she*instead of *Mommy; he* instead of *Dadda; it* instead of *cookie*. These words are called *pronouns*.

Here is a review of the four types of nouns:

CONCRETE	PROPER	ABSTRACT	PRONOUN
things you can see or touch	specific people, places, things	emotions, feelings, ideas	a noun substitute

Power Tip
To make your writing vivid and precise, it's often a good idea to choose concrete nouns over abstract ones. For more information, see Chapter 6, page 177.

ACTIVITY 1

For each word, identify the noun type.

EXAMPLE: jello concrete

1. water concrete
2. honesty abstract
3. Chicago proper
4. she pronoun
5. happiness abstract
6. Thomas Jefferson proper
7. we pronoun
8. potato concrete
9. ocean concrete
10. Jennifer proper

ACTIVITY 2

In each sentence, the nouns have been underlined. Above each underlined word, write the noun type.

EXAMPLE: Liz (proper) has a digital camera (concrete).

1. Michael (proper) has ordered a new computer (concrete).
2. Honesty (abstract) is important in friendship (concrete).
3. My cousin (concrete) owns a motorboat (concrete).
4. Determination (abstract) leads to success (abstract).
5. We (pronoun) are vacationing in Florida (proper).

Foundation Words: VERBS

Children quickly learn words to name actions: *run, cry, drink, talk,* and so on. These words are called **action verbs**, and they are easy to recognize.

ACTIVITY 3

In each sentence, circle the action verb.

EXAMPLE: For my birthday, my sister (baked) a cake.

1. Our team (played) well.
2. Michelle (called) me yesterday.
3. Elise (drove) the truck.
4. The contestant (chose) wisely.
5. Jose (opened) his birthday gift.

More difficult to learn, however, are two other types of verbs that do not identify actions. These are called **linking verbs** and **helping verbs**. Usually, these verbs must be followed by another word (or words) to make sense.

A linking verb is like a chain; it links one word to another word that describes or renames the first word. Take a look:

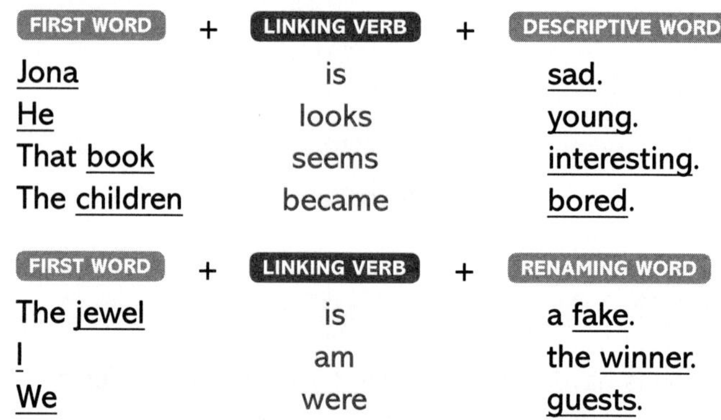

FIRST WORD	+	LINKING VERB	+	DESCRIPTIVE WORD
Jona		is		sad.
He		looks		young.
That book		seems		interesting.
The children		became		bored.

FIRST WORD	+	LINKING VERB	+	RENAMING WORD
The jewel		is		a fake.
I		am		the winner.
We		were		guests.

Common Linking Verbs

am, is, are, was, were (states of being)

appear, become, feel, get, grow, look, seem, smell, sound, taste

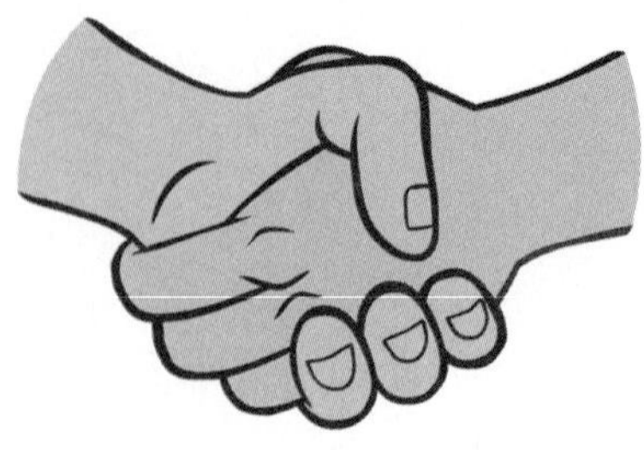

A helping verb is like a helping hand; it helps another verb. Take a look:

HELPING VERB	+	ANOTHER VERB
should		study
can		win
might		forget
will		exercise

Again, a linking verb or helping verb usually needs to be followed by another word or words:

LINKING VERB — Martha feels . . .

HELPING VERB — The team might . . .

Let's complete the sentences:

DESCRIPTIVE WORD — Martha feels energetic.

ANOTHER VERB — The team might practice.

Although there are many action verbs, there is only a small number of linking and helping verbs. You do not need to memorize these verbs, but you should be able to recognize them as verbs.

Common Helping Verbs

am, is, are, was, were

do, does, did

have, has, had

can, could, may, might, must, shall, should, will, would

Teaching Tip
Some students may find it helpful to think of nouns as *actors* and verbs as *actions*. Note that this text has a separate chapter dedicated to verbs (16). It also has a separate chapter on pronouns (17).

ACTIVITY 4

For each sentence, do the following:

- Circle the linking verb or helping verb.
- Underline the word that follows this verb.
- In the space after the sentence, write "linking" if the verb is followed by a descriptive word or a renaming word or "helping" if the verb is followed by another verb.

EXAMPLE: The guitar (sounds) mellow. linking

1. This milk (tastes) sour. linking
2. Our plane (is) leaving soon. helping
3. They (were) players. linking
4. The weather (turned) cold. linking
5. Deborah (is) speaking now. helping

Descriptive Words: ADJECTIVES and ADVERBS

Adjectives describe nouns or pronouns. Take a look:

old car — She is smart.

blue dress — They are late.

laptop computer

Adverbs describe verbs (actions). Take a look:

think carefully	sleep late
jump high	dance gracefully

Adverbs can also describe adjectives and other adverbs:

really pretty	very gracefully

Many adjectives can be changed to adverbs by adding *-ly:*

adjective describing the noun *voice*

Joan has a quiet voice.

adverb describing the verb *speaks*

Joan speaks quietly.

Here are some other examples:

beautiful	→	beautifully	quick	→	quickly
happy	→	happily	smooth	→	smoothly
loud	→	loudly	soft	→	softly

ACTIVITY 5

In each sentence, circle the word that describes the underlined word. Then, in the space after the sentence, write "adjective" or "adverb" as a label for the circled word. Your choice will depend on whether the underlined word is a noun or a verb.

EXAMPLE: Jeremy has (neat) handwriting. adjective

1. Nancy is holding a (yellow) rose. adjective
2. The wind is blowing (gently). adverb
3. A (loud) crash came from the kitchen. adjective
4. A dish crashed (loudly) to the floor. adverb
5. Rain falls (frequently) in Seattle. adverb

ACTIVITY 6

In each sentence, add a descriptive word. Then, write "adjective" or "adverb" in the space after the sentence to indicate whether the word describes a noun or a verb. Descriptive words will vary.

EXAMPLE: After a tune-up, the motor ran smoothly. adverb

1. Late for work, Blake walked quickly toward his office. adverb
2. Inside the gift box lay a (an) diamond ring. adjective

3. Blake drives a (an) ___red___ car. ___adjective___

4. The police chief spoke ___angrily___ about the arson case. ___adverb___

5. Maryann sang ___softly___ to the baby. ___adverb___

Connecting Words: PREPOSITIONS and CONJUNCTIONS

Prepositions (words like *at, by, for, in, on, to, with*) and **conjunctions** (words like *and, but, or, so*) are used to connect the other building blocks of language. Because these words are used for connecting, they are usually followed by other words.

PREPOSITION

Your wallet is on . . .

CONJUNCTION

Esther will make popcorn and . . .

In each example, you would need to add more information to complete the thought:

Your wallet is on the table.

Esther will make popcorn and cookies.

A preposition is usually part of a **prepositional phrase**. For example:

PREPOSITION

Your wallet is on the table.

PREPOSITIONAL PHRASE

A prepositional phrase always begins with a preposition, and it usually ends with a noun. As you will learn in Chapter 11, prepositional phrases tell us *when, where,* and sometimes *how* an action occurs.

Teaching Tip
Have a "parts-of-speech bee." Divide students into two teams and have one representative from each team step forward at a time. Call out a noun, verb, adjective, adverb, preposition, or conjunction. The first person to identify the word's correct part of speech scores a point for the team. Keep going until all students have taken a turn. The team that scores the most points wins. Alternatively, call out parts of speech and have students name appropriate words.

ACTIVITY 7

In each sentence, circle the one-word preposition. Then, underline the entire prepositional phrase.

EXAMPLE: (On) July 4th, we always have a barbecue.

1. Mattie's cat is stuck in a tree.
2. With you, I can do anything.
3. Michael made dinner for me.
4. At midnight, my alarm rang loudly.
5. Manuel is moving to Chicago.

Again, conjunctions, like prepositions, usually need to be followed by more information. Here are some examples:

NOUN + NOUN	Esther will make popcorn and cookies.
ACTION + ACTION	We will take a walk or go for a swim.
ADJECTIVE + ADJECTIVE	Jerry is handsome but shy.
CAUSE + OUTCOME	The actress was bored, so she left.

You will learn more about conjunctions in Chapters 12 and 13.

Teaching Tip
For test items on identifying various parts of speech, see the *Testing Tool Kit* CD available with this book.

ACTIVITY 8

In each sentence, circle the conjunction. Then, underline the two items that are connected by the conjunction.

EXAMPLE: The team lost the game but won the championship.

1. Are you happy or sad?
2. The waiter served our desserts and refilled our coffee cups.
3. For lunch, you may have chicken or roast beef.
4. Julia was sleepy, so she took a nap.
5. Ben is talented but humble.

In Chapter 11, you will build more sentences using the words you learned about in this chapter. Chapter 11 and later parts of this book include a key that identifies foundation, descriptive, and connecting words by the colors introduced in this chapter. This color coding will help you understand the various uses of these important words. The key is shown in the left margin.

FOUNDATION WORDS
NOUNS
VERBS
DESCRIPTIVE WORDS
ADJECTIVES
ADVERBS
CONNECTING WORDS
PREPOSITIONS
CONJUNCTIONS

Bringing It All Together

In this chapter, you have learned about the main building blocks of language: nouns, verbs, adjectives, adverbs, prepositions, and conjunctions. Check off each of the following statements that you understand. For any that you do not understand, review the appropriate pages in this chapter.

- ☐ **Nouns** and **verbs** are known as **foundation words** because they are the foundation of all verbal communication. (See page 267.)
- ☐ A noun is a word that identifies a person, place, or thing. There are three types of nouns (concrete, proper, and abstract) and a noun substitute (**pronoun**). (See page 268.)
- ☐ **Action verbs** name actions. (See page 270.) A **linking verb** links one word to another word that describes or renames the first word. (See page 270.) A **helping verb** helps another verb. (See page 270.)
- ☐ **Adjectives** and **adverbs** are **descriptive words**. Adjectives describe nouns. Adverbs describe verbs, adjectives, and other adverbs. (See page 271.)
- ☐ **Prepositions** and **conjunctions** are used to connect the other building blocks of language. Prepositions are often part of **prepositional phrases**, which always begin with a preposition and usually end with a noun. (See page 273.)

Chapter 11

The Simple Sentence

OVERVIEW OF THIS CHAPTER

Both of these are simple sentences. You'll find out why in this chapter.

NOUN + VERB + . = Students study.

PREPOSITIONAL PHRASE + , + ADJECTIVE + NOUN + VERB + ADVERB + .
= Before exams, good students study carefully.

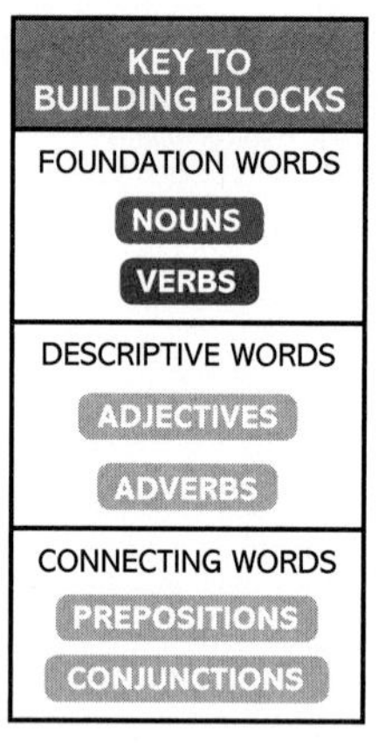

Building Simple Sentences

In the following sections, you will build longer and longer sentences using the building blocks described in Chapter 10.

BUILDING SHORT SIMPLE SENTENCES

In the last chapter, you were introduced to six building blocks of language. We identified two of these as the most important building blocks: **nouns** and **verbs**.

Every sentence that you write or speak will be a different combination of these six building blocks, but a simple sentence may have as few as **two words**. One of these words must be a noun, and the other must be a verb.

To restate, a sentence must have a noun and a verb; it must also express a complete thought. Look at these examples:

John laughed.

Planes fly.

She refused.

Yes, these are short, simple sentences, but they are complete and correct because they contain a noun (a person, place, or thing) and a verb (an action or state of being), and they express a complete thought. Most of us would probably choose to add more information to these sentences, but we don't have to.

Now, let's build some simple sentences.

ACTIVITY 1

In the following exercise, add one word in each blank to complete the sentence. *Answers will vary.*

A. Add a noun (person, place, or thing).

EXAMPLE: ___Sharks___ attack.

1. ___It___ exploded.
2. ___They___ sing.
3. ___Bill___ smokes.
4. ___Sheila___ listened.
5. ___We___ failed.

B. Add a verb (action).

EXAMPLE: Children ___play___.

1. Athletes ___run___.
2. Elizabeth ___cried___.
3. It ___stopped___.
4. Dogs ___bark___.
5. Rain ___fell___.

In some sentences, the verb needs to be followed by another noun to make sense. This noun usually answers the question "What?" Take a look:

Elevators carry ________. [What?]

In this case, the simple sentence must have at least **three words** to be complete.

NOUN VERB NOUN
Elevators carry passengers.

Often, verbs that are followed by nouns are action verbs. *Carry* is an action verb. (For more information, see Chapter 10, page 270.)

Let's build some sentences with action verbs that are followed by nouns.

Teaching Tip
If you think that your students will struggle with subject-verb agreement while completing Activity 1 or other activities in this chapter, you may want to refer them to page 466 of Chapter 16.

Terminology Tip
In English grammar, *passengers* is defined as an *object*. This means that it receives the action of the verb *carry*.

ACTIVITY 2

Fill in each blank to complete the sentence. *Answers will vary.*

A. Add another noun.

EXAMPLE: The letter carrier delivered ___the mail___.

1. The lawnmower cuts ___grass___.
2. Dexter watches ___TV___.
3. Cats love ___tuna___.
4. Wilma buys ___flowers___.
5. The bee stung ___Cathy___.

B. Add an action verb.

EXAMPLE: The crowd ___harassed___ the demonstrators.

1. The waiter ___served___ lunch.
2. My mother ___loves___ roses.
3. Bob ___sells___ boats.
4. He ___hates___ homework.
5. People ___filled___ the auditorium.

Common Linking Verbs

am, is, are, was, were (states of being)

appear, become, feel, get, grow, look, seem, smell, sound, taste

When the verb in a sentence is a linking or helping verb, the sentence must also have at least **three words** to be complete. Let's look at a sentence with a **linking verb**:

NOUN	LINKING VERB	ADJECTIVE
Cats	seem	wise.

In this simple sentence, the linking verb *seem* must be followed by an adjective, a word that describes a noun. Otherwise, the sentence will not make sense. (For more on linking verbs, see Chapter 10, page 270. For more on adjectives, see page 271.) Let's build some sentences with linking verbs.

ACTIVITY 3

Fill in each blank to complete the sentence. *Answers will vary.*

A. Add a noun.

EXAMPLE: *The customers* feel satisfied.

1. *Adam* appears upset.
2. *The student* is young.
3. *The crowd* became restless.
4. *The movie* sounds interesting.
5. *Ashley* seems happy.

B. Add a linking verb.

EXAMPLE: The spider *is* scary.

1. They *look* sad.
2. The soldier *seemed* scared.
3. I *feel* disgusted.
4. Jealousy *is* harmful.
5. The pie *tastes* good.

C. Add an adjective.

EXAMPLE: The gardens were *colorful*.

1. Maria became *ill*.
2. She looks *pretty*.
3. The marchers grew *tired*.
4. The child was *fussy*.
5. You seem *distracted*.

D. Add a linking verb and an adjective.

EXAMPLE: Miguel *sounded sick*.

1. We *feel satisfied*.
2. The roses *smelled nice*.
3. Jeremy *appeared pleased*.
4. The drink *tasted sweet*.
5. The house *looks messy*.

Common Helping Verbs

am, is, are, was, were

do, does, did

have, has, had

can, could, may, might, must, shall, should, will, would

Now, let's look at a sentence with a **helping verb**:

NOUN	HELPING VERB	ANOTHER VERB
Tim	should	study.

Terminology Tip
In English grammar, the verb that follows a helping verb is often called the *main verb*. Often, the main verb is an action verb.

In this simple sentence, the helping verb *should* must be followed by another verb; otherwise, the sentence will not make sense. (Remember that helping verbs *help* other verbs; for more information, see Chapter 10, page 270.)

Let's build some sentences with helping verbs.

ACTIVITY 4

Fill in each blank to complete the sentence. Answers will vary.

A. Add a noun.

EXAMPLE: ___We___ could swim.

1. ___They___ might jump.
2. ___The boys___ have fought.
3. ___The team___ will win.
4. ___Britney___ can come.
5. ___You___ must listen.

B. Add a helping verb.

EXAMPLE: I ___must___ clean.

1. He ___will___ laugh.
2. Tourists ___can___ visit.
3. The judge ___has___ ruled.
4. The box ___was___ opened.
5. I ___might___ sleep.

C. Add another verb.

EXAMPLE: They have ___played___.

1. Robert should ___go___.
2. The president might ___resign___.
3. Miguel has ___arrived___.
4. Passengers have ___complained___.
5. You could ___drive___.

D. Add a helping verb and another verb.

EXAMPLE: Our neighbors ___should come___.

1. It ___has happened___.
2. The student ___will study___.
3. Jessica ___must wait___.
4. The pilot ___was alerted___.
5. We ___can help___.

BUILDING LONGER SIMPLE SENTENCES

You already know that a sentence may have as few as two or three words. However, we usually write longer sentences that contain some of the other building blocks of language. In particular, **descriptive words** make sentences clearer and more specific for readers.

Here's a complete, correct sentence:

Children laugh.

Now, let's add an **adjective** (one word) to describe *what type* of children laugh.

Happy children laugh.

Next, let's add an **adverb** (one word) to describe *how* the children laugh.

Happy children laugh playfully.

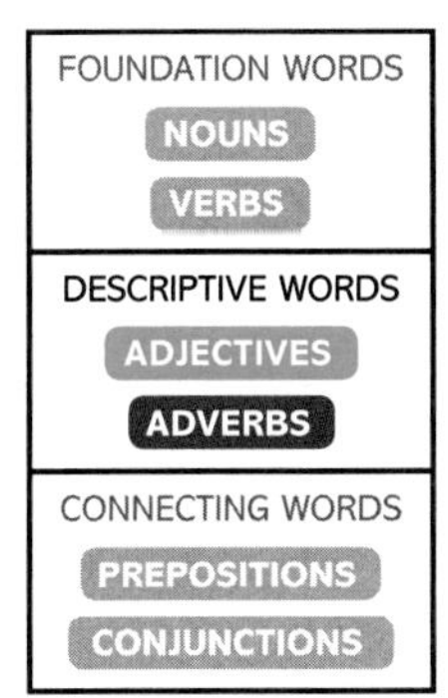

As these examples show, adjectives describe nouns, and adverbs usually describe verbs, telling *how, when, where,* or *why* an action occurs. (For more on adjectives and adverbs, see Chapter 10, page 271.)

Power Tip
Remember that an *ad*-verb adds meaning to a verb.

Additional Notes about Adverbs

Note that . . .

- adverbs can also describe adjectives (***Very** happy children laugh*) and other adverbs (*Happy children laugh* **very** *joyfully*).
- many, but not all, adverbs end in *-ly*. (See Chapter 10, page 272, for more examples.) In addition to *very,* adverbs that don't end in *-ly* include *first, last, more, less, soon, sooner, late, later, often,* and *sometimes.*
- people sometimes incorrectly use the adjective *good* instead of the adverb *well* to describe a verb.

INCORRECT	Even though the other team was stronger, we played good.
CORRRECT	Even though the other team was stronger, we played well. [Because *played* is a verb, it should be described by the adverb *well.*]

As a reminder, linking verbs like *feel, look,* and *smell* must be followed by adjectives, not adverbs:

INCORRECT	I feel badly.
CORRECT	I feel bad.
INCORRECT	You look sadly.
CORRECT	You look sad.

An exception is that *well* is used to describe a person's health:

I felt well after my swim.

Let's build some simple sentences with descriptive words.

ACTIVITY 5

Add **one word** in each blank to complete the sentence. *Answers will vary.*

A. Add an adjective.

EXAMPLE: Jill's ___new___ earrings sparkled.

1. The ___old___ car backfires.
2. My ___youngest___ brother called.
3. An ___annoyed___ passenger complained.
4. The ___town___ clock chimes.
5. The ___cotton___ shirt wrinkles.

B. Add an adverb.

EXAMPLE: Hector laughed ___loudly___.

1. We woke up ___early___.
2. Melissa worked ___hard___.
3. You play guitar ___beautifully___.
4. The days pass ___slowly___.
5. Jackson walked ___quickly___.

C. Add an adjective and an adverb.

EXAMPLE: A ___good___ doctor listens ___carefully___.

1. A ___skillful___ dancer moved ___gracefully___.
2. The ___shy___ teacher speaks ___softly___.
3. Her ___sports___ car runs ___smoothly___.
4. Edgar's ___first___ date ended ___badly___.
5. The ___new___ battery charged ___rapidly___.

D. Add two adjectives.

EXAMPLE: The ___old___ man was ___tired___.

1. The ___bank___ manager got ___upset___.
2. The ___damaged___ spaceship sounds ___strange___.
3. ___Rotten___ bananas smell ___bad___.
4. The ___blue___ chairs look ___comfortable___.
5. The ___little___ girl seems ___sick___.

BUILDING EVEN LONGER SIMPLE SENTENCES

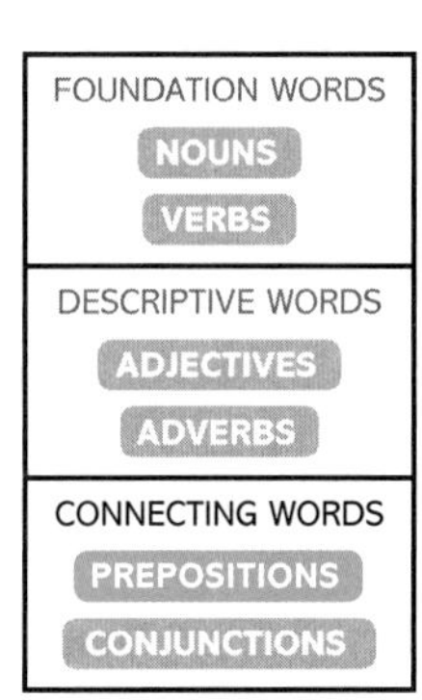

As you have seen, sentences become longer when we add descriptive words. Even longer sentences may have one or more **prepositional phrases** that tell us *when, where,* and sometimes *how* an action occurs. Let's take a look:

The book fell.

You should already know that this is a complete, correct sentence. However, we would probably add more information about where, when, or how the book fell. So, let's add a preposition:

The book fell in . . .

Now that we have added the preposition *in,* we must complete the thought. If we do not complete the thought, the sentence will not make sense.

The book fell in the water.

The preposition *in* connects the verb *fell* with information about *where* the book fell. The preposition **plus** the words that complete the thought are called the **prepositional phrase**. Usually, prepositional phrases end with nouns.

PREPOSITION NOUN

The book fell in the water.

Terminology Tip
The noun at the end of this prepositional phrase is known as the *object of the preposition.*

Power Tip
Because the phrase *in the water* describes the verb *fell,* it is functioning as an adverb. Prepositional phrases can also function as adjectives, as in this sentence: The cat on the bed is friendly. *On the bed* serves as an adjective describing the noun *cat.*

For online practice with building simple sentences, visit this book's Web site at **bedfordstmartins .com/steppingstones**.

Common Prepositions

about	before	for	on	to
above	behind	from	onto	toward
across	below	in	out	under
after	beneath	inside	outside	until
against	beside	into	over	up
along	between	like	past	upon
among	beyond	near	since	with
around	by	next	than	within
as	down	of	through	without
at	during	off	throughout	

ACTIVITY 6

In each item, circle the preposition and complete the prepositional phrase, ending it with a noun. *Answers will vary.*

EXAMPLE: The plane flew (over) our house.

1. Coconuts grow (on) palm trees.
2. (Before) dinner, I study.
3. The toy landed (in) the pond.
4. The slippers (under) the bed were dirty.
5. We can meet (in) the parking lot.

ACTIVITY 7

In each of the following sentences, add a prepositional phrase. *Answers will vary.*

Hints

- To write a prepositional phrase, start with a preposition and complete the thought, ending with a noun.
- The questions after each blank give clues about the type of prepositional phrase you might use.

EXAMPLE: We drove to the hospital. (Where?)

1. Janice lives near the park. (Where?)
2. In the morning, the children get dressed. (When?)
3. A car at my job caught on fire. (Where?)
4. I found my wallet on the floor. (Where?)
5. On Friday, we had a pop quiz. (When?)

ACTIVITY 8

Many long sentences may have two or more prepositional phrases. In each sentence that follows, add two prepositional phrases. Answers will vary.

EXAMPLE: After lunch, Bernice walked in the park.

1. On the porch, you will find the paint for the shutters.
2. In our grandmother's cookbook, my sister found a great recipe for pancakes.
3. The bus to New York stopped by the exit.
4. Since Wednesday, I have received three offers of help.
5. We live near the beach so that we can swim in the ocean.

ACTIVITY 9: Teamwork

Working with other students, add three prepositional phrases to each of the following items, filling in the blanks. Answers will vary.

EXAMPLE: During the earthquake, a pair of vases fell off the shelf.

1. Before dawn, the man in that house walks along the beach.
2. In autumn, the leaves from our trees blow into the street.
3. In a few minutes, the winner of the music award will speak to reporters.
4. In the park, a tall bronze statue of a soldier stands beside the playground.
5. In the evening, the jewelry store on Adams Street was damaged by high winds.

USING VARIOUS BUILDING BLOCKS OF SENTENCES

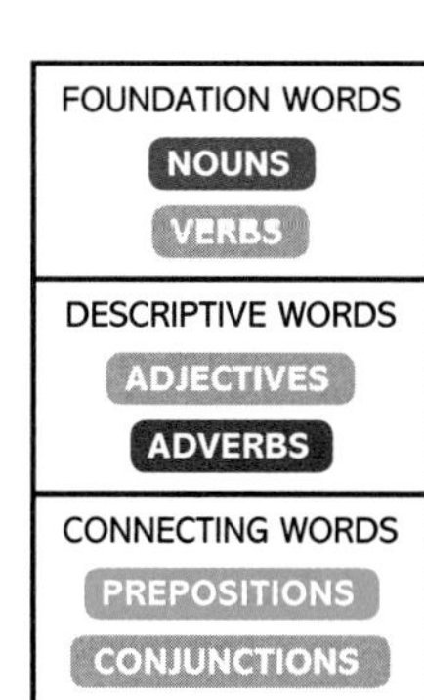

Often, we have a choice of how we will develop or complete a sentence. Take a look at the three different endings of the following sentences:

My grandfather ate breakfast.

My grandfather ate alone.

My grandfather ate at a restaurant.

- In the first sentence, the verb is followed by a **noun** that explains *what* my grandfather ate.
- In the second sentence, the verb is followed by an **adverb** that explains *how* my grandfather ate.
- In the third sentence, the verb is followed by a **prepositional phrase** that explains *where* he ate.

Now, we can build an even longer sentence by adding the noun, the adverb, and the prepositional phrase all together after the verb:

My grandfather ate breakfast alone at a restaurant.

Let's build some simple sentences using all three of these building blocks.

Power Tip
Notice the words *the* and *a* used in the examples. *The* is known as an *article,* and it signals specific, known nouns (***The** thief who stole **the** jewels was arrested*). *A* or *an,* also articles, usually signal general, unknown nouns (***A** thief stole the jewels; **An** intruder stole the jewels*). For more on articles, see Appendix C.

ACTIVITY 10

Complete each sentence as follows:

For item a, add a **noun**.

For item b, build onto the sentence by adding an **adverb**.

For item c, build the sentence further by adding a **prepositional phrase**.

Be as creative as possible in completing your sentences. Make them funny, serious, dramatic, or action-packed. Answers will vary.

EXAMPLE: **a.** The boy pulled a wagon.
b. The boy pulled a wagon quickly.
c. The boy pulled a wagon quickly along the sidewalk.

1. **a.** The soldier fired the gun.
   b. The soldier fired the gun rapidly.
   c. The soldier fired the gun rapidly at the target.
2. **a.** Beth wrote a letter.
   b. Beth wrote a letter daily.
   c. Beth wrote a letter daily to her son.
3. **a.** My dad lost weight.
   b. My dad lost weight quickly.
   c. My dad lost weight quickly during his diet.

We can build even longer sentences by using an **adjective**, an **adverb**, and more than one **prepositional phrase**. Here are four steps for writing such sentences:

1. Add an adjective to describe the noun.
2. Add an adverb to describe the verb.
3. Add prepositional phrases to the beginning and end of the sentence.
4. Add a prepositional phrase between the noun and the verb.

Here are examples of each step:

The vine grew.

1. The rose vine grew.
2. The rose vine grew quickly.
3. In the spring, the rose vine grew quickly up the wall.
4. In the spring, the rose vine beside my window grew quickly up the wall.

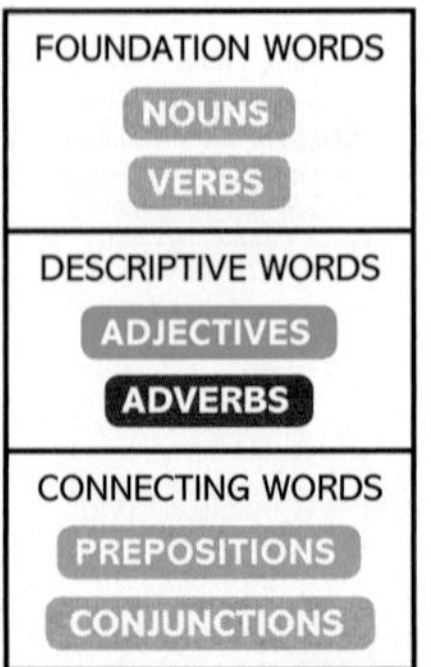

Notice that when a prepositional phrase begins the sentence, as in examples 3 and 4, this phrase is followed by a comma.

ACTIVITY 11: Teamwork

Working with some of your classmates, build each of the following simple sentences using the four-step method. Have a different student complete each step. Again, when a prepositional phrase begins the sentence, it is followed by a comma.
Answers will vary.

1. Music played.
   - **a.** Sweet music played.
   - **b.** Sweet music played softly.
   - **c.** At the dance, sweet music played softly in the ballroom.
   - **d.** At the dance, sweet music from another time played softly in the ballroom.
2. The wildcat leaps.
   - **a.** The angry wildcat leaps.
   - **b.** The angry wildcat leaps suddenly.
   - **c.** In the forest, the angry wildcat leaps suddenly from a tree.
   - **d.** In the forest, the angry wildcat with black stripes leaps suddenly from a tree.
3. The guest snored.
   - **a.** The tired guest snored.
   - **b.** The tired guest snored loudly.
   - **c.** At the wedding, the tired guest snored loudly during the ceremony.
   - **d.** At the wedding, the tired guest in the first row snored loudly during the ceremony.

Recognizing Simple Sentences

Now that you have practiced building simple sentences, you should be able to recognize the building blocks within a simple sentence. But before we go any further . . .

STOP! We have already seen that a complete, correct sentence must have a **noun** and a **verb** and express a complete thought. The main noun in a sentence is also known as the **subject**: the *main actor* of a sentence or *who* or *what* the sentence is about. Here's an example:

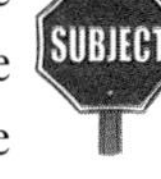

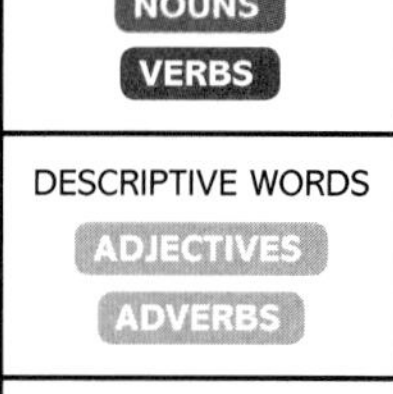

SUBJECT	VERB
Snow	melts.

Now, we can restate our general rule: Every complete sentence must have a **subject** and a **verb** and express a complete thought. Understanding this will help you write effective sentences and avoid some common problems discussed on page 294 of this chapter.

ACTIVITY 12

In the following sentences, circle the **subject** of each sentence. To identify the subject, ask yourself *Who or what is the main actor of the sentence?* OR *Who or what is this sentence about?*

A. Subject + Action Verb

EXAMPLE:
We walked.

1. Tom sneezed.
2. We forgot.
3. The mirror cracked.
4. New York buzzes.
5. You worry.

B. Subject + Linking Verb + Adjective

EXAMPLE:
The marchers grew tired.

1. Houses were expensive.
2. Stella seems unhappy.
3. It became difficult.
4. The dog looks hungry.
5. She felt guilty.

C. Subject + Helping Verb + Main Verb

EXAMPLE:
Dave has tried.

1. Turkeys can fly.
2. The rain might stop.
3. She will pass.
4. We should travel.
5. A disaster could happen.

IDENTIFYING SUBJECTS WHEN THERE IS MORE THAN ONE NOUN

As you already know, some simple sentences have *more than one* noun.

NOUN + VERB + NOUN
The store sells flowers.

Terminology Tip
In this example, *flowers* is the *object* of the sentence. It is not the main actor of the sentence; rather, it receives the action of the verb *sells*.

In this sentence, only one of these nouns is the **subject**. Because *the store* is the main actor (it is selling the flowers), it is the subject.

ACTIVITY 13

In each of the following sentences, underline the two nouns. Then, identify which is the subject of the sentence. Remember to ask yourself *Who or what is the main actor of the sentence?* OR *Who or what is this sentence about?*

EXAMPLE:
Angela washed the car. **Subject:** Angela

1. Dogs bury bones. **Subject:** Dogs
2. She fluffed the pillow. **Subject:** She
3. Tom threw the football. **Subject:** Tom
4. Computers save data. **Subject:** Computers
5. The babysitter heard noises. **Subject:** babysitter

IDENTIFYING SUBJECTS WHEN THERE ARE PREPOSITIONAL PHRASES

You have learned that prepositional phrases usually end in nouns. Another helpful hint to remember is that the noun in a prepositional phrase can never be the subject of a sentence.

SUBJECT — NOUN IN PREPOSITIONAL PHRASE

The girl in the pool swims well.

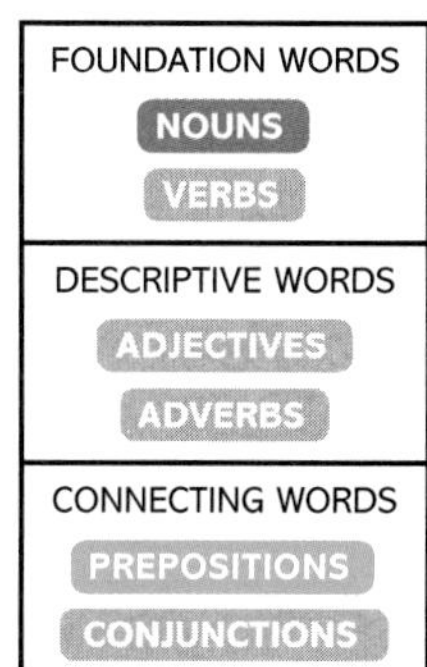

ACTIVITY 14

In each of the following sentences, underline the two nouns and identify which is the subject. One of the nouns will be in a prepositional phrase, but remember that *a noun within a prepositional phrase is* ***never*** *the subject of a sentence.*

EXAMPLE:

After class, we study. **Subject:** we

1. The motorcycle skidded on the ice. **Subject:** motorcycle
2. Before bed, I snacked. **Subject:** I
3. The snowman melted in the sun. **Subject:** snowman
4. Inside the cabin, the campers rested. **Subject:** campers
5. Rain fell during the ball game. **Subject:** Rain

ACTIVITY 15

In each of the following sentences, underline the three nouns and identify which is the subject. Remember that *a noun within a prepositional phrase is* ***never*** *the subject of a sentence.*

EXAMPLE:

With your help, I will make a cake. **Subject:** I

1. In the box, she found a puppy. **Subject:** she
2. After breakfast, Father washes the dishes. **Subject:** Father
3. That truck hauls fruit to the market. **Subject:** truck
4. During graduation, Jasmine tripped on stage. **Subject:** Jasmine
5. I hide money under my bed. **Subject:** I

ACTIVITY 16: Teamwork

Working with some of your classmates, underline the four nouns in each of the following sentences. Then, identify which noun is the subject of the sentence. Remember that *a noun within a prepositional phrase is* ***never*** *the subject of a sentence.*

EXAMPLE:

Before the day got too hot, I watered the plants behind the house. **Subject:** I

1. In the dugout, John told jokes to his teammates. **Subject:** John
2. Atlanta hosted the Olympics in the summer of 1996. **Subject:** Atlanta
3. On Monday, my professor gave a quiz on verbs. **Subject:** professor
4. My cat hides toys behind a dresser in the closet. **Subject:** cat
5. At lunch, we ordered pie for dessert. **Subject:** we

Teaching Tip

If you plan to teach subject-verb agreement (see Chapter 16, page 466), you might have students work through, or revisit, this section of Chapter 11 as preparation.

IDENTIFYING BOTH SUBJECTS AND VERBS

It is important to be able to identify the subject—and the verb that goes with it—in simple sentences because this will help you avoid errors as you write sentences of any length. The following sections will give you lots of practice in eliminating words that are not the subject or verb.

ACTIVITY 17

The following simple sentences contain one or more **prepositional phrases**. Remembering that a subject can *never* appear in these phrases, (1) cross out the prepositional phrase(s) and (2) identify the subject and the verb.

A. Cross out one prepositional phrase.

EXAMPLE:

The girl ~~with the injured dog~~ cried. **Subject:** girl **Action verb:** cried

1. A fight erupted ~~in the cafeteria~~. **Subject:** fight **Action verb:** erupted
2. ~~At the party,~~ we danced. **Subject:** we **Action verb:** danced
3. His fear ~~of snakes~~ is strong. **Subject:** fear **Linking verb:** is
4. ~~By noon,~~ Jimmy should arrive. **Subject:** Jimmy **Helping verb + Main verb:** should arrive
5. The lizard ~~on that rock~~ seems sleepy. **Subject:** lizard **Linking verb:** seems

B. Cross out two prepositional phrases.

EXAMPLE:

~~On Saturday,~~ we worked ~~in the house~~.	**Subject:** we	**Action verb:** worked
1. ~~At five o'clock,~~ the train arrived ~~in Baltimore~~.	**Subject:** train	**Action verb:** arrived
2. ~~During the party,~~ I talked ~~with Diana~~.	**Subject:** I	**Action verb:** talked
3. We had played ~~under the bridge for three days~~.	**Subject:** We	**Helping verb + Main verb:** had played
4. ~~At the reception,~~ Cecilia was lovely ~~in her black satin gown~~.	**Subject:** Cecilia	**Linking verb:** was
5. Conversations ~~about the war~~ should change his mind ~~about it~~.	**Subject:** Conversations	**Helping verb + Main verb:** should change

C. Cross out three prepositional phrases.

EXAMPLE:

~~In France,~~ I walked ~~out of a restaurant without paying~~.	**Subject:** I	**Action verb:** walked
1. ~~On New Year's Eve,~~ a bottle ~~of champagne~~ exploded ~~in my face~~.	**Subject:** bottle	**Action verb:** exploded
2. ~~Outside the store,~~ a line ~~of shoppers~~ snaked ~~around the corner~~.	**Subject:** line	**Action verb:** snaked
3. ~~In the afternoon,~~ we can see the sunset ~~over the ocean from the hilltop~~.	**Subject:** we	**Helping verb + Main verb:** can see
4. ~~After two nights of dancing at the club,~~ he was tired.	**Subject:** he	**Linking verb:** was
5. ~~At the school,~~ the children looked happy ~~about the new play area next to the parking lot~~.	**Subject:** children	**Linking verb:** looked

ACTIVITY 18

The following simple sentences contain one or more **descriptive words** (**adjectives** or **adverbs**). For each item, (1) cross out the descriptive word(s) and (2) identify the subject and the verb.

A. Cross out one descriptive word.

EXAMPLE:

That joke is ~~silly~~.	**Subject:** joke	**Linking verb:** is
1. The motor ran ~~quietly~~.	**Subject:** motor	**Action verb:** ran
2. That ~~raw~~ fish stinks.	**Subject:** fish	**Action verb:** stinks
3. The exam was ~~difficult~~.	**Subject:** exam	**Linking verb:** was

CONTINUED >

4. That cliff looks ~~dangerous~~. **Subject:** cliff **Linking verb:** looks
5. The ~~guilty~~ suspect might confess. **Subject:** suspect **Helping verb + Main verb:** might confess

B. Cross out <u>two</u> descriptive words.

EXAMPLE:
~~Light~~ rain fell ~~quietly~~. **Subject:** rain **Action verb:** fell

1. The ~~retired~~ nurse volunteers ~~often~~. **Subject:** nurse **Action verb:** volunteers
2. The ~~thin~~ man should eat ~~more~~. **Subject:** man **Helping verb + Main verb:** should eat
3. ~~Sticky~~ rice tastes ~~delicious~~! **Subject:** rice **Linking verb:** tastes
4. The ~~secret~~ operation ran ~~smoothly~~. **Subject:** operation **Action verb:** ran
5. The ~~popular~~ performer will sing ~~later~~. **Subject:** performer **Helping verb + Main verb:** will sing

C. Cross out <u>three</u> descriptive words.

EXAMPLE:
The ~~five exhausted~~ runners collapsed ~~dramatically~~. **Subject:** runners **Action verb:** collapsed

1. My ~~leather~~ suitcase is ~~somewhat heavy~~. **Subject:** suitcase **Linking verb:** is
2. ~~Sour~~ milk can smell ~~very bad~~. **Subject:** milk **Helping verb + Main verb:** can smell
3. ~~Hairy~~ spiders ~~often~~ scare ~~little~~ Ricky. **Subject:** spiders **Action verb:** scare
4. ~~Strangely,~~ he has ~~little common~~ sense. **Subject:** he **Action verb:** has
5. ~~Oddly,~~ Estelle dumped her ~~rich~~, ~~handsome~~ boyfriend. **Subject:** Estelle **Action verb:** dumped

ACTIVITY 19

The following simple sentences contain one or more **descriptive words** (**adjectives** or **adverbs**) and **prepositional phrases**. For each item, (1) cross out the descriptive word(s) and prepositional phrase(s) and (2) identify the subject and the verb.

A. Cross out <u>one</u> prepositional phrase and <u>one</u> adjective.

EXAMPLE:
~~Within three days,~~ the bananas turned ~~brown~~. **Subject:** bananas **Action verb:** turned

1. ~~After class,~~ the ~~substitute~~ teacher cried. **Subject:** teacher **Action verb:** cried

2. An ~~old~~ pipe leaks ~~under the sink~~. **Subject:** pipe **Action verb:** leaks
3. ~~On her birthday,~~ Angela seemed ~~sad~~. **Subject:** Angela **Linking verb:** seemed
4. The bread ~~in the pantry~~ became ~~stale~~. **Subject:** bread **Linking verb:** became
5. ~~Before a run,~~ you should stretch ~~tight~~ muscles. **Subject:** you **Helping verb + Main verb:** should stretch

B. Cross out one prepositional phrase and one adverb.

EXAMPLE:
~~For the dance,~~ Carlo dressed ~~formally~~. **Subject:** Carlo **Action verb:** dressed

1. ~~In summer,~~ the grass grows ~~quickly~~. **Subject:** grass **Action verb:** grows
2. We should eat ~~less~~ ~~at dinner~~. **Subject:** We **Helping verb + Main verb:** should eat
3. David called ~~repeatedly~~ ~~on his cell phone~~. **Subject:** David **Action verb:** called
4. ~~During the trial,~~ the lawyers argued ~~frequently~~. **Subject:** lawyers **Action verb:** argued
5. The kids ~~in the pool~~ might swim ~~more~~. **Subject:** kids **Helping verb + Main verb:** might swim

C. Cross out two prepositional phrases and one adjective or adverb.

EXAMPLE:
~~During the wedding,~~ the ~~annoying~~ guest laughed ~~behind his hand~~. **Subject:** guest **Action verb:** laughed

1. ~~At breakfast,~~ ~~hot~~ coffee spilled ~~on my lap~~. **Subject:** coffee **Action verb:** spilled
2. She whispered ~~softly~~ ~~in the ear of her friend~~. **Subject:** She **Action verb:** whispered
3. ~~After the concert,~~ the singer appeared ~~happy~~ ~~with her performance~~. **Subject:** singer **Linking verb:** appeared
4. The invitation ~~from Martino~~ floated ~~gently~~ ~~to the floor~~. **Subject:** invitation **Action verb:** floated
5. ~~Before church,~~ ~~young~~ volunteers will sell doughnuts ~~for the charity~~. **Subject:** volunteers **Helping verb + Main verb:** will sell

CONTINUED >

D. Cross out two prepositional phrases and two adjectives or adverbs.

EXAMPLE:

~~In the small tent,~~ the ~~uncomfortable~~ scouts fought ~~far into the night~~. Subject: scouts Action verb: fought

1. ~~During the earthquake,~~ the ~~frightened~~ children crawled ~~quickly under their desks~~. Subject: children Action verb: crawled
2. The ~~new~~ captain ~~of the team~~ must communicate ~~clearly with his teammates~~. Subject: captain Helping verb + Main verb: must communicate
3. ~~At night,~~ the ~~nervous~~ babysitter checked the lock ~~on the door twice~~. Subject: babysitter Action verb: checked
4. The ~~sexy~~ design ~~of the car~~ will make my ~~best~~ friend happy ~~about driving it~~. Subject: design Helping verb + Main verb: will make
5. The ~~cracked~~ concrete ~~on the bridge~~ appeared dangerous ~~to the inspector~~. Subject: concrete Linking verb: appeared

IDENTIFYING COMPOUND SUBJECTS AND VERBS

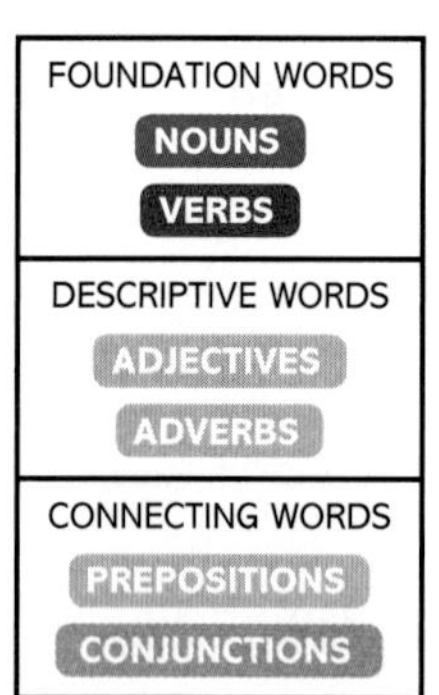

Some simple sentences have *more than one* subject or *more than one* verb. These are called **compound subjects** and **compound verbs**. We usually use the conjunction *and* when forming compound subjects or verbs. Let's take a look at a simple sentence:

SUBJECT VERB
Jason laughed.

Now, let's add another subject:

COMPOUND SUBJECT VERB
Emily and Jason laughed.

Now, let's add another verb:

SUBJECT COMPOUND VERB
Jason laughed and cried.

Note that a sentence can have *both* a compound subject and a compound verb.

COMPOUND SUBJECT COMPOUND VERB
Emily and Jason laughed and cried.

You will learn more about conjunctions and how they join parts of sentences in Chapters 12 and 13.

ACTIVITY 20

For each of the following sentences, circle the subject(s) and underline the verb(s). To avoid misidentifying the subjects, cross out any prepositional phrases first. (Remember that the subject of a sentence is *never* in a prepositional phrase.)

EXAMPLE:
Helena and her daughters sang and danced ~~in a family show~~. (2 subjects, 2 verbs)

1. Tyrone and his friends drove ~~to Las Vegas~~. (2 subjects, 1 verb)
2. Derek looked ~~in the mirror~~ and screamed. (1 subject, 2 verbs)
3. ~~After the race~~, the runners stretched and rested. (1 subject, 2 verbs)
4. Randy told a secret ~~about his sister~~ and got ~~in trouble~~. (1 subject, 2 verbs)
5. Barking and howling rang and echoed ~~throughout the halls of the kennel~~. (2 subjects, 2 verbs)

IDENTIFYING SUBJECTS AND VERBS IN WHOLE PARAGRAPHS

To build your awareness of complete sentences, it's a good idea to practice identifying subjects and verbs in whole paragraphs. The following activity will give you practice with this skill.

ACTIVITY 21

In each sentence of the following paragraphs:

- Circle the subject(s) and underline the verb(s).
- If you have trouble identifying a subject or a verb, remember to cross out any prepositional phrases in the sentence.
- If you are still having trouble, try crossing out any descriptive words.

The first sentence has been marked for you.

1. (1) The community garden is alive with activity. (2) Neighbors and volunteers pull weeds from the carrot bed. (3) A tall man digs holes for watermelon seeds. (4) Small children play games by the fence. (5) At daybreak, a rabbit hops toward the lettuce. (6) Songbirds perch on the phone lines above the garden. (7) They chirp sweetly. (8) Ladybugs fly and land on the tomato vines. (9) In the sky, even the clouds seem pleased with the happy scene. (10) Every town in America should have a community garden.

CONTINUED >

2. (1) Carlos wants an office job. (2) He applied for one on Tuesday. (3) The position is with a real estate company. (4) The company has an excellent reputation. (5) It pays its employees well and offers great benefits. (6) His girlfriend wrote a résumé for him. (7) In it, she emphasized his work qualities. (8) For example, he is punctual. (9) He is a strong team player and respects others. (10) His experience with computers and copy machines will be valuable in an office. (11) Carlos has a polite attitude. (12) Companies usually love these qualities. (13) His friends send good wishes to him. (14) Maybe he will get the job. (15) He would be a model employee!

Solving Problems in Simple Sentences: Fragments Caused by Incomplete Verbs or Missing Subjects

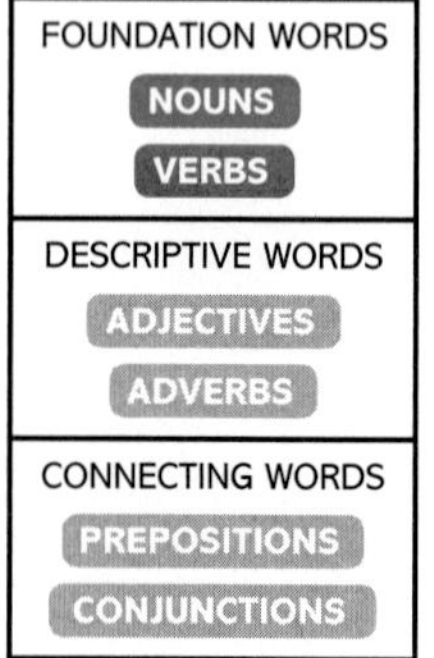

You already know that a complete sentence must have a *subject* and a *verb* and express a complete thought. If a sentence is **missing a subject or a verb**, it will be a **fragment** (an incomplete sentence).

Take a look at the following examples and see if you notice a problem.

The runner.

My job.

A person.

Each of these fragments is **missing a verb**. We don't know what is being said about the runner, the job, or the person. Now, let's add a verb to each fragment.

The runner won.

My job ended.

A person shouted.

Often, sentence fragments can be quite long when they include descriptive words and prepositional phrases. However, if the verb is missing, the sentence is still a fragment, regardless of length.

The fastest runner in the marathon.

My extremely boring job at the bank.

Behind me, a rude person.

Let's **add a verb** to each fragment to complete the thought.

> The fastest runner in the marathon won.
>
> My extremely boring job at the bank ended.
>
> Behind me, a rude person shouted.

ACTIVITY 22

In each of the following items, cross out one prepositional phrase and one descriptive word. (This will help you identify the subject.) Then, rewrite the complete word group—including the crossed-out parts—and add a subject to make it a complete sentence. You can also add other words to complete the thought. Answers will vary.

EXAMPLE:
The ~~beautiful~~ Persian cat ~~on the chair~~. The beautiful Persian cat on the chair likes catnip.

1. The ~~last~~ call ~~on my cell phone~~. The last call on my cell phone was from Elaine.
2. ~~In the morning,~~ the ~~tired~~ parents. In the morning, the tired parents slept late.
3. The ~~short~~ man ~~behind the curtain~~. The short man behind the curtain scared the children.
4. ~~At his computer,~~ the ~~serious~~ student. At his computer, the serious student worked on the project.
5. ~~In the distance,~~ ~~swirling~~ sand. In the distance, swirling sand danced across the desert.

FIXING FRAGMENTS THAT HAVE INCOMPLETE VERBS

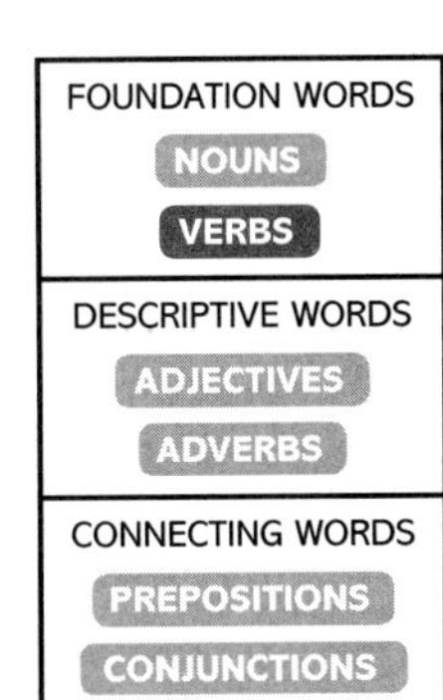

Sometimes, a sentence will contain only part of a verb. Any sentence with an **incomplete verb** is also a **fragment**. Take a look at the following examples and see if you notice a problem.

> John laughing at his brother.
>
> The police chasing a suspect.

Each of these examples is a fragment because the verb is incomplete. A verb ending with *-ing* is not a complete verb by itself. It needs one of the following helping verbs to make it complete: *am, is, are, was, were*. Take a look:

> John was laughing at his brother.
>
> The police are chasing a suspect.

For online practice with fixing fragments, visit this book's Web site at **bedfordstmartins .com/steppingstones**.

Each of these sentences is now complete and correct because it contains a subject and a complete verb (a helping verb plus the main verb). Now, take a look at the following examples and see if you notice a problem.

The kids lost in the mall.

Martha questioned by security.

Power Tip
The kids lost . . . could be the start of a complete sentence if the meaning is that the kids lost something: *The kids lost their mother in the mall.* However, the meaning here is that the kids themselves *were* lost. Therefore, another helping verb (*were*) needs to connect the kids to the description (*lost*). For more on using verbs, including *was* and *were,* see Chapter 16.

Each of these sentences is also a fragment because the verb is incomplete. To fix this type of incomplete verb, add one of the same helping verbs: *am, is, are, was, were.*

The kids were lost in the mall.

Martha was questioned by security.

ACTIVITY 23

Turn each of the following word groups into a sentence by adding *am, is, are, was,* or *were* to complete the verb. If you are unsure of what form of the verb (*am, is, are,* and so on) to use with each subject, see Chapter 16, page 456. Answers may vary.

EXAMPLE:

The letter mailed. The letter was mailed.

1. Dogs barking. Dogs were barking.
2. Wilma studying. Wilma is studying.
3. I caught. I was caught.
4. The tent destroyed. The tent was destroyed.
5. Voters complaining. Voters are complaining.

Teaching Tip
For test items on fragments, see the *Testing Tool Kit* CD available with this book.

ACTIVITY 24

The following fragments are longer because they contain prepositional phrases and descriptive words. However, the verb is still incomplete. Turn each fragment into a sentence by completing the verb. If you are unsure of what form of the verb (*am, is, are,* and so on) to use with each subject, see Chapter 16, page 456. Answers may vary.

EXAMPLE:

The ugly clown in the mini-car frightening the children.

The ugly clown in the mini-car is frightening the children.

1. A loud helicopter flying over my house.
   A loud helicopter is flying over my house.
2. In the dark sky, crying birds circling.
   In the dark sky, crying birds were circling.

3. My algebra teacher shocked by my perfect exam score.
   My algebra teacher was shocked by my perfect exam score.

4. The winning pitch thrown by my brother.
   The winning pitch was thrown by my brother.

5. A greedy executive suing the president of the company.
   A greedy executive is suing the president of the company.

FIXING FRAGMENTS THAT ARE MISSING SUBJECTS

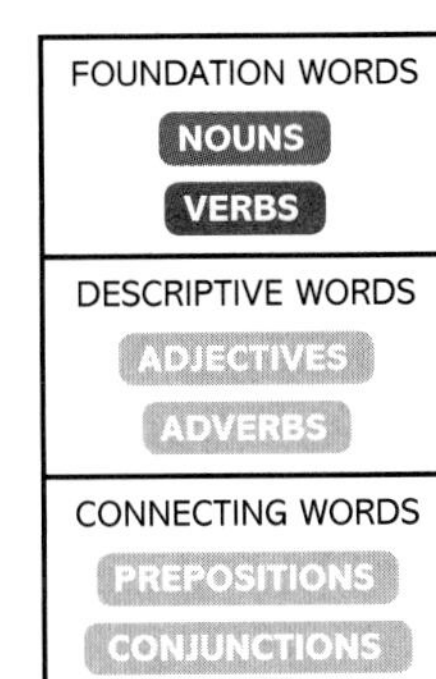

Remember that if a sentence is **missing a subject**, it will also be a **fragment**. Take a look at the following examples and see if you notice a problem.

> Plays the piano.
>
> Missed the bus.
>
> Will take the exam.

Each of these examples is a fragment because there is **no subject**. We don't know *who or what* plays the piano, missed the bus, or will take the exam. In each fragment, there is a complete verb—*plays, missed, will take*—so all we need to do is **add a subject**:

> He plays the piano.
>
> My father missed the bus.
>
> The students will take the exam.

ACTIVITY 25

Add a subject to turn each of the following fragments into a complete sentence. You do not need to change the verb. Answers will vary.

EXAMPLE: Played minor-league baseball. Luis played minor-league baseball.

1. Ran the race. Jayden ran the race.
2. Likes classical music. My mother likes classical music.
3. Will reschedule his appointment. Bruno will reschedule his appointment.
4. Wants to go home. The child wants to go home.
5. May borrow money. You may borrow money.

ACTIVITY 26

As you know, most fragments will contain some descriptive words and prepositional phrases, which may make the missing subject harder to identify. In each of the following fragments, cross out the prepositional phrases. Then you will see that there is a complete verb but **no subject**. When you write your answers, be sure to include all the prepositional phrases that were crossed out. Answers will vary.

A. Cross out two prepositional phrases. Then, turn the word groups into complete sentences by adding a subject.

EXAMPLE: ~~Across the street,~~ sold lemonade ~~for fifty cents~~.
Across the street, Jonah sold lemonade for fifty cents.

1. ~~After school,~~ practices ~~with the soccer team~~.
   After school, Natalie practices with the soccer team.
2. ~~At the bank,~~ deposited $400 ~~in her account~~.
   At the bank, Soon-Yee deposited $400 in her account.
3. ~~During the show,~~ will play two pieces ~~on the piano~~.
   During the show, he will play two pieces on the piano.
4. ~~At the mall,~~ watched a woman ~~with a pink mohawk~~.
   At the mall, we watched a woman with a pink mohawk.
5. ~~In the parking lot,~~ found a diamond ring ~~under her car~~.
   In the parking lot, my sister found a diamond ring under her car.

B. Cross out three prepositional phrases. Then, turn the word groups into complete sentences by adding a subject.

EXAMPLE: ~~Under a pot outside the front door,~~ kept a key ~~to her house~~.
Under a pot outside the front door, Lucy kept a key to her house.

1. ~~During his driver's test,~~ hit the curb ~~near the shoe store at the mall~~.
   During his driver's test, Ezra hit the curb near the shoe store at the mall.
2. ~~Before the divorce filing,~~ will search ~~in the phonebook for a lawyer~~.
   Before the divorce filing, Taylor will search in the phonebook for a lawyer.
3. ~~From a log in the swamp,~~ watches the fish ~~in the water~~.
   From a log in the swamp, the frog watches the fish in the water.
4. ~~At the meeting on Monday,~~ wore a black suit ~~with a crisp shirt~~.
   At the meeting on Monday, Chris wore a black suit with a crisp shirt.
5. ~~In the yard behind the house,~~ is hanging lights ~~for the party~~.
   In the yard behind the house, my friend is hanging lights for the party.

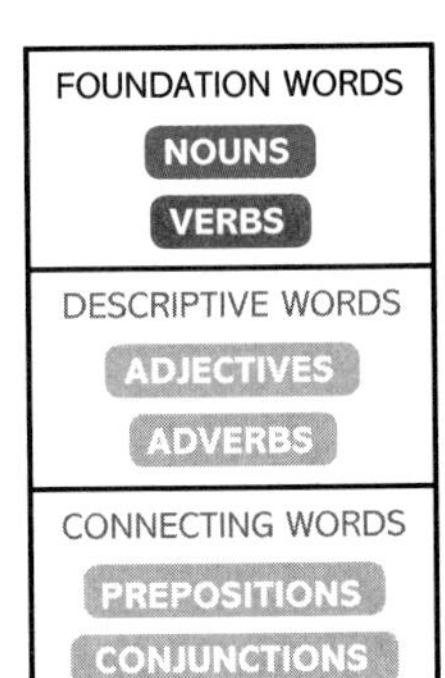

FIXING FRAGMENTS THAT HAVE MISSING SUBJECTS AND INCOMPLETE VERBS

Sometimes, a fragment may be **missing a subject** *and* have an **incomplete verb**. Take a look at the following examples and see if you notice the problems.

> Running to first base.
>
> To earn her degree.
>
> Hurt by his girlfriend.

Each fragment has an **incomplete verb**. Also, each fragment is **missing a subject**: we don't know *who or what* is running, earning, or being hurt. To fix this type of fragment, you must do two things: **add a subject** and **fix the verb**. If you add a subject but do not fix the verb, the sentence will not make sense. Take a look:

> The batter running to first base.
>
> Elizabeth to earn her degree.
>
> My brother hurt by his girlfriend.

Each of these examples is still a fragment because we have not fixed the verb. You may make the verb complete in a number of ways. For example, you may **change the verb** to the present, past, or future tense, or **add a helping verb** (*am, is, are, was, were,* or *will*) as needed. Take a look at the following complete sentences:

SIMPLE PRESENT	The batter runs to first base. Elizabeth earns her degree.
PRESENT WITH HELPING VERB	The batter is running to first base. Elizabeth is earning her degree. My brother is hurt by his girlfriend.
SIMPLE PAST	The batter ran to first base. Elizabeth earned her degree.
PAST WITH HELPING VERB	The batter was running to first base. Elizabeth has earned her degree. My brother was hurt by his girlfriend.
FUTURE WITH HELPING VERB	The batter will run to first base. Elizabeth will earn her degree.

Also, note that ***to* + a verb** cannot stand alone as a verb. This combination must be preceded by a verb or a verb and any other words needed for the sentence to make sense:

> Elizabeth wants to earn **her degree.**
>
> Elizabeth would like to earn **her degree.**
>
> Elizabeth hoped to earn **her degree.**
>
> Elizabeth is happy to earn **her degree.**

For more advice on using verbs and forming tenses, see Chapter 16. And for advice on finding and fixing other types of sentence fragments, see Chapters 13 and 14.

Teaching Tip
For a tutorial on finding and fixing fragments, see the *Make-a-Paragraph Kit* CD available with this book.

ACTIVITY 27

Rewrite each of the following fragments by doing two things: **add a subject** and **fix the verb**. Refer to the previous pages for more examples. Answers will vary.

EXAMPLE: To go to the mall. I hate to go to the mall.

1. Jumping for the ball. The outfielder is jumping for the ball.
2. To make the basketball team. Isabelle wants to make the basketball team.
3. Encouraged by the teacher. I was encouraged by the teacher.
4. To drive across the United States. Paul would like to drive across the United States.
5. Living in Seattle. Yolanda is living in Seattle.

ACTIVITY 28

The following fragments are longer because they contain more prepositional phrases and descriptive words. However, the subject is still missing and the verb is incomplete. Again, correct each sentence by doing two things: **add a subject** and **fix the verb**. Answers will vary.

EXAMPLE: In the aquarium pool, eaten by a shark.
In the aquarium pool, a seal was eaten by a shark.

1. On his sixteenth birthday, to pass his second driver's test.
On his sixteenth birthday, Kyle tried to pass his second driver's test.
2. Under the basement stairs, caught in a mousetrap.
Under the basement stairs, a mouse was caught in a mousetrap.
3. Along a dusty dirt road near the lake, ride our motorcycles.
Along a dusty dirt road near the lake, we like to ride our motorcycles.

4. Between you and me, wearing too much heavy cologne.
   Between you and me, our boss is wearing too much heavy cologne.

5. Behind the convenience store, discovered with a crowbar by an angry police officer.
   Behind the convenience store, a thief was discovered with a crowbar by an angry police officer.

FIXING FRAGMENTS IN WHOLE PARAGRAPHS

The following activity will give you practice with recognizing and fixing fragments in whole paragraphs—a valuable skill for improving your own writing.

ACTIVITY 29

Read each of the following paragraphs carefully, looking for fragments. Then, rewrite each fragment, turning it into a complete sentence. You may need to add a subject or a verb, or you may need to complete or rewrite a verb. However, do not join any sentences together in this practice. If a sentence is already complete and correct, write "OK" above it. The first sentence of each paragraph has been edited for you. Answers may vary.

The following paragraph has eleven fragments, including the one that has been edited for you.

1. (1) Jack [was] going to pitch in the big game. (2) ~~Had~~ [He had] practiced for three months. (3) His pitching arm [was] looking good. (4) [OK] The coach helped him with his form. (5) ~~Videotaped~~ [He videotaped] Jack pitching the ball. (6) [OK] They studied the video. (7) [OK] Jack corrected his posture and angle. (8) ~~Lifted~~ [He lifted] weights to improve his strength. (9) ~~Stretched~~ [He stretched] to increase his flexibility. (10) [He felt] Felt more confident than ever before. (11) The night of the big game, Jack [had an accident]. (12) [OK] The accident happened on the way to the game. (13) ~~Tripping~~ [Jack tripped] over a stump. (14) [OK] He landed on his left wrist. (15) As a result, [he was] unable to pitch in the game. (16) Fortunately, [his team] won anyway.

CONTINUED >

The following paragraph has eleven fragments, including the one that has been edited for you.

2. (1) Last summer, [Maya and her mother] traveled to Canada. (2) ~~Hoping~~ [They hoped] to save money. (3) ~~Stayed~~ [They stayed] in bed and breakfasts and inexpensive hotels. (4) Also, [they] cooked many of their own meals. (5) ~~To~~ [Maya and her mother tried to] take advantage of free attractions. (6) One afternoon, they [watched an outdoor performer.] (7) Another day, they went to a town festival. [OK] (8) They also looked for stores with inexpensive souvenirs. [OK] (9) ~~Sold~~ [One store sold] postcards and lapel pins. (10) Sometimes, ~~enjoying~~ [they enjoyed] just sipping coffee at outdoor cafés. (11) ~~Surprised~~ [The women were surprised] by all the fun they had for so little money. (12) ~~Realizing~~ [They realized] that great vacations do not have to be expensive. (13) Already, [they are] excited about taking another trip next summer!

The following paragraph has fourteen fragments.

3. (1) Melissa loves to go to the beach in winter. [OK] (2) For one thing, [she likes] seeing the snow on the sand dunes. (3) Also, the frost on the sea grass is beautiful. [OK] (4) Seals warm in their blubber [play] offshore. (5) In addition, almost no people [are] on the beach in winter time. (6) The shore [is] peaceful and quiet. (7) There [are] no tourists. (8) ~~Whipped~~ [Her clothes are whipped] by the cold wind. (9) However, the sky [is] clear and blue. (10) Often, [she] jogs along the water. (11) Sometimes, other people [are] taking walks. [OK] (12) One time, Melissa saw a famous actor. (13) He [was] picking up smooth black rocks. (14) ~~Putting~~ [He put] them in his pocket. (15) Mostly, [she] loves the sunset over the ocean. (16) It looks different in the winter. [OK] (17) ~~Is~~ [The beach is] lonely but quiet and beautiful. (18) ~~Her~~ [Winter is her] favorite time of year at the ocean.

ACTIVITY 30: TEAMWORK

When you have completed correcting one of the paragraphs from Activity 29, get together with two or three classmates. See if each of you can identify any fragments that the others missed. Also, did you fix any of the fragments differently? When you have finished, discuss any differences you found. If you still have any questions about fragments, ask your instructor.

ACTIVITY 31

Find a paper that you wrote recently but haven't turned in for a grade. Then, read the paper carefully, looking for any fragments; put a check by these. Next, correct the fragments.

Bringing It All Together

In this chapter, you have learned what a basic simple sentence is, how to build longer simple sentences, and how to avoid a common problem in these sentences: fragments. Check off each of the following statements that you understand. For any that you do not understand, review the appropriate pages in this chapter.

- ☐ A sentence must have a noun and a verb and express a complete thought. (See page 276.)
- ☐ In some sentences, the verb is followed by another noun (page 277), an adjective (in the case of linking verbs; page 278), or another verb (in the case of helping verbs; page 278).
- ☐ Descriptive words also build on simple sentences. These include **adjectives** (which describe nouns) and **adverbs** (which describe verbs, adjectives, and other adverbs). (See page 279.)
- ☐ Longer sentences may have one or more prepositional phrases that tell us *when, where,* and sometimes *how* an action occurs. (See page 281.)
- ☐ The main noun in a sentence is also known as the **subject**: the main actor of a sentence or who or what the sentence is about. This means that every complete sentence must have a subject and a verb and express a complete thought. (See page 285.)
- ☐ A noun within a prepositional phrase is *never* the subject of a sentence. (See page 287.)
- ☐ Some simple sentences have *more than one subject* or *more than one verb.* These are called **compound subjects** and **compound verbs**. (See page 292.)
- ☐ If a sentence is missing a subject or a verb, it will be a **fragment** (an incomplete sentence). (See page 294.) Any sentence with an *incomplete verb* is also a fragment. (See page 296.)

Chapter 12

The Compound Sentence

OVERVIEW OF THIS CHAPTER

This is a simple sentence:

NOUN + VERB + . = I study.

This is a compound sentence because it joins two simple sentences:

NOUN + VERB + , + CONJUNCTIONS + NOUN + VERB + .

= I study, and I learn.

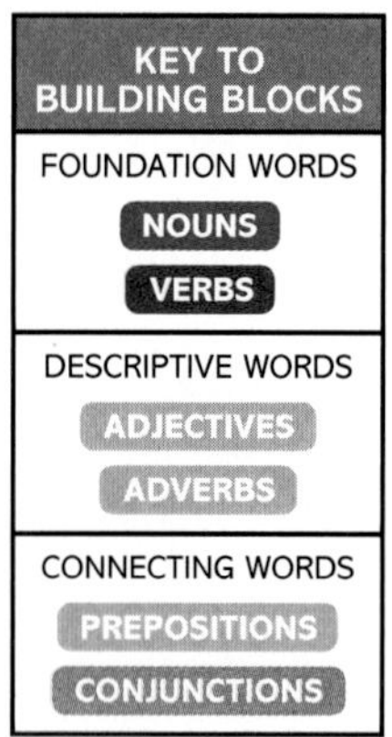

Power Tip

BOAS is a good abbreviation for remembering the common conjunctions *but, or, and,* and *so.* There are three more conjunctions: *yet, for, nor.* However, these conjunctions are used less frequently, so we will not address them in detail in this chapter. To practice using these three conjunctions, visit this book's Web site at **bedfordstmartins.com/steppingstones.**

Building Compound Sentences

In the previous chapter, you learned that a **simple sentence** may have as few as two words: a subject (noun) and a verb. Here are two examples:

We walked. They drove.

In this chapter, you will learn how to write and recognize compound sentences. A **compound sentence** is two or more related simple sentences joined together. Often, these sentences are joined using **a comma and a conjunction**.

The four most common conjunctions used to create compound sentences are *and, but, or,* and *so*. These are known as **coordinating conjunctions**.

Using the coordinating conjunction *and,* let's join the two simple sentences shown above:

SIMPLE SENTENCE 1 SIMPLE SENTENCE 2

We walked, and they drove.

COMMA AND CONJUNCTION

Notice that the word *they* does not start with a capital letter in this example because it no longer begins a sentence.

The compound sentence is one of the most important sentence forms. To master it, remember these two rules:

1. Each simple sentence must have its own subject and its own verb.
2. The sentences must be joined correctly. Often, you will use the conjunctions *and, but, or,* or *so,* and these conjunctions must be preceded by a comma.

ACTIVITY 1

Complete each of the following compound sentences by adding the missing items. Remember to add a comma before the conjunction. Answers will vary.

A. Add two subjects and a comma.

EXAMPLE: Lena sings, and Dan dances.

1. Dogs bark, and birds chirp.
2. Raheem won, but Vicky lost.
3. Terelle arrived, so I will leave.

B. Add two verbs and a comma.

EXAMPLE: You laugh, but I cry.

1. The rain pours, and the sun shines.
2. We drive, but they walk.
3. Julia disappeared, so Damien worried.

UNDERSTANDING THE MEANINGS OF DIFFERENT CONJUNCTIONS

Each conjunction expresses a *different type of relationship* between two simple sentences.

- Use **and** to combine two similar ideas:

  IDEA 1 IDEA 2

  Food nourishes, and exercise strengthens.

  These two ideas both express healthy influences on the body.

- Use **but** to contrast two different ideas:

  IDEA 1 IDEA 2

  Blanca forgot, but Edgar remembered.

  Each idea expresses a contrasting action.

- Use **so** to show a result:

  IDEA 1 IDEA 2

  The team won, so we celebrated.

  Here, the second idea is a result of the first idea.

- Use **or** to show alternatives:

  IDEA 1 IDEA 2

  The children must participate, or they will get bored.

  These two ideas express alternative options or possibilities.

Teaching Tip
Ask students to come up with more example sentences using the different conjunctions described in this section.

For online practice with compound sentences, visit this book's Web site at **bedfordstmartins.com/steppingstones**.

To sum up, the four types of relationships are **combination** (*and*), **contrast** (*but*), **result** (*so*), and **alternatives** (*or*). The following exercise will help you recognize the different relationships between two ideas in compound sentences.

ACTIVITY 2

First, add a conjunction (***and, but, so,*** or ***or***) to complete each compound sentence. Then, circle which type of relationship the conjunction suggests between the two ideas. Answers may vary.

EXAMPLE: You clean the bathroom, ___and___ I will clean the kitchen. (combination, contrast, result, alternatives)

1. Jonah inherited money, ___so___ he bought a house. (combination, contrast, result, alternatives)
2. Ida must stop gambling, ___or___ she will go broke. (combination, contrast, result, alternatives)
3. Asad dislikes peas, ___so___ he refuses to eat them. (combination, contrast, result, alternatives)
4. I will make a pie, ___and___ Dennis will bring cupcakes. (combination, contrast, result, alternatives)
5. I called Eric three times, ___but___ he did not call back. (combination, contrast, result, alternatives)

In a compound sentence, the conjunction that you use will determine the idea in the second sentence. For example:

COMBINATION	**They painted their garage, and they re-roofed the house.**
CONTRAST	**They painted their garage, but they did not paint the house.**
RESULT	**They painted their garage, so the neighbors stopped complaining.**

In each sentence, the first idea is the same. However, the second idea changes according to the conjunction used.

ACTIVITY 3

First, add a conjunction (***and, but, so,*** or ***or***) that makes sense to complete each compound sentence. Then, circle which type of relationship the conjunction suggests between the two ideas. Answers may vary.

EXAMPLE:

a. **Milo lost the race, ___but___ he won the championship. (combination, contrast, result, alternatives)**

b. **Milo lost the race, ___so___ he didn't win the medal. (combination, contrast, result, alternatives)**

c. **Milo lost the race, ___and___ he wrecked his car. (combination, contrast, result, alternatives)**

1. **a.** Diego lost his wallet, ___so___ he became upset. (combination, contrast, result, alternatives)
   b. Diego lost his wallet, ___but___ he found his keys. (combination, contrast, result, alternatives)
   c. Diego lost his wallet, ___or___ somebody stole it. (combination, contrast, result, alternatives)

2. a. My boss might fire me, ___or___ she might fire Bob. (combination, contrast, result, alternatives)
   b. My boss might fire me, ___so___ I should be careful. (combination, contrast, result, alternatives)
   c. My boss might fire me, ___but___ that is unlikely. (combination, contrast, result, alternatives)
3. a. Jessica needs a car, ___so___ she did some research. (combination, contrast, result, alternatives)
   b. Jessica needs a car, ___but___ she cannot afford one. (combination, contrast, result, alternatives)
   c. Jessica needs a car, ___and___ she will get one. (combination, contrast, result, alternatives)

ACTIVITY 4: Teamwork

With classmates, discuss what type of idea is necessary to complete each compound sentence. Then, write a simple sentence in the space provided to complete each sentence. Answers may vary.

EXAMPLE:

a. Leandra forgot Tim's birthday, so she called him to apologize.

b. Leandra forgot Tim's birthday, but she always remembered his anniversary.

c. Leandra forgot Tim's birthday, and she missed his party.

1. a. The dentist found cavities, and he filled them.
   b. The dentist found cavities, so he scolded the patient.
   c. The dentist found cavities, but he didn't scold the patient.
2. a. The puppy must eat, or he will become sick.
   b. The puppy must eat, but there is no food.
   c. The puppy must eat, so I will feed him.
3. a. Tamika likes the outdoors, so she visits parks.
   b. Tamika likes the outdoors, but she hates bugs.
   c. Tamika likes the outdoors, and she loves hiking.

Sometimes, *and* and *but* can both make sense in a compound sentence:

Planes fly, and boats float.

Planes fly, but boats float.

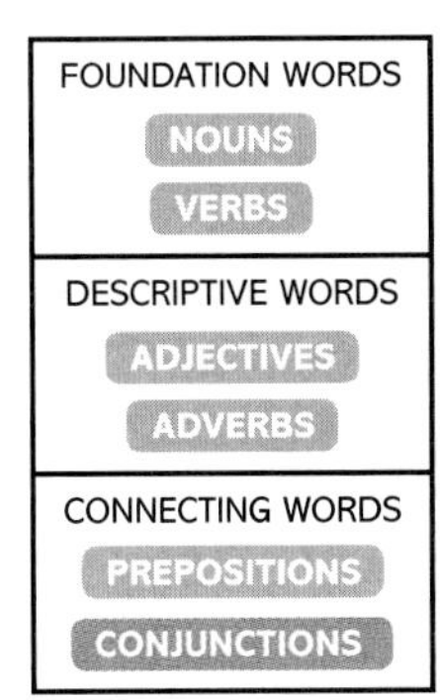

The first sentence suggests that planes and boats are similar because they are both modes of transportation. However, the second sentence suggests that planes and boats are different in the particular ways they move.

Let's consider another example:

My husband votes Republican, and I vote Democrat.

My husband votes Republican, but I vote Democrat.

The first sentence suggests that the husband and wife are similar because they both vote for a political party. The second sentence suggests that the husband and wife are different in the particular party they vote for. The writer would have to decide whether to highlight the similarity or the difference between the husband and wife.

ACTIVITY 5: Teamwork

With classmates, discuss how the sentences with ***and*** express a similarity and how the sentences with ***but*** express a difference. Then, write a brief explanation in the space provided. Answers may vary.

EXAMPLE:

a. The soccer team runs two miles, **and** the cross country team runs eight miles.
Similarity: Running is a part of both teams' training.

b. The soccer team runs two miles, **but** the cross country team runs eight miles.
Difference: The cross country team runs six miles more than the soccer team.

1. a. My sister jogs, **and** I run.
Similarity: Both people exercise.

b. My sister jogs, **but** I run.
Difference: One person moves faster than the other.

2. a. Blake drives a minivan, **and** Iris drives a pickup truck.
Similarity: Both Blake and Iris drive large vehicles.

b. Blake drives a minivan, **but** Iris drives a pickup truck.
Difference: Blake and Iris drive different types of vehicles.

3. a. Duane dislikes spinach, **and** he hates liver.
Similarity: Duane strongly dislikes both spinach and liver.

b. Duane dislikes spinach, **but** he hates liver.
Difference: Duane dislikes liver even more than spinach.

DISTINGUISHING COMPOUND SUBJECTS/VERBS AND COMPOUND SENTENCES

In Chapter 11, you learned about compound subjects and verbs. In this chapter, you are learning about compound sentences. It is very important that you do not confuse these two things. Compound subjects and verbs can appear in **one simple sentence**. On the other hand, compound sentences must contain **two or more simple sentences**.

First, let's review compound subjects and verbs found in **one simple sentence**.

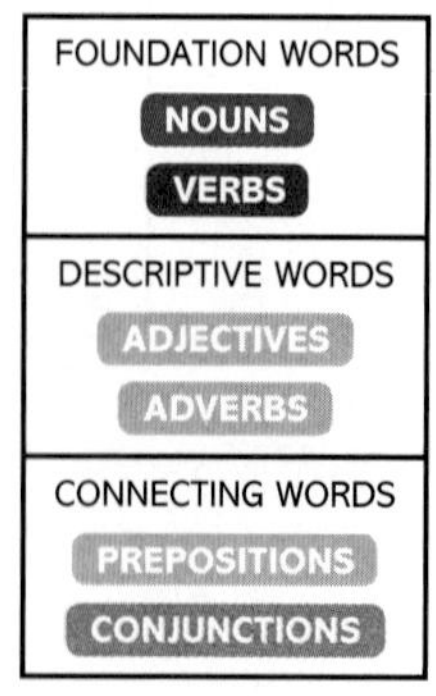

- A compound subject:

Rhonda and Bill danced.

Two subjects are performing the *same* action. Notice that when the conjunction (*and*) joins two simple subjects, **no comma is used.**

- A compound verb:

Rhonda danced and sang.

One subject is performing *two different* but connected actions. Notice that when the conjunction (*and*) joins two simple verbs, **no comma is used.**

- A compound subject and a compound verb:

ONE COMPOUND SUBJECT — ONE COMPOUND VERB

Rhonda and Bill danced and sang.

Two subjects are performing *two* different but connected actions. Notice that when the conjunction (*and*) joins two simple subjects or two simple verbs, **no comma is used.**

Next, let's look at a **compound sentence**, which must contain two or more simple sentences.

SENTENCE 1 — SENTENCE 2

Rhonda danced, and Bill sang.

1ST SUBJECT — 1ST VERB — 2ND SUBJECT — 2ND VERB

In a compound sentence, there will always be at least two separate subjects involved in at least two separate actions. Notice that when a conjunction joins two simple sentences, **a comma is required.** Here's another example, with the conjunction *but:*

Kent smoked, but he quit.

Power Tip

Note that you can also create compound adjectives (***Beautiful and talented*** *Rhonda danced*), compound adverbs (*Rhonda danced* ***smoothly and gracefully***), and compound prepositional phrases (*Rhonda danced* ***at home and at the ballet studio***).

ACTIVITY 6

For each simple sentence below, do the following:

- Underline the subjects, and circle the verbs.
- Rewrite the sentences, turning them into compound sentences by matching each subject to its own verb. Make sure to put a comma before the conjunction. Answers will vary.

EXAMPLE:

Simple sentence: The husband and wife cleaned the house and cooked dinner.

Compound sentence: The husband cleaned the house, and the wife cooked dinner.

1. **Simple sentence:** Jennifer and Minh swam laps and played tennis.

   Compound sentence: Jennifer swam laps, and Minh played tennis.

2. **Simple sentence:** The demonstrators and the police clashed and yelled.

   Compound sentence: The demonstrators clashed, and the police yelled.

3. **Simple sentence:** Bekka and Thomas enjoyed the picnic but left early.

   Compound sentence: Bekka enjoyed the picnic, but Thomas left early.

4. **Simple sentence:** The children and the adults like roller coasters but get sick on them.

   Compound sentence: The children like roller coasters, but the adults get sick on them.

ACTIVITY 7

Rewrite each of the following simple sentences, turning them into compound sentences. You will need to invent a second subject to complete the compound sentence. Remember to add a comma when you write the compound sentence. Answers will vary.

EXAMPLE:

Simple sentence: The bartender spilled a drink and got soaked.

Compound sentence: The bartender spilled a drink, and a customer got soaked.

1. **Simple sentence:** My sister told a joke and laughed.
   Compound sentence: My sister told a joke, and we laughed.
2. **Simple sentence:** The tennis star missed the ball and became angry.
   Compound sentence: The tennis star missed the ball, and her coach became angry.
3. **Simple sentence:** Marcus swerved off the road but did not crash.
   Compound sentence: Marcus swerved off the road, but his car did not crash.
4. **Simple sentence:** Jorge dressed in a chicken costume and put on a cowboy hat.
   Compound sentence: Jorge dressed in a chicken costume, and his friend put on a cowboy hat.
5. **Simple sentence:** Nina walked into the room and yelled, "Surprise!"
   Compound sentence: Nina walked into the room, and the guests yelled, "Surprise!"

ACTIVITY 8

Rewrite each of the following simple sentences, turning them into compound sentences. You will need to invent a second verb to complete the compound sentence. Remember to add a comma when you write the compound sentence. Answers will vary.

EXAMPLE:

Simple sentence: The clown and his dog rode a bike.

Compound sentence: The clown rode a bike, and his dog barked.

1. **Simple sentence:** Kristoff and his wife danced.
   Compound sentence: Kristoff danced, and his wife sang.
2. **Simple sentence:** The apartment building and library burned down.
   Compound sentence: The apartment building burned down, but the library remains.

3. **Simple sentence:** Clea and her husband told the truth.
   Compound sentence: Clea told the truth, but her husband lied.
4. **Simple sentence:** The brownies and cookies were rich.
   Compound sentence: The brownies were rich, and the cookies were buttery.
5. **Simple sentence:** The president and vice president traveled.
   Compound sentence: The president traveled, and the vice president stayed home.

In some cases, you can express the same ideas as *either* a simple sentence *or* a compound sentence. For example:

- A simple sentence:

ONE SUBJECT | ONE COMPOUND VERB

Andrea called but hung up.

This sentence has only one simple subject and one compound verb.

- A compound sentence:

This sentence has two separate subjects and two separate verbs. The pronoun *she* refers to *Andrea,* but it counts as a separate subject.

If both of these sentences express the same ideas, and both of them are grammatically correct, which is the best choice? The simple sentence states matter-of-factly that Andrea called and hung up; perhaps she never really intended to talk to the person she was calling. In the compound sentence, special emphasis is given to the fact that Andrea hung up; the author may be suggesting that Andrea changed her mind after calling and decided to hang up.

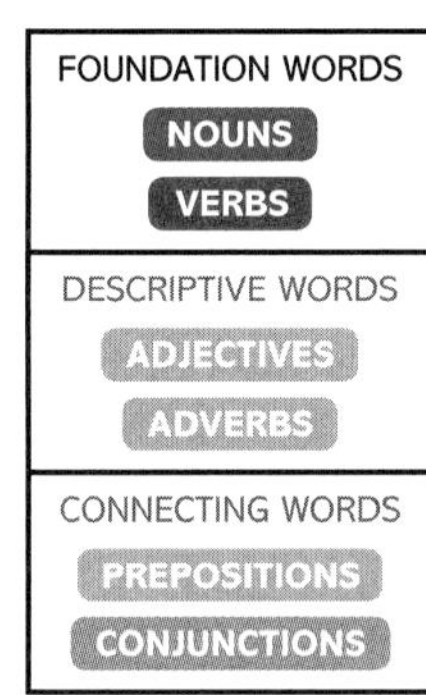

Power Tip
Notice that the second part of the sentence uses the singular (one person) feminine pronoun *she* to refer to *Andrea.* Whenever you include a pronoun in the second part of a compound sentence, make sure that it matches the subject in the first part: feminine pronouns for singular feminine subjects, masculine pronouns for singular masculine subjects, and so on. (For more on pronouns, see Chapter 10, page 269, and Chapter 17.)

ACTIVITY 9

Rewrite each of the following simple sentences as a compound sentence expressing the same idea. You will need to do the following:

- Add a pronoun as the second subject.
- Add a second verb, and make sure that this verb is complete.
- Add the required comma to the compound sentence.

CONTINUED >

EXAMPLE:

Simple sentence: You must floss your teeth or face health consequences.

Compound sentence: You must floss your teeth, or you may face health consequences.

1. **Simple sentence:** Many people floss their teeth but do not realize that flossing might help prevent heart disease.

   Compound sentence: Many people floss their teeth, but they do not realize that flossing might help prevent heart disease.

2. **Simple sentence:** Researchers suspected a connection between gum disease and heart disease and eventually found a link.

   Compound sentence: Researchers suspected a connection between gum disease and heart disease, and they eventually found a link.

3. **Simple sentence:** Mouth bacteria can build up and travel to the heart.

   Compound sentence: Mouth bacteria can build up, and it can travel to the heart.

4. **Simple sentence:** Pregnant women can be affected and deliver premature babies.

   Compound sentence: Pregnant women can be affected, and they can deliver premature babies.

5. **Simple sentence:** Flossing can prevent tooth and gum disease and improve one's overall health.

   Compound sentence: Flossing can prevent tooth and gum disease, and it can improve one's overall health.

ACTIVITY 10: Teamwork

With classmates, look at the sentences from Activity 9. In each case, discuss whether you prefer the simple sentence or the compound sentence. Try to explain why you prefer one version over the other. Remember that the compound sentence often gives special emphasis to the second idea.

ACTIVITY 11

From the two simple sentences provided, create (1) a simple sentence with a compound verb and (2) a compound sentence with a pronoun for the second subject. Make sure to include the required comma in the compound sentence. Answers may vary.

EXAMPLE:

Simple sentences: Derek buys hats. Derek never wears them.

Simple sentence with compound verb: Derek buys hats but never wears them.

Compound sentence: Derek buys hats, but he never wears them.

1. **Simple sentence:** Victoria buys fabric. Victoria makes quilts.

   Simple sentence with compound verb: Victoria buys fabric and makes quilts.

   Compound sentence: Victoria buys fabric, and she makes quilts.

2. **Simple sentence:** Farad plays the guitar. Farad does not sing.

   Simple sentence with compound verb: Farad plays the guitar but does not sing.

   Compound sentence: Farad plays the guitar, but he does not sing.

3. **Simple sentence:** The Jacobsons volunteer. The Jacobsons donate money.

   Simple sentence with compound verb: The Jacobsons volunteer and donate money.

   Compound sentence: The Jacobsons volunteer, and they donate money.

4. **Simple sentence:** The waiter dropped the tray. The waiter got fired.

   Simple sentence with compound verb: The waiter dropped the tray and got fired.

   Compound sentence: The waiter dropped the tray, and he got fired.

5. **Simple sentence:** The skier fell. The skier did not break her leg.

   Simple sentence with compound verb: The skier fell but did not break her leg.

   Compound sentence: The skier fell, but she did not break her leg.

ACTIVITY 12

Write five of your own compound sentences, using the sentences from Activity 11 (or earlier models) as examples. If you like, you can first write two simple sentences and then join them using a conjunction and a comma.

USING A SEMICOLON IN PLACE OF A CONJUNCTION

In some cases, you can use a semicolon (;) instead of a conjunction to connect two closely related simple sentences. Let's examine three possible ways to express the same pair of ideas:

1. Use a "hard" period:

   SENTENCE 1 SENTENCE 2

   Watching basketball is fun. Playing it is better.

The "hard" period separates the two ideas, suggesting that there is no special connection between them. This separation is reinforced by the capitalization of the first word in the second sentence.

2. Use a conjunction preceded by a comma:

SENTENCE 1 SENTENCE 2

Watching basketball is fun, but playing it is better.

The conjunction joins the two ideas, suggesting that there is a special connection between them.

3. Use a "soft" period (a semicolon):

SENTENCE 1 SENTENCE 2

Watching basketball is fun; playing it is better.

The "soft" period joins the two ideas, suggesting that there is a special connection between them. This connection is reinforced by the lack of capitalization of the first word in the second sentence.

Teaching Tip
You might also describe a semicolon as a "rolling stop" and a period as a "full stop."

The most important rule to remember as you start to use the semicolon is this: both "hard" and "soft" periods must always *follow* a complete sentence. Semicolons (and often periods) must also *be followed* by another complete sentence.

SENTENCE 1 SENTENCE 2

The music started. The dancers appeared.

SENTENCE 1 SENTENCE 2

The music started; the dancers appeared.

Power Tip
Although the semicolon has other uses as described in Appendix B, its main use is to connect two sentences with a "soft" period. We recommend that you master this use of the semicolon before attempting others.

Many students try to use the semicolon to replace commas. **Avoid this mistake!** As a "soft" period, the semicolon is nearly as powerful as a "hard" period, and you must respect its authority.

ACTIVITY 13

Form compound sentences from each pair of simple sentences by (1) using a comma and a conjunction and (2) using a semicolon. Answers may vary.

EXAMPLE:

Simple sentences: Thunderstorms are frightening. Hurricanes are terrifying.

Compound sentence with a conjunction: Thunderstorms are frightening, but hurricanes are terrifying.

Compound sentence with a semicolon: Thunderstorms are frightening; hurricanes are terrifying.

1. **Simple sentences:** Red is flattering. I wear it often.

   Compound sentence with a conjunction: Red is flattering, and I wear it often.

   Compound sentence with a semicolon: Red is flattering; I wear it often.

2. **Simple sentences:** Cheating is dishonest. Covering it up is worse.

   Compound sentence with a conjunction: Cheating is dishonest, but covering it up is worse.

   Compound sentence with a semicolon: Cheating is dishonest; covering it up is worse.

3. **Simple sentences:** I cheated at cards. I regret it.

   Compound sentence with a conjunction: I cheated at cards, and I regret it.

   Compound sentence with a semicolon: I cheated at cards; I regret it.

Many students have difficulty deciding when a semicolon is a better choice than a conjunction. Take a look at these two sentences:

> Slot machines require luck, but poker requires skill.
>
> Slot machines require luck; poker requires skill.

Some writers would say that the contrast between slot machines and poker is obvious, so the conjunction *but* is not necessary. Other writers would say that the conjunction emphasizes the contrast. Both versions are appropriate. If you were faced with this choice, you would have to decide which version you like best.

ACTIVITY 14: Teamwork

With classmates, look at the sentences that you wrote for Activity 13. In each case, discuss whether you prefer the compound sentence with the conjunction or the compound sentence with the semicolon. Try to explain why you prefer one version over the other.

In many compound sentences, the semicolon will not work effectively. How will you know when this is the case? First, remember that a conjunction provides information about the relationship between the two ideas that are being combined (combination, contrast, result, alternatives). However, **the semicolon does not provide this information** so it should be used only when that relationship is already clear. In general, you can use a semicolon in place of *and* (a simple combination) and sometimes in place of *but* (a simple contrast). Take a look:

COMBINATION	Slot machines require luck, and poker requires skill.

(Similiarity: Both forms of gambling require something from the gambler.)

SIMPLE CONTRAST	Slot machines require luck, but poker requires skill.

(Difference: Each form of gambling requires something different from the gambler.)

In both of these sentences, the relationship between the two ideas is very clear, so we can replace the conjunction with a semicolon:

> Slot machines require luck; poker requires skill.

Power Tip
Avoid using a semicolon to replace *so* (a result), *or* (alternatives), and *but* (when it expresses a strong contrast). In general, you will not use semicolons very often. In fact, most writers use many more conjunctions than semicolons.

With the semicolon, the relationship between the two parts is still clear and the sentence flows smoothly. However, if the relationship between the two parts of a sentence is more complicated, you will need to use a conjuction instead of a semicolon. Take a look:

RESULT	Slot machines require luck, so unlucky people should avoid them.
ALTERNATIVES	Slot machines require luck, or they may just require determination.
STRONG CONTRAST	Slot machines require luck, but some say skill is involved.

In each of these sentences, the conjunction provides useful information that helps connect the two ideas clearly. If we replace the conjuction with a semicolon, the relationship between the two ideas might not be completely clear, and the sentence might not flow smoothly. Take a look:

> Slot machines require luck; unlucky people should avoid them.
> Slot machines require luck; they may just require determination.
> Slot machines require luck; some say skill is involved.

ACTIVITY 15: Teamwork

For each item below, do the following:

- Work individually to form two compound sentences from each pair of simple sentences. Do this in two ways: (1) with a conjunction, and (2) with a semicolon. Make sure the conjunction is preceded by a comma.
- Working with classmates, decide which compound sentence is more effective.

Answers may vary.

EXAMPLE:

Simple sentences: Jamie loves baseball. His parents take him to many games.

Compound sentence with a conjunction: Jamie loves baseball, so his parents take him to many games.

Compound sentence with a semicolon: Jamie loves baseball; his parents take him to many games.

1. **Simple sentences:** Jamie likes a lot of teams. The Orioles are his favorite.

   Compound sentence with a conjunction: Jamie likes a lot of teams, but the Orioles are his favorite.

   Compound sentence with a semicolon: Jamie likes a lot of teams; the Orioles are his favorite.

2. **Simple sentences:** Jamie wanted a birthday surprise. His parents threw him a "baseball" party.

   Compound sentence with a conjunction: Jamie wanted a birthday surprise, so his parents threw him a "baseball" party.

   Compound sentence with a semicolon: Jamie wanted a birthday surprise; his parents threw him a "baseball" party.

3. **Simple sentences:** Jamie's mother baked a baseball-shaped cake. Jamie loved it.

   Compound sentence with a conjunction: Jamie's mother baked a baseball-shaped cake, and Jamie loved it.

   Compound sentence with a semicolon: Jamie's mother baked a baseball-shaped cake; Jamie loved it.

4. **Simple sentences:** It rained. The party guests played baseball.

   Compound sentence with a conjunction: It rained, but the party guests played baseball.

   Compound sentence with a semicolon: It rained; the party guests played baseball.

5. **Simple sentences:** Jamie wanted an autographed baseball. His parents got one from his favorite player.

   Compound sentence with a conjunction: Jamie wanted an autographed baseball, so his parents got one from his favorite player.

   Compound sentence with a semicolon: Jamie wanted an autographed baseball; his parents got one from his favorite player.

ACTIVITY 16: Teamwork

With classmates, discuss what type of idea is necessary to complete each of the following compound sentences. Then, write a simple sentence in the space provided to complete each sentence. Remember that the semicolon typically replaces *and* (combination) and sometimes *but* (simple contrast). Answers will vary.

EXAMPLE:

a. Our roof leaked, so we patched it.

b. Our roof leaked, but we did not fix it.

c. Our roof leaked; it needed repairs.

1. **a.** The car is beautiful, but the gas mileage is poor.
   b. The car is beautiful, and it is fast.
   c. The car is beautiful; I want it.
2. **a.** Daniel must lower his cholesterol, so he stopped eating meat.
   b. Daniel must lower his cholesterol, and he must also lose weight.
   c. Daniel must lower his cholesterol; his health depends on it.
3. **a.** It rained last night, but the fireworks were not canceled.
   b. It rained last night, so the golf course is soaked.
   c. It rained last night; the rain continues today.

Teaching Tip
You could treat Activity 16 as a game. Call out the first part of each sentence and have students take turns supplying different endings. You might break students into teams to see who can come up with the greatest variety of endings for one or two sentence beginnings.

BUILDING LONGER COMPOUND SENTENCES

So far, the sentences that you've written in this chapter have been rather short. In your academic writing, the compound sentences will sometimes be much longer. As with shorter sentences, it is important that you select the appropriate conjunction and use correct punctuation when writing longer compound sentences.

A compound sentence can become longer for three reasons:

Teaching Tip
Have students identify some of their favorite simple sentences from Chapter 11. Then, ask students to turn these sentences into longer and longer compound sentences using the strategies and examples in this chapter.

1. The two simple sentences in it include descriptive words and prepositional phrases.
2. The two simple sentences contain a compound subject and/or a compound verb.
3. The simple sentences are three in number instead of two.

Adding Descriptive Words and Prepositional Phrases

First, let's review how simple sentences become longer. In Chapter 11, you learned that a simple sentence can have as few as two words (a subject and a verb). When a writer adds descriptive words (adjectives and adverbs) and prepositional phrases, the simple sentence becomes longer. (As a reminder, a prepositional phrase begins with a preposition and typically ends with a noun; for more information, see Chapter 11, page 281.)

The longest simple sentences can have three or more prepositional phrases. Look at the following example:

SUBJECT AND A VERB INCLUDED	The bell rings.
DESCRIPTIVE WORDS ADDED	The tardy bell rings promptly.
PREPOSITIONAL PHRASES ADDED	The tardy bell rings promptly at eight o'clock in the morning.
ANOTHER PREPOSITIONAL PHRASE ADDED	At my high school, the tardy bell rings promptly at eight o'clock in the morning.

Notice that when a prepositional phrase begins a sentence, a comma usually follows it.

Similarly, compound sentences can contain descriptive words and prepositional phrases. Take a look:

SENTENCE 1

At my high school, the tardy bell rings promptly at eight o'clock in the morning, and late students complain angrily to each other.

SENTENCE 2

For a list of common prepositions, see Chapter 11, page 282.

ACTIVITY 17

For each pair of simple sentences below, do the following:

- Add a prepositional phrase to the end of each simple sentence.
- Use a conjunction to join the two sentences that you have created, making sure to precede it with a comma.

Even though the compound sentence will be longer, you will have only one comma, and it will be before the conjunction. Answers will vary.

EXAMPLE:

Simple sentences: The truck broke down. The driver called.

Add a prepositional phrase to sentence 1: The truck broke down on the highway.

Add a prepositional phrase to sentence 2: The driver called for help.

Combine the two previous sentences to make a compound sentence: The truck broke down on the highway, so the driver called for help.

1. **Simple sentences:** Randall lost his cell phone. He found it.

   Add a prepositional phrase to sentence 1: Randall lost his cell phone during his lunch break.

   Add a prepositional phrase to sentence 2: He found it in the cafeteria.

   Combine the two previous sentences to make a compound sentence: Randall lost his cell phone during his lunch break, but he found it in the cafeteria.

2. **Simple sentences:** Anna had a minor car accident. She missed her flight.

   Add a prepositional phrase to sentence 1: Anna had a minor car accident in the morning.

   Add a prepositional phrase to sentence 2: She missed her flight to Cleveland.

   Combine the two previous sentences to make a compound sentence: Anna had a minor car accident in the morning, so she missed her flight to Cleveland.

3. **Simple sentences:** The pitcher threw the baseball. The batter hit the ball.

   Add a prepositional phrase to sentence 1: The pitcher threw the baseball to the batter.

   Add a prepositional phrase to sentence 2: The batter hit the ball toward the stands.

   Combine the two previous sentences to make a compound sentence: The pitcher threw the baseball to the batter, and the batter hit the ball toward the stands.

ACTIVITY 18

First, write down each compound sentence from the previous exercise in the space provided. Then, make the sentence longer by

- adding another prepositional phrase to the beginning of the sentence, and
- adding another prepositional phrase to the end of the sentence.

Note: When a prepositional phrase starts a sentence, you usually put a comma after it. Therefore, each compound sentence will have two commas: one after the first prepositional phrase and one before the conjunction. Be sure to place your commas in the correct position. Answers will vary.

EXAMPLE:

Compound sentence: The truck broke down on the highway, so the driver called for help.

Add a prepositional phrase to the beginning and to the end: During rush hour, the truck broke down on the highway, so the driver called for help on his phone.

1. **Compound sentence:** Randall lost his cell phone during his lunch break, but he found it in the cafeteria.

   Add a prepositional phrase to the beginning and to the end: On Tuesday, Randall lost his cell phone during his lunch break, but he found it in the cafeteria after work.

2. **Compound sentence:** Anna had a minor car accident in the morning, so she missed her flight to Cleveland.

   Add a prepositional phrase to the beginning and to the end: With her usual luck, Anna had a minor car accident in the morning, so she missed her flight to Cleveland in the afternoon.

3. **Compound sentence:** The pitcher threw the baseball to the batter, and the batter hit the ball toward the stands.

   Add a prepositional phrase to the beginning and to the end: In the seventh inning, the pitcher threw the baseball to the batter, and the batter hit the ball toward the stands near third base.

ACTIVITY 19: Teamwork

Exchange books with another classmate. Then, proofread each other's sentences from Activity 18, making sure that the compound sentences with prepositional phrases have only <u>two commas</u> and that the commas are in the correct places.

ACTIVITY 20: Teamwork

Working with a classmate, look over the compound sentences with prepositional phrases that you wrote for Activity 18. Then, try to make the sentences longer by adding adjectives to describe the nouns and adverbs to describe the verbs. (For a review of adjectives and adverbs, see Chapter 10, page 271.) Have fun and be creative!

Note: You do not have to write these sentences; just discuss them out loud. *Answers will vary.*

Including Compound Subjects and Verbs

Earlier in this chapter, you studied the difference between two sentence types:

1. a simple sentence that contains a **compound subject** and/or a **compound verb**
2. a **compound sentence** that contains two simple sentences

Now, if we put these two types together, we get a third possibility:

3. a compound sentence made up of two simple sentences, each of which contains a compound subject and/or a compound verb

Let's take a closer look.

Here is a simple sentence with a compound subject and a compound verb:

A COMPOUND SUBJECT — A COMPOUND VERB

The players and the fans rushed to the field and embraced one another.

Both subjects are involved in two connected actions. Notice that no comma is used to join a compound subject or a compound verb.

Here is a compound sentence:

SENTENCE 1 — SENTENCE 2

The fans rushed to the field, and the players embraced one another.

1ST SUBJECT — 1ST VERB — CONJUNCTION — 2ND SUBJECT — 2ND VERB

These are two separate subjects involved in two separate actions. As you know, a comma is required when joining two simple sentences with a conjunction.

Here is a compound sentence in which each simple sentence has a compound subject and a compound verb:

1ST COMPOUND SUBJECT — 1ST COMPOUND VERB

The winning players and their fans rushed to the field and embraced one another, but the losing team and its coaches sat in silence and watched the celebration.

CONJUNCTION — 2ND COMPOUND SUBJECT — 2ND COMPOUND VERB

Teaching Tip
Encourage students to color-code or otherwise highlight subjects and verbs in their own writing to help them see the difference between simple and compound sentences. This will help them identify punctuation problems and other errors.

When we join simple sentences that have compound subjects and compound verbs, the resulting compound sentence can be quite long. Notice, however, that there is still only one comma in the previous sentence; we do not need a comma to join a compound subject or a compound verb.

ACTIVITY 21

Form a compound sentence from each pair of simple sentences, using an appropriate conjunction or a semicolon. (If you use a conjunction, remember to put a comma before it.) Write the compound sentence in the space provided. Answers may vary.

EXAMPLE:

Simple sentences: Katie and Jessica go to the same school and spend a lot of time together. They have poor judgment and sometimes get into trouble.

Compound sentence: Katie and Jessica go to the same school and spend a lot of time together, but they have poor judgment and sometimes get into trouble.

1. **Simple sentences:** Katie and Jessica skipped class on Thursday and claimed that they had the flu. Mrs. Fiskall listened to their excuse but didn't believe them.

   Compound sentence: Katie and Jessica skipped class on Thursday and claimed that they had the flu; Mrs. Fiskall listened to their excuse but didn't believe them.

2. **Simple sentences:** The Rag Dolls were in Denver and played only one concert Thursday night. Katie and Jessica had to see their favorite band.

   Compound sentence: The Rag Dolls were in Denver and played only one concert Thursday night, so Katie and Jessica had to see their favorite band.

3. **Simple sentences:** Katie and Jessica cut class and drove to Denver. They arrived late and had terrible seats in the back.

   Compound sentence: Katie and Jessica cut class and drove to Denver, but they arrived late and had terrible seats in the back.

4. **Simple sentences:** They left the concert at midnight and made up the flu story for the next day. They forgot one small detail and didn't realize it.

   Compound sentence: They left the concert at midnight and made up the flu story for the next day, but they forgot one small detail and didn't realize it.

5. **Simple sentences:** Mrs. Fiskall and the other students noticed and were surprised by the "Rag Dolls" stamps on Katie's and Jessica's hands. Mrs. Fiskall smirked and asked the girls if they enjoyed the concert.

   Compound sentence: Mrs. Fiskall and the other students noticed and were surprised by the "Rag Dolls" stamps on Katie's and Jessica's hands, and Mrs. Fiskall smirked and asked the girls if they enjoyed the concert.

ACTIVITY 22: Teamwork

With classmates, do the following for each set of simple sentences:

- Discuss how to combine each pair of simple sentences to make one simple sentence with a compound subject and/or a compound verb. Write the simple sentences in the spaces provided.
- Select a conjunction (or use a semicolon) to form a compound sentence from the simple sentences. Write the compound sentence in the space provided, making sure to place the comma correctly. *Answers may vary.*

EXAMPLE:

Simple sentences:

a. Snorkeling is a lot of fun. Scuba diving is a lot of fun.

b. Both activities can be dangerous. Both activities require special training.

Combined to form compound subjects/verbs:

a. Snorkeling and scuba diving are a lot of fun.

b. Both activities can be dangerous and require special training.

Compound sentence: Snorkeling and scuba diving are a lot of fun, but both activities can be dangerous and require special training.

1. **Simple sentences:**

   a. Snowboarding is great exercise. Skiing is great exercise.

   b. These sports can be expensive. These sports often require travel.

   Combined to form compound subjects/verbs:

   a. Snowboarding and skiing are great exercise.

   b. These sports can be expensive and often require travel.

   Compound sentence: Snowboarding and skiing are great exercise, but these sports can be expensive and often require travel.

2. **Simple sentences:**

   a. Shawn's truck was old. Shawn's truck needed a new engine.

   b. Shawn worked double shifts. Shawn bought a new truck.

   Combined to form compound subjects/verbs:

   a. Shawn's truck was old and needed a new engine.

   b. Shawn worked double shifts and bought a new truck.

   Compound sentence: Shawn's truck was old and needed a new engine, so Shawn worked double shifts and bought a new truck.

CONTINUED >

3. **Simple sentences:**
   a. The murder suspect struggled on the grass. The police officer struggled on the grass.
   b. The suspect broke free. The suspect escaped in a getaway car.

   Combined to form compound subjects/verbs:
   a. The murder suspect and the police officer struggled on the grass.
   b. The suspect broke free and escaped in a getaway car.

   Compound sentence: The murder suspect and the police officer struggled on the grass, but the suspect broke free and escaped in a getaway car.

4. **Simple sentences:**
   a. The bride exited the church and waved to the guests. The groom exited the church and waved to the guests.
   b. The bridesmaids threw rice and cheered. The ushers threw rice and cheered.

   Combined to form compound subjects/verbs:
   a. The bride and groom exited the church and waved to the guests.
   b. The bridesmaids and ushers threw rice and cheered.

   Compound sentence: The bride and groom exited the church and waved to the guests, and the bridesmaids and ushers threw rice and cheered.

5. **Simple sentences:**
   a. Two gorillas escaped from the zoo and fled to a suburban neighborhood. One baboon escaped from the zoo and fled to a suburban neighborhood.
   b. Zoo officers sped to the scene and captured the animals. Police sped to the scene and captured the animals.

   Combined to form compound subjects/verbs:
   a. Two gorillas and one baboon escaped from the zoo and fled to a suburban neighborhood.
   b. Zoo officers and police sped to the scene and captured the animals.

   Compound sentence: Two gorillas and one baboon escaped from the zoo and fled to a suburban neighborhood, so zoo officers and police sped to the scene and captured the animals.

Joining Three Simple Sentences Instead of Two

Most compound sentences join two simple sentences. Sometimes, however, a compound sentence will join three simple sentences. In this case, the sentence will have three separate subjects and three separate verbs. Also, two conjunctions will be needed to join the three sentences. In some instances, you may use a semicolon to replace one of the conjunctions.

FOUNDATION WORDS
NOUNS
VERBS

DESCRIPTIVE WORDS
ADJECTIVES
ADVERBS

CONNECTING WORDS
PREPOSITIONS
CONJUNCTIONS

Consider this example:

SIMPLE SENTENCE 1	Beth left early for the airport on Friday morning.
SIMPLE SENTENCE 2	The traffic was heavier than usual.
SIMPLE SENTENCE 3	She missed her flight and had to reschedule for the following day.
COMPOUND SENTENCE	Beth left early for the airport on Friday morning, but the traffic was heavier than usual, so she missed her flight and had to reschedule for the following day.
WITH SEMICOLON	Beth left early for the airport on Friday morning, but the traffic was heavier than usual; she missed her flight and had to reschedule for the following day.

ACTIVITY 23

Select appropriate conjunctions (or use a semicolon) to connect the following simple sentences. Start by joining the first two sentences, and then the third sentence should be easier to add. Write the complete compound sentence in the space provided.

Note: Each compound sentence will have at least two commas, unless you want to use a semicolon in place of one of the conjunctions. If the compound sentence begins with a prepositional phrase, the sentence will have an additional comma. Be sure that your commas are in the correct places. *Answers may vary.*

EXAMPLE: Lakwon is a talented singer. His friend Brandon is an experienced guitar player. They formed a band.

Compound sentence: Lakwon is a talented singer, and his friend Brandon is an experienced guitar player, so they formed a band.

1. Joan is a professional dancer. Her boyfriend is clumsy. They never go dancing together.

   Compound sentence: *Joan is a professional dancer, but her boyfriend is clumsy, so they never go dancing together.*

2. We have to water the yard. The grass and the plants will die. Our house will be the disgrace of the neighborhood.

   Compound sentence: *We have to water the yard, or the grass and the plants will die, and our house will be the disgrace of the neighborhood.*

CONTINUED >

3. Joseph can apply for a government loan. He can ask his family for tuition aid. His new college will not allow him to work during the semester.

   Compound sentence: Joseph can apply for a government loan, or he can ask his family for tuition aid; his new college will not allow him to work during the semester.

4. Some people like to rest and relax on their vacation. Other people want to climb mountains or scuba dive. Still other people prefer sightseeing and cultural activities.

   Compound sentence: Some people like to rest and relax on their vacation, but other people want to climb mountains or scuba dive; still other people prefer sightseeing and cultural activities.

5. During the long drought, the mayor and city officials were concerned about the water supply. They restricted the city's water use and banned citizens from watering their lawns. They threatened fines against violators.

   Compound sentence: During the long drought, the mayor and city officials were concerned about the water supply, so they restricted the city's water use and banned citizens from watering their lawns, and they threatened fines against violators.

ACTIVITY 24

Complete each of the following compound sentences by adding another conjunction and a third simple sentence. Answers will vary.

EXAMPLE: Jocelyn has an SUV, and she must drive 50 miles a day to and from her office, **so she decided to start a carpool with co-workers.**

1. Erika needed a gift for her boyfriend's birthday, and she had only one hour to shop, so she purchased a gift card.
2. Jon and Lori needed a new front porch and wanted a new car, but they couldn't afford both, so they fixed the porch and delayed the car purchase.
3. Randall's term paper was due on Monday, but his computer and printer were broken, so he will turn the paper in late.
4. After their company's expansion, Denise and Jacqueline might be promoted, or they might get higher-paying positions in the company's new offices; both possibilities excite them.
5. During the blaze at the electronics factory, firefighters brought all the workers to safety and delivered first aid to the injured, so no one perished, but several people suffered from smoke inhalation.

ACTIVITY 25: Teamwork

With classmates, unscramble each set of three simple sentences, following these steps:

- Discuss the sentences and put them in the correct order.
- Decide which conjunctions will join the sentences smoothly. You might use a semicolon in place of a conjunction.
- Working individually, write the compound sentence in the space provided. Make sure your commas are correctly placed. Answers may vary.

EXAMPLE: **We put our camping gear in the car and drove there. The tickets were too expensive. We waited until the last minute to look online for a flight to Alaska.**

Compound sentence: **We waited until the last minute to look online for a flight to Alaska, and the tickets were too expensive, so we put our camping gear in the car and drove there.**

1. Yvonne felt more at ease. Yvonne was nervous about her job interview. The interviewer was friendly and kind.

   Compound sentence: Yvonne was nervous about her job interview, but the interviewer was friendly and kind, so Yvonne felt more at ease.

2. It will be towed. You can park in the garage next to the bank. You can't leave your car on the street.

   Compound sentence: You can park in the garage next to the bank, but you can't leave your car on the street, or it will be towed.

3. Pamela's doctor advised her to become more active. She also signed up for a yoga class. She began walking two miles every morning.

   Compound sentence: Pamela's doctor advised her to become more active, so she began walking two miles every morning, and she also signed up for a yoga class.

4. He replaced their meals and gave them a complimentary dessert. William and Christine ordered steak. The waiter served them chicken by mistake.

   Compound sentence: William and Christine ordered steak, but the waiter served them chicken by mistake, so he replaced their meals and gave them a complimentary dessert.

5. Sleeping restfully is difficult. Mr. Cobb and Mrs. Brien argue loudly on the street every Saturday morning. Sleeping late is impossible.

   Compound sentence: Mr. Cobb and Mrs. Brien argue loudly on the street every Saturday morning, so sleeping restfully is difficult; sleeping late is impossible.

Teaching Tip
You might hold a contest to see who can write the longest sentence for Activity 26.

ACTIVITY 26

Write five compound sentences, trying to make them as long as you can. Use one or more of the strategies described earlier:

- Write two simple sentences that include descriptive words and prepositional phrases. (See page 318.)
- Write two simple sentences, each of which contains a compound subject and/or a compound verb. (See page 321.)
- Write simple sentences that are three in number instead of two. (See page 324.)

Recognizing Compound Sentences

Teaching Tip
If you plan to teach subject-verb agreement (see Chapter 16, page 466), you might have students work through, or revisit, this section of Chapter 12 as preparation.

Because compound sentences are one of the most frequently used and important sentence types, you should be able to recognize when you are writing one and write it correctly. With every compound sentence that you write, you should be able to identify the separate subjects and separate verbs and punctuate the sentence correctly. In this part of the chapter, you will increase your awareness of compound sentences by

- recognizing separate subjects and separate verbs in compound sentences.
- recognizing correct punctuation in compound sentences.

RECOGNIZING SEPARATE SUBJECTS AND SEPARATE VERBS IN COMPOUND SENTENCES

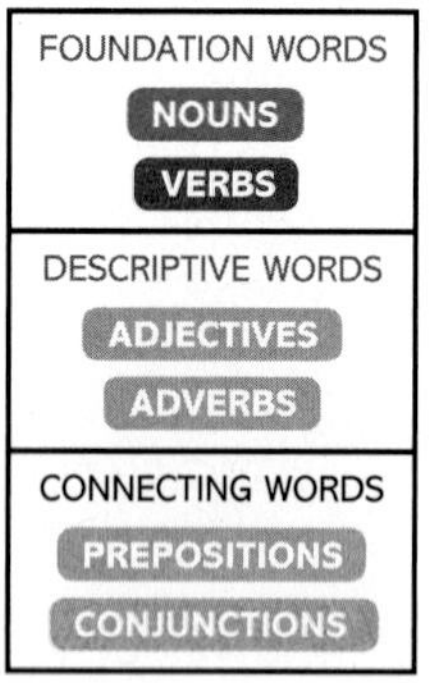

Remember that a compound sentence always joins two simple sentences; therefore, it must contain two separate subjects and two separate verbs. Here's an example to remind you:

The following activities will give you practice identifying separate subjects and verbs in short, longer, and very long compound sentences. As you complete them, keep these hints in mind:

- Remember from Chapter 11 that *subjects are never in prepositional phrases.* (Prepositional phrases start with prepositions and usually end with nouns. For a list of prepositions, see page 282.)
- Because compound sentences often have more than two nouns, make sure that any nouns that you identify as subjects are in fact subjects. Take a look:

SUBJECT + VERB + NOUN
The store sells flowers.

Power Tip
Notice that in this sentence, *flowers* is not identified as a subject. A subject is the main actor of a sentence or who or what the sentence is about. The actor in this sentence is *store,* not the *flowers.* Instead, *flowers* functions as an *object,* which receives the action of a verb. *What did the store sell?* → *flowers.*

ACTIVITY 27

In each of the following short compound sentences, underline the two separate subjects. Then, circle the two separate verbs.

Hint: Helping verbs (like ***can, must, was,*** and ***will***) are followed by another verb, so you will have to circle both. (For a review of helping verbs, see Chapter 10, page 270.)

EXAMPLE: My alarm rang, so I jumped out of bed.

1. These shoes feel comfortable, but they are expensive.
2. After dinner, we can have dessert, or we can take a walk.
3. Lisa's phone rang during the movie, and she answered it.
4. The rain fell all night, so practice was canceled in the morning.
5. Before she left, Gina said goodnight, and she kissed the children.

ACTIVITY 28

In each of the following longer compound sentences, cross out all the prepositional phrases. Then, underline the two separate subjects and circle the two separate verbs.

Hint: Helping verbs (like ***can, must, was,*** and ***will***) are followed by another verb, so you will have to circle both. (For a review of helping verbs, see Chapter 10, page 270.)

EXAMPLE: I studied ~~with my friend~~, and she helped me ~~with the problems~~.

1. Rick is at the mall, but he will return before lunch.
2. At noon, everyone gathered in the conference room, and our boss made an announcement.
3. The man behind the counter of the store must give the money to the robbers, or his life will be in danger.
4. For several hours, volunteers searched for the lost hikers without success, but just before sunset, they found the hikers beside a campfire on the bank of the river.
5. With enthusiasm, the fans at the front of the line ran to their seats near the stage, and they snapped pictures of the rock stars with their cell phones.

ACTIVITY 29

In each of the following long compound sentences, underline the separate subjects. (Some subjects may be compound.) Then, circle the separate verbs. (Some verbs may be compound.) If you have difficulty identifying the subjects and verbs, try crossing out all the prepositional phrases.

Hint: Helping verbs (like ***can, must, was,*** and ***will***) are followed by another verb, so you will have to circle both. (For a review of helping verbs, see Chapter 10, page 270.)

EXAMPLE: **Snow and rain are my favorite weather, but I hike and surf on sunny days.**

1. Cookies and cake are my favorite desserts, but carrots and apples are now my only treats.
2. Kevin and his brother borrowed their father's car and dented the fender, so they took the car to a body shop and got an estimate.
3. During the night, thieves entered the music shop and took several guitars, but within several hours, police found the suspects and arrested them.
4. The gambler and the card dealer jumped up from the table and grabbed each other's throats, so another player and a waitress ran from the table and brought security officers to the scene.
5. In the back of the classroom, Chad and Kristie whispered to each other and laughed at each other's jokes; the teacher and other students became annoyed and stared at the two of them for several icy moments.

ACTIVITY 30

Each of the following compound sentences contains three simple sentences. For each, underline the three separate subjects and circle the three separate verbs. If you have difficulty identifying the subjects and verbs, try crossing out all the prepositional phrases.

Hint: Helping verbs (like ***can, must, was,*** and ***will***) are followed by another verb, so you will have to circle both. (For a review of helping verbs, see Chapter 10, page 270.)

EXAMPLE: **The phone rang, and Jim answered it, but the line was dead.**

1. You can leave Tad, or you can stay with him, but you will be unhappy in either case.
2. A snowstorm closed the Denver airport, and Vanessa was stranded for several hours, but a helpful ticket agent found a hotel room for her.
3. Inside the cave, the explorers found large footprints on the damp floor, but they were uncertain of the source, so they investigated further.
4. A red truck in front of me stopped suddenly for a dog in the street, so I hit my brakes hard, and the bag of groceries in the passenger seat fell to the floor.
5. In a musty old trunk in her attic, Violet discovered a small black jewelry box, and she opened it; it contained a pair of spooky glass eyes.

ACTIVITY 31

Following is a mixture of the different compound sentence types from Activities 27–30. For each sentence, underline the separate subjects and circle the separate verbs.

Note: There may be two or three separate subjects and verbs, and some of these subjects and verbs may be compound. If you have difficulty identifying the subjects and verbs, try crossing out all the prepositional phrases. Also, if there is a helping verb (like ***can***, ***must***, ***was***, and ***will***), be sure to circle the verb after it.

EXAMPLE: **Bert and Aleesha planted the flower seeds, and their children cut and watered the grass.**

1. You won, and we lost.
2. The car sounds funny, so we will take it ~~to the repair shop on Monday~~.
3. ~~At work,~~ Elena stays busy and likes being productive, but ~~at home~~ she relaxes and enjoys quiet hobbies.
4. ~~From the back door of the restaurant,~~ the famous actress and her family hurried ~~toward a limousine~~ and dodged reporters, but the actress and her singer husband paused ~~for a moment~~ and signed autographs.
5. ~~In a small town in the Midwest,~~ Chelsea and her sister opened a quilt shop; the business was popular ~~among local quilters~~, so the sisters opened another location a year later.

RECOGNIZING CORRECT PUNCTUATION IN SIMPLE AND COMPOUND SENTENCES

In the first part of this chapter, you learned four rules for punctuating simple and compound sentences. Following is a review, with examples.

- If a sentence begins with a prepositional phrase, a comma usually follows this phrase:

PREPOSITIONAL PHRASE

At three in the morning, **the telephone started ringing.**

COMMA

- No comma is used when forming a compound subject or a compound verb:

COMPOUND SUBJECT, NO COMMA — COMPOUND VERB, NO COMMA

Liz and Ryan collect **antiques** and restore **furniture.**

- When a conjunction is used to join two simple sentences, a comma should precede the conjunction:

SENTENCE 1 — SENTENCE 2

My brother can have **my old car**, or he can buy **a new one.**

COMMA & CONJUNCTION

- The semicolon is a "soft" period; therefore, it should not be used to replace a comma:

INCORRECT	I returned **to college; and my** grades improved.
CORRECT	I returned **to college, and my** grades improved.
	I returned **to college. My** grades improved.
	I returned **to college; my** grades improved.

SEMICOLON REPLACES A HARD PERIOD

ACTIVITY 32

In this activity, you will need to add missing commas to compound sentences. For each sentence, do the following:

- Underline the subjects and circle the verbs. There will be some compound subjects and compound verbs.
- Decide whether the sentence is simple or compound. If the sentence is compound, write ***C*** next to it and add the missing comma to the sentence.

EXAMPLE: **Dietary changes can be difficult, but they are possible. C**

1. For years, Marcus and his friends ate a lot of meat and liked it.
2. Negative news reports about meat-heavy diets changed Marcus's views, and he became a vegetarian last spring. C
3. He has lost ten pounds since then, so he is pleased about making the change. C
4. At first, Marcus's parents and sister were puzzled by his vegetarianism, and they teased him. C
5. After a month or so, Marcus's mother searched the Internet and found some information on the health benefits of vegetarian diets.
6. She found and read an interesting article about the pros and cons of different diets, and it linked plant-based diets to reduced risks of heart disease and cancer. C
7. After reading the article, Marcus's mother grew concerned about her family's meat-rich diet, so she and her husband decided to make a change. C
8. For each meal, Marcus's mother and father now prepare and serve more vegetables and whole grains but minimize portions of meat.
9. Marcus's parents and sister feel better, so they are grateful to Marcus for helping them to change their lifestyle, and he is happy too. C
10. Now, Marcus has begun an exercise program, so he might start another trend in his family.

ACTIVITY 33

Carefully examine each of the following groups of sentences. Only one sentence has the correct punctuation. Put a check mark beside it.

EXAMPLE:

a. Modern life is demanding; and many people seek relief from stress.

b. Modern life is demanding, and many people seek relief from stress. ✓

c. Modern life is demanding and many people seek relief from stress.

1. **a.** In today's busy world many people fill their lives with too many activities.
   b. In today's busy world, many people fill their lives with too many activities. ✓
   c. In today's busy world; many people fill their lives with too many activities.
2. **a.** At home and at work; people struggle to find happiness.
   b. At home and at work people struggle to find happiness.
   c. At home and at work, people struggle to find happiness. ✓
3. **a.** They bring work home and they have little energy left for family and hobbies.
   b. They bring work home; and they have little energy left for family and hobbies.
   c. They bring work home, and they have little energy left for family and hobbies. ✓
4. **a.** Good time managers say "no" to extra commitments, they are not ashamed of this response.
   b. Good time managers say "no" to extra commitments; they are not ashamed of this response. ✓
   c. Good time managers say "no" to extra commitments they are not ashamed of this response.
5. **a.** Employees should leave work at closing time everyone needs relaxation time.
   b. Employees should leave work at closing time, everyone needs relaxation time.
   c. Employees should leave work at closing time; everyone needs relaxation time. ✓
6. **a.** Employees can spend less time at work; but that time can be more productive.
   b. Employees can spend less time at work, but that time can be more productive. ✓
   c. Employees can spend less time at work but that time can be more productive.

ACTIVITY 34: Teamwork

With classmates, discuss what is wrong with the punctuation in each of the following sentences. Then, individually, rewrite the entire sentence, correcting the punctuation.

EXAMPLE:

> Office romances may seem exciting but they are rarely a good idea.
> **Office romances may seem exciting, but they are rarely a good idea.**

1. Not all romances work out; and they can turn destructive.
   Not all romances work out, and they can turn destructive.
2. Co-workers may feel uncomfortable about the situation but they may be fearful about expressing their views.
   Co-workers may feel uncomfortable about the situation, but they may be fearful about expressing their views.
3. Romances can reduce the productivity of the couple; and other employees may be less productive, too.
   Romances can reduce the productivity of the couple, and other employees may be less productive, too.
4. In the worst situations office romances can result in sexual harassment cases or broken marriages.
   In the worst situations, office romances can result in sexual harassment cases or broken marriages.
5. With all the potential problems of office romances, employees should look elsewhere for romance, and leave office temptations alone.
   With all the potential problems of office romances, employees should look elsewhere for romance and leave office temptations alone.

Solving Problems in Compound Sentences: Run-ons and Comma Splices

So far in this chapter, you have learned that conjunctions are used to join other building blocks of language. Conjunctions can join two subjects to form a compound subject; they can join two verbs to form a compound verb; they can join two adjectives, two adverbs, or two prepositional phrases; and so on. Most important, conjunctions (preceded by a comma) can join two or more simple sentences to form a compound sentence. Remember this:

> **Conjunctions are the glue:** and, but, or, so **(+** for, nor, yet**).**

In this part of the chapter, you will see how to solve common problems in compound sentences by learning the following:

1. If you try to join two simple sentences without glue (a comma and a conjunction), you will have a major grammatical error, either a **run-on** or a **comma splice**.
2. A semicolon is also glue, but a comma by itself is not.
3. Often, we try to use other words like glue; however, these other words are not conjunctions, so they can cause run-ons and comma splices.
4. If you create a run-on or a comma splice, it is easy to fix: Just add glue!

UNDERSTANDING HOW RUN-ONS AND COMMA SPLICES OCCUR

There are just two types of glue for joining sentences in English: a conjunction (preceded by a comma) and a semicolon. Let's review:

1. A comma and conjunction as glue:

SENTENCE 1 SENTENCE 2

Class ended, so we left.

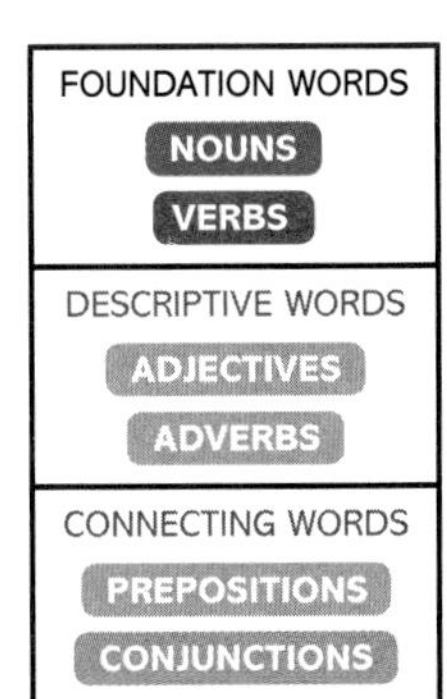

Although these sentences are very short, each one is a complete simple sentence with its own subject and verb. Therefore, if we want to join them to make a compound sentence, we must use glue. The glue we use most often is a **conjunction** preceded by a comma.

2. A semicolon as glue:

Class ended; we left.

Because the semicolon is really a type of period (a "soft" period), it has the strength of glue and can be used in place of a conjunction. A comma by itself, however, does not have this strength and can never be used as glue.

Run-ons and **comma splices** occur when we try to join two separate sentences without glue. Let's take a closer look at how this happens:

3. No glue:

Class ended we left.

Although these sentences are very short, they are two separate sentences with two separate subjects and two separate verbs. If we run them together without glue, we have a **run-on**.

4. Using a comma as glue:

Class ended, we left.

Because these sentences are so short, some writers believe that they can be joined with a comma. However, remember that a comma by itself is never glue. If we "splice" or join these two sentences with a comma only, we have a **comma splice**.

5. Using words that are not conjunctions as glue:

   Class ended **then** we left.

   Class ended, **then** we left.

Power Tip
A run-on and a comma splice are really the same grammatical error. In both cases, two separate sentences are joined without glue. In the case of a comma splice, the writer has added a comma as glue, but you now know that a comma by itself is never glue.

In English, there are many words that seem like glue but are not. In this example, *then* has been used in place of a conjunction, but it is not glue. As a result, the first example is a **run-on**. The second example is a **comma splice**. In both cases, the sentences do not have the glue they need to be joined correctly.

ACTIVITY 35: Teamwork

With classmates, examine each of the following items. Then, decide whether each

- has glue (a comma and conjunction or a semicolon),
- has no glue (run-on),
- tries to use a comma by itself as glue (comma splice),
- uses some other word as glue, or
- uses a comma and some other word as glue.

Write the appropriate label in the space next to the item.

EXAMPLE:

Pets are good company they can also improve people's health. has no glue

1. A pet cat can lower the blood pressure of a heart patient, a tropical fish can reduce stress. tries to use a comma by itself as glue
2. Elderly residents of retirement homes are often lonely, and they can also experience depression. has glue
3. At these homes, pets provide loving companionship depressed residents are cheered by their presence. has no glue
4. For very depressed patients, pets can provide a dramatic benefit they can be a step toward making more human contacts. has no glue
5. A patient may walk her dog around the halls then she may meet other people around the residence. uses some other word as glue
6. Some animals can be dangerous to sick and elderly patients caregivers should choose pets carefully. has no glue

For online practice with fixing run-ons and comma splices, visit this book's Web site at **bedfordstmartins.com/steppingstones**.

7. In most cases, animals can provide great benefits to the sick and elderly, that is an excellent reason for bringing pets and these patients together. tries to use a comma by itself as glue

ACTIVITY 36

Carefully examine each of the following items. Then, decide whether each is

- a correct compound sentence,
- a run-on, or
- a comma splice.

Write the appropriate label in the space provided. Then, fix incorrect sentences by adding glue (a comma and conjunction or a semicolon) or by forming two separate sentences. Revisions may vary.

EXAMPLE:

Staying focused on any task is not easy; it is harder for unpleasant chores. comma splice

1. No task is simple; anything can interrupt it. comma splice
2. Let's take the chore of laundry. It seems simple enough. run-on
3. You separate the clothes into piles, and you put one load into the washing machine. correct compound sentence
4. You see a stain on your red shirt, so you need a stain remover. run-on
5. On the top shelf of the laundry room closet, you find the stain remover, but the bottle is empty. correct compound sentence
6. The store is nearby, so you get in your car and drive toward town. comma splice
7. At the store, you find great bargains, so you fill your shopping cart with everything from lip balm to sandals. correct compound sentence
8. Electric ice-cream makers are on sale, so you buy one and all the ingredients for vanilla and mocha-almond ice cream. comma splice
9. You drive home with a smile on your face and with plans for ice cream parties with your friends. Life is good, very good. run-on
10. You walk in the door and see the washing machine. You have forgotten the bottle of stain remover. run-on

UNDERSTANDING WORDS THAT CAN CAUSE RUN-ONS AND COMMA SPLICES

Many run-ons and comma splices are caused when we try to use words that are not conjunctions as glue. What often confuses students is that there are only seven words that can truly be used as glue: *and, but, or, so, for, nor,* and *yet.* However, there are lots of other words that *seem* like glue.

Below are some words that are commonly *misused* as glue. They are divided into four groups to help you remember them.

Power Tip
The additive expressions listed here can also be used as transitional expressions. However, we distinguish them here because they cause run-ons and comma splices in a particular way.

Personal Pronouns	**Demonstrative Pronouns**	**Additive Expressions**	**Transitional Expressions**
I	this	also	as a result
you	that	for example	consequently
he	these	for instance	furthermore
she	those	next	however
it		plus	in addition
we		then	instead
they			moreover
			nevertheless
			otherwise
			therefore

Let's look at each of these groups individually to understand why the words often *seem like* glue.

Personal Pronouns

The personal pronouns in the previous list cause more run-ons and comma splices than any other group of words. Therefore, it is very important that you understand why. Take a look at the following run-on:

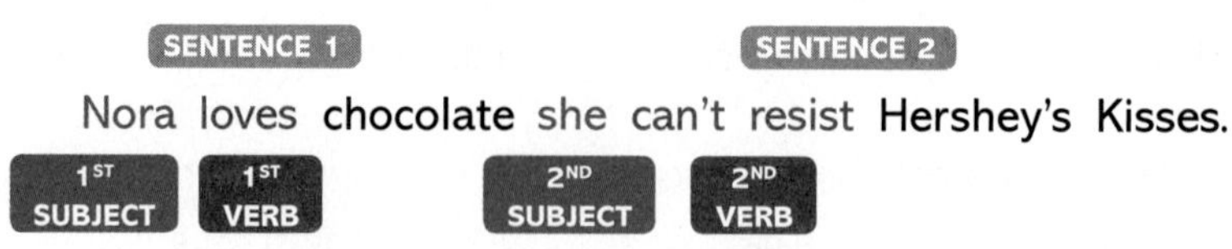

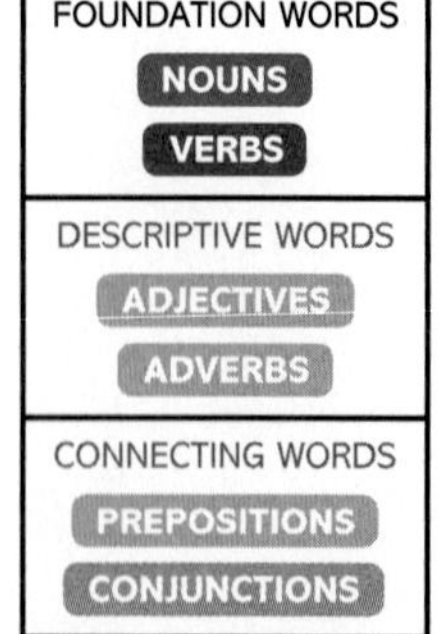

Notice that there are two separate sentences here with two separate subjects and two separate verbs. Therefore, we need some glue to join them.

Many of the sentences we write are about people. If the sentence is compound, the first subject will often name a person or persons. Then, the second subject will often be a personal pronoun that refers back to the first subject. Take a look:

Nora loves chocolate she can't resist Hershey's Kisses.

Because *she* refers to *Nora,* many writers believe that it is glue that can join the two simple sentences. However, as you already know, a personal pronoun can be the subject of its own sentence. Here, *she* is the subject of the second simple sentence, even though it refers back to Nora. Therefore, we still need some glue to join these sentences, or we need to break them into separate sentences:

COMMA AND COORDINATING CONJUNCTION ADDED	Nora loves chocolate, so she can't resist Hershey's Kisses.

or

SEMICOLON, OR "SOFT" PERIOD, ADDED	Nora loves chocolate; she can't resist Hershey's Kisses.

or

HARD PERIOD ADDED	Nora loves chocolate. She can't resist Hershey's Kisses.

The last option (the use of a hard period) does correct the run-on; however, it does not join the two simple sentences to form a compound sentence.

Remember: When you write a compound sentence with a personal pronoun as one of the subjects, the pronoun is not glue; you still need a conjunction or a semicolon to join the sentences.

Teaching Tip
For test items on run-ons and comma splices, see the *Testing Tool Kit* CD available with this book.

ACTIVITY 37

For each of the run-ons or comma splices below, do the following:

- Circle the personal pronoun.
- Draw an arrow connecting the pronoun to the subject to which it refers.
- Rewrite the run-on or comma splice in the space provided, adding a conjunction or a semicolon to make it a correct compound sentence. If you use a conjunction, don't forget the required comma. Rewrites may vary.

EXAMPLE:

Dining out seems luxurious it can be unpleasant.
Dining out seems luxurious, but it can be unpleasant.

1. Ted and Louisa were celebrating their tenth anniversary, they chose a special restaurant.
Ted and Louisa were celebrating their tenth anniversary, so they chose a special restaurant.

2. The Blue Sail served elegant dinners it was located close to the ocean.
The Blue Sail served elegant dinners, and it was located close to the ocean.

CONTINUED >

3. Ted and Louisa enjoyed the food, they will never go to the Blue Sail again.
Ted and Louisa enjoyed the food, but they will never go to the Blue Sail again.

4. The reason was not the food or service it was the other patrons.
The reason was not the food or service; it was the other patrons.

5. Three small children were seated with their family nearby, they were noisy throughout the evening.
Three small children were seated with their family nearby, and they were noisy throughout the evening.

6. The father ignored the children's behavior he was more interested in the messages on his cell phone.
The father ignored the children's behavior; he was more interested in the messages on his cell phone.

7. From time to time, the mother snapped at the children she annoyed Ted and Louisa with her sharp voice.
From time to time, the mother snapped at the children, and she annoyed Ted and Louisa with her sharp voice.

8. The children ignored their mother, they ran around the restaurant and bumped into other tables and diners.
The children ignored their mother, and they ran around the restaurant and bumped into other tables and diners.

9. At another nearby table, a woman held her cell phone to her ear and laughed repeatedly and loudly she did not see the cold stares from the serving staff and from other patrons in the restaurant.
At another nearby table, a woman held her cell phone to her ear and laughed repeatedly and loudly; she did not see the cold stares from the serving staff and from other patrons in the restaurant.

10. For their next anniversary, Ted will make a fancy meal for two, he and Louisa will dine alone in the peacefulness of their backyard.
For their next anniversary, Ted will make a fancy meal for two, and he and Louisa will dine alone in the peacefulness of their backyard.

FOUNDATION WORDS
NOUNS
VERBS
DESCRIPTIVE WORDS
ADJECTIVES
ADVERBS
CONNECTING WORDS
PREPOSITIONS
CONJUNCTIONS

Demonstrative Pronouns

These pronouns (*this, that, these, those*) work in a similar way as personal pronouns except that they refer to things, places, or ideas instead of people. Demonstrative pronouns do not cause as many run-ons and comma splices as personal pronouns do, but they are often more difficult to spot. Take a look at the following comma splice:

SENTENCE 1 SENTENCE 2

My teacher didn't read my essay, that upset me.

1ST SUBJECT 1ST VERB 2ND SUBJECT 2ND VERB

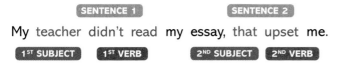

This example also contains two separate sentences with two separate subjects and two separate verbs. However, it may be difficult to recognize the pronoun *that* as a separate subject.

When a demonstrative pronoun is used as a subject in a compound sentence, it often refers back to a thing, a place, or an idea in the first part of the sentence. This thing, place, or idea may consist of more than one word. Take a look:

My teacher didn't read my essay, that upset me.

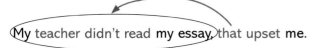

That is a pronoun, and just like all pronouns, it refers to something else (a person, place, thing, or idea). To understand what *that* refers to, ask yourself, "What upset me?" What upset you was the fact that your teacher did not read your essay. Because the pronoun *that* refers back to the idea in the first part of the sentence, many writers believe that it is glue, but it is not. We still need some glue to join these sentences, or we need to break them into separate sentences:

COORDINATING CONJUNCTION ADDED	My teacher didn't read my essay, and that upset me.
or	
SEMICOLON, OR "SOFT" PERIOD, USED	My teacher didn't read my essay; that upset me.
or	
HARD PERIOD USED	My teacher didn't read my essay. That upset me.

The last option (the use of a hard period) does correct the comma splice; however, it does not join the two simple sentences to form a compound sentence.

Power Tip
If there is any chance that a reader might not understand what you are referring to with a demonstrative pronoun, replace it with more specific words. For example, take a look at this replacement for *that*: *My teacher didn't read my essay, and her lack of interest in my work upset me.*

ACTIVITY 38

For each of the run-ons or comma splices below, do the following:

- Circle the demonstrative pronoun.
- Underline the thing, place, or idea to which the demonstrative pronoun refers.
- Rewrite the run-on or comma splice in the space provided, adding a conjunction or a semicolon to make it a correct compound sentence. If you use a conjunction, don't forget the required comma. Rewrites may vary.

CONTINUED >

EXAMPLE:

On Sundays, my father brings home jelly doughnuts these are my favorite.
On Sundays, my father brings home jelly doughnuts; these are my favorite.

1. My boss yelled at me every day that was only one reason behind my decision to quit.
My boss yelled at me every day, but that was only one reason behind my decision to quit.

2. I don't usually like mussels, these are the best I've tasted.
I don't usually like mussels, but these are the best I've tasted.

3. My boyfriend buys me flowers for every special occasion this always makes me happy.
My boyfriend buys me flowers for every special occasion, and this always makes me happy.

4. Brian took out an expensive mortgage on a new home, that became his financial downfall.
Brian took out an expensive mortgage on a new home, and that became his financial downfall.

5. For the holidays, I will make my famous mouse-shaped chocolates, those are big hits with my friends and family.
For the holidays, I will make my famous mouse-shaped chocolates; those are big hits with my friends and family.

Additive Expressions

Sometimes, we write a sentence and then decide to add more information to it. We often use additive expressions (*also, for example, next, plus, then,* and so on) to join this information to our sentence. However, if this additional information is expressed with a separate subject and a separate verb, it cannot be joined to the first simple sentence with an additive expression. Additive expressions are never glue. Look at the following comma splice:

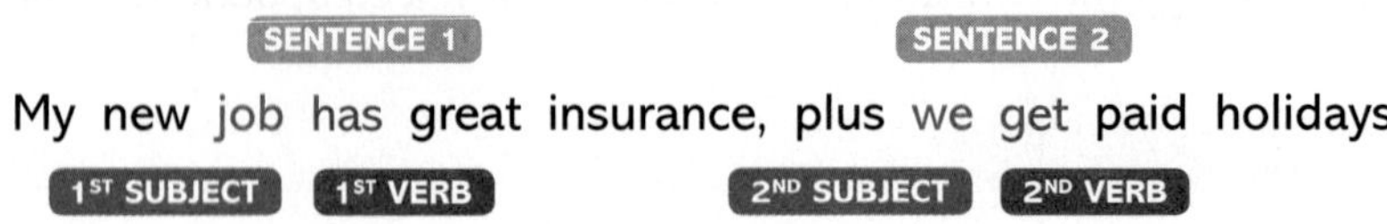

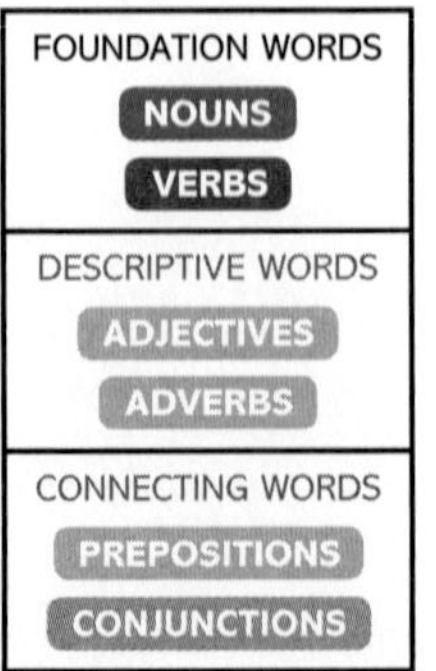

Additive expressions are tricky because they seem so much like glue! However, you know that in English, the only glue for joining sentences is (1) a conjunction (*and, but, or, so, for, nor,* or *yet*) preceded by a comma or (2) a semicolon. To fix the previous comma splice, you could use a conjunction in place of the additive expression or use a semicolon followed by the additive expression. If a conjunction is used, a comma must precede it. If an additive expression is used, a comma usually follows it. Take a look:

CONJUNCTION USED	My new job has great insurance, and we get paid holidays.

or

SEMICOLON AND ADDITIVE EXPRESSION USED	My new job has great insurance; plus, we get paid holidays.

In some cases—most commonly with *then*—you can use both a conjunction and an additive expression. Take a look:

I left my home in Dallas, and then I moved to San Francisco.

ACTIVITY 39

For each of the run-ons or comma splices below, do the following:

- Circle the additive expression (*also, for example, next, plus, then,* and so on).
- Rewrite the run-on or comma splice in the space provided, using the correction methods described previously. (If you add a conjunction, make sure to put a comma before it. If you use a semicolon followed by an additive expression, make sure that a comma follows this expression.)

Rewrites may vary.

EXAMPLE:

Scott is an adventurous person, for example, he likes traveling to distant places.

Scott is an adventurous person; for example, he likes traveling to distant places.

1. Scott quit his job at Burger Bun, then he went on the road.
   Scott quit his job at Burger Bun, and then he went on the road.
2. He wanted a new start also he wanted to live in the West.
   He wanted a new start; also, he wanted to live in the West.
3. Scott had heard about the beauty of California, for example, California is home to the Sierra Nevada mountain range.
   Scott had heard about the beauty of California; for example, California is home to the Sierra Nevada mountain range.
4. He gave his landlord thirty days' notice next he sold all his unneeded possessions at a yard sale.
   He gave his landlord thirty days' notice; next, he sold all his unneeded possessions at a yard sale.

CONTINUED >

5. Scott earned quite a bit of money from his yard sale, plus he had saved money from his job.

   Scott earned quite a bit of money from his yard sale; plus, he had saved money from his job.

6. On a cool September morning in Atlanta, Scott packed his remaining possessions in his truck then he turned west and headed for the mountains of California.

   On a cool September morning in Atlanta, Scott packed his remaining possessions in his truck, and then he turned west and headed for the mountains of California.

7. Along the way, Scott visited some interesting attractions for example, he stopped at the Grand Canyon in Arizona and spent one night in glittering Las Vegas.

   Along the way, Scott visited some interesting attractions; for example, he stopped at the Grand Canyon in Arizona and spent one night in glittering Las Vegas.

8. After driving across this country, Scott eventually stopped in a small town in a valley to the west of the Sierra Nevada Mountains then he smiled.

   After driving across the country, Scott eventually stopped in a small town in a valley to the west of the Sierra Nevada Mountains; then, he smiled.

Transitional Expressions

You already know that we use a conjunction to join two related simple sentences. Transitional expressions (*as a result, consequently, furthermore, however, in addition,* and so on) do exactly the same thing; in fact, transitional expressions are really just "grown-up" conjunctions. The only difference is that transitional expressions are never glue. A transitional expression by itself can never join two separate sentences. Take a look at this run-on:

SENTENCE 1 SENTENCE 2

My uncle refused to pay his gas bill furthermore he wrote a rude letter to the gas company.

1ST SUBJECT 1ST VERB 2ND SUBJECT 2ND VERB

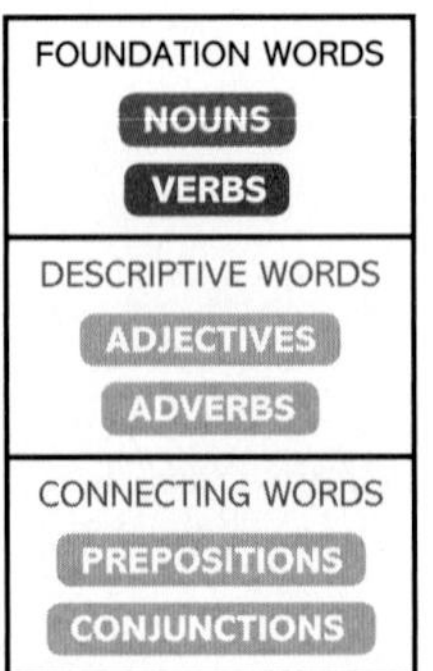

First, notice that this example consists of two separate sentences with two separate subjects and two separate verbs. The writer has tried to use *furthermore* as glue to join the two simple sentences, but we know that a transitional word can never be glue. Often, a writer will add a comma with the transitional word:

My uncle refused to pay his gas bill, furthermore he wrote a rude letter to the gas company.

COMMA & TRANSITIONAL EXPRESSION

However, you already know that a comma can never be glue. Even though the student has used a comma and a transitional word together here, there is still no glue to hold the two simple sentences together. If you want to use a transitional expression in a compound sentence, the best way to do so is with a semicolon. Take a look:

> **My uncle refused to pay his gas bill; furthermore, he wrote a rude letter to the gas company.**

This sentence is now a correct compound sentence; the semicolon is the glue that joins the two simple sentences. Now, notice the added comma after *furthermore.*

New comma rule: When a transitional expression begins a sentence (including a sentence that is part of a compound sentence), this expression should be followed by a comma. (Remember that this same rule applies to a prepositional phrase when it begins a sentence.) Also, recall that a comma usually follows an additive expression when it begins a sentence.

Power Tip
Transitions are an important tool for helping readers to follow your ideas. For more advice on using them, see Chapter 4, page 118, and Chapter 5, pages 158 and 159.

ACTIVITY 40

For each of the following run-ons or comma splices, do the following:

- Circle the transitional expression (*as a result, consequently, furthermore, however, in addition,* and so on).
- Rewrite the run-on or comma splice in the space provided, turning it into a correct compound sentence. Use a semicolon as glue, and remember to put a comma after the transitional expression. Rewrites may vary.

EXAMPLE:

Greedy people may save money, however they may lose friends and respect.
Greedy people may save money; however, they may lose friends and respect.

1. John has been called greedy, as a result people avoid him.
   John has been called greedy; as a result, people avoid him.
2. At restaurants with friends, he "forgets" his wallet, therefore someone else must pay his bill.
   At restaurants with friends, he "forgets" his wallet; therefore, someone else must pay his bill.
3. He rarely bought dinner for his former girlfriend instead he bought her a drink at happy-hour prices and "treated" her to the free appetizers.
   He rarely bought dinner for his former girlfriend; instead, he bought her a drink at happy-hour prices and "treated" her to the free appetizers.

CONTINUED >

4. In the office lunchroom, he helps himself to co-workers' lunches and snacks, in addition he takes office supplies home on a regular basis.

In the office lunchroom, he helps himself to co-workers' lunches and snacks; in addition, he takes office supplies home on a regular basis.

5. For a long time, John's friends have recommended counseling to him however John seems unaware of his problem and would find a counselor's fees too expensive anyway.

For a long time, John's friends have recommended counseling to him; however, John seems unaware of his problem and would find a counselor's fees too expensive anyway.

You have learned that transitional expressions are really just "grown-up" conjunctions. The following chart shows that conjunctions and transitional expressions are used to show the same *four types of relationships* between ideas. (Notice that the less commonly used conjunctions are in parentheses.)

Relationships Shown by Conjunctions and Transitional Expressions

	COMBINATION	CONTRAST	RESULT	ALTERNATIVES
Coordinating Conjunctions	and (nor)	but (yet)	so (for)	or
Transitional Expressions	furthermore	however	as a result	otherwise
	in addition	instead	consequently	instead
	moreover	nevertheless	therefore	

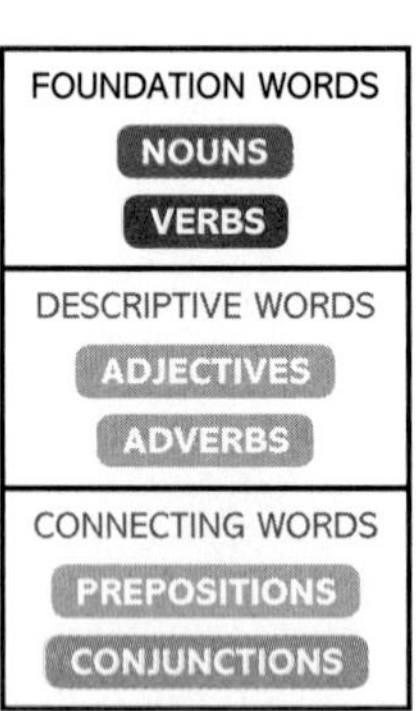

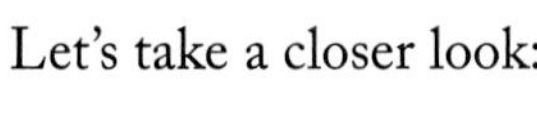

Let's take a closer look:

Combination

My sister was accepted to Stanford, and the university offered her a scholarship.

My sister was accepted to Stanford; furthermore, the university offered her a scholarship.

My sister was accepted to Stanford; in addition, the university offered her a scholarship.

My sister was accepted to Stanford; moreover, the university offered her a scholarship.

In the first sentence, the conjunction is the glue. In the next three sentences, the semicolon is the glue, not the transitional expressions.

All four compound sentences mean the same thing. Just like the conjunction *and,* the transitional expressions *furthermore, in addition,* and *moreover* **combine** two **similar** ideas.

If you were the writer of this sentence, you would have to choose the version you like best; it is a matter of personal style and taste.

Contrast

My sister was accepted to Stanford, but she decided to go to a local college.

My sister was accepted to Stanford; however, she decided to go to a local college.

My sister was accepted to Stanford; instead, she decided to go to a local college.

My sister was accepted to Stanford; nevertheless, she decided to go to a local college.

In the first sentence, the conjunction is the glue. In the next three sentences, the semicolon is the glue, not the transitional expressions.

All four compound sentences mean the same thing. Just like the conjunction *but,* the transitional expressions *however, instead,* and *nevertheless* **contrast** two **different** ideas.

If you were the writer of this sentence, you would have to choose the version you like best; it is a matter of personal style and taste.

Result

My sister was accepted to Stanford, so she declined UCLA's offer.

My sister was accepted to Stanford; as a result, she declined UCLA's offer.

My sister was accepted to Stanford; consequently, she declined UCLA's offer.

My sister was accepted to Stanford; therefore, she declined UCLA's offer.

In the first sentence, the conjunction is the glue. In the next three sentences, the semicolon is the glue, not the transitional expressions.

All four compound sentences mean the same thing. Just like the conjunction *so,* the transitional expressions *as a result, consequently,* and *therefore* show a **result** of one idea from another.

If you were the writer of this sentence, you would have to choose the version you like best; it is a matter of personal style and taste.

Alternatives

My sister might accept Stanford's offer, or she might wait for a better one.

My sister might accept Stanford's offer; otherwise, she might wait for a better one.

My sister might accept Stanford's offer; instead, she might wait for a better one.

In the first sentence, the conjunction is the glue. In the next two sentences, the semicolon is the glue, not the transitional expressions.

All three compound sentences mean the same thing. Just like the conjunction *or,* the transitional expressions *instead* and *otherwise* show **alternative** options or possibilities.

If you were the writer of this sentence, you would have to choose the version you like best; it is a matter of personal style and taste.

Teaching Tip
Have students write more examples of the various types of compound sentences described in this section. Encourage them to use a variety of additive and transitional expressions.

As a beginning writer, you should not feel pressured to use transitional expressions or semicolons. If you are more comfortable using conjunctions, focus your practice on writing compound sentences with conjunctions. Many excellent writers do not use transitional expressions or semicolons.

Teaching Tip
For a tutorial on finding and fixing run-ons and comma splices, see the *Make-a-Paragraph Kit* CD available with this book.

ACTIVITY 41

Correct each of the following run-ons or comma splices in two ways:

- For the first correction, add a conjunction. Make sure that a comma precedes the conjunction.
- For the second correction, add a semicolon and a transitional expression. Make sure that a comma follows the transitional expression.

Answers may vary.

EXAMPLE:

We can't avoid noise, we can avoid some of its unhealthy effects.

We can't avoid noise, but we can avoid some of its unhealthy effects.

We can't avoid noise; nevertheless, we can avoid some of its unhealthy effects.

1. This world is a busy place it is filled with noise.
   This world is a busy place, and it is filled with noise.
   This world is a busy place; moreover, it is filled with noise.
2. At home, the television blares, appliances beep and buzz.
   At home, the television blares, and appliances beep and buzz.
   At home, the television blares; in addition, appliances beep and buzz.
3. In our cars, we listen to the radio, we talk on our cell phones.
   In our cars, we listen to the radio, or we talk on our cell phones.
   In our cars, we listen to the radio; otherwise, we talk on our cell phones.
4. For many of us, solitude is not easy to find in our hectic lives, we must seek silence for the sake of our mental health.
   For many of us, solitude is not easy to find in our hectic lives, but we must seek silence for the sake of our mental health.
   For many of us, solitude is not easy to find in our hectic lives; nevertheless, we must seek silence for the sake of our mental health.
5. At busy times, we can take a walk in a peaceful place, we can just sit in a quiet room and close our eyes for a few minutes.
   At busy times, we can take a walk in a peaceful place, or we can just sit in a quiet room and close our eyes for a few minutes.
   At busy times, we can take a walk in a peaceful place; otherwise, we can just sit in a quiet room and close our eyes for a few minutes.

REVIEWING CAUSES AND CORRECTIONS OF RUN-ONS AND COMMA SPLICES

In this part of the chapter, you have learned about four groups of words that often cause run-ons and comma splices:

1. personal pronouns (*I, you, he, she, it, we, they*)
2. demonstrative pronouns (*this, that, these, those*)
3. additive expressions (*also, for example, for instance, next, plus, then*)
4. transitional expressions (*as a result, consequently, furthermore, however, in addition, instead, moreover, nevertheless, otherwise, therefore*)

Also, you have learned four ways to correct run-ons and comma splices:

1. Use a conjunction (preceded by a comma) to join simple sentences.
2. Use a semicolon (a "soft" period) to join the sentences.
3. Use a semicolon followed by an additive or transitional expression and a comma to join the sentences.
4. Use a "hard" period to form separate sentences.

The following activity includes all the types of words that can cause run-ons and comma splices, and it gives you more practice with the various correction methods.

ACTIVITY 42

For each of the run-ons or comma splices below, do the following:

- Circle the word or words that cause the problem.
- Above this expression, write ***PP*** for personal pronoun, ***DP*** for demonstrative pronoun, ***ADD*** for additive expression, or ***TRANS*** for transitional expression.
- Decide how to correct the error, and write the correct compound sentence on the line provided.

Try not to use a hard period; however, if you are not comfortable with any of the other methods, you may use a hard period. Be sure that commas are placed correctly. Answers may vary.

EXAMPLE:

ADD

Many consumers are concerned about gas mileage, (for example) more people are buying higher-mileage vehicles.

Many consumers are concerned about gas mileage; for example, more people are buying higher-mileage vehicles.

PP

1. Marianna was spending too much money on gasoline (she) did research on gas mileage.

Marianna was spending too much money on gasoline, so she did research on gas mileage.

CONTINUED >

DP
2. She found and tried many ideas for improving her gas mileage, these helped her save a significant amount of money.
She found and tried many ideas for improving her gas mileage, and these helped her save a significant amount of money.

ADD
3. Marianna's mechanic checked her engine's efficiency, then he tuned up her engine in an effort to improve the gas mileage.
Marianna's mechanic checked her engine's efficiency; then, he tuned up her engine in an effort to improve the gas mileage.

TRANS
4. On the freeway, Marianna avoids speeding moreover she accelerates and brakes her car more gently.
On the freeway, Marianna avoids speeding; moreover, she accelerates and brakes her car more gently.

5. She now keeps her vehicle's tires inflated to the recommended pressure, TRANS otherwise, her gas mileage will be decreased.
She now keeps her vehicle's tires inflated to the recommended pressure; otherwise, her gas mileage will be decreased.

FIXING RUN-ONS AND COMMA SPLICES IN WHOLE PARAGRAPHS

Remember, when you find a run-on or a comma splice in your writing, it is easy to fix:

Just add glue!

and, but, or, so (+ for, nor, yet)

The following activity will give you practice with recognizing and fixing run-ons and comma splices in whole paragraphs—a valuable skill for improving your own writing.

ACTIVITY 43

Read each of the following paragraphs carefully, looking for run-ons and comma splices. Then, rewrite each error to fix the problem, using one of the following methods: (1) adding a conjunction (with a comma, if one is missing), (2) adding a semicolon alone, (3) adding a semicolon followed by an additive or transitional expression and a comma, or (4) using a period. The first sentence of each paragraph has been edited for you. Answers may vary.

This paragraph has five comma splices (including the one that has been edited for you) and three run-ons.

1. (1) Most of us prefer a clutter-free place for paying bills and doing other tasks, ^but many of us suffer from messy workspaces. (2) Efficiency experts offer several ideas for reducing clutter, ^and anyone can get more organized by trying them. (3) A filing cabinet offers valuable

storage space furthermore the different drawers can help with organizing documents. (4) Hanging folders can be used for more than just letters and bills they can hold recipes, photographs, maps, and other documents. (5) Wire baskets are also useful for organizing materials, they can be stacked to save room on a desktop. (6) Shelves and drawers in the workspace should hold items commonly used for paperwork and studying, these items include envelopes, stamps, a calculator, a dictionary, pens, pencils, and paper clips. (7) Time management also plays a role in clutter control you should look at each piece of mail only once and act on it or throw it away. (8) With this practice, papers will not pile up, you will spend less time looking for important documents.

This paragraph has six comma splices (including the one that has been edited for you) and five run-ons.

2. (1) The Greece Athena High School basketball team was winning, it was the last game of the season. (2) With four minutes left in the game, the team had a comfortable lead spirits were high. (3) Coach Jim Johnson sent autistic student Jason McElwain onto the court this was Jason's first and only chance to play for his team. (4) Jason was only five feet, six inches tall, he was too small to make the team. (5) In spite of his size, he loved basketball and served as the team's manager also, he was one of the team's biggest fans. (6) Jason charged onto the court with enthusiasm, he shot an air ball and a layup that also missed. (7) Jason's teammates wanted him to make at least one basket they kept passing him the ball. (8) Then, something magical happened, it stunned the crowd. (9) Jason sunk one two-point basket and six three-point shots, within three minutes, he had scored twenty points for his team. (10) The news spread rapidly around the country, Jason quickly became a national hero. (11) He appeared on numerous television news programs he even met President Obama.

CONTINUED >

This paragraph has five comma splices and seven run-ons (including the one that has been edited for you).

3. (1) Sarah Breedlove Walker was a successful businesswoman moreover she became a role model for many African American women. (2) Sarah Breedlove was the daughter of freed slaves, she grew up in Louisiana at a very difficult time for African Americans. (3) After losing her parents and then her husband, Breedlove went north, in her new home, she worked as a washerwoman for little pay. (4) Eventually, Breedlove started selling beauty products for another woman she got restless and started her own beauty-products business in Denver, Colorado. (5) In Denver, she met advertising expert Charles J. Walker he became her second husband. (6) Charles Walker helped his wife create attractive advertisements for her products, he convinced her to use the fancy name "Madam C. J. Walker." (7) Advertising drew thousands of people to Sarah Breedlove Walker's products, it was the key to her success. (8) By the early 1900s, she had a 3,000-person sales force and yearly sales of more than $200,000 she had won the admiration of many. (9) In a relatively short time, Breedlove Walker became one of the largest employers of African American women, this is one of her most famous achievements. (10) She eventually purchased a large home and obtained other luxuries she never forgot the less fortunate. (11) Her generosity benefited many causes for example, she contributed to schools, orphanages, and civil-rights groups. (12) By the time of her death in 1919, Breedlove Walker had become an astonishing success she continues to inspire others.

ACTIVITY 44: Teamwork

When you have completed correcting one of the paragraphs from Activity 43, get together with two or three classmates. Then, compare the errors that you found and the correction methods that you used. If another student used a correction method that you like better than your own, feel free to change what you have written in your book. If you still have questions about run-ons or comma splices, ask your instructor.

ACTIVITY 45

Find a paper that you wrote recently but haven't turned in for a grade. Then, read the paper carefully, looking for any run-ons or comma splices; put a check by these. Next, correct the errors.

Bringing It All Together

In this chapter, you have learned what a compound sentence is, how to build compound sentences and punctuate them correctly, and how to avoid two common problems in these sentences: run-ons and comma splices. Check off each of the following statements that you understand. For any that you do not understand, review the appropriate pages in this chapter.

- ☐ A **compound sentence** is two or more related simple sentences joined together. Often, these sentences are joined using a **comma and a conjunction** (such as *and, but, or,* or *so*). (See page 304.)
- ☐ Each conjunction expresses a **different type of relationship** between simple sentences. *And* combines two similar ideas, *but* contrasts two different ideas, *so* shows a result, and *or* shows alternatives. (See page 305.)
- ☐ Compound **subjects and verbs** can appear in one simple sentence. On the other hand, compound **sentences** must contain **two or more simple sentences**. In a compound sentence, there will always be at least **two separate subjects** involved in **two separate actions**. No comma is used when forming a compound subject or a compound verb; however, a comma is used before a conjunction connecting two simple sentences. (See page 308.)
- ☐ In some cases, you can express the same idea as *either* a simple sentence *or* a compound sentence. (See page 311.)
- ☐ In addition to using a comma and a conjunction to join simple sentences, you can also use a "hard" period when there is no special connection between the sentences or a "soft" period (semicolon) when there is a special connection. Semicolons cannot be used to replace commas. (See page 313.)
- ☐ Compound sentences can join two simple sentences that each contain as few as two words. However, a compound sentence can become longer when (1) the two sentences in it include descriptive words and prepositional phrases (see page 318); (2) the two sentences contain a compound subject and/or a compound verb (see page 321); or (3) the simple sentences are **three** in number instead of two (see page 324).
- ☐ Different types of "glue" must be used to join simple sentences. A comma and a conjunction is glue, and a semicolon is glue. If you use no glue, you will have an error known as a **run-on**. If you use just a comma as glue, you will have an error known as a **comma splice**. Using words that are not conjunctions as glue can also result in these errors. (See page 328.)
- ☐ Words that often cause run-ons and comma splices because they are not conjunctions (glue) include personal pronouns (see page 338), demonstrative pronouns (see page 341), additive expressions (see page 342), and transitional expressions (see page 344).

Chapter 13

The Complex Sentence

OVERVIEW OF THIS CHAPTER

Both of these are complex sentences. They have the same basic meaning, but there are important differences. You'll learn why in this chapter.

CONJUNCTION + NOUN + VERB + , + NOUN + VERB + .
= Because I study, I learn.

NOUN + VERB + CONJUNCTION + NOUN + VERB + .
= I learn because I study.

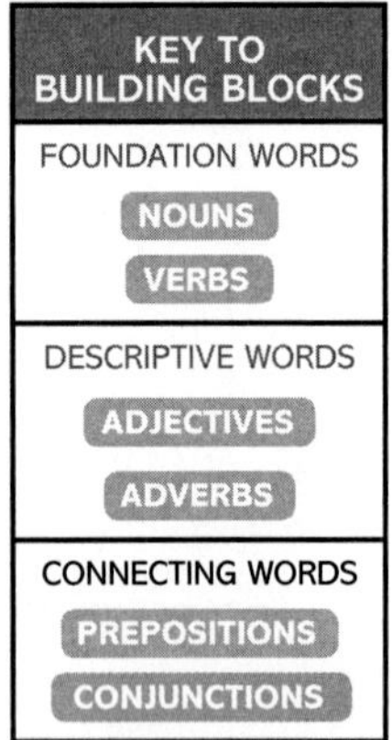

Teaching Tip

You might point out to students that *subordinate* means *lower in order or rank* or *under.* Ask them to call out other uses of *subordinate* that they have heard.

Building Complex Sentences

In the previous chapter, you learned that **coordinating conjunctions** (*and, but, or,* and *so,* and less commonly *for, nor,* and *yet*) work like glue to join simple sentences into **compound** sentences.

	SENTENCE 1	SENTENCE 2
SIMPLE SENTENCES	Our team won.	We celebrated.

	SENTENCE 1	SENTENCE 2
COMPOUND SENTENCE	Our team won, so	we celebrated.

COORDINATING CONJUNCTION PRECEDED BY COMMA

In this chapter, you will study **subordinating conjunctions**, another group of words that work like glue to join simple sentences into what are known as **complex sentences.**

	SENTENCE 1	SENTENCE 2
SIMPLE SENTENCES	Our team won.	We celebrated.

	SENTENCE 1	SENTENCE 2
COMPLEX SENTENCE	Since our team won,	we celebrated.

SUBORDINATING CONJUNCTION

From these examples, you can already see that coordinating and subordinating conjunctions work in a very similar way. However, you should keep some differences in mind:

- There are **more** subordinating conjunctions than coordinating conjunctions.
- Subordinating conjunctions may be **trickier** to use than coordinating conjunctions.
- Subordinating conjunctions have different rules for **punctuation.**
- If you do not correctly punctuate sentences with subordinating conjunctions, you can create a **sentence fragment.**

Subordinating conjunctions are like a glue gun. When you use a glue gun, you need to be especially careful because you have more power and more risk of making a mistake. Likewise, when you use subordinating conjunctions instead of coordinating conjunctions, you also have more power and more risk of making a mistake.

Subordinating Conjunctions

after, although, as, because, before, even, even if, if, since, though, unless, until, when, while

UNDERSTANDING COORDINATING VERSUS SUBORDINATING CONJUNCTIONS

From Chapter 12, you may remember that we use coordinating conjunctions to

- combine similar ideas
- contrast different ideas
- show a result
- show alternatives

This chart reviews the relationships shown by coordinating conjunctions, and those shown by subordinating conjunctions. Examples of these relationships follow.

Relationships Shown by Conjunctions

	COMBINATION	CONTRAST	RESULT	ALTERNATIVES/ POSSIBILITIES
Coordinating conjunctions	and (nor)	but (yet)	so (for)	or
Subordinating conjunctions	after as before when while	although even though	because since	if even if unless until

In each of the following sentence pairs, both sentences express the same idea. However, the first sentence uses a **coordinating conjunction**, and the second uses a **subordinating conjunction**. In the second (complex) sentence, the subordinating conjunction comes at the beginning of the sentence. The comma is in the middle of both sentences.

Combining two similar ideas

The clouds passed, and the moon appeared.

After the clouds passed, the moon appeared.

Contrasting two different ideas

Blanca always remembers, but Bert always forgets.

Although Blanca always remembers, Bert always forgets.

Showing a result

Our team won, so we celebrated.

Because our team won, we celebrated.

Showing alternatives or possibilities

You must study, or you will fail.

Unless you study, you will fail.

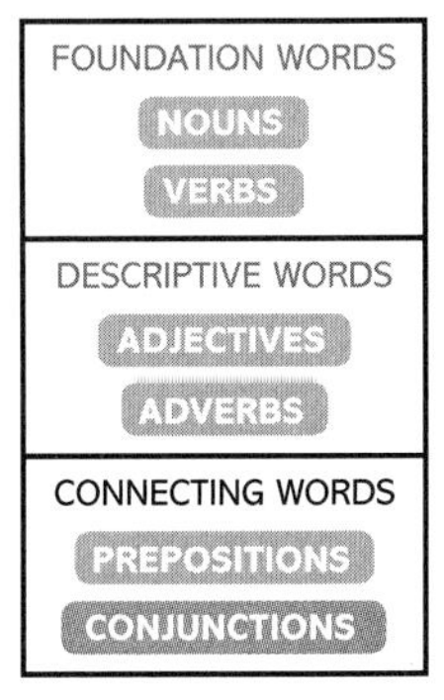

Power Tip

Avoid using both *although/even though* and *but* in the same sentence. You need just one of these expressions per sentence.

Incorrect: Although I left the house early, but I was still late for work.

Correct: Although I left the house early, I was late for work.

Terminology Tip
The part of the sentence that begins with the subordinating conjunction (*Unless you study*) is known as a **dependent clause** because it cannot stand alone as its own sentence. An **independent clause** (*you will fail*) can stand alone as a sentence. If a dependent/subordinate clause is not attached to a sentence, it is a sentence fragment. For more on fragments, see page 374.

Teaching Tip
Call out the first part of sentences that begin with subordinating conjunctions (for example, *Because I'm tired, . . .*). Have students take turns supplying different endings. You might break students into teams to see who can come up with the greatest variety of endings for one or two sentence beginnings.

Note that the parts of a sentence joined by a coordinating conjunction have equal weight:

You must study, or you will fail.

However, when you begin one sentence part with a subordinating conjunction, it often has less weight (emphasis) than the other part. In other words, it becomes *subordinate* (less important).

Unless you study,
you will fail.

Beginning a sentence with a subordinating conjunction can also give a sentence a more formal feeling, as discussed on page 366.

ACTIVITY 1

Combine each pair of simple sentences in two ways:

- as a compound sentence, using a coordinating conjunction, and
- as a complex sentence, using a subordinating conjunction.

For a list of conjunctions, see the chart on page 355. Answers may vary.

EXAMPLE: Greg is shy. He likes parties.

Compound sentence: Greg is shy, but he likes parties.

Complex sentence: Even though Greg is shy, he likes parties.

1. It was Greg's birthday. We baked him a cake.

   Compound sentence: It was Greg's birthday, so we baked him a cake.

   Complex sentence: Because it was Greg's birthday, we baked him a cake.

2. Greg's favorite flavor is pineapple. We baked him a chocolate cake.

   Compound sentence: Greg's favorite flavor is pineapple, but we baked him a chocolate cake.

   Complex sentence: Although Greg's favorite flavor is pineapple, we baked him a chocolate cake.

3. We called Greg's friends. We surprised him with a party.

   Compound sentence: We called Greg's friends, and we surprised him with a party.

   Complex sentence: After we called Greg's friends, we surprised him with a party.

4. Greg walked into his apartment. We all jumped up and yelled, "Surprise!"

Compound sentence: Greg walked into his apartment, and we all jumped up and yelled, "Surprise!"

Complex sentence: When Greg walked into his apartment, we all jumped up and yelled, "Surprise!"

5. Greg loved the chocolate cake. He loved the pineapple ice cream even more.

Compound sentence: Greg loved the chocolate cake, but he loved the pineapple ice cream even more.

Complex sentence: Even though Greg loved the chocolate cake, he loved the pineapple ice cream even more.

ACTIVITY 2

First, complete each compound sentence. Then, rewrite each compound sentence as a complex sentence, using a subordinating conjunction at the beginning. For a list of subordinating conjunctions, see page 365. Answers will vary.

Teaching Tip
For test items on subordination and other topics, see the *Testing Tool Kit* CD available with this book.

EXAMPLE:

Compound sentence: Don't shake the bottle, or it will explode.

Complex sentence: If you shake the bottle, it will explode.

1. **Compound sentence:** We must leave by noon, or we will be late.

   Complex sentence: If we do not leave by noon, we will be late.

2. **Compound sentence:** The exam was long, but it was easy.

   Complex sentence: Although the exam was long, it was easy.

3. **Compound sentence:** You should close the door, or flies will come inside.

   Complex sentence: If you do not close the door, flies will come inside.

4. **Compound sentence:** Beverly drove too quickly, and she received a speeding ticket

   Complex sentence: Because Beverly drove too quickly, she received a speeding ticket.

5. **Compound sentence:** We lost power on campus, so classes were canceled.

   Complex sentence: Since we lost power on campus, classes were canceled.

For online practice with complex sentences, visit this book's Web site at **bedfordstmartins .com/steppingstones**.

UNDERSTANDING RELATIONSHIPS SHOWN BY SUBORDINATING CONJUNCTIONS

Different subordinating conjunctions signal different meanings and relationships in complex sentences. The following sections describe the most common relationships.

Combinations with Time

We use the conjunctions *before, after, when, while,* and *as* to **combine** ideas. Each of these conjunctions shows a different time relationship between the two parts of the sentence. Consider the following examples:

BEFORE Before **the brakes failed, everything was fine.**

Here, we are combining two ideas: *The brakes failed. Everything was fine.* The conjunction *before* tells us the order in which these two things happened—one before the other.

AFTER After **the brakes failed, I pulled the emergency brake.**

Here, we are combining two ideas: *The brakes failed. I pulled the emergency brake.* The conjunction *after* tells us the order in which these two things happened—one after the other.

WHEN When **the brakes failed, I panicked.**

Here, we are combining two ideas: *The brakes failed. I panicked.* The conjunction *when* tells us that the two things happened at the exact same moment.

WHILE/AS As **the brakes failed, I looked for an exit.**

Here, we are combining two ideas: *The brakes failed. I looked for an exit.* The conjunctions *while* or *as* tell us that the two things were happening during the same period of time.

ACTIVITY 3

Join the following sentences with ***before***, ***after***, ***when***, ***while***, or ***as***. Answers may vary.

EXAMPLE: The door slammed. I jumped.

Complex sentence: When the door slammed, I jumped.

1. Lightning struck nearby. The house shook.

   Complex sentence: After lightning struck nearby, the house shook.

2. I was typing my report. The power went out.

   Complex sentence: While I was typing my report, the power went out.

3. They kissed their children. They left on their trip.

   Complex sentence: Before they left on their trip, they kissed their children.

4. Thomas was changing lanes. He struck another vehicle.

Complex sentence: As Thomas was changing lanes, he struck another vehicle.

5. Tammy sang off key. Her voice hurt our ears.

Complex sentence: When Tammy sang off key, her voice hurt our ears.

ACTIVITY 4: Teamwork

Pair up with another student. Then, each of you should write pairs of sentences that can be connected with ***before***, ***after***, ***when***, ***while***, or ***as*** (as in the previous activity). Next, exchange papers and join each other's sentences.

Expected and Unexpected Results

Now let's look at two usages of subordinating conjunctions that sometimes confuse writers. In the examples below, we will start with the same simple sentence: *My alarm clock did not ring.*

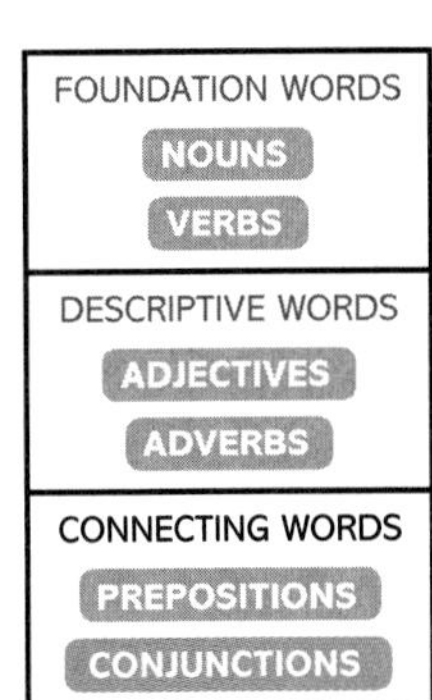

To show an expected result

Since **my alarm clock did not ring, I overslept.**

When we use *since* or *because* to form a complex sentence, we want to show an **expected** result. For example, when your alarm clock does not ring, you generally expect that you will oversleep.

Note that *since* and *because* mean the same thing. It does not matter which one you use.

Because **my alarm clock did not ring, I overslept.**

To show an unexpected result (contrast)

Although **my alarm clock did not ring, I woke up on time.**

When we use *although* or *even though* to form a complex sentence, we want to show an **unexpected** result (a contrast). For example, when your alarm clock does not ring, you generally do not expect to wake up on time.

Note that *although* and *even though* mean the same thing. It does not matter which one you use.

Even though **my alarm clock did not ring, I woke up on time.**

ACTIVITY 5

Examine each of the following pairs of complex sentences and decide whether each sentence shows an expected result or an unexpected result (a contrast). Then, use ***since/because*** or ***although/even though*** to complete the sentence. Answers may vary.

EXAMPLE:

a. ___Since___ my car ran out of gas, I was late for work.

b. ___Although___ my car ran out of gas, I was on time for work.

1. **a.** ___Although___ the watch was very expensive, I bought it.
   b. ___Since___ the watch was very expensive, I did not buy it.
2. **a.** ___Because___ the weather was cold, we did not go to the football game.
   b. ___Even though___ the weather was cold, we went to the football game.
3. **a.** ___Although___ the key lime pie looked delicious, we turned it down.
   b. ___Because___ the key lime pie looked delicious, we each had a slice.

ACTIVITY 6

For each of the following items, complete the first sentence with an expected result. Complete the second sentence with an unexpected result (a contrast). Answers will vary.

EXAMPLE:

a. Because Alexis lost her cell phone, she could not call her parents.

b. Even though Alexis lost her cell phone, she was able to reach her parents by pay phone.

1. **a.** Since the Willow Creek Bridge was under construction, Marta had to take a detour.
   b. Although the Willow Creek Bridge was under construction, Marta did not have to take a detour.
2. **a.** Because there was a terrible storm, we lost power during the night.
   b. Although there was a terrible storm, we did not lose power during the night.
3. **a.** Because Steven skipped lunch, he ate too much at dinner.
   b. Although Steven skipped lunch, he ate a light dinner.
4. **a.** Since the park opens at 8:00 A.M., we can leave very early.
   b. Even though the park opens at 8:00 A.M., we will not arrive until noon.
5. **a.** Because this restaurant has a dress code, we must go home and change into formal clothing.
   b. Even though this restaurant has a dress code, our casual clothing is acceptable.

Possibilities and Alternatives

We use the conjunctions *if, even if, unless,* and *until* to suggest **possibilities** and **alternatives.** Each complex sentence formed with one of these conjunctions must contain two possibilities. These possibilities can be either positive or negative, but they must make sense together. Take a look at these examples:

Using *if* to suggest possibilities/alternatives

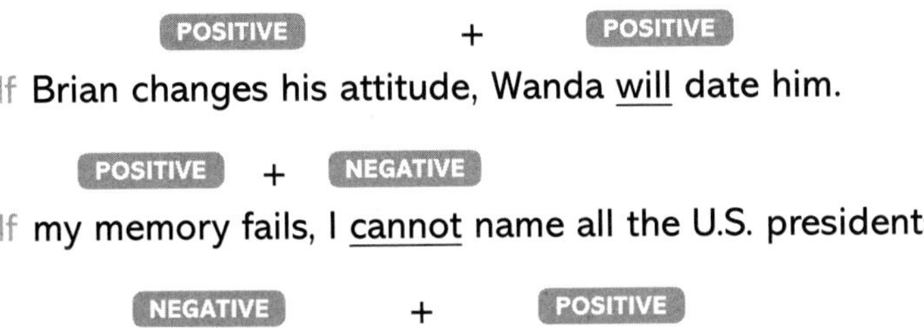

POSITIVE + POSITIVE
If Brian changes his attitude, Wanda will date him.
POSITIVE + NEGATIVE
If my memory fails, I cannot name all the U.S. presidents.
NEGATIVE + POSITIVE
If the bus does not come, the kids will walk to school.

Most writers have no difficulty using the conjunction *if.* Just be sure that the two possibilities make sense together.

FOUNDATION WORDS
NOUNS
VERBS
DESCRIPTIVE WORDS
ADJECTIVES
ADVERBS
CONNECTING WORDS
PREPOSITIONS
CONJUNCTIONS

ACTIVITY 7

Complete each of the following pairs of complex sentences with a second possibility that makes sense. Answers will vary.

EXAMPLE:

a. If my computer crashes, I will buy a new one.

b. If my computer does not crash, I will keep it for another year.

1. **a.** If Kaylee gets the job, she will buy a new car.
   b. If Kaylee does not get the job, she cannot buy a new car.
2. **a.** If we move to Denver, our rent will be high.
   b. If we do not move to Denver, our rent will still be high.
3. **a.** If it stops raining soon, our basement will not flood.
   b. If it does not stop raining soon, our basement will flood.
4. **a.** If we make cake for dessert, we must buy some ice cream.
   b. If we do not make cake for dessert, we do not need ice cream.
5. **a.** If I save money this summer, I can afford a new car.
   b. If I do not save money this summer, I cannot afford a new car.

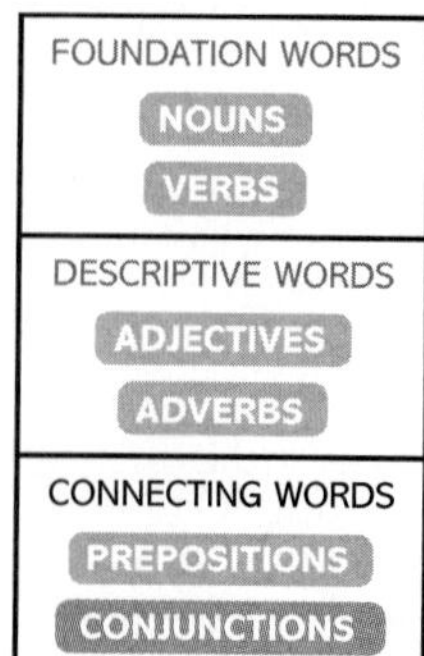

Using *even if* to suggest possibilities

POSITIVE + NEGATIVE

Even if Brian changes his attitude, Wanda will not date him.

POSITIVE + POSITIVE

Even if my memory fails, I can name all the U.S. presidents.

POSITIVE + POSITIVE

Even if the bus comes, the kids will walk to school.

Some writers have difficulty using the conjunction *even if.* Just remember that *even if* means *it doesn't matter whether. . . .* So, in the first example above, it doesn't matter whether Brian changes his attitude; Wanda still will not date him.

ACTIVITY 8

Complete each of the following pairs of complex sentences with a second possibility that makes sense. (Remember that *even if* means *it doesn't matter whether.*) Answers will vary.

EXAMPLE:

If Edgar passes the final exam, he will pass the class.

Even if Edgar passes the final exam, he will fail the class.

1. If Mary is going to Brad's party, I refuse to attend.
   Even if Mary is going to Brad's party, I will be there.
2. Even if this cell phone is expensive, I intend to buy it.
   If this cell phone is expensive, I will not buy it.
3. If apples are not on sale, we should buy some oranges.
   Even if apples are not on sale, we should buy some.

Using *unless* to suggest possibilities

Unless is typically used in two situations.

1. to suggest a necessary condition that may or may not be met:

NECESSARY + NEGATIVE

Unless Brian changes his attitude, Wanda will not date him.

Brian *must* change his attitude, or Wanda will not date him.

NECESSARY + NEGATIVE

Unless they train for the season, the athletes will not be in shape.

The athletes *must* train for the season, or they will not be in shape.

2. to suggest an unlikely possibility:

UNLIKELY + POSITIVE

Unless my memory fails, I can name all the U.S. presidents.

It is *not likely* that my memory will fail, so I will be able to name all the presidents.

UNLIKELY + POSITIVE

Unless the bus comes, the kids will walk to school.

It is *not likely* that the bus will come, so the kids will probably walk to school.

ACTIVITY 9

For each of the following sentences, decide whether the first possibility is *necessary* or *unlikely*. Then, complete each sentence with a second possibility that makes sense. Answers will vary.

EXAMPLES:

Unless it rains on the 4th of July, we will go to the beach.

Unless I pay my phone bill, my service will be disconnected.

1. Unless you earn an A on this essay, you will not pass the course.
2. Unless the store closes early, we will have plenty of time for shopping.
3. Unless Aunt Stella is out of town, we can visit her on Saturday.
4. Unless it stops snowing soon, the major highways will be closed.
5. Unless everyone dislikes chocolate, your dessert will be a hit.

Using *until* to suggest possibilities

We use the conjunction *until* to show a possibility *in the future*. It shows something that has not yet happened but needs to happen for something else to occur.

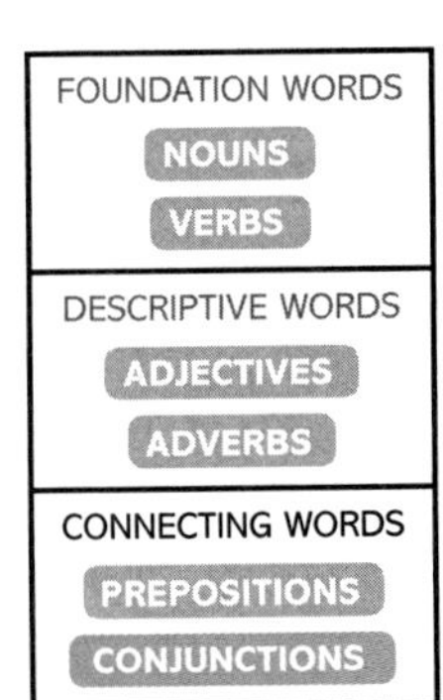

POSITIVE + NEGATIVE

Until Eddie finds his glasses, he will not be able to read.

POSITIVE + NEGATIVE

Until I find a new job, I cannot quit my old one.

POSITIVE + NEGATIVE

Until the engine is repaired, the car will not run.

ACTIVITY 10

Complete each of the following sentences with a second possibility that makes sense. Answers will vary.

EXAMPLE: Until we repair the roof, it will continue to leak.

1. Until we pay off the car, we cannot buy a new dishwasher.
2. Until Stephen graduates, he cannot accept a full-time job.
3. Until I buy more milk, I cannot eat this cereal.
4. Until we pay the light bill, our power will remain off.
5. Until Chan arrives at the office, we cannot begin the meeting.

CONTINUED >

ACTIVITY 11: Teamwork

With your classmates, discuss each of the following beginnings of complex sentences, considering what endings would make the most sense. The ending of the first sentence has been provided for you. Fill in the rest of the blanks with positive or negative versions of this ending, depending on the overall meaning of the sentence.

EXAMPLE:

If our team wins, we will be in the playoffs.

a. Even if our team wins, **we will not be in the playoffs.**

b. Unless our team wins, **we will not be in the playoffs.**

c. If our team loses, **we will not be in the playoffs.**

d. Even if our team loses, **we will be in the playoffs.**

e. Unless our team loses, **we will be in the playoffs.**

1. If Jessica gets a better-paying job, she will be able to buy her own home.
   - **a.** Even if Jessica gets a better-paying job, she will not be able to buy her own home.
   - **b.** Unless Jessica gets a better-paying job, she will not be able to buy her own home.
   - **c.** If Jessica does not get a better-paying job, she will not be able to buy her own home.
   - **d.** Even if Jessica does not get a better-paying job, she will be able to buy her own home.
   - **e.** Unless Jessica does not get a better-paying job, she will be able to buy her own home.
2. If the hurricane turns toward us, we will evacuate.
   - **a.** Even if the hurricane turns toward us, we will not evacuate.
   - **b.** Unless the hurricane turns toward us, we will not evacuate.
   - **c.** If the hurricane does not turn toward us, we will not evacuate.
   - **d.** Even if the hurricane does not turn toward us, we will evacuate.
   - **e.** Unless the hurricane does not turn toward us, we will evacuate.
3. If the children finish dinner, they can have ice cream.
   - **a.** Even if the children finish dinner, they cannot have ice cream.
   - **b.** Unless the children finish dinner, they cannot have ice cream.
   - **c.** If the children do not finish dinner, they cannot have ice cream.
   - **d.** Even if the children do not finish dinner, they can have ice cream.
   - **e.** Unless the children do not finish dinner, they can have ice cream.

REVIEW

You have now learned how to form complex sentences using the following subordinating conjunctions:

Relationships Shown by Subordinating Conjunctions

COMBINATION	CONTRAST	RESULT	ALTERNATIVES/ POSSIBILITIES
after as before when while	although even though	because since	if even if unless until

The following activity will give you more practice with these different conjunctions.

ACTIVITY 12

Complete each of the following complex sentences. Answers will vary.

EXAMPLE:

a. Since the movie is sold out, we can go to the arcade.

b. Although the movie is sold out, my friend has extra tickets.

c. Unless the movie is sold out, we can buy our tickets at the last minute.

1. a. Since it is raining outside, I cannot mow the lawn.

b. Even if it is raining outside, I can mow the lawn.

c. While it is raining outside, I cannot mow the lawn.

2. a. After the house burned down, the owners rebuilt it.

b. Unless the house burned down, it should be on this street.

c. Even though the house burned down, the land is still valuable.

3. a. Before you go to Germany, you have to get a passport.

b. If you go to Germany, you should visit a major city.

c. After you go to Germany, you will have learned some German.

4. a. Because Jackie's flight from Miami was late, she missed her flight to Seattle.

b. Although Jackie's flight from Miami was late, she did not miss her flight to Seattle.

c. Unless Jackie's flight from Miami was late, she should be on the plane to Seattle.

5. a. When I forgot Aaron's birthday, he was hurt.

b. Because I forgot Aaron's birthday, he was hurt.

c. Until I forgot Aaron's birthday, he was my good friend.

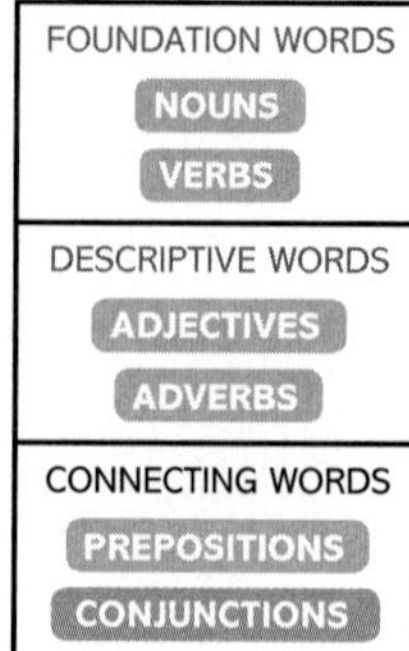

Teaching Tip
Ask students whether they prefer the formal or informal version for writing. You might point out that it's a good idea to use both kinds of structures to lend variety to writing.

FORMING AND PUNCTUATING COMPLEX SENTENCES

So far in this chapter, you have seen one way to form a complex sentence: by beginning the sentence with a subordinating conjunction:

> Because we were delayed at security, we missed our flight.

However, we can also put a subordinating conjunction in the middle of a sentence:

> We missed our flight because we were delayed at security.

Most students would write the second version of this sentence because it is more conversational or **informal**. The first version is more **formal**. However, both sentences emphasize the fact that the flight was missed. (For more on emphasis in sentences with subordinating conjunctions, see page 356.)

Now, notice the important difference in punctuation:

FORMAL Because we were delayed at security, we missed our flight.

CONJUNCTION IN THE MIDDLE; NO COMMA

INFORMAL We missed our flight because we were delayed at security.

When you begin a complex sentence with a subordinating conjunction, you must put a comma in the middle of the sentence. When the subordinating conjunction comes in the middle of the sentence, a comma doesn't usually need to come before it.

Note that a comma does not usually follow a subordinating conjunction regardless of this conjunction's position in a sentence:

INCORRECT

> Because, we were delayed at security, we missed our flight.

INCORRECT

> We missed our flight because, we were delayed at security.

ACTIVITY 13

Rewrite each of the following complex sentences, putting the conjunction at the beginning of the sentence if it's in the middle of the original sentence. Put the conjunction in the middle if it's at the beginning of the original sentence. Add or delete commas as necessary.

EXAMPLE: If it's up to me, I'll never go on another family cruise. *I'll never go on another family cruise if it's up to me.*

1. Our cruise to Mexico was a disappointment although we had expected to have a great time.
   Although we had expected to have a great time, our cruise to Mexico was a disappointment.

2. Our stateroom was not ready because the ship was understaffed.
   Because the ship was understaffed, our stateroom was not ready.

3. Before we could enter our room, we had to wait two hours.
   We had to wait two hours before we could enter our room.

4. Because the seas were rough, Aunt Anna and Uncle Rick became ill.
   Aunt Anna and Uncle Rick became ill because the seas were rough.

5. While she was taking a yoga class, Aunt Anna fell over a railing.
   Aunt Anna fell over a railing while she was taking a yoga class.

6. She was quite embarrassed when she landed in the swimming pool.
   When she landed in the swimming pool, she was quite embarrassed.

7. After we arrived on the island of Cozumel, Uncle Rick disappeared.
   Uncle Rick disappeared after we arrived on the island of Cozumel.

8. We were all worried until he returned to the ship with jewelry and pottery for everyone.
   Until he returned to the ship with jewelry and pottery for everyone, we were all worried.

9. After Aunt Anna was served an overdone steak, she marched into the kitchen to complain.
   Aunt Anna marched into the kitchen to complain after she was served an overdone steak.

10. I am not ready for another family cruise even if Aunt Anna and Uncle Rick stay home.
    Even if Aunt Anna and Uncle Rick stay home, I am not ready for another family cruise.

BUILDING SENTENCE VARIETY

In Chapter 12, you learned about two ways to form **compound** sentences: (a) with a comma and a coordinating conjunction, or (b) with a semicolon (alone or with a transitional expression followed by a comma):

COMMA AND COORDINATING CONJUNCTION

(a) Tom added lighter fluid, but the charcoal would not ignite.

SEMICOLON WITH TRANSITIONAL EXPRESSION AND COMMA

(b) Tom added lighter fluid; however, the charcoal would not ignite.

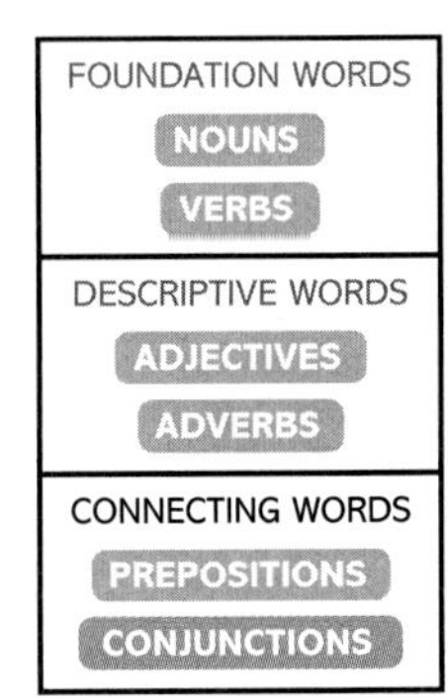

In this chapter, you have learned to form **complex** sentences in two ways: (c) formally, with the subordinating conjunction at the beginning of the sentence, and (d) informally, with the conjunction in the middle of the sentence.

COORDINATING CONJUNCTION AT BEGINNING

(c) Although Tom added lighter fluid, the charcoal would not ignite.

COORDINATING CONJUNCTION IN MIDDLE

(d) The charcoal would not ignite although Tom added lighter fluid.

In a basic sense, all four of these sentences express the same ideas. So which one is best for your writing? While there is no simple answer to this question, you should consider two things:

1. **Style:** If you like a more casual style of writing, you will probably prefer sentences **a** and **d**. Both of these sentences reflect the way we speak; they are more conversational in tone. If you like a more formal style of writing, you might prefer sentences **b** and **c**.
2. **Meaning:** Very thoughtful writers might notice a small difference in meaning among these sentences. Sentences **c** and **d** give a special emphasis to the fact that the charcoal would not ignite. Perhaps the writer wants to express surprise or frustration about this fact.

However, the best recommendation is to use a variety of these sentence types in your writing. Varied sentence patterns keep readers interested in the same way that music with varied rhythms holds our attention and pleases our ear. The more you practice and use these four sentence types, the more powerful your writing will become.

Let's review conjunctions and transitional expressions that can be used to create varied sentences.

Words Used for Sentence Variety

	COMBINATION	CONTRAST	RESULT	ALTERNATIVES/ POSSIBILITIES
Coordinating conjunctions	and (nor)	but (yet)	so (for)	or
Subordinating conjunctions	after as before when while	although even though	because since	if even if unless until
Transitional expressions (See Chapter 12.)	furthermore in addition moreover	however instead nevertheless on the other hand	as a result consequently therefore	on the other hand otherwise

ACTIVITY 14

Combine each pair of sentences in the four ways shown in the example. Remember: correct punctuation is absolutely necessary for the success of your sentences.

Answers may vary.

EXAMPLE: The bookshelf shook in the earthquake. Two books fell down.

Compound—with coordinating conjunction and comma: The bookshelf shook in the earthquake, and two books fell down.

Compound—with semicolon and transitional expression: The bookshelf shook in the earthquake; consequently, two books fell down.

Complex—with subordinating conjunction at beginning of sentence: When the bookshelf shook in the earthquake, two books fell down.

Complex—with subordinating conjunction in middle of sentence: Two books fell down when the bookshelf shook in the earthquake.

1. The factory closed. The warehouse stopped operating.

   Compound—with coordinating conjunction and comma: The factory closed, and the warehouse stopped operating.

   Compound—with semicolon and transitional expression: The factory closed; in addition, the warehouse stopped operating.

   Complex—with subordinating conjunction at beginning of sentence: After the factory closed, the warehouse stopped operating.

   Complex—with subordinating conjunction in middle of sentence: The warehouse stopped operating after the factory closed.

2. The homeowner reported a break-in. The police investigated.

   Compound—with coordinating conjunction and comma: The homeowner reported a break-in, so the police investigated.

   Compound—with semicolon and transitional expression: The homeowner reported a break-in; therefore, the police investigated.

   Complex—with subordinating conjunction at beginning of sentence: Since the homeowner reported a break-in, the police investigated.

   Complex—with subordinating conjunction in middle of sentence: The police investigated since the homeowner reported a break-in.

3. Randall cooks. We eat out.

   Compound—with coordinating conjunction and comma: Randall cooks, or we eat out.

   Compound—with semicolon and transitional expression: Randall cooks; otherwise, we eat out.

   Complex—with subordinating conjunction at beginning of sentence: If Randall cooks, we eat out.

   Complex—with subordinating conjunction in middle of sentence: We eat out if Randall cooks.

CONTINUED >

4. We had little rain. The flowers bloomed.

   Compound—with coordinating conjunction and comma: We had little rain, but the flowers bloomed.

   Compound—with semicolon and transitional expression: We had little rain; nevertheless, the flowers bloomed.

   Complex—with subordinating conjunction at beginning of sentence: Even though we had little rain, the flowers bloomed.

   Complex—with subordinating conjunction in middle of sentence: The flowers bloomed even though we had little rain.

ACTIVITY 15: Teamwork

Exchange books with a classmate. Then, proofread each other's sentences from the previous exercise. Be sure to check that each sentence makes sense and that the punctuation is correct.

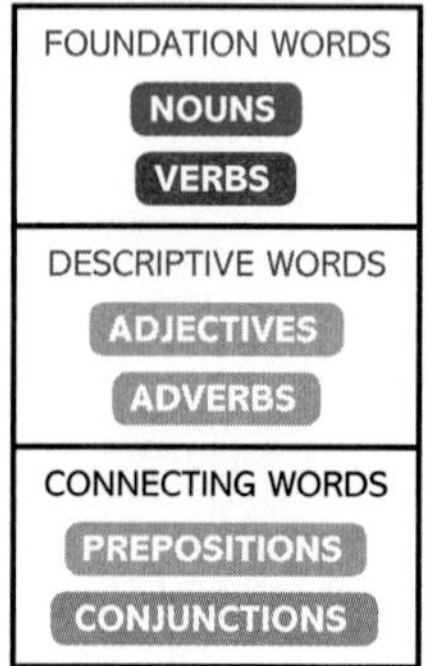

Recognizing Complex Sentences

In every complex sentence that you write, you should be able to identify the separate subjects and separate verbs and punctuate the sentence correctly. In this part of the chapter, you will increase your awareness of complex sentences by

1. recognizing separate subjects and separate verbs in complex sentences, and
2. recognizing correct punctuation in complex sentences.

RECOGNIZING SEPARATE SUBJECTS AND SEPARATE VERBS IN COMPLEX SENTENCES

Remember that a complex sentence joins two simple sentences; therefore, it must contain two separate subjects and two separate verbs. Here's an example:

Since it was raining, we took an umbrella.

Notice that *was raining* is a two-word verb: a helping verb (*was*) plus a main verb (*raining*). (For more on helping verbs, see Chapter 10, page 270.)

Power Tip
Notice that in sentence 2, *umbrella* is not identified as a subject. A subject is the main actor of a sentence or who or what the sentence is about. The actor in this sentence is *we*, not the umbrella. Instead, *umbrella* functions as an *object*, which receives the action of a verb. *What did we take?* → *an umbrella.*

ACTIVITY 16

In each of the following short complex sentences, underline the two separate subjects. Then, circle the two separate verbs.

HINTS:

- Helping verbs (like ***am/is/are/was, have/has, may, must, should,*** and ***will***) are followed by another verb, so you will have to circle both. For a review of helping verbs, see Chapter 10, page 270.
- Remember that the subject(s) in a sentence cannot be in a prepositional phrase. For more on prepositional phrases, see Chapter 11, page 281.

EXAMPLE: **Because the door was open, the burglar walked in.**

1. The baby sleeps after he eats.
2. Because the dog barked, the girl cried.
3. If the spider crawls up his leg, Marco will scream.
4. You should call when you arrive in town.
5. Daniel drove to Montana even though it was snowing.

ACTIVITY 17

In each of the following longer complex sentences, cross out all the prepositional phrases and any descriptive words. Then, underline the two separate subjects and circle the two separate verbs.

HINTS:

- For more on prepositional phrases and descriptive words, see Chapter 11.
- Remember that the subject(s) in a sentence cannot be in a prepositional phrase.
- Helping verbs (like ***am/is/are/was, have/has, may, must, should,*** and ***will***) are followed by another verb, so you will have to circle both. For a review of helping verbs, see Chapter 10, page 270.

EXAMPLE: Natalie reads ~~at a fourth-grade level~~ even though she is ~~in the second grade~~.

1. If I feel sick, I will stay ~~in bed for at least ten hours~~.
2. Although the ~~strawberry~~ ice cream was left ~~on the counter~~, it melted ~~only around the sides~~.
3. The neighbors seem ~~happy with the rosebush in their garden~~, so we should get one.
4. If you travel ~~to downtown Portland~~, you should try the ~~delicious~~ coffee ~~at the café beside the courthouse~~.
5. After Iris picked the ~~plump~~ blueberries ~~from the bush in the yard~~, she made seven jars ~~of jam for her friends~~.

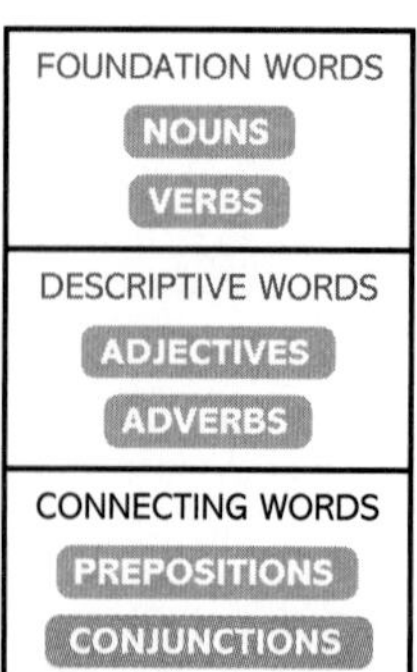

In Chapter 11, you learned that a simple sentence can have more than one subject or more than one verb:

ACT TOGETHER AS ONE COMPOUND SUBJECT

Bonnie and Carlo made **soothing noises.**

ACT TOGETHER AS ONE COMPOUND VERB

The babies cried and fussed.

Simple sentences like these can be joined with a subordinating conjunction, creating a complex sentence in which each part has more than one subject and/or more than one verb.

SUBORDINATING CONJUNCTION

Even though **Bonnie and Carlo made soothing noises, the babies cried and fussed.**

SUBORDINATING CONJUNCTION

The babies cried and fussed even though **Bonnie and Carlo made soothing noises.**

ACTIVITY 18

The following complex sentences have compound subjects and/or verbs. For each sentence, do the following:

- Underline the separate subjects.
- Circle the separate verbs.

If you have difficulty identifying the subjects and verbs, try crossing out all the prepositional phrases.

HINTS:

- For more on compound subjects and verbs and on prepositional phrases, see Chapter 11.
- Remember that the subject(s) in a sentence cannot be in a prepositional phrase.
- Helping verbs (like ***am/is/are/was, have/has, may, must, should,*** and ***will***) are followed by another verb, so you will have to circle both. For a review of helping verbs, see Chapter 10, page 270.

EXAMPLE: **Unless the landlord and the tenant agree on a solution, they may go to court.**

1. Before you arrive, we will cook and clean.
2. Sharelle and Tara screamed when they rode on the big rollercoaster.
3. The players ran back to the ball field after the rain stopped and the sun returned.
4. Before Michael's aunt and cousin visit his home in Florida, he and his wife must install air conditioning in their guest house and put a fence around their alligator pond.

5. While the wheat bread and yeast rolls bake and cool in the front kitchen, the chef and the assistants will peel the shrimp and wash the vegetables in the back kitchen.

RECOGNIZING CORRECT PUNCTUATION IN COMPLEX SENTENCES

So far in this chapter, you have learned three simple rules for punctuating complex sentences:

1. If the subordinating conjunction starts the sentence, a comma is required in the middle of the sentence:

   CONJUNCTION COMMA

   Unless we shout, they won't hear us.

2. If the subordinating conjunction comes in the middle of the sentence, a comma is not usually used:

   CONJUNCTION; NO COMMA

   They won't hear us unless we shout.

3. A comma does not usually follow a subordinating conjunction:

   INCORRECT Unless, we shout they won't hear us.

   They won't hear us unless, we shout.

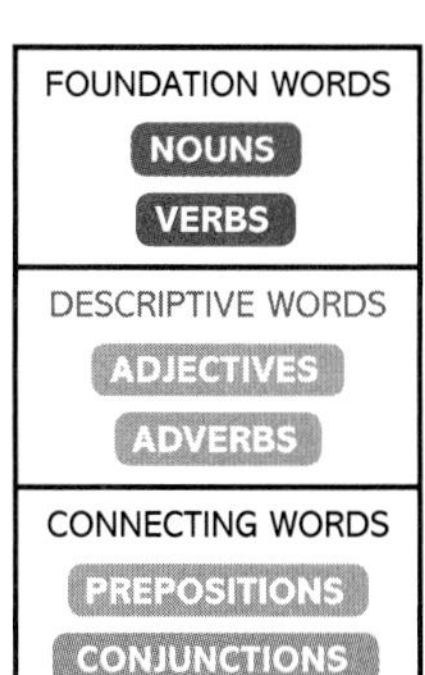

Now, let's add a fourth and final punctuation rule:

4. Never use a semicolon in a complex sentence:

   INCORRECT Unless we shout; they won't hear us.

   They won't hear us; unless we shout.

In the next section of this chapter, you will learn why a semicolon cannot be used in a complex sentence. For now, simply recognize that it is incorrect.

ACTIVITY 19

Examine each of the following sentences and determine whether the punctuation is correct. Write ***C*** next to the sentence if the punctuation is correct. Otherwise, rewrite the sentence, correcting the punctuation.

EXAMPLE: If, you don't call me I will call you.

If you don't call me, I will call you.

1. If you sleep until eleven you will miss the beautiful sunrise.

   If you sleep until eleven, you will miss the beautiful sunrise.

CONTINUED >

2. Felicia did not go to class; because she had the flu.
Felicia did not go to class because she had the flu.

3. Unless the computer goes on sale, it is too expensive for my budget. C

4. Elizabeth will forgive Bobby if, he apologizes.
Elizabeth will forgive Bobby if he apologizes.

5. Life became much more complicated and stressful for Jeremy; after he won the lottery.
Life became much more complicated and stressful for Jeremy after he won the lottery.

Solving Problems in Complex Sentences: Fragments Beginning with Subordinating Conjunctions

In Chapter 11, you learned about an error that writers sometimes make when writing simple sentences: fragments. A fragment is a word group that is missing a subject or verb or that doesn't express a complete thought. Fragments can also occur in complex sentences. The following sections explain common causes of fragments in complex sentences and how you can fix these errors.

PERIODS AND FRAGMENTS

By now, you should know that the following simple sentence is complete and correct:

I love **you**.

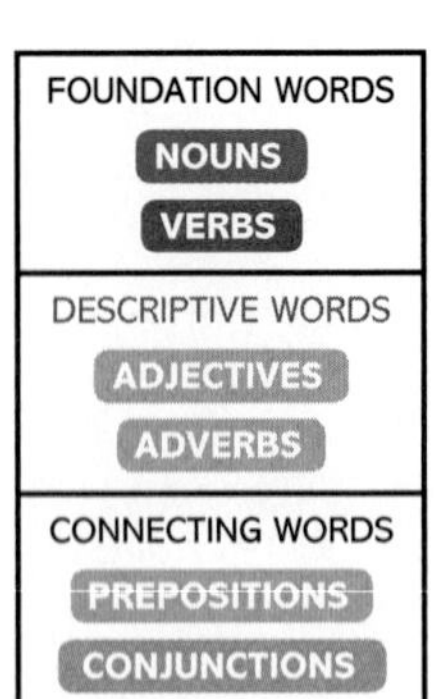

However, take a look at the following example:

I love **you** because.

Few people would write this fragment. It is obvious that this group of words is not a complete thought. Most writers would automatically complete the thought by adding more information:

I love **you** because you are **beautiful**.

On the other hand, many writers get confused when they begin a sentence with a subordinating conjunction. They might create the following fragment:

Because you are **beautiful**.

When we begin a simple sentence with a subordinating conjunction, we must add a comma and complete the thought:

Because you are beautiful, I love you.

Writers can create fragments accidentally when they add an unnecessary period. Take a look:

SIMPLE SENTENCE FRAGMENT

I love you. Because you are beautiful.

UNNECESSARY PERIOD

FRAGMENT SIMPLE SENTENCE

Because you are beautiful. I love you.

UNNECESSARY PERIOD

Fortunately, this type of fragment is very simple to correct. Just remove the period or replace it with a comma:

INFORMAL: Remove the period.

I love you because you are beautiful.

FORMAL: Replace the period with a comma.

Because you are beautiful, I love you.

Teaching Tip
For a tutorial on finding and fixing fragments, see the *Make-a-Paragraph Kit* CD available with this book.

ACTIVITY 20

In each of the following items, mark an ***F*** above the fragment. Then, correct the fragment by connecting it to a simple sentence. Remember to (1) remove the period between the fragment and the simple sentence to which you want to connect the fragment or (2) replace this period with a comma. Leave the other simple sentence alone.

Teaching Tip
For a tutorial on finding and fixing fragments, see the *Make-a-Paragraph Kit* CD available with this book.

EXAMPLE:

F

Credit-card debt can be frightening. Some cannot get free of it. Even though they try.

Credit-card debt can be frightening. Some cannot get free of it even though they try.

F

1. Doug was in debt. Because he had a large balance on his credit card. He felt depressed.

   Doug was in debt. Because he had a large balance on his credit card, he felt depressed.

F

2. Doug needed help. While visiting his friend Bill. He asked for advice.

   Doug needed help. While visiting his friend Bill, he asked for advice.

CONTINUED >

F

3. Bill needed help with a construction job. Doug could work for Bill. Until the job was done.

Bill needed help with a construction job. Doug could work for Bill until the job was done.

F

4. Since the construction job was during the day. Doug could keep his night job. He was relieved.

Since the construction job was during the day, Doug could keep his night job. He was relieved.

F

5. After Doug took the construction job. He put the money from this job in a separate account. He paid off the credit card from this account.

After Doug took the construction job, he put the money from this job in a separate account. He paid off the credit card from this account.

Teaching Tip
For test items on fragments, see the *Testing Tool Kit* CD available with this book.

ACTIVITY 21

In each of the following items, mark an ***F*** above the fragment. Then, correct the fragment by connecting it to a simple sentence. Remember to (1) remove the period between the fragment and the simple sentence to which you want to connect the fragment or (2) replace this period with a comma. Leave the other simple sentence(s) alone.

EXAMPLE:

F

Since our math professor is hard to understand. Many students are struggling in the class. My friend and I decided to hire a tutor. This should help us with the work.

Since our math professor is hard to understand, many students are struggling in the class. My friend and I decided to hire a tutor. This should help us with the work.

F

1. Visitors should not feed chipmunks in the park. If chipmunks become dependent on humans for food. They can starve during a long, cold winter. Then, the population may be lower in the spring.

Visitors should not feed chipmunks in the park. If chipmunks become dependent on humans for food, they can starve during a long, cold winter. Then, the population may be lower in the spring.

F

2. The volcanic mountain Mount St. Helens was once 9,677 feet high. After it erupted violently on May 18, 1980. It lost more than 1,000 feet in height.

The volcanic mountain Mount St. Helens was once 9,677 feet high. After it erupted violently on May 18, 1980, it lost more than 1,000 feet in height.

F

3. Even though fast food seems modern. Remains of fast-food restaurants have been found in ancient Roman ruins. People could sit down and eat at these restaurants or get their food "to go."

Even though fast food seems modern, remains of fast-food restaurants have been found in ancient Roman ruins. People could sit down and eat at these restaurants or get their food "to go."

F

4. Unfortunately, scandals have been common. Since sports have been popular. A very famous scandal occurred during the 1919 World Series. That year, members of the Chicago White Sox agreed to lose games in return for money.
Unfortunately, scandals have been common since sports have been popular. A very famous scandal occurred during the 1919 World Series. That year, members of the Chicago White Sox agreed to lose games in return for money.

F

5. In the 1800s, Levi Strauss invented denim jeans for miners in California. Because these workers wore through trousers quickly. They needed something more durable. Strauss made tough trousers from canvas and sold them to the miners.
In the 1800s, Levi Strauss invented denim jeans for miners in California. Because these workers wore through trousers quickly, they needed something more durable. Strauss made tough trousers from canvas and sold them to the miners.

SEMICOLONS AND FRAGMENTS

As you have seen, complex sentences can be informal (conversational) or formal:

INFORMAL I won't go unless you drive.

FORMAL Unless you drive, I won't go.

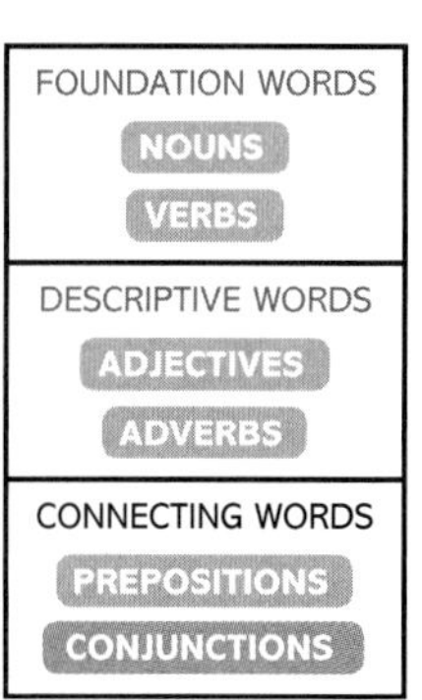

As noted earlier, less experienced writers sometimes add unnecessary periods to both types of sentences.

INCORRECT I won't go. Unless you drive. (FRAGMENT: Unless you drive.)

INCORRECT Unless you drive. I won't go. (FRAGMENT: Unless you drive.)

Another very common error when writing such sentences is to add a semicolon:

INCORRECT I won't go; unless you drive. (FRAGMENT: unless you drive.)

INCORRECT Unless you drive; I won't go. (FRAGMENT: Unless you drive;)

Remember that the semicolon functions as a "soft" period, so here it creates the same problem as a regular period. The rule is very simple: never use a semicolon in a complex sentence. You can correct the previous fragments in the following ways:

Remove the semicolon.	**Replace the semicolon with a comma.**
I won't go unless you drive.	Unless you drive, I won't go.

For online practice with fixing fragments, visit this book's Web site at **bedfordstmartins .com/steppingstones**.

ACTIVITY 22

In each of the following items, mark an ***F*** above the fragment. Then, correct the fragment by connecting it to a simple sentence. Remember to (1) remove the semicolon between the fragment and the simple sentence to which you want to connect the fragment or (2) replace this semicolon with a comma. Leave the other simple sentence alone.

EXAMPLE:

F

We hid in the dark; until the birthday girl arrived. Then, we yelled, "Surprise!"

We hid in the dark until the birthday girl arrived. Then, we yelled, "Surprise!"

F

1. It was snowing heavily. We drove very slowly up the mountain; because the roads were icy.

   It was snowing heavily. We drove very slowly up the mountain because the roads were icy.

F

2. Martin's tax return is due soon. He must mail his return by Monday; unless he files for an extension.

   Martin's tax return is due soon. He must mail his return by Monday unless he files for an extension.

F

3. We worked in the yard until noon. Even though we were tired; we finished the mowing and the weeding.

   We worked in the yard until noon. Even though we were tired, we finished the mowing and the weeding.

F

4. Before Amalia leaves her apartment; she turns on the television for her cat. The cat loves cartoons.

   Before Amalia leaves her apartment, she turns on the television for her cat. The cat loves cartoons.

F

5. Marianne handles the department budget; since she has a talent for math. Lorenzo handles creative decisions.

   Marianne handles the department budget since she has a talent for math. Lorenzo handles creative decisions.

FIXING FRAGMENTS IN WHOLE PARAGRAPHS

The following activity will give you practice with recognizing and fixing fragments in whole paragraphs—a valuable skill for improving your own writing.

ACTIVITY 23

In each of the following paragraphs, mark an ***F*** above any fragments that you find. Then, correct each fragment by connecting it to another sentence. Remember to remove incorrect periods or semicolons and replace them with commas when necessary. The first sentence of each paragraph has been edited for you.

The following paragraph has five fragments, including the one that has been marked for you.

1. (1) In October of 1973, Peter Jenkins began a long walk across America~~. Because~~ because he wanted to understand his country and himself better. (F) (2) He was a disillusioned young man. (3) It was a time of racial tensions and drug use among his peers. (4) Jenkins was also troubled about the Vietnam War~~. Although~~, although it was nearly over. (F) (5) His journey began in New York and ended~~;~~ when he reached New Orleans. (F) (6) For companionship and safety, he took his loyal dog, Cooper. (7) While Jenkins was on the road~~;~~, (F) he met many kind and interesting people. (8) His faith in America was eventually restored. (9) After he completed his long journey~~. He~~, he (F) wrote a book called *A Walk Across America*.

disillusioned: deeply disappointed

The following paragraph has seven fragments, including the one that has been marked for you.

2. (1) Since competition for good jobs can be fierce~~. Your~~, your (F) résumé must be correct, clear, and professional. (2) Although you may be well (F) qualified for the position~~;~~, your résumé can easily end up in the wastebasket. (3) Personnel managers become annoyed at several kinds of mistakes. (4) If your résumé is submitted on brightly colored or decorated paper~~. You~~, you (F) might be seen as unprofessional. (5) Even a carelessly chosen e-mail address can cost you an interview. (6) While an e-mail address such as (F) KutiePie or PartyBoy may seem clever~~. Such~~, such names might reflect unfavorably on your personality. (7) Before you submit your résumé~~;~~, (F) proofread it very carefully for errors. (8) Some applicants misspell the company's name or the city where the company is located. (9) Because an (F) employee represents the company to others~~. Employers~~, employers look for applicants

CONTINUED >

with a command of the English language. (10) A poorly written résumé can be your worst enemy; even if you are the best person for the job.

The following paragraph has eight fragments, including the one that has been marked for you.

3. (1) When TV personality Oprah Winfrey opened a school for disadvantaged girls near Johannesburg, South Africa. She made worldwide headlines. (2) She opened the Oprah Winfrey Leadership Academy for Girls in January of 2007; after she promised former South African President Nelson Mandela to give young women a brighter future. (3) Even though this academy cost about $40 million. Winfrey believes that the money is well spent. (4) She wants to help young girls in South Africa. Because many live in poverty and cannot afford an education. (5) Many schools in South Africa are overcrowded and cannot even provide books. (6) Even if girls can afford to go to school; they face gang violence and drugs there. (7) Also, HIV and AIDS have affected more than 5 million people in South Africa. (8) Many of the victims are female. (9) If girls are educated; they are less likely to become infected. (10) Winfrey considers this academy her best achievement. Although she has received sharp criticism from some people. (11) Unless Winfrey can first help the children of America, some say, she should not donate so much money to another country. (12) Winfrey dismisses the criticism; since she has donated millions to American charities.

ACTIVITY 24: Teamwork

When you have completed correcting one of the paragraphs from Activity 23, get together with two or three classmates. See if each of you can identify any fragments that the others missed. Also, did you fix any of the fragments differently? When you have finished, discuss any differences you found. If you still have any questions about fragments, ask your instructor.

ACTIVITY 25

Find a paper that you wrote recently but haven't turned in for a grade. Then, read the paper carefully, looking for any fragments; put a check by these. Next, correct the fragments.

Bringing It All Together

In this chapter, you have learned what subordinating conjunctions do, how they are used, and how they can cause problems in academic writing. Check off each of the following statements that you understand. For any that you do not understand, review the appropriate pages in this chapter.

- ☐ **Subordinating conjunctions** work like glue to join simple sentences into **complex sentences**. (See page 354 for a review, noting the chart of subordinating conjunctions on page 365.)
- ☐ Like coordinating conjunctions, subordinating conjunctions can indicate combinations, contrasts, results, and alternatives or possibilities. (See page 355.)
- ☐ Sentences that begin with a subordinating conjunction (*Unless we shout, they won't hear us.*) can sound more formal than those in which the conjunction comes in the middle (*They won't hear us unless we shout.*). (See page 366 for a review.) Writers sometimes mix these forms for sentence variety. (See page 367.)
- ☐ Each part of a complex sentence may have more than one subject and/or more than one verb. (See page 370.)
- ☐ Four simple rules apply to punctuating complex sentences: **(1)** If a subordinating conjunction starts the sentence, a comma is required in the middle of the sentence. **(2)** If a subordinating conjunction comes in the middle of the sentence, a comma is not usually used. **(3)** A comma does not usually follow a subordinating conjunction. **(4)** Never use a semicolon in a complex sentence. (See page 373.)
- ☐ Be aware that **unnecessary periods** can cause fragments—for example, *I won't go. Unless you drive.* OR *Unless you drive. I won't go.* Remove the period (*I won't go unless you drive.*) or replace it with a comma if the subordinating conjunction begins the sentence (*Unless you drive, I won't go.*). (See page 375.)
- ☐ Be aware that **improperly used semicolons** can cause fragments—for example, *They won't hear us; unless we shout.* OR *Unless we shout; they won't hear us.* Remove the semicolon (*They won't hear us unless we shout.*) or replace it with a comma if the subordinating conjunction begins the sentence (*Unless we shout, they won't hear us.*). (See page 377.)

Chapter 14

More Complex Sentences

OVERVIEW OF THIS CHAPTER

Descriptive clauses add more information to sentences. Also, they are another way to "glue" sentences together. You'll learn how to use them in this chapter.

NOUN + DESCRIPTIVE CLAUSE + VERB + .

= The students who study succeed.

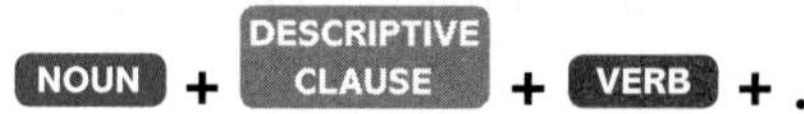

= The evening students, who are at school until 9 P.M., get home late.

KEY TO BUILDING BLOCKS

FOUNDATION WORDS
NOUNS
VERBS
DESCRIPTIVE WORDS
ADJECTIVES
ADVERBS
CONNECTING WORDS
PREPOSITIONS
CONJUNCTIONS

Building Complex Sentences with Clauses

In the previous two chapters, you learned that **coordinating conjunctions** (*and, but, or, so,* and so on) and **subordinating conjunctions** (*although, because, since, unless,* and so on) work like glue to join simple sentences. Here are some examples:

SENTENCE 1 SENTENCE 2

Our team won. We celebrated.

Joined with a Coordinating Conjunction

Our team won, so we celebrated.

Joined with a Subordinating Conjunction

Since our team won, we celebrated.

In this chapter, you will study other words that work like glue to join simple sentences. Here's an example:

SENTENCE 1 SENTENCE 2

The team won. The team celebrated.

Joined with a Pronoun

The team that won celebrated.

You can think of this type of sentence joining as putting one sentence within another. The main idea (expressed in what is known as the **main clause**) is that the team celebrated. The **descriptive clause** tells us which team celebrated.

The team that won celebrated.

Note that the descriptive clause always comes right after the word it describes (in this case, *team*). Like a jigsaw puzzle, a complex sentence formed with a descriptive clause must have all of its pieces connected in the right order to make sense.

Power Tip
Because the clause *that won* describes the noun *team*, it is functioning as an adjective. For more on adjectives, see Chapter 10, page 271. Descriptive clauses are also known as *modifiers*.

Terminology Tip
In English grammar, all the descriptive clauses discussed in this chapter are referred to as **dependent** or **subordinate clauses:** they cannot stand alone as a sentence but rather are *subordinate* to the main clause, which can stand alone as a sentence.

ACTIVITY 1

Join the following sentence pairs by making one a descriptive clause beginning with *that* and the other a main clause. Follow these steps:

- First, underline the repeated item in each simple sentence. Use this to begin your complex sentence.
- Form a descriptive clause using *that,* and put this in the middle of your new sentence.
- Double-underline the main clause and underline the descriptive clause in your new sentence.

EXAMPLE: The bird sings. The bird flew away.
The bird that sings flew away.

1. The vase fell. The vase broke.
   The vase that fell broke.
2. The cars sped. The cars crashed.
   The cars that sped crashed.
3. The monster breathes fire. The monster terrifies.
   The monster that breathes fire terrifies.
4. The puppy became tired. The puppy slept.
   The puppy that became tired slept.
5. A marriage is based on trust. A marriage succeeds.
   A marriage that is based on trust succeeds.

Terminology Tip
The glue words *that, which,* and *who* are known as *relative pronouns,* and descriptive clauses formed with them are known as *relative clauses.*

UNDERSTANDING GLUE WORDS USED IN CLAUSES

That is just one glue word that is used in descriptive clauses. The following chart reviews other words and their uses. Notice that in the joined sentences in the third column, the descriptive clauses come right after the words they describe.

GLUE WORD	COMMON USE	SAMPLE SENTENCE COMBINATIONS (descriptive clauses are underlined and main clauses are double-underlined)
that	**Refers to things:** *The house that . . . ; The test that . . .* Describes *which one* is meant	**Two sentences:** The pipe broke. The pipe was frozen. **Joined:** The pipe that broke was frozen. *Which* pipe was frozen? The one that broke.
which	**Refers to things:** *The bill, which I received . . . ; The holidays, which . . .* Adds details about things	**Two sentences:** The cookbook was a birthday gift. The cookbook has many color photos. **Joined:** The cookbook, which was a birthday gift, has many color photos. *What about* the cookbook? It was a birthday gift.
who	**Refers to people:** *The woman who . . . ; The coach who . . .* *Specifies who is meant*	**Two sentences:** The patient fainted. The patient fell down. **Joined:** The patient who fainted fell down. *Who fell down? The patient who fainted.*
where	**Refers to places:** *The restaurant where . . . ; The college where . . .* *Describes which place or where*	**Two sentences:** We danced at the club. The club closed down. **Joined:** The club where we danced closed down. *Which club closed down? The one where we danced.*
when	**Refers to time:** *The moment when . . . ; The season when . . .* *Describes a particular time/which time*	**Two sentences:** I graduated in the summer. That summer was fantastic. **Joined:** The summer when I graduated was fantastic. *Which summer was fantastic? The one when I graduated.*

Power Tip
Notice that *which* clauses are usually set off by commas. To learn more about punctuating these and other clauses, see page 390.

ACTIVITY 2

Using the examples from the previous chart as models, join each of the sentence pairs as directed. Then, double-underline the main clause and underline the descriptive clause.

HINT: Remember that ***which*** clauses are usually set off by commas.

EXAMPLE: The girl came in first. The girl won the prize.

Join the sentences with *who*: The girl who came in first won the prize.

1. The man left. The man was sick.

   Join the sentences with *who*: The man who left was sick.

2. The cat followed you home. The cat is in love with you.

   Join the sentences with *that*: The cat that followed you home is in love with you.

3. I won the Megabucks. The day is now a personal holiday.

   Join the sentences with *when*: The day when I won the Megabucks is now a personal holiday.

4. Chess is one of the most challenging board games. Chess is my brother's favorite hobby.

   Join the sentences with *which*: Chess, which is one of the most challenging board games, is my brother's favorite hobby.

5. We were born in the big red house. The house is now a bed-and-breakfast for visitors to Mt. Monadnock.

   Join the sentences with *where*: The big red house where we were born is now a bed-and-breakfast for visitors to Mt. Monadnock.

ACTIVITY 3

For each of the following items, underline the word that comes before the blank. Then, make up a clause to describe this word, using the explanations and examples from the previous chart as a guide. Answers will vary.

HINT: Remember that ***which*** clauses are usually set off by commas.

EXAMPLE: The day when I met you was the happiest day of my life.

1. The truck that my brother owned was stolen.
2. Sharks, which terrify me, often swim close to our local beach.
3. Within three months, the factory where Leonid works will be shut down.
4. The prisoner who escaped on Monday is armed and dangerous.
5. For me, the moment when the plane lands is the scariest part of flying.

USING VERBS AND/OR NOUNS IN CLAUSES

In some cases, descriptive clauses may consist of only a glue word and a verb. Take a look:

DESCRIPTIVE CLAUSE

The pipe that broke was frozen.

GLUE WORD + VERB

DESCRIPTIVE CLAUSE

Blue cheese, which stinks, is my brother's favorite.

GLUE WORD + VERB

DESCRIPTIVE CLAUSE

The patient who fainted fell down.

GLUE WORD + VERB

For online practice with complex sentences, visit this book's Web site at **bedfordstmartins .com/steppingstones.**

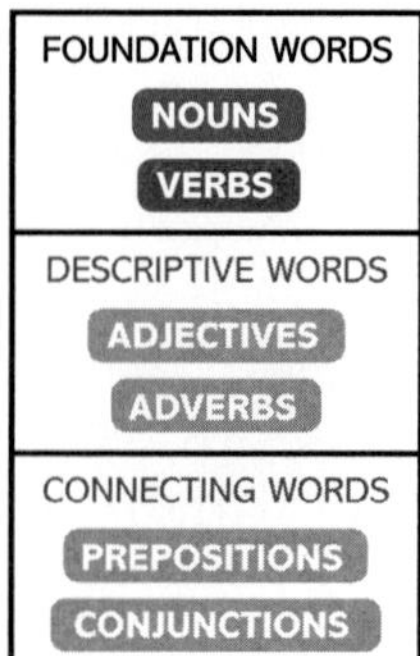

In other cases, descriptive clauses may consist of a glue word, a noun, and a verb.

DESCRIPTIVE CLAUSE

The pipe that we fixed broke again.

GLUE WORD + NOUN + VERB

DESCRIPTIVE CLAUSE

The bike, which Dan painted, is outside.

GLUE WORD + NOUN + VERB

DESCRIPTIVE CLAUSE

The girl whom Jim invited could not come.

GLUE WORD + NOUN + VERB

Notice that the last sentence uses *whom* instead of *who*. Usually, when this glue word is followed by a noun or another pronoun (as in the previous example), it becomes *whom*. Generally, when this glue word is followed by a verb, *who* is used.

Power Tip
Remember to use *who* instead of *that* when referring to people.

The boy who looks like Zac Efron is my son.

GLUE WORD + VERB

ACTIVITY 4

Fill in the blanks with a descriptive clause beginning with ***that***, ***which***, or ***who/whom***, following the cue below each sentence. For a reminder of the functions of these different glue words, see the chart on page 384. Answers will vary.

HINTS: Remember that ***which*** clauses are usually set off by commas. Also, when deciding between ***who*** or ***whom***, remember that you generally use ***who*** before a verb and ***whom*** before a noun or pronoun.

EXAMPLE: The job ___that I want___ is close to my home.

GLUE WORD + NOUN + VERB

1. Teens ___who smoke___ endanger their health.

   GLUE WORD + VERB

2. Saturday cartoons ___, which children love,___ often bore adults.

   GLUE WORD + NOUN + VERB

3. The handsome stranger ___whom you kissed___ is my brother.

   GLUE WORD + NOUN + VERB

4. The puppy ___that I trained___ behaves like a gentleman.

   GLUE WORD + NOUN + VERB

5. The car ___that you hit___ belongs to the police commissioner.

   GLUE WORD + NOUN + VERB

When a noun + verb combination follows the glue word *that* or *whom*, you can leave out the glue word in most cases. Look at these examples:

The pipe ~~that~~ we fixed broke again.

The girl ~~whom~~ Jim invited could not come.

However, do not leave out these glue words before verbs alone.

The pipe ~~that~~ broke was frozen.

In this example, omitting *that* makes the sentence difficult to understand.

ACTIVITY 5: Teamwork

Working with a classmate, look back at your answers to Activity 4. Individually, identify sentences in which you could eliminate ***that*** or ***whom.*** Then, compare your answers. If you find any differences between your answers, try to decide who is correct. It may be helpful to read the sentences aloud.

So far, we have looked at descriptive clauses beginning with *that, which,* and *who/whom.* These glue words can be followed by a verb alone or by a noun and a verb. However, descriptive clauses beginning with the glue word *where* or *when* always include *both* a noun and a verb.

DESCRIPTIVE CLAUSE

The club where we danced closed down.

GLUE WORD + NOUN + VERB

DESCRIPTIVE CLAUSE

The summer when I graduated was fantastic.

GLUE WORD + NOUN + VERB

Often, we can use *that* instead of *when* to describe time.

The summer that I graduated was fantastic.

ACTIVITY 6

Fill in the blanks with a descriptive clause beginning with ***where*** or ***when,*** remembering that these glue words must always be followed by both a noun and a verb. For a reminder of the functions of these glue words, see the chart on page 384.

EXAMPLE: The restaurant where I worked closed last month.

1. The time when you were sick was frightening.
2. The gym where we worked out is now a private club.

CONTINUED >

3. The skating rink where we met is still popular with young people.
4. The winter when the blizzard hit will always be in my memories.
5. The pool where I swim was closed during the water shortage.

PLACING CLAUSES IN SENTENCES

The descriptive clauses that we've looked at so far can be in the middle or at the end of a sentence. The important thing is that they appear directly after the word they describe.

Take a look at the following examples, in which the same descriptive clause appears first in the middle and then at the end of a sentence. The words being described are underlined.

DESCRIPTIVE CLAUSE IN THE MIDDLE	The pipe that broke was frozen.
DESCRIPTIVE CLAUSE AT THE END	We cannot fix the pipe that broke.
DESCRIPTIVE CLAUSE IN THE MIDDLE	Monopoly, which I hate, is my in-laws' favorite game.
DESCRIPTIVE CLAUSE AT THE END	My in-laws like to play Monopoly, which I hate.
DESCRIPTIVE CLAUSE IN THE MIDDLE	The club where we danced closed down.
DESCRIPTIVE CLAUSE AT THE END	I recommended the club where we danced.

Power Tip
Notice that when a *which* clause is in the middle of a sentence, commas are used both before and after it. However, when a *which* clause is at the end of a sentence, we need only one comma: the one before the clause.

ACTIVITY 7: Teamwork

Working with a classmate, write two sentences for each of the following descriptive clauses: one in which the clause is in the middle and one in which the clause is at the end. Make sure that the clause comes right after the word that it describes. Answers will vary.

HINT: Remember that when a ***which*** clause is in the middle of a sentence, commas are used both before and after it. However, when a ***which*** clause is at the end of a sentence, we need only one comma: the one before the clause.

EXAMPLE: who sneezed

Sentence with descriptive clause in the middle: The girl who sneezed went home sick.

Sentence with descriptive clause at the end: I know the girl who sneezed.

1. where you play soccer

   Sentence with descriptive clause in the middle: The field where you play soccer flooded.

   Sentence with descriptive clause at the end: Storms flooded the field where you play soccer.

2. which Catherine loves

   Sentence with descriptive clause in the middle: Pizza, which Catherine loves, is my specialty.

   Sentence with descriptive clause at the end: I will make pizza, which Catherine loves.

3. when we went fishing

   Sentence with descriptive clause in the middle: The day when we went fishing was rainy.

   Sentence with descriptive clause at the end: It rained the day when we went fishing.

4. whom you like

   Sentence with descriptive clause in the middle: The boy whom you like is coming to the party.

   Sentence with descriptive clause at the end: I have not met the boy whom you like.

5. that we made

   Sentence with descriptive clause in the middle: The rice that we made tasted like sawdust.

   Sentence with descriptive clause at the end: No one will eat the rice that we made.

6. who lie

   Sentence with descriptive clause in the middle: Witnesses who lie face penalties.

   Sentence with descriptive clause at the end: The legal system frowns on witnesses who lie.

A final note: When you include descriptive clauses, be sure that the *order* of the ideas makes sense. For example, the ideas in the following sentence make sense in either order:

> The barrel that turned over was full of tomatoes.
>
> The barrel that was full of tomatoes turned over.

However, in some cases, only one order will make perfect sense. Take a look:

The phone that rang disturbed the class.

The phone that disturbed the class rang.

The second version does not make perfect sense because it is not clear that the phone rang first, thus disturbing the class.

PUNCTUATING COMPLEX SENTENCES WITH CLAUSES

You have already learned that *which* clauses are usually set off by commas. When a *which* clause is in the middle of a sentence, commas are used both before and after it.

DESCRIPTIVE CLAUSE WITH *WHICH*

Monopoly, which I hate, is my in-laws' favorite game.

However, when a *which* clause is at the end of a sentence, we need only one comma: the one before the clause.

DESCRIPTIVE CLAUSE WITH *WHICH*

My in-laws like to play Monopoly, which I hate.

With other glue words, you may or may not need to set off the descriptive clause with **commas**. Compare these two sentences (the descriptive clause is underlined in each):

The deliveryman, who usually shows up at 8 A.M., was an hour late today.

The deliveryman who usually shows up at 8 A.M. was an hour late today.

Terminology Tip
The clause in the second sentence is said to be **restrictive** because it controls the meaning of the sentence. Without it, the main point of the sentence would not be clear. However, the clause in the first sentence is said to be **nonrestrictive** because it does not control the meaning of the sentence. In other words, it provides optional (nonessential) information.

The commas in the first sentence signal that the descriptive clause adds **optional** (extra) information about the deliveryman; the necessary (essential) information is that he was an hour late.

The lack of commas in the second sentence signals that the descriptive clause provides **necessary** (essential) information. The sentence suggests that there is more than one deliveryman, and the one who usually shows up at 8 A.M. was an hour late. If this information were left out, your co-workers might ask, "Which deliveryman was late?"

Let's take a closer look at the various descriptive clauses and how they are punctuated.

That *and* Which *Clauses*

Many writers have trouble deciding whether to use *that* or *which* when forming a descriptive clause. To make the right choice, you need to consider *the information* contained in a descriptive clause and how this information relates to the sentence as a whole. Let's look at two examples:

DESCRIPTIVE CLAUSE

The answer that the president gave disappointed the audience.

DESCRIPTIVE CLAUSE

The answer, which took almost ten minutes, disappointed the audience.

In these sentences, the writer uses punctuation to help us understand which ideas are necessary to the main meaning of the sentence and which ideas are optional.

In the first sentence, there are **no commas,** so we know that the information contained in the descriptive clause is necessary to understand the writer's main idea: Not just *any* answer disappointed the audience but *specifically* the answer that the president gave.

In the second sentence, the writer uses a *which* clause set off **with commas,** telling us that the information in the descriptive clause is optional. In this version of the sentence, the fact that the answer took almost ten minutes is interesting but not essential to the writer's main point: that the answer was disappointing.

Deciding whether information is necessary or optional can be tricky. However, with practice your ability to judge should improve.

Power Tip
Descriptive clauses beginning with *that* are nearly always essential to the meaning of a sentence, so they are not set off by commas.

ACTIVITY 8: Teamwork

For each sentence pair below, do the following:

- First, working individually, circle the descriptive clause in each complex sentence.
- Next, discuss with classmates whether the information in the descriptive clause is necessary or optional for the meaning of the sentence.
- Then, write down the reason why the information is necessary or optional.

Answers may vary.

EXAMPLE:

a. The book that is required for my math class costs sixty dollars.
Necessary: The information tells us specifically which book is required.

b. The book, which costs sixty dollars, is useless.
Optional: The main point of the sentence is that the book is useless. How much it costs is optional information.

1. a. The movie that we saw last night was hilarious.
Necessary: The information tells us specifically which movie was seen.

b. The movie, which starred Jack Black, was a comedy set at a private school.
Optional: The main point of the sentence is that the movie was a comedy set at a private school. The fact that it starred Jack Black is optional information.

CONTINUED >

2. a. Boiled cabbage, which smells bad, makes my son sick.
Optional: The main point of the sentence is that boiled cabbage makes him sick. The fact that it smells bad is optional information.

b. The foods that my son likes have nothing green in them.
Necessary: The information makes it clear that we're considering only the foods that the son likes.

3. a. Chess, which requires much skill, is a good way to keep the brain sharp.
Optional: The main point of the sentence is that chess is a good way to keep the brain sharp. The fact that the game requires much skill is optional information.

b. The chess game that we watched on television ended in a fight.
Necessary: The information makes it clear that the particular chess game that was seen on television ended in a fight.

ACTIVITY 9

Combine each pair of simple sentences to make a complex sentence.

- First, underline the repeated item in each simple sentence. Use this noun to begin your complex sentence.
- Form a descriptive clause using ***that*** or ***which,*** and put this descriptive clause in the middle of the sentence.
- If you use ***which,*** set off the descriptive clause with commas.
- Circle the descriptive clause in your complex sentence. Answers may vary.

EXAMPLE: **My homework was a masterpiece. My homework fell in the water.**
My homework, which was a masterpiece, fell in the water.

1. Markeese's computer was overloaded. Markeese's computer crashed.
Markeese's computer, which was overloaded, crashed.

2. The truck has red stripes. The truck was the one my aunt chose.
The truck that has red stripes was the one my aunt chose.

3. Pauline's vacuum cleaner was cheap and unreliable. Pauline's vacuum cleaner chewed up her rug.
Pauline's vacuum cleaner, which was cheap and unreliable, chewed up her rug.

4. The boat hit our boat. The boat was speeding.
The boat that hit our boat was speeding.

5. The fireworks were loud and colorful. The fireworks made the children cheer.
The fireworks, which were loud and colorful, made the children cheer.

ACTIVITY 10

Combine each pair of simple sentences to make a complex sentence.

- First, form a descriptive clause using ***that*** or ***which,*** and put this descriptive clause at the end of the sentence.
- If you use ***which,*** set off the descriptive clause with a comma.
- Circle the descriptive clause in your complex sentence. Answers may vary.

EXAMPLE: Ricardo bought the coat. The coat was on sale.
Ricardo bought the coat that was on sale.

1. We took the subway. The subway is cheaper than a taxi.
   We took the subway, which is cheaper than a taxi.
2. Rebecca saw the movie. The movie was recommended by her best friend.
   Rebecca saw the movie that was recommended by her best friend.
3. We ate the pizza. The pizza was left over from the party.
   We ate the pizza that was left over from the party.
4. I try to avoid spiders and snakes. Spiders and snakes have frightened me since I was a child.
   I try to avoid spiders and snakes, which have frightened me since I was a child.
5. I like dark chocolate. Dark chocolate is bolder in flavor than milk chocolate.
   I like dark chocolate, which is bolder in flavor than milk chocolate.

ACTIVITY 11

Complete each descriptive clause in the following pairs of complex sentences. Answers will vary.

EXAMPLE:

a. The bus that we take every day was late.

b. The bus, which is usually on time, was late.

1. **a.** The dream that I had last night seemed real.
   b. The dream, which took place at my job, seemed real.
2. **a.** Movies that are set on spaceships bore me.
   b. Movies, which can run for two or more hours, bore me.
3. **a.** Seashells that have unusual shapes and colors are fun to collect.
   b. Seashells, which are common on this beach, are fun to collect.
4. **a.** The blue suit that you wore to my party was stunning.
   b. The blue suit, which had silver buttons and gray trim, was stunning.
5. **a.** Dance shows that feature celebrities are on television almost every night.
   b. Dance shows, which my husband hates, are on television almost every night.

Who *and* Whom *Clauses*

Descriptive clauses formed with *who* or *whom* can also contain necessary or optional information. Take a look:

DESCRIPTIVE CLAUSE

The runner who won the marathon was from Ethiopia.

DESCRIPTIVE CLAUSE

The runner, who claimed to be an amateur, won the marathon.

In these sentences, the writer uses punctuation to help us understand which ideas are necessary to the main meaning of the sentence and which ideas are optional.

In the first sentence, there are **no commas,** so we know that the information contained in the descriptive clause is necessary to understand the writer's main idea: Not just *any* runner was from Ethiopia but *specifically* the runner who won the marathon.

In the second sentence, the writer sets off the descriptive clause **with commas,** telling us that the information in this clause is optional. In this version of the sentence, the fact that the runner claimed to be an amateur is interesting but not essential to the writer's main point: that the runner won the marathon.

Power Tip

A semicolon (a "soft" period) should not appear in a complex sentence. Take a look:
Incorrect: We elected Justine Campbell; who has a good record of public service.
For more on semicolon usage, see Chapter 12, page 313.

ACTIVITY 12

Combine each pair of simple sentences to make a complex sentence.

- First, underline the repeated item in each simple sentence. Use this noun to begin your complex sentence.
- Form a descriptive clause using ***who,*** and put this clause in the middle of the sentence.
- If the information in the descriptive clause is necessary, do not use commas. If the information in the descriptive clause is optional, set off the descriptive clause with commas.
- Circle the descriptive clause in your complex sentence. Answers may vary.

EXAMPLE: The fireman retired. The fireman received a lifetime achievement award.
The fireman who retired received a lifetime achievement award.

1. Yolanda quit. Yolanda was the best player on our team.
Yolanda, who was the best player on our team, quit.

2. The child painted the classroom walls. The child was sent home.
The child who painted the classroom walls was sent home.

3. Babies are not shown affection. Babies can grow up with emotional problems.
Babies who are not shown affection can grow up with emotional problems.

4. Milo was the most popular student in high school. Milo became the mayor of our town.

   Milo, who was the most popular student in high school, became the mayor of our town.

5. Billy is terrified of clowns and performing animals. Billy refuses to go to the circus.

   Billy, who is terrified of clowns and performing animals, refuses to go to the circus.

ACTIVITY 13

Combine each pair of simple sentences to make a complex sentence.

- Turn the second sentence into a descriptive clause beginning with ***who,*** and put it at the end of your complex sentence.
- If the information in the descriptive clause is necessary, do not use a comma. If the information in the descriptive clause is optional, set off the descriptive clause with a comma.
- Circle the descriptive clause. Answers may vary.

EXAMPLE: I made the cake for John. John is the birthday boy.

I made the cake for John, who is the birthday boy.

1. I will plan the party for Taki. Taki is my best friend.

   I will plan the party for Taki, who is my best friend.

2. We will not put peanuts in the cookies for Betty. Betty is allergic to nuts.

   We will not put peanuts in the cookies for Betty, who is allergic to nuts.

3. I want to pay the kid. The kid shoveled our driveway after the snowstorm.

   I want to pay the kid who shoveled our driveway after the snowstorm.

4. The fraud charges will be a blow to the president. The president has already been accused of misusing funds.

   The fraud charges will be a blow to the president, who has already been accused of misusing funds.

5. The detective gave the crime-scene information to the officer. The officer was in charge of investigating the murder.

   The detective gave the crime-scene information to the officer who was in charge of investigating the murder.

Remember that when *who* is followed by a noun or another pronoun, it usually becomes *whom*. Take a look:

Hillary Clinton, whom my mother admires, was first lady from 1993 to 2001.

GLUE WORD + NOUN

ACTIVITY 14

Combine each pair of simple sentences to make a complex sentence.

- Turn the second sentence into a descriptive clause beginning with ***whom,*** and put it in the middle or at the end of your complex sentence.
- If the information in the descriptive clause is necessary, do not use a comma. If the information in the descriptive clause is optional, set off the descriptive clause with commas.
- Circle the descriptive clause. Answers may vary.

EXAMPLE: Albert Einstein became a U.S. citizen in 1940. People called Einstein the smartest man in the world.

Albert Einstein, whom people called the smartest man in the world, became a U.S. citizen in 1940.

1. The man just walked into the room. You like the man.
   The man whom you like just walked into the room.
2. Christine has become president of our bank. We do not trust Christine.
   Christine, whom we do not trust, has become president of our bank.
3. The suspect was found innocent. The prosecutors charged the suspect with the crime.
   The suspect whom prosecutors charged with the crime was found innocent.
4. You will be trained by Bob. You will meet Bob later.
   You will be trained by Bob, whom you will meet later.
5. The doctor is my best friend's doctor. You recommended the doctor.
   The doctor whom you recommended is my best friend's doctor.

Where *and* When *Clauses*

Descriptive clauses formed with *where* and *when* can also contain necessary or optional information. Again, punctuation helps us understand which ideas are necessary to the main meaning of the sentence and which ideas are optional. Take a look:

DESCRIPTIVE CLAUSE

My father eats at the restaurant where my mother works.

DESCRIPTIVE CLAUSE

I'll never forget the Saturday night when you proposed to me.

In these sentences, there are **no commas,** so we know that the information contained in the descriptive clauses is necessary to understand the main meaning of the sentence. In the first sentence, the father doesn't eat at just *any* restaurant; he eats *specifically* at the restaurant where the mother works. In the second sentence, it's not just *any* Saturday night that the writer will never forget but *specifically* the Saturday night when the writer was proposed to.

Now, look at these sentences:

DESCRIPTIVE CLAUSE

The restaurant, where people sit for hours, never has an empty table.

DESCRIPTIVE CLAUSE

On Saturday nights, when most of my friends go out, I study.

In these sentences, the writer has set off the descriptive clauses **with commas**, telling us that the information in these clauses is optional. In the first sentence, the fact that people sit in the restaurant for hours is interesting but not essential to the writer's main point: that the restaurant is always full. In the second sentence, the fact that most of the writer's friends go out on Saturday night is interesting but not essential to the writer's main point: that he studies on Saturday nights.

Teaching Tip

Ask students to write two sentences: one with *necessary* information and one with *optional* information. (They can use the examples in this section as models.) Then, have some students read their sentences aloud, pausing at the commas in the sentences with optional information. Do students agree about what information is necessary versus optional?

ACTIVITY 15

Combine each pair of simple sentences to make a complex sentence.

- Turn the second sentence into a descriptive clause beginning with ***where*** or ***when,*** and put it in the middle or at the end of your complex sentence.
- If the information in the descriptive clause is necessary, do not use commas. If the information in the descriptive clause is optional, set off the descriptive clause with commas.
- Circle the descriptive clause. Answers may vary.

EXAMPLE: The library has Internet access. We study at the library.

The library where we study has Internet access.

1. Nauset Beach is home to Nauset Lighthouse. My sister was married on Nauset Beach.

   Nauset Beach, where my sister was married, is home to Nauset Lighthouse.

2. Sarah arrived at that instant. I opened the door at that instant.

   Sarah arrived at the instant when I opened the door.

3. On Saturdays, Jack works long hours. Many people relax on Saturdays.

   On Saturdays, when many people relax, Jack works long hours.

4. We rented an apartment on Bridge Street. You live on Bridge Street.

   We rented an apartment on Bridge Street, where you live.

5. Dan plays guitar at the bar. His brother works at the bar.

   Dan plays guitar at the bar where his brother works.

BUILDING LONGER SENTENCES WITH CLAUSES

We started this chapter by looking at complex sentences with few words. Let's go back to an earlier example:

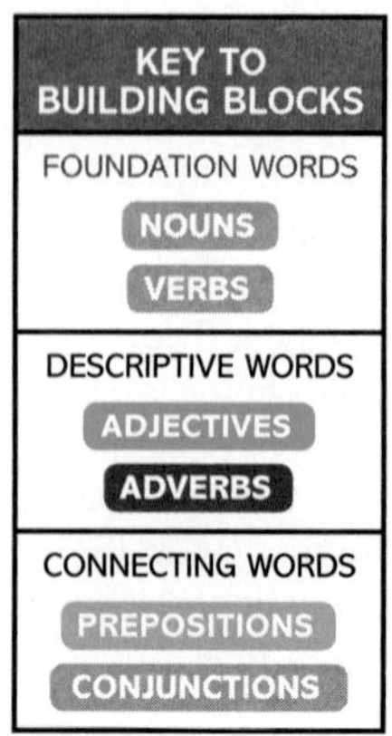

TWO SENTENCES	The team won. The team celebrated.
JOINED WITH A DESCRIPTIVE CLAUSE	The team that won celebrated.

We can make complex sentences more informative by adding descriptive words (adjectives and adverbs) and prepositional phrases to the different parts of the sentence.

The team	that won	celebrated.
WHICH TEAM?	HOW DID IT WIN?	HOW DID IT CELEBRATE?
The varsity football team	narrowly by one point	late into the night.

Now, let's put the pieces of the puzzle together:

> The varsity football team that won narrowly by one point celebrated late into the night.

For a review of adjectives and adverbs, see Chapter 10, page 272. For more on prepositions and prepositional phrases, see Chapter 11, page 281.

ACTIVITY 16: Teamwork

Working in a group of three students, expand each of the sentences below, following these steps:

- Each student should take one part of the sentence.
- Working individually, each student should think of descriptive words and/or a prepositional phrase to add to that part of the sentence.
- Starting at the beginning of the sentence, each student should read his or her part aloud, including the added words.
- When everyone has finished, each student should write down the complete sentence, being sure to include any necessary commas. *Answers will vary.*

EXAMPLE: The car + that crashed + exploded.

The bright red sports car that crashed violently into a tree exploded into a ball of flames.

1. The night + when we danced + is a happy memory.
   The warm night when we danced together on the back patio is a happy memory for me.

2. The building + where we work + was evacuated.
   The old and dangerous building where we work every day was evacuated quickly during the tornado warning.

3. The moon + that rose + dazzled us.
   The large yellow moon that rose over the lake dazzled us with its pale beauty.

4. Adam, + who exercises, + is healthy.
   My friend Adam, who exercises vigorously for three hours every day, is very healthy.

5. Danice + will make fish and chips, + which she cooked for last year's picnic.
   My co-worker Danice will make deliciously greasy and crunchy fish and chips, which she cooked for last year's company picnic at the state park.

ACTIVITY 17

Combine each pair of sentences into one complex sentence, remembering to include any necessary commas. Answers may vary.

EXAMPLE: **The publishers of the literary magazine awarded the poetry prize to a young author. The young author had never been published before, other than a short poem in a local newspaper.**

The publishers of the literary magazine awarded the poetry prize to a young author who had never been published before, other than a short poem in a local newspaper.

1. The odd-looking man ran into a waiting car and left the scene. The odd-looking man left the mysterious little package on our front porch.
   The odd-looking man who left the mysterious little package on our front porch ran into a waiting car and left the scene.

2. The children's spring play left the audience sweaty, thirsty, and exhausted. The play lasted for three long hours in a hot gym with no air conditioning.
   The children's spring play, which lasted for three long hours in a hot gym with no air conditioning, left the audience sweaty, thirsty, and exhausted.

3. The angry note made me hop up and down with fury. My nosy neighbor left the note on my car windshield in the morning.
   The angry note that my nosy neighbor left on my car windshield in the morning made me hop up and down with fury.

4. The long summer was full of thrilling discoveries about flowering plants, towering trees, and creepy bugs. I went to science camp in the long summer.
   The long summer when I went to science camp was full of thrilling discoveries about flowering plants, towering trees, and creepy bugs.

5. Detective Daniels ducked into the dark, smoke-filled club. The famous actress was last seen at the club before she disappeared.
   Detective Daniels ducked into the dark, smoke-filled club where the famous actress was last seen before she disappeared.

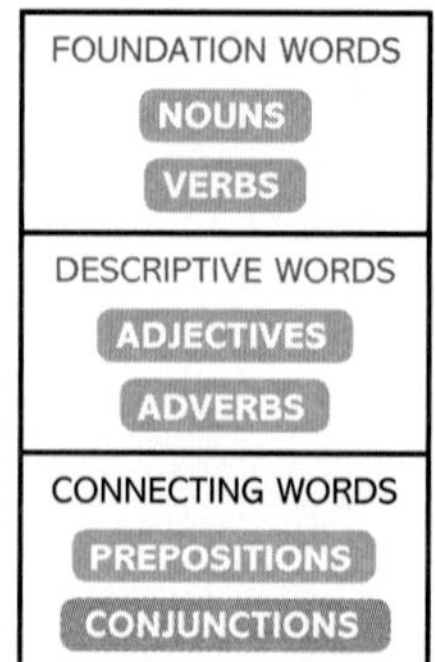

BUILDING SENTENCE VARIETY

In Chapter 12, you learned to form **compound** sentences in two ways: (1) with a comma and a coordinating conjunction and (2) with a semicolon (alone or with a transitional expression followed by a comma):

1. My father is an excellent carpenter, but he doesn't like home repair.
2. My father is an excellent carpenter; however, he doesn't like home repair.

In Chapter 13, you learned to form **complex** sentences in two ways: (1) with a subordinating conjunction at the beginning of the sentence and (2) with a subordinating conjunction in the middle of the sentence:

1. Although my father is an excellent carpenter, he doesn't like home repair.
2. My father doesn't like home repair although he is an excellent carpenter.

In this chapter, you have learned to form **complex** sentences with descriptive clauses:

My father, who is an excellent carpenter, doesn't like home repair.

Remember to use . . .

that or **which** for *things* **where** for *places*
who or **whom** for *people* **when** for *time*

Notice that although the previous sentences have similar meanings, they vary in word order and word choice, giving them different rhythms. Using sentences with varying patterns adds life to your writing, just as varying melodies, voices, and instruments adds life to music.

To complete the following activity, you might want to refer to this chart, which you first saw in Chapter 13:

Words Used for Sentence Variety

	COMBINATION	CONTRAST	RESULT	ALTERNATIVES/ POSSIBILITIES
Coordinating conjunctions	and (nor)	but (yet)	so (for)	or
Subordinating conjunctions	after as before when while	although even though	because since	if even if unless until
Transitional expressions (See Chapter 12.)	furthermore in addition moreover	however instead nevertheless on the other hand	as a result consequently therefore	on the other hand otherwise

ACTIVITY 18

Combine each pair of simple sentences in the four ways suggested, remembering to use correct punctuation. You can refer to the previous chart for coordinating conjunctions, subordinating conjunctions, and transitional expressions. Answers may vary.

EXAMPLE: I want the car. The car is too expensive.

Complex—with descriptive clause: The car that I want is too expensive.

Compound—with coordinating conjunction and comma: I want the car, but it is too expensive.

Compound—with semicolon and transitional expression: I want the car; however, it is too expensive.

Complex—with subordinating conjunction at beginning of sentence: Although I want the car, it is too expensive.

1. Darla loves pets. She collects them.

   Complex—with descriptive clause: Darla loves pets, which she collects.

   Compound—with coordinating conjunction and comma: Darla loves pets, so she collects them.

   Compound—with semicolon and transitional expression: Darla loves pets; therefore, she collects them.

   Complex—with subordinating conjunction at beginning of sentence: Because Darla loves pets, she collects them.

2. I like chilies. They are very spicy.

   Complex—with descriptive clause: I like chilies that are very spicy.

   Compound—with coordinating conjunction and comma: I like chilies, but they are very spicy.

   Compound—with semicolon and transitional expression: I like chilies; however, they are very spicy.

   Complex—with subordinating conjunction in the middle of sentence: I like chilies even though they are very spicy.

3. The fan broke into the star's apartment. She was arrested.

   Complex—with descriptive clause: The fan who broke into the star's apartment was arrested.

   Compound—with coordinating conjunction and comma: The fan broke into the star's apartment, and she was arrested.

   Compound—with semicolon and transitional expression: The fan broke into the star's apartment; as a result, she was arrested.

   Complex—with subordinating conjunction at the beginning of sentence: As the fan broke into the star's apartment, she was arrested.

ACTIVITY 19: Teamwork

Exchange books with a classmate. Then, proofread each other's sentences from Activity 18. Be sure to check that each sentence makes sense and that the punctuation is correct.

Recognizing Clauses

It is important to recognize when you are using a clause so that you can control the ideas and punctuation in your complex sentence. (This awareness will also help you avoid some common errors discussed on page 407.)

Early in this chapter, you learned that a complex sentence can be thought of as putting one sentence within another:

(1) The team won. + (2) The team celebrated. = (3) The team that won celebrated.

Sentence 3 is created by turning sentence 1 into a descriptive clause (*that won*) and embedding it in sentence 2.

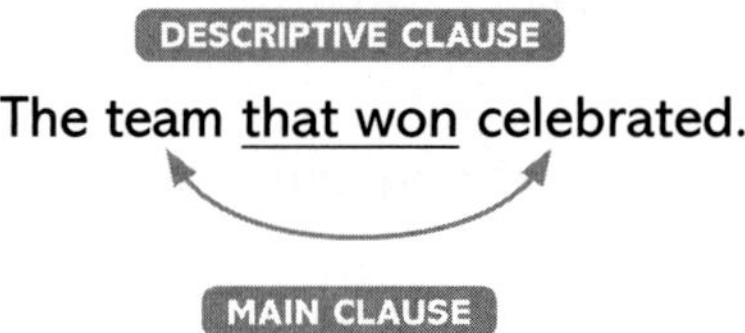

We can also look at complex sentences as having two separate subjects and two separate verbs. Consider this example:

Let's identify the **subject** and **verb** of each clause:

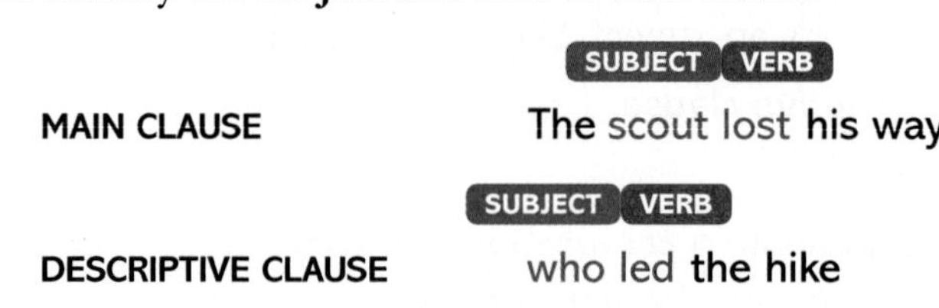

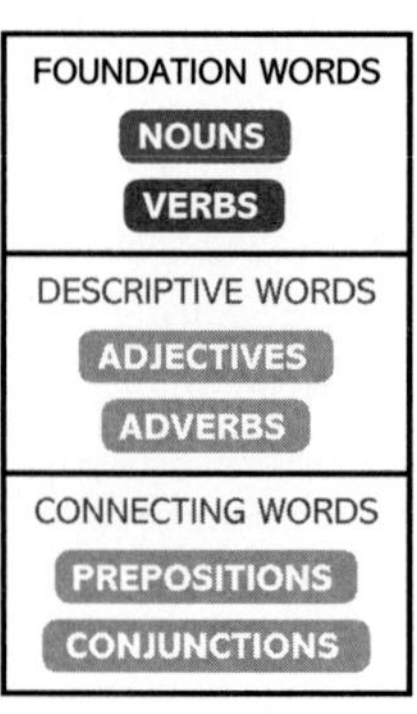

We can tell that the glue word *who* is the subject of the descriptive clause because it replaces *scout*. This becomes clearer if we look at the two simple sentences from which this complex sentence was formed:

The scout lost his way.

The scout led the hike.

WHO

The following activities will give you more practice with recognizing descriptive versus main clauses.

ACTIVITY 20

Follow these steps to recognize short descriptive clauses:

- First, put brackets around the descriptive clause.
- Next, circle the subject and the verb in the descriptive clause.
- Then, underline the subject and the verb in the main clause. Draw an arrow from this subject to connect it to the verb.
- Last, write the two simple sentences from which the complex sentence was formed.

EXAMPLE: The outfielder [who slipped] missed the ball.

The outfielder slipped. The outfielder missed the ball.

1. The glass [that fell] broke.
   The glass fell. The glass broke.

2. The student [who studied] passed the test.
   The student studied. The student passed the test.

3. The stock market, [which fell,] rose again.
   The stock market fell. The stock market rose again.

4. The horse [that jumped] cleared the fence.
   The horse jumped. The horse cleared the fence.

5. The boy [who laughed] woke the baby.
   The boy laughed. The boy woke the baby.

ACTIVITY 21

Follow these steps to recognize longer descriptive clauses:

- First, put brackets around the descriptive clause.
- Next, circle the subject and verb in the descriptive clause. If necessary, cross out any prepositional phrases or descriptive words.
- Then, underline the subject and verb in the main clause. Draw an arrow from this subject to connect it to the verb. If necessary, cross out any prepositional phrases or descriptive words.
- Last, write the two simple sentences from which the complex sentence was formed.

CONTINUED >

EXAMPLE: ~~In the fall, my cousin~~ Deirde, [who reads ~~easily at a fourth-grade level~~], was promoted ~~to a higher grade~~.

In the fall, my cousin Deirdre was promoted to a higher grade.

My cousin Deirdre reads easily at a fourth-grade level.

1. ~~During the violent rainstorm~~, the gutters, [which were ~~clogged with dead leaves~~,] overflowed ~~with brown water~~.

   During the violent rainstorm, the gutters overflowed with brown water. The gutters were clogged with dead leaves.

2. The ~~old peach~~ tree [that stands ~~proudly at the edge of the meadow~~] produces ~~sweet, juicy~~ fruit ~~in the summer~~.

   The old peach tree produces sweet, juicy fruit in the summer. The old peach tree stands proudly at the edge of the meadow.

3. ~~After a long day of work, my friend~~ Andre, [who works ~~in my department~~,] invited me ~~to dinner with him and some other co-workers~~.

   After a long day of work, my friend Andre invited me to dinner with him and some other co-workers. My friend Andre works in my department.

4. ~~At lunchtime~~, the ~~little burger~~ stand [that opened ~~next to the busy computer factory~~] has a ~~long~~ line ~~of hungry customers~~.

   At lunchtime, the little burger stand has a long line of hungry customers. The little burger stand opened next to the busy computer factory.

5. ~~Patient~~ Doreen, [who drives the ~~loud and out-of-control~~ school bus ~~every day~~,] remains ~~calm in every situation~~.

   Patient Doreen remains calm in every situation. Patient Doreen drives the loud and out-of-control school bus every day.

In some cases, a word other than a glue word will be the subject of the descriptive clause.

DESCRIPTIVE CLAUSE

The book that Nancy wanted was checked out.

In this sentence, *that* is not the subject of the descriptive clause. We can tell this by looking at the two simple sentences from which this complex sentence was formed:

The book was checked out.

Nancy wanted the book.

From this example, we can see that *Nancy* is the subject of the descriptive clause.

ACTIVITY 22

Follow these steps to recognize short descriptive clauses:

- First, put brackets around the descriptive clause.
- Next, circle the subject and verb in the descriptive clause.
- Then, underline the subject and verb in the main clause. Draw an arrow from this subject to connect it to the verb.
- Last, write the two simple sentences from which the complex sentence was formed.

EXAMPLE: The hotel [where we stay] has weekend specials.
The hotel has weekend specials. We stay at the hotel.

1. Jill, [whom I adore,] has arrived.
   Jill has arrived. I adore Jill.

2. The dress [that I bought] ripped.
   The dress ripped. I bought the dress.

3. The house [where Grandma lives] has a barn.
   The house has a barn. Grandma lives in the house.

4. The day [when we voted] was a Tuesday.
   The day was a Tuesday. We voted on a Tuesday.

5. Nuts, [which you hate,] are healthful.
   Nuts are healthful. You hate nuts.

ACTIVITY 23

Follow these steps to recognize longer descriptive clauses:

- First, put brackets around the descriptive clause.
- Next, circle the subject and verb in the descriptive clause. If necessary, cross out any prepositional phrases or descriptive words.
- Then, underline the subject and verb in the main clause. Draw an arrow from this subject to connect it to the verb. If necessary, cross out any prepositional phrases or descriptive words.
- Last, write the two simple sentences from which the complex sentence was formed.

EXAMPLE: The ~~fifty-year-old bank~~ teller, [whom the police had suspected ~~for weeks,~~] ~~finally~~ surrendered ~~to the authorities~~.
The fifty-year-old bank teller finally surrendered to the authorities.
The police had suspected the fifty-year-old bank teller for weeks.

Power Tip
In the example for Activity 23, you may wonder why *the police* and not *whom* is circled as the subject of the descriptive clause. Turn the first part of the sentence (including the clause) around, and you'll see: ***The police** had suspected the fifty-year-old bank teller*. You can also ask, "Who is doing the suspecting?" The police are.

CONTINUED >

1. My best friend from high school lives in Darwin, Minnesota, [where many tourists visit a 17,400-pound ball of twine.]

   My best friend from high school lives in Darwin, Minnesota. Many tourists visit a 17,400-pound ball of twine in Darwin, Minnesota.

2. During the test, my new cell phone, [which I programmed with a siren-like ring,] went off loudly in my pocket.

   During the test, my new cell phone went off loudly in my pocket. I programmed my new cell phone with a siren-like ring.

3. In the evening, the cute little parrot [that I got for my last birthday] screeches obnoxiously.

   In the evening, the cute little parrot screeches obnoxiously. I got the cute little parrot for my last birthday.

4. The tall and handsome man [whom you drove to the bus station] is the star of our community theater production.

   The tall and handsome man is the star of our community theater production. You drove the tall and handsome man to the bus station.

5. The summer [when I drove to Vermont with my ex-husband and five cats] was unforgettable for several unpleasant reasons.

   The summer was unforgettable for several unpleasant reasons. I drove to Vermont with my ex-husband and five cats that summer.

Solving Problems in Sentences with Clauses: Descriptive Clause Fragments and Misplaced Modifiers

In this section, you will learn how to find and fix two common problems in sentences with clauses: fragments and misplaced modifiers. Remember from earlier chapters that fragments are word groups that are missing a subject or verb or that do not express a complete thought.

FRAGMENTS

By now, you know that the following sentence is complete and correct:

The phone rang.

Now, decide whether the following example is a complete, correct sentence:

The phone that rang.

The answer is *no.* By adding *that,* we have created a **descriptive clause:** it is part of a sentence but it can't stand alone as a sentence. In other words, it is a **fragment.**

To fix this fragment, we must complete the thought by adding a verb to the main clause:

MISSING VERB

The phone [that rang] ________

In other words, we must answer the question, *What happened with the phone that rang?* Take a look:

The phone [that rang] interrupted the teacher.

To check whether you have successfully completed the complex sentence, cover the descriptive clause and read the main clause:

The phone [ ] interrupted the teacher.

This makes sense. The main clause has been completed successfully.

Power Tip
You might be wondering why this sentence needs another verb in addition to *rang.* The reason is that *rang* is no longer the main verb in the sentence. The words *that rang* function as an adjective describing the phone: *What phone? The phone that rang.*

Now, let's review:

A CORRECT SIMPLE SENTENCE	The phone rang.
A DESCRIPTIVE CLAUSE FRAGMENT	The phone that rang.
A CORRECT COMPLEX SENTENCE	The phone that rang interrupted the teacher.
TWO CORRECT SIMPLE SENTENCES	The phone rang. The phone interrupted the teacher.

Teaching Tip
For test items on fragments, see the *Testing Tool Kit* CD available with this book.

Notice that you cannot correct a descriptive clause fragment by adding descriptive words:

The phone [that rang] repeatedly.

To see why, remove the descriptive clause and read the main clause:

The phone [ ] repeatedly.

This does not make sense. The adverb *repeatedly* describes how the phone *rang,* so it belongs in the descriptive clause:

The phone [that rang repeatedly] ____________.

Teaching Tip
To check for fragments, students can cover descriptive clauses with a finger or a small slip of paper.

To complete this sentence, add a verb to the main clause:

The phone [that rang repeatedly] interrupted the teacher.

Also, you cannot complete a descriptive clause fragment with a prepositional phrase:

The phone [that rang] during the lecture.

To see why, remove the descriptive clause and read the main clause:

The phone [ ] during the lecture.

This does not make sense. The prepositional phrase *during the lecture* describes when the phone *rang*, so it belongs in the descriptive clause:

The phone [that rang during the lecture] ____________.

To complete this sentence, add a verb to the main clause:

The phone [that rang during the lecture] interrupted the teacher.

ACTIVITY 24

For each item below, do the following:

- Decide whether the word group is a complete sentence or a fragment. (First, put brackets around the descriptive clause.)
- If the word group is a complete sentence, write ***correct*** on the line provided.
- If the word group is a fragment, rewrite it as a complete, correct sentence on the line provided. Answers will vary.

EXAMPLE: The majorette [who marched in the Fourth of July parade.]

The majorette who marched in the Fourth of July parade dropped her baton.

1. The hiker [who was trapped under the boulder.]
   The hiker who was trapped under the boulder survived.
2. Cape Cod, [where I first met my husband.]
   Cape Cod, where I first met my husband, is our favorite vacation spot.
3. The concert ticket [that I purchased online] is a fake.
   correct
4. Florence, [who lives in the big yellow house.]
   Florence, who lives in the big yellow house, likes to garden.
5. The summer [when we lived in the cabin.]
   The summer when we lived in the cabin was uncomfortable.
6. Nelson, [which is my father's name.]
   Nelson, which is my father's name, is also my brother's name.
7. The diner [where we worked in our youth] has been closed by the health department.
   correct

Remember that the *length* of a word group does not determine whether it is a complete and correct sentence. When descriptive clause fragments are long, they can be tricky to recognize. Take a look:

> **The National Rifle Association headquarters, [where the congressman gave his famous speech on the right to bear arms].**

If we remove the descriptive clause, we can see that the word group that is left is not a complete sentence:

> **The National Rifle Association headquarters, [ ].**

Now, let's form a complete sentence by adding a verb and other words to complete the thought:

> **The National Rifle Association headquarters, [where the congressman gave his famous speech on the right to bear arms], is hosting a rally in support of the Second Amendment.**

ACTIVITY 25

For each item below, do the following:

- Decide whether the word group is a complete sentence or a fragment. (First, put brackets around the descriptive clause.)
- If the word group is a complete sentence, write ***correct*** on the line provided.
- If the word group is a fragment, rewrite it as a complete, correct sentence on the line provided. Answers will vary.

EXAMPLE: **The new president of the college, [whom the board of trustees approved in a unanimous vote on Tuesday,] will be sworn into office on Friday.** correct

1. The fragile old dinosaur skeleton,[which the researchers found in a narrow cave in the desert.]
   The fragile old dinosaur skeleton, which the researchers found in a narrow cave in the desert, was fifty feet long.

2. The cold and rainy week[when we took our family vacation at the beach.]
   The cold and rainy week when we took our family vacation at the beach was not a happy time.

3. For lunch, my aunt,[who caught ten pounds of fresh trout in the stream.]
   For lunch, my aunt, who caught ten pounds of fresh trout in the stream, fried the fish in butter.

4. Talented poet and essayist Chris Santos,[whom you met at the college's literary awards dinner in May.]
   Talented poet and essayist Chris Santos, whom you met at the college's literary awards dinner in May, will teach here next year.

CONTINUED >

5. The empty riverbed, [where high school students used to race cars dangerously on Saturday nights.]

The empty riverbed, where high school students used to race cars dangerously on Saturday nights, has been filled in with cement.

6. After digging in the yard for several hours, my oldest son discovered a small metal box [that someone had buried under a rosebush on the side of the house.]

correct

Often, writers create descriptive clause fragments accidentally, by putting a period where it does not belong. Take a look:

DESCRIPTIVE CLAUSE FRAGMENT

INCORRECT My father and I cleaned out the garage. Where we found a squirrel's nest with two baby squirrels in it.

When you find a descriptive clause fragment in your writing, usually the easiest way to fix it is to join it to another sentence—either the sentence that comes before it or the sentence that comes after it.

CORRECT My father and I cleaned out the garage, where we found a squirrel's nest with two baby squirrels in it.

Sometimes, when you connect the fragment to another sentence, you may have to remove an extra word. For example:

DESCRIPTIVE CLAUSE FRAGMENT

INCORRECT The stadium where we played our final game. It had bad lighting and old Astroturf.

When joining this fragment to the sentence that follows, we must remove the extra subject *it*. Take a look:

CORRECT The stadium where we played our final game had bad lighting and old Astroturf.

ACTIVITY 26

For each item below, do the following:

- First, mark an ***F*** above the fragment.
- Then, correct the fragment by connecting it to a simple sentence. Remember to remove the period or replace the period with a comma. Also, you may need to remove an extra word.
- Leave the other simple sentence alone.

F

EXAMPLE: The paint that we bought. It was the wrong kind. We needed a weather-resistant paint.

The paint that we bought was the wrong kind. We needed a weather-resistant paint.

F

1. I like to swim. When it's warm outside. The pool is the perfect temperature.

   I like to swim when it's warm outside. The pool is the perfect temperature.

F

2. The hall where we met to plan the party. It had a leaky roof. Therefore, we met at my house.

   The hall where we met to plan the party had a leaky roof. Therefore, we met at my house.

F

3. Dan likes stamps. Which he has collected since he was a child. He gets stamps for every birthday.

   Dan likes stamps, which he has collected since he was a child. He gets stamps for every birthday.

F

4. The people who live next door. They have loud parties every Friday night. We have had to call the police.

   The people who live next door have loud parties every Friday night. We have had to call the police.

F

5. My daughter and I shop at Marconi's. Where we find many good bargains. Last week, we both bought shoes there.

   My daughter and I shop at Marconi's, where we find many good bargains. Last week, we both bought shoes there.

Sometimes, you will not be able to fix a descriptive clause fragment by joining it to another sentence. Take a look:

DESCRIPTIVE CLAUSE FRAGMENT

> **Our coach asked for volunteers to pick up lunch. Ernie, who was the first to volunteer. However, the coach had another job for him.**

If we try to connect this descriptive clause fragment to one of the other sentences, the results will not make sense. In this case, there are two other methods for correcting the fragment. First, we could simply delete the glue word *who:*

CORRECT SIMPLE SENTENCE

> **Our coach asked for volunteers to pick up lunch. Ernie was the first to volunteer. However, the coach had another job for him.**

The second method is to add more information to the fragment to make it a complete, correct sentence:

> **Our coach asked for volunteers to pick up lunch. Ernie, who was the first to volunteer, was not chosen. The coach had another job for him.**

ADDED INFORMATION

ACTIVITY 27

In each item below, do the following:

- First, mark an ***F*** above the fragment.
- Then, correct the fragment by (1) deleting the glue word or (2) adding more information to make the fragment a complete sentence.
- Leave the other simple sentence(s) alone. Answers will vary.

EXAMPLE: **For my physical education requirement, I chose tae kwon do. The martial arts, which build strength and discipline. Also, my brother has enjoyed taking karate.**

F (above "The martial arts, which build strength and discipline.")

For my physical education requirement, I chose tae kwon do. The martial arts build strength and discipline. Also, my brother has enjoyed taking karate.

1. In September, we pick apples at my uncle's farm. The apples that fall to the ground. We pick them up and save them for applesauce.

   F (above "The apples that fall to the ground.")

   In September, we pick apples at my uncle's farm. The apples that fall to the ground are still useful. We pick them up and save them for applesauce.

2. Miklos's debt, which is growing and growing. He plans to see a credit counselor. Also, he has gotten rid of two of his credit cards.

   F (above "Miklos's debt, which is growing and growing.")

   Miklos's debt is growing and growing. He plans to see a credit counselor. Also, he has gotten rid of two of his credit cards.

3. The media are blamed for many wrongs. My friend Portia, who writes for our local paper. She is upset by people's criticism.

   F (above "My friend Portia, who writes for our local paper.")

   The media are blamed for many wrongs. My friend Portia, who writes for our local paper, gets negative comments sometimes. She is upset by people's criticism.

4. When we moved to our new apartment. The mechanic across the street worked on cars until midnight. The children down the street played loudly throughout the day.

   F (above "When we moved to our new apartment.")

   When we moved to our new apartment, we were surprised by the noise. The mechanic across the street worked on cars until midnight. The children down the street played loudly throughout the day.

5. My mother goes jogging every morning before work. Exercise that gets her blood flowing. She also lifts weights at the gym.

   F (above "Exercise that gets her blood flowing.")

   My mother goes jogging every morning before work. Exercise that gets her blood flowing is her favorite. She also lifts weights at the gym.

CONTINUED >

F

6. Our math professor is hard to understand. Some students who are struggling in the class. They have decided to hire a tutor. This assistance should improve their grades.

Our math professor is hard to understand. Some students are struggling in the class. They have decided to hire a tutor. This assistance should improve their grades.

F

7. Where the stolen car was hidden. Branches had been placed on top of it. A tarp covered the side closest to the street. I called the police.

I saw where the stolen car was hidden. Branches had been placed on top of it. A tarp covered the side closest to the street. I called the police.

F

8. We have found many talented people to perform at the benefit concert. Sam, who sings in his church choir every Sunday. Madeleine will play the piano. Her sister Maria will dance to a song that she composed herself.

We have found many talented people to perform at the benefit concert. Sam, who sings in his church choir every Sunday, will do a solo. Madeleine will play the piano. Her sister Maria will dance to a song that she composed herself.

F

9. Cucumbers, which do not agree with me. They hurt my stomach and make me burp. I do not put them in salads. Also, I ask waiters to leave them out of my meals.

Cucumbers do not agree with me. They hurt my stomach and make me burp. I do not put them in salads. Also, I ask waiters to leave them out of my meals.

F

10. The party was a disaster. First, the hostess split her pants up the seam. Then, a potted plant that fell from a shelf. Finally, the cake collapsed in the oven.

The party was a disaster. First, the hostess split her pants up the seam. Then, a potted plant that fell from a shelf knocked out a guest. Finally, the cake collapsed in the oven.

FIXING FRAGMENTS IN WHOLE PARAGRAPHS

The following activity will give you practice with recognizing and fixing fragments in whole paragraphs—a valuable skill for improving your own writing.

ACTIVITY 28

Read each of the following paragraphs carefully, looking for fragments. Then, rewrite each error to fix the problem, using one of the following methods:

- Connect the fragment to another sentence.
- Delete the glue word.
- Add more information to make the fragment a complete sentence.
- If the revised sentences require commas, be sure to include them.

CONTINUED >

The first item in each paragraph has been edited for you. *Answers may vary.*

The following paragraph has six fragments (including the one that has been edited for you).

1. (1) The number of Americans who have been asked to make sacrifices in the wars in Iraq and Afghanistan~~.~~ (2) ~~It~~ has been relatively small. (3) Soldiers and their families have carried the full burden~~.~~, (4) ~~Which~~ which many people believe to be unfair. (5) In other wars, however, ~~when~~ more Americans were asked to contribute. (6) For example, during World War II, citizens were asked to limit their use of gasoline, sugar, certain cloth, and other materials~~.~~, (7) ~~Which~~ which helped the government supply troops and the defense industry with necessary goods. (8) Also, the "Victory Gardens" that many private citizens grew~~.~~ (9) ~~They~~ accounted for about 40 percent of vegetables consumed during the war. (10) Most significant, a draft required all eligible men to register for military service. (11) As a result, not just thousands but millions of Americans ~~who~~ faced the possibility of losing a loved one—or their own life.

The following paragraph has six fragments (including the one that has been edited for you).

2. (1) People who have a positive, optimistic outlook on life~~.~~ (2) ~~They~~ are likely to be healthier than negative people, researchers report. (3) Studies have found that optimistic people are less likely to get infectious diseases, heart disease, and other illnesses than people with a negative outlook. (4) One study, which was done among college students~~.~~, (5) ~~It~~ found that positive students reported having more energy and fewer minor illnesses than negative students. (6) When researchers looked for the reasons for the better health of positive people~~.~~, (7) ~~They~~ they found a few possible answers. (8) First, positive people tend to be more connected to others~~.~~, (9) ~~Which~~ which makes it easier for them to get the help and support that they need. (10) Also, negative emotions ~~that~~ can cause high blood pressure, harm the immune system, and even raise blood sugar. (11) In other words,

negative emotions may wear down the body over time. (12) Regardless of the reason for the link between optimism and health, it is a good idea to adopt a positive attitude toward even bad events~~.~~ (13) ~~That~~ that come our way.

The following paragraph has eight fragments (including the one that has been edited for you).

3. (1) Most of us know people~~.~~ (2) ~~Who~~ who like to collect certain objects, like dolls, baseball cards, or stamps. (3) However, some people feel compelled to fill their homes with things~~.~~ (4) ~~That~~ that many others would consider worthless—even garbage. (5) These people~~, who~~ are known as *hoarders*. (6) Psychologists are learning more about what causes hoarding. (7) It may be a response to stress or isolation from others. (8) It may also occur~~.~~ (9) ~~When~~ when people become unusually attached to objects. (10) Additionally, some hoarding may result from a chemical imbalance in the brain. (11) Whatever the cause, hoarding is a serious problem~~.~~ (12) ~~That~~ that can cause difficulties in the lives of sufferers and their families. (13) For example, some hoarders have lost important papers or other valuable possessions. (14) Others have even been buried under piles of boxes~~.~~ (15) ~~That~~ that were stacked dangerously high. (16) Mental health professionals ~~who~~ can help hoarders with their problem. (17) For example, these professionals can recommend psychotherapy~~.~~, (18) ~~Which~~ which can help hoarders explore and change their behavior. (19) Also, doctors can prescribe helpful medications, such as antidepressants.

ACTIVITY 29: Teamwork

When you have finished correcting one of the paragraphs from Activity 28, get together with two or three classmates. Then, compare the errors that you found and the correction methods that you used. If another student used a correction method that you like better than your own, feel free to change what you have written in your book. If you still have questions about descriptive clause fragments, ask your instructor.

ACTIVITY 30

Find a paper that you wrote recently but haven't turned in for a grade. Then, read the paper carefully, looking for any descriptive clause fragments; put a check by these. Next, correct the fragments.

MISPLACED MODIFIERS

As you already know, a descriptive clause adds information to a sentence. Whether this information is necessary or optional, it changes, or "modifies," the meaning of the main clause. For example, look at the following simple sentence:

My father married a woman.

Now, when we add a descriptive clause to this sentence, it modifies the meaning of the main clause:

DESCRIPTIVE CLAUSE

My father married a woman who was pregnant.

In this sentence, the descriptive clause modifies *woman*. However, suppose that you were writing quickly and put the modifier in the wrong place:

My father who was pregnant married a woman.

In this funny example, the descriptive clause modifies *father*. Clearly, the writer did not want to say that his father was pregnant. Instead, the descriptive clause must be placed right next to the item it is modifying (in other words, right after *woman*).

If you put a descriptive clause in the wrong place, you can end up with a **misplaced modifier** and possibly a very strange sentence.

ACTIVITY 31

For each sentence below, do the following:

- First, put brackets around the descriptive clause.
- Next, decide where the descriptive clause needs to be placed.
- Then, rewrite the sentence with the descriptive clause in the correct place.

If the sentence requires commas, be sure to include them.

EXAMPLE: The scout lost his way [who led the hike.]

The scout who led the hike lost his way.

Teaching Tip
For test items on misplaced and dangling modifiers, see the *Testing Tool Kit* CD available with this book. (Dangling modifiers are covered in Chapter 15 of this book.)

1. The lion roared [that we saw at the zoo.]
   The lion that we saw at the zoo roared.
2. In spring, [where we live] the farm is full of baby animals.
   In spring, the farm where we live is full of baby animals.
3. Valerie takes care of five horses [whom you met at my wedding.]
   Valerie, whom you met at my wedding, takes care of five horses.
4. The eggs were served on a silver dish [that I ate for breakfast.]
   The eggs that I ate for breakfast were served on a silver dish.

For online practice with fixing fragments and misplaced modifiers, visit this book's Web site at **bedfordstmartins .com/steppingstones**.

5. The restaurant is next to a jail [where we had our first date.]
The restaurant where we had our first date is next to a jail.

6. Boris, [which is Anna's favorite treat,] hates rice pudding.
Boris hates rice pudding, which is Anna's favorite treat.

7. The thief was captured by police [who stole the jewels.]
The thief who stole the jewels was captured by police.

8. The field was full of big, ripe pumpkins [where the spaceship landed.]
The field where the spaceship landed was full of big, ripe pumpkins.

9. The answer disappointed the audience, [which took almost ten minutes.]
The answer, which took almost ten minutes, disappointed the audience.

10. The deep and comfortable bathtub is next to a large window, [which is my favorite place to relax,] with a view of the park.
The deep and comfortable bathtub, which is my favorite place to relax, is next to a large window with a view of the park.

FIXING MISPLACED MODIFIERS IN WHOLE PARAGRAPHS

The following activity will give you practice with recognizing and fixing misplaced modifiers in whole paragraphs—a valuable skill for improving your own writing.

Power Tip
You will learn about other types of misplaced modifiers in Chapter 15.

ACTIVITY 32

Read each of the following paragraphs carefully, looking for misplaced modifiers. Then, follow these steps:

- First, underline misplaced modifiers.
- Then, correct the misplaced modifiers, putting the descriptive clause in the correct place.
- If the revised sentences require commas, be sure to include them.

The first sentence in each paragraph has been edited for you. Answers may vary.

The following paragraph has eight misplaced modifiers (including the one that has been edited for you).

1. (1) The day [when we had my daughter Abby's birthday party] didn't go as I had planned ~~when we had my daughter Abby's birthday party~~, but Abby had fun anyway. (2) First, Abby's best friend [, who baked cupcakes for the event,] tripped and dropped the treats in a mud puddle~~, who baked cupcakes for the event~~. (3) Then, the tent [where we were planning to hold the party] collapsed in a heap ~~where we were planning to hold the party~~. (4) Next, the pony [that we hired to give rides] ran into the neighbor's

CONTINUED >

garage ~~that we hired to give rides~~ and wouldn't come out. (5) Finally, the
whom we had hired to juggle and sing for the children
actor ^ called my husband ~~whom we had hired to juggle and sing for the children~~ to cancel. (6) On the positive side, the five-layer coconut
that I baked for Abby
cake ^ was delicious ~~that I baked for Abby~~. (7) Also, we learned that the
who lives next door
boy ^ is training to be an acrobat ~~who lives next door~~. (8) He came over and performed for Abby and her friends. (9) The happiest moment was ~~when we presented Abby with a Gibson guitar~~ at the end of the party, ^ which she
when we presented Abby with a Gibson guitar,
has wanted for a long time.

The following paragraph has six misplaced modifiers (including the one that has been edited for you).

2. (1) The health insurance crisis in the United States ~~that has drawn more attention in recent years~~ is a serious problem ^. (2) Surprisingly, many
that has drawn more attention in recent years
who have no health insurance
of the 47 million Americans ^ work full time, and nearly 20 percent of them are children ~~who have no health insurance~~. (3) These frightening
, which are worsening every year,
numbers ^ have led to attempts~~, which are worsening every year,~~ to establish national health insurance. (4) However, many small employers
, who are concerned about the costs of providing insurance to all workers,
^ are fearful about such attempts~~, who are concerned about the costs of providing insurance to all workers~~. (5) Politicians and organizations have offered various plans to address the insurance crisis. (6) For example, some politicians ~~that would help employers and individuals pay for health insurance~~ have proposed tax cuts. ^ (7) Also, the government and private
that would help employers and individuals pay for health insurance
insurers may have to cooperate more closely to make sure that all citizens are covered. (8) The insurance crisis has no easy solutions. (9) However, if America does not find a way to address the problem, the number of
who do not have insurance
citizens ^ will likely grow ~~who do not have insurance~~.

ACTIVITY 33: Teamwork

When you have finished correcting one of the paragraphs from Activity 32, get together with two or three classmates. Then, compare the errors that you found and the correction methods that you used. If another student used a correction method that you like better than your own, feel free to change what you have written in your book. If you still have questions about misplaced modifiers, ask your instructor.

ACTIVITY 34

Find a paper that you wrote recently but haven't turned in for a grade. Then, read the paper carefully, looking for any misplaced modifiers; put a check by these. Next, correct the errors.

Bringing It All Together

In this chapter, you have learned what descriptive clauses are, how they are used, and how they can cause problems in academic writing. Check off each of the following statements that you understand. For any that you do not understand, review the appropriate pages in this chapter.

- ☐ Like coordinating conjunctions and subordinating conjunctions, the words *that, which, who, where,* and *when* can also work like glue to join simple sentences. These words are used in **descriptive clauses,** which describe certain nouns in sentences. (See page 384.)
- ☐ In some cases, descriptive clauses may consist of only a glue word and a verb. In other cases, they may consist of a glue word, a noun, and a verb. Descriptive clauses that contain the glue words *where* and *when* always include both a noun and a verb. (See page 385.)
- ☐ Descriptive clauses can appear both in the middle and at the end of sentences. (See page 388.)
- ☐ When a *which* clause is in the middle of a sentence, commas are used both before and after it. However, when a *which* clause is at the end of a sentence, only one comma is needed. With other glue words, you may or may not need to set off descriptive clauses with commas. In general, commas signal clauses with **optional** information, while no commas signal clauses with **necessary** information. (See page 390.)
- ☐ We can make complex sentences more informative by adding descriptive words (adjectives and adverbs) and prepositional phrases to the different parts of the sentence. (See page 398.)
- ☐ Like coordinating and subordinating conjunctions, descriptive clauses can add variety to sentences. (See page 400.)
- ☐ A common problem in sentences with descriptive clauses is **fragments.** Verbs in descriptive clauses do not count as the main verb in the sentence. If the only verb in a word group is in the descriptive clause, the word group is a fragment; you must add a verb to the main clause to have a complete sentence. (See page 407.)
- ☐ Writers frequently create descriptive clause fragments accidentally, by putting a period where it does not belong. Often, you can connect such fragments to other sentences. Sometimes, however, you will not be able to fix a descriptive clause fragment by joining it to another sentence. In this case, you may need to delete a glue word or add more information to the fragment to make it a complete, correct sentence. (See page 410.)
- ☐ Another common problem in sentences with descriptive clauses is **misplaced modifiers:** when a descriptive clause is placed somewhere other than next to the word(s) it modifies. (See page 416.)

Chapter 15

Sentences with Modifiers

OVERVIEW OF THIS CHAPTER

Modifying words and phrases offer other ways to add information to different sentence parts. You'll learn how to use them in this chapter.

MODIFYING PHRASE + , + NOUN + VERB + .

= Prepared for the exam, I succeeded.

NOUN + , + MODIFYING PHRASE + , + VERB + .

= The students, studying together for long hours, succeeded.

Building Sentences with Modifying Phrases

In Chapters 12 through 14, you learned how to combine simple sentences into compound or complex sentences. In this chapter, you will learn a new and useful method of combining simple sentences. Let's begin with a brief review.

SIMPLE SENTENCE 1 — SIMPLE SENTENCE 2

My dog howls at the moon. He wakes up all the neighbors.

You already know that these two simple sentences can be combined to form a **compound** sentence. Take a look:

My dog howls at the moon, and he wakes up all the neighbors.

My dog howls at the moon; as a result, he wakes up all the neighbors.

Or, you can combine the two simple sentences to make a **complex** sentence:

When my dog howls at the moon, he wakes up all the neighbors.

My dog, who howls at the moon, wakes up all the neighbors.

As you have learned, both compound and complex sentences always have two separate subjects and two separate verbs. However, if we do not want to repeat a subject, we can combine the two simple sentences by turning one of them into a **modifying phrase**.

MODIFYING PHRASE — SIMPLE SENTENCE

Howling at the moon, my dog wakes up all the neighbors.

SUBJECT BEING DESCRIBED

Terminology Tip

A **phrase** is a word group that does not have both a subject and a verb. *Howling at the moon* is a phrase because it is missing a subject—we don't know who or what is howling at the moon.

When you begin a sentence with a phrase, the phrase works like a coat hanger: You will hang the rest of your sentence on it.

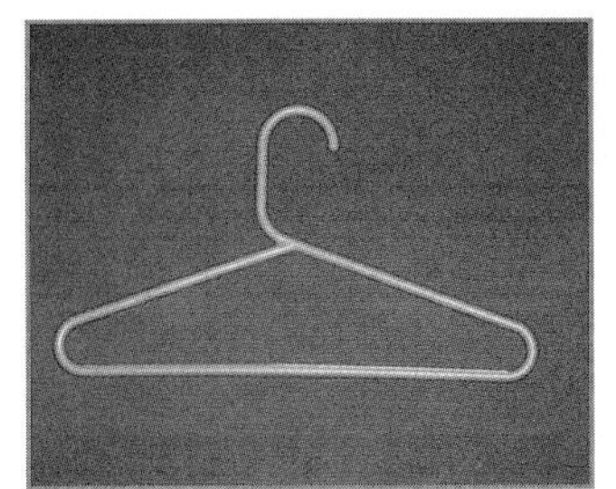

In the first part of this chapter, you will learn to begin sentences with three types of modifying phrases:

- an *-ing* phrase (*present participle* phrase)
- a *to* phrase (*infinitive* phrase)
- an *-ed* phrase (*past participle* phrase)

These phrases all work in the same basic way, but their meanings vary somewhat. Later in this chapter, you will learn how to use *-ing, to,* and *-ed* phrases in the middle or at the end of sentences.

PLACING MODIFYING PHRASES AT THE BEGINNING OF A SENTENCE

Beginning a sentence with a modifying phrase is a good way to add variety to your writing, especially if a lot of your sentences start with subjects and verbs.

Read these two examples aloud. Can you hear a difference between them?

SUBJECT VERB SUBJECT VERB

The criminal entered the courtroom. He smiled at the jury.

MODIFYING PHRASE SUBJECT VERB

Entering the courtroom, the criminal smiled at the jury.

The first example sounds almost robot-like. The second example sounds more musical. The following sections of this chapter will help you make your writing more "musical" by showing you how to begin sentences with different modifying phrases.

Teaching Tip
Have students pair up and write, individually, a series of sentences following the subject-verb pattern. Then, have them rewrite each other's sentences to introduce more varied patterns, using the strategies in this chapter.

Beginning a Sentence with an -ing *Phrase*

Verbs ending in *-ing* (*dancing, sleeping, driving,* and so on) are typically used for one action that is **ongoing** at the same time as another. In the following sentence, the *-ing* verb (*Running*) leads into or sets up the second action, so the *-ing* verb comes first, followed by the second action (*tripped*) that occurs as the first action is taking place.

ONGOING ACTION SECOND ACTION

Running for the bus, Dominic tripped on a garden hose.

If you wish to combine two simple sentences by turning one of the sentences into an *-ing* phrase, begin by identifying the verb in each simple sentence:

Dominic ran for the bus. He tripped on a garden hose.

Next, use the base form of the first verb (*run* in this case) and add *-ing* to it. Begin your sentence with the *-ing* phrase:

Running for the bus . . .

Power Tip
Some writers prefer to add the word *while* to the beginning of an *-ing* phrase. For example: *While running for the bus, Dominic tripped on a garden hose.*

Now, add a comma and "hang" the rest of your sentence onto the phrase:

Running for the bus, Dominic tripped on a garden hose.

The second part of the sentence begins with the subject *Dominic* instead of *he* because *Dominic* doesn't appear in the first part of the sentence, and it is a more specific name for the subject.

ACTIVITY 1

Complete each sentence below by following these steps:

- Add a verb to the subject.
- Add any additional information to complete the thought. Answers will vary.

EXAMPLE: Sliding into second base, Jason twisted his ankle.

1. Opening the door to his apartment, Dewayne was surprised by his friends.
2. Seeing a strange light in the sky, the farmer ran home to tell his wife.
3. Making lasagna for dinner, Stephen burned his hand.
4. Jogging around the block, Jolina saw her neighbor's new deck.
5. Chasing the neighbor's cat, my dog got covered in mud.

ACTIVITY 2

Combine each pair of simple sentences by turning the first sentence into an *-ing* phrase. Follow these steps:

- Underline the verb in each simple sentence.
- Put the first verb in the *-ing* form and use it to write an *-ing* phrase that will begin your new sentence.
- Add a comma after the phrase.
- Hang the rest of your sentence onto the phrase. (You may need to change the subject of the second part of the sentence.)

EXAMPLE: Nicole noticed a problem. She sprung into action.

Noticing a problem, Nicole sprung into action.

1. Nicole heard screeching tires. She looked out her window.
   Hearing screeching tires, Nicole looked out her window.
2. She saw a badly damaged car in the ditch. She called 911.
   Seeing a badly damaged car in the ditch, she called 911.
3. Nicole wanted to help. She grabbed her first aid kit.
   Wanting to help, Nicole grabbed her first aid kit.
4. Nicole arrived at the crash site. She calmed the injured driver.
   Arriving at the crash site, Nicole calmed the injured driver.
5. The driver trembled with fear. He thanked Nicole for her help.
   Trembling with fear, the driver thanked Nicole for her help.

For online practice with using modifiers, visit this book's Web site at **bedfordstmartins .com/steppingstones**.

ACTIVITY 3: Teamwork

For each of the following items, use the two verbs and subject provided to write a sentence that begins with an *-ing* phrase. Follow these steps:

- Put the first verb in the *-ing* form and use it to begin your sentence with a phrase.
- Add a comma after the phrase.
- Use the subject and the second verb to complete the thought. (You may put the second verb in the past, present, or future tense.) Answers will vary.

Power Tip
For advice on forming various verb tenses, see Chapter 16.

EXAMPLE:

First verb: sneak **Subject:** Laura **Second verb:** surprise

Sneaking into the house, Laura surprised her roommates.

1. **First verb:** drive **Subject:** Miguel **Second verb:** listen
   Driving to work, Miguel listened to the radio.
2. **First verb:** wash **Subject:** Blake **Second verb:** cut
   Washing her car, Blake cut her foot.
3. **First verb:** investigate **Subject:** detective **Second verb:** question
   Investigating a burglary, the detective questioned nearby residents.
4. **First verb:** sip **Subject:** Melinda **Second verb:** burn
   Sipping her coffee, Melinda burned her tongue.
5. **First verb:** throw **Subject:** pitcher **Second verb:** hurt
   Throwing a fast ball, the pitcher hurt his shoulder.

Beginning a Sentence with a to *Phrase*

When a verb is written in the *to* form (*to dance, to sleep, to drive,* and so on), it often shows a **desired action** or goal. In such cases, you will find a desired action or goal (the *to* phrase) in the first part of the sentence and a necessary action in the second part of the sentence:

Terminology Tip
A verb that is written in the *to* form is called an **infinitive**. The *to* in an infinitive should not be confused with the preposition *to,* which typically shows direction: *I went to the store.*

DESIRED ACTION — ACTION THAT MUST BE TAKEN

To get to work on time, I catch the six o'clock train.

When you begin sentences like these with a *to* phrase, it is the same as beginning the sentence with *In order to* . . . Take a look:

To get to work on time, I catch the six o'clock train.

In order to get to work on time, I catch the six o'clock train.

Both of these sentences are correct, and they have the same meaning. You may use either form you prefer.

If you wish to combine two simple sentences by turning one of the sentences into a *to* phrase, begin by identifying the *to* + verb combination in the first simple sentence:

My cousin wants to find a girlfriend. He tried an online dating service.

Use this combination to form the phrase that will begin your new sentence:

To find a girlfriend . . .

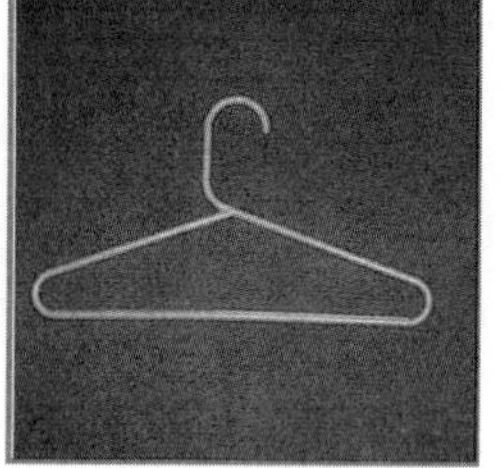

Now, add a comma and "hang" the rest of your sentence onto the phrase:

To find a girlfriend, my cousin tried an online dating service.

The second part of the sentence begins with *my cousin* instead of *he* because *my cousin* doesn't appear in the first part of the sentence, and it is a more specific name for the subject.

ACTIVITY 4

Complete each sentence below by following these steps:

- Add a verb to the subject.
- Add any additional information to complete the thought. Answers will vary.

EXAMPLE: To teach the spoiled child a lesson, the babysitter took away his PlayStation.

1. To get to work on time, Frank gets up at 5 A.M.
2. To receive a free coupon, the customer answered the telemarketer's questions.
3. To repair the broken lamp, you will need a new switch.
4. To comfort the lost child, the police officer gave her a teddy bear.
5. To learn her lines, the actress rehearsed them with her roommate.

ACTIVITY 5

Combine each pair of simple sentences by turning the first sentence into a *to* phrase. Follow these steps:

- Underline the *to* + verb combination in the first simple sentence.
- Use this combination to form the phrase that will begin your new sentence.
- Add a comma after the phrase.
- Hang the rest of your sentence onto the phrase. (You may need to change the subject of the second part of the sentence.)

EXAMPLE: Many homeowners want to keep remodeling costs low. They do the work themselves.

To keep remodeling costs low, many homeowners do the work themselves.

1. David and Muriel decided to remodel their home. They took out a small loan.
To remodel their home, David and Muriel took out a small loan.

2. They wanted to find the best price for carpeting. They compared prices in the area.
To find the best price for carpeting, they compared prices in the area.

3. David wanted to learn how to lay the carpet himself. He took a free class at a building supply store.
To learn how to lay the carpet himself, David took a free class at a building supply store.

4. David decided to save even more money. He would redo the plumbing himself.
To save even more money, David would redo the plumbing himself.

5. Muriel decided to stay out of the way. She visited her sister in Lake Tahoe.
To stay out of the way, Muriel visited her sister in Lake Tahoe.

ACTIVITY 6: Teamwork

For each of the following items, use the two verbs and subject provided to write a sentence that begins with a *to* phrase. Follow these steps:

- Put the first verb in the *to* form and use it to begin your sentence with a phrase.
- Add a comma after the phrase.
- Use the subject and the second verb to complete the thought. (You may put the second verb in the past, present, or future tense.) Answers will vary.

EXAMPLE:

First verb: improve **Subject:** the high school senior **Second verb:** hire

To improve his SAT scores, the high school senior hired a tutor.

1. **First verb:** win **Subject:** the mayor **Second verb:** promise
To win the election, the mayor promised lower taxes.

2. **First verb:** annoy **Subject:** Benjamin **Second verb:** talk
To annoy his classmates, Benjamin talked in a squeaky voice.

3. **First verb:** study **Subject:** many students **Second verb:** review
To study for exams, many students review their notes.

4. **First verb:** qualify **Subject:** applicants **Second verb:** apply
To qualify for the scholarship, applicants must apply before October 1.

5. **First verb:** reduce **Subject:** yoga students **Second verb:** breathe
To reduce stress, the yoga students breathe deeply.

Beginning a Sentence with an -ed Phrase

When a verb in a modifying phrase is written in the *-ed* form (*embarrassed, married, angered,* and so on), it indicates the **condition** of someone or something. In a sentence that begins with an *-ed* phrase, you will find the description of the condition in the first part of the sentence and the person or thing being described, and what the person/thing did, in the last part of the sentence:

CONDITION — PERSON DESCRIBED — PERSON'S ACTION

Injured during the tryouts, the gymnast could not compete in the Olympics.

Injured is known as a *past participle.* Keep in mind that not all past participles end in *-ed*. (You will learn more about the irregular forms in Chapter 16.) Take a look:

PAST PARTICIPLE OF *LOSE*

Lost in the amusement park, the child started to cry.

PAST PARTICIPLE OF *STEAL*

Stolen on New Year's Day, my car was never found.

Power Tip
For more on identifying complete verbs (including helping verbs and the verbs that follow them), see Chapter 10, page 270, and Chapter 11.

If you wish to combine two simple sentences by turning one of the sentences into an *-ed* phrase (or other past-participle form), begin by identifying the complete verb in the first simple sentence:

Our antique clock was damaged during the move. It will not keep the correct time.

Drop the helping verb *was* and use the part participle to form the phrase that will begin your new sentence:

Damaged during the move . . .

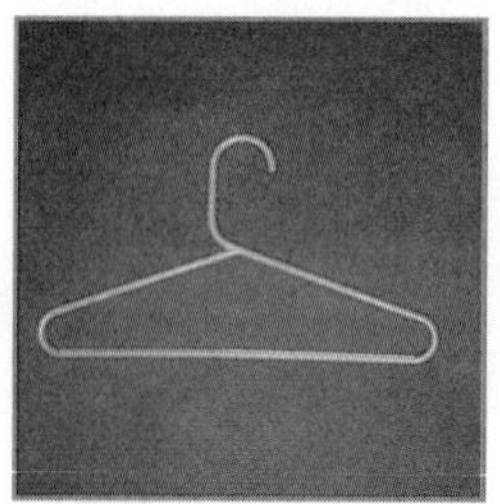

Now, add a comma and "hang" the rest of your sentence onto the phrase:

Damaged during the move, our antique clock will not keep the correct time.

The second part of the sentence begins with the subject *our antique clock* instead of *it* because *our antique clock* doesn't appear in the first part of the sentence, and it is a more specific name for the object.

ACTIVITY 7

Complete each sentence by following these steps:

- Add a verb to the subject.
- Add any additional information to complete the thought. Answers will vary.

EXAMPLE: Punctured by a nail, the tire flapped loudly.

1. Confused by the numerous signs, the driver got lost.
2. Exhausted by the huge wedding, the mother of the bride collapsed onto the couch.
3. Excited about his new job, Isaac called his friends.
4. Annoyed by the noisy children, the neighbor told them to be quiet.
5. Frightened by the large spider, Professor Stevens jumped onto a chair.

ACTIVITY 8

Combine each pair of simple sentences by turning the first sentence into an *-ed* phrase. Follow these steps:

- Underline the complete verb in the first simple sentence.
- Drop the helping verb and use the past participle to form the phrase that will begin your new sentence.
- Add a comma after the phrase.
- Hang the rest of your sentence onto the phrase. (You may need to change the subject of the second part of the sentence.)

EXAMPLE: Some students are motivated by a desire to improve their skills. They seek help.

Motivated by a desire to improve their skills, some students seek help.

1. Gregory was discouraged about his poor writing skills. He talked to his instructor.

   Discouraged about his poor writing skills, Gregory talked to his instructor.

2. Professor Adams was pleased about Gregory's devotion. He recommended a tutor.

   Pleased about Gregory's devotion, Professor Adams recommended a tutor.

3. Gregory was determined to pass his writing course. He made an appointment with the tutor.

   Determined to pass his writing course, Gregory made an appointment with the tutor.

4. The tutor was talented in language skills. She helped Gregory with grammar.

   Talented in language skills, the tutor helped Gregory with grammar.

5. Gregory was convinced that he could pass the course. He thanked the tutor and his instructor.

   Convinced that he could pass the course, Gregory thanked the tutor and his instructor.

ACTIVITY 9: Teamwork

For each of the following items, use the two verbs and subject provided to write a sentence that begins with an *-ed* phrase.

- Put the first verb in the *-ed* form and use it to begin your sentence with a phrase.
- Add a comma after the phrase.
- Use the subject and the second verb to complete the thought. (You may put the second verb in the past, present, or future tense.) Answers will vary.

EXAMPLE:

First verb: identify **Subject:** the suspect **Second verb:** confess

Identified in a lineup, the suspect confessed to the robbery.

1. **First verb:** diagnose **Subject:** the patient **Second verb:** ask
   Diagnosed with a bad sprain, the patient asked for crutches.
2. **First verb:** damage **Subject:** the seafood restaurant **Second verb:** close
   Damaged in the hurricane, the seafood restaurant closed.
3. **First verb:** satisfy **Subject:** the customer **Second verb:** thank
   Satisfied with the refund, the customer thanked the manager.
4. **First verb:** anger **Subject:** our neighbor **Second verb:** complain
   Angered by our barking dog, our neighbor complained to the police.
5. **First verb:** cover **Subject:** the boxer **Second verb:** collapsed
   Covered with lumps and bruises, the boxer collapsed.

The following activities mix the three different modifying phrases that we have discussed so far: *-ing* phrases, *to* phrases, and *-ed* phrases.

ACTIVITY 10

Combine each pair of simple sentences by turning the first sentence into an *-ing* phrase, a *to* phrase, or an *-ed* phrase. Follow these steps:

- Decide whether the beginning phrase should express an ongoing action, a desired action, or a condition.
- Create this phrase using the guidance provided earlier in this chapter. (Use *-ing* phrases for ongoing actions, *to* phrases for desired actions, and *-ed* phrases for conditions.)
- Add a comma after the phrase.
- Hang the rest of your sentence onto the phrase. (You may need to change the subject of the second part of the sentence.)

EXAMPLE: Many employees are faced with difficult co-workers. These employees may not know what to do.

Faced with difficult co-workers, many employees do not know what to do.

1. Employees can follow a few tips. They can deal with most difficult colleagues.
   Following a few tips, employees can deal with most difficult colleagues.

2. Employees can recognize that a difficult person may be insecure. They can acknowledge his or her positive traits.
   Recognizing that a difficult person may be insecure, employees can acknowledge his or her positive traits.

3. A difficult co-worker will be encouraged by such praise. He or she may become less defensive.
   Encouraged by such praise, a difficult co-worker may become less defensive.

4. Employees need to deal with a know-it-all. They should recognize that arguing with such a person is useless.
   To deal with a know-it-all, employees should recognize that arguing with such a person is useless.

5. It is a good idea to avoid misunderstandings through e-mail. Employees should discuss difficult situations face to face.
   To avoid misunderstandings through e-mail, employees should discuss difficult situations face to face.

PLACING MODIFYING PHRASES IN OTHER PARTS OF A SENTENCE

So far in this chapter, you have practiced placing modifying phrases at the beginning of sentences.

An *-ing* phrase at the beginning

Listening to classical music, Deirdre fell into a deep sleep.

A *to* phrase at the beginning

To enlist in the army, my cousin visited his local recruiting office.

An *-ed* phrase at the beginning

Annoyed by the attorney, the judge called a recess.

Teaching Tip
Have students read these examples aloud. Which position(s) of the modifying phrases do they prefer and why? You might also have them say aloud some alternative versions not shown here—for example, *The judge called a recess, annoyed by the attorney.* Can they hear why this sentence is awkward?

However, modifiers can also appear in the middle or at the end of sentences. Consider the following examples:

A modifying phrase in the middle

Deirdre, listening to classical music, fell into a deep sleep.

The judge, annoyed by the attorney, called a recess.

A modifying phrase at the end

Deirdre fell into a deep sleep listening to classical music.

My cousin visited his local recruiting office to enlist in the army.

Notice that when a modifying phrase is in the middle of a sentence, commas are used before and after it. When a modifying phrase comes at the end, commas generally are not used. (For more on punctuating modifying phrases, see page 431.)

You will have to decide on the best position for a modifying phrase. In most cases, though, it is a good idea to place the modifying phrase right before or right after the word(s) that the phrase is describing. Otherwise, you may create a problem known as a *misplaced modifier.* (For more information, see page 444 of this chapter and page 416 of Chapter 14.)

ACTIVITY 11

For each of the following modifying phrases, write different sentences that place the phrase as directed. Remember these rules:

- When a modifying phrase starts a sentence, a comma comes after it.
- When the phrase is in the middle of a sentence, commas are used before and after it.
- When a modifying phrase comes at the end, commas generally are not used. Answers will vary.

EXAMPLE:

Modifying phrase: to get to Phoenix by 5 A.M.

Phrase at the beginning: To get to Phoenix by 5 A.M., we'll have to drive through the night.

Phrase at the end: We'll have to drive through the night to get to Phoenix by 5 A.M.

1. **Modifying phrase:** driving to the dinner party

   Phrase at the beginning: Driving to the dinner party, Roseanne got lost.

   Phrase at the end: Roseanne got lost driving to the dinner party.

2. **Modifying phrase:** wounded in a fight with another dog

   Phrase at the beginning: Wounded in a fight with another dog, our German shepherd limped back to our house.

   Phrase in the middle: Our German shepherd, wounded in a fight with another dog, limped back to our house.

3. **Modifying phrase:** to get tickets to the concert

   Phrase at the beginning: To get tickets to the concert, I stood in line for five hours.

   Phrase at the end: I stood in line for five hours to get tickets to the concert.

4. **Modifying phrase:** interrupting our romantic meal

   Phrase at the beginning: Interrupting our romantic meal, the loud thunderclap made me jump in my seat.

   Phrase in the middle: The loud thunderclap, interrupting our romantic meal, made me jump in my seat.

5. **Modifying phrase:** captured as he retreated from a firefight

   Phrase at the beginning: Captured as he retreated from a firefight, the enemy soldier refused to provide information on his mission.

   Phrase in the middle: The enemy soldier, captured as he retreated from a firefight, refused to provide information on his mission.

PUNCTUATING MODIFYING PHRASES: MORE DETAILS

As you have learned, how and whether you punctuate modifying phrases depend on whether the phrase comes at the beginning, middle, or end of a sentence. The following sections give more details and practice.

Modifying Phrases at the Beginning of Sentences

In most of the sentences that we write, we begin with a subject and a verb. Beginning a sentence with a subject and a verb is perhaps the most common and "natural" (conversational) way to order the ideas in a sentence. Here are three examples:

SUBJECT VERB

My truck gets 16 miles per gallon in the city.

SUBJECT VERB

Meditation helps relieve stress.

SUBJECT VERB

Doctors recommend annual checkups for people over fifty.

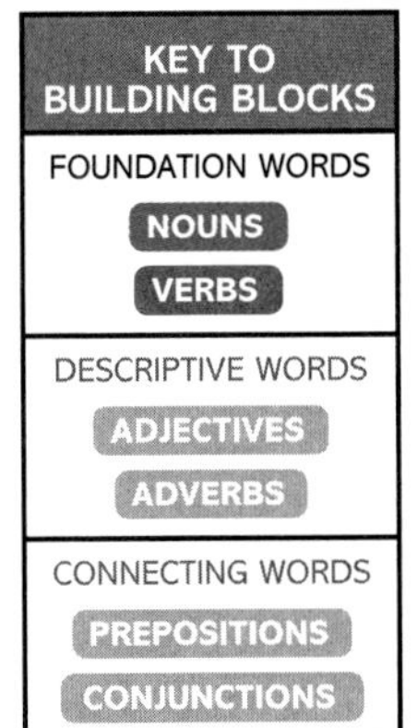

However, as we have discussed, we may begin our sentences with introductory words and phrases to add more variety or "music" to our writing. In these cases, the subject and verb come later in the sentence. Whenever this happens, **a comma must always follow the word or phrase that opens the sentence**. For example, in this chapter, you have seen that when a sentence begins with an *-ing* phrase, a *to* phrase, or an *-ed* phrase, this phrase must be followed by a comma. Take a look:

-ING PHRASE + COMMA SUBJECT VERB

Backing down the driveway, the car ran over a tricycle.

TO PHRASE + COMMA SUBJECT VERB

To escape from the handcuffs, the magician picked the lock.

-ED PHRASE + COMMA SUBJECT VERB

Disappointed with his salary, Jaime looked for a new job.

In addition to *-ing* phrases, *to* phrases, and *-ed* phrases, you have learned about other phrases and expressions that we use to begin sentences. All of these must be followed by commas.

Transitional expressions
(see Chapter 5, page 149, and Chapter 12, page 344)

In the first place, athletes need to be team players.
More important, the building failed to meet safety codes.
Last, you should find a good financial adviser.
However, the prom was canceled because of the hurricane.
Nevertheless, she will apply for the scholarship.
Furthermore, China hosted the summer Olympics.

Prepositional phrases
(see Chapter 11, page 281)

In the morning, light fills my bedroom.
After the party, we will go dancing.
Under her pillow, Joanne found a diamond necklace.

You can also use a simple adverb (see Chapter 10, page 272) to begin a sentence:

Sadly, our hamster escaped from its cage.
Suddenly, the lights went out in the stadium.
Reluctantly, James signed the new contract.

Modifying Phrases in Other Parts of Sentences

If the modifier follows the subject and the verb, a comma generally is not required. This happens when a modifier appears at the end of a sentence:

	MODIFYING PHRASE
NO COMMA	Missy found Rob locked in the closet.

Finally, if the modifier separates the subject from the verb, two commas are required to set off the modifier. This happens when a modifier appears in the middle of a sentence:

	MODIFYING PHRASE
COMMAS OFFSET MODIFYING PHRASE	The professor, returning to his office, found two students waiting.

ACTIVITY 12

For each sentence below, do the following:

- If a comma or commas are required, rewrite the complete sentence, adding the comma or commas.
- If no comma is required, write "OK" on the line provided.

EXAMPLE: Tired of our daily routines many of us look for change.

Tired of our daily routines, many of us look for change.

1. Ringing up purchases in a grocery store Sarah looked longingly out the window at people who seemed happier.

   Ringing up purchases in a grocery store, Sarah looked longingly out the window at people who seemed happier.

2. Sarah bored with her dull job wanted a change in her life.

   Sarah, bored with her dull job, wanted a change in her life.

3. She asked for suggestions from friends and family to get ideas about different jobs.

   OK

4. Feeling more and more excited about the possibilities for her life Sarah decided to apply for a flight-attendant position.

   Feeling more and more excited about the possibilities for her life, Sarah decided to apply for a flight-attendant position.

5. Sarah pleased that she took control of her life got the job and now flies from city to city.

   Sarah, pleased that she took control of her life, got the job and now flies from city to city.

Recognizing Sentences with Modifying Phrases

As you already know, every sentence must contain a subject and a verb. Here's a familiar example:

My dog wakes up all the neighbors.

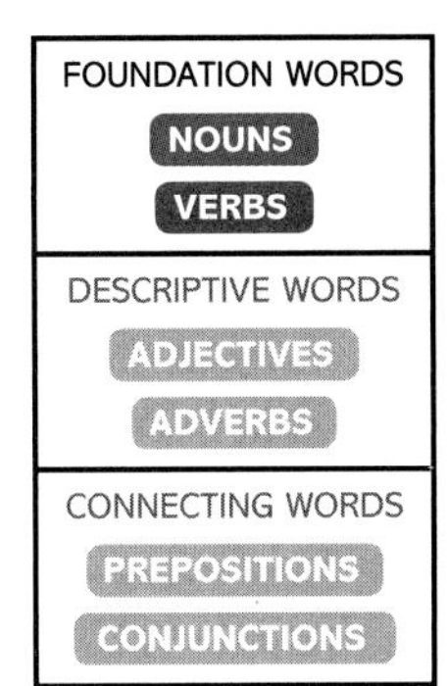

The information in this sentence is limited: we know that the dog wakes up the neighbors, but we do not know how, why, or when this happens. The author of this sentence could provide more information by beginning the sentence with a phrase describing *how* the dog wakes up the neighbors:

SUBJECT BEING DESCRIBED

Howling at the moon, my dog wakes up all the neighbors.

This *-ing* phrase tells us that the dog wakes up the neighbors because it howls at the moon. This phrase is called a **modifying phrase**, or simply a **modifier**, because it changes or adds to the meaning of the original sentence. Notice that the subject (*dog*) comes right after the phrase that modifies it.

Most writers use modifiers frequently without even knowing it. As a college writer, you will want to build your awareness of modifiers in order to use them correctly and effectively.

In this section of the chapter, you will practice recognizing subjects and verbs in sentences with modifying phrases. If we look for the subject and verb in modifying phrases, we will find that they never appear. Take a look:

Power Tip
Looking for subjects, especially, will help you decide whether your sentence is missing a subject that makes sense, among other problems. (These problems are discussed in more depth on page 435 of this chapter.)

Terminology Tip
You might think that *listening, to enlist,* and *annoyed* should be labeled as verbs in these sentences. Remember, however, that they are *modifying* or *describing* elements in the sentence that includes the color-coded subjects and verbs. This sentence is known as a **main clause**.

A sentence with an *-ing* phrase

MODIFIER SUBJECT VERB

Listening to classical music, Deirdre fell into a deep sleep.

SUBJECT VERB MODIFIER

Deirdre fell into a deep sleep listening to classical music.

A sentence with a *to* phrase

To enlist in the army, my cousin visited his local recruiting office.

My cousin visited his local recruiting office to enlist in the army.

A sentence with an *-ed* phrase

Annoyed by the attorney, the judge called a recess.

The judge, annoyed by the attorney, called a recess.

ACTIVITY 13

For each sentence below, do the following:

- Underline the modifying phrase.
- Draw a circle around the subject.
- Double-underline the verb.

EXAMPLE: Noreen, taking her mother's advice, brought her umbrella.

1. To keep her apartment tidy, Jennifer spends an hour each day on housework.
2. Disturbed by the stranger's behavior, Alise moved to the other end of the subway car.
3. The bride, gliding slowly down the aisle, tripped on the plush carpeting.
4. You should take the Hill Street Bridge to get to the mall.
5. Muttering about nosy reporters, Senator Smith left the news conference.

Solving Problems in Sentences with Modifying Phrases: Dangling Modifiers and More Misplaced Modifiers

In this section, you will learn how to find and fix two common problems in sentences with modifying phrases: dangling modifiers and misplaced modifiers. (For more on misplaced modifiers, see Chapter 14, page 416.)

Teaching Tip
For test items on dangling modifiers and misplaced modifiers, see the *Testing Tool Kit* CD available with this book.

DANGLING MODIFIERS

Take a look at the following sentence and see if you can spot a problem with its meaning:

Delayed in traffic, the sun got hotter and hotter.

There is something odd about this sentence, but you may have to look very closely to figure out the problem. Let's begin by examining a simple sentence:

The sun got hotter and hotter.

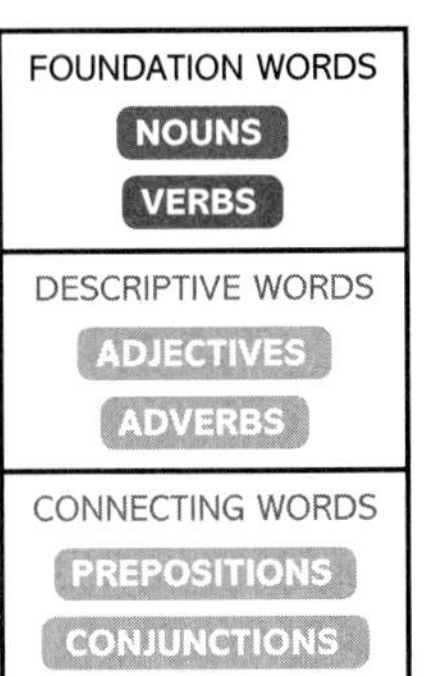

The meaning of this sentence is clear and simple. However, if we add a modifying phrase to the beginning of the sentence, we have to be sure that the two parts of the sentence fit together. Sometimes, especially when we are writing quickly, we may write a sentence where the two parts do not fit together; as a result, the sentence will not make perfect sense:

Delayed in traffic, the sun got hotter and hotter.

According to this sentence, who or what was delayed in traffic? While your imagination may tell you that a person was delayed in traffic, the sentence actually says that *the sun* was delayed in traffic. This is an odd idea. Take a look at the following pair of illustrations to understand *what you imagine* when you read this sentence and *what the sentence actually says.*

What you imagine

What the sentence actually says

Teaching Tip
Ask students to draw pictures of other dangling modifiers in this chapter. Emphasize that they should illustrate what the sentence actually says, not what they imagine the sentence to say.

To be absolutely clear, we must add a subject that makes sense:

Delayed in traffic, Mark felt the sun get hotter and hotter.

When you begin a sentence with a modifier, remember two rules:

- The subject of the sentence must come immediately after the comma.
- This subject must connect with the action in the modifier.

Take a look:

> **Waking up on Friday morning, (subject) + (verb) + (other words to complete the thought).**

Now, look at the following two sentences and decide which subject fits with the action in the modifier (*waking up*):

> A. Waking up on Friday morning, my blanket was on the floor.

> B. Waking up on Friday morning, I discovered my blanket on the floor.

According to sentence A, the *blanket* woke up, which doesn't make sense. When we write or read such a sentence, we usually allow our imagination to fill in the *real* subject of the action. Instead, we should use our grammar awareness to recognize that the sentence does not make sense and needs to have a *real* subject added. Sentence B is correct because it tells us that *I* woke up on Friday morning. In this case, the subject of the action is 100% clear.

When the *real* subject is missing or unclear, we cannot be 100% sure who or what is connected to the action in the modifier. So, the action is left **dangling** or unattached to a subject that makes sense.

ACTIVITY 14: Teamwork

Working with two or three classmates, do the following for each group of sentences below:

- Read all three sentences.
- In the space provided, write a question that will help you identify the correct subject. (See the example below.)
- Circle the subject or subjects that fit with the action in the modifier. If none of the subjects fit, write "none" in the margin. Questions may vary.

EXAMPLE:

Locked out of the house, Antonia's keys would not work.

Locked out of the house, an open window was Antonia's only option.

Locked out of the house, Antonia's luck ran out. none

Question: Who or what was locked out of the house?

1. Seated in the dentist's chair, the dentist prepared to drill.

   Seated in the dentist's chair, the (patient) nervously awaited the drill.

   Seated in the dentist's chair, the drill came closer.

   Question: Who or what was seated in the dentist's chair?

2. Barking wildly, Jennifer told the dog to be quiet.

   Barking wildly, the dog's owner told the dog to be quiet.

   Barking wildly, Jennifer's patience with the dog was wearing thin. none

   Question: Who or what was barking wildly?

3. Returning to the car, one of the tires was flat.

   Returning to the car, a slash had flattened one of the tires.

   Returning to the car, Jake and I discovered a flat tire.

   Question: Who or what was returning to the car?

4. Injured during a football tackle, Victor's grandmother forbade him to play again.

   Injured during a football tackle, Victor's shoulder required surgery.

   Injured during a football tackle, Victor suffered a broken shoulder.

   Question: Who or what was injured?

5. Landing the airplane during a storm, the passengers were nervous.

   Landing the airplane during a storm, the flight attendants calmed the passengers.

   Landing the airplane during a storm, the pilot avoided an accident.

   Question: Who or what was landing the plane?

When we write a sentence that begins with an *-ing* phrase, a *to* phrase, or an *-ed* phrase, the subject of the sentence is really connected with two actions. Take a look:

To memorize the new vocabulary, the students used flash cards.

You already know that *used* must be the verb in this sentence because the verb can never appear within a modifier. However, the subject (*students*) is still connected to two related actions: *memorizing* and *using*. Understanding this idea will help you to control the sentences that you write with modifiers.

ACTIVITY 15

For each sentence below, do the following:

- First, circle the subject.
- Next, underline the two actions that are connected to the subject.
- Last, draw arrows from the subject to each of the actions.

EXAMPLE: Hiding in the tall grass, the crocodile waited for lunch.

1. Concerned about the rash on his arm, Kevin called his physician.

2. Pouring hot fudge sauce on her ice cream, Michelle grinned widely.

CONTINUED >

3. To save money on airline tickets, you should fly in the middle of the week.

4. Overwhelmed by the wedding plans, Ann hired a wedding planner.

5. To enter the building, employees must have a valid identification card.

ACTIVITY 16

Complete each of the following sentences by adding a verb and any additional information that you want. Answers will vary.

EXAMPLE: Swollen to twice its normal size, my ankle throbbed with pain.

1. Running backwards to catch a fly ball, the right-fielder bumped into the stands.
2. Excited about his vacation plans in Las Vegas, Grandpa bought three guide books.
3. Turning left onto Colorado Avenue, the taxi driver saw a man roller-skating in a clown suit.
4. To train for the marathon, Chris ran fifteen miles every other day.
5. Stung by an angry hornet, the small child cried and ran home.

ACTIVITY 17

Complete each of the following sentences by adding a subject, a verb, and any additional information that you want. Be sure that your subject fits with the action in the modifier. Answers will vary.

EXAMPLE: To reach his desired body weight, the body builder ate only tuna for lunch.

1. Frightened by the loud thunder, the dog crawled under the bed.
2. Wearing a brand-new suit, Diego looked more handsome than ever.
3. To save money for a house, Karin took a second job.
4. Wanting to impress his girlfriend, Marcus cleaned her apartment.
5. Opening up the morning newspaper, we were shocked by the photos of the huge downtown fire.

If you find that you have written a dangling modifier, you will need to do one of the following things:

1. Change the second part of the sentence by adding a subject.
2. Change the first part of the sentence (the modifier) by adding a subject and a complete verb.

Let's consider these options one at a time.

Changing the Second Part of the Sentence

Take a look at a new example:

> **Standing in line, the hours seemed to drag.**

Clearly, it does not make sense to say that *the hours* stood in line. As you read sentences like this, *do not let your imagination do the work that the sentence should be doing.* The first way to fix this error is to leave the modifier the same but change the second half of the sentence. In doing this, we must add a subject that fits with the action *standing.* For example:

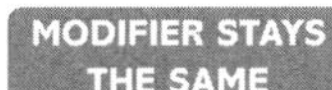

> **Standing in line, Bill felt the hours dragging.**

Now it is clear that *Bill* was standing in line. This makes perfect sense. Notice, too, that the new subject, *Bill,* requires a new verb, *felt.* Bill did what? He felt the hours dragging.

Teaching Tip

Have students write one or two sentences with dangling modifiers, making them as humorous as possible. Then, select some students to read their sentences aloud to the class. Finally, have students exchange their papers and correct each other's dangling modifiers.

ACTIVITY 18

Correct each dangling modifier below by following these steps:

- Copy the modifying phrase that opens the sentence, leaving it the same.
- Put a comma after this phrase.
- Add a subject that fits with the action in the modifier.
- Add a verb and complete the thought. Answers will vary.

Note: You may need to change other words in the second part of the sentence.

EXAMPLE: Entering the subway, a huge *Shrek* poster caught my attention.
Entering the subway, I noticed a huge Shrek poster.

1. Walking to work one morning, a briefcase fell from a skyscraper onto the sidewalk.
   Walking to work one morning, Salina saw a briefcase fall from a skyscraper onto the sidewalk.
2. To repair the engine, the mechanic's best skills will be needed.
   To repair the engine, the mechanic must use her best skills.
3. Seated in the back row, the performers were difficult to see and hear.
   Seated in the back row, we found it difficult to see and hear the performers.
4. Riding a skateboard down the street, a poodle danced on its hind legs.
   Riding a skateboard down the street, Chris saw a poodle dancing on its hind legs.
5. Exhausted by the long drive, the hotel bed looked inviting.
   Exhausted by the long drive, Jake found the hotel bed inviting.

Changing the Modifier

The second method for correcting a dangling modifier is to change the modifier but leave the second half of the sentence the same. In doing this, we must add a subject that fits with the action in the modifier. We must also make sure that there is a complete verb. Let's return to a familiar example:

Standing in line, the hours seemed to drag.

Now, we will add a subject to the first part of this sentence. We will also add the helping verb *was* before *standing* to make the verb complete. (For more on helping verbs, see Chapter 10, page 270.) Notice that the second half of the sentence remains unchanged:

While Bill was standing in line, the hours seemed to drag.

Notice also that the subordinating conjunction *while* has been added to the opening phrase. By adding this information to the modifier, we have created a complex sentence with two separate subjects and two separate verbs.

1ST SUBJECT 1ST VERB 2ND SUBJECT 2ND VERB

While Bill was standing in line, the hours seemed to drag.

Now it is clear that *Bill* was standing in line.

ACTIVITY 19

Correct each dangling modifier below by following these steps:

- Rewrite the modifier, adding a subordinating conjunction (see the Subordinating Conjunctions box) and a new subject. Change the verb as necessary.
- Add a comma.
- Leave the second half of the sentence the same. Answers will vary.

EXAMPLE: **Lying on his application, the loan request was denied.**
Because Hugo lied on his application, the loan request was denied.

1. Fishing for salmon, Matt's fishing line became snagged on a branch.
While he was fishing for salmon, Matt's fishing line became snagged on a branch.

2. Crossing a shallow stream, Betty's foot slipped on a rock.
As she was crossing a shallow stream, Betty's foot slipped on a rock.

3. Baking oatmeal cookies, the pan must first be sprayed with vegetable oil.
Before you bake oatmeal cookies, the pan must first be sprayed with vegetable oil.

Subordinating Conjunctions

after	*if*
although	*since*
as	*unless*
because	*until*
before	*when*
even if	*while*
even though	

4. Determined to get her pilot's license, her weekends were devoted to flying lessons.
   Because Rhonda was determined to get her pilot's license, her weekends were devoted to flying lessons.

5. To get her passport by May, the application must be submitted by March.
   If Shelley wants to get her passport by May, the application must be submitted by March.

ACTIVITY 20

Correct each of the following dangling modifiers in two ways:

- First, leave the opening modifier the same but change the second half of the sentence.
- Next, add more information to the opening modifier but leave the second half of the sentence the same.

EXAMPLE: **Dangling modifier:** Sledding downhill, a wolf appeared behind a snow bank.

First revision: Sledding downhill, Maria saw a wolf appear behind a snow bank.

Second revision: As Maria was sledding downhill, a wolf appeared behind a snow bank.

1. Writing the last paragraph of his essay, his cat stepped on the delete key.

   First revision: Writing the last paragraph of his essay, Larry saw his cat step on the delete key.

   Second revision: While Larry was writing the last paragraph of his essay, his cat stepped on the delete key.

2. Covered with hot fudge and whipped cream, the guests admired the dessert.

   First revision: Covered with hot fudge and whipped cream, the dessert thrilled the guests.

   Second revision: Because it was covered with hot fudge and whipped cream, the guests admired the dessert.

3. To be eligible for the athletic scholarship, a college coach must recommend the athlete.

   First revision: To be eligible for the athletic scholarship, the athlete must be recommended by a college coach.

   Second revision: If the athlete is to be eligible for the athletic scholarship, a college coach must recommend the athlete.

FIXING DANGLING MODIFIERS IN WHOLE PARAGRAPHS

Activity 21 will give you practice with recognizing and fixing dangling modifiers in whole paragraphs—a valuable skill for improving your own writing.

ACTIVITY 21

Read each of the following paragraphs carefully, looking for dangling modifiers. Then, rewrite each error to fix the problem, using one of the following methods:

- Leave the opening modifier the same, but change the second half of the sentence.
- Add more information to the opening modifier, but leave the second half of the sentence the same.

Be sure to put any commas in the correct places. The first error in each paragraph has been edited for you. *Answers will vary.*

The following paragraph has five dangling modifiers (including the one that has been edited for you).

1. (1) My best friend, Marta, a full-time security guard and mother, has great ideas for eating well on a budget. (2) First, she's a smart shopper. (3) To get the best deals, ~~bulk purchases are essential~~ [she purchases items in bulk]. (4) Marta looks for sales on spaghetti sauce, ground turkey, toilet paper, and other common items and then buys large quantities to get the best price. (5) Driving to the store, ~~a snack of~~ [she snacks on] carrot sticks or peanut butter on crackers ~~keeps her~~ [to keep] from shopping while hungry: a major cause of over-purchasing. (6) ~~Committed~~ [Because Marta is committed] to her family's health and her budget, chips and soda are a no-no. (7) She knows that junk food is not only bad for the body but costlier than healthier foods. (8) At home, Marta saves time and money by cooking meals in advance and saving them in a large freezer. (9) On busy nights when she's too tired to cook, she defrosts a pre-cooked meal instead of spending money on fast-food takeout. (10) ~~Stretching~~ [Because Marta stretches] meat portions by adding rice or beans, her meals are flavorful, nutritious, and economical. (11) To save more money, ~~Marta is a role model for me~~ [I want to follow Marta's good example].

The following paragraph has seven dangling modifiers (including the one that has been edited for you).

most of us are unaware of
2. (1) Watching movies, ^ the effort and history behind motion pictures ~~go unnoticed~~. (2) Some historians trace the history of movies to as far back as the 1400s, when entertainers used lanterns and puppets to create moving shadows on a wall. (3) Much later, in 1878, the English inventor Eadweard Muybridge took a sequence of photographs of a running horse.
When a user spun
(4) These were put in a circular device. (5) ^ ~~Spinning~~ the device, the pictures ran together to create the illusion of real motion. (6) To create
inventors developed
longer sequences of movement, ^ special film and cameras ~~were developed~~. (7) Eventually, some of these "moving pictures" were shown to large audiences. (8) Fascinated by short scenes of dancers, actors, and even traffic at city intersections, ~~short films were popular among~~ people seeking
attended short films in large numbers
something new and different. ^ (9) Wanting to take advantage of this new
business people opened in the United States
interest, ^ ~~the United States saw~~ hundreds of movie theaters ^ ~~open~~ through the early years of the twentieth century. (10) Originally, motion pictures had no sound. (11) Words on the screen showed the actors' lines, and music from an orchestra, piano, or organ would sometimes accompany the film. (12) Eventually, however, the next big invention transformed motion pictures: sound. (13) Experimenting with
inventors matched
"gramophones" (record players) and film, ^ recorded sounds ~~were matched~~ with motions on the screen. (14) Released in 1927,
The Jazz Singer, the first feature-length "talkie" film, thrilled audiences.
^ ~~audiences were thrilled by the first feature-length "talkie" film, *The Jazz Singer*.~~ (15) This movie included both dialogue and singing.

ACTIVITY 22: Teamwork

When you have finished correcting one of the paragraphs from Activity 21, get together with two or three classmates. Then, compare the errors that you found and the correction methods that you used. If another student used a correction method that you like better than your own, feel free to change what you have written in your book. If you still have questions about dangling modifiers, ask your instructor.

ACTIVITY 23

Find a paper that you wrote recently but haven't turned in for a grade. Then, read the paper carefully, looking for any dangling modifiers; put a check by these. Next, correct the dangling modifiers.

MISPLACED -*ING* AND -*ED* PHRASES

Take a look at the following sentence and see if you can spot a problem with its meaning:

> Dominic tripped on a garden hose running for the bus.

There is something odd about this sentence, but you may have to look very closely to figure out the problem. Let's begin by examining a simple sentence:

> Dominic tripped on a garden hose.

The meaning of this sentence is clear and simple. However, when we add a modifier to the middle or the end of a sentence, we have to be sure that the modifier is attached to the specific item it is meant to modify. Sometimes, especially if we are writing quickly, we may connect a modifier to some other item in the sentence; as a result, the sentence will not make perfect sense:

> Dominic tripped on a garden hose running for the bus.

According to this sentence, who or what was running for the bus? While your imagination may tell you that Dominic was running for the bus, the sentence actually says that *the garden hose* was running for the bus. This is an odd idea.

As we have seen, a misplaced modifier happens when a modifier is attached to the wrong item in a sentence. In the previous example, *running for the bus* is connected to *garden hose,* but it should be connected to *Dominic.*

The easiest way to correct a misplaced modifier is to move it, attaching it to the specific item it is meant to modify:

> Running for the bus, Dominic tripped on a garden hose.

In fixing a misplaced modifier, you may feel more confident adding additional information to the sentence or using a different sentence form. Here is the same idea expressed as a complex sentence:

> While he was running for the bus, Dominic tripped on a garden hose.

And here is the same idea expressed as a simple sentence with a compound verb:

> Dominic was running for the bus and tripped on a garden hose.

All three sentences correct the misplaced modifier, and you may use whichever one you like. Now, let's look at an example with an *-ed* phrase:

> The child never knew her biological mother adopted at six months.

It may seem obvious to you that *the child* was adopted at six months; however, this sentence actually tells us that *the mother* was adopted at six months. The modifier *adopted at six months* needs to be attached to *child.*

Once again, there are several ways to correct this misplaced modifier. The easiest method is to move the modifier, connecting it to the specific item it is meant to modify:

> Adopted at six months, the child never knew her biological mother.

> The child, adopted at six months, never knew her biological mother.

Power Tip

Again, notice that a comma is used after an opening modifier (*Running for the bus, . . .*), after an opening subordinate clause in a complex sentence (*While he was running for the bus, . . .*), and to set off a modifier in the middle of a sentence (*The child, adopted at six months, . . .*).

Once again, you can also change the sentence form if this approach is more comfortable for you:

> Because the child was adopted at six months, she never knew her biological mother.
>
> The child was adopted at six months and never knew her biological mother.

ACTIVITY 24

Underline the misplaced modifiers in the following sentences. Then, use two methods to correct them:

- Rewrite the sentence, moving the modifier and connecting it to the specific item it is meant to modify.
- Rewrite the sentence again but change its form (complex sentence or simple sentence with a compound verb).

You may need to add commas. Answers may vary.

EXAMPLE: Jessica saw an accident driving on the freeway.

First revision: Driving on the freeway, Jessica saw an accident.

Second revision: While Jessica was driving on the freeway, she saw an accident.

1. Melissa was thinking about Brad Pitt biking down the street.

First revision: Biking down the street, Melissa was thinking about Brad Pitt.

Second revision: As Melissa was biking down the street, she was thinking about Brad Pitt.

CONTINUED >

2. We were worried that no one would hear our cries locked in the cellar.

First revision: Locked in the cellar, we were worried that no one would hear our cries.

Second revision: We were worried that no one would hear our cries because we were locked in the cellar.

3. Rescuers spotted the missing hikers by the river using infrared cameras.

First revision: Using infrared cameras, rescuers spotted the missing hikers.

Second revision: Rescuers, because they used infrared cameras, spotted the missing hikers by the river.

4. We saw a herd of elk traveling through northern Idaho.

First revision: Traveling through northern Idaho, we saw a herd of elk.

Second revision: We saw a herd of elk while we were traveling through northern Idaho.

5. Grandpa carved the rib roast seated at the head of the table.

First revision: Grandpa, seated at the head of the table, carved the rib roast.

Second revision: Grandpa carved the rib roast because he was seated at the head of the table.

OTHER MISPLACED MODIFIERS

In Chapter 14, you learned that a descriptive clause is a type of modifier that can be misplaced in a sentence:

The student impressed the teacher who knew the answer.

Teaching Tip
Pair up students and ask each of them to write a modifying phrase on one scrap of paper and the rest of the sentence on another scrap. Next, have them trade scraps and put the sentences in both correct and incorrect orders. How does the meaning change with the different orders? Ask volunteers to share their findings with the class.

The placement of the underlined modifier suggests that the teacher knew the answer. While this is probably true, here's what the writer of this sentence really meant to say:

The student who knew the answer impressed the teacher.

Remember, the modifier must be attached to the specific item it is meant to describe.

In this chapter, you have learned that an *-ing* phrase or an *-ed* phrase is a type of modifier that can be misplaced in a sentence:

The car hit a pedestrian running a red light.

A pedestrian cannot really *run a red light,* so this sentence does not make perfect sense. We need to attach the modifier to the specific thing it is meant to modify:

Running a red light, the car hit a pedestrian.

Now, you'll learn about two other types of modifiers that are frequently misplaced.

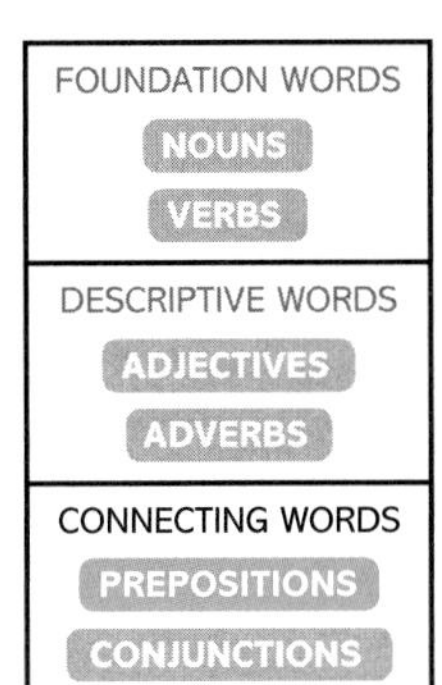

Prepositional Phrases

The first type of modifier that is often misplaced is a prepositional phrase. Look at this example.

> The truck was stopped on the side of the road with a flat tire.

If you read this sentence quickly, it seems to make sense; your imagination joins all the pieces of the puzzle. However, the sentence really tells us that *the road* had a flat tire! To fix this error, move the misplaced modifier and connect it to the specific item it is meant to modify:

> The truck with a flat tire was stopped on the side of the road.

Remember that if a modifying phrase begins a sentence, you will need to put a comma after it:

> At the circus, the sword swallower amazed the children.

As you learned in Chapter 11, we often use two or three prepositional phrases in a sentence. When including several prepositional phrases in a sentence, be sure that they are placed correctly so that the sentence makes sense.

ACTIVITY 25

In each sentence below, identify and correct the misplaced modifier by following these steps:

- Underline the prepositional phrase that is misplaced.
- Rewrite the sentence in the space provided, moving the prepositional phrase so that it's connected to the item it is supposed to modify. Add any commas that are necessary. *Answers may vary.*

EXAMPLE: Corinne saw the lady who taught her to swim <u>at the movies</u>.

At the movies, Corinne saw the lady who taught her to swim.

1. I chased my cat <u>in my best work shoes</u>.
   In my best work shoes, I chased my cat.

2. Thomas pulled up in his brand-new Corvette <u>with a huge grin</u>.
   With a huge grin, Thomas pulled up in his brand-new Corvette.

3. The principal announced that students could receive free counseling <u>over the loudspeaker</u>.
   The principal announced over the loudspeaker that students could receive free counseling.

4. Jamaal asked Tiffany to marry him <u>on his cell phone</u>.
   On his cell phone, Jamaal asked Tiffany to marry him.

5. The patient sat for two hours in the doctor's waiting room <u>with a rash</u>.
   The patient with a rash sat for two hours in the doctor's waiting room.

Adverbs

Another type of modifier that is frequently misplaced is a simple adverb. Look at this example:

The runner almost ran thirty miles.

According to this sentence, the runner did not really run at all. He *almost ran,* which suggests that he may have been thinking about running thirty miles, but he did not follow through on his plan. Now, here is what the writer of this sentence really wants to say:

The runner ran almost thirty miles.

Here, the modifier is attached to the specific item it is supposed to modify (*thirty miles*); as a result, it is 100 percent clear that the runner really ran and that he ran almost thirty miles. When an adverb is misplaced in this way, it can be very tricky to spot. Certain adverbs tend to be misplaced more than others: *nearly, almost, hardly, only, even,* and *often* are some frequently misplaced adverbs.

ACTIVITY 26

In each sentence below, identify and correct the misplaced modifier by following these steps:

- Underline the adverb that is misplaced.
- Rewrite the sentence in the space provided, moving the adverb so that it's connected to the item it is supposed to modify. (The clues in brackets tell you the intended meanings of the sentences.)

EXAMPLE: We only made three dollars. [The meaning is that we made no more than three dollars.]

We made only three dollars.

1. At the garage sale, Tiffany nearly earned $500. [The meaning is that Tiffany's earnings fell slightly short of $500.]

   At the garage sale, Tiffany earned nearly $500.

2. Professor Chang only assigns homework on Mondays. [The meaning is that Monday is the only day on which Professor Chang assigns homework.]

   Professor Chang assigns homework only on Mondays.

3. My lazy roommate even takes out the trash. [The meaning is that the roommate, though lazy, manages to take out the trash.]

   Even my lazy roommate takes out the trash.

4. Police officers saved almost three people who drowned. [The meaning is that the people were close to drowning.]
Police officers saved three people who almost drowned.

5. We had hardly driven three miles when the tire went flat. [The meaning is that the tire went flat at around the three-mile mark.]
We had driven hardly three miles when the tire went flat.

FIXING MISPLACED MODIFIERS IN WHOLE PARAGRAPHS

The following activity asks you to recognize and fix, in whole paragraphs, the various types of misplaced modifiers that you have learned about in this chapter: misplaced *-ing* and *-ed* phrases, misplaced prepositional phrases, and misplaced adverbs. This activity will give you valuable practice in editing misplaced modifiers in your own writing.

ACTIVITY 27

Read each of the following paragraphs carefully, looking for misplaced modifiers. Then, edit the misplaced modifiers, connecting them to the items they are supposed to modify. Be sure to put any commas in the correct places. The first error in each paragraph has been edited for you. Answers may vary.

The following paragraph has six misplaced modifiers (including the one that has been edited for you).

1. (1) Most of us know about the health problems that can result from smoking: cancer, heart disease, even wrinkles. (2) Why, then, do almost all smokers ~~almost~~ have a difficult time quitting? (3) The main reason is that tobacco contains the stimulant nicotine. (4) People can become addicted to this substance, and they feel driven to supply their body with it every day ~~with it~~. (5) Even cigarettes ~~Cigarettes even~~ labeled as "light" can contain enough nicotine to hook users. (6) Unfortunately, smokers build up a nicotine tolerance over time. (7) Compelled to get "their fix," they ~~They~~ smoke more and more cigarettes ~~compelled to get "their fix."~~. (8) Trying to quit, many ~~Many~~ smokers turn to products like patches and gum ~~trying to quit~~. (9) Many of these products contain nicotine replacements to treat withdrawal symptoms. (10) Smokers with a very serious addiction may need psychotherapy ~~with a very serious addiction~~.

CONTINUED >

The following paragraph has eight misplaced modifiers (including the one that has been edited for you).

2. (1) Today, it seems common knowledge that germs cause certain
Baffled by the causes of infectious diseases, many
illnesses, but this wasn't always the case. (2) ~~Many~~ ^ ancient peoples
pointed to evil spirits, "foul winds," and other factors ~~baffled by the causes of infectious diseases~~. (3) In 1840s Vienna, doctor Ignaz Semmelweis
among new mothers
began to suspect that an "invisible agent" was causing a deadly fever ^ at
Observing behaviors in the hospital, he
his hospital ~~among new mothers~~. (4) ^ ~~He~~ saw that doctors were delivering
babies right after performing autopsies ~~observing behaviors in the hospital~~.
Nearly all
(5) ^ ~~All~~ of the doctors ~~nearly~~ failed to wash their hands between the
autopsies and the deliveries. (6) Semmelweis didn't have proof that an
invisible agent was being transferred from the dead bodies to the mothers.
(7) However, he began to require that all doctors wash their hands
with a special solution
^ before seeing patients ~~with a special solution~~. (8) As a result, the death
among patients
rate ^ dropped from more than 12 percent ~~among patients~~ to just over
2 percent. (9) Eventually, however, doctors and medical authorities began
to object to sanitation measures recommended by Semmelweis. (10) Later,
Angered by the reactions to his efforts to improve sanitary conditions, he
he was fired from the hospital. (11) ^ ~~He~~ abruptly left Vienna ~~angered by the reactions to his efforts to improve sanitary conditions~~. (12) Frequent
hand washing is now considered essential for limiting ~~in hospitals~~ the
in hospitals
spread of disease ^ and among the general public.

ACTIVITY 28: Teamwork

When you have finished correcting one of the paragraphs from Activity 29, get together with two or three classmates. Then, compare the errors that you found and the correction methods that you used. If another student used a correction method that you like better than your own, feel free to change what you have written in your book. If you still have questions about misplaced modifiers, ask your instructor.

ACTIVITY 29

Find a paper that you wrote recently but haven't turned in for a grade. Then, read the paper carefully, looking for any misplaced modifiers; put a check by these. Next, correct the errors.

Bringing It All Together

In this chapter, you have learned how to add various modifiers to sentences. Check off each of the following statements that you understand. For any that you do not understand, review the appropriate pages in this chapter.

- ☐ Another way to combine simple sentences is to turn one of them into a **modifying phrase** beginning with *-ing, to,* or *-ed.* Typically, *-ing* phrases are used for one action that is **ongoing** at the same time as another, while *to* phrases often show a **desired action** or goal. Usually, *-ed* phrases indicate the **condition** of someone or something. Often, these modifying phrases begin sentences. (See page 420.)
- ☐ Additionally, modifying phrases sometimes appear in the middle or at the end of sentences. (See page 429.)
- ☐ When a modifying phrase appears at the beginning of a sentence (before the subject and verb), it must be followed by a comma. If the modifier follows the subject and the verb, a comma generally is not required. Finally, if the modifier separates the subject from the verb, two commas are required to set off the modifier. (See page 431.)
- ☐ One common problem in sentences with modifying phrases is **dangling modifiers:** modifiers that seem to refer to a subject that is not clearly stated in the sentence. To fix this problem, you can leave the dangling modifier as is and add a subject to the second part of the sentence, also adding or adjusting the verb as needed. Or you can change the dangling modifier itself, adding a subject and fixing the verb as needed. (See page 435.)
- ☐ Another common problem is **misplaced modifiers:** modifiers attached to some item other than what they are intended to describe. The easiest way to correct a misplaced modifier is to move it, attaching it to the specific item it is meant to modify. Misplaced modifiers can include *-ing* or *-ed* phrases, prepositional phrases, or simple adverbs. (See pages 444, 446, and 448.)

Chapter 16

Using Verbs Correctly

OVERVIEW OF THIS CHAPTER

Verbs tell us when something happens or happened. You'll learn more details in this chapter.

PRESENT TENSE

The students study.

PAST TENSE

The students studied.

PRESENT PERFECT TENSE

The students have studied for many hours.

PAST PERFECT TENSE

The students had studied for many hours by the time of the exam.

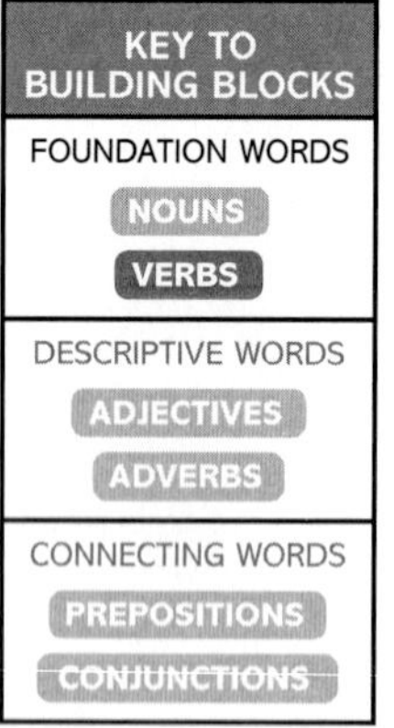

Introduction

As you have learned, **verbs** often express actions, although some of them have other functions. (See Chapter 10 for a review.) In this chapter, you will learn about how verbs change form to express different times, and you will also learn about some problems that can occur with verbs.

First, though, we'll consider some everyday uses of verbs that you may be familiar with. We'll also disprove a myth about verbs that may be holding you back from mastering them. (You *can* master them!)

STANDARD VERSUS NONSTANDARD VERBS

When we speak, we sometimes use *nonstandard English,* which does not follow the rules of written academic English. Take a look at this example:

NONSTANDARD ENGLISH	Alex be smart. He don't need to study.
STANDARD ENGLISH	Alex is smart. He doesn't need to study.

You may hear nonstandard English in television shows, movies, and music as well. Rap and hip-hop artists, for example, often mix standard and nonstandard English in their songs. Look at the lyrics of "Hard Times," by hip-hop group Run-D.M.C. (The nonstandard verbs—and their standard versions—appear in red.)

Hard times spreading just like the flu	(standard English: are spreading)
Watch out, homeboy, don't let it catch you	
P-p-prices go up, don't let your pocket go down	
When you got short money you're stuck on the ground	(standard English: have)
Turn around, get ready, keep your eye on the prize	
And be on point for the future shock	
Hard times are coming to your town	
So stay alert, don't let them get you down	
They tell you times are tough, you hear that times are hard	
But when you work for that ace you know you pulled the right card	
Hard times got our pockets all in chains	(standard English: have)
I'll tell you what, homeboy, it don't have my brain	(standard English: doesn't)
All day I have to work at my peak	
Because I need that dollar every day of the week	
Hard times can take you on a natural trip	
So keep your balance, and don't you slip	
Hard times is nothing new on me	(standard English: are)
I'm gonna use my strong mentality	(standard English: going to)
Like the cream of the crop, like the crop of the cream	
B-b-beating hard times, that is my theme	
Hard times in life, hard times in death	
I'm gonna keep on fighting to my very last breath	(standard English: going to)

This song communicates a powerful message, and Run-D.M.C. shows that breaking the rules of grammar can sometimes be empowering in our personal and artistic lives. However, if you know *only* nonstandard English, you may be limiting your opportunities for personal and professional success.

Standard English (which follows the rules of written academic English) helps you to express your ideas with great precision and clarity, and it is the form of English expected in most school and work settings. Therefore, as a college writer, you should commit to learning and using standard English. Doing so will help you achieve academic success and allow you to communicate more effectively in your personal and professional lives.

If you are more comfortable with nonstandard English than with standard English, you can improve your academic writing simply by focusing on verbs, as you'll do in this chapter.

Teaching Tip
Play "Hard Times," or another song, like the Rolling Stones' "(I Can't Get No) Satisfaction," that uses nonstandard English, in class. Ask students to listen for nonstandard verbs. Discuss how they contribute to the message of the song. Then, ask students how the same verb usages might be perceived if used during a job interview or in a college paper.

THE "MYTH" OF LEARNING VERBS

Many students mistakenly believe that learning standard verb usage is very difficult. Some students are even convinced that they will *never* learn to use verbs correctly because they've been embarrassed by verb errors throughout their school years, and their grades may have suffered. In truth, however, learning correct verb usage doesn't have to be difficult; it just requires some *awareness* and *self-discipline* based on the following principles:

1. Some **memorization** will be necessary. Many students dislike memorization because it can be dull. In this chapter, however, you will learn memorization strategies that minimize the dullness while providing faster results. Keep in mind that the memorization will not go on forever; after mastering the most common verbs, you can look up the rest in your textbook or in a dictionary as needed.
2. **Daily practice** with verbs is the key to your success. A small amount of practice each day (about ten minutes) is the quickest and most effective way to build your skills. If you do an hour's worth of practice only one day a week, the information won't "stick." Training yourself to practice each day requires some self-discipline. If possible, try to do your ten minutes at the same time every day—right after breakfast or lunch, for example. Once you sit down, you'll see that the ten minutes will fly by.
3. **Online exercises** are the best resource for your daily practice. Unlike exercises in your textbook, online practices can provide immediate feedback on your answers and almost endless practice. Plenty of exercises on verbs and other topics are available on this book's Web site at **bedfordstmartins.com/steppingstones**, and immediate feedback is provided. If you do not have a computer at home, plan to use one at your school or local public library.

Once you understand these principles, it is time for you to make a personal decision. Are you ready to dedicate yourself to learning correct verbs? Keep in mind that you can dramatically improve your skills if you are willing to follow the principles. To ensure your success, check each of the following statements that apply to you:

Teaching Tip
Collect students' responses to the checklists. (They should sign their names first.) If some students have left boxes unchecked, you may want to arrange private conferences with them to get a better sense of what their issues are and how these could be addressed. For instance, if a student says she doesn't have time to practice, help her brainstorm strategies for finding time. If several students have left the same box unchecked, you might want to have a class discussion about strategies for addressing this particular issue.

- ☐ Yes, I want to use correct verbs in my writing.
- ☐ Yes, I will use the memorization strategies in this chapter.
- ☐ Yes, I will find ten minutes each day to practice my verbs.
- ☐ Yes, I will use online exercises for my practice. If necessary, I will use a computer at my school or public library.

If you checked all four boxes, you are ready to move on to the next section of this chapter. If you did not check one or more of the boxes, you should discuss your plans with your instructor before you move on to the next section of this chapter.

Understanding Basic Verb Usage: Present and Past Tense

As you have learned, every sentence must have a subject and a verb. The verb must be in the correct form to match

- the tense (time) of the action in a sentence *and*
- the subject. (More on this later.)

The simple present tense is used for regular actions (*I* ***take*** *the train every day*), for facts (*Jonas* ***likes*** *rich desserts*), and for actions happening right now (*I* ***hear*** *the doorbell*). The simple past tense is used for actions completed in the past (*I* ***walked*** *four miles every day*).

The correct form of a verb is determined by the spelling. About 90 percent of all verb problems are caused by two simple errors: the absence or unnecessary addition of an ***-s*** or an ***-ed*** ending. You will learn more about these problems and other common mistakes later in this chapter.

Power Tip
To make sure that you are using the correct verbs in your sentences, it is very important that you know how to identify subjects versus verbs. If you are unsure about how to do this, consider reviewing the instruction and exercises in Chapter 11.

USING THE PRESENT TENSE

Again, the simple present tense is used for regular actions, for facts, and for actions happening right now. Present tense verbs follow a very simple spelling rule. Take a look:

Subject	Verb	Subject	Verb
I / **you** / **we** / **they** / **the girls**	play	**he** / **she** / **it/the iPod** / **Terri** / **everyone**	plays

Terminology Tip
In English grammar, *I* and *we* are said to be in the *first person; you* in the *second person;* and *he, she, it, they,* and other "third parties" (for example, *the girls, Terri*) in the *third person.*

Grabbing onto the Slippery -s

Notice that the only difference in the two forms of the verb *play* is that an *-s* comes at the end when the subject is *he, she,* or *it* (or some equivalent). We call this "the slippery *-s*" because, like a snake or a lizard, it can slip out of sight easily when we are not paying attention. Most students know how to spell verbs in the present tense, but they sometimes forget to write the *-s*. (And sometimes they add it when it's not needed.) Because the slippery *-s* is a major cause of verb errors, you should grab a hold of it in your mind and not let go.

The Slippery -s

Power Tips

Often, the *-s* ending moves from the verb to the subject when the subject becomes plural (more than one in number):

Singular Subject: The girl plays.

Plural Subject: The girls play.

You will have to add an *-es* instead of an *-s* to the end of some verbs, such as those that end in *-ch* or *-sh: teach* → *teaches; catch* → *catches; fish* → *fishes; wish* → *wishes.*

ACTIVITY 1

For each sentence below, do the following:

- In the space provided, write the correct present tense form of the verb in parentheses.
- If the verb ends in -*s*, circle the *s* or mark it with a highlighter.

EXAMPLE: We ___need___ (need) six sources for our research project.

1. Enrico ___walks___ (walk) three miles every day.
2. We ___believe___ (believe) Bradley's wild story.
3. The city park ___remains___ (remain) open from dawn until dusk.
4. Petra ___wants___ (want) a satisfying career.
5. The Rodriguez sisters ___visit___ (visit) Mexico every summer.

Recognizing Irregular Present Tense Verbs: Be, Have, *and* Do

You should be aware of three "irregular" verbs that we use frequently. These verbs are irregular because they follow different spelling rules from regular verbs (like *play, walk,* and *bake*). Fortunately, most students use and spell them correctly.

Power Tip

In everyday speech, we sometimes leave out *be* verbs (*am/is/are/was/were*). Avoid this error in writing.

Incorrect: I sick.
He happy.

Revised: I am sick.
He is happy.

Be		***Have***		***Do***	
I	am	I	have	I	do
you / we / they / students	are	you / we / they / students	have	you / we / they / students	do
he / she / it / everyone	is	he / she / it / everyone	has	he / she / it / everyone	does

Notice that the slippery *-s* is found in the same place even with these irregular verbs.

Teaching Tip

Have a "verbs bee" with *be, have,* and *do.* Call out a subject and a base verb (for example, *I* and *be*), and see who can be the first to call out both the subject and the correct verb (*I am*).

ACTIVITY 2

For each sentence, do the following:

- In the space provided, write the correct present tense form of the verb in parentheses.
- If the verb ends in -*s*, circle the *s* or mark it with a highlighter.

For online practice with present tense verbs, visit this book's Web site at **bedfordstmartins .com/steppingstones**.

EXAMPLE: I ___am___ (be) excited about going on vacation next month.

1. Margaret ___has___ (have) a bad headache.
2. He ___does___ (do) a good job painting.
3. The band members ___are___ (be) on stage.
4. Marco ___is___ (be) a flight attendant.
5. Our neighbors ___have___ (have) a vacation home in Colorado.
6. The students ___do___ (do) well on tests after class reviews.
7. My boss ___is___ (be) hard to please sometimes.
8. Randall ___has___ (have) a new job.
9. Maria ___does___ (do) dishes twice a day.
10. I ___am___ (be) confused about the new tax laws.

Power Tip
If English is not your first language, see Appendix C for special advice on verb usage and other grammar topics.

ACTIVITY 3

For the passage below, do the following:

- In the spaces provided, write the correct present tense forms of the verbs in parentheses.
- If a verb ends in *-s,* circle the *s* or mark it with a highlighter.

The first space in the passage has been filled in for you.

(1) Road trips ___are___ (be) a great way to see the country, but keep some travel tips in mind. (2) First, gasoline prices ___are___ (be) sure to remain high for some time. (3) Therefore, you might want to rent a small car if you don't own a fuel-efficient vehicle. (4) Often, lodging ___is___ (be) expensive, too. (5) However, some motels ___have___ (have) discounts for advance or off-season bookings, so ask about special rates. (6) Also, long hours on the road can be exhausting. (7) Rather than trying to see several sights in one trip, smart travelers focus on one or two major destinations. (8) Yosemite National Park in California, for instance, ___is___ (be) a great place for varied activities, such as hiking, rafting, horse-back riding, and camping. (9) Big cities ___have___ (have) great restaurants, historic sites, and nightlife. (10) Finally, while they're on the road, smart travelers ___do___ (do) stretches and take breaks to stay alert. (11) With the right planning and pacing, a road trip ___does___ (do) wonders for tired spirits.

USING THE PAST TENSE

Power Tip
Remember these spelling points:

If a verb already ends in *e*, you usually add just a *d* to form the past tense.

If a verb ends in a consonant (*b, c, d, f, g*, and so on), both the *e* and the *d* must be added.

A final *y* usually must change to *i* before *ed* is added, unless a vowel precedes the *y*—for example, *convey* → *conveyed*.

Again, the simple past tense is used for actions completed in the past (*I* ***walked*** *four miles every day*). All regular past tense verbs follow a simple rule. Take a look:

Base Form		Past Tense
look laugh spell	+ ed	looked laughed spelled
love type refuse	+ d	loved typed refused
cry try marry	− y + ied	cried tried married

elusive: difficult to see, find, or grasp

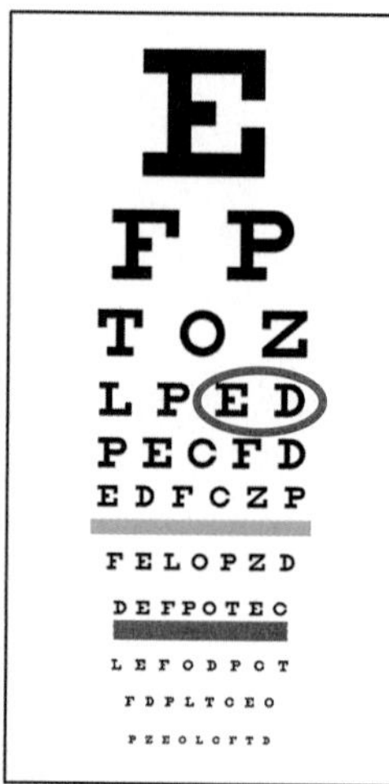

The Elusive *-ed*

Keeping an Eye on the Elusive -ed

Notice that all of these verbs—regardless of their present tense spelling—end in ***-ed*** in the past tense. Most students know this, but they may forget to add the ***-ed.*** (Often, they *hear* the ***-ed*** in their head, but they don't *see* that it's missing on the page.) For this reason, we call this the "elusive ***-ed.***" Like the "slippery ***-s,***" it is another major cause of verb errors, so remember to keep a close eye on it in your writing.

ACTIVITY 4

For each sentence below, write the correct past tense form of the verb in parentheses.

EXAMPLE: In 2003, the nation ___watched___ (watch) as authorities ended two famous criminal careers.

1. Craig Pritchert and Nova Guthrie ___robbed___ (rob) banks for a living.
2. Authorities ___compared___ (compare) them to the 1930s bank robbers Bonnie Parker and Clyde Barrow.
3. While Pritchert robbed the banks, Nova ___waited___ (wait) in the getaway car.
4. The outlaw couple ___lived___ (live) a luxurious lifestyle.
5. They ___rented___ (rent) a condo in an Oregon ski resort for two months.
6. They also ___vacationed___ (vacation) in Belize.
7. Naturally, Pritchert and Guthrie's crime spree ___ended___ (end).
8. The police finally ___located___ (locate) the couple in Cape Town, South Africa.
9. They ___arrested___ (arrest) them in 2003 and returned them to the United States to be tried.
10. The judge ___sentenced___ (sentence) them both to long prison terms.

For online practice with regular past tense verbs, visit this book's Web site at **bedfordstmartins .com/steppingstones**.

Recognizing Irregular Past Tense Verbs

Now, it is time to prepare for some memorization work. Many past tense verbs have an "irregular" form that is not spelled with an *-ed* ending. Some of these irregular spellings you already know by heart. The following pre-test will help you identify the forms that you do not know so that you can focus on these in your memorization work.

CHECKING YOUR KNOWLEDGE: PRE-TEST

For each sentence pair, do the following:

- Look at the underlined verb in the first sentence.
- Then, in the second sentence, fill in the blank with the correct past tense form of this verb. Your answer should consist of only one word: the past tense verb. Do not add any words to the sentence or change any words in the sentence.
- When you have finished this pre-test, check your answers by using the chart on page 462.

If you want this test to work for you, do it honestly. Do not look for the answers while you're taking it.

EXAMPLE:

My son brings me a flower on my birthday.	**My son __brought__ me a flower on my birthday.**
1. I am happy about the raise.	I __was__ happy about the raise.
2. You are a good student.	You __were__ a good student.
3. The children become restless.	The children __became__ restless.
4. The playoffs begin on Friday.	The playoffs __began__ on Friday.
5. Our dog bites letter carriers.	Our dog __bit__ letter carriers.
6. The wind blows.	The wind __blew__.
7. The fragile vases break.	The fragile vases __broke__.
8. The guests bring gifts.	The guests __brought__ gifts.
9. My cousin builds porches.	My cousin __built__ porches.
10. The teenagers buy jeans.	The teenagers __bought__ jeans.
11. The vacationers catch fish.	The vacationers __caught__ fish.
12. You choose wisely.	You __chose__ wisely.
13. They come to our parties.	They __came__ to our parties.
14. Shoes cost a lot now.	Even when I was a child, shoes __cost__ a lot.
15. We dive into the pool.	We __dived/dove__ into the pool.
16. The kids do the laundry.	The kids __did__ the laundry.
17. Bernice draws well.	Bernice __drew__ well.
18. We drink lots of water.	We __drank__ lots of water.
19. The truckers drive all night.	The truckers __drove__ all night.
20. The Changs eat healthfully.	The Changs __ate__ healthfully.

CONTINUED >

21.	The books fall from the shelf.	The books __fell__ from the shelf.
22.	Shontelle feeds the dog.	Shontelle __fed__ the dog.
23.	The boys feel sick.	The boys __felt__ sick.
24.	The boxers fight aggressively.	The boxers __fought__ aggressively.
25.	I find mushrooms in the woods.	I __found__ mushrooms in the woods.
26.	We fly to Kentucky.	We __flew__ to Kentucky.
27.	The rain puddles freeze.	The rain puddles __froze__.
28.	My sister gets an employee discount.	My sister __got__ an employee discount.
29.	We give to charity.	We __gave__ to charity.
30.	My roommates go to the gym.	My roommates __went__ to the gym.
31.	The vegetables grow quickly.	The vegetables __grew__ quickly.
32.	You have a cold.	You __had__ a cold.
33.	The babysitter hears strange noises.	The babysitter __heard__ strange noises.
34.	We hide the children's presents.	We __hid__ the children's presents.
35.	The box holds a precious gem.	The box __held__ a precious gem.
36.	Jason hurts his knees running.	Jason __hurt__ his knees running.
37.	The Grimaldis keep their house clean.	The Grimaldis __kept__ their house clean.
38.	The students know the answer.	The students __knew__ the answer.
39.	Chris lay the tablecloth on the table.	Chris __laid__ the tablecloth on the table.
40.	The mountaineer leads our hike.	The mountaineer __led__ our hike.
41.	I leave my shoes in the hall.	I __left__ my shoes in the hall.
42.	We let the boys play outside every day.	We __let__ the boys play outside yesterday.
43.	The sunbathers lie on the beach.	The sunbathers __lay__ on the beach.
44.	Cassie lights the candles before dinner.	Cassie __lit__ the candles before dinner.
45.	We lose every time we play.	We __lost__ every time we played.
46.	James makes the bed.	James __made__ the bed.
47.	I know what the note means.	I know what the note __meant__.
48.	Our class meets on Tuesdays.	Our class __met__ on Tuesdays.
49.	My job pays well.	My job __paid__ well.
50.	I always put the glasses on the top shelf.	Yesterday, I __put__ the glasses on the top shelf.
51.	Dan quits his job every few years.	Yesterday, Dan __quit__ his fifth job.
52.	I read the newspaper every day.	I __read__ the newspaper yesterday.
53.	We ride the subway.	We __rode__ the subway.
54.	The church bells ring over the city.	The church bells __rang__ over the city.
55.	The dough rises in the warm oven.	The dough __rose__ in the warm oven.
56.	Lisette runs every day.	Lisette __ran__ every day.
57.	My daughter says she's tired.	My daughter __said__ she was tired.

58.	Jo sees a movie every week.	Jo ___saw___ a movie every week.
59.	The lost travelers seek help.	The lost travelers ___sought___ help.
60.	Karin sells jewelry.	Karin ___sold___ jewelry.
61.	I send funny cards to my sister.	I ___sent___ funny cards to my sister.
62.	Carrie sets the table every night.	Last summer, Carrie ___set___ the table every night.
63.	The bartender shakes the drinks.	The bartender ___shook___ the drinks.
64.	That theater shows old movies.	That theater ___showed___ old movies.
65.	The clothes shrink in the wash.	The clothes ___shrank___ in the wash.
66.	I shut the windows at night.	I ___shut___ the windows last night.
67.	Darnell sings beautifully.	Darnell ___sang___ beautifully.
68.	My heart sinks when you leave.	My heart ___sank___ when you left.
69.	Grandpa sits in that chair.	Grandpa ___sat___ in that chair.
70.	My son sleeps late on Saturdays.	My son ___slept___ late on Saturday.
71.	The mayor speaks at most town events.	The mayor ___spoke___ at most town events.
72.	We spend our vacations at the beach.	We ___spent___ our vacations at the beach.
73.	Flowers spring from the ground in May.	Flowers ___sprang___ from the ground in May.
74.	I stand by my decision.	I ___stood___ by my decision.
75.	Ian steals candy from his brother.	Ian ___stole___ candy from his brother.
76.	Our shoes stick to the dirty floor.	Our shoes ___stuck___ to the dirty floor.
77.	The bees sting the picnickers.	The bees ___stung___ the picnickers.
78.	Lightning strikes the barn often.	Lightning ___struck___ the barn often.
79.	I swim at the community pool.	I ___swam___ at the community pool.
80.	I take doughnuts to work.	I ___took___ doughnuts to work.
81.	Mr. Vega teaches my daughter.	Mr. Vega ___taught___ my daughter.
82.	Betsy tears tickets at the concert hall.	Betsy ___tore___ tickets at the concert hall.
83.	Constance tells the truth.	Constance ___told___ the truth.
84.	I think of you often.	I ___thought___ of you often.
85.	The quarterback throws the ball.	The quarterback ___threw___ the ball.
86.	We understand the directions.	We ___understood___ the directions.
87.	Luis wakes the baby.	Luis ___woke/waked___ the baby.
88.	We wear casual clothes to work.	We ___wore___ casual clothes to work.
89.	Aziza wins every card game.	Aziza ___won___ every card game.
90.	The soldier writes to his family every day.	The soldier ___wrote___ to his family every day.

As you check your work on the pre-test against the following chart, put a check mark beside each irregular verb that you spelled incorrectly in the past tense.

Power Tip
For an expanded list of irregular verbs, you might consult online resources, such as **www.englishpage.com**.

Irregular Verbs

BASE FORM	PAST TENSE FORM
☐ be	was/were
(I *am;* you/we/they *are;* he/she/it *is*)	(I/he/she/it *was;* you/we/they *were*)
☐ become	became
☐ begin	began
☐ bite	bit
☐ blow	blew
☐ break	broke
☐ bring	brought
☐ build	built
☐ buy	bought
☐ catch	caught
☐ choose	chose
☐ come	came
☐ cost	cost
☐ dive	dived, dove
☐ do	did
(I/you/we/they *do;* he/she/it *does*)	(I/you/we/he/she/it/they *did*)
☐ draw	drew
☐ drink	drank
☐ drive	drove
☐ eat	ate
☐ fall	fell
☐ feed	fed
☐ feel	felt
☐ fight	fought
☐ find	found
☐ fly	flew
☐ freeze	froze
☐ get	got
☐ give	gave
☐ go	went

For online practice with irregular past tense verbs, visit this book's Web site at **bedfordstmartins .com/steppingstones**.

BASE FORM	PAST TENSE FORM
☐ grow	grew
☐ have (I/you/we/they *have;* he/she/it *has*)	had (I/you/we/he/she/it/they *had*)
☐ hear	heard
☐ hide	hid
☐ hold	held
☐ hurt	hurt
☐ keep	kept
☐ know	knew
☐ lay (*to put down*)	laid
☐ lead	led
☐ leave	left
☐ let	let
☐ lie (*to recline*)	lay
☐ light	lit
☐ lose	lost
☐ make	made
☐ mean	meant
☐ meet	met
☐ pay	paid
☐ put	put
☐ quit	quit
☐ read	read
☐ ride	rode
☐ ring	rang
☐ rise	rose
☐ run	ran
☐ say	said
☐ see	saw
☐ seek	sought
☐ sell	sold
☐ send	sent
☐ set	set
☐ shake	shook
☐ show	showed

CONTINUED >

BASE FORM	PAST TENSE FORM
☐ shrink	shrank
☐ shut	shut
☐ sing	sang
☐ sink	sank
☐ sit	sat
☐ sleep	slept
☐ speak	spoke
☐ spend	spent
☐ spring	sprang
☐ stand	stood
☐ steal	stole
☐ stick	stuck
☐ sting	stung
☐ strike	struck
☐ swim	swam
☐ take	took
☐ teach	taught
☐ tear	tore
☐ tell	told
☐ think	thought
☐ throw	threw
☐ understand	understood
☐ wake	woke, waked
☐ wear	wore
☐ win	won
☐ write	wrote

Memorizing Irregular Past Tense Verbs

Once you have identified the irregular past tense forms that you do not know, it's time to use some memorization strategies to help the correct forms "stick" in your mind. These strategies work best in combination, so plan to use as many of them as possible.

Priority Lists. Review the chart on pages 462–464 and pick the three to five verbs that you use most frequently but missed on the pre-test. This will be your **priority list**. Practice only these words for two or three days (or more, if necessary) until you know them by heart. To practice, invent sentences using these verbs, say the correct forms out loud, and complete online practices (visit **bedfordstmartins.com/steppingstones**). You can also try some of the other strategies that we'll discuss later in this section.

Next, go back to the chart and pick three to five more verbs that you missed on the pre-test. Add these words to your priority list. Then, practice *all* the words on your priority list until you know them by heart.

Repeat this process until you have incorporated all the verbs that you missed on the pre-test into your practice. Remember not to rush; practice each new group for as many days as you need to until you can say and write the correct past tense form without hesitation.

Teaching Tip
Suggest that students make up stories with verbs that challenge them. Then, they can share those stories with classmates or friends for feedback. Simply using challenging verbs more often will help students build their skills.

Visual Aids. For each new word on your priority list, make a **flash card**. To do this, use small index cards that you can hold comfortably in your hand. On one side of a card, write the present tense verb in large, bold print. (Write only one word per card to increase the visual impact.) On the back of the card, write the past tense form in large, bold print. Keep your cards with you as often as possible throughout the day (in your backpack, in a convenient place at work, or other convenient location) and review them whenever you have a few free minutes: on the bus, eating breakfast, on a break at work, waiting for your class to start. These moments of practice will add up to make a big difference in your mastery of verbs.

You might also buy a pack of medium or large **sticky notes**. On the front of each note, write the past tense form of a different verb from your priority list. Then, stick these notes on surfaces in your daily environment: one on the refrigerator, one on the bathroom mirror, one on your dashboard, one on your boyfriend's or girlfriend's forehead, and so on. Each time you see one of the sticky notes, pause to pronounce the verb and spell it out loud so that your brain records each letter. These few seconds of concentration can really boost your mastery of verbs.

Auditory Aids. For some of the verbs that you find especially challenging, create a **rhyme** using the past tense form. For example, *I **bit** the **pit** of a perfect peach.* If you have made flash cards for these verbs (see Visual Aids), write the rhyme under the past tense form. Each time you review the flash cards, say the rhymes out loud. Often, rhymes are easier to remember than isolated words.

Also, review the chart of irregular verbs, looking for two or more past tense verbs that rhyme with one another. For example, *fought* and *bought* rhyme. Now, create a rhyming sentence using both of these words: *The couple **fought** about the house they **bought**.* Write this rhyme on the flash cards for both verbs, under the past tense form, and say it out loud each time you review the flash cards.

If you have trouble thinking of rhymes, ask your family or friends to help you: many people love to make up sayings.

Tactile Aids. For this strategy, you will need to make small **letter blocks**. Cut out 1-by-1-inch squares of cardboard and use a marker to write one bold letter on each block. Look at the verbs on your first priority list (see page 464) and make sure that you have all the letter blocks necessary to spell each of these words,

Teaching Tip
You might bring in a *Scrabble* game so that small groups of students can work with the pieces while others experiment with the other memorization strategies described here.

one at a time. (If you own the *Scrabble* game, you can use the letter tiles for this strategy.) Put all of these letter blocks into a pile.

Now, it's time to practice. Select one of the words from your first priority list, using flash cards if you made them (see Visual Aids). First, look at the present tense verb. Then, pick the letter blocks necessary to spell the past tense form, placing the letters side by side. Then, check the spelling by flipping over the flash card or referring to the irregular verbs chart. Mix the letter blocks back into the pile and move on to another verb from your priority list. Manipulating these letter blocks will help you remember the verbs more easily.

As you add new verbs to your priority list, create new letter blocks that you will need to spell each additional past tense verb. You can keep the letter blocks in a plastic Baggie and carry them with you.

ACTIVITY 5: Teamwork

Working with two or three classmates, identify five to ten irregular past tense verbs that you all have trouble with. Then, as a group, try one or more of the memorization strategies. For example, you might

- have each person create a flash card for two or three different verbs, with the present tense on one side and the past tense on the other. Then, have someone collect the cards, keeping the cards present-tense-up, and scramble them. Going through one card at a time, see who can call out the past tense form the fastest.
- have each person pick a verb and make up a rhyme with it. Decide whose rhyme is the funniest or most original.

Avoiding Common Verb Problems

The following sections discuss some errors that often occur with use of the present and past tenses.

SUBJECT-VERB AGREEMENT ERRORS

A verb is said to "agree" with its subject when it is in the correct form for that subject according to the rules of English grammar. As you have already learned, when the subject is *he, she,* or *it* (or some equivalent of *he, she,* or *it,* such as *Terri* or *the iPod*), the verb must end in *-s* in the present tense (*plays*).

Making sure that verbs agree with their subjects can be tricky in certain instances, such as with the verbs *be, have,* and *do* (see page 456). Here, we'll look at some other situations where agreement problems may occur. As you'll see, these errors are often made in the present tense.

Verbs Separated from the Subject

As you learned in earlier chapters, words or word groups often separate the subject of a sentence from its verb. Let's look at some examples.

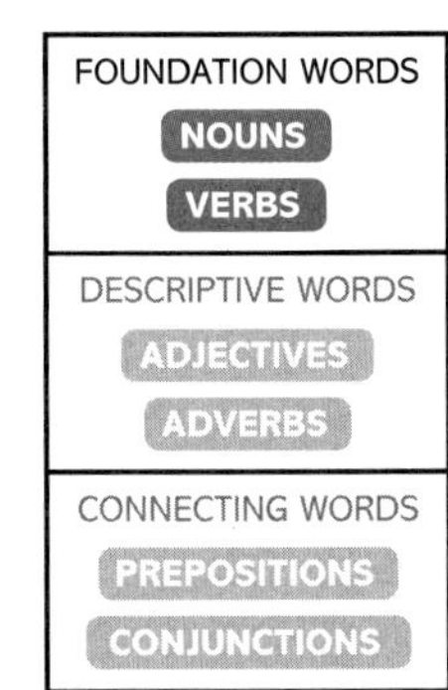

PREPOSITIONAL PHRASE

The workers on the first shift eat lunch early.

For more on prepositional phrases, see Chapter 10.

DESCRIPTIVE CLAUSE

The veterinarian who cares for my dogs recommends all-natural pet food.

For more on descriptive clauses, see Chapter 14.

MODIFYING PHRASE

Global climate change, worsening every year, continues to draw concern.

For more on modifying phrases, see Chapter 15.

When words come between the subject and verb, you need to make the verb agree with the subject, not with the word that comes right before the verb. Crossing out prepositional phrases, descriptive clauses, modifying phrases, and other such word groups can help you identify the subject and its verb. Take a look:

INCORRECT The babysitter who watches my children are friendly.

HE/SHE EQUIVALENT — *-S* ENDING ON VERB

REVISED The babysitter ~~who watches my children~~ is friendly.

The subject of the sentence is *babysitter,* not *children,* as we can see by crossing out the prepositional phrase. The verb *is* agrees with *babysitter.*

Power Tip
On pages 467–469, only subjects (not other nouns) are highlighted in blue.

Teaching Tip
If you want to give students more practice with eliminating prepositional phrases and descriptive words, you might refer them to Chapter 11, page 288.

ACTIVITY 6

For each sentence below, do the following:

- Cross out any prepositional phrases, descriptive clauses, or modifying phrases.
- Underline the subject, and circle the verb.
- If the verb agrees with the subject, write "OK" in the space provided.
- If the verb does not agree with the subject, rewrite the sentence in the space provided, using the correct form of the verb.

EXAMPLE: The clothes ~~at P.J.'s Discount~~ (is) hipper than most expensive brands.
The clothes at P.J.'s Discount are hipper than most expensive brands.

1. The coffee ~~at work~~ (tastes) like varnish.
OK

2. The bread ~~that I purchased for my children's lunches~~ (look) moldy.
The bread that I purchased for my children's lunches looks moldy.

CONTINUED >

3. Identity theft ~~on online shopping sites~~ (are) increasingly common.
Identity theft on online shopping sites is increasingly common.

4. The police officer ~~who parks in the CVS lot~~ (tickets) many speeders each morning.
OK

5. The children, ~~tired after their long days of school and homework,~~ (collapses) on the couch every night.
The children, tired after their long days of school and homework, collapse on the couch every night.

Verbs before the Subject

In some sentences, the verb comes before the subject. For example, such reversals happen in questions and in statements that begin with *There is* or *There are.*

Take a look at the following questions:

Where is the entrance?

Who are your favorite athletes?

Notice that the subjects are the words in blue; they are not *Who* or *Where.* If you are confused about how to identify subjects in questions, turn the questions around:

The entrance is . . .

Your favorite athletes are . . .

Teaching Tip
For tutorials on subject-verb agreement and verb usage in general, see the *Make-a-Paragraph Kit* CD available with this book.

As we can see, the subjects and verbs in these examples agree. Now, take a look at the following statements:

There is a big bug on the wall.

There are three infants at my daughter's daycare.

Again, the subjects are the words in blue. If you are confused about how to identify subjects in statements that begin with *There is* or *There are,* turn the statements around:

A big bug is on the wall.

Three infants are at my daughter's daycare.

As we can see, the subjects and verbs in these examples agree.

For online practice on subject-verb agreement, visit this book's Web site at **bedfordstmartins .com/steppingstones**.

ACTIVITY 7

For each sentence below, do the following:

- Underline the subject, and circle the verb. If you have trouble identifying the subject, you may want to turn the question or statement around.
- If the verb agrees with the subject, write "OK" in the space provided.
- If the verb does not agree with the subject, rewrite the sentence in the space provided, using the correct form of the verb.

EXAMPLE: There (is) two doctors on this plane.
There are two doctors on this plane.

1. What (is) your children's names?
   What are your children's names?
2. There (are) chicken in the oven.
   There is chicken in the oven.
3. Where (are) the children's coats?
   OK
4. Who (is) the best doctors in our town?
   Who are the best doctors in our town?
5. There (is) several good crime shows on television.
   There are several good crime shows on television.

Verbs with Compound Subjects

As you learned in Chapter 11, **compound subjects** consist of more than one subject. Often, compound subjects are joined with the conjunction *and*. Take a look:

COMPOUND SUBJECT

Emily and Jason laugh.

However, if *or* instead of *and* is used as the conjunction, the verb needs to agree with the subject that is closest to the verb. Consider these examples:

THEY EQUIVALENT — NO *-S* ENDING ON VERB

The guard or the prisoners complain.

HE/SHE EQUIVALENT — *-S* ENDING ON VERB

The prisoners or the guard complains.

HE/SHE EQUIVALENT — *-S* ENDING ON VERB

The warden, prisoners, or the guard complains.

ACTIVITY 8

For each sentence below, do the following:

- In the space provided, write the correct present tense form of the verb in parentheses.
- If the verb ends in *-s,* circle the *s* or mark it with a highlighter.

EXAMPLE: Sandro and Ellen ___are___ (be) worried about their finances.

1. Grandma and the children ___watch___ (watch) movies together.
2. Jonathan and Chanda ___are___ (be) in love.
3. The Morettis or their son ___parks___ (park) in this space.
4. Roy, Janice, and Tanya ___cook___ (cook) delicious food for every neighborhood picnic.
5. The parents or the child ___fills___ (fill) out the form.

Indefinite-Pronoun Subjects

Indefinite pronouns refer to general people or things. Most indefinite pronouns, like those in the following list, take the *he/she/it* form of the verb; in other words, there is an *-s* at the end of the verb. (See the chart in Chapter 17, page 504 as a reminder.)

anybody	**neither**
anyone	**no one**
anything	**nobody**
each	**nothing**
either	**one**
everybody	**somebody**
everyone	**someone**
everything	**something**

Everyone is **excited about the game.**

Nothing bothers **me more than mosquitoes.**

However, some indefinite pronouns (such as *many, several,* and *few*) take the *they* form of the verb; in other words, there is no *-s* at the end of the verb.

Few plan **to attend the meeting.**

It's a good idea to minimize your use of indefinite pronouns, not only because they can cause agreement problems but also because they can lead to generalizations. (For more information, see Chapter 17, page 512.)

ACTIVITY 9

For each sentence, do the following:

- In the space provided, write the correct present tense form of the verb in parentheses.
- If the verb ends in *-s,* circle the *s* or mark it with a highlighter.

EXAMPLE: Everything ___is___ (be) fine.

1. Everybody ___likes___ (like) pizza.
2. Many ___are___ (be) called, but few ___are___ (be) chosen.
3. No one ___wants___ (want) to deliver bad news.
4. Somebody ___leaves___ (leave) muddy footprints across our driveway every morning.
5. Most members of my church contribute to charities, and several ___volunteer___ (volunteer) at local organizations.

ERRORS BASED ON PRONUNCIATION

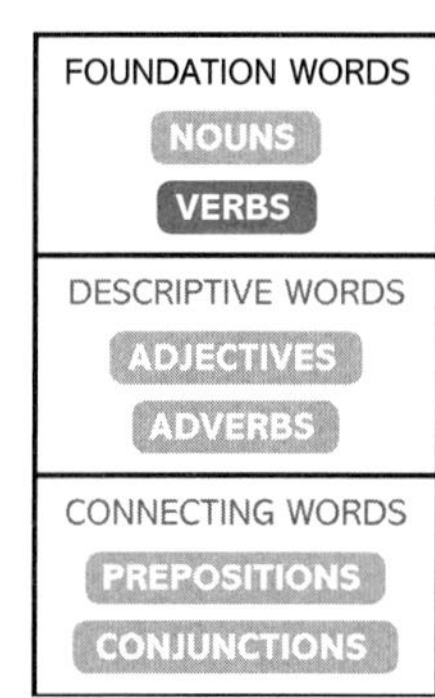

When we speak, we sometimes run words together in our pronunciation. Then, when we write these words, we try to spell them the way we pronounce them. This is how we end up with nonstandard verbs like ***gonna, wanna, gotta, should of, would of,*** and ***could of.*** Study the following examples:

NONSTANDARD ENGLISH	STANDARD ENGLISH
Our team is gonna win the game.	Our team is going to win the game.
I wanna lose some weight.	I want to lose some weight.
They gotta find a new apartment.	They have to find a new apartment.
Julio should of studied.	Julio should have studied.
We would of forgotten the date.	We would have forgotten the date.
Sheila could of found a better job.	Sheila could have found a better job.

It is common to see these nonstandard verb forms in personal e-mails. However, you should eliminate them from your academic and professional writing.

ACTIVITY 10

Rewrite each of the following sentences to eliminate nonstandard verbs. There may be more than one nonstandard verb in each sentence.

EXAMPLE: We gotta leave or we're gonna be late.
We have to leave or we're going to be late.

1. Do you wanna try my recipe for lasagna?
   Do you want to try my recipe for lasagna?
2. We gotta finish this report if we're gonna leave early on Friday.
   We have to finish this report if we're going to leave early on Friday.
3. Ernest would of won the lottery if he had played his number this week.
   Ernest would have won the lottery if he had played his number this week.
4. We could of taken that shortcut, and we should of.
   We could have taken that shortcut, and we should have.
5. Nobody is gonna believe your story; you should of made up a better one.
   Nobody is going to believe your story; you should have made up a better one.

SHIFTS

Some errors result from accidental shifts (inconsistencies) in verb tense or in other verb usages. The following sections will examine these shifts and how they happen.

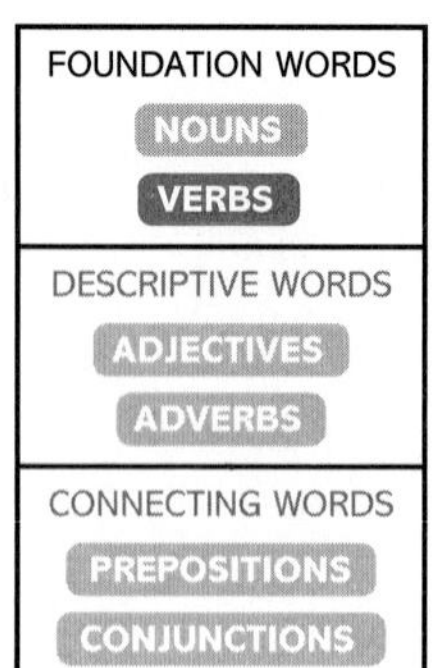

Shifts in Verb Tense

As you have learned, we use verb tenses to show when an action took (or takes) place. Take a look at these examples:

AN ACTION IN THE PAST	The airplane landed on the wrong runway.
A REGULAR ACTION (PRESENT TENSE)	I cash my paycheck on Friday afternoon.

If we are describing several actions that took (or take) place *together*, we need to be sure that the verb tenses match. Take a look:

TWO RELATED ACTIONS IN THE PAST	The airplane landed on the wrong runway and narrowly missed another plane.
TWO RELATED, REGULAR ACTIONS (PRESENT TENSE)	I cash my paycheck on Friday afternoon and buy food for the weekend.

For online practice with fixing nonstandard verbs, visit this book's Web site at **bedfordstmartins .com/steppingstones**.

In both sentences, the verbs are consistent (the same) in tense. However, if we change one of the verbs to a different tense without a good reason for doing so, the sentence will not make sense:

Incorrect Shift in Verb Tense

PAST — PRESENT

The airplane landed on the wrong runway and narrowly misses another plane.

PAST — PRESENT

I cashed my paycheck on Friday afternoon and buy food for the weekend.

This unnecessary change in verb tense usually happens when we are not paying close attention to the spelling of our verbs.

Sometimes, a sentence may contain two actions that happen at different times. In this case, a change in verb tense may make sense:

AN ACTION IN THE PAST — A CURRENT STATE (PRESENT TENSE)

Rebecca joined the National Guard, but she regrets her decision.

Rebecca joined the National Guard at some point in the past, but she regrets her decision now, in the present. This change in verb tense makes perfect sense.

ACTIVITY 11

For each sentence below, do the following:

- Decide whether or not the verb tense is consistent.
- If the tense is consistent, write a ***C*** in the margin.
- If the tense is inconsistent, cross out one of the verbs and write the correct verb tense above it.

EXAMPLE: The children lost their way and ~~decide~~ *decided* to ask a stranger for help.

1. Water rose over the river bank and ~~floods~~ *flooded* the basements of many homes.
2. Jessica works the night shift every Friday and always ~~came~~ *comes* home after midnight.
3. Maurey drove through a red light and ~~hits~~ *hit* another car broadside.
4. At first, I thought Brad was arrogant, but now I like him. *C*
5. Last night the waiter ~~walks~~ *walked* up to our table and slammed down a basket of rolls.

For online practice with using consistent verb tense, visit this book's Web site at **bedfordstmartins .com/steppingstones**.

Incorrect shifts in verb tense commonly occur when we are describing historical events or telling stories because these descriptions may involve multiple sentences and multiple verbs. In these instances, it is important to pay close attention to verbs, keeping them consistent.

In describing a historical event, most writers relate the facts in the past tense. Here is a description of the Boston Tea Party:

Boston Tea Party: an act of protest of colonial Americans against Britain's policy of taxing the colonists without giving them government representation. The Boston Tea Party is one of the events that led to the Revolutionary War (1775–1783), which resulted in America's independence from Britain.

> On an icy December evening in 1773, Boston's Old South Meeting House was ablaze with the fury of revolution. Samuel Adams led the revolt against the British government's taxation of colonists. He convinced a group of Boston patriots to disguise themselves as Mohawk Indians and attack three British cargo ships carrying tea for which colonists would be taxed. The patriots, known as the Sons of Liberty, stormed out of the meeting house and descended on Boston Harbor. There, they boarded the ships and destroyed 342 crates of tea by throwing them into the water. The hoots and howls of the revolutionaries were heard late into the night.

However, a writer may choose to narrate a historical event in the present tense to give it more dramatic impact. Here is an example:

> On an icy December evening in 1773, the Old South Meeting House is ablaze with the fury of revolution. Samuel Adams leads the revolt against the British government's taxation of colonists. He convinces a group of Boston patriots to disguise themselves as Mohawk Indians and attack three British cargo ships carrying tea for which the colonists would be taxed. The patriots, known as the Sons of Liberty, storm out of the meeting house and descend on Boston Harbor. There, they board the ships and destroy 342 crates of tea by throwing them into the water. The hoots and howls of the revolutionaries are heard late into the night.

Power Tip
If you are writing about past events for a history class, ask your professor what tense he or she prefers. In writing about events in a work of literature, it is conventional to use the present tense. For example, *In The Scarlet Letter, Hester Prynne* ***maintains*** *her dignity despite being branded with the letter* A, *for* adultery.

Both of these descriptions of the Boston Tea Party are grammatically correct because the verb tense is consistent in each one. Notice that the first sentence of each narrative establishes the tense that the entire story will use. Always be sure that the verbs in the first sentence of any narrative that you write are in the tense you really intend. In most cases, you will want to stay with this tense to avoid confusing shifts like the following:

> On an icy December evening in 1773, the Old South Meeting House was ablaze with the fury of revolution. Samuel Adams led the revolt against the British government's taxation of colonists. He convinces . . .

When telling a personal story, many writers use the past tense. Take a look:

> My happiest memory was leading my high school basketball team to victory in the regional championship. Imagine this scene: just thirty seconds remained on the clock. The gymnasium was packed with fans. My team, Lincoln Heights, and the rival team, Bonaventure, struggled for control of the ball as Bonaventure fought to hold onto its one-point lead. Sweat dripped in my eyes and nearly blinded me. Suddenly, the ball flew in front of me, and I intercepted it. I saw three seconds on the clock and made a wild, half-blind toss toward the net—SCORE!

However, the writer could also tell this story in the present tense to heighten the dramatic energy:

Power Tip
For more information on narration, see Appendix A.

My happiest moment is leading my high school basketball team to victory in the regional championship. Imagine this scene: just thirty seconds remain on the clock. The gymnasium is packed with fans. My team, Lincoln Heights, and the rival team, Bonaventure, struggle for control of the ball as Bonaventure fights to hold onto its one-point lead. Sweat drips in my eyes and nearly blinds me. Suddenly, the ball flies in front of me, and I intercept it. I see three seconds on the clock and make a wild, half-blind toss toward the net—SCORE!

Shifting Tense in the Middle of a Story. Sometimes, we may begin a story in the *past* tense but then get so involved in the actions or details that we shift to the *present* tense without realizing it. Here is an example:

My happiest memory was leading my high school basketball team to victory in the regional championship. Imagine this scene: just thirty seconds remained on the clock. The gymnasium was packed with fans. My team, Lincoln Heights, and the rival team, Bonaventure, struggle for control of the ball as Bonaventure fights to hold onto its one-point lead. Sweat drips in my eyes and nearly blinds me. Suddenly, the ball flies in front of me, and I intercept it. I see three seconds on the clock and make a wild, half-blind toss toward the net—SCORE!

Here, the writer begins in the past tense. By the fourth sentence, however, he gets so involved in his own story that he loses track of the verb tense. In revising this narrative, he will need to select one tense and make all the verbs consistent.

Jumping Back and Forth between Tenses in a Story. Sometimes, writers get so swept up in the drama of a story that they jump back and forth between tenses. Read this version of the basketball story and notice how the verb tenses start shifting back and forth.

My happiest memory was leading my high school basketball team to victory in the regional championship. Imagine this scene: just thirty seconds remained on the clock. The gymnasium was packed with fans. My team, Lincoln Heights, and the rival team, Bonaventure, struggle for control of the ball as Bonaventure fights to hold onto its one-point lead. Sweat dripped in my eyes and nearly blinded me. Suddenly, the ball flies in front of me, and I intercepted it. I see three seconds on the clock and made a wild, half-blind toss toward the net—SCORE!

This sort of "out of control" shift in verb tense is a common problem for inexperienced writers. If you are ever unsure about your use of verb tense when writing a story, ask your instructor for guidance.

ACTIVITY 12

For the passage below, do the following:

- Read the first sentence and decide whether the story is in the past or present tense.
- Read the rest of the passage, crossing out any verbs that are not in the correct tense.
- In each place where you have crossed out a verb, write the correct verb form above it.

You should find five verb tense errors.

(1) Isabella Baumfree, who later took the name Sojourner Truth, was a former slave who became a passionate spokesperson for African American and women's rights. (2) Born in 1797 to slave parents in New York, she spent half her life as a slave. (3) She endured savage treatment, and her young son Peter ~~is~~ was sold to another family who abused him. (4) Finding refuge in religion, Baumfree ~~becomes~~ became an inspiring preacher and abolitionist. (5) In 1843, she ~~changes~~ changed her name to Sojourner Truth and spread her message everywhere she went. (6) In 1854, at a women's rights convention in Akron, Ohio, she ~~delivers~~ delivered a now famous speech in which she asked, "Ain't I a woman?" (7) In this speech, this genuine, plain-speaking woman ~~drives~~ drove home the point that women should be regarded as equals to men. (8) In 1883, Sojourner Truth died, leaving a powerful legacy.

abolitionist: someone who fought for the elimination of slavery

Interrupting a Story with Current Information or Facts. Again, most stories are told in the past tense. Sometimes, however, we may want to interrupt the action of a story with current information or facts. This information may make more sense in the present tense. As you read the following story, notice that the action is in the past tense (the verbs highlighted in yellow) and that current information and facts are in the present tense (highlighted in blue):

When the patrol car flashed its lights behind my brother and me, I sensed that something wasn't right. My brother, who was driving, has a spotless record and drives conservatively. He also keeps his registration tags and his vehicle maintenance up to date, so I knew that the cops hadn't chosen us because of a traffic violation, old tags, or an extinguished taillight. My brother pulled carefully onto the shoulder of the road and turned off the engine. As the cops approached from both sides, they aimed their flashlights in the backseat like they were searching for something. Suddenly, I remembered what my cousin always said about the police in our town: they are often guilty of racial profiling, stopping innocent drivers just because of their race. My brother and I happen to be Latino, so I prepared myself for the worst . . .

The brother's driving record and responsible behavior, the profiling by police, and the race of the writer and his brother are *current* and *factual* details, so it makes sense to keep them in the present tense. Interrupting a story with current information in the present tense can be tricky. Check any story you write carefully to make sure that any shifts to the present tense are justified. If you are uncertain about whether a shift to the present tense is correct, ask your instructor for guidance.

ACTIVITY 13

For the passage below, do the following:

- Read the passage to confirm that it's generally in the past tense.
- Look for any sentences that contain current information or facts.
- In these sentences, cross out any verbs that are in the past tense. Above them, write the correct present tense verbs.

You should find three sentences that contain current information or facts.

(1) Of all NASA's space missions, one of the most familiar to Americans ~~was~~ is Apollo 13 even though it never reached its destination. (2) The three-man crew of Apollo 13 lifted off on April 11, 1970, bound for the moon. (3) Official NASA records ~~showed~~ show that almost 56 hours into the flight, oxygen tank 2 on the spacecraft blew up. (4) That explosion caused oxygen tank 1 to fail also. (5) As a result, the craft lost oxygen and critical electrical power. (6) The moon landing was canceled, and all attention was turned to bringing the astronauts home safely. (7) The crew deactivated some systems to preserve power needed for re-entry and landing. (8) During the crisis, the crew endured loss of cabin heat and limited water supplies. (9) In the end, a NASA team led the three astronauts safely back to Earth. (10) This true space drama ~~continued~~ continues to fascinate people. (11) It inspired the 1995 film *Apollo 13,* starring Tom Hanks as astronaut Jack Swigert.

NASA: the National Aeronautics and Space Administration, the U.S. government agency responsible for space exploration

Terminology Tip
Helping verbs "help" other (main) verbs. For more information, see Chapter 10, page 270.

Using *Can/Could* and *Will/Would*. Most students have no trouble using the helping verbs *can* and *will*. *Can* shows an ability to do something, and *will* shows an intention (plan) to do something. Take a look:

AN ABILITY TO BALANCE	I can balance a spoon on my nose.
AN INTENTION TO BUY	I will buy three lottery tickets.

Power Tip
Notice that when you use *can, could, will,* and *would,* the verb that appears after these helping verbs does not change form; instead, it is always in the base form (for example, *balance*, not *balanced*).

Could and *would* are often used to express an ability or an intention in the past tense:

AN ABILITY TO BALANCE	When I was six years old, I could balance a spoon on my nose.
AN INTENTION TO BUY	I told my mother I would buy three lottery tickets.

In the following passage, you can see how the writer keeps the verb tense consistent, using *can* and *will*. Notice that the highlighted verbs in the first sentence establish this story in the present tense:

I am still a student, so I have to follow my parents' house rules. For example, I can go out only two nights a week, Friday and Saturday. On the other nights, I can invite friends to the house to study. My parents will allow me to have a part-time job, but I can work up to only twenty hours per week. If my grades start to slip, I will have to cut back on hours at work or quit. My parents will also let me participate in one extracurricular activity at college, like a sports team or student government. However, if I neglect my studies because of this activity, I will have to give it up. These rules may seem strict, but I know they can help me succeed, so I will obey them. When I live on my own, I can make my own house rules, but as long as I live at home, I will respect my parents' wishes.

extracurricular: occurring outside of class

Teaching Tip
Ask students to write their own stories using *can/could* and *will/would*. Then, have them exchange papers with peers to check for consistency of tense.

Now, watch what happens when this story changes to the past tense. The helping verbs change to *could* and *would*, and they stay consistent. Once again, notice how the highlighted verbs in the first sentence establish this story in the past tense:

When I was a high school student, I had to follow my parents' house rules. For example, I could go out only two nights a week, Friday and Saturday. On the other nights, I could invite friends to the house to study. My parents would allow me to have a part-time job, but I could work up to only twenty hours per week. If my grades started to slip, I would have to cut back on hours at work or quit. My parents would also let me participate in one extracurricular activity at college, like a sports team or student government. However, if I neglected my studies because of this activity, I would have to give it up. These rules may have seemed strict, but I knew they could help me succeed, so I would obey them. I knew that when I lived on my own, I could make my own house rules, but as long as I lived at home, I would respect my parents' wishes.

Some writers have difficulty staying consistent when using these helping verbs. In conversation, we often jump back and forth between *can/could* and *will/would*, and most people don't notice. In our writing, we then repeat this error without recognizing it. As an example, read the following passage and notice that it *sounds* correct:

I am still a student, so I have to follow my parents' house rules. For example, I can go out only two nights a week, Friday and Saturday. On the other nights, I can invite friends to the house to study. My parents would allow me to have a part-time job, but I could work up to only twenty hours per week. If my grades start to slip, I will have to cut back on hours at work or quit. My parents would also let me participate in one extracurricular activity at college, like a sports team or student government. However, if I neglect my studies because of this activity, I would have to give it up. These rules may seem strict, but I know they could help me succeed, so I will obey them. When I live on my own, I could make my own house rules, but as long as I live at home, I will respect my parents' wishes.

Although this passage may sound correct, by now you know that it contains inconsistent verb tenses. The writer begins the story in the present tense but then jumps back and forth between *can/could* and *will/would.*

ACTIVITY 14

For the passage below, do the following:

- Read the first sentence and decide whether the writing is in the past or present tense.
- Read the rest of the passage, crossing out any ***can/could/will/would*** helping verbs that are not in the correct tense.
- In each place where you have crossed out a helping verb, write the correct verb form above it.

You should find three errors.

(1) More and more women are entering trades like plumbing, construction, and vehicle repair. (2) There are several reasons for this trend. (3) For one thing, women can earn a good living in these jobs. (4) Experienced plumbers, construction workers, and mechanics ~~could~~ can earn $100,000 a year or more. (5) Also, workers can sometimes choose their hours. (6) For example, a plumber with young children might be able to accept jobs only when her children are in school. (7) Also, working in the trades ~~could~~ can provide a lot of satisfaction and a sense of accomplishment. (8) If some people think that females can't weld iron or install an engine, women in the trades ~~would~~ will prove them wrong

CONTINUED >

again and again. (9) Finally, there will never be a shortage of dripping faucets, leaky roofs, and squealing brakes. (10) Therefore, job security is practically guaranteed for skilled workers.

Could and *would* are also used when we express wishes or possibilities:

A WISH I wish I could balance a spoon on my nose.

A POSSIBILITY If I had some money, I would buy three lottery tickets.

In college, some writing topics ask you to express your wishes or imagine possibilities. You can recognize these topics by the presence of *could* and *would:*

If you **could** travel anywhere, which country **would** you like to visit?
If you **could** spend a day with one famous person, who **would** it be?
If you **could** change one thing about the world, what **would** it be?
If you **could** have the career of your dreams, what **would** it be?

When you express a wish or possibility, you should use *could* and *would* consistently; do not jump back and forth unnecessarily between *can/could* and *will/would*. In the following paragraph, the writer has made this mistake:

If I could spend a day with one famous person, it would be Bill Gates, chairman and former CEO of Microsoft. For starters, I would like him to give me an "insider's" tour of the Microsoft headquarters. I would like to start my tour in Bill's executive office. I can sit in his chair and pretend that I am in command of the world's greatest software empire. I can also pick up the phone and surprise my girlfriend with a call from Bill's office. Then, I would like Bill to escort me to the "inner sanctum," where top-secret software design takes place. I will meet with Microsoft's elite designers—some of the highest-paid engineers in the world—and tell them what I don't like about Vista, the newest version of Windows. I could give them some tips on how to improve it. I would like to finish my tour by viewing exhibits on Microsoft's products and history at the company's visitor center. Bill can guide me through the exhibits, sharing the details of his many inventions.

When we read this passage quickly, it may *sound* correct because we are used to shifting verb tenses in our casual conversation. However, if you turn in a paper with tense shifts like this, it will likely be marked down. Here is the same passage revised for consistent verb tense:

If I could spend a day with one famous person, it would be Bill Gates, chairman and former CEO of Microsoft. For starters, I would like him to give me an "insider's" tour of the Microsoft headquarters. I would like to start my tour in Bill's executive office. I could sit in his chair and pretend that I am in command of the world's greatest software empire. I could also pick up the phone and surprise my girlfriend with a call from Bill's office. Then, I would like Bill to escort me to the "inner sanctum," where top-secret software design takes place. I would meet with Microsoft's elite designers—some of the highest-paid engineers in the world—and tell them what I don't like about Vista, the newest version of Windows. I could give them some tips on how to improve it. I would like to finish my tour by viewing exhibits on Microsoft's products and history at the company's visitor center. Bill could guide me through the exhibits, sharing the details of his many inventions.

ACTIVITY 15

For the passage below, do the following:

- Read the passage and determine the general tense of the writing.
- Cross out any ***can/could/will/would*** helping verbs that are not in the correct tense.
- In each place where you have crossed out a helping verb, write the correct verb form above it.

You should find three errors.

(1) Stephen recently received his associate's degree in business, and he got an offer for an accounting job. (2) However, if he could do anything in the world, it would be to make pottery. (3) To earn extra money while attending college, Stephen worked in his friend Pablo's pottery studio. (4) Under Pablo's guidance, Stephen developed a passion for making clay vases and plates, and he learned how to make creative sculptures. (5) If Stephen ^could^ can have any job he wanted, he would become a partner in Pablo's studio, perhaps opening his own studio later on. (6) He ^would^ will work late into the evening on beautiful but practical creations like bowls, vases, and platters. (7) He would also create more sculptures, using unusual shapes and different-colored glazes. (8) To get more ideas, he ^could^ can take classes at a local arts college. (9) The pottery work would not pay nearly as much as the accounting job, but Stephen has concluded that he might be happier making less money while doing something he loves.

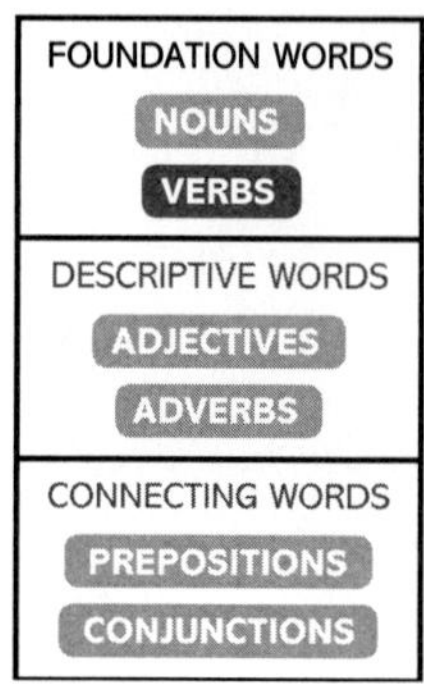

Shifts in Voice

In most sentences that we write, the subject takes some kind of action. Take a look:

> SUBJECT
>
> Judy Hernandez received the employee-of-the-month award.

These sentences are said to be in the **active voice**.

In some cases, however, the subject is acted upon:

> SUBJECT
>
> The employee-of-the-month award was received by Judy Hernandez.

These sentences are said to be in the **passive voice**. Notice that when we form the passive voice, a *be* helping verb precedes the main verb (*received* in this example).

Generally, it's a good idea to avoid the passive voice because it is less direct than the active voice. However, writers may choose the passive voice when they want to emphasize an object over a human actor or when they do not know who the human actor is:

> Some dirty plates were left in the sink.

Also, avoid shifting between the active and passive voices. Take a look at these examples:

SHIFT IN VOICE	Judy Hernandez received the employee-of-the-month award, and the sales award was also received by her.
REVISED	Judy Hernandez received the employee-of-the-month award, and she also received the sales award.

ACTIVITY 16

Edit the following passage to eliminate four shifts to the passive voice. (In other words, the entire passage should be in the active voice.)

(1) All of the Talanians contributed something to make their family reunion special. (2) Adam prepared a refreshing salad of cucumbers, lettuce, carrots, and peppers, while ^his sister, Anna, made^ a spicy appetizer of beans, garlic, and herbs ~~was made by his sister, Anna~~. (3) Adam and Anna's parents grilled fish and roasted lamb, and ^Aunt Marie prepared^ a special yogurt sauce for the lamb ~~was prepared by their Aunt Marie~~. (4) For dessert, Aunt Marie baked a fruit-and-walnut cake. (5) ^Other guests provided many^ ~~Many~~ additional desserts ~~were provided by other guests~~. (6) After the meal, the youngest Talanian, Zakar, played

his guitar while [Anna hummed] romantic tunes ~~were hummed by Anna~~. (7) Most agreed that the music was their favorite part of the event, and couples danced under the moonlight until late into the evening.

FIXING MIXED VERB ERRORS IN WHOLE PARAGRAPHS

The following activity will give you more practice with recognizing and fixing the verb problems that you have learned about so far in this chapter. You will correct these errors in whole paragraphs—a valuable skill for improving your own writing.

ACTIVITY 17

Read the following paragraphs carefully, looking for verb errors. Then, rewrite each error to fix the problem. The errors will include:

- missing *-s* endings and other subject-verb agreement problems. (See pages 455 and 466.)
- missing *-ed* endings on regular past tense verbs. (See page 458.)
- incorrect forms of irregular verbs, both present and past tense. (See pages 459 and 462.)
- some of the verb errors based on pronunciation. (See page 471.)
- inconsistent tense and/or voice. (See page 472.)

The first error in each paragraph has been edited for you.

The following paragraph has ten verb errors (including the one that has been edited for you).

1. (1) If I could magically make one change in America, it would be to have more gardens. (2) I [know] ~~knows~~ that gardens may not seem important, especially given all the pressing problems in the world. (3) However, I think that they would do a lot of good. (4) For one thing, we hear a lot about how Americans [are] is isolated from their neighbors and from the world. (5) Community gardens would allow more people, from all backgrounds, to get to know each other and work together. (6) Even if people [have] has very different views and opinions, most can appreciate the beauty of plants and the rewards of working in the soil. (7) Also, we

CONTINUED >

continue to hear bad news about the obesity problem in America. (8) (Recently, the news ~~report~~ *reported* that 66 percent of American adults ~~is~~ *are* overweight.) (9) Gardening ~~provide~~ *provides* great exercise, and it would help many people to lose weight. (10) Finally, by growing at least some of their own food, people ~~will~~ *would* reduce their reliance on packaged food that is shipped over long distances. (11) These reductions would cut down on waste and the use of fossil fuels, helping the environment. (12) Our ancestors ~~knowed~~ *knew* about the value of gardening, and now it's time for all of us to reclaim those benefits for a better future. (13) Recently, I helped to establish a garden in my own neighborhood, and I wish I would ~~of~~ *have* done it sooner. (14) Last week, we picked our first tomatoes, and *everyone enjoyed* the delicious harvest and sense of community ~~were enjoyed by everyone~~.

The following paragraph has sixteen verb errors (including the one that has been edited for you).

hoax: an attempt to trick others

2. (1) It happens every day: someone ~~get~~ *gets* a forwarded e-mail from a friend that contains a serious-sounding warning or "news" item. (2) Often, the e-mail ~~say~~ *says* "This is not a hoax!" or "Forward this to everyone you can!" (3) In many cases, such e-mails are in fact hoaxes. (4) Since e-mail ~~beginned~~ *began* to be used widely, many hoaxes have circulated. (5) One recent "news flash" ~~claim~~ *claimed* that using a cell phone while it is charging could lead to electrocution. (6) Another ~~suggest~~ *suggested* that boycotting major gasoline providers like Mobil and Exxon would bring gas prices down. (7) Investigators ~~finded~~ *found* these items—and many others—to be false. (8) If you ~~wanna~~ *want to* avoid being taken in by Internet hoaxes, you ~~does~~ *do* not have to be an expert, but you ~~gotta~~ *have to* be a critical consumer. (9) First, if an e-mail ~~shout~~ *shouts* "This is not a hoax!" it may very well be one. (10) Also, be suspicious if the e-mail ~~report~~ *reports* something that you have never heard of before or that has not been confirmed by a trusted news source. (11) Most important, if an e-mail ~~ask~~ *asks* for money, your credit card information, or any other personal information, do not respond, even if the sender

claims to be a bank or another trustworthy-sounding organization. (12) Consumers who provide personal information in these cases ~~faces~~ face financial losses or even identity theft. (13) Consumer affairs offices in many states ~~says~~ say that Internet fraud is mounting, and they ~~recommended~~ recommend that people report potential scams to the authorities. (14) Finally, if you ~~suspects~~ suspect that you have received a hoax e-mail, be courteous and do not forward it to others.

scams: deceptions, often aimed at making money

ACTIVITY 18: Teamwork

When you have finished correcting one of the paragraphs from Activity 17, get together with two or three classmates. Then, compare the errors that you found and the corrections that you made. If you corrected errors differently, discuss why this might be. If you still have questions about the verbs covered in the activity, ask your instructor.

ACTIVITY 19

Find a paper that you wrote recently but haven't turned in for a grade. Then, read the paper carefully, looking at the verbs. Put a check by any errors that you identify in these verbs. Then, correct the problems.

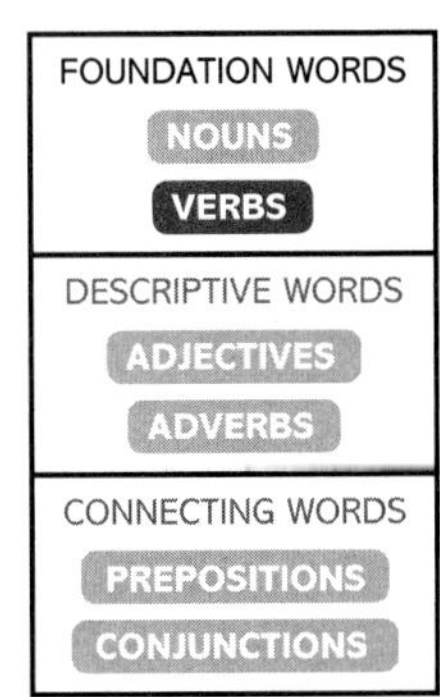

Understanding Advanced Verb Usage: Perfect Tenses

In the first part of this chapter, you studied some basic verb tenses: the simple present and the simple past. In this section, you will learn about some advanced verb tenses, called the *perfect* tenses. They are trickier to use because they show more complex time relationships.

Perfect tense verbs are made by combining a helping verb (*have*) and what is known as a **past participle**. If the helping verb is in the present tense (*have* or *has,* depending on the subject), you will get the present perfect.

As you will learn later, the present perfect is often used for actions that occurred over a duration of time as opposed to those that were completed at a specific time:

PRESENT TENSE | PAST PARTICIPLE FORM OF *PROVIDE*

As a volunteer at the Humane Society, Muriel has provided comfort to many abandoned animals.

If the helping verb is in the past tense (*had*), you will get the past perfect. As you will learn later, the past perfect is used for a past action that happened before another past action.

PRESENT TENSE

By the time she quit as a volunteer at the Humane Society, Muriel had provided comfort to many abandoned animals.

PAST PARTICIPLE FORM OF *PROVIDE*

Although perfect tenses are used much less frequently than simple tenses, you will need to master both as you advance in your college career. To achieve this goal, you will need to

1. Learn the past participle form of the following:
   - regular verbs
   - irregular verbs
2. Understand when these tenses should be used:
   - the present perfect
   - the past perfect

LEARNING THE PAST PARTICIPLE FORMS OF REGULAR VERBS

Just like verbs in the simple tenses, past participle forms can be *regular* or *irregular.* Regular past participles follow the same spelling rule as for regular past tense verbs: they end in *-ed.* Here is a chart showing just a few examples of these regular verbs.

BASE FORM	PAST TENSE	PAST PARTICIPLE (with *have* or *has*)
answer	answered	answered
call	called	called
dance	danced	danced
decide	decided	decided
look	looked	looked
walk	walked	walked
and so on . . .		

ACTIVITY 20

For each of the following sentences, write the perfect tense form of the regular verb in parentheses. The past participle should be preceded by ***have*** or ***has***.

EXAMPLE: The investigators ***have searched*** (search) for evidence.

1. The interior design company has earned (earn) many prestigious awards.
2. The administrative assistant has worked (work) for Ms. Brown for six years.
3. For the past several years, Maggie has lived (live) on a houseboat.
4. As a pilot, Katherine has learned (learn) how to predict the weather by studying clouds.
5. Researchers have discovered (discover) a link between consumption of dark chocolate and reductions in blood pressure.

LEARNING THE PAST PARTICIPLE FORMS OF IRREGULAR VERBS

Because regular past participles are spelled the same as regular past tense verbs, few students have trouble forming them. However, *irregular* past participles may require some serious memorization work. The following pre-test will help you identify the forms that you do not know so that you can focus on these in your memorization work.

CHECKING YOUR KNOWLEDGE: PRE-TEST

For each sentence pair, do the following:

- Look at the underlined verb in the first sentence.
- Then, in the second sentence, fill in the blank with the correct past participle form of this verb. Your answer should consist of only one word: the past participle. Do not add any words to the sentence or change any words in the sentence.
- When you have finished this pre-test, check your answers by using the chart on page 490.

If you want this test to work for you, do it honestly. Do not look for the answers while you're taking it.

EXAMPLE:

I often find money in the seat of my car. **By the time we finished cleaning the car, we had *found* several quarters in the seats.**

1. I am tired. I had been tired before I went on vacation.
2. She becomes angry easily. Since she was laid off, Cara has become angry.

CONTINUED >

For online practice with regular past participles, visit this book's Web site at bedfordstmartins .com/steppingstones.

3. The play begins at 7. The play has begun.
4. The snake bites. Before the hiker knew it, the snake had bit/bitten his friend.
5. The wind blows loudly. The wind has blown loudly all night.
6. I break lots of earrings. I have broken several pairs of earrings.
7. I bring the car to the garage. I had brought the car in before the garage opened.
8. Katy builds birdhouses. Katy has built fifteen birdhouses.
9. Our parents buy many gifts. Our parents have bought many gifts over the years.
10. The baby catches colds. The baby has caught many colds this winter.
11. I choose ice cream over cake. I had chosen ice cream before you persuaded me not to.
12. Gerald comes here often. Gerald has come here often.
13. This gym costs a lot. This gym membership has cost a lot over the years.
14. Rick dives for the team. Rick has dived for the team for six months.
15. Ava does the little girl's hair. By the time Joe arrived, Ava had done his daughter's hair.
16. Ming draws pictures of the lake. Ming has drawn various pictures of the lake.
17. I drink tea for breakfast. I have drunk tea since I was a little girl.
18. Sal drives to work. Sal had driven to work before subway service started.
19. The kids eat pizza. By the time I got home, the kids had eaten all of the pizza.
20. Leaves fall from the trees. Leaves have fallen all month.
21. My husband feeds the children. My husband has fed the children all week.
22. Leonid feels sick. Leonid has felt sick since he ate that hamburger.
23. The boys fight. The boys have fought every day.
24. I find my car key whenever I lose it. I had found my car key by the time Bill arrived with a spare.
25. I fly to Ohio regularly. I have flown to Ohio many times to see family.
26. The pond freezes at night. The pond has frozen and thawed three times this winter.
27. Marianne gets cable. Marianne has gotten/got cable for years.
28. Our friendship gives me joy. Our friendship has given me much joy.
29. You go to the movies often. You had gone to the movies by the time I arrived.
30. Avram grows huge squash. Avram has grown many types of squash in his garden.
31. Lou has a headache. Lou has had a headache all week.
32. We hear rumors. We have heard a number of rumors.
33. Tina hides the chocolate. Tina had hidden the chocolate before the kids got home.
34. Miguel holds the baby. Miguel has held the baby all evening.

35. Bob hurts his arm regularly.	Bob has ___hurt___ his arm four times since he started pitching.
36. You keep secrets.	You have ___kept___ many secrets.
37. I know Shorelle.	I have ___known___ Shorelle since we were children.
38. Margo lays her glasses on the table.	Margo has ___laid___ her glasses on this table for years.
39. Our boss leads the team.	Our boss had ___led___ the team before he was fired.
40. We leave good tips.	We have always ___left___ good tips at this restaurant.
41. I let the dogs out.	I have ___let___ the dogs out three times today.
42. Josie lies in bed until noon.	Josie has ___lain___ in bed all day.
43. Mark lights the birthday candles.	Mark has ___lit___ all of the birthday candles.
44. The Rockets lose regularly.	The Rockets have ___lost___ every game.
45. Asad makes dinner.	By the time we arrived, Asad had ___made___ dinner.
46. I mean to write.	Our relationship has ___meant___ a lot to me.
47. The lovers meet at the bridge.	The lovers have ___met___ at the bridge every night.
48. We pay Ross for his work.	We had ___paid___ Ross by the time his rent was due.
49. We put out the trash.	For a year, we have ___put___ out the trash on Tuesdays.
50. Felicia quits unhealthy habits.	By her thirtieth birthday, Felicia had ___quit___ smoking.
51. The children read a lot.	The children have ___read___ ten books.
52. I ride horses.	I have ___ridden___ horses all my life.
53. My ears ring after I swim.	My ears have ___rung___ since I swam this morning.
54. The sun rises at 6 now.	The sun has ___risen___ earlier and earlier every day.
55. Alicia runs on the track team.	Alicia has ___run___ track since she was in grade school.
56. You say you don't like fish.	You have ___said___ several times that you don't like fish.
57. Jan sees Marco daily.	Jan has ___seen___ Marco every day this week.
58. I seek friendship.	I had ___sought___ your friendship long before you knew me.
59. Horace sells cars.	Horace has ___sold___ cars since he graduated from high school.
60. We send the kids home.	By the start of the storm, we had ___sent___ the kids home.
61. I set the plates down gently.	I have ___set___ the table with care.
62. The boy shakes the soda bottle.	The boy has ___shaken___ every soda bottle here.
63. You show courage.	You have ___shown___ courage in every act.
64. I shrink all my T-shirts.	The T-shirt had ___shrunk___ by the time I opened the drier door.
65. Tia shuts the door gently.	Tia has ___shut___ the door gently every time.
66. Jorge sings with feeling.	Jorge has ___sung___ the same song for years.
67. Tom's boat always sinks.	Tom's boat has ___sunk___ every time we go fishing.
68. The travelers sit patiently.	The travelers have ___sat___ in the bus terminal for hours.

CONTINUED >

69. The dog sleeps on the floor. The dog has ___slept___ on the floor since we kicked him out of our bed.

70. I speak honestly. I had ___spoken___ to Bob about the problem before he quit.

71. Boris spends money freely. Boris has ___spent___ his whole paycheck.

72. Ideas spring from Alex's mind. Many ideas have ___sprung___ from Alex's fertile mind.

73. Caitlin stands by the fire. Caitlin has ___stood___ by the fire for a long time.

74. Those kids steal cars. Those kids had ___stolen___ my car long before I got home.

75. Mike sticks notes on my door. Mike has ___stuck___ twelve notes on my door this month.

76. The bees sting the children. The bees have ___stung___ every child in this camp.

77. The soldiers strike with force. The soldiers have ___struck/stricken___ the enemy base.

78. Yvette swims laps daily. Yvette has ___swum___ fifty laps already today.

79. The children take the bus. The children have ___taken___ the bus since first grade.

80. Corey teaches painting. Corey has ___taught___ painting for twenty years.

81. Mia tears her pants often. Mia has ___torn___ her pants three times since working at the cactus nursery.

82. I tell the truth. I had ___told___ the truth before you asked me to.

83. You think Paul is mistaken. You have ___thought___ about this a long time.

84. Jan throws horseshoes. Jan has ___thrown___ horseshoes every summer.

85. We understand the problem. We have ___understood___ the problem for months.

86. I wake up before anyone else. I have ___waked/woken___ early for all of my life.

87. Jason wears strong cologne. Jason has ___worn___ that cologne for too long.

88. The Red Sox win often. The Red Sox had ___won___ by the time we turned on the TV.

89. Michelle writes long e-mails. Michelle has ___written___ many long e-mails.

As you check your work on the pre-test against the following chart, put a check mark beside each irregular verb for which you formed the past participle incorrectly.

Irregular Verbs

BASE FORM	PAST TENSE FORM	PAST PARTICIPLE FORM
☐ be	was / were	been
☐ become	became	become
☐ begin	began	begun
☐ bite	bit	bitten, bit
☐ blow	blew	blown
☐ break	broke	broken

For online practice with irregular past participles, visit this book's Web site at **bedfordstmartins .com/steppingstones**.

BASE FORM	PAST TENSE FORM	PAST PARTICIPLE FORM
☐ bring	brought	brought
☐ build	built	built
☐ buy	bought	bought
☐ catch	caught	caught
☐ choose	chose	chosen
☐ come	came	come
☐ cost	cost	cost
☐ dive	dived, dove	dived
☐ do	did	done
☐ draw	drew	drawn
☐ drink	drank	drunk
☐ drive	drove	driven
☐ eat	ate	eaten
☐ fall	fell	fallen
☐ feed	fed	fed
☐ feel	felt	felt
☐ fight	fought	fought
☐ find	found	found
☐ fly	flew	flown
☐ freeze	froze	frozen
☐ get	got	gotten, got
☐ give	gave	given
☐ go	went	gone
☐ grow	grew	grown
☐ have	had	had
☐ hear	heard	heard
☐ hide	hid	hidden
☐ hold	held	held
☐ hurt	hurt	hurt
☐ keep	kept	kept
☐ know	knew	known
☐ lay (*to put down*)	laid	laid
☐ lead	led	led

CONTINUED >

BASE FORM	PAST TENSE FORM	PAST PARTICIPLE FORM
☐ leave	left	left
☐ let	let	let
☐ lie (*to recline*)	lay	lain
☐ light	lit	lit
☐ lose	lost	lost
☐ make	made	made
☐ mean	meant	meant
☐ meet	met	met
☐ pay	paid	paid
☐ put	put	put
☐ quit	quit	quit
☐ read	read	read
☐ ride	rode	ridden
☐ ring	rang	rung
☐ rise	rose	risen
☐ run	ran	run
☐ say	said	said
☐ see	saw	seen
☐ seek	sought	sought
☐ sell	sold	sold
☐ send	sent	sent
☐ set	set	set
☐ shake	shook	shaken
☐ show	showed	shown
☐ shrink	shrank	shrunk
☐ shut	shut	shut
☐ sing	sang	sung
☐ sink	sank	sunk
☐ sit	sat	sat
☐ sleep	slept	slept
☐ speak	spoke	spoken
☐ spend	spent	spent
☐ spring	sprang	sprung

BASE FORM	PAST TENSE FORM	PAST PARTICIPLE FORM
☐ stand	stood	stood
☐ steal	stole	stolen
☐ stick	stuck	stuck
☐ sting	stung	stung
☐ strike	struck	struck, stricken
☐ swim	swam	swum
☐ take	took	taken
☐ teach	taught	taught
☐ tear	tore	torn
☐ tell	told	told
☐ think	thought	thought
☐ throw	threw	thrown
☐ understand	understood	understood
☐ wake	woke, waked	woken, waked
☐ wear	wore	worn
☐ win	won	won
☐ write	wrote	written

Memorizing Irregular Past Participles

Once you have identified the irregular past participles that you do not know, it's time to use some memorization strategies to help the correct forms "stick" in your mind. If you practiced these strategies to learn irregular past tense verbs (see page 464), you already know how fun and effective they can be. Remember that they work best in combination, so plan to use as many of them as possible.

Priority Lists. Construct and practice your priority list the same way that you did for the irregular past tense verbs. If you've forgotten how to do this, look back at page 464 for instructions.

Visual Aids. If a verb is irregular in *both* the past tense and the past participle, write both of these forms on the back of your **flash card** for that verb. This way, you will get in the habit of pronouncing both forms together.

Likewise, write *both* the irregular past tense and past participle forms on each **sticky note**. Each time you see a sticky note in your environment, pause to pronounce and spell both forms out loud to yourself so that your brain records each letter.

Auditory Aids. For some of the irregular past participles that you find especially challenging, create a **rhyme**. For example, *The party **had begun**, and we were having **fun**.*

Tactile Aids. Make any additional **letter blocks** that you will need to spell the irregular past participles. Practice with these letter blocks the same way that you did for the irregular past tense verbs. If you've forgotten how to do this, look back at page 465 for instructions.

UNDERSTANDING WHEN TO USE THE PRESENT PERFECT

To understand when to use the present perfect, you should do two things:

1. Compare it with the simple past tense.
2. Start recognizing "time tags."

A "time tag" is a word or phrase that shows a time frame for an action. Basically, there are two types of time frames:

- a specific point in time (*in 2001, at four o'clock, last month, yesterday*)
- a duration of time (*over the years, until now, since then, for some time*)

In the following sentences, you will see that the *simple past tense* is usually connected with a specific point in time; on the other hand, the *present perfect* is usually connected with a duration of time. In the following examples, the time tags are underlined.

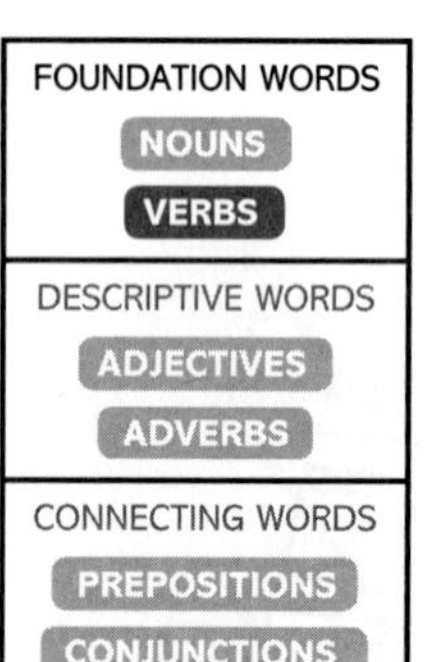

SIMPLE PAST

SPECIFIC POINT IN TIME Josephine and Ricardo met in 2004.

PRESENT PERFECT

DURATION OF TIME Josephine and Ricardo have been a couple for several years.

In the first sentence, the action was completed at a specific point in time: the meeting began and ended in 2004. In the second sentence, the action began in the past but is *ongoing:* Josephine and Ricardo are *still* a couple. Look at these additional examples:

SIMPLE PAST

SPECIFIC POINT IN TIME On Thursday, the judge dismissed three cases.

PRESENT PERFECT

DURATION OF TIME So far this week, the judge has dismissed three cases.

In the first sentence, the action took place at a specific point in time: the cases were dismissed on Thursday. In the second sentence, the action was completed sometime during the week, but we don't know exactly when: the cases were dismissed at an unspecified point in time.

From the examples above, we can identify two main uses of the present perfect tense:

1. to show an action that began in the past but is ongoing:

   Josephine and Ricardo have been a couple for several years.

   (They continue to be a couple.)

2. to show an action that was completed at an unspecified point in time:

   So far this week, the judge has dismissed three cases.

   (We don't know exactly when.)

Note that time tags are often left out when the time frame is unknown or already clear:

The judge has dismissed three cases.

The following chart will help you remember some time tags that show duration. Often, you will find these words and phrases used with the present perfect.

Power Tip
The simple past tense is sometimes used to refer to actions that occurred over a duration of time, but only if we are certain that those actions are *fully completed.* For example: *Vladimir* ***took*** *piano lessons for ten years.*

Time Tags That Show Duration

PREPOSITIONAL PHRASES		
For . . .	**Over . . .**	**Since . . .**
For some time . . .	Over several weeks . . .	Since this morning . . .
For several weeks . . .	Over a long period of time . . .	Since last week . . .
For many years . . .	Over the course of my life . . .	Since 1994 . . .
For days . . .	Over the last few minutes . . .	Since I was four . . .
For as long as I can remember . . .	Over and over again . . .	Since yesterday . . .
ADVERBS AND ADVERBIAL PHRASES		
lately		
recently		
already	**Douglas has already accepted an athletic scholarship.**	
often		
repeatedly	**The parole officer has repeatedly warned his client.**	
frequently		
time and time again		
ever	**The most I have ever paid for a cell phone is $50.**	
never		
not yet	**They have not yet signed the papers.**	

ACTIVITY 21

For each pair of sentences below, do the following:

- Underline the time tag in each sentence.
- Above each time tag, write ***P*** for point in time or ***D*** for duration of time.
- In each blank, write the correct form of the verb, either the simple past tense or the present perfect.

EXAMPLE:

Verb: earn

P
a. Last year, our company ___earned___ $60,000.

D
b. Over the years, our company ___has earned___ $60,000.

1. **Verb:** wreck

   P
   a. Two weeks ago, David ___wrecked___ his car.

   D
   b. Over the past six months, David ___has wrecked___ his car two times.

2. **Verb:** travel

   D
   a. Since 1999, Katy ___has traveled___ to eight different states.

   P
   b. In 1999, Katy ___traveled___ to eight different states.

3. **Verb:** work

   P
   a. In 2007, Jennifer ___worked___ for her father.

   D
   b. For the past few years, Jennifer ___has worked___ for her father.

4. **Verb:** spend

   D
   a. Since the start of the year, our department ___has spent___ 70 percent of the yearly furniture budget.

   P
   b. In one month, our department ___spent___ 70 percent of the yearly furniture budget.

5. **Verb:** collect

   D
   a. Recently, Mother ___has collected___ skunk figurines.

   P
   b. During her vacation, Mother ___collected___ skunk figurines.

For online practice with present perfect tense, visit this book's Web site at **bedfordstmartins .com/steppingstones**.

FOUNDATION WORDS
NOUNS
VERBS
DESCRIPTIVE WORDS
ADJECTIVES
ADVERBS
CONNECTING WORDS
PREPOSITIONS
CONJUNCTIONS

UNDERSTANDING WHEN TO USE THE PAST PERFECT

The past perfect is used to show a *past action* that happened before *another past action.* One of these actions will be in the simple past tense; the other will be in the past perfect (with a past participle). Take a look:

SIMPLE PAST — PAST PERFECT

By the time we arrived, the party had already begun.

PAST PERFECT — SIMPLE PAST

The rescuers had searched for forty-eight hours by the time they found the survivors.

The following time line shows when these actions occurred:

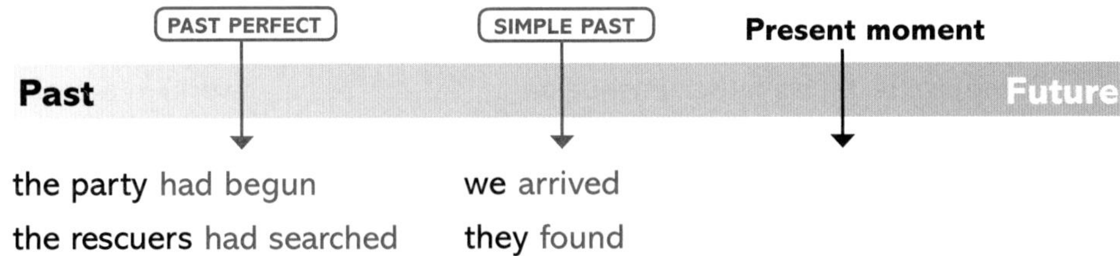

Teaching Tip
Have students draw time lines for the sentences in Activity 22 or for any other sentences using the past perfect.

ACTIVITY 22

For each of the following sentences, write the correct verb forms in the spaces provided. One verb will be in the simple past tense; the other will be in the past perfect.

EXAMPLE: We <u>had extinguished</u> (extinguish) the fire before the fire truck <u>showed</u> (show) up.

1. By the time we <u>arrived</u> (arrive) at the potluck dinner, all the fried chicken <u>had disappeared</u> (disappear).
2. We <u>performed</u> (perform) poorly on the exam because we <u>had spent</u> (spend) the previous evening at a party.
3. We <u>had seen</u> (see) Beck in concert before last night's show, but his latest performance <u>exceeded</u> (exceed) all the others.
4. Because he <u>had studied</u> (study) Spanish in college, Julian <u>communicated</u> (communicate) well with the people he met in Mexico.
5. Looters <u>had stolen</u> (steal) nearly all the electronics by the time police <u>reached</u> (reach) the scene.

USING PERFECT TENSES IN WHOLE PARAGRAPHS

The following activity will give you practice using perfect tenses (and other verb forms) in whole paragraphs—a valuable skill for your own writing.

For online practice with past perfect tense, visit this book's Web site at **bedfordstmartins .com/steppingstones**.

Teaching Tip
For test items on the various verb issues covered in this chapter, see the *Testing Tool Kit* CD available with this book.

ACTIVITY 23

In the following paragraphs, fill in each blank with the correct form of the verb in parentheses, depending on the meaning of the sentence. You will need to choose among

- the simple present tense,
- the simple past tense,
- the present perfect tense, or
- the past perfect tense.

The first blank in each paragraph has been filled in for you.

1. (1) In 1922, my grandfather was born into poverty, and the experience **has shaped** (shape) his entire life. (2) At the time of Grandpa's birth, his father, Pasquale, had worked (work) in a coal mine for many years. (3) Pasquale didn't make much money in the mine, so eventually he got (get) a job on a construction crew. (4) He had been (be) on the crew for about seven years when the Depression, a serious economic downturn, occurred. (5) Many people, including Pasquale, lost (lose) their jobs. (6) Pasquale could not pay the rent, and so the landlord threw (throw) the family's belongings out on the street while my grandfather and his sisters watched. (7) After the family had moved (move) to a less expensive place, my grandfather got a job selling newspapers, while Pasquale looked for work. (8) Also, Grandpa helped (help) his mother, Angela, grow a garden and pick berries, mushrooms, and dandelion greens. (9) The family tried (try) not to buy much food at the store. (10) Also, to save money, my grandfather and everyone in his family kept (keep) everything they might reuse, from old clothes to soap pieces to string. (11) To this day, my grandfather saves (save) almost everything. (12) Over time, he has passed (pass) some of these habits on to me and my daughter, saying, "Now you need to save things to help the environment." (13) For many years, I have heard (hear) my grandfather's stories, but they never cease to move me.

2. (1) For many years, social scientists **have asked** (ask) an intriguing question: what makes people successful learners? (2) Over time, several researchers have explored (explore) this question, but

they have found (find) specific answers only recently. (3) In 2002, Richard B. Gunderman, M.D., published (publish) a paper on this topic, based on observations about doctors-in-training. (4) His advice is (be) relevant to just about anyone who wants to succeed or help others to succeed. (5) First, learners do (do) best with tasks that are challenging but not so difficult that they seem unachievable. (6) In other words, learners need (need) to push themselves, but not so much that they give up. (7) Second, they need (need) to be prepared, getting study resources and other advice in advance of challenging learning situations. (8) Over the long term, students who have had (have) the most support tend to do the best. (9) Additionally, learners who see (see) themselves as being responsible for their own success do better than those who believe that others are in control. (10) Through years of experience, educators have discovered (discover) that students can take more responsibility for their learning by "thinking about their thinking." (11) For example, they can ask, "Why don't I understand this task? What might I do to master it? What kind of help do I need to seek?" (12) In 2008, some colleges tried out these strategies with new students who had struggled (struggle) in high school. (13) By the time the students had completed (complete) the program, they reported greater confidence and an improvement in their grades.

ACTIVITY 24: Teamwork

When you have filled in all of the blanks for one of the paragraphs from Activity 23, get together with two or three classmates. Then, compare the answers that you provided. If you provided different answers in any cases, discuss why this might be. If you still have questions about perfect tenses, ask your instructor.

ACTIVITY 25

Find a paper that you wrote recently but haven't turned in for a grade. Then, read the paper carefully, looking at all the verbs. Can you see places where the perfect tenses should be used but are not? If so, decide in each case whether the present perfect or past perfect tense should be used, and edit your work accordingly.

Bringing It All Together

In this chapter, you have learned how verbs change form to express different times. You have also learned about some common verb errors. Check off each of the following statements that you understand. For any that you do not understand, review the appropriate pages in this chapter.

- ☐ When we speak, we sometimes use **nonstandard** English, which does not follow the rules of written academic English. However, as a college writer, you should commit to learning and using **standard** English, which will help you achieve academic success and allow you to communicate more effectively in your personal and professional lives. (See page 452.)
- ☐ The **simple present tense** is used for regular actions, for facts, and for actions happening right now. Often, verb errors in the present tense occur because of the absence or unnecessary addition of an *-s* ending. (See page 455.)
- ☐ Be aware of the irregular present tense verbs *be, have,* and *do,* which follow different spelling rules from regular verbs. (See page 456.)
- ☐ The **simple past tense** is used for actions completed in the past. All regular past tense verbs end in *-ed.* Often, verb errors in the regular past tense occur because we forget to add the *-ed* ending. (See page 458.)
- ☐ Many past tense verbs have an "irregular" form; that is, they are not spelled with an *-ed* ending. You can use certain memorization strategies to help these irregular forms "stick" in your mind. (See page 464.)
- ☐ Some problems that can occur when forming the present and past tenses include subject-verb agreement errors, errors based on pronunciation, and shifts in verb tense and voice. (See pages 466, 471, and 472.)
- ☐ **Perfect tenses** are made by combining a **helping verb** (*have*) and a **past participle**. Just like verbs in the simple tenses, past participle forms can be regular or irregular. The regular forms end in *-ed* (see page 486), while the irregular forms use different spellings and have to be memorized. You can use certain memorization strategies to help these irregular forms "stick" in your mind. (See page 493.)
- ☐ The **present perfect tense** is used to show (1) an action that began in the past but is ongoing or (2) an action completed at an unspecified point in time. Certain words known as "time tags" help us understand when the actions took place. (See page 494.)
- ☐ The **past perfect** is used to show a past action that happened before another past action. One action will be in the simple past tense; the other will be in the past perfect (with a past participle). (See page 497.)

Chapter 17

Using Pronouns Correctly

Pronouns (noun substitutes) take different forms. You'll learn these forms—and how to avoid errors in them—in this chapter.

SUBJECT OBJECT

I study with him.

POSSESSIVE

His grades are improving.

OVERVIEW OF THIS CHAPTER

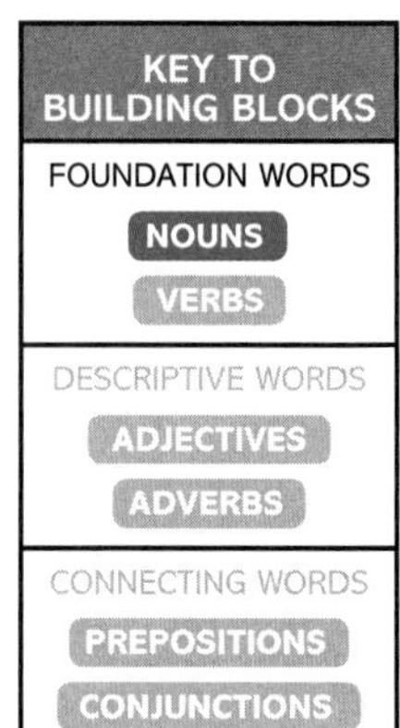

Understanding Pronoun Usage

A **pronoun** is a word that takes the place of a noun (a person, place, or thing):

~~Alonzo~~ enjoys ~~espresso~~.

He enjoys it.

PRONOUN PRONOUN

Often, a pronoun refers back to (renames) a specific noun that has already been mentioned:

Alonzo enjoys espresso. It is his favorite drink.

Pronouns can also replace and refer to *noun phrases* (a noun plus descriptive words or a prepositional phrase). Take a look:

The whole class liked the idea of a take-home exam.

Everybody liked that.

PRONOUN PRONOUN

Terminology Tip

As you learned in Chapter 10, a pronoun is a type of noun that functions as a noun substitute. In English grammar, the noun that a pronoun refers back to is known as an *antecedent*.

Power Tip

In the sentence examples in this chapter, not all nouns are in blue. Instead, the blue highlighting is used for pronouns and for the words that pronouns replace.

TYPES OF PRONOUNS

The goal of this chapter is to help you avoid common pronoun errors. To achieve this goal, we will focus on three major groups of pronouns:

1. specific and general pronouns
2. subject and object pronouns
3. possessive pronouns

Specific versus General Pronouns

Pronouns can be used to identify both specific people and things and general people and things. Look at the examples in the following chart:

SPECIFIC		GENERAL	
People	**Things**	**People**	**Things**
I	it	anybody	anything
you	this	anyone	everything
he	that	everybody	nothing
she	they	everyone	one
we	these	no one	something
they	those	nobody	
		one	
		somebody	
		someone	

Teaching Tip
If your students haven't worked through Chapter 10, where pronouns were introduced, you might want to refer them to it at this time.

Later, we will explore two basic guidelines for using these pronouns in academic writing:

1. Pronouns that identify specific people and things can help your academic writing.
2. Pronouns that identify general people and things can sometimes weaken your academic writing.

ACTIVITY 1

In each of the following sentences, underline the pronoun(s). Then, label the pronouns as follows:

- Write ***SP*** above the pronouns that refer to specific people.
- Write ***ST*** above the pronouns that refer to specific things.
- Write ***GP*** above the pronouns that refer to general people.
- Write ***GT*** above the pronouns that refer to general things.

For online practice with pronouns, visit this book's Web site at **bedfordstmartins .com/steppingstones**.

ST
EXAMPLE: Many citizens want to make a difference; this is a natural desire.

GT
1. Malika wanted to do something to help people in need.

SP
2. She wasn't sure what deed would have the most impact.

SP
3. Therefore, she asked for advice from several people, but the best advice

ST GT GT
came from a poster on poverty; it read, "Just do something . . . anything."

SP
4. Malika and three friends organized a food drive at school, and they collected

many boxes of canned goods and other foods.

GP
5. Everyone at the local homeless shelter was pleased when Malika delivered

the donations.

ACTIVITY 2: Teamwork

Working with two or three classmates, pick a reading from Part 3 of this book. Working separately, see how many specific and general pronouns each of you can circle in the reading in three minutes. When time is up, work together to label the pronouns as identifying specific people, specific things, general people, or general things.

Subject versus Object Pronouns

Specific pronouns can take subject or object forms, depending on their role in the sentence. Subject pronouns act as the subject of the sentence: who or what the sentence is about. Look at these examples:

SUBJECT	Marianne **fears horses.**
SUBJECT PRONOUN (REPLACES *MARIANNE*)	She **fears horses.**

Objects receive the action of a verb:

OBJECT	**A horse kicked** Marianne.
OBJECT PRONOUN (REPLACES *MARIANNE*)	**A horse kicked** her.

In these examples, *Marianne* and *her* receive the action of *kicked.* Notice that the object pronoun has a different form from the subject pronoun: *her* instead of *she.*

Power Tip
Note that the pronouns *she/her* and *he/him* identify someone as male or female; *she* and *her* can refer only to females, and *he* and *him* can refer only to males.

Objects can also complete prepositional phrases:

OBJECT PRONOUN

The snoring man was behind me.

PREPOSITIONAL PHRASE (UNDERLINED)

For more on prepositions and prepositional phrases, see Chapter 11, page 281.

Teaching Tip
Have students pick paired subject/object pronouns (such as *I/me* and *we/us*), and ask them to use each word in the pair in a different sentence. (In other words, one sentence will have a pronoun subject, and the other will have a pronoun object.) Then, have students check each other's work to see that they've used the subject and object forms correctly.

Subject and Object Pronouns

PEOPLE			THINGS		
Subject		**Object**	**Subject**		**Object**
I	→	me	it	→	it
we	→	us	this	→	this
you	→	you	that	→	that
he/she	→	him/her	they	→	them
they	→	them	these	→	them
who	→	whom	those	→	them

ACTIVITY 3

In each of the following sentences, label the underlined pronouns as ***S*** for subject pronoun or ***O*** for object pronoun.

EXAMPLE: Small children often challenge us. (O)

1. We (S) think that we (S) are in control, but sometimes our children seem to control us (O).
2. I (S) want my three-year-old, Celia, to learn independence, but she (S) has other ideas.
3. When I (S) leave her (O) at daycare, she (S) cries and says she (S) wants to go to work with me (O).
4. The daycare providers jiggle toys and try to distract Celia when I (S) leave, and I (S) am grateful to them (O) for helping.
5. I (S) know that Celia will adjust eventually, but her crying still upsets me (O).

ACTIVITY 4

In each sentence below, circle the correct subject or object form of the pronoun in parentheses.

EXAMPLE: **Recently, (I / me) moved to a new town, and (I / me) would like to meet more people.**

1. It would be nice to meet people to date, but (I / me) would like to make friends, too.
2. My sister tells (I / me) to talk to more people at work and school, but I am shy.
3. I met a nice person, Randi, at school, and (she / her) is going to study with (I / me) on Friday.
4. I would also like to invite (she / her) to the movies since (we / us) both like the same kinds of films.
5. Also, some co-workers have asked (I / me) to go for walks with (they / them) at lunch; (that / them) would be a great way for me to stay in shape and get to know new people.

ACTIVITY 5: Teamwork

Working with two or three classmates, pick a reading from Part Three of this book. Working separately, see how many subject and object pronouns each of you can circle in the reading in three minutes. When time is up, work together to label the pronouns as subject versus object.

Possessive Pronouns

Possessive pronouns (*my, mine, ours, yours,* and so on) show ownership. Take a look at the following examples (the possessive pronouns are in blue):

> That is my car. That car is mine.
>
> Our house is old and drafty, but yours is warm.
>
> The shark flashed its sharp teeth.

Possessive Forms of Specific Pronouns

SUBJECT PRONOUNS	POSSESSIVE FORMS
I	my, mine
we	our, ours
you	your, yours
he	his
she	her, hers
it	its
they	their, theirs

Power Tip
You do not need to add an apostrophe (') to show possession when you use a possessive pronoun.
Incorrect: This cabin is your's; our's is across the lake.
Revised: This cabin is yours; ours is across the lake.

ACTIVITY 6

In each of the following sentences, underline the possessive pronoun(s).

EXAMPLE: **Last week, our neighborhood had a huge yard sale to benefit a local elementary school.**

1. My father brought his old baseball gloves and other sports equipment from our garage.
2. My mother brought some of her old jewelry and a television that we don't use anymore.
3. I contributed some of my old toys, including a clown that laughs when a string is pulled in its back.
4. "You are going to scare someone with that old thing," my mom said, shaking her head.
5. However, one of our neighbors paid five dollars for this treasure.

WHY WE USE PRONOUNS

We use pronouns for convenience, so that we do not have to repeat a noun or a noun phrase over and over. Take a look at the following passage, in which two noun phrases are repeated in every sentence:

My cousin Angel from Puerto Rico bought a classic 1968 Ford Mustang. My cousin Angel from Puerto Rico won the classic 1968 Ford Mustang on eBay. When the classic 1968 Ford Mustang arrived by ship, my cousin Angel from Puerto Rico inspected the classic 1968 Ford Mustang. My cousin Angel from Puerto Rico discovered that the classic 1968 Ford Mustang was not the classic 1968 Ford Mustang shown on eBay. My cousin Angel from Puerto Rico called the seller about the classic 1968 Ford Mustang and learned that the wrong classic 1968 Ford Mustang had been shipped. My cousin Angel from Puerto Rico returned the classic 1968 Ford Mustang and waited for the right classic 1968 Ford Mustang to be shipped.

Of course, most people would substitute single-word nouns (*Angel, Mustang*) and shorter noun phrases (*my cousin, the car*) for the longer noun phrases:

My cousin Angel from Puerto Rico bought a classic 1968 Ford Mustang. My cousin won the car on eBay. When the Mustang arrived by ship, Angel inspected the car. Angel discovered that the car was not the Mustang shown on eBay. Angel called the seller about the Mustang and learned that the wrong car had been shipped. My cousin returned the car and waited for the right Mustang to be shipped.

This version is more efficient, but it still sounds wordy and repetitive. The most efficient way to communicate this information is to replace some of the nouns and noun phrases with pronouns (*he, it,* and so on):

My cousin Angel from Puerto Rico bought a classic 1968 Ford Mustang. He won it on eBay. When the car arrived by ship, Angel inspected it. He discovered that it was not the Mustang shown on eBay. He called the seller about this and learned that the wrong car had been shipped. Angel returned the Mustang and waited for the right one to be shipped.

In this version, the writer has achieved a nice balance of nouns and pronouns to make the information smoother and easier to digest.

In conversation, we use pronouns as a shortcut to communicate quickly and efficiently. Pronouns are common in academic writing, too; however, in the writing that we do for college, we must use pronouns with extra care, making sure to balance the need for efficiency with the need for *clarity* at all times.

Avoiding Common Pronoun Problems

The final passage in the previous section shows how an experienced writer uses pronouns to identify specific people and things. When used with care, these pronouns can make your academic writing clear and efficient.

Be aware, however, that even specific pronouns, which are friends of the academic writer, can cause problems if used carelessly. The following sections discuss common problems connected with pronouns.

UNCLEAR REFERENCE

You have learned that a pronoun refers to a noun—a specific person, place, or thing. However, if we use pronouns carelessly, the reference (what the pronoun refers to) may not be 100 percent clear to our reader. In a conversation, we can always ask for or provide clarification if a pronoun does not make sense. Take a look:

Vince: I had a blind date with a girl named Kirsten on Saturday night. I took her to dinner at a new restaurant. It was a disaster.

Earl: Yeah, I went on a blind date once, and it was a disaster too.

Vince: No, I mean the restaurant was a disaster. The service was slow. It took almost forty minutes to get our food, and it was cold.

Earl: What about Kirsten?

Vince: She's awesome. We had two margaritas while waiting for dinner and had a deep conversation. We're going out again this weekend.

Teaching Tip
As a class, listen to a podcast, a radio news broadcast, or other programming. Have students write down pronouns as they are used. Can they identify any pronouns that seem unclear?

Here, the pronoun *it* has an unclear reference: it might refer to *the date* or to *the restaurant*. When Earl gets confused, Vince is able to clarify that the pronoun refers to *the restaurant*. In our conversations, this sort of clarification happens all the time.

However, when we use unclear pronouns in our writing, the reader may not have the opportunity to ask for clarification. Read the following passage and see how difficult it is to follow the writer's ideas:

> The hardest thing I ever had to do was put my dog Chester to sleep. To begin with, making the decision to end Chester's life was tough. For a long time, I was in denial about it. They told me to learn more about this. I read a book on it and even saw a documentary on that. It helped me understand our responsibility to them. She explained that allowing it to suffer should not be an option. We decided to make an appointment with the vet to discuss this. This was the first step in coming to terms with it.

This passage is confusing because most of the pronouns have an unclear reference: we don't know *exactly* what they mean. Take a look:

> . . . in denial about it (In denial about what, exactly?)
> . . . They told me (Who told, exactly?)
> . . . to learn more about this (About what, exactly?)
> . . . I read a book on it (A book on what, exactly?)
> . . . saw a documentary on that (A documentary on what, exactly?)
> . . . It helped me understand (What helped, exactly?)
> . . . our responsibility to them (Our responsibility to whom, exactly?)
> . . . She explained (Who explained, exactly?)
> . . . allowing it to suffer (Allowing what to suffer, exactly?)
> . . . We decided (Who decided, exactly?)
> . . . to discuss this (To discuss what, exactly?)
> . . . This was the first step (What was the first step, exactly?)
> . . . in coming to terms with it (Coming to terms with what, exactly?)

The reader should not have to pause to guess about what a pronoun means. If you suspect that a pronoun in your writing is unclear, replace it with a noun or noun phrase that clarifies your meaning. Compare the following version of the passage to its original:

euthanasia: ending the life of a very ill creature

The hardest thing I ever had to do was put my dog Chester to sleep. To begin with, making the decision to end Chester's life was tough. For a long time, I was in denial about Chester's terminal condition. My family told me to learn more about cancer in animals. I read a book on cancer in dogs and even saw a documentary on pet euthanasia. The film helped me understand our responsibility to our terminally ill pets. The author of the book explained that allowing a pet to suffer should not be an option. My family and I decided to make an appointment with the vet to discuss Chester's situation. Making this appointment was the first step in coming to terms with my responsibility to Chester.

ACTIVITY 7

For the paragraph below, do the following:

- Underline any pronouns that have an unclear reference.
- Using your imagination, rewrite the paragraph, adding more specific words in place of the unclear pronouns. Answers will vary.

the phone
(1) Late on Friday, it rang in the dark house. (2) Mark picked it up
a voice
and heard silence at first. (3) Then, it asked, "Is this Mark Ranco?"
Mark
(4) He replied, "Who wants to know?" (5) The caller laughed in an
Mark
evil-sounding way. (6) He looked out the window, beginning to feel that

a mysterious-looking van
someone might be watching the house. (7) Then, he saw ~~it~~ parked
The sight of the van Mark
outside. (8) ~~This~~ made him upset. (9) ~~He~~ asked the caller, "Who are you?"
The caller
(10) ~~He~~ replied, "I'm from Tri-Cities Motors, and I understand that it's your birthday. (11) I'm in the van out front, and I have a new motorcycle
Mark
for you—a gift from your Grandma Marie." (12) ~~He~~ still felt suspicious,
the driver taking a shiny red motorcycle out of the van
until he stepped outside and saw ~~it~~.

OVERUSE OF *YOU*

In conversation, we often use the pronoun *you* to mean "people in general." In academic writing, however, be careful when using *you.* In the following passage, notice that the writer begins by narrating a personal experience, using the pronouns *I, me,* and *my* (see the words highlighted in yellow). Then, unexpectedly, she shifts to the pronouns *you* and *your* to refer to people in general (see the words highlighted in blue).

> Doing research for my history assignment was easier than I had expected. First, I found all the materials that I needed online. For instance, the librarian showed me how to use a database called LexisNexis, which contains thousands of articles and documents. All you have to do is type in keywords related to your topic, and you get hundreds of professional articles on that topic. Also, my local library now has whole books in digital format. I was able to read a digital version of Women and Slavery by Gwyn Campbell. You can also Google your topic, but you have to be careful about the quality of the Web sites you find with this search engine.

This shift in pronoun usage is considered nonstandard English. Such shifts are so common in conversational English that many students repeat them in their academic writing without even realizing the error. However, if the subject of a sentence or a paragraph is a specific person, place, or thing, the pronouns referring to that subject should be consistent with it. Take a look at this revision of the previous paragraph:

Terminology Tip
The pronoun error described here is called a **shift in person** because the pronoun shifts unexpectedly from a specific person to the generalized *you.*

> Doing research for my history assignment was easier than I had expected. First, I found all the materials that I needed online. For instance, the librarian showed me how to use a database called LexisNexis, which contains thousands of articles and documents. All I had to do was type in keywords related to my topic, and I got hundreds of professional articles on that topic. Also, my local library now has whole books in digital format. I was able to read a digital version of Women and Slavery by Gwyn Campbell. I also Googled my topic, but I had to be careful about the quality of the Web sites I found with this search engine.

There are really only two situations in which the pronoun *you* is useful in academic writing:

1. In a direct quotation:

   My boss said to me, "You are going to be president of this company one day."

   Here, *you* refers to a specific person, not to people in general.

2. In a paragraph or essay in which you are addressing the reader directly to explain a process:

   To prepare for the SAT exam, you should first consider enrolling in a special training class.

   Here, *you* refers to a specific person, the reader.

Power Tip
Some instructors may prefer that students do not use *you* even when explaining a process. If you are in doubt about your instructor's preference, it's always a good idea to ask.

ACTIVITY 8

For each sentence below, do the following:

- Cross out each *you* pronoun that refers to people in general.
- Above this crossed-out word, write in the pronoun that is consistent with the specific subject of the sentence. (See Chapter 11 for more on identifying subjects.)

Teaching Tip
Consider mentioning that the use of *you* can be off-putting to readers if the writer is discussing something uncomfortable or controversial.

EXAMPLE: My father likes the view from the hills because ~~you~~ he can see for miles.

1. We have always loved Artie's Seafood Restaurant because ~~you~~ we can get delicious red snapper there.
2. I'm nervous about the final exam because ~~you~~ I need to pass the exam in order to pass the course.
3. As we drove over the summit of the mountain, ~~you~~ we could see all the lights of Las Vegas glittering in the valley.
4. Students are pleased with the new class schedule options because ~~you~~ they can take classes on weekends.
5. Samantha wants to work on a cruise ship because ~~you~~ she will be able to meet so many different people there.

ACTIVITY 9

For the paragraph on page 511, do the following:

- Cross out each *you* pronoun that refers to people in general.
- Above each crossed-out word, write in the pronoun that is consistent with the specific subject of the paragraph.

(1) When Annika set out to ride her bicycle across the United States, she was not prepared for the dangers and hardships that ~~you~~ she would encounter. (2) First, she didn't realize that ~~you~~ she would have to climb so many steep hills or that ~~your~~ her bicycle would feel like a heavy burden going up the hills. (3) Also, Annika didn't realize how close cars would come to ~~you~~ her as they passed on the highway. (4) She was also unprepared for the dull trip through the plains of Kansas. (5) Despite all the hardships, Annika experienced many rewarding moments on her journey. (6) She is proud of her accomplishment, and she told a newspaper reporter that it was an experience ~~you~~ she will never forget.

OVERUSE OF *IT*

The pronoun *it* is sometimes called the "king of the pronouns" because it is used so frequently. However, the careless use or overuse of this pronoun in academic writing can confuse readers. Take a look:

Dropping out of high school can lead to a number of problems. To begin with, a teenager can experience a sense of isolation and loneliness without the social opportunities that high school provides. For example, it really made my brother crazy when he quit school in the eleventh grade. He watched television all day to try to forget about it. Even though he still saw his old buddies on the weekends, it was painful. Worst of all, the girls stopped calling, and it became unbearable for him. it proves that dropping out of high school can be a risky choice.

In this passage, each use of the pronoun *it* leads to a lack of clarity:

... it really made my brother crazy (What made him crazy, exactly?)
... to forget about it (To forget about what, exactly?)
... it was painful (What was painful, exactly?)
... it became unbearable for him (What became unbearable, exactly?)
... It proves (What proves, exactly?)

The answers to these questions might be clear *in the writer's mind,* but the reader will have to guess, which can result in confusion and frustration. A more experienced writer avoids the careless use of *it,* replacing this pronoun with more specific nouns and noun phrases. Let's see how the previous paragraph could be revised:

Teaching Tip
For test items on pronouns, see the *Testing Tool Kit* CD available with this book.

Dropping out of high school can lead to a number of problems. To begin with, a teenager can experience a sense of isolation and loneliness without the social opportunities that high school provides. For example, the sudden isolation really made my brother crazy when he quit school in the eleventh grade. He watched television all day to try to forget about his growing sense of loneliness. Even

CONTINUED >

though he still saw his old buddies on the weekends, losing daily contact with them was painful. Worst of all, the girls stopped calling, and the loss of dates became unbearable for him. My brother's example proves that dropping out of high school can be a risky choice.

ACTIVITY 10

For the paragraph below, do the following:

- Underline unclear uses of *it.*
- Using your imagination, replace the unclear pronouns with more specific words. You may need to replace other words, too. Answers will vary.

(1) A job interview can be stressful, but applicants can take certain steps to make the experience better. (2) For example, they can do research on ~~it~~ the job they're interested in. (3) Also, applicants can prepare for ~~it~~ the interview by thinking of questions to ask. (4) ~~It~~ Such questions will show their interest in the job. (5) Applicants should also think about questions that the interviewer might ask. (6) These questions might include, "Why do you want this job?" "What skills would you bring to this job?" and "Where do you see yourself in two to five years?" (7) ~~Doing it~~ Practicing answers to these questions in front of a mirror will help an applicant respond confidently during the interview. (8) ~~It~~ The interview doesn't have to be scary; applicants just need to be ready. (9) For those who prepare well, ~~it~~ interviewing for a job can be a life-changing experience.

OVERUSE OF INDEFINITE PRONOUNS

The following pronouns are used to identify general people or things:

Indefinite Pronouns

GENERAL	
People	**Things**
anybody anyone everybody everyone no one nobody one somebody someone	anything everything nothing one something

Using indefinite pronouns to identify general people and things can harm your academic writing for two reasons:

1. They can lead to generalizations.
2. They can lead to awkward agreement.

Next, we'll discuss both reasons in more detail.

Indefinite Pronouns and Generalizations

Pronouns that identify people or things in general are called *indefinite* because they do not identify a *definite* (specific) person or thing. Take a look:

> Everybody would like to win the lottery. (Who, exactly?)

If we make this statement, we are saying that *most people* or *people in general* would like to win the lottery. However, this statement is weak because it is not universally true: certainly, there are individuals who would not want to win the lottery or who do not care about it.

Such *generalizations* are common in spoken language; however, in academic writing, specifics are preferable to generalizations. Therefore, whenever possible, it's a good idea to replace indefinite pronouns with nouns or noun phrases that are more specific:

WEAK	Everybody would like to win the lottery.
BETTER	Many people would like to win the lottery.
MORE SPECIFIC	The average working-class person would like to win the lottery.
	Most lottery players would like to win the lottery.
	All of my best friends would like to win the lottery.

Here is another example of an indefinite pronoun that leads to a generalization:

> Nothing upsets me.

If I make this a statement, I mean that *not one single thing upsets me*, with "thing" being a nonspecific term. However, it's hard to imagine that this statement is always true: certainly, a tragedy or a catastrophic event is likely to upset me.

In your academic writing, be careful to find specific nouns or noun phrases to express your thoughts:

WEAK	Nothing upsets me.
BETTER	Very few things upset me.
MORE SPECIFIC	Ordinary human difficulties do not upset me.
	Day-to-day problems do not upset me.
	Small failures do not upset me.

Teaching Tip
Call out some general statements to the class, such as "Everyone likes chocolate" or "Anybody can pass this course." Then, ask students to identify the indefinite pronouns and replace them with more specific words. Encourage students to come up with as many specific alternatives as they can.

As you can see from these examples, indefinite pronouns can lead to generalizations: weak statements that are not universally true or that are hard to prove. For this reason, you should avoid using indefinite pronouns in your academic writing. Whenever possible, replace an indefinite pronoun with a more specific noun or noun phrase.

ACTIVITY 11

For each sentence below, do the following:

- Underline the indefinite pronoun.
- Using your imagination, rewrite the sentence to replace the pronoun with more specific words. You may need to rewrite other parts of the sentence, too. Answers will vary.

EXAMPLE: With five seconds left on the clock, everyone was anxious.

With five seconds left on the clock, the fans were anxious.

1. In my history class, someone always knows the answer.
   In my history class, the A students always know the answer.
2. Everybody will be going to Janeese's party.
   Most of Janeese's friends and neighbors will be going to her party.
3. If we leave the house unlocked, anything could happen.
   If we leave the house unlocked, a burglar could steal our valuables.
4. Anybody can quit smoking.
   People with enough willpower and persistence can quit smoking.
5. No one can beat Barry's home run record.
   No member of this year's rival teams can beat Barry's home run record.

Indefinite Pronouns and Awkward Agreement

If you decide to use an indefinite pronoun as the subject of a sentence, you may encounter another common problem. Take a look:

Nobody **wants to have** their **taxes raised.**

SUBJECT (Nobody) — PRONOUN REFERRING BACK TO SUBJECT (their)

Terminology Tip
When singular pronouns refer back to singular nouns/pronouns and plural pronouns refer back to plural nouns/pronouns, these words are said to agree in **number**.

Although this sentence *sounds* correct, it contains a common pronoun error: the possessive pronoun *their* (plural) does not match the subject *nobody* (singular); in other words, the pronoun *their* does not *agree* with the subject.

Remember that most indefinite pronouns are singular even though many of them have plural meanings (*everybody, everyone, everything*). If you want to use a singular indefinite pronoun as the subject of a sentence, there are just three ways to fix the pronoun error just described:

Singular subject + Singular pronoun

1. Nobody wants to have his or her taxes raised.
2. Nobody wants to have her taxes raised.
3. Nobody wants to have his taxes raised.

Each of these sentences is now grammatically correct. However, each one sounds awkward:

1. *His or her* is wordy, and if you use it over and over, your writing can become cluttered.
2. *Her* by itself sounds odd because not all taxpayers are women.
3. *His* by itself also sounds odd because not all taxpayers are men.

The best way to correct the problem may be to change *nobody* to a more specific subject. Take a look:

Plural subject + Plural pronoun

Few taxpayers want to have their taxes raised.

This sentence is a better choice for academic writing because it has a more specific subject, it has a plural pronoun to match a plural subject, and it is not awkwardly worded.

Power Tip

Don't think that you can *never* use indefinite pronouns, but be aware of the problems they can cause. Whenever you are tempted to use such a pronoun, ask yourself if you can find a more specific noun or noun phrase. If you still want to use an indefinite pronoun, make sure it agrees with (matches) the noun it refers back to.

ACTIVITY 12

Each sentence below has a pronoun agreement error. For each one, underline the subject pronoun and the possessive pronoun that refers back to the subject pronoun. Then rewrite the sentence in two ways:

- First, replace the possessive pronoun, but leave the subject pronoun alone.
- Second, replace the subject pronoun, but leave the possessive pronoun alone.

You may need to change other words as well. For example, if you make the subject plural, you may need to change the verb to agree with it. (For more information, see Chapter 16.) Answers will vary.

EXAMPLE: Somebody left their shoes on the porch.

Somebody left her shoes on the porch.

The children left their shoes on the porch.

CONTINUED >

1. Everyone brings their kids to the company outing.
   Everyone brings his or her kids to the company outing.
   All employees bring their kids to the company outing.
2. No one wants to have their identity stolen.
   No one wants to have his or her identity stolen.
   No citizens want to have their identity stolen.
3. Someone dumps their garbage on the street every week.
   Someone dumps his or her garbage on the street every week.
   Strangers dump their garbage on the street every week.
4. With enough time and patience, anyone can paint their own house.
   With enough time and patience, anyone can paint his or her own house.
   With enough time and patience, homeowners can paint their own house.
5. Everybody wants their children to succeed.
   Everybody wants his or her children to succeed.
   Concerned parents want their children to succeed.

OTHER PRONOUN PROBLEMS

Finally, we'll look at some other problems that can occur with pronouns. We'll begin with errors in the use of subject versus object pronouns. To remind yourself of the differences between these types of pronouns, see page 503.

Problems with Subject versus Object Forms

In most sentences with a single subject or object, we have no trouble understanding what type of pronoun to use. Take a look:

SINGLE SUBJECT PRONOUN	I shop for groceries every week.
SINGLE OBJECT PRONOUN	Robin gave the books to me.

When there is more than one subject or object, however, it's sometimes harder to "hear" what pronouns are correct. Take a look at the following sentences, in which the pronoun usage is incorrect:

COMPOUND SUBJECT	Bob and me shop for groceries every week.
COMPOUND OBJECT	Robin gave the books to Maura and I.

Remember, if a pronoun is acting as a subject, the subject form must be used, and if a pronoun is acting as an object, the object form must be used. Let's look at corrected versions of the previous sentences:

SUBJECT PRONOUN

Bob and I shop for groceries every week.

OBJECT PRONOUN

Robin gave the books to Maura and me.

Teaching Tip

Some students, eager to use correct grammar, write *X and I* even when they should be using the object pronoun *me*—for example, *The children went with my husband and I.* Express appreciation for their desire to use correct grammar, and remind them that the object form is correct in such cases.

ACTIVITY 13

In the following paragraph, circle the correct pronouns from the choices in parentheses.

(1) My sister, Martha, and (I / me) spend a lot of time together. (2) Because Martha lives close to me, (she / her) and (I / me) are able to get together a few times a week. (3) Sometimes, we go for walks together, while other times, we go to the movies or just sit in a café and talk. (4) Occasionally, Martha comes over and has dinner with my children and (I/ me). (5) My daughter says that she wants to have a sister so that she can have someone like Martha in her life. (6) I tell (she / her) and my son that I am not having any more babies. (7) However, I encourage both of my children to form close friendships with others.

When we make comparisons, we may also have trouble deciding between a subject or an object pronoun. What pronoun would you choose to complete the following sentence?

Bill drives faster than (I / me).

The object pronoun *me* might sound right, but it is incorrect. How can we tell? Let's add words to flesh out the second part of the sentence:

Bill drives faster than (I / me) drive.

or

Bill drives faster than (I / me) do.

It may be clearer now that the subject pronoun *I* is the correct choice. It is correct because *I* is the subject that goes with the added-on verbs (*drive, do*).

Whenever you are in doubt about whether to use a subject or an object pronoun in a comparison, flesh out the comparison.

ACTIVITY 14

In each of the following sentences, circle the correct pronoun from the choices in parentheses.

EXAMPLE: Rodney is nicer than (I / me).

1. You are more experienced than (I / me).
2. I wish I could be as tall as (he / him).
3. Grace is generous; no one I know has donated more money than (she / her).
4. My son was upset because the other children got more candy than (he / him).
5. Anita's strength is admirable; not many people have faced as many difficulties as (she / her).

A reminder about *who* and *whom*. *Who* and *whom* are often misused in writing. *Who* is the subject form of the pronoun, and *whom* is the object form. As you may remember from Chapter 14 (see page 386), *who* is usually used before verbs, while *whom* is usually used before nouns and pronouns:

VERB

The person who made lunch used too much pepper.

PRONOUN

The woman whom I met at the party knows you.

Problems with Collective Nouns

Collective nouns refer to groups of people or things. Here are some examples:

Teaching Tip
Ask students if they can think of other collective nouns.

audience	company
crowd	family
class	jury
committee	team

In everyday conversation, we often use the plural possessive *their* to refer to collective nouns, but this usually is incorrect in academic writing. Take a look:

The company laid off half of their employees.

In most cases, like this one, the members of a group described by a collective noun act as one. Therefore, collective nouns usually are treated as singular. This means that pronouns referring to them usually are singular too.

Let's look at the corrected version of the previous sentence.

The company laid off half of its employees.

COLLECTIVE NOUN

And here's another correct example:

The team won its third straight championship.

COLLECTIVE NOUN — SINGULAR POSSESSIVE PRONOUN

However, collective nouns may be referred to by a plural pronoun if the members of a group are acting as individuals. In the following example, different family members picked up different swimsuits; they acted individually, not as one. Thus, the collective noun has a plural meaning and takes a plural possessive pronoun.

The family picked up their wet swimsuits and hung them on the line.

ACTIVITY 15

For each sentence below, do the following:

- Underline the collective noun. If the members of the collective noun are acting as one, write **O** next to the sentence.
- If they are acting as individuals, write ***I*** next to the sentence.
- Circle the possessive pronoun (singular or plural) that goes with the collective noun.

EXAMPLE: **The jury shared (its / their) decision with the court. O**

1. Because of severe weather, the committee decided to delay (its / their) vote. O
2. The class turned in (its / their) notebooks to be graded. I
3. The audience clapped loudly to show (its / their) appreciation for the performance. O
4. The crowd repeated (its / their) angry cheer several times: "Senator Joe must go!" O
5. Over the summer, the junior-high team outgrew (its / their) uniforms. I

FIXING MIXED PRONOUN ERRORS IN WHOLE PARAGRAPHS

The following activity will give you more practice with recognizing and fixing pronoun errors in whole paragraphs—a valuable skill for improving your own writing.

ACTIVITY 16

Read the following paragraphs carefully, looking for pronoun errors. Then, rewrite each error to fix the problem. The errors will include:

- unclear pronoun references (see page 507)
- shifts from specific subjects to *you* (see page 509)
- incorrect pronoun agreement (see pages 514 and 518)
- incorrect use of subject versus object pronouns (see page 516)

The first error in each paragraph has been edited for you. *Edits may vary.*

The following paragraph has ten pronoun errors (including the one that has been edited for you).

1. (1) My roommate, Shawn, and ~~me~~ I have had several disagreements over the past few weeks. (2) For example, he says that I use more lights and heat than ~~him~~ he because my room is bigger. (3) Therefore, he claims, I should pay a higher share of the electricity bill than ~~him~~ he. (4) I disagree, of course. (5) As for me, I am tired of asking Shawn to wash his dirty dishes and to remove his hair from the shower drain. (6) Also, ~~you~~ I can't believe what a mess he leaves in the living room. (7) Every day after work, Shawn takes off his coat and shoes and leaves them right in the middle of the floor. (8) Later, while watching TV, ~~him~~ he throws peanut shells and candy wrappers on the floor. (9) ~~It~~ His lack of consideration really bothers me. (10) ~~Everyone has~~ Many people have problems with their roommates, but Shawn and ~~me~~ I have reached a crisis point. (11) I am going to suggest that ~~him~~ he and I have a serious discussion to try to resolve our conflicts. (12) Can we continue to live in the same place? (13) My family back in Texas has given me ~~their~~ its decision already: absolutely not.

The following paragraph has thirteen pronoun errors (including the one that has been edited for you).

2. (1) Imagine this situation: a biker hits a pothole and flies from her bike, landing on the sidewalk. (2) Clearly, ~~her~~ she is injured. (3) ~~Whom~~ Who would help her, and ~~whom~~ who would stand on the sidelines? (4) A research team

has investigated these questions, and ~~their~~ its answers are quite interesting. (5) First, witnesses who feel positive or fortunate are more likely to help than those experiencing more negative emotions. (6) Also, witnesses who are feeling guilty about something may be more likely to help, perhaps to make up for the act that prompted their guilt. (7) ~~It~~ The guilt could stem from anything—from a dishonest act at work to a fight with a friend. (8) Finally, ~~if you~~ people who see others who are willing to help~~, you~~ are more likely to come to a stranger's aid than ~~if you are a lone witness.~~ lone witnesses. (9) ~~It~~ Seeing the concern of others might inspire witnesses to act. (10) My personal experience suggests that these observations are true. (11) Once, my husband and ~~me~~ I saw a pedestrian get bumped by a car. (12) We had just had a disagreement, and ~~me~~ I, personally, was feeling guilty. (13) Also, we saw another person coming to the pedestrian's aid. (14) In seconds, the two of us ran to help. (15) The other person arrived at the scene faster than ~~us~~ we, but we were all able to help. (16) Fortunately, the pedestrian had experienced only minor injuries. (17) Based on this experience and the research findings, I conclude that ~~everybody has~~ all people have the ability to help their fellow citizens. (18) Some of us are just more motivated than others, for various reasons.

ACTIVITY 17: Teamwork

When you have finished correcting one of the paragraphs from Activity 16, get together with two or three classmates. Then, compare the errors that you found and the corrections that you made. If you corrected errors differently, discuss why this might be. If you still have questions about the pronoun problems covered in the activity, ask your instructor.

ACTIVITY 18

Find a paper that you wrote recently but haven't turned in for a grade. Then, read the paper carefully, looking at the pronouns. Put a check by any errors that you identify in these pronouns. Then, correct the problems.

Bringing It All Together

In this chapter, you have learned what pronouns are, how they are used, and how they can cause problems in academic writing. Check off each of the following statements that you understand. For any that you do not understand, review the appropriate pages in this chapter.

- ☐ A **pronoun** is a word that takes the place of a noun. Often, a pronoun refers back to a specific noun that has already been mentioned. (See page 501.) We use pronouns for convenience, so that we do not have to repeat a noun or a noun phrase over and over. (See page 506.)
- ☐ Three major groups of pronouns are **specific** versus **general** pronouns, **subject** versus **object** pronouns, and **possessive** pronouns. (See pages 502, 503, and 505.)
- ☐ Pronouns that identify specific people, places, and things are generally acceptable in academic writing. However, follow these guidelines:
  - ____ Be sure that it is clear what each pronoun refers to. (See page 507.)
  - ____ Avoid overusing the pronouns *you* and *it.* (See page 509.)
- ☐ Pronouns that identify general persons and things may cause special problems in your academic writing. Remember these guidelines for using indefinite pronouns:
  - ____ Whenever possible, replace an indefinite pronoun with a specific noun or noun phrase. (See page 513.)
  - ____ Most indefinite pronouns are singular, so in most cases, you cannot use the plural possessive pronoun *their* to refer to them. (See page 514.)
- ☐ In sentences with compound subjects or objects or in sentences that make comparisons, it can be tricky to decide between subject and object pronouns. Be careful in these cases, making sure to use the right pronouns for each situation. (See page 516.)
- ☐ **Collective nouns** refer to groups of people or things. In most cases, the members of the group described by a collective noun act as one. Therefore, pronouns that refer to them usually are singular, too. (See page 518.)

PART THREE

A Writer's Reader

Chapter 18

Empathy and Kindness

READINGS

Empathy is the ability to identify with the feelings of others—to "put ourselves in another's shoes," as the saying goes. Some argue that empathy and kindness are now in shorter supply than ever, given the growing demands of daily life and the increasing distractions—such as iPods and computer games and videos—that can pull us away from others. On the other hand, most of us continue to empathize with others, from friends or family members who are going through hard times to struggling characters in television dramas. Furthermore, many of us, at one time or another, have depended on the kindness of others, even strangers. And if we think back on just the previous week or month, most of us can probably identify at least a few kind deeds—large or small—that we've done.

As you read the following essays, think of all the different ways in which kindness and empathy are shown. How do kind acts affect not only the recipient but also the giver? Do you think that we, as a society, are becoming more or less caring toward others? Does it matter either way? Why or why not?

Pius Kamau

A Duty to Heal

Pius Kamau was born in Kenya, Africa, sometime in 1941. Although he doesn't know his exact birthday, he chose September 1 because, he says, it sounded like a good day. Kamau studied in Mombasa until he was fourteen years old, when he dropped out of school to earn money as a railway clerk. He later continued his studies in Spain, England, and Kenya, earning a degree in medicine before moving to the United States in 1971. Kamau currently lives in Aurora, Colorado, where he works as a surgeon and writes a weekly column for the *Denver Post.*

In "A Duty to Heal," Kamau tells the story of a patient who tested his values of empathy and kindness. He wrote the essay for *This I Believe,* a National Public Radio project that invites people to share the basic philosophies that guide their daily lives.

Reading Tips: Notice how the author blends storytelling with reflections on the meaning of events in the story.

Power Tip

In the readings in this part of the book, many challenging words are defined. However, you may be unsure of the meanings of other words. Put a check mark by these words and guess their meanings as you read. Then, after you have finished reading, look these words up in a dictionary. Also, consider recording new vocabulary in a special log. (See Chapter 7, page 222, for advice on keeping a vocabulary log.)

Martin Luther King, Jr. (1929–1968): an African American minister who became a key figure in the American civil-rights movement of the 1960s

Teaching Tip
If you teach in a computer classroom, show a video clip from Martin Luther King's "I Have a Dream" speech. Alternatively, bring in the text of the speech.

white supremacist: someone who believes that whites are superior to all other races

Nazi: originally a political party in World War II–era Germany. Nazis hold white-supremacist beliefs and espouse hatred of Jews, African Americans, and other minorities.

swastika: symbol of Nazism

Teaching Tip
Ask students to describe a time when a stranger reacted negatively to them. How did it affect them?

Growing up in the grinding poverty of colonial Africa, America was my shining hope. Martin Luther King's nonviolent political struggle made freedom and equality sound like achievable goals. America's ideals filled my head. Someday, I promised myself, I would walk on America's streets. 1

But, as soon as I set foot in America's hospitals, reality—and racism—quickly intruded on the ideals. My color and accent set me apart. But in a hospital I am neither black nor white. I'm a doctor. I believe every patient that I touch deserves the same care and concern from me. 2

In 1999, I was on-call when a nineteen-year-old patient was brought into the hospital. He was coughing up blood after a car accident. He was a white supremacist, an American Nazi with a swastika tattooed on his chest. 3

The nurses told me he would not let me touch him. When I came close to him, he spat on me. In that moment, I wanted no part of him, either, but no other physician would take him on. I realized I had to minister to him as best as I could. 4

I talked to him, but he refused to look at me or acknowledge me. He would only speak through the white nurses. Only they could check his body for injury. Only they could touch his tattooed chest. 5

As it turned out, he was not badly hurt. We parted strangers. 6

I still wonder: Was there more I could have done to make our encounter different or better? Could I have approached him differently? Could I have tried harder to win his trust? 7

I can only guess his thoughts about me, or the beliefs he lived by. His racism, I think, had little to do with me, personally. And, I want to think it had little to do with America, with the faith of Martin Luther King and other great men whose words I heard back in Africa, and who made me believe in this nation's ideals of equality and freedom. 8

My hands—my black hands—have saved many lives. I believe in my duty to heal. I believe all patients, all human beings, are equal, and that I must try to care for everyone, even those who would rather die than consider me their equal. 9

CHECK YOUR UNDERSTANDING

1. How did the author feel about America before going to work in an American hospital?
   - **a.** pessimistic
   - **b.** hopeful
   - **c.** distrustful
   - **d.** uncertain
2. How did the author react to the accident victim's racism?
   - **a.** He refused to treat the patient and left his care to the nurses.
   - **b.** He ignored the patient's behavior and began to treat his bleeding.
   - **c.** He decided that he would have to treat the patient as well as he could.
   - **d.** He smiled and expressed hope that he and the patient could overcome their differences.

3. What did the author learn about the patient's thoughts and beliefs?
   a. Nothing; he could only guess the patient's thoughts.
   b. The patient had strong personal feelings against the author.
   c. The patient deeply opposed the beliefs of Martin Luther King.
   d. The patient wasn't really racist; he was merely fearful of medical treatment.
4. What conclusion did the author come to after the experience described in this essay?
   a. If another patient with racist tattoos were to need treatment, he would pass the case on to another doctor.
   b. He would cheerfully treat every patient, even those whose beliefs are "dramatically different" from his own.
   c. Medicine might not be the best career for those who hesitate to treat patients whose beliefs and values differ strongly from their own.
   d. It is his duty to care for everyone, even patients "who would rather die than consider [him] their equal."

DISCUSS WITH YOUR PEERS

1. Look at paragraphs 4 and 5. Even though the patient had been coughing up blood, he does not let the author treat him. Furthermore, he spits on the author. With your peers, try to imagine what the patient might actually be thinking and feeling when he sees the author. Do you think the author could have done anything differently to improve the situation? Finally, discuss whether this sort of racism is unusual in America or whether it represents a fairly common reality.
2. Even after the incident, the author continues to search his soul: "Could I have tried harder to win his trust?" (para. 7). First, discuss with your peers how you would react if someone spat on you for racist reasons. Would you fight back or be forgiving? Then, discuss the doctor's character. What kind of person is he to be so devoted to forgiveness and human equality? In your opinion, are there many people in America like this doctor, or is he more like a saint than a real person?
3. In paragraph 8, the author says that he "want[s] to think" that the patient's racism "had little to do with America, with the faith of Martin Luther King and other great men whose words I heard back in Africa." In other words, he would like to believe that racism is not an essential or permanent part of America's reality. Discuss whether you agree or disagree with the author's optimism. In your opinion, has racism always been—and will it always be—woven into the fabric of American society? Or is it reasonable to believe that it has been, or will be, overcome?

IDENTIFY THE PATTERNS

For more on the various writing patterns referenced here, see Appendix A.

1. The author uses **narration** to develop his writing. Notice how his story is organized into three general parts: background, the incident, and reflections on the incident. Identify which paragraphs belong to each of these parts.
2. In paragraph 5, the author uses **exemplification** to show how the patient refuses the doctor's help. Identify the four examples that he gives. Then, discuss whether these four examples, given back-to-back, are effective in re-creating the scene and its emotional impact.
3. In paragraph 9, the author uses **definition** to clarify what he has learned from the incident and to define his beliefs. Reread this paragraph and identify the main parts of his definition.

WRITE A PARAGRAPH

1. Discuss whether doctors should be required to care for any patient who needs their immediate assistance regardless of the patient's attitude or behavior.
2. Describe a situation in which you (1) behaved in a racist manner, (2) were a victim of racist behavior, or (3) observed a racist exchange between others. Explain what happened, how the participants behaved, and how the situation ended.

Sarah Adams

Be Cool to the Pizza Dude

Sarah Adams was born in 1968 in New London, Connecticut, and grew up in Wisconsin. She holds a B.A. in English and an M.A. in literature from the University of Wisconsin. Adams currently teaches English composition at Olympic College in Bremerton, Washington.

Adams's first published piece of writing, the following essay was originally broadcast on *This I Believe,* a National Public Radio project highlighting the values and beliefs that guide people in their everyday lives. Empathy and kindness are at the core of Adams's guiding philosophy, as she illustrates in "Be Cool to the Pizza Dude." Although she has never delivered pizza herself, she has held a variety of jobs, including telemarketer, factory worker, hotel clerk, and flower shop cashier.

Teaching Tip
Ask if any students in the class have ever delivered pizza or done some similar service job. Do they agree with Adams's views of the job? Do they think she idealizes the work in any way? Why or why not?

Reading Tips: The author breaks her essay down into four principles. To help you understand the reading, briefly summarize (put into your own words) these principles as you read.

If I have one operating philosophy about life, it is this: "Be cool to the pizza delivery dude; it's good luck." Four principles guide the pizza dude philosophy. 1

humility: modesty; not seeing oneself as overly important

Principle 1: Coolness to the pizza delivery dude is a practice in humility and forgiveness. I let him cut me off in traffic, let him safely hit the exit ramp 2 from the left lane, let him forget to use his blinker without extending any of my digits out the window or toward my horn because there should be one moment in my harried life when a car may encroach or cut off or pass and I let it go. Sometimes when I have become so certain of my ownership of my lane, daring anyone to challenge me, the pizza dude speeds by in his rusted Chevette. His pizza light atop his car glowing like a beacon reminds me to check myself as I flow through the world. After all, the dude is delivering pizza to young and old, families and singletons, gays and straights, blacks, whites, and browns, rich and poor, and vegetarians and meat lovers alike. As he journeys, I give safe passage, practice restraint, show courtesy, and contain my anger.

harried: troubled; worry-filled

encroach: to intrude into someone's "space"

beacon: a guiding or warning light, like that in a lighthouse

3 Principle 2: Coolness to the pizza delivery dude is a practice in empathy. Let's face it: We've all taken jobs just to have a job because some money is better than none. I've held an assortment of these jobs and was grateful for the paycheck that meant I didn't have to share my Cheerios with my cats. In the big pizza wheel of life, sometimes you're the hot bubbly cheese and sometimes you're the burnt crust. It's good to remember the fickle spinning of that wheel.

fickle: unreliable or constantly changing

4 Principle 3: Coolness to the pizza delivery dude is a practice in honor, and it reminds me to honor honest work. Let me tell you something about these dudes: They never took over a company and, as CEO, artificially inflated the value of the stock and cashed out their own shares, bringing the company to the brink of bankruptcy, resulting in twenty thousand people losing their jobs while the CEO builds a home the size of a luxury hotel. Rather, the dudes sleep the sleep of the just.

Teaching Tip

Ask students how they define "honest work." Alternatively, how do they define "dishonest work"?

5 Principle 4: Coolness to the pizza delivery dude is a practice in equality. My measurement as a human being, my worth, is the pride I take in performing my job—any job—and the respect with which I treat others. I am the equal of the world not because of the car I drive, the size of the TV I own, the weight I can bench-press, or the calculus equations I can solve. I am the equal to all I meet because of the kindness in my heart. And it all starts here—with the pizza delivery dude.

6 Tip him well, friends and brethren, for that which you bestow freely and willingly will bring you all the happy luck that a grateful universe knows how to return.

bestow: to give

CHECK YOUR UNDERSTANDING

1. What is part of the author's philosophy about being cool to the pizza delivery dude?
   a. It ensures excellent service.
   b. It's good luck.
   c. It makes her feel good about herself.
   d. It makes her feel closer to others.

CONTINUED >

2. Why does the author tolerate bad driving behavior from pizza deliverers?
   a. She is a bad driver herself; therefore, she is more forgiving of others' bad driving habits.
   b. She is worried that if she is not tolerant, the pizza deliverers might act angrily—even violently.
   c. She got into an accident once with a speeding pizza deliverer.
   d. She believes there should be times in her busy life when she is forgiving about such behavior.
3. What does the author suggest about the work behavior of pizza deliverers?
   a. They behave ethically and honestly and do not harm others.
   b. Some of them are dishonest, but most of them act ethically.
   c. Most of them are working toward management positions.
   d. They work constantly and well even though they earn little.
4. What is the author's final advice to readers?
   a. Tip the pizza delivery dude well.
   b. Never cut off the pizza delivery dude in traffic.
   c. Always greet the pizza delivery dude pleasantly.
   d. Work as hard as the pizza delivery dude does.

DISCUSS WITH YOUR PEERS

1. In paragraph 2, the author says that the light on the pizza dude's car is "like a beacon" that reminds her to be humble and forgiving. First, underline the one sentence in the paragraph that describes what the pizza deliverers do that makes them a model for human behavior. Then, discuss the sentence and explain why the author believes that the pizza dude's job is far more important than simply delivering pizza.
2. Remember from Chapter 6 that a *metaphor* is a creative comparison of two items with similar characteristics. In paragraph 3, the author uses strong metaphorical details to describe the human condition: "In the big pizza wheel of life, sometimes you're the hot bubbly cheese and sometimes you're the burnt crust." First, discuss what the author means by this metaphor. In your own experience, have you ever felt like "the hot bubbly cheese" or "the burnt crust"? Finally, discuss why the author says that empathy is necessary, given this reality.
3. In paragraph 5, underline or highlight the sentence in which the author states how she determines her worth as a person. What are the two ways she measures this worth? Do you agree that these two measures are sufficient for determining a person's value? Would you eliminate one or both of them? By what other standards would you measure a person's worth as a human being?

IDENTIFY THE PATTERNS

For more on the various writing patterns referenced here, see Appendix A.

1. The author uses **definition** as the main pattern of development for her writing. In paragraphs 2 through 5, she defines her "pizza dude philosophy." Each of these paragraphs begins with a *topic sentence* in which the author states a main idea or part of the definition. Read each of these topic sentences and underline or highlight the key words that contribute to her definition.
2. In paragraph 2, the author uses **exemplification** to develop her writing. Underline or highlight some examples of how she is humble and forgiving toward the pizza dude in traffic. Do you think these examples are effective? Why or why not?
3. In paragraph 4, the author uses **comparison and contrast** to develop her writing. First, identify what two things are being compared and/or contrasted. Then, discuss how these things are similar and/or different. Finally, discuss whether this use of comparison and contrast makes the writing more powerful and interesting.

WRITE A PARAGRAPH

1. Discuss whether you ever feel empathy for people doing certain types of jobs. Describe what these jobs are, how you feel about the people doing them, and what you do, if anything, to honor those people and their work.
2. Discuss a time in your life when you felt like "the burnt crust." Describe what made you feel this way and whether the empathy of others helped you in this situation.

Angela Adkins

Dr. Dana

Angela Adkins, born in 1972, wrote the following essay as a student at Wayne College in Orville, Ohio, where she graduated in 2007 with a B.A. in sociology and anthropology. She is working toward an M.A. in sociology at the University of Akron and plans to pursue doctoral studies. Eventually, she would like to teach sociology at the university level and begin a mentorship program for teenage mothers who wish to continue their education. In addition to being a student, she volunteers as a tutor to adults who are preparing for the GED test. When she is not studying or tutoring, she spends as much time as possible with her husband and three children.

Adkins wrote "Dr. Dana" in response to an assignment for an English composition class. The assignment asked students to write a "tribute paper" about someone who had inspired or influenced them in some way. As her subject, Adkins chose a doctor who showed tremendous compassion for her at a very difficult time in her life. Adkins's instructor encouraged her to submit the paper to a Wayne College writing contest, and she later received a Student Writing Award for it. (For an essay by another Wayne College Student Writing Award winner, see page 584.)

Adkins's advice to other student writers is to write a little every day, whether in a notebook, a journal, or a blog. "It's great writing practice," she says, "and it serves as a reference list of ideas when you need a topic for a paper. Also, reading your writing out loud is very helpful when editing papers. It feels weird at first, but actually hearing what you've written is a great way to catch errors."

Reading Tips: Notice how the writer uses transitions (see Chapter 5, page 158) to move the reader through different parts of the story. You might want to put a check mark by these as you read.

prenatal: before birth
requisite: required
snide: nasty
gaudy: flashy; showy
stifle: to stop or muffle

Teaching Tip
Ask students to describe memorable first impressions of others—especially impressions that turned out to be wrong.

albatross: burden

There I sat alone in an exam room in the women's clinic, a very pregnant seventeen-year-old girl on the day of her first prenatal visit. Clad in a requisite paper gown—feeling much smaller inside than my bulging middle would suggest—I tried to calm my nervous anticipation. I knew that this would be just another uncomfortable experience among the months of curious stares, snide remarks, and well-intended but too-late lectures. Yet, I had already endured so many, what was one more? 1

After a brief knock sounded, the door opened and the scent of rosewater swept into the room. Glancing down, I saw my new doctor: a short and wrinkled, wispy-haired woman with pudgy cheeks and bright pink lipstick. A gold chain held her glasses close around her neck, and a gaudy rhinestone pin jutted from beneath her jacket. Surprisingly, she offered no disapproving stare, no cluck of pity—only a warm and toothy smile accompanied by a genuine, "Hi, I'm your doctor. Call me Dana. Tell me, how are you today?" 2

What an odd sight, this tiny grandma outfitted with a lab coat and stethoscope; I paused for a moment while trying to stifle my laughter. We had only just met, but surely her gentle face would uphold my trust and dignity. At last, I let my hands drop to my sides, knuckles no longer held tightly together. I told her of my plans and goals, at least what they used to be, and then I confided about the embarrassment and alienation by people who were supposed to be my friends and my family. Self-doubt and uncertainty about my life's course poured forth in a mixture of relief and dreadful finality. Dana said nothing as she listened and wrote. She remained delicately perched on her pink step stool, silently reading her notes long after I had finished speaking. 3

"Well, we can't change what's happened," she finally said, "only how we learn from it. Someone who can't see past that is not worth your time—no person escapes this life without making their share of missteps. The choice is yours to turn a situation into an albatross or a blessing." She patted my tummy with a soft, shaking hand. "I think you've definitely counted this little angel as a blessing. Sounds like now you need some new friends. But it's hard to see into someone's heart while they're feeling sorry for themselves, dear." She lifted my chin and gave my cheek a slight squeeze, but her unwavering voice was full of sincerity. Dana made no judgment on my condition or my character, nor did she tell me what to do. I was entrusted with the burden of making my own decision. 4

The rest of the initial exam was spent chatting about diet, exercise, and 5
expectations; mother and baby were both pronounced healthy. Dana strongly recommended taking a course of Lamaze classes to help prepare for labor and birth. She said I should know what to expect because "fear is the enemy!" Although I disliked the thought of being an unwed mother in a place full of happy couples, I halfheartedly agreed to go to the first class. I didn't really think it would be helpful, but already there was a strong need not to discourage her obvious faith in me.

Lamaze classes: These classes inform women and their partners about strategies for successful childbirth.

On the Saturday afternoon of my first Lamaze class, I arrived in the hos- 6
pital room with no pillow, no comfort music, and no partner. I intended to stay only half an hour, just long enough to get some general information and fulfill the promise to my new doctor. Suddenly, I felt a tap on my shoulder and cringed slightly before turning around to face the unknown. There before me stood Dana in jeans and a bright pink sweatshirt. "Hey!" she said with a grin. "I was waiting for a seminar and just thought I would grab some coffee . . . and look who I find? Mind if I pass the time with you? I could probably use a brushup on the new coaching techniques." All I could do was nod my head while wiping away the single rolling tear that betrayed my thanks. She gave me a fast hug, and then just as quickly waved it off with the back of her hand.

Teaching Tip
Call students' attention to the use of quotations in paragraph 6. Ask them how the writing would be different if the author had just summarized Dr. Dana's words instead of quoting them.

With a renewed sense of hope and confidence, I completed not only 7
that class but also five others in the following weeks, with my new coach in tow. Our weekly date ended with stops for cocoa to discuss worldly things like politics and newspaper articles. After snacks, we faithfully returned to her office to learn the basics of diapering, feeding, and coping from an old pro.

Occasionally, Dana would stop by my apartment to drop off "lost and 8
found" articles from her office—blankets, toys, and baby bottles that were always suspiciously pink. It was not long before I stopped looking at the floor and started meeting the gaze of others. I saw reflected there what Dana had seen in my downcast eyes: kindness, strength, and worth.

When I gave birth to a healthy little girl, one look into her tiny face 9
confirmed the absolute rightness of my decision. I realized the road ahead of us wouldn't be always smooth, but I knew we could travel it successfully. With Dana's subtle guidance, I had forged a wonderful support system and a strong belief in my own abilities.

Just before my daughter's first birthday, we received a package in the 10
mail. Inside I found a beautiful pink toddler dress, a month's supply of diapers, and a small unsigned note. I couldn't help but smile as I saw the distinctive and familiar handwriting that conveyed best wishes. Printed on the bottom of the stationery in trademark pink script were the words, "Friends are the family we choose for ourselves."

I chose well. 11

CHECK YOUR UNDERSTANDING

1. What was the author's reaction on first seeing Dr. Dana?
   a. She was worried about the professional competence of Dr. Dana.
   b. She was impressed by Dr. Dana's serious and authoritative manner.
   c. She was surprised and amused by Dr. Dana's grandmotherly appearance.
   d. She was frightened by the prospect of being treated by someone who didn't look like a doctor.
2. When the author shared her feelings on the first visit with Dr. Dana, how did Dr. Dana react?
   a. She listened silently and then responded in an accepting and supportive manner.
   b. She expressed a strongly negative judgment about the author's life choices.
   c. She assured the author that everything was going to be fine.
   d. She shared stories about other young, expectant mothers whom she'd treated.
3. After the author's first visit with Dr. Dana, Dr. Dana does something that moves the author greatly. What is it?
   a. She offers to drive the author to various other appointments.
   b. She tells the author that she will not charge her for medical visits.
   c. She offers to babysit after the author's baby is born.
   d. She appears at the author's first Lamaze class and provides support.
4. How did Dana's friendship and support change the author?
   a. It gave her new respect for the medical profession.
   b. It made her more confident and able to get the support she needed.
   c. It helped her see that her difficulties were no greater than anyone else's.
   d. It helped her become a better friend to everyone in her life.

DISCUSS WITH YOUR PEERS

1. In paragraph 4, what advice does Dana give the author about friendship? Discuss whether you agree or disagree with her strong opinions. Are the author's family and friends "not worth [her] time" anymore because of their unsupportive behavior?
2. In paragraph 6, Dana claims that she "was waiting for a seminar and just thought [she] would grab some coffee." Do you believe that Dana encountered the author accidentally, or did she plan the encounter? In your opinion, what motivates Dana to attend all six classes with her patient? Are you surprised that a "tiny grandma outfitted with a lab coat" might go out of her way to befriend a pregnant seventeen-year-old? Explain why or why not.

3. In paragraph 8, what is it that the author discovers about herself? Given her situation, how valuable is this self-realization? Discuss exactly what Dr. Dana has done to bring about this change. In your opinion, is Dana's contribution especially remarkable or just a normal act of kindness? Explain your position.

IDENTIFY THE PATTERNS

For more on the various writing patterns referenced here, see Appendix A.

1. Primarily, the author uses **narration** to tell this story of an unusual friendship. She organizes the story according to the important "steps" in the development of the friendship. Try to identify four main "steps" that take this friendship from first encounter to ultimate bonding.
2. In paragraphs 2 and 3, the author uses **description** to develop a powerful portrait of Dr. Dana. Underline or highlight some of the colorful details that bring Dr. Dana to life.
3. The author uses **cause and effect** to develop her writing. When Dr. Dana enters the life of an insecure seventeen-year-old, she is a powerful force of change. First, identify the *cause:* who is Dana, and what does she do to bring about changes in the author? Then, looking at paragraphs 8 and 9, identify the *effect:* how has the author changed?

WRITE A PARAGRAPH

1. Describe an "unusual" friendship that you've had with someone who was not of your age or background. Discuss how the friendship developed, what made it unusual, and what finally happened to the friendship.
2. Tell about a time when you went out of your way to help someone who was in need. Describe the person's situation, what you did to help the person, and what motivated you to perform those acts of kindness.
3. Tell about a time when you were in need and someone went out of his or her way to help you. Describe your situation, what that person did for you, and how those acts of kindness affected you.

MAKE CONNECTIONS

1. In all three reading selections in this chapter, we learn how empathy can benefit human beings. In a paragraph or essay, discuss what empathy means to you and how it improves people's lives. You may use ideas and examples from the readings and from your own knowledge and experience.
2. In all three essays, we meet narrators or characters with remarkable empathy. In your opinion, do these examples give a realistic picture of the world? In a paragraph or essay, discuss whether there is enough empathy in the world today. Be sure to state your position clearly, and provide reasons and examples to support your position. You may use ideas and examples from the readings and from your own knowledge and experience.

Be aware of other readings that relate to the theme of empathy and kindness:

- "Unforgettable Miss Bessie" by Carl T. Rowan (page 537)
- "The Sanctuary of School" by Lynda Barry (page 547)
- "Under the Influence" by Scott Russell Sanders (page 572)
- "My Ecumenical Father" by Jose Antonio Burciaga (page 591)
- "We Are Each Other's Business" by Eboo Patel (page 599)
- "Why Couldn't My Father Read?" by Enrique Hank Lopez (page 603)
- "Fish Cheeks" by Amy Tan (page 607)
- "Raising a Son—with Men on the Fringes" by Robyn Marks (page 610)

Chapter 19

School and Learning

READINGS

- "Unforgettable Miss Bessie"
- "The Joy of Reading and Writing: Superman and Me"
- "The Sanctuary of School"

All of us have been shaped by educational experiences—both good and bad, both inside of the classroom and beyond it. Some of us have felt inspired and cared for in school, while others of us have felt unconnected to our teachers, fellow students, and the work we have been asked to do. Some of us may even have had to rely on our own motivation and efforts to become educated. Our home life also influences our education; whether or not we feel supported and secure at home can dramatically affect our attitude toward school and our prospects for success there and beyond.

At some point during our schooling, a few of us have been fortunate enough to have benefited from the wisdom, compassion, toughness, humor, or persistence of an unusually gifted teacher. In some cases, our lives have changed dramatically as a result.

As you read the following essays, think about your own educational experiences, positive and negative. Which of those experiences changed your life, for better or worse? How has your home life supported or worked against your efforts to become educated? Finally, what does it even mean to "become educated"? How far can teachers and classroom lessons take us in this effort, and what responsibility must we take on ourselves?

Carl T. Rowan

Unforgettable Miss Bessie

Carl T. Rowan (1925–2000) grew up in McMinnville, Tennessee, during the Depression, a severe economic downturn that lasted from 1929 through the 1930s. Although his family faced severe poverty—they had no electricity, running water, telephone, or radio—he graduated as valedictorian and class president of his high school. After serving in the U.S. Navy during World War II, Rowan earned a B.A. in mathematics from Oberlin College in Ohio and a master's degree in journalism from the University of Minnesota. He went on to become a journalist for the *Chicago Sun-Times,* writing a nationally syndicated column on race relations, civil rights, and other political and social issues for more than thirty years. He also wrote eight books, including the memoir *Breaking Barriers* (1991) and the biographies *Wait Till Next Year: The Life Story of Jackie Robinson* (1960) and *Dream Makers, Dream Breakers: The World of Justice Thurgood Marshall* (1993). In addition to his writing career, Rowan served as ambassador to Finland and director of the U.S. Information Agency in the 1960s.

In the following essay, which first appeared in *Reader's Digest* in 1985, Rowan pays tribute to a memorable high school teacher. Using vivid detail to bring Miss Bessie to life, Rowan shows how her passion for teaching had lasting effects on many students.

Reading Tips: Rowan's essay includes several historical and literary references: the Battle of Hastings, the Magna Carta, Milton, Voltaire, and so on. Even if you are not familiar with these references, you can still appreciate the basic story. However, as a college student, it is a good habit to look up references you do not know either online or in an encyclopedia. This practice will help you build your "cultural literacy" so that you can understand more topics as you progress in college. Highly motivated students might also want to record these references in a special notebook.

Beowulf: a long poem/story written in eighth-century England

She was only about five feet tall and probably never weighed more than 110 pounds, but Miss Bessie was a towering presence in the classroom. She was the only woman tough enough to make me read *Beowulf* and think for a few foolish days that I liked it. From 1938 to 1942, when I attended Bernard High School in McMinnville, Tennessee, she taught me English, history, civics—and a lot more than I realized. 1

I shall never forget the day she scolded me into reading *Beowulf.* 2

"But Miss Bessie," I complained, "I ain't much interested in it." 3

Her large brown eyes became daggerish slits. "Boy," she said, "how dare you say 'ain't' to me! I've taught you better than that." 4

"Miss Bessie," I pleaded, "I'm trying to make first-string end on the football team, and if I go around saying 'it isn't' and 'they aren't,' the guys are gonna laugh me off the squad." 5

Teaching Tip
As an outside project, ask students to interview a grandparent or other elderly relative or acquaintance about his or her educational experiences, inside or outside of the classroom. Students can use the interview material as the basis of an extended paragraph. For advice on interviewing, refer students to Chapter 2, page 43.

"Boy," she responded, "you'll play football because you have guts. But do you know what *really* takes guts? Refusing to lower your standards to those of the crowd. It takes guts to say you've got to live and be somebody fifty years after all the football games are over." 6

I started saying "it isn't" and "they aren't," and I still made first-string end—and class valedictorian—without losing my buddies' respect. 7

mediocrity: the state of being average or not outstanding

During her remarkable 44-year career, Mrs. Bessie Taylor Gwynn taught hundreds of economically deprived black youngsters—including my mother, my brother, my sisters, and me. I remember her now with gratitude and affection—especially in this era when Americans are so wrought-up about a "rising tide of mediocrity" in public education and the problems of finding competent, caring teachers. Miss Bessie was an example of an informed, dedicated teacher, a blessing to children, and an asset to the nation. 8

Born in 1895, in poverty, she grew up in Athens, Alabama, where there was no public school for blacks. She attended Trinity School, a private institution for blacks run by the American Missionary Association, and in 1911 graduated from the Normal School (a "super" high school) at Fisk University in Nashville. Mrs. Gwynn, the essence of pride and privacy, never talked about her years in Athens; only in the months before her death did she reveal 9 that she had never attended Fisk University itself because she could not afford the four-year course.

At Normal School she learned a lot about Shakespeare, but most of all about the profound importance of education—especially, for a people trying to move up from slavery. "What you put in your head, boy," she once said, "can never be pulled out by the Ku Klux Klan, the Congress, or anybody." 10

Ku Klux Klan: a name given to several organizations that have persecuted African Americans for nearly 150 years

Miss Bessie's bearing of dignity told anyone who met her that she was "educated" in the best sense of the word. There was never a discipline problem in her classes. We didn't dare mess with a woman who knew about the Battle of Hastings, the Magna Carta, and the Bill of Rights—and who could also play the piano. 11

This frail-looking woman could make sense of Shakespeare, Milton, Voltaire, and bring to life Booker T. Washington and W. E. B. Du Bois. Believing that it was important to know who the officials were that spent taxpayers' money and made public policy, she made us memorize the names of everyone on the Supreme Court and in the President's Cabinet. It could be embarrassing to be unprepared when Miss Bessie said, "Get up and tell the class who Frances Perkins is and what you think about her." 12

Frances Perkins (1880–1965): U.S. secretary of labor during the presidency of Franklin D. Roosevelt (1933–1945) and the first woman to serve in a presidential cabinet

Miss Bessie knew that my family, like so many others during the Depression, couldn't afford to subscribe to a newspaper. She knew we didn't even own a radio. Still, she prodded me to "look out for your future and find some way to keep up with what's going on in the world." So I became a delivery boy for the Chattanooga *Times*. I rarely made a dollar a week, but I got to read a newspaper every day. 13

Teaching Tip

Do students agree with Miss Bessie that it's important to "keep up with what's going on in the world"? Ask them whether or how they follow current events—whether through newspapers, Web sites, blogs, broadcasts or podcasts, or even conversations with friends.

Miss Bessie noticed things that had nothing to do with schoolwork, but were vital to a youngster's development. Once a few classmates made fun of my frayed, hand-me-down overcoat, calling me "Strings." As I was leaving school, Miss Bessie patted me on the back of that old overcoat and said, "Carl, never fret about what you *don't* have. Just make the most of what you *do* have—a brain." 14

Among the things that I did not have was electricity in the little frame house that my father had built for $400 with his World War I bonus. But because of her inspiration, I spent many hours squinting beside a kerosene lamp reading Shakespeare and Thoreau, Samuel Pepys and William Cullen Bryant. 15

Power Tip

Paragraph 16 includes some literary terms that might be unfamiliar to you. For definitions, visit an online glossary at **bedfordstmartins.com/literature/bedlit/glossary_a.htm**.

No one in my family had ever graduated from high school, so there was no tradition of commitment to learning for me to lean on. Like millions of youngsters in today's ghettos and barrios, I needed the push and stimulation of a teacher who truly cared. Miss Bessie gave plenty of both, as she immersed me in a wonderful world of similes, metaphors and even onomatopoeia. She led me to believe that I could write sonnets as well as Shakespeare, or iambic-pentameter verse to put Alexander Pope to shame. 16

barrios: neighborhoods inhabited mostly by Spanish-speaking people

In those days the McMinnville school system was rigidly "Jim Crow," and poor black children had to struggle to put anything in their heads. Our high school was only slightly larger than the once-typical little red schoolhouse, and its library was outrageously inadequate—so small, I like to say, that if two students were in it and one wanted to turn a page, the other one had to step outside. 17

Jim Crow: separation of blacks from whites, as mandated by various laws in place in the United States until the mid-1960s

Negroes, as we were called then, were not allowed in the town library, except to mop floors or dust tables. But through one of those secret Old South arrangements between whites of conscience and blacks of stature, Miss Bessie kept getting books smuggled out of the white library. That is how she introduced me to the Brontës, Byron, Coleridge, Keats and Tennyson. "If you don't read, you can't write, and if you can't write, you might as well stop dreaming," Miss Bessie once told me. 18

So I read whatever Miss Bessie told me to, and tried to remember the things she insisted that I store away. Forty-five years later, I can still recite her "truths to live by," such as Henry Wadsworth Longfellow's lines from "The Ladder of St. Augustine": 19

> The heights by great men reached and kept
> Were not attained by sudden flight,
> But they, while their companions slept,
> Were toiling upward in the night.

cajoling: persuading

osmotic: referring to the transfer of something from one place to another, as if through a cell membrane

Years later, her inspiration, prodding, anger, cajoling, and almost osmotic infusion of learning finally led to that lovely day when Miss Bessie dropped me a note saying, "I'm so proud to read your column in the Nashville *Tennessean*." 20

Miss Bessie was a spry 80 when I went back to McMinnville and visited her in a senior citizens' apartment building. Pointing out proudly that her building was racially integrated, she reached for two glasses and a pint of bourbon. I was momentarily shocked, because it would have been scandalous in the 1930s and '40s for word to get out that a teacher drank, and nobody had ever raised a rumor that Miss Bessie did. 21

I felt a new sense of equality as she lifted her glass to mine. Then she revealed a softness and compassion that I had never known as a student. 22

common carrier: a public transportation system

"I've never forgotten that examination day," she said, "when Buster Martin held up seven fingers, obviously asking you for help with question number seven, 'Name a common carrier.' I can still picture you looking at your exam paper and humming a few bars of 'Chattanooga Choo Choo.' I was so tickled, I couldn't punish either of you." 23

Miss Bessie was telling me, with bourbon-laced grace, that I never fooled her for a moment. 24

When Miss Bessie died in 1980, at age 85, hundreds of her former students mourned. They knew the measure of a great teacher: love and motivation. Her wisdom and influence had rippled out across generations. 25

Teaching Tip
If an influential teacher or other individual inspired you to become a teacher, you might want to share your story with the class.

Some of her students who might normally have been doomed to poverty went on to become doctors, dentists, and college professors. Many, guided by Miss Bessie's example, became public-school teachers. 26

"The memory of Miss Bessie and how she conducted her classroom did more for me than anything I learned in college," recalls Gladys Wood of Knoxville, Tennessee, a highly respected English teacher who spent 43 years in the state's school system. "So many times, when I faced a difficult classroom problem, I asked myself, *How would Miss Bessie deal with this?* And I'd remember that she would handle it with laughter and love." 27

No child can get all the necessary support at home, and millions of poor children get *no* support at all. This is what makes a wise, educated, warm-hearted teacher like Miss Bessie so vital to the minds, hearts, and souls of this country's children. 28

CHECK YOUR UNDERSTANDING

1. What action by the author led to a memorable scolding from Miss Bessie?
   - **a.** his absence from class for football practice
   - **b.** his use of the word *ain't*
   - **c.** his failure to do the assigned homework
   - **d.** his cheating on a test
2. Why did the author become a delivery boy for the Chattanooga *Times*?
   - **a.** so that he could read the paper to keep up on world events, as Miss Bessie had advised
   - **b.** so that he could earn extra money for his struggling family and save for college
   - **c.** so that he could begin to learn the workings of the newspaper industry in which he eventually advanced
   - **d.** to make Miss Bessie proud of him
3. What did Miss Bessie do to make sure that her students read works by the Brontës, Byron, Coleridge, and so on?
   - **a.** She brought in books from her personal library.
   - **b.** She got books smuggled out of the white library in town.
   - **c.** She persuaded the school to purchase the books for its library.
   - **d.** She took her students on field trips to the white library in town.
4. What "lovely day" did Miss Bessie's inspiring and tough teaching lead to?
   - **a.** the author's graduation from college
   - **b.** the author's receipt of a prestigious journalism prize
   - **c.** the author's receipt of a note from her expressing her pride in reading his newspaper column
   - **d.** the author's marriage to a schoolteacher

DISCUSS WITH YOUR PEERS

1. In paragraph 16, the author says that he grew up in a home with "no tradition of commitment to learning." Discuss whether you believe that this sort of home environment can be a significant disadvantage to youngsters in school. Then, discuss why an especially dedicated teacher can make all the difference for students who are the first in their families to get a formal education or to pursue a college degree. Can you think of any students or teachers you've known who are like the author or Miss Bessie?

CONTINUED >

2. Look at paragraph 18, and discuss why Miss Bessie believes so strongly in books and literature. Considering your own education and life, do you believe that reading the poetry of the Brontës, Byron, Coleridge, and so on would help you succeed? Finally, discuss whether you agree or disagree with Miss Bessie's philosophy that "If you don't read, you can't write, and if you can't write, you might as well stop dreaming." Do you believe there is some truth in this idea, or is the teacher exaggerating?
3. In paragraph 23, Miss Bessie recalls an episode when the author and his classmate were cheating on an exam. Although she saw and heard them cheating, she reports that "I was so tickled, I couldn't punish either of you." Discuss whether her reaction seems consistent or inconsistent with everything that you know about her character. Given that Miss Bessie cares so much about the future of her students—and given that cheating is a serious act—should she have handled the situation differently? Explain your opinions.

IDENTIFY THE PATTERNS

For more on the various writing patterns referenced here, see Appendix A.

1. The author uses **narration** as the main pattern of development. The whole essay tells a story, but look at paragraphs 9 and 21 for "concentrated" examples of storytelling. Underline or highlight some of the details in these paragraphs that make the stories they tell precise and interesting.
2. The author also uses **cause and effect** to show how a dedicated teacher can have a powerful influence on her students' lives. Reread paragraphs 6–7, 13, 15–16, and 26. In each case, underline or highlight what Miss Bessie does (the cause) and the behavior that this brings about in the students (the effect).
3. The author uses **exemplification** to illustrate Miss Bessie's teaching philosophy and techniques. Without these examples, the reader might not be able to believe the author's claims about this teacher's remarkable power. Reread paragraphs 12–14 and 18–20 and underline or highlight some of the examples the author gives to help us understand Miss Bessie's teaching strategies.

WRITE A PARAGRAPH

1. Describe a strongly influential or inspirational teacher you have known. Discuss what made this teacher powerful and what effects he or she had on you.
2. Discuss whether you have experienced any obstacles to learning in your school life. Describe these obstacles and explain whether you were able to overcome them.

Sherman Alexie

The Joy of Reading and Writing: Superman and Me

Sherman Alexie is a poet, fiction writer, and filmmaker known for his portrayals of contemporary Native American life. Born in 1966, he grew up on the Spokane Indian Reservation in Wellpinit, Washington. Soon after graduating from Washington State University with a B.A. in American studies, Alexie published two critically acclaimed poetry collections, *The Business of Fancydancing* (1991) and *I Would Steal Horses* (1991). His first collection of short stories, *The Lone Ranger and Tonto Fistfight in Heaven* (1993) won the PEN/Hemingway Award for Best First Book of Fiction, and he has gone on to win numerous other awards for his writing. Alexie's most recent works include the short story collections *The Toughest Indian in the World* (2000) and *Ten Little Indians* (2003); the novel *Flight* (2007); the young adult novel *The Absolutely True Diary of a Part-Time Indian* (2007); and the screenplay for *Smoke Signals* (1999), which received two Sundance Film Festival Awards and was the first feature film to be entirely written, directed, and produced by Native Americans.

In the essay that follows, first published in 1998, Alexie recalls how a Superman comic book transformed his education and his life.

Reading Tips: In paragraphs 5, 6, and 8, the author describes some of the educational and psychological challenges faced by Native American (Indian) children living on reservations. Without a general awareness of these challenges, it may be hard to follow these ideas. Thus, in preparation for reading this selection, you might want to do a quick Internet search, using the key words "Indian reservation schools." Reading even a small amount of background information may boost your ability to follow the author's thinking.

I learned to read with a Superman comic book. Simple enough, I suppose. 1
I cannot recall which particular Superman comic book I read, nor can I remember which villain he fought in that issue. I cannot remember the plot, nor the means by which I obtained the comic book. What I can remember is this: I was 3 years old, a Spokane Indian boy living with his family on the Spokane Indian Reservation in eastern Washington state. We were poor by most standards, but one of my parents usually managed to find some minimum-wage job or another, which made us middle-class by reservation standards. I had a brother and three sisters. We lived on a combination of irregular paychecks, hope, fear, and government surplus food.

Teaching Tip
Ask students to share their own stories of how they learned to read. You might want to tell your own story first to make students feel more comfortable.

My father, who is one of the few Indians who went to Catholic school 2
on purpose, was an avid reader of westerns, spy thrillers, murder mysteries, gangster epics, basketball player biographies, and anything else he could find. He bought his books by the pound at Dutch's Pawn Shop, Goodwill, Salvation Army, and Value Village. When he had extra money, he bought new novels at supermarkets, convenience stores, and hospital gift shops. Our house was filled with books. They were stacked in crazy piles in the bathroom, bedrooms, and living room. In a fit of unemployment-inspired creative energy, my father built a set of bookshelves and soon filled them with a random assortment of books about the Kennedy assassination, Watergate,

avid: enthusiastic
epics: long, involved tales

the Vietnam War, and the entire 23-book series of the Apache westerns. My father loved books, and since I loved my father with an aching devotion, I decided to love books as well.

Teaching Tip
Ask students to come up with their own metaphors for what a paragraph is or what its role is in a larger piece of writing.

I can remember picking up my father's books before I could read. The words themselves were mostly foreign, but I still remember the exact moment when I first understood, with a sudden clarity, the purpose of a paragraph. I didn't have the vocabulary to say "paragraph," but I realized that a paragraph was a fence that held words. The words inside a paragraph worked together for a common purpose. They had some specific reason for being inside the same fence. This knowledge delighted me. I began to think of everything in terms of paragraphs. Our reservation was a small paragraph within the United States. My family's house was a paragraph, distinct from the other paragraphs of the LeBrets to the north, the Fords to our south, and the Tribal School to the west. Inside our house, each family member existed as a separate paragraph but still had genetics and common experiences to link us. Now, using this logic, I can see my changed family as an essay of seven paragraphs: mother, father, older brother, the deceased sister, my younger twin sisters, and our adopted little brother. 3

At the same time I was seeing the world in paragraphs, I also picked up that Superman comic book. Each panel, complete with picture, dialogue, and narrative, was a three-dimensional paragraph. In one panel, Superman breaks through a door. His suit is red, blue, and yellow. The brown door shatters into many pieces. I look at the narrative above the picture. I cannot read the words, but I assume it tells me that "Superman is breaking down the door." Aloud, I pretend to read the words and say, "Superman is breaking down the door." Words, dialogue, also float out of Superman's mouth. Because he is breaking down the door, I assume he says, "I am breaking down the door." Once again, I pretend to read the words and say aloud, "I am breaking down the door." In this way, I learned to read. 4

The Grapes of Wrath: a classic American novel written by John Steinbeck (1902–1968) and published in 1939

Dick and Jane: main characters in a series of children's books aimed at teaching basic reading skills

prodigy: a child with unusual talent

This might be an interesting story all by itself. A little Indian boy teaches himself to read at an early age and advances quickly. He reads "Grapes of Wrath" in kindergarten when other children are struggling through "Dick and Jane." If he'd been anything but an Indian boy living on the reservation, he might have been called a prodigy. But he is an Indian boy living on the reservation and is simply an oddity. He grows into a man who often speaks of his childhood in the third person, as if it will somehow dull the pain and make him sound more modest about his talents. 5

powwow: a Native American ceremony

monosyllabic: consisting of one syllable

submissively: meekly; obediently

A smart Indian is a dangerous person, widely feared and ridiculed by Indians and non-Indians alike. I fought with my classmates on a daily basis. They wanted me to stay quiet when the non-Indian teacher asked for answers, for volunteers, for help. We were Indian children who were expected to be stupid. Most lived up to those expectations inside the classroom but subverted them on the outside. They struggled with basic reading in school but could remember how to sing a few dozen powwow songs. They were monosyllabic in front of their non-Indian teachers but could tell complicated stories and jokes at the dinner table. They submissively ducked their heads 6 when confronted by a non-Indian adult but would slug it out with the Indian bully who was 10 years older. As Indian children, we were expected to fail in the non-Indian world. Those who failed were ceremonially accepted by other Indians and appropriately pitied by non-Indians.

7 I refused to fail. I was smart. I was arrogant. I was lucky. I read books late into the night, until I could barely keep my eyes open. I read books at recess, then during lunch, and in the few minutes left after I had finished my classroom assignments. I read books in the car when my family traveled to powwows or basketball games. In shopping malls, I ran to the bookstores and read bits and pieces of as many books as I could. I read the books my father brought home from the pawnshops and secondhand. I read the books I borrowed from the library. I read the backs of cereal boxes. I read the newspaper. I read the bulletins posted on the walls of the school, the clinic, the tribal offices, the post office. I read junk mail. I read auto-repair manuals. I read magazines. I read anything that had words and paragraphs. I read with equal parts joy and desperation. I loved those books, but I also knew that love had only one purpose. I was trying to save my life.

arrogant: proud; having an attitude of superiority

8 Despite all the books I read, I am still surprised I became a writer. I was going to be a pediatrician. These days, I write novels, short stories, and poems. I visit schools and teach creative writing to Indian kids. In all my years in the reservation school system, I was never taught how to write poetry, short stories, or novels. I was certainly never taught that Indians wrote poetry, short stories, and novels. Writing was something beyond Indians. I cannot recall a single time that a guest teacher visited the reservation. There must have been visiting teachers. Who were they? Where are they now? Do they exist? I visit the schools as often as possible. The Indian kids crowd the classroom. Many are writing their own poems, short stories, and novels. They have read my books. They have read many other books. They look at me with bright eyes and arrogant wonder. They are trying to save their lives. Then there are the sullen and already defeated Indian kids who sit in the back rows and ignore me with theatrical precision. The pages of their notebooks are empty. They carry neither pencil nor pen. They stare out the window. They refuse and resist. "Books," I say to them. "Books," I say. I throw my weight against their locked doors. The door holds. I am smart. I am arrogant. I am lucky. I am trying to save our lives.

Teaching Tip
Invite a local writer to your classroom to talk about his or her own education and the role of reading in it. The writer might be a faculty member, a newspaper reporter, or some other local literary figure.

sullen: silent and resentful

CHECK YOUR UNDERSTANDING

1. How did the author learn to read?
   - **a.** He studied Superman comic books and also listened along while a family member recited great works of literature.
   - **b.** He decided to look through at least three Superman comics a day until he understood the words.
   - **c.** He looked at the pictures in a Superman comic book and guessed, based on the pictures, what the written dialogue was saying.
   - **d.** He took part in a special school program for gifted students.

CONTINUED >

2. How does the author describe his father?
   a. as an "occasional reader" of westerns and spy thrillers
   b. as an "avid reader" of many different types of books
   c. as a "snob" who would read only literary classics
   d. as a nonreader
3. What, according to the author, were the expectations for the Indian children at his school?
   a. They were expected to overcome difficult obstacles to succeed.
   b. They were expected to get well-paying jobs to better themselves and their families.
   c. They were expected to go to college.
   d. They were expected to fail in the outside world.
4. When the author visits reservation schools, how do the children react?
   a. Some are interested in the author and in writing; others "refuse and resist."
   b. All of the children are impressed that a famous author would choose to visit them.
   c. The children are eager to "show off" their writing to the author.
   d. Most of the children ignore him and his advice about reading and writing.

DISCUSS WITH YOUR PEERS

1. In paragraph 3, what metaphor (creative comparison) does the author use to describe "the purpose of a paragraph"? Discuss whether his understanding of the paragraph has a useful and important purpose in his life. As a student, do you believe that your ability to organize and write coherent paragraphs will help you succeed in other areas of your life? Explain your opinions, providing some examples.
2. In paragraph 6, underline or highlight examples of how the Indian children hide their intelligence from the non-Indian teachers. Then, discuss the first and last sentences of the paragraph. Explain what motivates the Indian children to keep up an appearance of ignorance. Does their behavior make sense to you? Discuss why a child might choose to *play* stupid in an environment where all the adults expect that child to *be* stupid.
3. First, reread paragraph 8. Then, discuss how the reservation school system failed the author when he was a boy. Next, discuss how the author tries to compensate for the failures of this system when he grows up. Pay close attention to the following sentences: "I throw my weight against their locked doors. . . . I am trying to save our lives." What does the author know about these children that motivates him? If he is already a successful author, why does he say, "save *our* lives"? Do you agree or disagree that books can save a person's life? Explain your opinions.

IDENTIFY THE PATTERNS

For more on the various writing patterns referenced here, see Appendix A.

1. The author uses **narration** as his main pattern of development. In the first sentence of paragraph 1, identify the main idea for the story. Then, keeping this main idea in mind, try to identify the important "parts" of the story. What happens? What is the time frame? Who are the main characters?
2. In paragraphs 2–3 and 6–7, the author uses **exemplification** to develop his writing. First, select one or two of these paragraphs to work with. Next, identify the main idea of each paragraph. Then, underline or highlight some of the examples that the author gives to support each main idea.
3. In paragraph 4, the author uses both **process** and **description**. Because Alexie learned to read by looking at pictures in comic books, he wants to make this process as visual as possible for readers. First, he uses descriptive details to help us visualize the images in the comic book. Underline or highlight some of these details. Next, he specifies each step in the learning process. On a separate sheet of paper, list these steps.

WRITE A PARAGRAPH

1. Discuss the role of reading in your life.
2. Discuss your feelings about your own intelligence and how these feelings have affected your school experiences. Are you secure or insecure about your intelligence? Do you hide your intelligence or show it off? Can you, like Alexie, proclaim, "I refused to fail. I was smart. I was arrogant. I was lucky" (para. 7)? Or are you more like the young Indians who "stare out the window" and "refuse and resist" (para. 8)?

Lynda Barry

The Sanctuary of School

Cartoonist and author Lynda Barry was born in Wisconsin in 1956 and raised in Seattle, Washington. Her work focuses on the complexities of growing up, touching on everything from bad haircuts and first crushes to racism and drugs. Barry studied fine art at Evergreen State College in Olympia, Washington, where her work caught the eye of classmate Matt Groening, creator of *The Simpsons.* Impressed by her crudely sketched characters and sense of humor, Groening submitted her comic strip *Ernie Pook's Comeek* to the college newspaper; soon, it was picked up by the *Chicago Reader.* In addition to her weekly strip, which now appears in alternative newspapers across the country, Barry has published numerous collections of her comics as well as the novels *The Good Times Are Killing Me* (1988) and *Cruddy* (1999).

First published in the *New York Times* in 1992, the following essay brings to life a defining experience from Barry's childhood. Sneaking out of her house before daybreak, Barry discovers that school is the one place she feels safe and secure.

Reading Tips: Notice that the essay is broken into two major parts: a story about the author's experiences in school and a commentary about current attitudes toward public schools. As you read, consider how the parts work together.

I was 7 years old the first time I snuck out of the house in the dark. It was winter and my parents had been fighting all night. They were short on money and long on relatives who kept "temporarily" moving into our house because they had nowhere else to go. 1

My brother and I were used to giving up our bedroom. We slept on the couch, something we actually liked because it put us that much closer to the light of our lives, our television. 2

Steve Allen (1921–2000) and **Johnny Carson** (1925–2005): popular comedians and late-night talk-show hosts

At night when everyone was asleep, we lay on our pillows watching it with the sound off. We watched Steve Allen's mouth moving. We watched Johnny Carson's mouth moving. We watched movies filled with gangsters shooting machine guns into packed rooms, dying soldiers hurling a last grenade and beautiful women crying at windows. Then the sign-off finally came and we tried to sleep. 3

The morning I snuck out, I woke up filled with a panic about needing to get to school. The sun wasn't quite up yet but my anxiety was so fierce that I just got dressed, walked quietly across the kitchen and let myself out the back door. 4

It was quiet outside. Stars were still out. Nothing moved and no one was in the street. It was as if someone had turned the sound off on the world. 5

I walked the alley, breaking thin ice over the puddles with my shoes. I didn't know why I was walking to school in the dark. I didn't think about it. All I knew was a feeling of panic, like the panic that strikes kids when they realize they are lost. 6

nondescript: bland; not distinctive or interesting

Teaching Tip

Ask students if, as children, they ever turned to some institution outside of home for support. They might mention a school, a church, a community center, sports program—anything.

That feeling eased the moment I turned the corner and saw the dark outline of my school at the top of the hill. My school was made up of about 15 nondescript portable classrooms set down on a fenced concrete lot in a rundown Seattle neighborhood, but it had the most beautiful view of the Cascade Mountains. You could see them from anywhere on the playfield and you could see them from the windows of my classroom—Room 2. 7

I walked over to the monkey bars and hooked my arms around the cold metal. I stood for a long time just looking across Rainier Valley. The sky was beginning to whiten and I could hear a few birds. 8

In a perfect world my absence at home would not have gone unnoticed. I would have had two parents in a panic to locate me, instead of two parents in a panic to locate an answer to the hard question of survival during a deep financial and emotional crisis. 9

But in an overcrowded and unhappy home, it's incredibly easy for any child to slip away. The high levels of frustration, depression and anger in my house made my brother and me invisible. We were children with the sound turned off. And for us, as for the steadily increasing number of neglected children in this country, the only place where we could count on being noticed was at school. 10

"Hey there, young lady. Did you forget to go home last night?" It was Mr. Gunderson, our janitor, whom we all loved. He was nice and he was funny and he was old with white hair, thick glasses and an unbelievable number of keys. I could hear them jingling as he walked across the playfield. I felt incredibly happy to see him. 11

He let me push his wheeled garbage can between the different portables as he unlocked each room. He let me turn on the lights and raise the window shades and I saw my school slowly come to life. I saw Mrs. Holman, our school secretary, walk into the office without her orange lipstick on yet. She waved. 12

I saw the fifth-grade teacher, Mr. Cunningham, walking under the breezeway eating a hard roll. He waved. 13

And I saw my teacher, Mrs. Claire LeSane, walking toward us in a red coat and calling my name in a very happy and surprised way, and suddenly my throat got tight and my eyes stung and I ran toward her crying. It was something that surprised us both. 14

It's only thinking about it now, 28 years later, that I realize I was crying from relief. I was with my teacher, and in a while I was going to sit at my desk, with my crayons and pencils and books and classmates all around me, and for the next six hours I was going to enjoy a thoroughly secure, warm and stable world. It was a world I absolutely relied on. Without it, I don't know where I would have gone that morning. 15

Mrs. LeSane asked me what was wrong and when I said "Nothing," she seemingly left it at that. But she asked me if I would carry her purse for her, an honor above all honors, and she asked if I wanted to come into Room 2 early and paint. 16

She believed in the natural healing power of painting and drawing for troubled children. In the back of her room there was always a drawing table and an easel with plenty of supplies, and sometimes during the day she would come up to you for what seemed like no good reason and quietly ask if you wanted to go to the back table and "make some pictures for Mrs. LeSane." We all had a chance at it—to sit apart from the class for a while to paint, draw and silently work out impossible problems on 11 × 17 sheets of newsprint. 17

Drawing came to mean everything to me. At the back table in Room 2, I learned to build myself a life preserver that I could carry into my home. 18

We all know that a good education system saves lives, but the people of this country are still told that cutting the budget for public schools is necessary, that poor salaries for teachers are all we can manage and that art, music and all creative activities must be the first to go when times are lean. 19

Before- and after-school programs are cut and we are told that public schools are not made for baby-sitting children. If parents are neglectful temporarily or permanently, for whatever reason, it's certainly sad, but their unlucky children must fend for themselves. Or slip through the cracks. Or wander in a dark night alone. 20

We are told in a thousand ways that not only are public schools not important, but that the children who attend them, the children who need 21

Teaching Tip
You may want to share more information with students on the state of funding for public schools in the United States. One good resource is a "backgrounder" from PBS's *NewsHour*, at **pbs.org/newshour/backgrounders/school_funding.html**.

a thousand points of light: a term used by the first President George Bush in his 1989 inaugural speech. The "thousand points of light" are community and volunteer organizations.

them most, are not important either. We leave them to learn from the blind eye of a television, or to the mercy of "a thousand points of light" that can be as far away as stars.

I was lucky. I had Mrs. LeSane. I had Mr. Gunderson. I had an abundance of art supplies. And I had a particular brand of neglect in my home that allowed me to slip away and get to them. But what about the rest of the kids who weren't as lucky? What happened to them? 22

By the time the bell rang that morning I had finished my drawing and Mrs. LeSane pinned it up on the special bulletin board she reserved for drawings from the back table. It was the same picture I always drew—a sun in the corner of a blue sky over a nice house with flowers all around it. 23

Mrs. LeSane asked us to please stand, face the flag, place our right hands over our hearts and say the Pledge of Allegiance. Children across the country do it faithfully. I wonder now when the country will face its children and say a pledge right back. 24

CHECK YOUR UNDERSTANDING

1. Which of the following most accurately describes the author's home life during her childhood?
   - **a.** It was peaceful.
   - **b.** It was full of stress, conflict, and unhappiness.
   - **c.** It was educationally stimulating.
   - **d.** It was full of loving and caring adults.
2. What, for the author, were the differences between home and school?
   - **a.** She was punished at home and praised at school.
   - **b.** She was the center of attention at home and ignored at school.
   - **c.** She was invisible at home and noticed at school.
   - **d.** She was calm at home but full of stress at school.
3. What "healing" thing did Mrs. LeSane do for her students?
   - **a.** She let them paint and draw.
   - **b.** She let them carry her purse.
   - **c.** She let them open the classroom for her.
   - **d.** She listened to all of their problems.
4. What is the author's attitude toward budget cuts for public schools?
   - **a.** She disagrees with them but understands that they are necessary in tough economic times.
   - **b.** She reluctantly accepts them, as long as art, music, and other creative activities are preserved.
   - **c.** She accepts them without reservations.
   - **d.** She thinks that they harm children—especially those who do not have a lot of support at home.

DISCUSS WITH YOUR PEERS

1. In paragraph 3, the author explains that she and her brother watched television "with the sound off." Then, in paragraph 5, she repeats this idea when she says, "It was as if someone had turned the sound off on the world." Finally, in paragraph 10, she states, "We were children with the sound turned off." Discuss with your peers what the author means by these descriptions. What are the problems in the child's home environment? Do you think the impact of this environment on the child is very serious or not? Explain your opinion.
2. Reread paragraph 14 and discuss why the author starts crying. Does this reaction make sense to you? Does Mrs. LeSane do something that causes the author to cry? Discuss what powerful force the teacher represents that would make a child react so dramatically.
3. Reread paragraph 17 and discuss the teacher's belief in the "natural healing power of painting and drawing for troubled children." Do you think that allowing students to paint and draw in class would be effective in helping them work through their personal problems? Why or why not?
4. Discuss whether you agree or disagree with the author's views, expressed in paragraphs 19 and 20, that public schools are often neglected in the United States. Do you believe that a role of the education system is to "save lives" and that public schools should be given greater funding and support for this reason? If possible, use examples from your own school experiences.

IDENTIFY THE PATTERNS

For more on the various writing patterns referenced here, see Appendix A.

1. The first sentence of paragraph 1 makes it clear that the author is using **narration** to develop her writing. Explain why this sentence clearly indicates the use of narration. Then, in your own words, describe the story that the author tells. What happens? What is the time frame? Who are the main characters?
2. Throughout this essay, the author uses **comparison and contrast** to develop her writing. In particular, she shows how the home environment and the school environment are dramatically different. Reread paragraphs 1–6 and 9–10 and underline or highlight some of the key details that help you understand the home environment. Then, reread paragraphs 11–18, underlining or highlighting some of the key details that help you understand the school environment. Finally, discuss some of the key elements that are contrasted, including the people, the places, the activities, and the emotions.
3. In paragraphs 17 and 18, the author uses **cause and effect** to show how Mrs. LeSane's teaching had a powerful effect on her life. First, discuss the cause: what does the teacher do to help her students? Then, discuss the particular effect that this strategy has on the author. Is this effect an important and lasting one?

CONTINUED >

4. In paragraphs 19–22, the author uses **argument** to develop her writing. What general argument does the author make about the attitude toward public schools in the United States? Underline or highlight some of the key points that she makes to support her argument. Then, underline or highlight some of the emotional details that the author uses to help convince the reader that her argument is a valid one.

WRITE A PARAGRAPH

1. Discuss your earliest feelings about school, when you were in the elementary grades. Did you love going to school? Was it a sort of "sanctuary" for you? Or, was it something altogether different? How did people treat you? What sort of activities did you participate in?
2. Discuss how your home environment made you feel when you were a child.
3. Discuss whether you agree or disagree with the idea that "a good education system saves lives" (para. 19).

MAKE CONNECTIONS

1. In all three reading selections in this chapter, we see examples of dedicated and powerful teachers: Miss Bessie, Mrs. LeSane, and Sherman Alexie when he returns to teach writing to the Indian children. In a paragraph or essay, discuss what makes a teacher a great teacher. You may use ideas and examples from the readings and from your own experiences and knowledge.
2. In all three reading selections, we see that a child's home environment and family background can affect his or her ability to succeed in school. For some children, poverty and prejudice can be *obstacles* to success in school; for other children, these same factors can be *motivators* for success in school. In a paragraph or an essay, discuss how important a child's home environment and family background are for succeeding in school. You may use ideas and examples from the readings and from your own experiences and knowledge.

Be aware of other readings that relate to the theme of school and learning:

- "Our Religious Diversity" by Sandy Sasso (page 595)
- "Why Couldn't My Father Read?" by Enrique Hank Lopez (page 603)
- "Raising a Son—with Men on the Fringes" by Robyn Marks (page 610)

Chapter 20

Marriage

READINGS

- "What Makes Marriages Work"
- "The 'M-Word': Why It Matters to Me"
- "Like Mexicans"

Marriage is one of the oldest and most honored of human bonds. A couple, traditionally a man and a woman of similar ethnic background, unite and vow to spend the rest of their lives together. For many, marriage is the realization of a lifelong dream, but for others it's a disappointment, or worse. Now, with divorce rates approaching 50 percent worldwide, some people are questioning traditional assumptions about marriage. At the same time, the drive to marry remains strong, and relatively new forms of marriage, such as gay and interracial marriage, are gaining acceptance.

As you read the following selections, consider your own beliefs about marriage. Perhaps you plan to honor your parents' guidelines for marriage, or maybe you plan to decide your own requirements for marriage. If you are already married (or if you have been married), consider how your beliefs about the institution may have changed over time. Also, consider the issue beyond yourself: do you believe that others should marry as they please, or should all people be expected to follow some basic rules for marriage?

Kathleen Stassen Berger

What Makes Marriages Work

Kathleen Stassen Berger is chair of the Social Science Department at Bronx Community College of the City University of New York, where she has taught psychology for the past thirty-five years. Berger earned her undergraduate degrees from Stanford University and Radcliffe College and then received an M.A.T. from Harvard University and an M.S. and Ph.D. from Yeshiva University. She is the author of three college-level psychology textbooks and has written articles for the American Association of Higher Education, the National Education Association, and the *Wiley Encyclopedia of Psychology.* Her research focuses on adolescent identity, sibling relationships, and bullying.

In this excerpt from her textbook *The Developing Person Through the Life Span,* Berger examines the ingredients of a successful marriage. Note how she supports her points with facts and statistics from various sources. (For another reading from this textbook, see page 580.)

Reading Tips: In this piece of academic writing, the author uses statistics and scientific vocabulary (*homogamy, heterogamy,* and so on) to discuss her topic. Be prepared to read slowly and reread when necessary to grasp the author's ideas. Also, notice that she gives credit to other experts, whose names are in parentheses immediately after the ideas that they contributed. Full information on these experts' publications can be found at the end of this excerpt.

prelude: something that comes before something else

Teaching Tip
Some of your students might be married. You might ask if any of them feel comfortable sharing their reactions to this piece with the class. Based on their own experiences, do they agree with the author's observations, or do they take exception to any of her findings?

Marriage is not what it once was—a legal and religious arrangement sought as the *exclusive* avenue for sexual expression, the *only* legitimate prelude for childbearing, and a *lifelong* source of intimacy and support. Here are some U.S. statistics that make this point: 1

- The proportion of adults who are unmarried is higher than at any time in the past century.
- Only 10 percent of brides are virgins.
- Nearly one-half of all first births are to single mothers, who are increasingly unlikely to marry the fathers of their babies.
- At least another 20 percent of all first births are conceived before marriage.
- The divorce rate is 49 percent of the marriage rate.
- The rate of first marriages in young adulthood is the lowest in 50 years (Bachu, 1999; Zavodny, 1999). Most adults aged 20 to 30 are not yet married (62 percent) (U.S. Bureau of the Census, 2002).

Low marriage rates in young adulthood are by no means limited to the United States: Adults in many developed countries now spend, on average, half of the years between ages 20 and 40 unmarried, with men less likely to marry before age 30 than women (Iacovou, 2002). 2

Nevertheless, marriage remains a personal as well as public commitment, celebrated in every culture of the world by a ceremony with special words, clothes, blessings, food, drink, and often many guests and great expense. The hoped-for outcome is a love that deepens over the years as the couple's bond is cemented by bearing and raising children, weathering economic and emotional turbulence, surviving serious illness or other setbacks, and sharing social and financial commitments. 3

turbulence: unrest

Research from all over the world finds that married people are happier, healthier, and richer (Stack & Eshleman, 1998). Although gender roles have changed over the years, U.S. couples in 2000 rated their marriages as satisfying as did couples in 1980 (Amato et al., 2003). Let's look at some ingredients of that satisfaction. 4

* * *

From a developmental perspective, marriage is a useful institution: 5
Children generally thrive when two parents are directly committed to their well-being, and adults thrive if one other person satisfies their need for intimacy and for generativity. Yet, clearly, not all marriages accomplish these goals. Why do some marriages work well, while others do not?

generativity: a need to nurture others, especially young people

One developmental factor that influences the success of a marriage is 6
the maturity of the partners. In general, the younger the bride and groom, the less likely their marriage is to succeed (Amato et al., 2003). That may be because, as Erikson pointed out, intimacy is hard to establish until identity is secure. Thus, in a series of studies, college students who were less advanced on Erikson's identity and intimacy stages tended to define love in terms of passion, not intimacy or commitment—butterflies and excitement, not openness, trust, and loyalty (Aron & Westbay, 1996).

Erikson's identity and intimacy stages: necessary stages in human development as defined by German psychologist Erik Erikson (1902–1994)

A second influence on marital success is the degree of similarity between 7
husband and wife. Anthropologists distinguish between **homogamy**, or marriage within the same tribe or ethnic group, and **heterogamy**, or marriage outside the group. Traditionally, homogamy meant marriage between people of the same cohort, religion, socioeconomic status, ethnicity, and education. For contemporary marriages, homogamy and heterogamy refer to similarity in interests, attitudes, and goals (Cramer, 1998).

cohort: a group of people who share some characteristic

One study of 168 young couples found that **social homogamy**, defined 8
as similarity in leisure interests and role preferences, is particularly important to marital success (Houts et al., 1996). For instance, if both spouses enjoyed (or hated) picnicking, dancing, swimming, going to the movies, listening to music, eating out, or entertaining friends, the partners tended to be more "in love" and more committed to the relationship. Similarly, if the two agreed on who should make meals, pay bills, shop for groceries, and so on, then ambivalence and conflict were reduced.

Teaching Tip
Ask students about their own "leisure interests" and "role preferences" in terms of dating, marriage, or other committed relationship.

ambivalence: uncertainty; conflicting feelings

The authors of this study do not believe that "finding a mate compatible 9
on many dimensions is an achievable goal." In reality, "individuals who are seeking a compatible mate must make many compromises if they are to marry at all" (Houts et al., 1996). They found that, for any young adult, fewer than 1 in 100 potential mates provides minimal social homogamy, defined as sharing three favorite leisure activities and three role preferences. Most successful couples learn to compromise, adjust, or agree to disagree about many things.

A third factor affecting the success of a marriage is *marital equity*, the 10
extent to which the two partners perceive a rough equality in the partnership. According to **social exchange theory**, marriage is an arrangement in which each person contributes something useful to the other (Edwards, 1969). Historically, the two sexes traded gender-specific commodities: Men provided social status and financial security, while women provided homemaking, sex, and children (Townsend, 1998).

social exchange theory: the view of human interaction as an exchange aimed at maximizing an individual's advantages or benefits while minimizing his or her disadvantages or costs

In many modern marriages, the equity that is sought is not an exchange 11
but rather shared contributions of a similar kind: Instead of husbands earning all the money and wives doing all the domestic work, both are now expected to do both. Similarly, both partners expect equality and sensitivity to their needs regarding dependence, sexual desire, shared confidences, and so on, and happier

equity: fairness

adept: skilled

marriages are those in which both partners are adept at emotional perception and expression (Fitness, 2001). Evidence for the new form of exchanges is that over the past few decades wives have begun earning more money and husbands have begun doing more housework—with the result that overall marital satisfaction has improved (Amato et al., 2003). What matters most, however, is the perception of fairness, not absolute equality (Sanchez, 1994; Wilkie et al., 1998).

References

Amato, Paul R., Johnson, David R., Booth, Alan, & Rogers, Stacy J. (2003). Continuity and change in marital quality between 1980 and 2000. *Journal of Marriage and Family, 65,* 1–22.

Aron, Arthur, & Westbay, Lori. (1996). Dimensions of the prototype of love. *Journal of Personality and Social Relationships, 70,* 535–551.

Bachu, A. (1999). Trends in premarital childbearing: 1930 to 1994. *Current Population Reports, 1999,* Series P-23, No. 197.

Cramer, Duncan. (1998). *Close relationships: The study of love and friendship.* New York: Oxford University Press.

Edwards, John N. (1969). Familiar behavior as social exchange. *Journal of Marriage and Family, 31,* 518–526.

Fitness, Julie. (2001). Intimate relationships. In Joseph Ciarrochi, Joseph R. Forgas, & John D. Mayer (Eds.), *Emotional intelligence in everyday life: A scientific inquiry* (pp. 98–112). Philadelphia: Psychology Press.

Houts, Renate M., Robins, Elliot, & Huston, Ted L. (1996). Compatibility and the development of premarital relationships. *Journal of Marriage and Family, 58,* 7–20.

Iacovou, Maria. (2002). Regional differences in the transition to adulthood. *Annals of the American Academy of Political and Social Science, 580,* 40–69.

Sanchez, Laura. (1994). Gender, labor allocations, and the psychology of entitlement within the home. *Social Forces, 73*(2), 533–553.

Stack, Steven, & Eshleman, J. Ross. (1998). Marital status and happiness: A 17-nation study. *Journal of Marriage and Family, 60,* 527–537.

Townsend, John Marshall. (1998). *What women want—What men want: Why the sexes still see love and commitment so differently.* New York: Oxford.

U.S. Bureau of the Census. (2002). *National Vital Statistics Reports, 50*(5).

Wilkie, Jane R., Ferree, Mayra M., & Ratcliff, Kathryn S. (1998). Gender and fairness: Marital satisfaction in two-earner couples. *Journal of Marriage and Family, 60,* 577–594.

Zavodny, Madeline. (1999). Do men's characteristics affect whether a nonmarital pregnancy results in marriage? *Journal of Marriage and Family, 61,* 764–773.

CHECK YOUR UNDERSTANDING

1. Marriage was once the "*exclusive* avenue for sexual expression." Which current statistic shows that this is no longer true?
   - **a.** The divorce rate is 49 percent of the marriage rate.
   - **b.** The rate of first marriages in young adulthood is the lowest in 50 years.
   - **c.** Only 10 percent of brides are virgins.
   - **d.** The proportion of adults who are unmarried is higher than at any time in the past century.

2. If you are an immature individual with an identity that is not yet secure, how are you likely to define love?
   a. in terms of openness
   b. in terms of passion and excitement
   c. in terms of commitment
   d. in terms of physical attractiveness
3. What are the chances that a young adult will find a mate who shares three similar leisure activities and three role preferences?
   a. very low
   b. good
   c. fairly high
   d. very high
4. Which of the following is part of the "new form of exchanges" in modern marriages?
   a. wives do all the housework
   b. husbands do some of the housework
   c. husbands earn most of the money
   d. wives do most of the child-raising

DISCUSS WITH YOUR PEERS

1. According to the author, what customs are used to celebrate the marriage and to set the stage for the hoped-for outcome of deeper love (para. 3)? Do you agree that such customs help to encourage deeper love in a couple, or are they more likely to hurt the relationship?
2. In paragraph 6, the author states that "intimacy is hard to establish until identity is secure." What does this mean, and do you agree with the idea? Explain your opinion.
3. What is it that both partners expect in a modern marriage (para. 11)? Do you agree that these are reasonable expectations for both husbands and wives? Do you know any couples who have achieved these goals in their marriage?

IDENTIFY THE PATTERNS

For more on the various writing patterns referenced here, see Appendix A.

1. In paragraph 1, the author uses **definition** to explain what marriage "once was." Underline or highlight the key parts of the definition. Discuss whether this is a complete and interesting definition for traditional marriage.
2. In paragraph 5, the author uses **cause and effect** to make a point about the usefulness of marriage. Underline or highlight two positive *effects* of a good marriage and the two *causes* of these positive outcomes.

CONTINUED >

3. In paragraph 8, the author uses **exemplification** to discuss factors behind successful marriages. Underline or highlight some of the specific examples that the author provides to illustrate her ideas. Discuss whether these examples strengthen the writing.
4. In paragraphs 10 and 11, the author uses **comparison and contrast**. Identify the two things that are being compared and contrasted. Then, explain how these things are similar and different. Does the author provide enough information and details for this to be an effective use of comparison and contrast?

WRITE A PARAGRAPH

1. What do you, personally, see as the ingredients of a successful marriage? You can draw on the author's research and on your own experiences and observations.
2. At the end of her piece, the author discusses how marriage has changed over time. Do you see marriage continuing to change? In what ways? What changes would be for the good, and what changes might be harmful to couples, their families, or society?

Andrew Sullivan

The "M-Word": Why It Matters to Me

Andrew Sullivan is a writer known for his outspoken opinions on gay rights and other social and political topics. Born in England in 1963, Sullivan received a B.A. in modern history from Oxford University and a Ph.D. in government from Harvard University. He began his journalism career as an intern for *The New Republic,* quickly moving up to become the youngest editor in the magazine's history. After leaving *The New Republic* in 1996, Sullivan wrote for a variety of publications, including the *New York Times,* the *Washington Post, Esquire,* and *Time* magazine. Sullivan is currently a contributing editor at *The Atlantic* and the author of *The Daily Dish,* one of the most widely read blogs on the Web. Sullivan also has published several books, including *Virtually Normal: An Argument about Homosexuality* (1995), *Love Undetectable: Notes on Friendship, Sex and Survival* (1999), and *The Conservative Soul: How We Lost It, How to Get It Back* (2006).

In this essay from a 2004 issue of *Time* magazine, Sullivan passionately defends same-sex marriage. Marriage isn't about religion, he claims, but about two people's right to celebrate and affirm their love and commitment to family values.

Reading Tips: Many of us have very strong opinions about homosexuality and gay lifestyles. As you read this essay, try to keep an open mind about the author's experiences. Even if you do not agree with his position on gay rights, can you empathize with his struggles for self-esteem, love, and acceptance?

What's in a name? 1

Perhaps the best answer is a memory. 2

As a child, I had no idea what homosexuality was. I grew up in a tradi- 3
tional home—Catholic, conservative, middle class. Life was relatively simple: education, work, family. I was brought up to aim high in life, even though my

parents hadn't gone to college. But one thing was instilled in me. What matters is not how far you go in life, how much money you make, how big a name you make for yourself. What really matters is family, and the love you have for one another. The most important day of your life was not graduation from college or your first day at work or a raise or even your first house. The most important day of your life was when you got married. It was on that day that all your friends and all your family got together to celebrate the most important thing in life: your happiness, your ability to make a new home, to form a new but connected family, to find love that puts everything else into perspective.

instilled: gradually put into someone's mind

Teaching Tip
What do students and their families see as the most important day of one's life, and why?

But as I grew older, I found that this was somehow not available to 4
me. I didn't feel the things for girls that my peers did. All the emotions and social rituals and bonding of teenage heterosexual life eluded me. I didn't know why. No one explained it. My emotional bonds to other boys were one-sided; each time I felt myself falling in love, they sensed it, pushed it away. I didn't and couldn't blame them. I got along fine with my buds in a non-emotional context; but something was awry, something not right. I came to know almost instinctively that I would never be a part of my family the way my siblings one day might be. The love I had inside me was unmentionable, anathema—even, in the words of the Church I attended every Sunday, evil. I remember writing in my teenage journal one day: "I'm a professional human being. But what do I do in my private life?"

anathema: something that is hated

So, like many gay men of my generation, I retreated. I never discussed 5
my real life. I couldn't date girls and so immersed myself in schoolwork, in the debate team, school plays, anything to give me an excuse not to confront reality. When I looked toward the years ahead, I couldn't see a future. There was just a void. Was I going to be alone my whole life? Would I ever have a "most important day" in my life? It seemed impossible, a negation, an undoing. To be a full part of my family I had to somehow not be me. So like many gay teens, I withdrew, became neurotic, depressed, at times close to suicidal. I shut myself in my room with my books, night after night, while my peers developed the skills needed to form real relationships, and loves. In wounded pride, I even voiced a rejection of family and marriage. It was the only way I could explain my isolation.

negation: denial

It took years for me to realize that I was gay, years later to tell others, 6
and more time yet to form any kind of stable emotional bond with another man. Because my sexuality had emerged in solitude—and without any link to the idea of an actual relationship—it was hard later to reconnect sex to love and self-esteem. It still is. But I persevered, each relationship slowly growing longer than the last, learning in my twenties and thirties what my straight friends found out in their teens. But even then, my parents and friends never asked the question they would have asked automatically if I were straight: So when are you going to get married? When is your relationship going to be public? When will we be able to celebrate it and affirm it and support it? In fact, no one—no one—has yet asked me that question.

persevered: persisted; continued with determination

When people talk about "gay marriage," they miss the point. This isn't 7
about gay marriage. It's about marriage. It's about family. It's about love. It isn't about religion. It's about civil marriage licenses—available to atheists

as well as believers. These family values are not options for a happy and stable life. They are necessities. Putting gay relationships in some other category—civil unions, domestic partnerships, civil partnerships, whatever—may alleviate real human needs, but, by their very euphemism, by their very separateness, they actually build a wall between gay people and their own families. They put back the barrier many of us have spent a lifetime trying to erase.

alleviate: to relieve or satisfy

euphemism: a term that is misleading, often because it uses a pleasant- or bland-sounding word for a distasteful thing

Teaching Tip

If you know or suspect that certain students in your class are gay, be careful not to "out" them accidentally to the class. Singling out such students can sometimes make them feel more isolated, especially if they are just starting to come to terms with their homosexuality.

It's too late for me to undo my own past. But I want above everything else to remember a young kid out there who may even be reading this now. I want to let him know that he doesn't have to choose between himself and his family any more. I want him to know that his love has dignity, that he does indeed have a future as a full and equal part of the human race. Only marriage will do that. Only marriage can bring him home. 8

CHECK YOUR UNDERSTANDING

1. For the author's family, what is the most important day in one's life?
   a. the day you graduate
   b. the day you begin your first job
   c. the day you get married
   d. the day you move into your first house
2. As a gay teenager, how did the author react to the "void" he saw in his future?
   a. He formed new friendships.
   b. He sought help from a counselor.
   c. He became argumentative.
   d. He withdrew.
3. How does the author regard civil unions, domestic partnerships, and civil partnerships?
   a. They are completely unacceptable substitutes for marriage.
   b. They create barriers between gay people and their families.
   c. They are "good enough" for gays who want official recognition of their marriage in states where gay marriage is illegal.
   d. They are an ideal way for gay couples to show their commitment to one another.
4. What is one of the messages that the author wants to send to young gays?
   a. They have no hope of ever marrying.
   b. They do not have to choose between their families and their own desires.
   c. They should devote all their efforts to advocating for gay marriage.
   d. They should "work tirelessly" for the institution of civil unions.

DISCUSS WITH YOUR PEERS

1. In paragraph 5, how does the author describe the life of many gay teenagers? Sullivan was a teenager in the 1970s. Discuss whether gay teenagers today have an easier time. What social changes might be making life easier for gay teenagers? Do you think gay teens will face fewer or less severe challenges in the future? Why or why not?
2. In paragraph 6, the author suggests that heterosexual teenagers may have some advantages over gay teenagers in their ability to develop healthy relationships. He says: "But I persevered, each relationship slowly growing longer than the last, learning in my twenties and thirties what my straight friends found out in their teens." Discuss whether you agree or disagree with this claim. Do straight teens really have advantages in their social and sexual development, or do straight and gay teens face more or less the same challenges? Explain your opinions.
3. In paragraph 7, the author argues that granting gay partners all the *rights* of marriage is not enough; instead, we must use the *word marriage.* If we use other terms for gay unions (*civil unions, domestic partnerships, civil partnerships*), we continue to "build a wall between gay people and their families." Discuss whether you agree or disagree that a single word really has the power to harm or improve people's lives. Should gay couples be satisfied with the rights of marriage and stop worrying about the word *marriage*? If the word causes so much trouble, should we discontinue its use and find a neutral term—such as *domestic partnership*—for all unions, gay and straight?
4. In paragraph 8, the author argues that "only marriage" will allow a gay person to be "a full and equal part of the human race." Discuss whether you agree or disagree with this claim. Is the author giving too much importance to marriage? Is he looking at reality merely from the perspective of his own upbringing? If a gay person—or any person—doesn't believe in marriage, can that person still be "a full and equal part of the human race"? Explain your opinion.

IDENTIFY THE PATTERNS

For more on the various writing patterns referenced here, see Appendix A.

1. The author uses **narration** as the main pattern of development. What story does the author tell? What are the main parts of this story? Does the author provide enough information and details to make this a successful narrative?
2. In paragraph 4, the author uses **comparison and contrast**. First, identify what things are being compared and contrasted. Then, decide whether the paragraph contains more comparison or more contrast. Highlight or underline specific details to prove your point. Discuss whether the author's use of comparison and contrast strengthens his writing.
3. In paragraph 5, the author uses **cause and effect**. Underline or highlight some of the *effects* or consequences of being a gay man of his generation. Discuss whether identifying these effects strengthens his writing.
4. In paragraphs 7 and 8, the author makes a few different **arguments**. Underline or highlight these arguments. Then, decide whether the author has given enough information and evidence in his essay to persuade you that his arguments are valid.

WRITE A PARAGRAPH

1. Imagine that you are a gay teenager or young adult. Discuss the sorts of challenges you think you might face. Be specific in describing the challenges, the people involved, and your ability to handle the situations. If you decided to marry your significant other, would the marriage present other challenges?
2. Tell the story of a gay person (yourself or someone you have known) who has struggled for social acceptance. What sorts of challenges has the person faced, how did he or she handle the challenges, and what are some of the outcomes of those struggles?
3. Compare and contrast the relationship of a gay couple (yourself and your partner or a couple you have known) to the relationship of straight couples. Are the couples more similar or different? Could you apply the term *marriage* equally to both relationships?

Gary Soto

Like Mexicans

Gary Soto was born in Fresno, California, in 1952. After his father died in a factory accident, Soto spent much of his childhood working in the fields of the San Joaquin Valley to help support his family. Although he admits to having been a poor student in high school, he went on to earn a B.A. in English from California State University–Fresno and an M.F.A. in creative writing from the University of California–Irvine. Soto's first collection of poems, *The Elements of San Joaquin* (1977), won the United States Award of the International Poetry Forum, and a later collection, *New and Selected Poems* (1995), was nominated for a National Book Award. Soto's other honors include the Andrew Carnegie Medal, the Bess Hokin Prize and the Levinson Award from *Poetry* magazine, and fellowships from the Guggenheim Foundation, the National Endowment for the Arts, and the California Arts Council. In addition to his many poetry collections, Soto has written children's and young-adult books, novels, and the memoir *Living up the Street* (1985), which won an American Book Award. He also helps promote the work of California Rural Legal Assistance and the United Farm Workers of America, organizations that assist farm workers and the rural poor.

Like much of Soto's writing, the following essay draws on his experiences growing up in a working-class Mexican American family. Questioning his decision to marry a woman of a different ethnicity, Soto is relieved by a discovery he makes as he gets to know her better.

Reading Tips: The first half of this essay describes Soto's upbringing in a Mexican family; the second half describes his introduction to the family of his Japanese girlfriend. As you read the first half, try to identify the beliefs and values he receives from his family. Then, while reading the second half of the story, be aware of how his beliefs and values change or stay the same.

My grandmother gave me bad advice and good advice when I was in my early teens. For the bad advice, she said that I should become a barber because they made good money and listened to the radio all day. "Honey, they don't work como burros," she would say every time I visited her. She made the sound 1

como burros [Spanish]: like donkeys

of donkeys braying. "Like that, honey!" For the good advice, she said that I should marry a Mexican girl. "No Okies, hijo"—she would say—"Look my son. He marry one and they fight every day about I don't know what and I don't know what." For her, everyone who wasn't Mexican, black, or Asian were Okies. The French were Okies, the Italians in suits were Okies. When I asked about Jews, whom I had read about, she asked for a picture. I rode home on my bicycle and returned with a calendar depicting the important races of the world. "Pues si, son Okies tambien!" she said, nodding her head. She waved the calendar away and we went to the living room where she lectured me on the virtues of the Mexican girl: first, she could cook and, second, she acted like a woman, not a man, in her husband's home. She said she would tell me about a third when I got a little older.

hijo [Spanish]: son

"Pues si, son Okies tambien!" [Spanish]: "Then they are also Okies!"

Teaching Tip
Ask students about both bad and good advice that family members have given them about relationships and/or marriage.

I asked my mother about it—becoming a barber and marrying Mexican. 2
She was in the kitchen. Steam curled from a pot of boiling beans, the radio was on, looking as squat as a loaf of bread. "Well, if you want to be a barber—they say they make good money." She slapped a round steak with a knife, her glasses slipping down with each strike. She stopped and looked up. "If you find a good Mexican girl, marry her of course." She returned to slapping the meat and I went to the backyard where my brother and David King were sitting on the lawn feeling the inside of their cheeks.

"This is what girls feel like," my brother said, rubbing the inside of his 3
cheek. David put three fingers inside his mouth and scratched. I ignored them and climbed the back fence to see my best friend, Scott, a second-generation Okie. I called him and his mother pointed to the side of the house where his bedroom was a small aluminum trailer, the kind you gawk at when they're flipped over on the freeway, wheels spinning in the air. I went around to find Scott pitching horseshoes.

I picked up a set of rusty ones and joined him. While we played, we 4
talked about school and friends and record albums. The horseshoes scuffed up dirt, sometimes ringing the iron that threw out a meager shadow like a sundial. After three argued-over games, we pulled two oranges apiece from his tree and started down the alley still talking school and friends and record albums. We pulled more oranges from the alley and talked about who we would marry. "No offense, Scott," I said with an orange slice in my mouth, "but I would never marry an Okie." We walked in step, almost touching, with a sled of shadows dragging behind us. "No offense, Gary," Scott said, "but I would *never* marry a Mexican." I looked at him: a fang of orange slice showed from his munching mouth. I didn't think anything of it. He had his girl and I had mine. But our seventh-grade vision was the same: to marry, get jobs, buy cars and maybe a house if we had money left over.

meager: small or weak

We talked about our future lives until, to our surprise, we were on the 5
downtown mall, two miles from home. We bought a bag of popcorn at Penneys and sat on a bench near the fountain watching Mexican and Okie girls pass. "That one's mine," I pointed with my chin when a girl with eyebrows arched into black rainbows ambled by. "She's cute," Scott said about a girl with yellow hair and a mouthful of gum. We dreamed aloud, our chins busy pointing out girls. We agreed that we couldn't wait to become men and lift them onto our laps.

Teaching Tip
Students may be confused about whether "the brown girl in a white dress" (para. 6) is real. Although she is probably a vividly imagined ideal, the comment is open to interpretation. Ask students if they have ever imagined a person so vividly that he or she seems like a real person they might actually meet.

But the woman I married was not Mexican but Japanese. It was a surprise to me. For years, I went about wide-eyed in my search for the brown girl in a white dress at a dance. I searched the playground at the baseball diamond. When the girls raced for grounders, their hair bounced like something that couldn't be caught. When they sat together in the lunchroom, heads pressed together, I knew they were talking about us Mexican guys. I saw them and dreamed them. I threw my face into my pillow, making up sentences that were good as in the movies. 6

But when I was twenty, I fell in love with this other girl who worried my mother, who had my grandmother asking once again to see the calendar of the Important Races of the World. I told her I had thrown it away years before. I took a much-glanced-at snapshot from my wallet. We looked at it together, in silence. Then grandma reclined in her chair, lit a cigarette, and said, "Es pretty." She blew and asked with all her worry pushed up to her forehead: "Chinese?" 7

I was in love and there was no looking back. She was the one. I told my mother who was slapping hamburger into patties. "Well, sure if you want to marry her," she said. But the more I talked, the more concerned she became. Later I began to worry. Was it all a mistake? "Marry a Mexican girl," I heard my mother say in my mind. I heard it at breakfast. I heard it over math problems, between Western Civilization and cultural geography. But then one afternoon while I was hitchhiking home from school, it struck me like a baseball in the back: my mother wanted me to marry someone of my own social class—a poor girl. I considered my fiancee, Carolyn, and she didn't look poor, though I knew she came from a family of farm workers and pull-yourself-up-by-your-bootstraps ranchers. I asked my brother, who was marrying Mexican poor that fall, if I should marry a poor girl. He screamed "Yeah" above his terrible guitar playing in his bedroom. I considered my sister who had married Mexican. Cousins were dating Mexican. Uncles were remarrying poor women. I asked Scott, who was still my best friend, and he said, "She's too good for you, so you better not." 8

Teaching Tip
Ask students why the author's best friend would say of the author's new girlfriend, "She's too good for you." Does the friend seem to be jealous? Protective? Something else?

I worried about it until Carolyn took me home to meet her parents. We drove in her Plymouth until the houses gave way to farms and ranches and finally her house fifty feet from the highway. When we pulled into the drive, I panicked and begged Carolyn to make a U-turn and go back so we could talk about it over a soda. She pinched my cheek, calling me a "silly boy." I felt better, though, when I got out of the car and saw the house: the chipped paint, a cracked window, boards for a walk to the back door. There were rusting cars near the barn. A tractor with a net of spiderwebs under a mulberry. A field. A bale of barbed wire like children's scribbling leaning against an empty chicken coop. Carolyn took my hand and pulled me to my future mother-in-law who was coming out to greet us. 9

We had lunch: sandwiches, potato chips, and iced tea. Carolyn and her mother talked mostly about neighbors and the congregation at the Japanese Methodist Church in West Fresno. Her father, who was in khaki work clothes, excused himself with a wave that was almost a salute and went outside. I heard a truck start, a dog bark, and then the truck rattle away. 10

Carolyn's mother offered another sandwich, but I declined with a shake of my head and a smile. I looked around when I could, when I was not saying over and over that I was a college student, hinting that I could take care of her daughter. I shifted my chair. I saw newspapers piled in corners, dusty cereal boxes and vinegar bottles in corners. The wallpaper was bubbled from rain that had come in from a bad roof. Dust. Dust lay on lamp shades and window sills. These people are just like Mexicans, I thought. Poor people. 11

Carolyn's mother asked me through Carolyn if I would like a *sushi.* 12
A plate of black and white things was held in front of me. I took one, wide-eyed, and turned it over like a foreign coin. I was biting into one when I saw a kitten crawl up the window screen over the sink. I chewed and the kitten opened its mouth of terror as she crawled higher, wanting in to paw the leftovers from our plates. I looked at Carolyn who said that the cat was just showing off. I looked up in time to see it fall. It crawled up, then fell again.

We talked for an hour and had apple pie and coffee, slowly. Finally, 13
we got up with Carolyn taking my hand. Slightly embarrassed, I tried to pull away but her grip held me. I let her have her way as she led me down the hallway with her mother right behind me. When I opened the door, I was startled by a kitten clinging to the screen door, its mouth screaming "cat food, dog biscuits, *sushi*. . . ." I opened the door and the kitten, still holding on, whined in the language of hungry animals. When I got into Carolyn's car, I looked back: the cat was still clinging. I asked Carolyn if it were possibly hungry, but she said the cat was being silly. She started the car, waved to her mother, and bounced us over the rain-poked drive, patting my thigh for being her lover baby. Carolyn waved again. I looked back, waving, then gawking at a window screen where there were now three kittens clawing and screaming to get in. Like Mexicans, I thought. I remembered the Molinas and how the cats clung to their screens—cats they shot down with squirt guns. On the highway, I felt happy, pleased by it all. I patted Carolyn's thigh. Her people were like Mexicans, only different.

Teaching Tip
Ask students to imagine an alternative scene in which the author discovers Carolyn's home to be expensive and lavishly decorated and her parents to be wealthy and highly educated. How might he describe the scene and react to it? How might his relationship with Carolyn change as a result? Have students write out their imagined scenes, inventing as many vivid details as they can. They might also include dialogue. (Students might want to work in small groups to generate ideas for this assignment.)

gawking: staring in a stupid-looking way

CHECK YOUR UNDERSTANDING

1. Why does the author's grandmother want him to marry a Mexican girl?
   - **a.** because Mexican girls are good cooks
   - **b.** because Mexican girls act feminine
   - **c.** for some reason she will tell him about later
   - **d.** all of the above
2. How do the author's grandmother and mother first react when they learn that he's fallen in love with a Japanese girl?
   - **a.** They insist that he not marry her.
   - **b.** They accept the news but have some concerns.
   - **c.** They admire his decision as an act of independence.
   - **d.** They tell him that they cannot accept the girl into the family.

CONTINUED >

3. What does the girlfriend's (Carolyn's) home suggest about her family and upbringing?
   a. Carolyn comes from a poor family, like his own.
   b. Carolyn's family is even poorer than his own.
   c. Carolyn's family is quite well-off.
   d. Carolyn has a strongly religious background.
4. How does the author feel at the end of his visit with Carolyn's family?
   a. confused
   b. depressed
   c. frightened
   d. happy

DISCUSS WITH YOUR PEERS

1. Reread paragraph 1 and discuss whether the grandmother's attitude about other races is racist. Then, discuss whether her advice about marriage is racist or simply traditional. Finally, are her claims about Mexican girls sexist and potentially harmful? If you are a woman, would you like to be described in this way? Explain your opinions.
2. Notice from paragraph 8 that the author's family members tend to date and marry within their own ethnic group (Mexican) and socioeconomic class (poor). Moreover, they encourage him to do the same thing. Discuss what some advantages and disadvantages of this practice might be.
3. Look closely at the description of the kitten in paragraphs 12–13. The author seems fixated on the kitten as he struggles to feel comfortable in the unfamiliar environment. Discuss how the kitten is an illustration of Soto himself and what he is going through at that moment. What terrifies Soto? In what way is Soto trying to "crawl higher" and then falling and crawling up again? What is he clinging to? What is he starved for?

IDENTIFY THE PATTERNS

For more on the various writing patterns referenced here, see Appendix A.

1. The author uses **narration** as the main pattern of development. What is the story he tells? What are the main events of the story? Does the author effectively re-create the settings and the characters? Provide specific examples.
2. Soto also uses **description** to develop his writing. Almost every sentence contains strong action verbs, colorful adjectives, and concrete nouns. Reread paragraphs 4 and 9 in particular, and underline or highlight some of the powerful details that bring the scenes and the characters to life.
3. In paragraphs 10–13, the author uses **comparison and contrast**. First, identify what two things are being compared and/or contrasted. Then, identify some of the ways in which these two things are similar and/or different. Does the author use more comparison, more contrast, or an equal amount of both? Does he provide enough information and details to make this an effective comparison and contrast?

WRITE A PARAGRAPH

1. Discuss whether people should try to marry someone of their own race, ethnicity, or socioeconomic class. Support your position with specific reasons and examples.
2. Describe the relationship of an interracial couple or a couple from different socioeconomic backgrounds (you and your partner or a couple you have known). What sorts of challenges does the couple face, how do they handle the challenges, and what are some of the outcomes of those situations?

MAKE CONNECTIONS

1. The traditional, Western idea of marriage is of a permanent, monogamous bond between a man and woman for the purpose of forming a larger family. Typically, the man and woman are of the same race and social background. However, all of the writers in this chapter suggest—in different ways—that traditional views of marriage don't always match reality, and they can even be limiting. Do you think it is important for marriage to hold to traditional definitions, or should individuals have more freedom to redefine the institution on their own terms? In an extended paragraph or brief essay, defend your position with specific reasons and examples. You can draw on the readings in this chapter and on your own experiences and observations.
2. Write a letter to a son, daughter, niece, nephew, or imagined young person about what you hope he or she will find in a committed relationship with a romantic partner—whether or not that relationship will be a marriage. (If you think such a relationship would have to be marriage, say so.) What do you see as the qualities of a healthy and satisfying relationship? What advice would you provide to help him or her face challenges and doubts? You can draw on the readings in this chapter and on your own experiences and observations.

Chapter 21

Addiction

READINGS

- "As They Say, Drugs Kill"
- "Under the Influence"
- From *Don't Eat This Book*

Addiction is a word now used so often that, some argue, it has lost its original power. We often hear people say that they are addicted to caffeine, chocolate, or certain TV shows. A popular 1980s song describes the symptoms of being "addicted to love."

Even so, there are many serious forms of dependence aside from those connected to alcohol or drugs. For years now, news reports have sounded alarms about an obesity epidemic in America, affecting even young children. Addiction to cheap, widely available junk food is at the root of the epidemic, many experts say. Also, Americans are increasingly concerned about addiction to gambling and Internet use. Meanwhile, dependence on drugs and alcohol remains a serious concern.

As you read the following selections, consider your own views about addiction. Do you think the term *addiction* should be used only for certain forms of dependence, or can it be applied fairly to any harmful behavior that is beyond our control? What are the consequences of addiction, both for the addict and for those close to him or her? How should we, as a society, react to addiction and its effects?

Laura Rowley

As They Say, Drugs Kill

Laura Rowley is a print and television journalist who writes a biweekly column on money and happiness for Yahoo! Finance. Born in 1965 in Chicago, Rowley earned an undergraduate degree in journalism from the University of Illinois at Urbana-Champaign. She went on to receive graduate degrees from the New York Theological Seminary and the University of Burgundy in France. Before joining Yahoo!, Rowley worked as a reporter and producer for CNN, a personal finance columnist for *Self* magazine, and an adjunct professor of religious studies at Seton Hall University. Her writing has appeared in publications including the *New York Times* and *Parents* magazine. She has also published two books, *On Target: How the World's Hottest Retailer Hit a Bull's-eye* (2003) and *Money and Happiness: A Guide to Living the Good Life* (2005).

In the following essay, first published in *Newsweek on Campus* in 1987, Rowley reflects on the dangers of substance abuse. Drawing on a personal experience from her college days, she makes a compelling argument.

Reading Tips: Read just the first sentence of this piece and pause. What do you think the essay is going to be about? How do you think the writer will develop her ideas (through exemplification, description, narration, some other method)?

The fastest way to end a party is to have someone die in the middle of it. 1

At a party last fall I watched a 22-year-old die of cardiac arrest after he had used drugs. It was a painful, undignified way to die. And I would like to think that anyone who shared the experience would feel his or her ambivalence about substance abuse dissolving. 2

ambivalence: uncertainty; conflicting feelings

This victim won't be singled out like Len Bias as a bitter example for "troubled youth." He was just another ordinary guy celebrating with friends at a private house party, the kind where they roll in the keg first thing in the morning and get stupefied while watching the football games on cable all afternoon. The living room was littered with beer cans from last night's party—along with dirty socks and the stuffing from the secondhand couch. 3

Len Bias (b. 1963): college basketball star who died of a cocaine overdose in 1986

And there were drugs, as at so many other college parties. The drug of choice this evening was psilocybin, hallucinogenic mushrooms. If you're cool you call them "'shrooms." 4

This wasn't a crowd huddled in the corner of a darkened room with a single red bulb, shooting needles in their arms. People played darts, made jokes, passed around a joint and listened to the Grateful Dead on the stereo. 5

Teaching Tip
Some students may have witnessed an event similar to the one described in this essay. (The substance may have been alcohol, not drugs.) If they feel comfortable talking about their experiences, have them share their stories with the class. How did they react at the time? Looking back on the event, is there anything they would have done differently?

Suddenly, a thin, tall, brown-haired young man began to gasp. His eyes rolled back in his head, and he hit the floor face first with a crash. Someone laughed, not appreciating the violence of his fall, thinking the afternoon's festivities had finally caught up with another guest. The laugh lasted only a second, as the brown-haired guest began to convulse and choke. The sound of the stereo and laughter evaporated. Bystanders shouted frantic suggestions: 6

"It's an epileptic fit, put something in his mouth!" 7

"Roll him over on his stomach!" 8

"Call an ambulance; God, somebody breathe into his mouth." 9

A girl kneeling next to him began to sob his name, and he seemed to moan. 10

"Wait, he's semicoherent." Four people grabbed for the telephone, to find no dial tone, and ran to use a neighbor's. One slammed the dead phone against the wall in frustration—and miraculously produced a dial tone. 11

semicoherent: somewhat capable of thought and speech

But the body was now motionless on the kitchen floor. "He has a pulse, he has a pulse." 12

"But he's not breathing!" 13

"Well, get away—give him some f—ing air!" The three or four guests gathered around his body unbuttoned his shirt. 14

"Wait—is he OK? Should I call the damn ambulance?" 15

A chorus of frightened voices shouted, "Yes, yes!" 16

"Come on, come on, breathe again. Breathe!" 17

Over muffled sobs came a sudden grating, desperate breath that passed through bloody lips and echoed through the kitchen and living room. 18

Teaching Tip
A number of graphic antidrug advertisements are appearing on television and online. If you teach in a computerized classroom, you might want to show one or more of these ads to students. (For example, see the ad clips produced by the Montana Meth Project, at **http://montanameth.org/View_Ads/index.php**. Because these clips are very disturbing, it's a good idea to view them yourself before you decide to show them in class.) Ask students to compare antidrug video ads with antidrug writing. Which is more effective? Or do both have a place?

"He's had this reaction before—when he did acid at a concert last spring. But he recovered in 15 seconds . . . ," one friend confided. 19

The rest of the guests looked uncomfortably at the floor or paced purposelessly around the room. One or two whispered, "Oh, my God," over and over, like a prayer. A friend stood next to me, eyes fixed on the kitchen floor. He mumbled, just audibly, "I've seen this before. My dad died of a heart attack. He had the same look. . . ." I touched his shoulder and leaned against a wall, repeating reassurances to myself. People don't die at parties. People don't die at parties. 20

Eventually, no more horrible, gnashing sounds tore their way from the victim's lungs. I pushed my hands deep in my jeans pockets wondering how much it costs to pump a stomach and how someone could be so careless if he had had this reaction with another drug. What would he tell his parents about the hospital bill? 21

Two uniformed paramedics finally arrived, lifted him onto a stretcher and quickly rolled him out. His face was grayish blue, his mouth hung open, rimmed with blood, and his eyes were rolled back with a yellowish color on the rims. 22

The paramedics could be seen moving rhythmically forward and back through the small windows of the ambulance, whose lights threw a red wash over the stunned watchers on the porch. The paramedics' hands were massaging his chest when someone said, "Did you tell them he took psilocybin? Did you tell them?" 23

"No, I . . ." 24

"My God, so tell them—do you want him to die?" Two people ran to tell the paramedics the student had eaten mushrooms five minutes before the attack. 25

irreverent: disrespectful

It seemed irreverent to talk as the ambulance pulled away. My friend, who still saw his father's image, muttered, "That guy's dead." I put my arms around him half to comfort him, half to stop him from saying things I couldn't believe. 26

The next day, when I called someone who lived in the house, I found that my friend was right. 27

Teaching Tip
Students who are parents may have different reactions to this piece than other, younger students. If they feel comfortable sharing their reactions, encourage them to speak. Have they had conversations with their children about recreational drug use? Do they think that reading an account like Rowley's would deter their children from using drugs? Why or why not?

My hands began to shake and my eyes filled with tears for someone I didn't know. Weeks later the pain has dulled, but I still can't unravel the knot of emotion that has moved from my stomach to my head. When I told one friend what happened, she shook her head and spoke of the stupidity of filling your body with chemical substances. People who would do drugs after seeing that didn't value their lives too highly, she said. 28

But others refused to read any universal lessons from the incident. Many of those I spoke to about the event considered him the victim of a freak accident, randomly struck down by drugs as a pedestrian might be hit by a speeding taxi. They speculated that the student must have had special physical problems; what happened to him could not happen to them. 29

Couldn't it? Now when I hear people discussing drugs I'm haunted by the image of him lying on the floor, his body straining to rid itself of substances he chose to take. Painful, undignified, unnecessary—like a wartime casualty. But in war, at least, lessons are supposed to be learned, so that old mistakes are not repeated. If this death cannot make people think and change, that will be an even greater tragedy. 30

CHECK YOUR UNDERSTANDING

1. What traumatic event did the author witness at a party?
   a. an epileptic seizure that nearly killed one of the guests
   b. a young man's overdose on hallucinogenic mushrooms
   c. a young man's overdose on heroin and cocaine
   d. the incompetence of paramedics in treating an overdose victim
2. What is the most accurate description of the guests' reactions to the traumatic event?
   a. They were indifferent to the victim's suffering.
   b. They were angry that the victim hadn't exercised more self-control.
   c. They were frightened but confident about what to do.
   d. They were frightened and confused about what to do.
3. What happened to the victim?
   a. He died.
   b. He survived but lost most brain function.
   c. He survived but had slurred speech.
   d. He made a full recovery.
4. According to the author, what would be "an even greater tragedy" than the victim's fate?
   a. the legalization of marijuana, cocaine, and other recreational drugs
   b. the closing of the college drug treatment facility that might have helped the victim
   c. if what happened to the victim didn't deter the party guests from attending future parties
   d. if what happened to the victim didn't make people change their attitudes toward recreational drug use

DISCUSS WITH YOUR PEERS

1. Look at paragraphs 7–20 and 23–25. Discuss whether the reactions of the party guests seem reasonable and responsible. Do you think their responses to the emergency were affected by their own drug use? Might they have handled the situation more successfully? How? What do you think you would do in a similar situation?
2. In paragraph 21, the author wonders how "someone could be so careless if he had had this reaction with another drug." Discuss what may have motivated the young man to use drugs again. Do you believe that this sort of careless behavior is fairly common among teenagers and young adults, or is this a truly exceptional case? Explain your opinions.
3. Look at paragraphs 28 and 29. Discuss whether recreational drug users would be likely to change their habits if they witnessed a similar scene, or whether they would be more likely to explain the victim's death as a "freak accident" and continue their drug use. Finally, would *reading* about this event be likely to change the thinking or behavior of a recreational drug user? In your opinion, might this story actually save lives? Why or why not?

IDENTIFY THE PATTERNS

For more on the various writing patterns referenced here, see Appendix A.

1. The author uses **narration** as the main pattern of development. In your own words, retell the main events of the story. In your opinion, what makes this a powerful story? (If you don't think the story is powerful, explain why.)
2. The author also uses vivid **description** to develop her writing. Reread paragraphs 6, 22, and 23. Underline or highlight some of the powerful descriptive details that bring this story to life.
3. Additionally, the author uses **argument** to develop her writing. Both the second paragraph and the last sentence of the essay argue that people should change their attitude and behavior after learning about such a tragic event. For the author, the details of the young man's death are powerful *evidence* that using drugs is stupid and dangerous. Do you believe that the author's argument is successful? Will readers be moved to change their behavior based on the evidence in this essay?

WRITE A PARAGRAPH

1. Tell a story that might convince people to stay away from drug use.
2. Discuss whether you are totally against recreational drug use or whether it should be allowed in certain circumstances.

Scott Russell Sanders

Under the Influence

Scott Russell Sanders is best known for his personal essays on nature, family, and spirituality. Born in 1945, Sanders grew up on a farm in Tennessee until his father took a job at a military arsenal in Ohio. These two childhood homes had a great impact on his writing, which often focuses on the contrast between the beauty of nature and the destructiveness of human technology. Sanders studied physics in college before switching his focus to English, receiving a B.A. from Brown University and a Ph.D. from Cambridge University. His numerous essay collections include *The Paradise of Bombs* (1987), *Staying Put* (1993), *Hunting for Hope* (1998), *The Country of Language* (1999), and *The Force of Spirit* (2000). He has also written several novels, short story collections, and children's books. In 1995, Sanders received the Lannan Literary Award for his collected work in nonfiction, and his essays have been selected four times for *The Best American Essays* series. Sanders is currently Distinguished Professor of English at Indiana University, where he has taught for more than thirty years. His most recent book is the memoir *A Private History of Awe* (2006).

The following is an excerpt from "Under the Influence," which first appeared in *Harper's* magazine in 1989. In the piece, Sanders reflects on the effects of his father's alcoholism.

Reading Tips: The author uses some vocabulary that may be unfamiliar to you, so be prepared to read slowly and look up words that you do not know. You will understand the basic story without looking up these words; however, as a college student, it is a good idea to start building your vocabulary. Try recording new vocabulary in a special log. (See Chapter 7, page 222, for advice on keeping a vocabulary log.)

Soon after my parents moved back to Father's treacherous stomping ground, my wife and I visited them in Mississippi with our five-year-old daughter. Mother had been too distraught to warn me about the return of the demons. So when I climbed out of the car that bright July morning and saw my father napping in the hammock, I felt uneasy, for in all his sober years I had never known him to sleep in daylight. Then he lurched upright, blinked his bloodshot eyes, and greeted us in a syrupy voice. I was hurled back helpless into childhood. 1

distraught: upset

lurched: swayed or staggered

"What's the matter with Papaw?" our daughter asked. 2

Papaw: Grandpa

"Nothing," I said. "Nothing!" 3

Like a child again, I pretended not to see him in his stupor, and behind my phony smile I grieved. On that visit and on the few that remained before his death, once again I found bottles in the workbench, bottles in the woods. Again his hands shook too much for him to run a saw, to make his precious miniature furniture, to drive straight down back roads. Again he wound up in the ditch, in the hospital, in jail, in treatment centers. Again he shouted and wept. Again he lied. "I never touched a drop," he swore. "Your mother's making it up." 4

stupor: a state of numbness or reduced sensibility

Teaching Tip
Call students' attention to the use of dialogue in paragraphs 2–4 and in paragraph 6. What does it add to the essay? Encourage them to use dialogue (quoted details) in their own writing whenever someone's actual speech would be more vivid than describing the person's words. For guidelines on using quoted details, see Chapter 6, page 187.

I no longer fancied I could reason with the men whose names I found on the bottles—Jim Beam, Jack Daniels—nor did I hope to save my father by burning down a store. I was able now to press the cold statistics about alcoholism against the ache of memory: ten million victims, fifteen million, twenty. And yet, in spite of my age, I reacted in the same blind way as I had in childhood, ignoring biology, forgetting numbers, vainly seeking to erase through my efforts whatever drove him to drink. I worked on their place twelve and sixteen hours a day, in the swelter of Mississippi summers, digging ditches, running electrical wires, planting trees, mowing grass, building sheds, as though what nagged at him was some list of chores, as though by taking his worries on my shoulders I could redeem him. I was flung back into boyhood, acting as though my father would not drink himself to death if only I were perfect. 5

redeem: to save someone or make up for their shortcomings

I failed of perfection; he succeeded in dying. To the end, he considered himself not sick but sinful. "Do you want to kill yourself?" I asked him. "Why not?" he answered. "Why the hell not? What's there to save?" To the end, he would not speak about his feelings, would not or could not give a name to the beast that was devouring him. 6

In silence, he went rushing off the cliff. Unlike the biblical swine, however, he left behind a few of the demons to haunt his children. Life with him and the loss of him twisted us into shapes that will be familiar to other sons and daughters of alcoholics. My brother became a rebel, my sister retreated into shyness, I played the stalwart and dutiful son who would hold the family together. If my father was unstable, I would be a rock. If he squandered money on drink, I would pinch every penny. If he wept when drunk—and only when drunk—I would not let myself weep at all. If he roared at the Little League umpire for calling my pitches balls, I would throw 7

biblical swine: a reference to a Bible story in which Jesus commands a group of demons to enter a herd of swine (hogs) and depart. The swine then jump off a cliff.

stalwart: strong and brave

squandered: wasted

flounder: to struggle

banish: to send away

humiliation: shame

futile: useless

nothing but strikes. Watching him flounder and rage, I came to dread the loss of control. I would go through life without making anyone mad. I vowed never to put in my mouth or veins any chemical that would banish my everyday self. I would never make a scene, never lash out at the ones I loved, never hurt a soul. Through hard work, relentless work, I would achieve something dazzling—in the classroom, on the basketball floor, in the science lab, in the pages of books—and my achievement would distract the world's eyes from his humiliation. I would become a worthy sacrifice, and the smoke of my burning would please God.

8 It is far easier to recognize these twists in my character than to undo them. Work has become an addiction for me, as drink was an addiction for my father. Knowing this, my daughter gave me a placard for the wall: WORKAHOLIC. The labor is endless and futile, for I can no more redeem myself through work than I could redeem my father. I still panic in the face of other people's anger, because his drunken temper was so terrible. I shrink from causing sadness or disappointment even to strangers, as though I were still concealing the family shame. I still notice every twitch of emotion in the faces around me, having learned as a child to read the weather in faces, and I blame myself for their least pang of unhappiness or anger. In certain moods I blame myself for everything. Guilt burns like acid in my veins.

9 I am moved to write these pages now because my own son, at the age of ten, is taking on himself the griefs of the world, and in particular the griefs of his father. He tells me that when I am gripped by sadness he feels responsible; he feels there must be something he can do to spring me from depression, to fix my life. And that crushing sense of responsibility is exactly what I felt at the age of ten in the face of my father's drinking. My son wonders if I, too, am possessed. I write, therefore, to drag into the light what eats at me—the fear, the guilt, the shame—so that my own children may be spared.

10 I still shy away from nightclubs, from bars, from parties where the solvent is alcohol. My friends puzzle over this, but it is no more peculiar than for a man to shy away from the lions' den after seeing his father torn apart. I took my own first drink at the age of twenty-one, half a glass of burgundy. I knew the odds of my becoming an alcoholic were four times higher than for the sons of nonalcoholic fathers. So I sipped warily.

11 I still do—once a week, perhaps, a glass of wine, a can of beer, nothing stronger, nothing more. I listen for the turning of a key in my brain.

Teaching Tip
You might ask students to write about the role they play (or played) in their own family. Were they comfortable with this role? Why or why not? Did they assume the role by their own choice, or did circumstances force it upon them?

CHECK YOUR UNDERSTANDING

1. According to the author, what did he fail at, and what did his father succeed in?
   - **a.** The author failed at fighting his own addiction, and his father succeeded in overcoming his alcoholism.
   - **b.** The author failed at improving his father's property, and his father succeeded in getting counseling for his alcoholism.
   - **c.** The author failed at being perfect, and the father succeeded in dying of alcoholism.
   - **d.** None of the above.

2. Growing up, what role did the author play in his family?
   a. He was a rebel.
   b. He was the son who held the family together.
   c. He was a distant loner.
   d. He was the family comedian.
3. What addiction does the author suffer from?
   a. an addiction to work
   b. an addiction to alcohol
   c. an addiction to gambling
   d. an addiction to drugs
4. What inspired the author to write the essay?
   a. a desire to unburden himself of his problems
   b. a desire to reach out to other children of alcoholics
   c. a desire to record important memories for his family
   d. his own son's concern for him

DISCUSS WITH YOUR PEERS

1. Reread paragraph 5 and discuss the author's determination to save his father from alcoholism. Does his behavior seem reasonable? Why does he ignore the facts and statistics about alcoholism and react as he did when he was a boy? Discuss his belief that "my father would not drink himself to death if only I were perfect." Why might a child feel this way about his parent's addiction?
2. In paragraph 8, the author describes a legacy of addiction that he inherits from his father. Discuss at least three ways in which the son's life is marked by his father's addiction. Then, discuss whether most children of addicts also live with a similar legacy of addiction. If you wish, provide examples from your personal experience and knowledge.
3. Reread paragraph 9 and discuss why the author writes. What does he hope to achieve from the act of writing? If his children were to read this essay, do you think they might "be spared" in some ways from the legacy of addiction? Finally, discuss whether writing has ever helped you or someone you know survive a difficult situation. Can you imagine that writing might someday serve this purpose in your life? Why or why not?

IDENTIFY THE PATTERNS

For more on the various writing patterns referenced here, see Appendix A.

1. In paragraph 5, the author uses **exemplification** to explain how he tries to save his father from alcoholism. Underline or highlight some of the examples he uses. Do you think these examples show the son's desperation in a vivid way? Why or why not?

CONTINUED >

2. In paragraph 7, the author uses **cause and effect** to show the powerful influence of the father's alcoholism on the child. First, underline or highlight details about the father's behavior (the *cause*); then, underline or highlight details about the son's behavior (the *effects*). Does this paragraph adequately show the strong cause-and-effect relationship between a parent's alcoholism and the consequences for a child?
3. In paragraph 9, the author uses **comparison and contrast** to develop his writing. First, identify what two things are being compared and/or contrasted. Then, decide how these things are similar and/or different.

WRITE A PARAGRAPH

1. Discuss the consequences of addiction that you or someone you know lives with.
2. Discuss how a family member with an addiction (alcohol, drugs, gambling, or something else) can affect the rest of the family.

Morgan Spurlock

From Don't Eat This Book

Morgan Spurlock was born in 1970 in Parkersburg, West Virginia. After graduating with a degree in film from New York University's Tisch School for the Arts, Spurlock spent several years as a production assistant on movies including *Bullets over Broadway* and *Terminator 2.* In 1999, his play *The Phoenix* won awards at the New York International Fringe Festival and the Route 66 American Playwriting Competition. Spurlock is best known, however, for his 2004 documentary film *Supersize Me,* which follows Spurlock through an experiment in which he ate nothing but McDonald's food for one month. It earned him a Sundance Film Festival award and an Academy Award nomination—along with an extra twenty-five pounds and other negative health effects. Currently, Spurlock directs and produces the television program *30 Days.* The show follows people who immerse themselves in a living situation outside their comfort zone; for example, an atheist spends thirty days living with fundamentalist Christians, and Spurlock himself spends thirty days as an inmate in a county prison. He is currently working on a new documentary titled *What Would Jesus Buy?*

In this excerpt from *Don't Eat This Book* (2005), Spurlock examines the role of supersized portions in America's addiction to unhealthy food.

Reading Tips: This essay mixes both casual language and facts and statistics. The casual language engages readers, while the facts support the author's point about overeating in America. Be prepared to read slowly and consider *both* the casual and factual language.

gluttons: people who eat excessive amounts

Have we all become compulsive eaters? Are we all gluttons? Are we actually, 1
physically hungrier than we used to be? Or will we simply eat more if you put it in front of us, whether we're really hungry or not?

A study done at Penn State suggests the latter. Volunteers were served a series of lunches that kept increasing in size and "as portions increased, all participants ate increasingly larger amounts," no matter how hungry they were. A University of Illinois study found that if you hand the average person a one-pound bag of M&Ms, he'll eat 80 pieces; hand him a two-pound bag, and he'll eat 112 in the same period of time. 2

If you put it there, we will eat it. Just keep your hands away from our mouths. 3

John Robbins, author of *Diet for a New America* and *The Food Revolution,* offers a wise, and I think true, explanation. "The quality of food that we're eating is degrading so rapidly," he told me. "We're eating more of it, because it's advertised so massively and it's so convenient. . . . So we're always wanting to eat more and more and more, because there's something inside us that's saying we're not getting what we need and want. . . . We lose touch with that inner compass by which we can sense what's good for us. Instead, we give up control over what we eat to the corporations and the fast-food companies." 4

The evidence is clear, America. We don't really need to eat more. We're not really hungrier than we were thirty years ago, and God knows we're not more physically active. No, friends, we've been *trained* to eat more. Conditioned to do it. Have you seen that commercial where the pizza guy rings the doorbell and the guys in the house go running like Pavlov's dogs, literally salivating and slobbering all over themselves? It was played for laughs, but I saw that commercial and thought, "What the hell is *funny* about that?" That's what we've become—lab rats for the junk-food industry! 5

We're not only eating more food, we're eating more food that's bad for us, that doesn't satisfy us and that makes us hungry for more soon after. Fast food is terrible for you. It shouldn't even be called "food." It should be called more like what it is: a highly efficient delivery system for fats, carbohydrates, sugars and other bad things. Most of those extra calories we're putting on come in the form of carbohydrates. Especially fries. The average American now wolfs down 30 pounds of french fries annually—up from only 3.5 pounds in 1960. And don't forget sodas. Soft-drink consumption in the United States increased 135 percent between about 1977 and 2001. It's highest, not surprisingly, among kids: American kids now drink twice as much soda as they did twenty-five years ago. 6

The average American teen drinks two or more 12 ounce sodas a day. How much sugar is in a single 12-ounce soda? Ten teaspoons. *That kid is consuming the equivalent of twenty teaspoons of sugar every day.* Just in soda. Throw in all the other sugar the average kid consumes in fast food, junk food and snacks. Then ask me again why we're seeing an epidemic of type 2 diabetes in America's children. 7

Teaching Tip
Ask students to identify and describe other fast-food commercials that they have seen. What types of characters and settings are featured in the commercials? What message does the advertiser seem to be communicating about its food and the people who eat it? Do students find the commercials appealing, or do they have other reactions?

Pavlov's dogs: participants in experiments conducted by Russian scientist Ivan Pavlov (1849–1936). Pavlov found that when a bell was struck when the dogs were fed, the animals came to associate the sound of the bell with food, salivating whenever they heard it.

Teaching Tip
If students express special interest in the topic of food addiction and fast food, you might want to read them excerpts from *Fast Food Nation* by Eric Schlosser. This book explores not only the negative health consequences of fast food but also other social consequences, such as urban sprawl.

CHECK YOUR UNDERSTANDING

1. According to this essay, which of the following statements is accurate?
   - **a.** Most of us will eat only until we are full, unless the food is french fries.
   - **b.** We will eat smaller portions if we put our food on smaller plates.
   - **c.** We will eat as much as is put before us, even if we are not hungry.
   - **d.** None of the above.
2. What does author John Robbins believe?
   - **a.** Even low-quality food can satisfy our needs.
   - **b.** We eat more because we feel dissatisfied.
   - **c.** Americans should try to become vegetarians.
   - **d.** Fast-food companies should be fined out of business.
3. What ingredient accounts for most of the extra calories Americans are consuming?
   - **a.** carbohydrates
   - **b.** fats
   - **c.** salt
   - **d.** all of the above
4. According to Spurlock, how much sugar is the average soda-drinking teen consuming every day?
   - **a.** ten teaspoons
   - **b.** twenty teaspoons
   - **c.** twenty tablespoons
   - **d.** three cups

DISCUSS WITH YOUR PEERS

1. Look at paragraph 5. Discuss whether you agree or disagree with the author's characterization of Americans as "Pavlov's dogs" or "lab rats." Have we really been "trained" or "conditioned" by the food industries to consume food without thinking about the consequences? Is this a realistic or an exaggerated image of American consumers? Support your position with examples from your personal experience or knowledge.
2. Discuss whether you agree or disagree with the author's definition and description of fast food in paragraph 6. Do you believe that fast food is really all bad? If so, why do so many Americans continue to eat it? Do you think that fast food will continue to be popular in ten or twenty years? Explain your opinion.
3. At the end of paragraph 7, the author refers to an "epidemic of type 2 diabetes in America's children." (Type 2 diabetes used to develop mostly in older people, often after many years of overeating.) Discuss why so many Americans continue to consume large quantities of junk food—and allow their children to consume such food—even when they know about the health risks.

IDENTIFY THE PATTERNS

For more on the various writing patterns referenced here, see Appendix A.

1. The author uses **argumentation** as the main pattern of development. Look in paragraph 1 for his main argument, which he states as a question. Then, underline or highlight the *evidence* that he provides to support his argument. Consider, for example, the statistics in paragraphs 2, 6, and 7 and the expert opinion in paragraph 4.
2. In paragraph 6, the author uses **definition** to make a point. Underline or highlight his definition of "fast food." Then, discuss whether this definition is important and powerful even though it is short.
3. The author uses **cause and effect** throughout the essay. Underline or highlight both a cause and an effect (outcome) in the following paragraphs: 2, 5, and 7.

WRITE A PARAGRAPH

1. Discuss whether you might be "addicted" to junk food. Give reasons and examples to show why your intake of junk food does or does not indicate an addiction.
2. Some people believe that compulsive junk food consumption is not a serious form of addiction, like alcoholism or drug abuse. Tell a story that might convince others that excessive junk food consumption is a very serious type of addiction.

MAKE CONNECTIONS

1. The three readings in this chapter describe different forms of addiction and some of the consequences of these addictions, such as guilt, shame, obesity, diabetes, and death. In a paragraph or essay, discuss whether you believe that all forms of addiction are equally serious and should be treated with equal concern. Compare and contrast several types of addiction to prove that they are equal or not equal in their seriousness. You may use ideas and examples from the readings and from your own experience and knowledge.
2. The essays by Rowley (page 568) and Sanders (page 572) suggest that an addict's family and friends can be hurt by the addictive behavior just as much as the addicts themselves. In a paragraph or essay, discuss how addiction hurts the family and friends of the addict. You may use ideas and examples from the readings and from your own experience and knowledge.

Be aware of another reading that relates to the theme of addiction: "Weighing Risks and Benefits: Adolescent Decision Making" by Kathleen Stassen Berger (page 580).

Chapter 22

Making Mistakes

READINGS

- "Weighing Risks and Benefits: Adolescent Decision Making"
- "King of the Road"
- "Nothing to Lose"

Making mistakes, large and small, is part of being human. In fact, many scientists, writers, and other great thinkers have said that mistakes are not only common but essential for personal growth and creative insight. As the famously inventive Irish writer James Joyce once remarked, "Mistakes are the portals of discovery." At the same time, our instinct is often to protect ourselves and those we care about from the negative consequences of bad decisions and risky behavior.

As you read the following selections, consider your own views about mistakes. When and under what circumstances are people most likely to take risks and make mistakes? When and what can we learn from bad decisions?

Kathleen Stassen Berger

Weighing Risks and Benefits: Adolescent Decision Making

Kathleen Stassen Berger is chair of the Social Science Department at Bronx Community College of the City University of New York, where she has taught psychology for the past thirty-five years. Berger earned her undergraduate degrees from Stanford University and Radcliffe College. Then, she received an M.A.T. from Harvard University and an M.S. and Ph.D. from Yeshiva University. She is the author of three college-level psychology textbooks and has written articles for the American Association of Higher Education, the National Education Association, and the *Wiley Encyclopedia of Psychology.* Her research focuses on adolescent identity, sibling relationships, and bullying.

The following is an excerpt from Berger's textbook *The Developing Person through the Life Span.* In it, Berger examines adolescent decision making, citing research to explain why teenagers are particularly prone to making mistakes. (For another reading from this textbook, see page 553.)

Reading Tips: Because this excerpt is a piece of academic writing, the paragraphs tend to be long. Also, because it includes some academic language, you may need to read slowly and reread difficult sections. Notice that the author gives credit to other experts, whose names are in parentheses immediately after the ideas that they contributed. Full information on these experts' publications can be found at the end of this excerpt.

Adults are not necessarily wiser than teenagers in calculating the risks and benefits of various decisions (Gruber, 2001). In fact, adults do not necessarily decide wisely for themselves: In almost every nation in the world, the worst outcomes (drug addiction, homicide, accidental death) are far more common after age 20 than before (Heuveline, 2002). Adult decision making is often based on mistaken assumptions, damaging ignorance, and questionable priorities, just as adolescent thought is (Allwood & Selart, 2001; Byrnes, 1998; Ranyard et al., 1997). 1

Nevertheless, teenagers need special protection from poor judgment, for several reasons (O'Donoghue & Rabin, 2001): 2

Teaching Tip
Assign students to find one of the articles mentioned in paragraph 2, using the reference list at the end of this excerpt. Ask them to read the article and highlight two or three additional findings that interested them. Have them share their findings with the rest of the class. You might point out that most scholarly articles (such as the ones they looked up) cite additional sources. These cited publications can serve as additional sources for student researchers.

- The younger a person is, the more serious are the consequences of risk taking. A year in prison, for example, is much more damaging at age 16 than at age 46.
- Adolescent choices are long-lasting. "A significant determinant of the well-being of many older persons will be the risky decisions that they made in their youth," such as dropping out of school, having a baby, or joining a gang (Gruber, 2001, p. 25).
- Adolescents are particularly likely to overrate the joys of the moment and disregard the risks of a mind-altering drug, a sexually arousing situation, a disrespectful police officer, a dangerous dare, and the like. They discount consequences, miscalculate probabilities, and risk their futures (O'Donoghue & Rabin, 2001).

Every decision requires the weighing of risk against opportunity. How should risk itself be weighed? Some people are "risk-averse"—they never do anything that might end in disaster. Others "throw caution to the wind"; they enjoy the thrill of spontaneity, of impulse, of being close to danger. Good decision making avoids both extremes, rejecting both overly risky and overly cautious choices. Personality, culture, and situation are all factors in risk assessment, but age is probably the strongest influence of all. The allure of risky behavior increases from age 11 to age 18. 3

averse: avoiding or opposing

spontaneity: acting without a plan or without restraint

There are also interesting sex differences. Boys are more inclined than girls to seek thrills, such as parachuting or roller coasting, and to rebel against adult authority, as by engaging in secret drinking or illicit sex (Gullone et al., 2000). But adolescent girls admire risk-taking boys, which encourages the boys to be even more daring. For both sexes, behaviors that adults consider foolhardy (skipping school, using drugs, breaking the law, having unprotected sex, driving too fast, and so on) are ways to gain status and respect, to become sexually attractive, to strengthen friendship bonds, and to demonstrate freedom from parental restraints (Lightfoot, 1997). In adolescent culture, risk taking is viewed as brave, while caution is considered "goody-goody" or wimpish. 4

foolhardy: foolish or thoughtless

Teaching Tip
Ask students if they believe that they have become better decision makers as they've matured. What factors, aside from age, have changed their decision-making behavior?

Good decision-making skills take time to develop. This was shown by 5
a study in which life dilemmas were posed to 204 subjects aged 14 to 37. Among the adolescents, wiser, more mature analysis was evident with each passing year. This gradual improvement suggests that "adolescents are acquiring reasoning capacities that may support both the acquisition and expression of wisdom-related knowledge and judgment" (Pasupathi et al., 2001, p. 358).

References

Allwood, Carl Martin, & Selart, Marcus (Eds.). (2001). *Decision making: Social and creative dimensions.* Norwell, MA: Kluwer Academic Publishers.

Byrnes, James P. (1998). *The nature and development of decision-making: A self-regulation model.* Mahwah, NJ: Erlbaum.

Gruber, Jonathan. (2001). Introduction. In Jonathan Gruber (Ed.), *Risky behavior among youth: An economic analysis* (pp. 1–28). Chicago: University of Chicago Press.

Gullone, Eleonora, Moore, Susan, Moss, Simon, & Boyd, Candace. (2000). The Adolescent Risk-Taking Questionnaire: Development and psychometric evaluation. *Journal of Adolescent Research, 15,* 231–250.

Heuveline, Patrick. (2002). An international comparison of adolescent and young adult mortality. *Annals of the American Academy of Political and Social Science, 580,* 172–200.

Lightfoot, Cynthia. (1997). *The culture of adolescent risk-taking.* New York: Guilford Publications.

O'Donoghue, Ted, & Rabin, Matthew. (2001). Risky behavior among youths: Some issues from behavioral economics. In Jonathan Gruber (Ed.), *Risky behavior among youth: An economic analysis* (pp. 29–67). Chicago: University of Chicago Press.

Pasupathi, Monisha, Staudinger, Ursula M., & Baltes, Paul B. (2001). Seeds of wisdom: Adolescents' knowledge and judgment about difficult life problems. *Developmental Psychology, 37,* 351–361.

Ranyard, Rob, Crozier, W. Ray, & Svenson, Ola (Eds.). (1997). *Decision making: Cognitive models and explanations.* New York: Routledge.

CHECK YOUR UNDERSTANDING

1. According to the author, what is true about decision making in adults compared with teenagers?
   - **a.** It is clear that adults make better decisions than teenagers do.
   - **b.** Teenagers with strong family bonds will make better decisions than many adults will.
   - **c.** Adults do not always make better decisions than teenagers do.
   - **d.** None of the above.
2. Why, according to the author, do teenagers need "special protection" from making poor decisions?
   - **a.** They are more likely than adults to harm others by making poor decisions.
   - **b.** They are more likely than adults to focus on the thrills of an activity and ignore the risks.

c. If they are not prevented from making poor decisions, they will grow into resentful, even violent, adults.

d. All of the above.

3. According to the author, what is true about good decision making?

a. It favors caution over risk taking in most situations.

b. It avoids risk at all costs.

c. It requires careful consideration of all the available information.

d. It strikes a balance between caution and risk taking.

4. Why do teenagers engage in risky behavior despite the possibly negative consequences?

a. It is a way to gain status and respect.

b. It is a way to become sexually attractive.

c. It is a way to demonstrate freedom from parental control.

d. All of the above.

DISCUSS WITH YOUR PEERS

1. In paragraph 2, the author quotes another expert as saying, "A significant determinant of the well-being of many older persons will be the risky decisions that they made in their youth, such as dropping out of school, having a baby, or joining a gang." Discuss whether you agree or disagree that risky decisions made during a person's youth can have significant long-term effects on that person's life. Give examples of people you know who were or were not affected by risky decisions that they made when they were young.
2. In paragraph 3, the author defines three different approaches to decision making and risk assessment. First, identify the three approaches (two extreme and one moderate). Then, discuss which approach best describes your own decision-making behavior. If you like, give examples from your own experiences to support your claim.
3. In paragraph 4, the author states, "Boys are more inclined than girls to seek thrills, such as parachuting or roller coasting, and to rebel against adult authority, as by engaging in secret drinking or illicit sex." Do you agree that girls and boys are essentially different in their risk-taking behavior, or do you think that this claim stereotypes female and male behavior? Give examples from your own experiences to support your opinion.

IDENTIFY THE PATTERNS

For more on the various writing patterns referenced here, see Appendix A.

1. In paragraph 2, the author uses **exemplification** to show that poor decision making can be especially harmful to teenagers. Underline or highlight some of the specific examples of harm that she gives. Then, discuss whether you agree or disagree that teenagers are especially likely to be harmed when they take big risks.

CONTINUED >

2. In paragraph 3, the author uses **definition**. Underline or highlight the three definitions that she gives for the ways people make decisions and weigh risks.
3. In paragraph 4, the author uses **comparison and contrast**. Identify the two things that are being compared and contrasted. Then, explain how these things are similar and/or different.

WRITE A PARAGRAPH

1. Discuss whether the decisions that a person makes in his or her youth can have serious consequences for the future.
2. Tell the story of a person you know who took a big risk in his or her youth. Describe what happened, and then tell how the person's future was or was not affected by the decision.

Brian Rickenbrode

King of the Road

Brian Rickenbrode, born in 1968, wrote the following essay as a student at Wayne College (Orville, Ohio), where he graduated in 2008. He currently works as a painting contractor but plans to enter the field of computer networking. Rickenbrode says, "My life goal is to prove to myself and others that dreams have no expiration date, and even when they only exist in the back of your thoughts for decades, they still can be achieved." His current interests include spending time with his daughter, Lauren; rooting for the Cleveland Browns, Cavaliers, and Indians; and computer gaming.

Rickenbrode wrote "King of the Road" in response to an assignment that asked students to tell a story from their lives. As his fortieth birthday approached, he observed: "I look back on the experiences that have brought me this far and I often wander down two paths of thought—nostalgia and regret—and though they are different they often merge, as they did for 'King of the Road.' I feel nostalgic for the carefree days of my youth but also regretful for how the carelessness often hurt others and especially my mother. . . . I felt 'King of the Road' would allow me to relive a truly thrilling moment while also acknowledging my mother's struggle."

Rickenbrode submitted the essay to a writing contest at Wayne College and later received a Student Writing Award for it. (For an essay by another Wayne College Student Writing Award winner, see page 531.)

His advice to other student writers is to challenge themselves: "If you go into a situation thinking you can't write or you can't do any better, you won't—but if you push yourself beyond that initial draft, you'll be more satisfied with the final product." Rickenbrode adds: "Read as much as you can. Understand how great authors use words to tell a story, and find a style that inspires you."

Reading Tips: To fully appreciate why this essay is successful, pay close attention to the author's word choice: almost every sentence contains precise verbs, colorful adjectives, and concrete nouns. This language brings the writing to life, keeping the reader involved.

In the fall of 1984, I turned sixteen years old. My status of "cool" had plummeted among my clique of friends. The guys who owned cars drew all of the attention. Not only did the girls notice them, but the other boys saw them as an opportunity for a ride. I certainly held a disadvantage, being a wiry boy with a thin, blond, curling mullet. I sported a paper-thin mustache and a pair of glasses that now rest in a history museum. Somehow, I needed to surpass my competition. 1

plummeted: fell dramatically

clique: social group

wiry: thin and muscular

mullet: a hairstyle that is short on the top and in front and long in the back

My family did not have much money. When I was thirteen, my parents divorced and my mother struggled greatly to raise me and my siblings. The fear of asking her to buy me a car was prohibitive. It was not out of respect for her situation, because I definitely took advantage of living in a fatherless environment. I did not want to hear her nagging that I was not mature enough to drive. 2

prohibitive: so great that it discourages action

Employment offered me a solution. I applied at the local supermarket and landed a job as a bagger. I would earn $3.35 an hour and work every night after school. I could soon look forward to buying a car. 3

My older brother, Alan, four inches taller than I, took pride as the local hooligan with tattoos strewn across his body. He was a menacing sight in a black leather coat and dark sunglasses, constantly in trouble with the law. One night I came home after work and overheard him on the phone telling a friend about a great deal on a hot ride. My ears perked up as I listened eagerly. I waited for his conversation to end and approached him about the news. Alan nearly choked on his cigarette as his laughter filled the air. "You, in that car?" he kept cackling. He assured me, "It's way too powerful a machine for a little wimp." I bartered with him; it appeared that a finder's fee would change his mind. After paying my brother ten dollars, we hopped in his car and drove to his friend's house. The trip seemed to take hours, and I could not contain my excitement; I was about to become a man. 4

hooligan: troublemaker

menacing: threatening or intimidating

cackling: laughing wickedly

bartered: made a deal

Tony, a little Italian man who always smelled of gasoline, looked like a greaser from head to toe. He had helped Alan with all his auto repairs, and my brother admired him as a mechanic. Upon our arrival, Tony led me to his garage and opened the door; I instantly caught a whiff of fresh paint and grease. That is when I saw her and fell in love. She was the most beautiful thing I had ever seen. A 1972 Chevy Monte Carlo, painted candy apple red with a vinyl black top, greeted me with her chrome wheels shining brightly in the spring sunshine. Tony tossed me the keys and said, "Take it for a spin." He jumped in the passenger seat, and I fired up the ignition. We drove around the block, checking everything over. This lady knew how to perform, but I needed the permission of a more important lady to be able to purchase this car. 5

greaser: mechanic

The aroma of fresh coffee woke me early the next day. I found my mother in the kitchen, a gorgeous woman in her youth, whose red hair and perfect smile had turned the heads of many men. That morning she showed signs of aging; a divorce and three children could do that to any woman. I felt sure she had had several sleepless nights wondering about my brother's safety. We sat down to enjoy our coffee, and I explained to her my intentions. She would approve of the purchase only if I would help transport my sister and run other household errands. I agreed to her requests, and she drove me to the bank to withdraw a season's worth of wages. 6

Teaching Tip

Ask students about things that they saved toward when they were in high school. Did they end up getting what they saved for? If so, did the things live up to their expectations? Why or why not?

Everything I had wished for at sixteen was finally happening. I imagined my friends' jealousy and became elated. That weekend I drove around, showing off my new trophy. My stock had risen and I was cool again. I quickly realized the power this awesome car possessed. I was King of the Road, and I challenged everyone to a race; I could not be beaten. 7

Teaching Tip
Some states have debated raising the driving age to reduce accidents and deaths linked to teen drivers. Do students think that such policies would be a good idea, or would they unfairly penalize young people? If you would like to provide students with statistics on car accidents involving young drivers, you can access a Centers for Disease Control and Prevention report at **www.cdc.gov/ncipc/factsheets/teenmvh.htm**.

Monday arrived and I raced to work. As I accelerated up a hill, I approached two vehicles traveling much too slowly for me. Common traffic laws were for the weak and inexperienced; I was a man and made my own rules. I darted up the left lane; the initial vehicle posed no challenge, and I passed it with ease—the first of many victories, or so I thought. My car raced beside the second vehicle. A kid no older than sixteen looked at me with pride and contempt as he sped up. I pushed the gas pedal harder; I was flying, going almost 90 mph. The other car kept pace, and I could not catch him. 8

Then I saw it, cresting the top of the hill, a semi-truck headed straight toward me. I panicked. I looked over to my right, and there was no room to fit between the two cars I was attempting to pass. Seconds flew by; I had to react as the truck barreled closer. He was approaching too quickly and would crush me if I tried to brake. I jerked the steering wheel to the right, not knowing what would happen. My cherished possession squeezed between the two cars, surely the sign of an expert driver. Then momentum carried me on. I veered off the road, a telephone pole doing what my brakes could not: bringing me to a dead halt. 9

carnage: slaughter (In this case, the author is referring to the messy aftermath of his accident.)

heckles: harassing statements or taunts

pertains: relates

I sat there for a moment, amazed at what had happened. I cleared my head and opened the door. As I looked at the carnage, Alan's heckles echoed in my head. I thought about my mother, knowing that her signs of age from years of stress were not just the fault of my brother. I knew she deserved better. I turned my back as the wreck was towed away, realizing how much more could have been lost. That brief experience taught me more than years of nagging ever could. Manhood does not consist of speed and status; instead, it pertains to respect and responsibility. Now, more than twenty years later, I pass that spot after visiting my mother. I acknowledge the double-yellow line and glance with a thrill at the still-red gash in that telephone pole. 10

CHECK YOUR UNDERSTANDING

1. At the time he turned sixteen, what was the author's social status?
   - **a.** He was one of the most popular kids at school.
   - **b.** He was viewed as a "nerd" because of his high grades.
   - **c.** He was not popular.
   - **d.** He was a loner.
2. How did the author learn about the car that he eventually purchased?
   - **a.** He saw an advertisement in the local paper.
   - **b.** His brother told him about it.
   - **c.** He heard his brother telling a friend about it over the phone.
   - **d.** His best friend at school told him about it.

3. How did the author act after he first purchased the car?
   a. with pride and carelessness
   b. with caution
   c. with protectiveness
   d. with fearfulness
4. What did the car accident teach the author?
   a. that he should purchase less flashy cars in the future
   b. that he should treat his mother with greater kindness
   c. that there are more important things in life than material possessions
   d. that responsibility is an important part of manhood

DISCUSS WITH YOUR PEERS

1. In paragraph 5, the author writes as if the car is a human being, referring to it as "she" and "her." After taking the car for a test drive, he says, "This lady knew how to perform." Some readers might argue that this description is sexist because it likens machines to women: both must perform well for men to feel like men. Discuss with your peers whether this description is sexist or simply good writing.
2. Reread paragraphs 7 and 8 and discuss what factors motivate the author to drive recklessly. Underline or highlight some of the details that explain his mental state. In your experience, do similar factors motivate other young adults to engage in risky behavior? Do these factors apply more to girls or boys, or are they equally relevant for both genders?
3. Discuss what life-changing lessons the author learns after the accident (para. 10). Then, discuss whether such an accident would really be sufficient to change the behavior of an average teenager who likes to take risks. Think of some young adults you know who have a history of high-risk behavior; what sort of event would be necessary to get them to stop such behavior?

IDENTIFY THE PATTERNS

For more on the various writing patterns referenced here, see Appendix A.

1. The main pattern of development in this essay is **narration**: the author tells the story of a serious mistake that he made. Effective narration usually includes strong, colorful characters and a clear sequence of events leading up to a climax. First, underline or highlight some of the details that bring the mother and the brother to life. Next, reread the carefully constructed sequence of events in paragraphs 8 and 9. Underline or highlight the precise and powerful verbs that the author uses to show action. Then, notice how the author uses lots of short sentences to establish a quick pace for the action. Circle the semicolons that he uses to briefly pause but not stop as he moves the story forward.
2. The author also uses **description** to develop his writing. In paragraph 5, underline or highlight some of the powerful descriptive details that appeal to the different senses (sight, hearing, smell, and so on).

WRITE A PARAGRAPH

1. Tell the story of the biggest mistake you ever made. Include the significant events leading up to the mistake, the details of the mistake itself, and the consequences of the mistake, including any lessons you may have learned.
2. Discuss factors that motivate young adults or adults to engage in risky behavior.

Susan Gobin

Nothing to Lose

Born in 1946, Susan Gobin grew up in San Antonio, Texas. She is the author of *Love Is the Healer; Death Is a Vehicle,* a book about the life lessons that can come from the death of a loved one. She has volunteered as a personal caretaker and hospice worker, spending time with patients in the last stages of their lives. Gobin currently lives in Austin, Texas, where she teaches workshops on spirituality and meditation.

This brief selection is from the January 2007 issue of *The Sun* magazine. Each month, the magazine features a "Readers Write" column that invites readers to submit a short piece of writing in response to a particular theme. The theme for this issue was "Nothing to Lose." In her piece, Gobin takes a positive view of what most people would consider mistakes. She explains how certain life lessons helped her become a more spiritual person.

Teaching Tip
Ask students how the impact of this essay might be different if the author had used dialogue—for example, dialogue between herself and her parents in paragraph 1. You might ask them to invent some dialogue for one or more parts of the narrative. Students can refer to Chapter 6, page 187, for advice on using dialogue (quoted details).

Reading Tips: As you read Gobin's short narrative, notice how she condenses the major episodes of her life into four short paragraphs or "chapters": early childhood, adolescence, adulthood, and late maturity.

Growing up Catholic and being the only one in my family to take the religion seriously was not easy. I attended a Catholic girls' school, and in first grade I kept track of my mortal sins, the kind that send you to hell: I didn't go to Mass on Sundays. (My parents wouldn't take me.) I ate meat on Fridays. (My parents would punish me if I didn't eat what they served.) 1

strove: tried

Though in high school I strove to be a good girl and worthy of Jesus' love, deep down I wanted to be like the bad girls who didn't care what the nuns thought. In my senior year I rebelled: I skipped school, went to parties, and had sex. But there was still a way out of damnation. Every Saturday afternoon I went to confession, hoping I could restrain myself that night so I could take Communion on Sunday. Even when I got pregnant, I found a way out: marriage. 2

confession: the practice, in the Catholic church, of admitting to one's sins and being forgiven for them

Communion: a ritual in which bread and wine are consumed in remembrance of Jesus' death

reprieve: a delay in or relief from punishment

I went on to have three children, a beautiful home, and everything else that defined the perfect family life. Then, at the age of thirty, I got divorced. The Church dictated that marriage was a lifetime commitment and divorce was a mortal sin: no way out. If I was going to hell with no hope of reprieve, I decided, I would taste every pleasure I could find on the way there. I was free. 3

Now, at the age of sixty, married for twenty-four years, I know that the judging of good and evil is the biggest sin. If I had stayed the "good" little girl, I would never have gotten to experience the vastness of God. 4

CHECK YOUR UNDERSTANDING

1. What statement is true about the author's childhood?
   - **a.** She grew up in a strictly Catholic household.
   - **b.** She was the only serious Catholic in her family.
   - **c.** She refused to go to church.
   - **d.** She wanted to become a nun.
2. How did the author's behavior change during her senior year of high school?
   - **a.** She gave up religion.
   - **b.** She became a more serious student.
   - **c.** She rebelled.
   - **d.** She tried to follow her parents' rules.
3. What did the author decide to do after her divorce, which was a "mortal sin" according to her religion?
   - **a.** to withdraw from society
   - **b.** to remarry
   - **c.** to change her religion
   - **d.** to seek pleasure
4. What, according to the author, is "the biggest sin"?
   - **a.** getting a divorce
   - **b.** judging what is good and evil
   - **c.** denying pleasure to oneself
   - **d.** disobeying God

DISCUSS WITH YOUR PEERS

1. As a young girl, the author seems trapped in a world of inconsistencies (para. 1). On the one hand, she is convinced that she is bad because she eats meat on Fridays, something prohibited by her religion. On the other hand, her parents seem insensitive to her religious beliefs, indirectly causing her "sinful" behavior. Discuss how this situation might make it difficult for a child to understand the difference between good and bad and to take full responsibility for her choices and actions.
2. Discuss why the author feels a need to rebel (para. 2). Do you believe the author takes full responsibility for her actions? Why or why not?
3. Discuss why the author is finally able to move beyond the church's definition of "good" and "bad" behavior (para. 4). Do you agree that religions can sometimes prevent people from having a full or true experience of God?

IDENTIFY THE PATTERNS

For more on the various writing patterns referenced here, see Appendix A.

1. In paragraph 1, the author uses **exemplification**. Underline or highlight two examples of "mortal sins." Explain why these are powerful examples, even though they are short.
2. In paragraph 2, the author uses **comparison and contrast**. Using details from the paragraph, explain how "good girls" are different from "bad girls."
3. In paragraph 3, the author uses **cause and effect** to explain a major turning point in her life. First, explain what *causes* this turning point. Then, explain how her life changes dramatically (the *effect*).

WRITE A PARAGRAPH

1. Discuss whether boys and girls have similar attitudes toward teenage sexual relationships and the risk of pregnancy.
2. Discuss whether religion is effective in helping young adults make wise decisions and avoid risky behavior.

MAKE CONNECTIONS

1. In "Weighing Risks and Benefits: Adolescent Decision Making" (page 580), the author suggests that mistakes made in a person's youth can be especially damaging. However, in two of the readings, "King of the Road" (page 584) and "Nothing to Lose" (page 588), the authors' youthful mistakes lead to important realizations that help them become more responsible individuals. In a paragraph or an essay, discuss whether youthful mistakes are a useful and necessary part of growth and maturation. You may use ideas and examples from the readings and from your own knowledge and experience.
2. The article "Weighing Risks and Benefits: Adolescent Decision Making" suggests that there are some differences and some similarities in risk-taking behavior among boys and girls. On the other hand, "King of the Road" focuses on male risk-taking behavior, and "Nothing to Lose" focuses on female risk-taking behavior. In a paragraph or essay, discuss whether young men and women are truly different in their risk-taking attitudes and behavior. You may use ideas and examples from the readings and from your own knowledge and experience.

Be aware of other readings that relate to the theme of addiction:

- "Dr. Dana" by Angela Adkins (page 531)
- "As They Say, Drugs Kill" by Laura Rowley (page 568)
- "Under the Influence" by Scott Russell Sanders (page 572)
- Excerpt from *Don't Eat This Book* by Morgan Spurlock (page 576)
- "Raising a Son—with Men on the Fringes" by Robyn Marks (page 610)

Chapter 23

Religious Diversity

READINGS

As noted by rabbi Sandy Sasso, one of the authors in this chapter, the United States is now a country not just of Christians and Jews but also of Muslims, Buddhists, Hindus, and people of other faiths. For years, religious and political leaders have preached tolerance for various religious beliefs, but is tolerance alone enough in an increasingly diverse—yet divided—world?

As you read the following selections, consider the ways in which different religions can coexist. Do all of us need to take a more active role in connecting with those whose beliefs are different from our own?

José Antonio Burciaga

My Ecumenical Father

ecumenical: accepting of all faiths

José Antonio Burciaga (1940–1996) was a Mexican American writer, artist, and activist. Born and raised in El Paso, Texas, Burciaga lived in Iceland and Spain for several years while serving in the U.S. Air Force. After earning a degree in fine arts from the University of Texas, he began a career as a graphic illustrator. Burciaga went on to become a resident fellow at Stanford University, where he became known for the murals he painted in Casa Zapata, a student dormitory that was (and still is) the center of activity for Stanford's Chicano student community. His collections of poetry and drawings include *Restless Serpents* (1976) and *Undocumented Love: A Personal Anthology of Poetry* (1992), for which he received an American Book Award. He also published the essay collections *Weedee Peepo* (1988), *Drink Cultura: Chicanismo* (1993), and *Spilling the Beans: Loteria Chicana* (1995).

In this essay from *Drink Cultura,* Burciaga describes how his father, a Mexican immigrant who worked as a custodian for a Jewish synagogue, taught him to respect religious and cultural diversity.

Reading Tips: Because this story contains some words from foreign languages, be prepared to read slowly and to reread when necessary. Although you can understand the basic story without knowing the meaning of these words, don't skip over them; instead, read their translations or ask your instructor for clarification.

Feliz Navidad [Spanish]: Merry Christmas

¡Feliz Navidad! Merry Christmas! Happy Hanukkah! As a child, my season's greetings were tricultural—Mexicano, Anglo and Jewish. 1

Our devoutly Catholic parents raised three sons and three daughters in the basement of a Jewish synagogue, Congregation B'nai Zion in El Paso, Texas. José Cruz Burciaga was the custodian and *shabbat goy.* A shabbat goy is Yiddish for a Gentile who, on the Sabbath, performs certain tasks forbidden to Jews under orthodox law. 2

Every year around Christmas time, my father would take the menorah out and polish it. The eight-branched candleholder symbolizes Hanukkah, the commemoration of the first recorded war of liberation in that part of the world. 3

pagan idols: images or figures of non-Jewish deities

In 164 B.C., the Jewish nation rebelled against Antiochus IV Epiphanes, who had attempted to introduce pagan idols into the temples. When the temple was reconquered by the Jews, there was only one day's supply of oil for the Eternal Light in the temple. By a miracle, the oil lasted eight days. 4

My father was not only in charge of the menorah but for 10 years he also made sure the Eternal Light remained lit. 5

As children we were made aware of the differences and joys of Hanukkah, Christmas and Navidad. We were taught to respect each celebration, even if they conflicted. For example, the Christmas carols taught in school. We learned the song about the twelve days of Christmas, though I never understood what the hell a partridge was doing in a pear tree in the middle of December. 6

O Tannenbaum [German]: a Christmas song (*O Christmas Tree* in English)

"Adeste Fideles" [Latin]: The common English translation for the name of this Christmas song is "O Come All Ye Faithful."

Español [Spanish]: Spanish

Noche de paz, noche de amor [Spanish]: Night of peace, night of love

We also learned a German song about a boy named Tom and a bomb—*O Tannenbaum.* We even learned a song in the obscure language of Latin, called "Adeste Fideles," which reminded me of, *Ahh! d'este fideo,* a Mexican pasta soup. Though 75% of our class was Mexican-American, we never sang a Christmas song in *Español.* Spanish was forbidden. 7

So our mother—a former teacher—taught us "Silent Night" in Spanish: *Noche de paz, noche de amor:* It was so much more poetic and inspirational. 8

While the rest of El Paso celebrated Christmas, Congregation B'nai Zion celebrated Hanukkah. We picked up Yiddish and learned a Hebrew prayer of thanksgiving. My brothers and I would help my father hang the Hanukkah decorations. 9

Teaching Tip

Ask students if they celebrate any religious holidays with special food, songs, and other customs. What are their customs?

At night, after the services, the whole family would rush across the border to Juarez and celebrate the *posadas,* which takes place for nine days before Christmas. They are a communal re-enactment of Joseph and Mary's search for shelter, just before Jesus was born. 10

To the posadas we took candles and candy left over from the Hanukkah celebrations. The next day we'd be back at St. Patrick's School singing, "I'm dreaming of a white Christmas." 11

One day I stopped dreaming of the white Christmases depicted on greeting cards. An old immigrant from Israel taught me Jesus was born in desert country just like that of the West Texas town of El Paso. 12

On Christmas Eve, my father would dress like Santa Claus and deliver gifts to his children, nephews, godchildren and the little kids in orphanages. 13

The next day, minus his disguise, he would take us to Juarez, where we delivered gifts to the poor in the streets.

My father never forgot his childhood poverty and forever sought to 14
help the less fortunate. He taught us to measure wealth not in money but in terms of love, spirit, charity and culture.

We were taught to respect the Jewish faith and culture. On the Day of 15
Atonement, when the whole congregation fasted, my mother did not cook, lest the food odors distract. The respect was mutual. No one ever complained about the large picture of Jesus in our living room.

Through my father, leftover food from B'nai B'rith luncheons, Bar 16
Mitzvahs and Bat Mitzvahs, found its way to Catholic or Baptist churches or orphanages. Floral arrangements in the temple that surrounded a Jewish wedding *huppah* canopy many times found a second home at the altar of St. Patrick's Cathedral or San Juan Convent School. Surplus furniture, including old temple pews, found their way to a missionary Baptist Church in *El Segundo Barrio.*

B'nai B'rith: a Jewish organization that promotes human rights and other humanitarian causes

Bar Mitzvahs (for boys); **Bat Mitzvahs** (for girls): religious ceremonies that welcome young teenagers as adult members of the Jewish community

It was not uncommon to come home from school at lunch time and 17
find an uncle priest, an aunt nun and a Baptist minister visiting our home at the same time that the Rabbi would knock on our door. It was just as natural to find the president of B'nai Zion eating beans and tortillas in our kitchen.

My father literally risked his life for the Jewish faith. Twice he was 18
assaulted by burglars who broke in at night. Once he was stabbed in the hand. Another time he stayed up all night guarding the sacred Torahs after anti-Semites threatened the congregation. He never philosophized about his ecumenism, he just lived it.

Torahs: texts, often scrolls, of Jewish scripture

anti-Semites: people who oppose Jews or the Jewish faith

Cruz, as most called him, was a man of great humor, a hot temper 19
and a passion for dance. He lived the Mexican Revolution and rode the rails during the Depression. One of his proudest moments came when he became a U.S. citizen.

September 23, 1985, sixteen months after my mother passed away, 20
my father followed. Like his life, his death was also ecumenical. The funeral was held at Our Lady of Peace, where a priest said the mass in English. My cousins played mandolin and sang in Spanish. The president of B'nai Zion Congregation said a prayer in Hebrew. Members of the congregation sat with Catholics and Baptists.

Mexican Revolution (1910–1920): a period of political unrest and armed conflict in Mexico, beginning with an uprising against dictator and longtime president Porfirio Díaz (1830–1915). It caused many Mexicans to migrate to the United States.

Depression: a severe economic downturn that lasted from 1929 through the 1930s

Observing Jewish custom, the cortege passed by the synagogue one last 21
time. Fittingly, father was laid to rest on the Sabbath. At the cemetery, in a very Mexican tradition, my brothers, sisters and I each kissed a handful of dirt and threw it on the casket.

cortege: a procession (train) of people taking part in some type of ceremony, often a funeral

I once had the opportunity to describe father's life to the late, great 22
Jewish American writer Bernard Malamud. His only comment was, "Only in America!"

CHECK YOUR UNDERSTANDING

1. As a *shabbat goy*, what did the author's father do at the synagogue for which he was the custodian?
   - **a.** He studied the Jewish religion with the goal of converting from Catholicism to Judaism.
   - **b.** He lit the menorah during Hanukkah.
   - **c.** He performed certain tasks that Jews could not do themselves on the Sabbath.
   - **d.** None of the above.
2. What attitude did the father take—and teach his children to take—toward beliefs different from his own?
   - **a.** one of reluctant acceptance
   - **b.** one of respect
   - **c.** one of outrage
   - **d.** one of fear and suspicion
3. Why did the author stop dreaming of "the white Christmases depicted on greeting cards"?
   - **a.** As a native of Texas, he had never seen actual snow.
   - **b.** His family never personally received such Christmas cards.
   - **c.** He came to see such views of Christmas as childish.
   - **d.** He learned from a Jewish immigrant that Jesus was born in a desert climate.
4. What is the best description of the father's funeral?
   - **a.** It involved people of different religions and different religious customs.
   - **b.** As the father wished, it was a strictly Catholic ceremony.
   - **c.** It closely followed Jewish religious custom.
   - **d.** It avoided religious ceremonies altogether.

DISCUSS WITH YOUR PEERS

1. Reread paragraphs 2, 5, and 9 and discuss the father's commitment to his work. In your opinion, is he just doing a good job, or has his sense of duty become a sense of devotion? In other words, is he simply protecting the property and practices of his Jewish employers, or is he participating in their beliefs?
2. Reread paragraphs 6, 14, and 15 and discuss the values that the father teaches his children. Are any of these values specifically religious, or are they more general ethical principles? Explain your position.
3. Throughout the essay, the author provides examples of how the different religious cultures coexist peacefully, sharing food, decorations, music, and so on. However, the father's funeral (paras. 20–21) is a sacred rite, which makes it a more serious example of cultural exchange. Discuss whether the father's funeral goes beyond mere cultural sharing and indicates real changes in the religious traditions involved. Are such changes even possible?

Teaching Tip

In paragraph 18, the author writes of his father, "He never philosophized about his ecumenism, he just lived it." Ask students if they know of anyone who lives (or lived) a belief instead of just talking about it. They can name a famous person or someone in their own life. Encourage them to provide detailed support for their choices.

IDENTIFY THE PATTERNS

For more on the various writing patterns referenced here, see Appendix A.

1. The author uses **narration** as the main pattern of development. What is the main point of the story he tells? What are the main parts of the story? Does the story have strong characters? In your opinion, is the author successful in telling his story?
2. In paragraphs 6–11, the author uses **comparison and contrast**. First, identify the three things that are being compared and/or contrasted. Then, identify some of the ways these things are similar and/or different. Does the author use more comparison, more contrast, or an equal amount of both? Does the author provide enough details for an effective use of comparison and contrast?
3. In paragraphs 20–21, the author uses **exemplification** to show that the father's funeral is ecumenical. Underline or highlight some examples of the different religious traditions involved in the funeral. Does the author provide enough precise details to make this a successful use of exemplification?

WRITE A PARAGRAPH

1. Describe some religious traditions that you have participated in other than your own. Explain the purpose or meaning of those traditions, what you appreciated or disliked about them, and whether you would be interested in learning more about them.
2. Discuss a person you know or have known who loves bringing different cultures and their traditions together.
3. Discuss why it is often very difficult for people of different religions to coexist peacefully. What prevents them from being like the people in this story?

Sandy Sasso

Our Religious Diversity

Born in 1947 in Philadelphia, Sandy Sasso received bachelor's and master's degrees from Temple University and became the first woman ordained from Reconstructionist Rabbinical College. She also holds a doctor of ministry degree from Christian Theological Seminary. Sasso has written eleven children's books on religion and spirituality, including *God's Paintbrush* (1992), *God Said Amen* (2000), and *Cain and Abel: Finding the Fruits of Peace* (2001). Sasso recently published her first book for adults, *God's Echo: Exploring Scripture with Midrash* (2007), and she also writes a weekly column for *The Indianapolis Star.* For the past twenty years, Sasso and her husband have been rabbis at the Congregation Beth-El Zedeck in Indianapolis.

In her writings for both children and adults, Sasso encourages readers to understand and accept each other's religions. In the following essay, first published in *The Indianapolis Star* in 2004, Sasso discusses how religious diversity can become a source of strength—rather than a cause of division—in the United States.

Reading Tips: This essay includes some difficult vocabulary and some deep arguments about American religious, social, and constitutional customs. Be prepared to reread individual paragraphs several times until you get a clear sense of what the author is saying. For some especially difficult paragraphs, it may be useful to rewrite the author's sentences *in your own words* to simplify and clarify their meaning.

Sikh: a religion that originated in Punjab, a region now split between India and Pakistan

cardamom: a spice, related to ginger, often used in Indian cooking

Tandoori: a style of Indian cooking in which food is baked in a clay oven

microcosm: miniature version

I remember a hot day in July when my husband, Dennis, and I met a Sikh friend at an Indian restaurant. There we greeted a Muslim physician, a professor of Christian theology, a Methodist pastor, and a congregant from our synagogue. There we were—Jew, Muslim, Sikh, and Christian—sipping sweet Indian tea mixed with milk and spiced with cardamom. Hebrew, Punjabi, and English mixed freely with curried rice and Tandoori cooking. What happened around that lunch table is but a microcosm of what is happening across our country. 1

When the sociologist Will Herberg wrote a seminal book in 1955 titled *Protestant, Catholic, and Jew,* he was reflecting on what he saw were the primary religious affiliations in the United States. He wrote of ethnic divisions fading against a backdrop of three primary faith expressions that made up the American landscape. 2

Teaching Tip

There are many intriguing quotations about religion. Consider, for example, this one from the late Egyptian statesman Mohammed Neguib: "Religion is a candle inside a multicolored lantern. Everyone looks through a particular color, but the candle is always there." Ask students to respond briefly in writing to this quotation or to another quotation of your choice. (A good source is www.quotationspage.com.)

That landscape has changed significantly since his writing. We can no longer claim to be merely a "Christian" or even a "Judeo-Christian" country. We are a country of Christians and Jews, but also Muslims, Sikhs, Buddhists, and Hindus, among the many religious groups who have made a home in America. Diana Eck in her book *A New Religious America* affirms that the United States is the most religiously diverse nation in the world. Religious freedom and the separation of church and state enshrined in our Bill of Rights helped to ensure that we would also be the "most religious" nation in the world. 3

cohesive: unified

Even as our country is home to more religions and is "more religious" than other nations, we have still to decide what the reality of this diversity will mean for America. Despite the increasing variety of religious expressions, few Americans have been to a mosque or Buddhist temple. How can we learn to live together, to understand one another's concerns, if we don't even know each other? How can we build a cohesive national identity without listening to the many voices that make up our nation? 4

Religion is often the cause of division and tension. If we are to make it a source of strength and a resource for a critical discussion of values, then we will need not simply to agree to tolerate one another, to live together because we have no other choice, but to understand each other and how we are different. So much of the so-called public prayer offered at civic occasions fails to respect and speak for the diverse public for whom it is offered. Too often the words spoken in the name of God who includes us all are insensitive and exclusive. 5

doctrinal: related to the basic fundamentals, rules, or principles of something

abysmally: extremely; hopelessly

Our public schools have been reluctant to teach religion for fear that teaching will become preaching. We do not need doctrinal instruction in our schools, but we do need to teach youth about religions in a way that does not seek to promote conversion but to advance knowledge. We are abysmally ignorant about the religious and cultural traditions of our neighbors, and that ignorance has led not merely to misunderstandings but to prejudice, hateful rhetoric, and overt violence. 6

To be a truly pluralistic nation, and not merely a diverse one, we need to learn from one another, to appreciate our differences and to value our distinctiveness. Our faith commitments are not threatened through dialogue with other religious or even secular ideas and values. On the contrary, such encounters enrich us. Through the study of world religions, my own faith has been expanded and deepened. And because I believe that no one faith has a monopoly on God, that we are all created in divine image, viewing the divine through the eyes of others has broadened my own comprehension of God. 7

There is a lot of talk about religion, but not the right kind of talk. We spend our time and efforts arguing about placing religious symbols in our public squares, bringing prayer back to the schools and the Ten Commandments to the lawns of courthouses. We should spend more time and effort learning about one another, honoring the many traditions that make up the spiritual fabric of our nation. 8

The founders of our country learned that at the heart of independence was interdependence, the ability not only to co-exist but to cooperate with one another. The challenge today is to respond to a new call to interdependence and cooperation among the diverse faces and faiths that are the new America. 9

pluralistic: granting equal measures of tolerance and respect to different religions, beliefs, ethnic groups, and so on

monopoly: sole claim to

Ten Commandments: ten moral and religious rules central to Judaism and Christianity

Teaching Tip

Some students will have views that are starkly different from Sasso's. For example, some may see what she views as the "wrong" kind of talk about religion (para. 8) as just the right kind of talk. Encourage students to share their views if they feel comfortable doing so.

CHECK YOUR UNDERSTANDING

1. According to the author, what is now true about the religious landscape of the United States?
   - **a.** It is growing less and less diverse.
   - **b.** It is more diverse than ever.
   - **c.** It is becoming dominated by religions other than Christianity and Judaism.
   - **d.** Humanism is replacing religious belief.
2. What is lacking in the United States, according to the author?
   - **a.** tolerance for religious beliefs other than our own
   - **b.** an understanding of various religious faiths and how they are different
   - **c.** enough places of worship for various religious faiths
   - **d.** public policy that respects religious diversity
3. What kind of religious education is needed in public schools, according to the author?
   - **a.** one that teaches the doctrines of various religions
   - **b.** one that encourages memorization of religious texts
   - **c.** one that teaches different faiths' religious and cultural traditions
   - **d.** none of the above
4. What, according to the author, is the "wrong" kind of talk about religion?
   - **a.** discussions about placing religious symbols in public places
   - **b.** discussions about bringing prayer back to the schools
   - **c.** discussions about displaying the Ten Commandments in public places
   - **d.** all of the above

DISCUSS WITH YOUR PEERS

1. In paragraph 3, the author claims that our religious "rights" in the United States have helped us to become the "most religious" nation in the world. Discuss whether you agree or disagree with this claim. First, what does it mean to be the "most religious" nation? How would you measure this? Does it have more to do with the number of faithful or the depth of their faith? If you can agree on a definition of "most religious," discuss whether or not the United States deserves this title. Keep in mind that other countries might argue that America's greatest faith is in the "almighty dollar."
2. In paragraph 6, the author claims that public schools should teach religion—not as faith but as knowledge. Discuss whether you agree or disagree that classes in religion would be beneficial to students and the country. Do you believe that religion could be taught as "knowledge" without the faith of instructors and students interfering? Would you support "Religion 101" becoming a general education requirement? Explain your opinions.
3. In paragraph 7, the author suggests that a person's faith is strengthened and enriched when it is receptive to other religious traditions. Discuss whether you agree or disagree with this idea. Do you think that knowledge of and experience with different religions would strengthen your faith or weaken it? Do you worry that you might be confused by other religions or tempted to change your beliefs?
4. In paragraph 5, the author suggests that much "public prayer" in the United States is insensitive to people who are not of the dominant faith (Christianity). Now, look at paragraph 7, where the author claims that "we are all created in divine image." Discuss whether an atheist would be likely to agree with this claim. Do you think the author is being insensitive to atheists? Is she guilty of the same sort of insensitivity that she criticizes in paragraph 5?

IDENTIFY THE PATTERNS

For more on the various writing patterns referenced here, see Appendix A.

1. The author uses **argumentation** as the main pattern of development. She states her main argument or claim at least three times. In paragraphs 5, 7, and 8, underline or highlight one sentence that contains the author's main argument. Decide whether these three sentences all express the same idea. Finally, does the author provide enough information to convince you that her argument is valid?
2. In paragraph 3, the author uses **definition**. She says that America can no longer be defined as a "Christian" or "Judeo-Christian" country; then, she provides what she sees as a more accurate definition. Underline or highlight the key parts of the new definition. Does she provide enough information to make this an effective use of definition?
3. In paragraph 7, the author uses **cause and effect**. Underline or highlight some of the things that will cause America to become a "truly pluralistic nation" (the effect). Does the author focus more on causes or effects here? Does she provide enough information to make this an effective use of cause and effect?

WRITE A PARAGRAPH

1. Discuss whether a "Religion 101" course should be a general requirement for college students. Be sure to give sufficient reasons and examples to support your position.
2. Discuss whether the United States is the "'most religious' nation in the world" (para. 3). Be sure to give sufficient reasons and examples to support your position.
3. Discuss whether atheism should be considered a type of religion. Be sure to give sufficient reasons and examples to support your position.

Eboo Patel

We Are Each Other's Business

The son of Muslim Indian immigrants, Eboo Patel was born in 1975 and grew up in Glen Ellyn, Illinois. After receiving his undergraduate degree from the University of Illinois at Champaign-Urbana and a doctorate in the sociology of religion from Oxford University, Patel traveled through impoverished areas of India and South Africa performing volunteer work. He then founded Interfaith Youth Core, an organization that builds trust and respect among young people of different religions by bringing them together to serve their communities. In 2002, the magazine *Utne Reader* named Patel one of "thirty social visionaries under thirty changing the world" for his work with youth. His writing has appeared in the *Chicago Tribune, The Journal of Muslim Law and Culture,* and the *Harvard Divinity School Bulletin,* and he serves as an online panelist for the "On Faith" blog co-hosted by the *Washington Post* and *Newsweek* magazine. A frequent speaker on youth and religion, Patel gave the keynote address at the 2004 Nobel Peace Prize Forum. He recently published the memoir *Acts of Faith: The Story of an American Muslim, the Struggle for the Soul of a Generation* (2007).

In "We Are Each Other's Business," from National Public Radio's *This I Believe* series, Patel describes a time when he failed to act on his belief in religious diversity. The incident, he writes, was the "single most humiliating experience" of his life.

Reading Tips: Notice how the author weaves an argument into a personal story. You might want to highlight or otherwise mark where he moves between narrative and argumentative writing.

I am an American Muslim. I believe in pluralism. In the Holy Quran, God tells us, "I created you into diverse nations and tribes that you may come to know one another." I believe America is humanity's best opportunity to make God's wish that we come to know one another a reality. 1

In my office hangs Norman Rockwell's illustration *Freedom to Worship.* A Muslim holding a Quran in his hands stands near a Catholic woman fingering her rosary. Other figures have their hands folded in prayer and their eyes filled with piety. They stand shoulder-to-shoulder facing the same direction, comfortable with the presence of one another and yet apart. It is a vivid depiction of a group living in peace with its diversity, yet not exploring it. 2

pluralism: a condition in which equal measures of tolerance and respect are granted to different religions, beliefs, ethnic groups, and so on

Quran (also Koran): the sacred text of the Muslim faith

piety: religious feeling or respect

We live in a world where the forces that seek to divide us are strong. To overcome them, we must do more than simply stand next to one another in silence. 3

I attended high school in the western suburbs of Chicago. The group I ate lunch with included a Jew, a Mormon, a Hindu, a Catholic, and a Lutheran. We were all devout to a degree, but we almost never talked about religion. Somebody would announce at the table that they couldn't eat a certain kind of food, or any food at all, for a period of time. We all knew religion hovered behind this, but nobody ever offered any explanation deeper than "my mom said," and nobody ever asked for one. 4

hovered: floated

A few years after we graduated, my Jewish friend from the lunchroom reminded me of an experience we both wish had never happened. A group of thugs in our high school had taken to scrawling anti-Semitic slurs on classroom desks and shouting them in the hallway. 5

thugs: cruel or evil-acting people

anti-Semitic: against Jews or the Jewish faith

I did not confront them. I did not comfort my Jewish friend. Instead I averted my eyes from their bigotry, and I avoided the eyes of my friend because I couldn't stand to face him. 6

bigotry: intolerance

My friend told me he feared coming to school those days, and he felt abandoned as he watched his close friends do nothing. Hearing him tell me of his suffering—and my complicity—is the single most humiliating experience of my life. 7

complicity: association with a harmful act

humiliating: shameful

My friend needed more than my silent presence at the lunch table. I realize now that to believe in pluralism means I need the courage to act on it. Action is what separates a belief from an opinion. Beliefs are imprinted through actions. 8

Teaching Tip

Some students will understand the author's reluctance, as a high school student, to bring up religion, even when his friend faced harassment based on his religion. In fact, many of us have been advised to "avoid religion and politics" in conversation. You might discuss this advice with students. When are religious and political topics counterproductive in conversation, and when are they worth taking on?

In the words of the American poet Gwendolyn Brooks: "We are each other's business; we are each other's harvest; we are each other's magnitude and bond." 9

I cannot go back in time and take away the suffering of my Jewish friend, but through action I can prevent it from happening to others. 10

CHECK YOUR UNDERSTANDING

1. According to the author, what is needed to overcome the forces that seek to divide us as a country?
   - **a.** more religious education
   - **b.** quiet tolerance of beliefs that are different from our own
   - **c.** the courage to speak up for and act on our beliefs
   - **d.** none of the above
2. What is true about the author's interactions with high school friends at lunch?
   - **a.** They never talked about religion.
   - **b.** They constantly talked about religion.
   - **c.** They shared food from their different cultures.
   - **d.** They had lively political discussions.

3. What happened to the author's Jewish friend during high school?
   a. He was harassed by the other students at the lunch table.
   b. He witnessed and heard anti-Semitic remarks.
   c. He was physically assaulted.
   d. He was expelled for fighting with students who teased him.
4. At the time, how did the author react to the events that troubled his Jewish friend?
   a. He reported them to school authorities.
   b. He discussed them with the friend.
   c. He confronted those responsible.
   d. He ignored the events.

DISCUSS WITH YOUR PEERS

1. In paragraph 2, the author describes different religious groups living in peace with one another. However, he suggests that mutual respect and tolerance may not be enough in today's world; instead, we need to explore one another's religions actively. Discuss whether you agree or disagree that people should be responsible for actively exploring each other's religions. Do you believe that this is a necessary and reasonable requirement for people in today's world?
2. Discuss why the author calls the episode described in paragraph 7 the "single most humiliating experience" of his life. Do the author's feelings make sense to you? Why or why not?
3. In paragraph 9, the author quotes poet Gwendolyn Brooks. What do you think Brooks means by the metaphors (creative comparisons) "we are each other's harvest; we are each other's magnitude and bond"? Discuss whether you agree or disagree with Brooks's claims about who we are (or should be) to one another. Is Brooks being realistic or idealistic?

IDENTIFY THE PATTERNS

For more on the various writing patterns referenced here, see Appendix A.

1. The author uses **argumentation** to develop his writing. Identify his main arguments or claims by underlining or highlighting one sentence in each of the following paragraphs: 1, 3, and 8. Do you think that each of these claims is equally important to the author's purpose? Why or why not?
2. The author also uses **narration** to develop his writing. In the middle of the essay, he tells a story. Identify the paragraph in which he begins telling the story. What is the main event of the story? What is the author's purpose in telling this story? Does the author provide enough information and details to make this a successful narration?
3. In paragraph 2, the author uses **description**. What is it that he describes? Underline or highlight some of the details of this description. Does the author provide adequate descriptive details to create a clear mental image for the reader? Is this a successful use of description?

WRITE A PARAGRAPH

1. Tell the story of a time when you or someone you know was a victim of religious prejudice. Explain what happened, how the person handled the situation, and what lessons might be learned from the experience.
2. Discuss whether you have "the courage to act on" your religious beliefs (or on your atheistic beliefs).

MAKE CONNECTIONS

1. All three readings in this chapter praise the United States as a special place where religious diversity can flourish. In a paragraph or essay, argue for or against the claim that the United States is an ideal place for religious diversity to grow and endure. You may use ideas and examples from the readings and from your own knowledge and experience.
2. All three readings suggest that peaceful coexistence, respect, and tolerance may not be powerful enough to protect and encourage religious diversity in the world today. Instead, the authors argue that we must actively explore one another's religions. Discuss whether an "active exploration" of other religious beliefs and traditions is essential to the growth and survival of religious diversity and peace. You may use ideas and examples from the readings and from your own knowledge and experience.

Be aware of other readings that relate to the theme of religion:

- "The 'M-Word': Why It Matters to Me" by Andrew Sullivan (page 558)
- "Nothing to Lose" by Susan Gobin (page 588)

Chapter 24

Parents and Parenting

READINGS

- "Why Couldn't My Father Read?"
- "Fish Cheeks"
- "Raising a Son—with Men on the Fringes"

Parenting comes with a great burden of responsibility. As journalist Robyn Marks says of raising her young son, Jason, as a single mother: ". . . at the end of the day, everything Jason is, everything he trusts about who and what he can become, will come from me."

While most people do the best they can for their children, parents have flaws—just like every other human being. Children can be unforgiving of these flaws, sometimes loudly expressing resentment or embarrassment.

As you read the following selections, consider the sources of conflict between parents and children. What causes children to be resentful of or embarrassed by their parents? When are these emotions justified, and when might they be immature reactions? When is conflict between children and their parents not only unavoidable but necessary? And what about the inner conflicts that nearly every parent experiences? Can they ever be resolved?

Enrique Hank Lopez

Why Couldn't My Father Read?

Enrique Hank Lopez (1920–1985) grew up in Denver, Colorado. After earning his undergraduate degree from the University of Denver, he went on to become the first Hispanic-American to graduate from Harvard Law School. Lopez taught at Yale University, Harvard University, and the University of California at Berkeley, focusing on immigrants' rights and bilingual education, and from 1962 to 1967, he edited the Hispanic literary journal *Dialogos.* His books include the novel *The Hidden Magic of Uxmal* (1980) and the nonfiction books *The Harvard Mystique* (1979) and *Conversations with Katherine Anne Porter* (1981).

In the essay that follows, first published in the *Cleveland Plain Dealer* in 1979, Lopez describes the experience of growing up with a father who couldn't read or write. While most people know what it feels like to be embarrassed by a parent, the shame that Lopez felt over his father's illiteracy was particularly painful.

Reading Tips: The author uses some English and Spanish vocabulary that may not be familiar to you. Be prepared to read slowly and to use a dictionary to look up unfamiliar English words. Also, take a moment to read the translations of Spanish words, or you might miss the precise meaning of the essay. Consider recording new vocabulary in a special log. (See Chapter 7, page 222, for advice on keeping a vocabulary log.)

articulate: clear and effective in expressing one's thoughts

proficient: skilled

Bachimba Chihuahua: a village in northern Mexico

Recent articles on immigration and education remind me of my father, who was an articulate, fascinating storyteller but totally illiterate. By the time I entered fourth grade in Denver, I was a proud, proficient reader—and painfully aware of my father's inability to read a single word in either Spanish or English. Although I'd been told there were no schools in his native village of Bachimba Chihuahua, I found it hard to accept the fact that he didn't even know the alphabet. 1

Consequently, every night as I watched my mother read to him, I would feel a surge of resentment and shame. Together they bent over *La Prensa* from San Antonio—the only available Spanish language newspaper. "How can he be so dumb?" I would ask myself. "Even a little kid can read a damned newspaper." Of course many adults in our barrio couldn't read or write, but that was no comfort to me. Nor did it console me that my hero Pancho Villa was also illiterate. After all, this was my own father, the man I considered to be smarter than anyone else, who could answer questions not even my mother could answer, who would take me around the ice factory where he worked and show me how all the machinery ran, who could make huge cakes of ice without any air bubbles, who could fix any machine or electrical appliance, who could tell me all those wonderful stories about Pancho Villa. 2

barrio: neighborhood inhabited mostly by Spanish-speaking people

Pancho Villa (1878–1923): a hero of the Mexican Revolution (1910–1920), a period of political unrest and armed conflict in Mexico, beginning with an uprising against dictator and longtime president Porfirio Díaz (1830–1915)

Teaching Tip

Do students have strong memories of learning to read or write? Encourage them to share their stories. What were their emotions at the time?

But he couldn't read. Not one damned word! 3

Whenever I saw my mother reading to him—his head thrust forward like a dog waiting for a bone—I would walk out of the kitchen and sit on the back porch, my stomach churning with a swelling anger that could easily have turned to hatred. So bitter was my disappointment, so deep was my embarrassment, that I never invited my friends into the house during that after-dinner hour when my mother habitually read to him. And if one of my friends had supped with us, I would hastily herd them out of the kitchen when my mother reached for *La Prensa.* 4

supped: shared a meal

Once, during a period of deepening frustration, I told my mother that we ought to teach him how to read and write. And when she said it was probably too late to teach him—that it might hurt his pride—I stomped out of the house and ran furiously down the back alley, finally staggering behind a trash can to vomit everything I'd eaten for supper. 5

Standing there in the dark, my hand still clutching the rim of the can, I simply couldn't believe that anyone as smart as my dad couldn't learn to read, couldn't learn to write "cat" or "dog" or even "it." Even I, who could barely understand the big words he used when he talked about Pancho Villa (revolucion, libertad), even I, at the mere age of ten, could write big words in both English and Spanish. So why couldn't he? 6

revolucion [Spanish]: revolution

libertad [Spanish]: liberty

Eventually, he did learn to write two words—his name and surname. Believing that he would feel less humble if he could sign his full name rather than a mere "X" on his weekly paycheck, my mother wrote "José Lopez" 7 on his Social Security card and taught him to copy it letter by letter. It was a slow, painstaking process that usually required two or three minutes as he drew each separate letter with solemn tight-lipped determination, pausing now and then as if to make sure they were in the proper sequence. Then he would carefully connect the letters with short hyphen-like lines, sometimes failing to close the gaps or overlapping letters.

I was with him one Friday evening when he tried to cash his paycheck at a furniture store owned by Frank Fenner, a red-faced German with a bulbous nose and squinty eyes. My father usually cashed his check at Alfredo Pacheco's corner grocery store, but that night Pacheco had closed the store to attend a cousin's funeral, so we had crossed the street to Fenner's place. 8

bulbous: bulging

"You cambiar this?" asked my father, showing him the check. 9

"He wants you to cash it," I added, annoyed by my father's use of the word *cambiar*. 10

cambiar [Spanish]: to change; in this case, to cash

"Sure, Joe," said Fenner. "Just write your signature on the back of it." 11

"Firme su nombre atrás," I told my father, indicating that Fenner wanted him to sign it. 12

"Okay, I put my name," said my father, placing his Social Security card on the counter so he could copy the "José Lopez" my mother had written for him. 13

With Fenner looking on, a smirk building on his face, my father began the ever-so-slow copying of each letter as I literally squirmed with shame and hot resentment. Halfway through "Lopez," my father paused, nervously licked his lips, and glanced sheepishly at Fenner's leering face. "No write too good," he said. "My wife teach me." 14

smirk: a mean smile

sheepishly: with embarrassment or shyness

leering: having a cruel or malicious expression

Then, concentrating harder than before, he wrote the final "e" and "z" and slowly connected the nine letters with his jabby little scribbles. But Fenner was not satisfied. Glancing from the Social Security card to the check, he said, "I'm sorry, Joe, that ain't the same signature. I can't cash it." 15

"You bastard!" I yelled. "You know who he is! And you just saw him signing it." 16

Then suddenly grabbing a can of furniture polish, I threw it at Fenner's head but missed by at least six inches. As my father tried to restrain me, I twisted away and screamed at him, "Why don't you learn to write, goddamn it! Learn to write!" 17

He was trying to say something, his face blurred by my angry tears, but I couldn't hear him, for I was now backing and stumbling out of the store, my temples throbbing with the most awful humiliation I had ever felt. My throat dry and sour, I kept running and running down Larimer Street and then north on 30th Street toward Curtis Park, where I finally flung myself on the recently watered lawn and wept myself into a state of complete exhaustion. 18

humiliation: shame

Hours later, now guilt-ridden by what I had yelled at my dad, I came home and found him and my mother sitting at the kitchen table, writing tablet between them, with the alphabet neatly penciled at the top of the page. 19

"Your mother's teaching me how to write," he said in Spanish, his voice so wistful that I could hardly bear to listen to him. "Then maybe you won't be ashamed of me." 20

wistful: sad or longing

Teaching Tip
Ask students to imagine and write a letter from the author, as a grown man, to his father. What might the son say to his father to help him understand the angry reactions of a child to a parent's limitations? How might the son show compassion and respect for the father?

But for reasons too complex for me to understand at that time, he never learned to read or write. Somehow, the multisyllabic words he had always known and accurately used seemed confusing and totally beyond his grasp when they appeared in print or in my mother's handwriting. So after a while, he quit trying. 21

CHECK YOUR UNDERSTANDING

1. According to the essay, what is true about the author's father?
   - **a.** He is reasonably bright but illiterate.
   - **b.** He is very smart but illiterate.
   - **c.** He is neither intelligent nor literate.
   - **d.** He is fully literate in Spanish.
2. What did the father eventually learn to write?
   - **a.** the names of his wife and children
   - **b.** reports at the factory where he worked
   - **c.** his name and surname
   - **d.** poetry about his native Mexico
3. What reason did the owner of the furniture store give for not cashing the father's check?
   - **a.** He didn't have the necessary cash to do so.
   - **b.** He didn't want to do business with Mexican immigrants.
   - **c.** He was still upset about a fight that he and the father had had.
   - **d.** The father's signature on the check didn't look like the signature on his Social Security card.
4. What was the author's reaction to the events at the furniture store?
   - **a.** He felt deep shame followed by guilt.
   - **b.** He felt pride that his father had attempted to sign his name.
   - **c.** He felt renewed determination to teach his father English.
   - **d.** He became determined to get as much education as he could.

DISCUSS WITH YOUR PEERS

1. Based on the evidence in paragraphs 2 and 6, do you agree or disagree that the author's father was an exceptionally smart person? Or do you think that he simply appeared that way through the eyes of a child? Then, look at paragraphs 5 and 21. Discuss why the father never learned to read. What might have been the main obstacles to his success? Does the fact that he never learned to read suggest that he might not have been so intelligent after all? Explain your opinions.
2. Look at paragraphs 2, 14, 18, and 19, and underline or highlight descriptions of the son's emotions in response to his father's illiteracy. Discuss whether these emotions seem reasonable and fair. Or is the son being childish and selfish? If you wish, discuss some limitations of your own parents that caused you similar emotions. Do you still feel these emotions, or have you moved beyond them?

3. Reread paragraphs 8–17, describing what happens when the son and father go to the furniture store to cash a check. Discuss whether the son fails his father in this situation. Is he right to yell at the owner, or is he simply venting his frustration? How might he have handled the situation more effectively? Then, discuss whether children of immigrant parents need exceptional maturity to help their parents cope in U.S. society. If possible, share examples from your own experience and knowledge.

IDENTIFY THE PATTERNS

For more on the various writing patterns referenced here, see Appendix A.

1. In paragraph 2, the author uses **exemplification** to show that his father is "smarter than anyone else." Underline or highlight the examples of his father's intelligence. Are these examples a powerful illustration of how the son sees his father? Why or why not?
2. In paragraph 7, the author uses **process** to develop his writing. Underline or highlight some of the details that show the father's process of learning to write his name. Does the author do a good job showing the parts of this process and bringing it to life? Why or why not?
3. The author also uses powerful **description** to develop his writing. For example, take a close look at paragraphs 14 and 18. Underline or highlight some of the action verbs, vivid adjectives, and concrete nouns that give readers a strong mental image of the events.

WRITE A PARAGRAPH

1. Discuss some limitations of your own parents that were difficult for you to accept.
2. Discuss whether you supported or failed your parents in their times of difficulty. If you could relive those difficult times with your parents, would you do anything differently?

Amy Tan

Fish Cheeks

Amy Tan was born in Oakland, California, in 1952. Although her mother pushed her to become a doctor or a concert pianist, Tan followed her own path, graduating from San Jose State University with a B.A. in English and an M.A. in linguistics. Tan began her career as a business writer and language development specialist, writing fiction in her spare time. A trip to China in 1987 inspired her to complete her first novel, *The Joy Luck Club.* Published in 1989, the book quickly became a popular and critical success. Since then, she has written the novels *The Kitchen God's Wife* (1991), *The Hundred Secret Senses* (1995), *The Bonesetter's Daughter* (2001), and *Saving Fish from Drowning* (2005). She has also published two children's books and a memoir, *The Opposite of Fate: A Book of Musings* (2003).

In "Fish Cheeks," which originally appeared in *Seventeen* magazine in 1987, Tan recalls a memorable Christmas dinner from her childhood. This brief narrative shows some of the cultural conflicts Tan faced as the American-born daughter of Chinese parents.

Reading Tips: In this essay, the author uses vivid details to describe a fancy meal. However, the deeper meaning of the story concerns the characters' behavior, which is not always easy to recognize or understand. As you read, enjoy the colorful descriptions of the food, but pay special attention to the attitudes and actions of the characters.

Mary in the manger: a reference to Mary, mother of Jesus, who is often shown as being white in pictures and statues

I fell in love with the minister's son the winter I turned fourteen. He was not Chinese, but as white as Mary in the manger. For Christmas I prayed for this blond-haired boy, Robert, and a slim new American nose. 1

When I found out that my parents had invited the minister's family over for Christmas Eve dinner, I cried. What would Robert think of our shabby Chinese Christmas? What would he think of our noisy Chinese relatives who lacked proper American manners? What terrible disappointment would he feel upon seeing not a roasted turkey and sweet potatoes but Chinese food? 2

prawns: shellfish similar to shrimp

appalling: horrifying

On Christmas Eve I saw that my mother had outdone herself in creating a strange menu. She was pulling black veins out of the backs of fleshy prawns. The kitchen was littered with appalling mounds of raw food: A slimy rock cod with bulging eyes that pleaded not to be thrown into a pan of hot oil. Tofu, which looked like stacked wedges of rubbery white sponges. A bowl soaking dried fungus back to life. A plate of squid, their backs crisscrossed with knife markings so they resembled bicycle tires. 3

And then they arrived—the minister's family and all my relatives in a clamor of doorbells and rumpled Christmas packages. Robert grunted hello, and I pretended he was not worthy of existence. 4

Teaching Tip

Chinese food and foods from many other cultures are now more widely available than they were when the events of this essay took place (in the 1960s). Ask students whether the guests might react more enthusiastically to the food if this meal had taken place today instead of the 1960s. What kinds of ethnic foods do students like that their parents or grandparents might consider strange?

Dinner threw me deeper into despair. My relatives licked the ends of their chopsticks and reached across the table, dipping them into the dozen or so plates of food. Robert and his family waited patiently for platters to be passed to them. My relatives murmured with pleasure when my mother brought out the whole steamed fish. Robert grimaced. Then my father poked his chopsticks just below the fish eye and plucked out the soft meat. "Amy, your favorite," he said, offering me the tender fish cheek. I wanted to disappear. 5

At the end of the meal my father leaned back and belched loudly, thanking my mother for her fine cooking. "It's a polite Chinese custom to show you are satisfied," explained my father to our astonished guests. Robert was looking down at his plate with a reddened face. The minister managed to muster up a quiet burp. I was stunned into silence for the rest of the night. 6

After everyone had gone, my mother said to me, "You want to be the same as American girls on the outside." She handed me an early gift. It was a miniskirt in beige tweed. "But inside you must always be Chinese. You must be proud you are different. Your only shame is to have shame." 7

And even though I didn't agree with her then, I knew that she understood how much I had suffered during the evening's dinner. It wasn't until many years later—long after I had gotten over my crush on Robert—that I was able to fully appreciate her lesson and the true purpose behind our particular menu. For Christmas Eve that year, she had chosen all my favorite foods. 8

CHECK YOUR UNDERSTANDING

1. What important guests joined the author's family for Christmas Eve dinner?
   - **a.** one of the author's school friends and his family
   - **b.** the minister's family
   - **c.** new neighbors
   - **d.** the author's teacher and the teacher's family
2. What kind of food did the author's mother prepare for the meal?
   - **a.** American classics, such as turkey and sweet potatoes
   - **b.** a combination of Chinese and American foods
   - **c.** food that was "strange" for typical American tastes
   - **d.** food that was new to both the author's family and the guests
3. How did the guests react to the meal and the behavior of the author's family?
   - **a.** with quiet astonishment
   - **b.** with humor and understanding
   - **c.** with disgust and outrage
   - **d.** with outspoken disrespect
4. What were the author's true feelings about the food her mother served?
   - **a.** She hated everything.
   - **b.** She liked only a few dishes.
   - **c.** She was disgusted by the fish cheeks.
   - **d.** She liked the dishes; they were her favorites.

DISCUSS WITH YOUR PEERS

1. Discuss whether the narrator of this essay seems like a typical American teenager. In your opinion, what makes her similar to or different from other fourteen-year-old American girls?
2. Reread the last sentence of paragraphs 5 and 6, and discuss whether the author's reaction seems reasonable or exaggerated. Should she have had more pride in her Chinese culture and traditions? The events of this essay took place in the 1960s. Do you think that most teenagers today are more comfortable with their family background and ethnic heritage? Why or why not? If possible, give examples from your own experiences.
3. Even though this essay shows the Chinese parents as somewhat naïve, what does the ending (para. 8) suggest about the mother's intelligence, awareness, and concern as a parent?

IDENTIFY THE PATTERNS

For more on the various writing patterns referenced here, see Appendix A.

1. The author uses **narration** as the main pattern of development. What are the key events of the story? What is the time frame? Who are the principal characters? Do you think this is a powerful story even though it is short? If you think it is powerful, what makes it so?
2. In paragraph 3, the author uses **exemplification** and **description**. First, underline or highlight five examples of the "strange menu" that the mother is preparing. Then, circle some of the descriptive details that bring these menu items to life.
3. In paragraphs 2, 5, and 6, the author uses **comparison and contrast** to develop her writing. First, identify the two things that are being compared and/or contrasted. Then, identify the ways in which these two things are similar and/or different. Is the author using more comparison, more contrast, or an equal amount of both?

WRITE A PARAGRAPH

1. Tell the story of a time when you were very embarrassed by your family's customs or behavior. Describe what happened, why you were embarrassed, and how you handled the situation.
2. Discuss whether your parent or parents were wise in understanding your needs as a child, teenager, or young adult. What special things did they do—or intentionally not do—to help you through the difficulties of growing up?
3. Discuss a time when you tried to be someone you were not. Describe the situation, what you wanted to change—or tried to change—about yourself, and the outcome of the situation.

Robyn Marks

Raising a Son—with Men on the Fringes

Born in 1974 in Baltimore, Maryland, Robyn Marks earned a B.A. in communications from Morgan State University in Baltimore. A freelance journalist, Marks has written about hip-hop and sports culture for publications including *Vibe* magazine, *Dime* magazine, and *Sports*. She has also worked in radio and television as a sports reporter and news anchor.

In the following selection, which first appeared in *Newsweek* magazine, Marks writes about the challenges of being a single mother. The essay won the 2004 New York Association of Black Journalists Award for personal commentary.

Reading Tips: Although the author focuses on her son in this essay, she also considers larger factors that may influence his life. You might want to highlight or otherwise mark these other factors as you read.

1 Despite my best efforts, I am a single mother. It's a title I'm not too fond of, a repeat of my urban family's legacy of strong black women raising a black boy with men on the fringes. My grandmother eventually became a single mother, as did my mother and now me.

legacy: something handed down from the past

2 My son, a gigantic 4-year-old with big, bright eyes, doesn't even yet realize that he's a future "black man" and, before that, a "black male teenager," but I do. I am so panicked at the thought that every single solitary thing has to be *just so* over these next 20 years in order for me to produce a solid, productive adult who understands the world in which he lives, both the realities and the possibilities.

Teaching Tip
If you have parents in your class, some of them may willingly share their experiences with and insights about parenting. How have they dealt with worries about wanting to do the best for their children?

3 Studies show that African-American women have been outpacing our men in education and corporate America for two generations now. Almost half of black boys wind up a grade behind in school, and only a third of 20-year-old black men are enrolled in college. All the more daunting is the fact that the majority of these boys and men were just like Jason, raised in a home by a single black mother. I have a lot of work to do to ensure that my child clears these hurdles, but they are hurdles that are so elusive, I have yet to get a firm grip on where exactly they lie.

daunting: intimidating or discouraging

4 I am a journalist who has covered crime and urban blight, and I love my job. My background, I believe, allows me a certain compassion and sensibility toward the subjects of my articles. But that doesn't mean that when I head home into suburbia, I am not completely awestruck at the fact that my son is only a couple of generations and a few miles away from poverty, crime and abject desperation. He has no idea. Do I tell him? Show him? How? How much? He has to know eventually, for his own good.

abject: hopeless

5 I remember my brother, who is a few years younger than me, not being aware of the subtle snubs and racist attitudes he occasionally faced while attending a prestigious private school, and being dumbfounded when he and a pack of friends were all taken in by the police for drinking in a public park and he (the only black kid) was the only one not just released to his parents. How do you explain that?

snubs: insults

dumbfounded: startled or puzzled

6 The plan for Jason, of course, is private school, at a cost of close to $20,000 a year. But then I owe it to him to balance that with a hefty dose of African-American culture—the culture he will surely miss out on at an elite boarding or country day school. Added to the mix is the fact that I am a Generation-X child of hip-hop who embraces rap music and identifies with the likes of Allen Iverson. How do I balance all that? I imagine conversations that will go something like, "OK, Jason, *general* bling-bling is fine and has its place if you work hard for it . . . but not watching videos of booty-shaking objectified women!"

Generation-X: people born between the mid-1960s and the early 1980s

Allen Iverson (b. 1975): star basketball player for the Denver (Colorado) Nuggets

7 He comes from an athletic background, so naturally everybody is attempting to put a basketball or football in his hands and get him signed to Reebok tomorrow, but I shun the pressure, until I realize that I have put my own pressures on him, too. I could read at the age of 2, and called his pediatrician when he couldn't (she laughed at me). I skipped grades and breezed through school, and want him to do the same. All he wants right now, the summer before pre-K, is Thomas the Tank Engine.

bling-bling: jewelry or other ornamentation

objectified: treated like objects rather than human beings

shun: to refuse or avoid

I talk to my mom all the time about raising a black man, and there's good and bad news. The good news is she did a pretty good job; the bad news is she's far from done, and my brother is 25. We worry that he moved to a bad neighborhood and may become a victim of crime or, worse yet, accused of one; that he isn't assertive enough at a job where he may be hindered by his race; that black women intimidate him, and that he'll be profiled by police because his pants are baggy. Times are ever changing, so even my mom's experience is slightly different from what mine will be. 8

hindered: blocked from advancing

Blessedly, there are great men all over the place who love and nurture Jason: my uncle, who drives 40 miles round trip out of his way each Tuesday to take Jason to the barbershop; my dad, who relishes getting it right with his only grandchild. And there are even books intended to coach me on issues like black male masculinity, peer pressure, academic achievement, the lack of fathers and goal setting. I appreciate and seek out all of it. But I still realize that at the end of the day, everything Jason is, everything he trusts about who and what he can become, will come from me. So at night—especially when I have just returned from a long work trip that has taken me away for days—I peek in at him, asleep in his room surrounded by trains and DVDs and basketballs, and I think about all the things I know I have to do for him. And then I get to the real work: I pray. 9

Teaching Tip

Ask students about adults, other than parents, who had a strong influence on them when they were growing up. What did these adults do or say that made them so influential?

CHECK YOUR UNDERSTANDING

1. What central challenge concerns the author?
   - **a.** giving her son a private-school education
   - **b.** finding a man who can be a father to her son
   - **c.** raising her son on one income
   - **d.** raising an African-American son as a single mother
2. What statement is true based on this essay?
   - **a.** African-American women have been advancing beyond African-American men in business and education.
   - **b.** Nearly 50 percent of African-American boys fall behind by a grade in school.
   - **c.** Only one-third of twenty-year-old African-American males are enrolled in college.
   - **d.** All of the above.
3. What is one of the "pressures" that the author has put on her son?
   - **a.** She wants him to succeed in athletics.
   - **b.** She wants him to become a good reader and a good student.
   - **c.** She wants him to enter an elite college.
   - **d.** She wants him to take care of her when she is old.
4. What is true about the son's connection with men?
   - **a.** No men take any interest in the son's life.
   - **b.** Certain men have taken an interest in the son.
   - **c.** The son has come to mistrust men.
   - **d.** None of the above.

DISCUSS WITH YOUR PEERS

1. In paragraph 2, the author discusses her concerns about all that she must do for her four-year-old son, and later (para. 7), she remarks that all he cares about is Thomas the Tank Engine. Discuss whether the mother is overthinking and overimagining the future. In your opinion, should she just relax, enjoy her son's childhood, and address future issues as they arise? Or are her concerns about his future reasonable and necessary? Explain your opinions.
2. Discuss whether the cultural influences mentioned in paragraph 6 will be more likely to help or hurt the son as he matures. If you grew up around cultural diversity, do you think it strengthened you or made your life more difficult?
3. Although the author's brother is twenty-five years old, their mother's parenting duty is "far from done" (para. 8). Discuss whether parents should continue parenting when their children become adults. Do successful parents guide their children throughout life, or do they let go, allowing their children to fly with their own wings?
4. From the details in paragraph 9, it is clear that the son's uncle and grandfather are extremely devoted to him. Discuss whether male relatives can ever fully replace an absent father. Why or why not? If possible, support your opinions with examples from your personal experience or knowledge.

IDENTIFY THE PATTERNS

For more on the various writing patterns referenced here, see Appendix A.

1. In paragraph 2, the author uses **argumentation** to develop her writing. Underline or highlight the author's main argument about being the single mom of a black son. In the rest of the essay, the author provides evidence to show that her argument is valid. By the end of the essay, has the author convinced you that her concerns and strategies are justified?
2. In paragraph 3, the author uses **comparison and contrast** to develop her writing. First, identify what two things are being compared and/or contrasted. Then, identify how these things are similar and/or different. Does the author use more comparison, more contrast, or an equal amount of both? Could the author have provided more information to make this use of comparison and contrast more effective?
3. In paragraph 8, the author uses **exemplification** to show the challenges of being a successful black man. Underline or highlight the examples of challenges that a young black man might face. Do these examples provide a powerful illustration of the realities of being a young black man? Why or why not?
4. In paragraph 9, the author uses **exemplification** and **argumentation** again. First, underline the examples that the author gives. Then, underline the one sentence that contains the author's most powerful argument in this paragraph.

WRITE A PARAGRAPH

1. Discuss the challenges of being raised by a single parent.
2. Discuss whether child rearing is more successful when the larger, extended family (uncles, aunts, grandparents, cousins, and so on) is involved. Or, is the extended family more likely to create problems and interference in the raising of children?

MAKE CONNECTIONS

Teaching Tip

After students have read all the selections in this chapter, you might ask them to call out definitions and examples of good parenting. Write the ideas on the board as students provide them. Then, ask students to write their own extended definitions of good parenting, incorporating ideas that the class generated, information from this chapter's readings, and details from their own experience and knowledge.

1. All three readings in this chapter show examples of successful parenting. In a paragraph or an essay, explain what makes a parent successful. You may use ideas and examples from the readings or from your own experiences and knowledge.
2. All three reading selections show how parents are only human; sometimes, they can fail their children, in spite of good intentions. As children, we are sometimes disappointed in our parents' decisions and behavior; however, as we grow older, we often understand their wisdom or forgive their mistakes. In a paragraph or essay, explain what you would keep the same and what you would change about the way your parents raised you. Explain the wisdom of your parents' (or parent's) good decisions and state whether you forgive them for any mistakes they made.

Be aware of other readings that relate to the theme of parents and parenting:

- "The Joy of Reading and Writing: Superman and Me" by Sherman Alexie (page 543)
- "The Sanctuary of School" by Lynda Barry (page 547)
- "The 'M-Word': Why It Matters to Me" by Andrew Sullivan (page 558)
- "Like Mexicans" by Gary Soto (page 562)
- "Under the Influence" by Scott Russell Sanders (page 572)
- "King of the Road" by Brian Rickenbrode (page 584)
- "My Ecumenical Father" by José Antonio Burciaga (page 591)

Appendix A

Patterns of Development

APPENDIX OVERVIEW

You can develop a paragraph or an essay based on one or more recognizable patterns. As you saw in Chapter 1 (see pages 26–32), writers may use a single pattern or a combination of patterns.

Let's start with the basic patterns, which you may recall from Chapter 1:

- description
- exemplification
- narration
- process
- definition

Many college writing assignments involve describing details (description), giving some examples (exemplification), telling stories (narration), explaining how something happens or is done (process), or defining a word or idea (definition). We can consider these patterns the fundamental ingredients of effective writing.

Once you understand how to use these basic patterns of development, you will be able to master the advanced ones more effectively. Here are the advanced patterns:

- cause and effect
- comparison and contrast
- argumentation

Teaching Tip
If students have not worked through pages 26–32 of Chapter 1, you might want to have them do so now.

Terminology Tip
The patterns of development are sometimes called the *modes* or *rhetorical modes.*

Basic Writing Patterns

Again, the basic writing patterns are description, exemplification, narration, process, and definition. The following pages discuss the main features of these patterns and provide student examples of each.

DESCRIPTION

In descriptive writing, you describe what you see, hear, smell, taste, or feel. The subject of your description might be a person, a place, or an object. **The key to good descriptive writing is finding colorful and precise adjectives and nouns that will create a strong sensory experience for your reader.** (For more on adjectives and nouns, see Chapter 10, pages 268 and 271. For more on developing powerful sensory details, see Chapter 6, page 183.)

A Student Writer Uses Description

In the following paragraph, a student describes a photograph of two giraffes. Notice the colorful and precise adjectives and nouns that she uses to create a vivid picture in words.

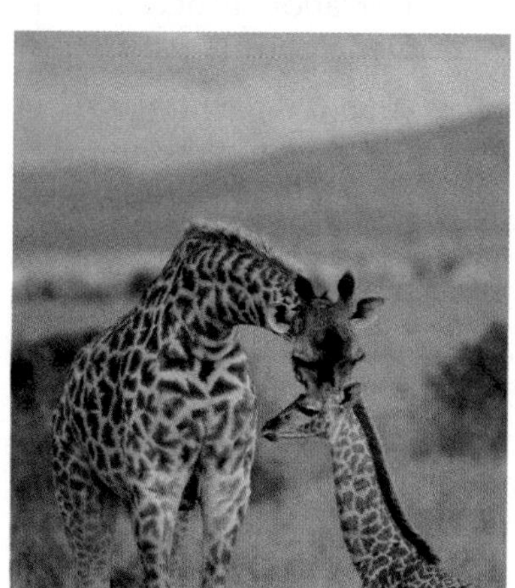

Power Tip
Notice that some of the transitions in this paragraph (*Far back in the picture, Closer up,* and so on) move the reader through space. For more on transitions, see Chapter 5, page 158.

> A beautiful day welcomes a mother giraffe and her new baby. Far back in the picture are a soothing blue sky and blue hills. The blueness is layered with shades of light and dark. The darkest part is the hills. However, some parts of the hills look lighter, as if there might be grass or trees growing in places. Closer up is a field. In the part of the field next to the hills are some shapes that are difficult to see. These might be village huts or tents. Closer to the front of the picture is green and brown grass. There are also some bushes and other dark shapes. The background is slightly blurry because the photographer is focusing on the giraffes. Both have acorn-brown spots on a cream background. There is short, bristly, acorn-brown hair on the back of the mother's and baby's necks, and the mother is bending her head down, almost as if she is whispering in the baby's ear; her oval ears point up alertly. The giraffes' eyes are nothing but black blurs, but you can still see that there is love in both their eyes. The emotions of these two are clearly love, closeness, and a feeling of nurturing and protection. As their faces touch, they can feel each other's warmth through thin, soft fur. They can also feel the cool air lightly brushing their fur and tickling them, cooling them off on a hot day in July.

In developing her description, this student focused on one part of the image at a time. This strategy helped her organize her paragraph and describe each section in precise detail.

ACTIVITY 1

Read the previous paragraph carefully, underlining or highlighting precise and colorful adjectives and nouns.

ACTIVITY 2

Working from the previous paragraph, complete the following outline. (Part of it has already been filled in for you.) The outline will help you see how the writer divides her description into three major parts and then uses a series of descriptive details to develop each part. Answers may vary.

MAIN IDEA A beautiful day welcomes a mother giraffe and her new baby.

PART 1
far background: blue sky and blue hills
layered blueness: light and dark
hills are darkest part
lighter parts within dark hills

PART 2
closer up: field
shapes like huts or tents
green and brown grass
bushes and other dark shapes

PART 3
focus (up front): mother and baby giraffes
brown spots on cream background
bristly hair
mother's bent neck and alert ears
black eyes
feelings of love, closeness, and nurturing
physical sensations

Power Tip
For an example of a description by a professional writer, see paragraph 3 of "Fish Cheeks" by Amy Tan (page 607).

ACTIVITY 3

For each of the following prompts, list precise and colorful adjectives and nouns.

1. Describe what you see when you look in the mirror.
2. Describe the sound of one type of music that you love or hate.
3. Describe the worst smell you have ever encountered.

When to Use the Pattern

Many writing tasks in college and at work may require you to use description as the main pattern of development. Assignments calling for description may use words like *describe, show, discuss the features,* or *discuss the type.*

ACTIVITY 4: Teamwork

With classmates, discuss why each of the following projects might require description as the main pattern of development. Then, for each category (college and workplace), work together to invent a third assignment that would also use description.

College Assignments

1. **Art history:** Write a paragraph describing painter Vincent van Gogh's *Starry Night.*
2. **Biology:** Write a paragraph describing the lungs of the frog that you dissected during lab.
3. **Anthropology:** ____.

Workplace Assignments

Teaching Tip
Encourage students to bring in writing assignments from other classes, or bring in assignments from your colleagues in other disciplines. See if they can identify the pattern(s) of development required.

1. Write a memo in which you discuss the strange odor that you've detected several times in the warehouse.
2. As the head of a modeling agency, discuss the type of models that you want to hire.
3. As a representative for a cruise ship company, write ____.

EXEMPLIFICATION

In exemplification writing, you provide a series of examples to support or illustrate your main idea. Depending on the topic of your writing assignment, the examples may come from your personal experience or from information that you have read or studied. **The key to good exemplification writing is finding colorful and precise examples that will capture your reader's interest and imagination.**

A Student Writer Uses Exemplification

In the following paragraph, a student explains why reading is important to her, giving several examples.

> Reading is important to me because it excites my imagination as well as challenges my intelligence, and in the end it makes me forget my problems. First of all, reading excites my imagination like nothing else can. For instance, the passage I am reading becomes real to me. Things are not just in my mind; it is as if they were right in front of me, unfolding before my eyes. Also, colors come alive. The way that colors are described in some books makes them so much more vivid than they are in real life. Purple is not just purple; it's a purple you have never seen before. Green is not just green; it's like neon green but much brighter and clearer. Reading also excites my imagination when I picture myself as one of the

characters. Whether it's the main character or a minor character, I just let myself go free and flow with the story. For instance, I can feel as if I'm in the midst of a battle or running through a meadow with the love of my life or locked in a passionate embrace. In the second place, reading challenges my intelligence and broadens my thoughts. When I read different styles of writing, I think outside the box. I try to think not just about what's in front of me but "between the lines." Some books challenge what I believe or what I think I believe. They may put questions in my mind and make me think long and hard as to what I really believe. If I am biased about a topic, I try to think the way the writer is thinking, or I try to be open about what the writer is trying to get across. Last but not least, reading helps me pass the time and escape all my worries and problems. Reading helps me pass the time on road trips, on flights, or during boring days at home. Once I am engrossed in a book, time flies by, and I don't even realize that I have sat in one place all day. Alone in my own little world of reading, I forget my problems and doubts. Without reading, my life would be much less rich.

In this paragraph, the student's examples all come from her personal experience. They are memorable examples because they reflect the student's genuine love of reading.

ACTIVITY 5

Working from the previous paragraph, complete the following outline. (Part of it has already been filled in for you.) The outline will help you see how the student uses a series of examples to illustrate her main idea. Answers may vary.

MAIN IDEA Reading excites my imagination, challenges my intelligence, makes me forget my problems.

EXAMPLE 1 Reading excites my imagination like nothing else can.
Things become real.
Colors come alive.
I picture myself as one of the characters.

EXAMPLE 2 Reading challenges my intelligence and broadens my thoughts.
It helps me think outside the box/between the lines.
It challenges my beliefs/thoughts.
It helps me be open-minded.

EXAMPLE 3 Reading helps me pass the time and escape all my worries and problems.
It helps me pass the time on road trips, on flights, and during boring days.
In my own world, I forget my problems and doubts.

Power Tip
For an example of exemplification by a professional writer, see paragraph 2 of "Be Cool to the Pizza Dude" by Sarah Adams (page 528).

Power Tip
For more on brainstorming, see Chapter 3, page 55.

Teaching Tip
You might have volunteers from each group share their examples with the class.

ACTIVITY 6: Teamwork

With classmates, make a list of examples to support each of the following topics. Then, working individually, select one of the topics and brainstorm for ten minutes, getting down all the ideas you can.

1. Ways to enjoy yourself on the Internet
2. Difficulties of being a college student
3. Characteristics of a good friend

When to Use the Pattern

Many writing tasks in college and at work may require you to use exemplification as the main pattern of development. Assignments calling for exemplification may use words like *give examples, illustrate, show, explain, list,* or *discuss why.*

ACTIVITY 7: Teamwork

With classmates, discuss why each of the following projects might require exemplification as the main pattern of development. Then, for each category (college and workplace), work together to invent a third assignment that would also use exemplification.

College Assignments

1. **General:** Write a paragraph discussing why some students make a good first impression on their instructors.
2. **Health:** Write a paragraph discussing the benefits of regular exercise.
3. **History:** ____
____.

Workplace Assignments

1. Write a memo in which you discuss why the working conditions in your office are unsanitary.
2. Write a letter of recommendation for an employee who deserves a raise.
3. To advertise for a pizza delivery job at your father's pizza parlor, write ____.

NARRATION

In narrative writing, you relate the key events and important details of a story. Depending on the topic of your writing assignment, this may be a true personal story, a fictional story, or perhaps a current event or historical episode. **The key to good storytelling is including the major events or actions of the story and using colorful details to bring the characters, settings, and actions to life.**

A Student Writer Uses Narration

The following paragraph tells one student's story of growing up with a difficult mother during a difficult time in the United States. (The student was born during the Depression, a severe economic downturn that lasted from 1929 through the 1930s.)

> On reflection, I can see how my relationship with my mother shaped my life. My mother was a victim of her own childhood. She was very headstrong, and everyone in the family was afraid of her. I seemed to be the target mostly because I was Daddy's favorite. For example, she gave me pennies once to buy candy for myself and my brothers. I bought the candy and ate it all. It tasted so good. I didn't think of my brothers until it was all gone. I was only six years old and rarely had candy. When I came home from school, my mother asked, where is the candy? She beat me. My little girl's sin of candy eating was punished so hard that Daddy said, "Oh, stop! Can't you see she's just a kid?" I went outside to cry. My dogs came running to comfort me. They licked my face clean of tears, and they wagged their tails for me. I said to them, "You are so lucky you never get into trouble. I wish I was a dog." But they had to sleep outside, and I was afraid of the dark. I think my mother's abuse and neglect showed outside the home because my teacher would check my legs for bruises. Children didn't have much protection in those days. Once, when I was a teenager, my mother beat me with a club. I ran away from home for a few days. In much later years, I divorced my husband. I came to realize that I needed professional help to sort things out. During this therapy, I talked out old hurts. Apparently, though my mother's anger hurt, I got enough mothering to be whole. In many ways, this time in childhood helped me to have a wonderful relationship with my own daughter. In other words, the old conflict taught me not to put my child through that type of pain. My daughter calls me every day and sometimes several times a day. We live in the same city, and we see each other very often.

In developing her narration, the student first identified key events in the story. With this understanding of her narrative, she was then able to add colorful details and dialogue to bring the characters, settings, and actions to life.

ACTIVITY 8

The author of the previous piece devotes most of her paragraph to one traumatic experience. Name the experience. Then, list all the events that were part of this experience. The last event has been filled in for you. Answers may vary.

The experience: A daughter being punished by her mother for eating all the candy meant for both her and her brothers

The events

1. Mother gives daughter pennies to buy candy for herself and her brothers.
2. Daughter buys candy and eats it all.
3. Daughter comes home from school and mother asks where candy is.
4. Mother beats daughter.
5. Father tells mother to stop.
6. Daughter goes outside to cry.
7. Dogs comfort the daughter.

Power Tip
For an example of narration by a professional writer, see "Dr. Dana" by Angela Adkins (page 531).

ACTIVITY 9

For each of the following topics, list the major events in the story.

1. The best or worst date you've ever been on
2. A nightmare or dream that you've had
3. Your favorite children's story

When to Use the Pattern

Many writing tasks in college and at work may require you to use narration as the main pattern of development. Assignments calling for narration may use words like *narrate, tell how, describe the events leading to,* or *discuss/explain how.*

ACTIVITY 10: Teamwork

With classmates, discuss why each of the following projects might require narration as the main pattern of development. Then, for each category (college and workplace), work together to invent a third assignment that would also use narration.

College Assignments

1. **American history:** Describe the events that led to South Carolina's decision to secede from the Union before the American Civil War.
2. **Biology:** Discuss how Alexander Fleming discovered penicillin.
3. **Current events:** ____
____.

Workplace Assignments

1. Write a memo explaining events leading to a factory accident.
2. Prepare a history of your work experience for a job interview.
3. To explain how you successfully trained a new employee, write ________________________________.

PROCESS

In process writing, you explain or describe each step in a series of actions. There are two types of process writing: the "how to" approach and the "how it happens" approach.

In the "how to" approach, you give specific instructions to the reader, teaching him or her how to do something. The following are "how to" writing topics:

How to prepare for a job interview
How to apply for financial aid
How to decorate a wedding cake

In "how to" writing, the reader is an imaginary *participant* in the process. In order for the reader to complete the process successfully, you must provide clear step-by-step instructions and precise details.

In the "how it happens" approach, you describe how an event occurs. The following are "how it happens" writing topics:

How a solar eclipse occurs
How cell division occurs
How a tsunami occurs

In "how it happens" writing, the reader is an imaginary *observer* of the process. In order for the reader to understand fully how the process occurs, you must provide clear step-by-step descriptions and precise details.

In both approaches, the key to good process writing is providing clear step-by-step explanations and precise details.

A Student Writer Uses Process ("How To")

In the following paragraph, a student writer explains how to get a good night's sleep.

> In today's stressful world, many of us have trouble sleeping the seven to nine hours that we need to feel rested. Fortunately, you can take some steps to become a better sleeper. First, make sure that your mattress and pillows are comfortable, and try to replace them if they are worn. Ideally, a mattress should be somewhat firm to provide support and prevent backaches in the morning. Next, try to start going to bed at the same time every night. This way, you will get your body into a routine and help it to "expect" to sleep at a certain time. When you have established your bedtime, count

Teaching Tip
Remind students that a process often is a specific sequence leading to an end result, not just a list of examples. The paragraph shown here provides a clear sequence.

back two hours from it. During this two-hour period, avoid stimulating activities such as exercising, viewing violent or humorous TV shows, listening to loud or upbeat music, arguing, or thinking about work or other responsibilities. Instead, you might do light reading in a quiet room or listen to soft music. Also, be careful about what you eat and drink before bedtime. Avoid coffee, chocolate, and other foods or beverages containing caffeine. If you want a little snack before bed, try drinking warm milk. Once it's time for bed, make sure that your room will be dark and fairly cool during the night. Draw your shades or blinds to make sure that streetlights or other lights don't keep you up or wake you up prematurely. You can cover your eyes with a bandana or eye mask if your window coverings aren't adequate. Ideally, your room should be no warmer than 65 degrees. Finally, turn off your light and let drowsiness wash over you. If it doesn't, try counting back from one hundred, or try counting imaginary sheep as they leap a fence one by one. Believe it or not, this old trick works for some!

The paragraph takes readers step-by-step through the process of preparing for a good night's sleep, providing precise details.

ACTIVITY 11

Working from the previous paragraph, list the major steps of preparing for a good night's sleep. The first step has been filled in for you. Answers may vary.

1. Make sure that your mattress and pillows are comfortable; try to replace them if they are worn.
2. Try to start going to bed at the same time every night.
3. During the two hours before bedtime, avoid stimulating activities. (Instead, do light reading in a quiet room or listen to soft music.)
4. Avoid coffee, chocolate, and other foods or beverages containing caffeine. (Instead, try drinking warm milk.)
5. Make sure that your room will be dark and fairly cool during the night.
6. Turn off your light and let drowsiness wash over you.
7. If you still can't sleep, try counting back from one hundred, or try counting imaginary sheep.

A Student Writer Uses Process ("How It Happens")

In this paragraph, a student writer describes the steps in the grieving process.

Teaching Tip
Remind students that the number of major steps in a process will vary. The process described here, for example, has five major steps.

Psychiatrist Elisabeth Kübler-Ross, in her 1969 book *On Death and Dying*, describes the process a person undergoes when grieving for a loved one who has died or is dying, when coming to terms with one's own terminal illness, or when facing some other great difficulty, such as job loss, breakup, divorce, or life-changing injury (such as amputation or paralysis). The first stage is denial or shock. Initially, the loss (or the idea that the loss will soon occur) is so overwhelming that a person cannot even believe it is happening. It's a natural defense mechanism to at first refuse to accept the facts and attempt to avoid a sad situation. After the person goes through denial, he or she usually comes to the anger stage. For example, if the individual has lost someone to death, he or she may be angry with the person who died for letting it happen (even if the death was unavoidable). Survivors may also be angry with themselves and think they could have somehow prevented a loved one's death. It is important to keep this stage in mind when someone you know is going through it and not judge this anger as wrong. After anger, the person goes through the bargaining stage. He or she may want to make a deal with God or the universe or *someone*. If, for instance, the individual is terminally ill, he or she may say, "Just let me stay around long enough to see my daughter graduate from college," or "If I could just get well, I'll go to church every Sunday." In cases of romantic separation, a grieving person may say to his or her former partner, "Why don't we at least remain friends?" The next stage is depression. In this stage, the individual is filled with sadness and hopelessness and may think, "What's the use of doing anything?" This step is important because it means the person is working through to the final stage, which is acceptance. The person may not be happy about the situation, but he or she realizes that reality will not change. The loss is inescapable or unchangeable, so the best response is to be ready for it or to come to terms with it. According to therapists, it is best to allow oneself to go through each of these stages, however long they may take.

The paragraph explains each stage of the grieving process, with examples, so that readers understand how this process happens.

ACTIVITY 12

Working from the previous paragraph, list the major steps of the grieving process.

1. denial or shock
2. anger
3. bargaining
4. depression
5. acceptance

Power Tip
For an example of "how it happens" process writing by a professional writer, see paragraph 4 of "The Joy of Reading and Writing: Superman and Me" by Sherman Alexie (page 543).

ACTIVITY 13: Teamwork

With classmates, list the steps for each of the following processes. Then, working individually, select one of the topics and brainstorm for ten minutes, getting down all the details you can.

1. Explain how to bathe a child or a pet.
2. Explain how to use the college learning center or writing center.
3. Explain how to find and download songs from the Internet.

When to Use the Pattern

Many writing tasks in college and at work may require you to use process as the main pattern of development. Assignments calling for process may use words like *explain/discuss how, describe the process,* or *explain/discuss the steps.*

ACTIVITY 14: Teamwork

With classmates, discuss why each of the following projects might require process as the main pattern of development. Then, for each category (college and workplace), work together to invent a third assignment that would also use process.

College Assignments

1. **Art:** Explain how to prepare clay to make a pot.
2. **Biology:** Write a paragraph explaining how photosynthesis works.
3. **Writing class:** ______________________________.

Workplace Assignments

1. As a Taco Bell employee, explain how to make a burrito.
2. As a Gap employee, explain how to fold a sweater for the display table.
3. As a computer repair technician, explain how to ____________________.

DEFINITION

In writing a definition, you explain the meaning of a word or idea. Most people think of definitions as short, formal explanations of meaning like those found in a dictionary. However, if you are writing a paragraph or an essay, a short dictionary-style definition will not allow you to develop your assignment adequately.

Instead, you will probably be asked to develop a more complex and creative definition. For example, a *technical* definition may require you to define the full meaning of a scientific or technical term, such as *symbiosis* or *photosynthesis.* A *personal* definition might ask you to define what a particular term, such as *success* or *love,* means for you. A *contextual* definition may ask you to define a term in a specific framework, such as *depression in postpartum women* or *capitalism in modern Russia.* In each case, **the key to good definition is discussing as many levels of meaning as possible and using precise vocabulary and examples to discuss each level.**

Teaching Tip
You might want to spend some time discussing the link between **definition** and **exemplification**. Emphasize to students that it is difficult to develop an effective extended definition without using specific examples.

A Student Writer Uses Definition

In the following paragraph, a student provides a *personal* definition of the term *freedom.*

The word "freedom" may mean freedom of speech or freedom of religion to some people, but to me it means freedom from people

> telling me how to live my life. First, I choose jobs that allow me to be free to do things the way I choose. For instance, I could never work at a fast-food restaurant where I'd have to weigh each burger, bean, or tomato to make a perfect cookie-cutter version of some item. Currently, I work as an in-home care companion, and I can do what feels right to help each individual, and no one tells me to be more precise or do anything differently. Each experience is created on the spot, the result of my sense of what's needed, not the result of some individual with an instruction manual. Second, I don't want my parents telling me how to live my life. Now that I'm nineteen, I feel it's important to make my own choices, even if it means making a mistake now and then. I choose my own hours to come and go, make my own choices about what classes to take and what jobs to accept, and manage my own money. While I will listen to my parents' suggestions, I make decisions that feel right for me, not because they've told me I have to. Finally, I enjoy being free from cultural pressure. I don't adhere to fashion trends, hang with cliques, or buy products everyone else buys. I don't allow society, whether it's through magazines, television, or pushy friends, to tell me how to be. I dress the way that feels true to me and comfortable, regardless of this season's style. The friends I spend time with come from different social and economic circles. Also, despite the urgings of friends, I still don't own a cell phone or iPod—even though every one of my friends owns them, I simply don't want them and won't buy them just to conform. The freedom I have allows me to be confident and comfortable in my own skin.

In developing her definition of *freedom,* this student identifies several levels of meaning and gives examples for each.

ACTIVITY 15

Working from the previous paragraph, complete the following outline. (Part of it has already been filled in for you.) The outline will help you see how the writer identifies different levels of meaning for *freedom* and explores each one. Answers may vary.

MAIN IDEA "Freedom" means no one telling me how to live my life.

PART 1 I choose jobs that give me freedom.

I avoid jobs that require creation of a cookie-cutter product.

I do what feels right in my current job as an in-home companion.

Each experience at my current job is created on the spot.

CONTINUED >

PART 2

I don't want my parents telling me how to live my life.
I make my own choices, even if I make mistakes.
I choose my own hours, classes, and jobs and manage my own money.
I listen to my parents' suggestions, but I'm in control.

PART 3

I enjoy being free from cultural pressure.
I dress the way I want to, regardless of fashion trends.
I spend time with people from different social and economic circles.
I don't buy things that everyone else buys (like cell phones and iPods).

Power Tip
For an example of a definition by a professional writer, see paragraph 1 of "What Makes Marriages Work" by Kathleen Stassen Berger (page 553).

ACTIVITY 16: Teamwork

With classmates, make a list of possible definitions for the following words or ideas. Then, working individually, select one of the topics and brainstorm for ten minutes, getting down all the details you can.

1. Define what it means to be "cool."
2. Define *beauty*.
3. Define *adventure*.

When to Use the Pattern

Many writing tasks in college and at work may require you to use definition as the main pattern of development. Assignments calling for definition may use words like *define* or *explain the meaning of*.

ACTIVITY 17: Teamwork

With classmates, discuss why each of the following projects might require definition as the main pattern of development. Then, for each category (college and workplace), work together to invent a third assignment that would also use definition.

College Assignments

1. **Political science:** Define *human rights*.
2. **Music appreciation:** Define *classical*.
3. **Psychology:** ______________________.

Workplace Assignments

1. As a team leader, prepare a talk for your employees in which you define *team spirit.*
2. For a new group of firefighters, define a *code red.*
3. For the nursing staff at your hospital, define ______________________.

Advanced Writing Patterns

Again, the advanced writing patterns are cause and effect, comparison and contrast, and argument. The following pages discuss the main features of these patterns and provide student examples of each.

CAUSE AND EFFECT

In cause-and-effect writing, you explain the origin and the outcome of a particular event or occurrence. There are three approaches to this writing pattern: pure cause, pure effect, or combined cause and effect.

In pure cause, you show only the causes or origins of something. Look at these examples:

> **There are several causes of lung cancer.**
> **Three factors prompted the rapid development of the Internet.**

In pure effect, you show only the results or outcomes of something. Look at these examples:

> **Global warming has many harmful effects on the planet.**
> **I have noticed several benefits from my new workout routine.**

In combined cause and effect, you show both the origin and the outcome of something. Consider these examples:

> **Several factors are responsible for the AIDS pandemic in Africa; furthermore, the effects of the disease are threatening the survival of the continent and its inhabitants.**

> **Currently, about 20% of the world's adult population is illiterate. What allows for this outrageous figure, and what does it mean to be an illiterate person in today's world? The causes of illiteracy are both political and economic, and the effects of illiteracy on the illiterate can be devastating.**

The key to successful cause-and-effect writing is to clarify the main origins and/or outcomes and to provide sufficient details to illustrate them.

Power Tip
Many of the professional readings in Part Three of this book blend causes and effects. Examples include "Dr. Dana" by Angela Adkins (page 531), "Unforgettable Miss Bessie" by Carl T. Rowan (page 537), "The Sanctuary of School" by Lynda Barry (page 547), and "Under the Influence" by Scott Russell Sanders (page 572).

pandemic: a disease that is prevalent throughout an entire region or population

A Student Writer Uses Pure Cause

In the following paragraph, a student writer explains what caused him to be a poor student during his freshman year of college.

> As I look back on my freshman year of college, I now see clearly the causes for my lack of success. For one thing, I didn't pay attention to my physical health. For the first time in my life, I had total control over my eating habits, and I childishly chose to eat only what I wanted to—what tasted good, not what was healthy for me. I lived on beer, Domino's pizza, Oreos, and Fritos. For months, nothing green could be found on my plate. I also stayed up late watching movies and soon became sleep-deprived, meaning that I slept during class. My poor health affected my concentration and my class attendance. Furthermore, I ignored my instructors' studying advice. I never read assignments before class, so often I couldn't follow the lecture and didn't have questions about the reading that I didn't do. Because I was ill-prepared for class, I would sit in the very back of the room, away from the blackboard; therefore, the few notes I would take were always incomplete. I would cram the night before exams and become overwhelmed by so much material that was new to me (but shouldn't have been), so even if I managed to pick up some information, I would feel panicked or tired during the exam and forget what little I did learn. Finally, I lacked discipline in the new social environment of college. Meeting new people or bonding with new friends always seemed more important than studying for an exam. I found a club I liked to dance at and went there almost every night, often staying until closing time. Also, I went to a lot of parties. As a result of my active social life, my grades plummeted. Poor decisions about my health, lousy study habits, and always choosing socializing over school led to a freshman-year GPA that I'm still working to make up for.

For each case of the student's lack of academic success, he provides plenty of details.

ACTIVITY 18

Working from the previous paragraph, complete the following outline. (Part of it has already been filled in for you.) The outline will help you see how the writer identifies various causes of his unsuccessful freshman year and provides details to explain each cause. *Answers may vary.*

MAIN IDEA As I look back on my freshman year of college, I now see clearly the causes for my lack of success.

CAUSE 1 I didn't pay attention to my physical health.

I ate what I wanted to (beer, pizza, and so on), not what was healthy for me.

I stayed up late and became sleep-deprived.

CAUSE 2

I ignored my instructors' studying advice.
I never read assignments before class.
I sat in the back of the room, so my notes were always incomplete.
I crammed for exams and became overwhelmed.

CAUSE 3

I lacked discipline in the new social environment of college.
Meeting new people and bonding with new friends seemed more important than studying.
I went to a club almost every night, staying late.
I went to a lot of parties.

A Student Writer Uses Pure Effect

In the following paragraph, a student writer explains the effects (results or outcomes) of the AIDS pandemic in the region of Africa south of the Sahara Desert.

> AIDS continues to have a devastating effect on sub-Saharan Africa. To begin with, it is a merciless killer. Currently, AIDS is the most common cause of death in sub-Saharan Africa. Additionally, in 2007, more than three-fourths of AIDS-related deaths worldwide occurred in this region of Africa, according to UNAIDS (the Joint United Nations Programme on HIV/AIDS). That year, nearly 23 million people in the region were living with HIV, with 1.6 million deaths occurring. Furthermore, AIDS has orphaned large numbers of children, with severe consequences. UNAIDS estimates that 11.4 million children in sub-Saharan Africa have lost both parents as a result of the disease, and this number is projected to approach 16 million by 2010. Many orphaned children are forced to seek help in the streets, begging for money and food. Also, many orphaned girls turn to prostitution to survive, greatly raising their chances of contracting HIV. Finally, AIDS causes hunger. In Malawi, Zambia, and Zimbabwe, it is increasingly common for grandparents to be caring for ten or more children because the children's parents have died of AIDS-related illness; those children often go hungry because their grandparents can't provide enough food for everyone. Another reason that HIV has a big impact on food availability is that it takes the greatest toll on the most productive members of the community, those who work to provide food or earn money for food purchases. Former South African president Nelson Mandela eloquently summarized the economic impact of AIDS on his country, saying, "AIDS kills those on whom society relies to grow the crops, work in the mines and factories, run the schools and hospitals and govern countries." Even when AIDS does not kill, it weakens providers in families, with serious consequences. Years after AIDS started making national headlines, it remains a powerfully destructive force in sub-Saharan Africa.

In this paragraph, the author examines each effect of AIDS, providing details and explanations.

ACTIVITY 19

Working from the previous paragraph, complete the following outline. (Part of it has already been filled in for you.) The outline will help you see how the writer identifies and explains various effects of HIV/AIDS in sub-Saharan Africa. Answers may vary.

MAIN IDEA AIDS continues to have a devastating effect on sub-Saharan Africa.

EFFECT 1 It is a merciless killer.
AIDS is the most common cause of death in sub-Saharan Africa.
In 2007, more than three-fourths of AIDS-related deaths worldwide occurred in the region.
In 2007, nearly 23 million people in the region were living with HIV, with 1.6 million deaths occurring.

EFFECT 2 AIDS has orphaned large numbers of children, with severe consequences.
UNAIDS estimates that 11.4 million children in sub-Saharan Africa have lost both parents as a result of the disease, and this number is expected to approach 16 million by 2010.
Many orphaned children are forced to beg for money and food.
Many orphaned girls turn to prostitution to survive, greatly raising their chances of contracting HIV.

EFFECT 3 AIDS causes hunger.
Grandparents can't provide enough food for large numbers of orphaned children.
HIV takes the greatest toll on the most productive members of the community.
Even when AIDS does not kill, it weakens providers in families.

ACTIVITY 20: Teamwork

With classmates, list causes or effects for each of the following events or occurrences. Then, working individually, select one of the topics and brainstorm for ten minutes, getting down all the details you can.

1. Causes of divorce
2. Causes of traffic accidents
3. Causes of depression
4. Effects of identity theft
5. Effects of getting a college degree
6. Effects of having unprotected sex

When to Use the Pattern

Many writing assignments in college and at work may require you to use cause and effect as the main pattern of development. Assignments calling for cause-and-effect writing may use words like *explain the causes/effects, trace the causes/effects, discuss the causes/effects,* or *trace the origins/outcomes.*

ACTIVITY 21: Teamwork

With classmates, discuss why each of the following projects might require cause and effect as the main pattern of development. Then, for each category (college and workplace), work together to invent a third assignment that would also use cause and effect.

College Assignments

1. **Health:** Discuss the causes and effects of type 2 diabetes in children.
2. **Physical education:** Explain the primary causes of sports-related injuries.
3. **Speech:** ______________________________.

Workplace Assignments

1. As a hair stylist, discuss the effects of using too much bleach when coloring someone's hair.
2. As a real estate agent, explain the causes of losing a sale.
3. As a bar manager, discuss ____________________ with your employees.

COMPARISON AND CONTRAST

In comparison-and-contrast writing, you identify the similarities and/or differences between things (usually two). There are three approaches to this writing pattern: pure comparison, pure contrast, or combined comparison and contrast.

In pure comparison, you show only the similarities between items. Look at these examples:

> **Spanish and Italian are very similar languages.**
> **Halloween and Day of the Dead have important similarities.**

In pure contrast, you show only the differences between items. Look at these examples:

> **High school and college are very different academic experiences.**
> **Ancient Athens and ancient Sparta were extremely different cultures.**

Power Tip
Many of the professional readings in Part Three of this book blend comparison and contrast. Examples include "Like Mexicans" by Gary Soto (page 562), "My Ecumenical Father" by José Antonio Burciaga (page 591), and "Fish Cheeks" by Amy Tan (page 607).

In combined comparison and contrast, you show both the similarities and differences between items. Consider these examples:

> American baseball and British cricket are both similar and different.
> Jazz and bluegrass have some similarities and some differences.

The key to successful comparison-and-contrast writing is to clarify the main similarities and/or differences and to provide sufficient details to illustrate them.

A Student Writer Uses Pure Comparison

In the following paragraph, a student uses pure comparison to show how she is similar to Rosa Parks (1913–2005). Parks, an African American, became an inspiring figure in the U.S. civil-rights movement when, in 1955, she refused a command to give up her seat on a Montgomery, Alabama, bus to a white passenger. Parks was arrested as a result, triggering a 381-day bus boycott among African Americans and drawing national attention to the cause of ending racial segregation, the forced separation of blacks from whites.

Rosa Parks's arrest in Alabama, 1955

dialysis: a blood-cleaning procedure used in patients with kidney failure

> Rosa Parks and I are similar in various ways. First, our childhoods were similar because we were raised by a single female parent. Parks's parents separated when she was very young, after her brother was born. My father walked out when I was four years old, right after my brother was born. Both Parks and I are the older of two children, with one younger brother, and we grew up needing paternal love and a father figure. In addition, as the older children, we had to take on more responsibilities. Parks took care of her ill grandmother and then her ill mother, and she had to do home chores. When I was young, I took care of my ill grandmother and went with her to dialysis. Also, I had to help with all the household chores. Having many responsibilities and seeing the coldness of the world made me grow up at a young age. Second, both Parks and I have a positive attitude toward life and are willing to stand up for what we believe in. Although Parks faced segregation and obstacles to getting an education, she didn't give up. In fact, she took advantage of all the opportunities she could to become educated. When I was young, negative people around me told me that I could not go to college, yet I did, and I've tried to learn as much as I can. Like Parks, I didn't let negative people and thoughts get to me and destroy my dreams. Parks stood up for her beliefs: she took a stand that started the Alabama bus boycott, even though it caused her to lose her job and receive threatening phone calls. I have also stood up for what is important to me. When I was young, I loved going to the Christian church with my grandmother, although I knew my mother hated that religion. When I would get home from church, she would punish me,

yet I kept going to that church. Both Parks and I were successful in our efforts: the bus boycott that Parks started helped to end segregation on Alabama buses, and after five years of my prayers, my mother became a Christian. Finally, both Parks and I are hard-working women. Before becoming a civil-rights leader, Rosa Parks had worked as a salesperson, office clerk, housekeeper, and seamstress. During summer vacations when I was young, I worked for my uncle at his auto shop. When my stepfather's daughter moved in with us, he took my job and gave it to her. At that point, I was forced to find a new job, so I worked as a salesperson at a mall. Although Parks and I might not have liked the jobs that we had to do, we showed responsibility in working to help our families. All of our struggles and accomplishments have shaped both of our personalities.

Notice that the author of this paragraph lays out three different points of similarity. For each point, she compares herself fully to Rosa Parks before moving on to the next point. This is known as *point-by-point comparison*. (As you will see, the Albert Einstein paragraph on page A-22 uses point-by-point contrast.) Another way to organize the paragraph would have been to describe only Parks's qualities in the first part of the paragraph and then present the author's similar qualities in the second part of the paragraph.

ACTIVITY 22

Working from the previous paragraph, complete the following outline. (Part of it has already been filled in for you.) The outline will help you see how the writer identifies various similarities between herself and Rosa Parks and then provides details to illustrate these similarities. Answers may vary.

MAIN IDEA Rosa Parks and I are similar in various ways.

SIMILARITY 1
We were raised by a single female parent.
Both of us were left without fathers at an early age.
Both of us needed paternal love and a father figure.
Both of us had to take on significant responsibilities at an early age.

SIMILARITY 2
Both Parks and I have a positive attitude toward life and are willing to stand up for what we believe in.
We both pursued an education despite obstacles and negative influences.
Standing up for our beliefs is important to both of us (bus incident for Parks; churchgoing for me).

SIMILARITY 3
Both Parks and I are hard-working women.
Parks worked as a salesperson, office clerk, and so on, while I worked in my uncle's auto shop.
I also worked as a salesperson at a mall.
Both of us were responsible workers, even though we might not have liked our jobs.

A Student Writer Uses Pure Contrast

In the following paragraph, a student uses pure contrast to show how he is different from Albert Einstein (1879–1955), a German-born physicist best known for his theories of relativity. Relativity holds that measurements of time and distance vary with the speed at which the observer is traveling relative to what is being observed. Einstein's study of relativity led to his famous formula describing the conversion of energy into mass and vice versa: $E = mc^2$. This formula was the scientific basis for the development of the atomic bomb.

Albert Einstein

Although I, like Albert Einstein, have a strong interest in mathematics, he and I are different in several important ways. To begin with, Einstein was a free thinker; he was not bound by the limits set by his colleagues or by books. He was able to think "outside the box," like a visionary. He could not be taught like ordinary children; he did better when he was self-taught. I, on the other hand, do better when things are explained or taught to me. For example, in college math, I do exceptionally well and find many solutions for one problem, but I'm bound by the rules put before me, unable to think around them, over them, under them. I do not question why the rules are there as long as they can be proven; they are like the word of God. Another way that I am different from Einstein is in our backgrounds. Einstein was a Jewish man from Germany who traveled to faraway places. These places included Milan, Italy; Zurich, Switzerland, where he studied at the Federal Polytechnic Institute; and Princeton, New Jersey, where he eventually settled. In contrast, I have never been anywhere besides Southern California for my studies or pleasure. Additionally, I'm a Roman Catholic and have been raised so since I was old enough to talk. The final difference between Einstein and me is that he became famous, while I am not—not yet, anyway. Einstein is widely known for his theory of relativity, which led to his formula $E = mc^2$, and he won the Nobel Prize for physics. His work has aided understanding of time and space, and some even believe that his theories can provide a basis for time travel. I, myself, have taken only a small step by going to college. I have taken Calculus 1 but have not yet scratched the surface of Calculus 3. However, I hope to further my studies in science and mathematics, allowing me to better understand Einstein's theory of relativity. I even hope to one day study with renowned physicist Michio Kaku, who has his own theory about time travel.

Teaching Tip
As an additional assignment, ask students to compare or contrast themselves with a famous person.

ACTIVITY 23

Working from the previous paragraph, complete the following outline. (Part of it has already been filled in for you.) The outline will help you see how the writer identifies various differences between himself and Albert Einstein and then provides details to illustrate these differences. *Answers may vary.*

MAIN IDEA

Albert Einstein and I are different in several important ways.

DIFFERENCE 1

Einstein was a free thinker, while I am not. Einstein wasn't bound by colleagues or books; he could think outside the box and did better when he was self-taught. I do better when things are explained to me; I'm bound by the rules and do not question them.

DIFFERENCE 2

Einstein and I have very different backgrounds. Einstein was a German Jew who traveled widely. I am a Roman Catholic who has never been outside of Southern California.

DIFFERENCE 3

Einstein became famous, while I am not—yet. Einstein is known for his theory of relativity and $E = mc^2$, and he won a Nobel Prize; also, his work has aided the understanding of time and space and may allow for time travel. Although I hope to further my studies in science and mathematics, I have taken only small steps so far.

ACTIVITY 24: Teamwork

With classmates, list similarities and/or differences for each of the following pairs. Then, working individually, select one of the topics and brainstorm for ten minutes, getting down all the details you can.

1. Compare Frankenstein and Dracula.
2. Compare the Grand Canyon and Niagara Falls (or two other vacation spots).
3. Contrast a CD player and an iPod.
4. Contrast writing an in-class exam by hand and writing an in-class exam on the computer.
5. Compare and contrast shopping in a store and shopping online.
6. Compare and contrast snow skiing and waterskiing.

When to Use the Pattern

Many writing tasks in college and at work may require you to use comparison and contrast as the main pattern of development. Assignments calling for comparison and contrast may use words like *compare, contrast,* or *describe/discuss/explain similarities or differences.*

ACTIVITY 25: Teamwork

With classmates, discuss why each of the following projects might require comparison and contrast as the main pattern of development. Then, for each category (college and workplace), work together to invent a third assignment that would also use comparison and contrast.

College Assignments

1. **Computer technology:** Compare and contrast Mozilla and Internet Explorer.
2. **Anthropology:** Compare and contrast the Aztec and Mayan cultures.
3. **Poetry:** ______________________________.

Workplace Assignments

1. In your position as a taxi driver, compare and contrast two routes to the airport.
2. In your position as a vacation planner, compare and contrast two possible travel destinations for a customer.
3. In your position as a wedding planner, compare and contrast

   ______________________________.

ARGUMENTATION

In argumentation, you state and defend your position on an issue. Look at the underlined issues in the following examples:

> **I am against experimentation on animals.**
> **Steroid use in professional sports should be legalized.**
> **College professors should be required to dress professionally.**
> **I am in favor of granting driver's licenses to illegal immigrants.**

Defending your position means providing your *best reasons* for being for or against an issue. Look at the reasons given for the following position on steroid use:

> **Steroid use in professional sports should be legalized because . . .**
> **—it results in better performance.**
> **—it helps athletes recover from injuries.**
> **—it helps athletes have longer careers.**

When explaining your reasons, try to keep in mind *counterarguments* that might be used to challenge your position. Anticipating how others might oppose your argument can help you explain your position more carefully.

For example, some readers might have concerns about the negative health effects of steroids. The writer might acknowledge these concerns in a statement like the following:

Teaching Tip
Ask students if they can come up with other counterarguments for the reasons for legalizing steroid use in professional sports.

> **Although some people are concerned about the negative health effects of steroids, moderate use of them can actually help athletes recover from injuries.**

The key to successful argumentation is to state your position clearly, to give sufficient reasons for it, and to provide precise details to illustrate your reasons.

A Student Writer Uses Argumentation

In the following paragraph, a student writer makes a convincing argument for worker-provided daycare.

> To benefit workers and improve performance, as many businesses as possible should provide onsite daycare. First, onsite daycare reduces absenteeism and improves productivity. According to a report by the National Conference of State Legislatures (NCSL), 80 percent of the companies surveyed by the NCSL said that child care problems cause reduced workdays among their employees. With onsite daycare, employees would not have to worry about such problems, allowing them to work full, productive days. Also, knowing that a company cares enough to provide daycare is a morale booster. When morale is high, workers tend to be more productive and more willing to "go the extra mile" in their jobs. Second, onsite daycare helps to attract and retain workers. In a personal interview, Helen Dobbs, president of Maywood Technology, said, "There's no question that our daycare facility has helped us to attract top talent, both men and women. It sets us apart from the competition in a tight market for highly skilled technology workers." Dobbs and other employers report that onsite daycare also contributes to worker satisfaction, meaning less employee turnover. Finally, onsite daycare may actually benefit companies' financial health. The biggest argument against such a benefit has been that it is too expensive and that only the biggest and most profitable businesses can afford it. However, in their recent book *Kids at Work: The Value of Employer-Sponsored On-Site Child Care Centers,* Rachel Connelly, Deborah S. DeGraff, and Rachel A. Willis argue that onsite daycare can actually be profitable for companies. Two daycare-providing companies studied by the authors realized savings of $150,000 and $250,000 in wages. The authors also found that workers were willing to contribute up to $225 per year to help pay for company daycare, whether or not they themselves would make use of it. These workers seemed to realize that onsite daycare would help to make everyone happier and more productive. Although setting up onsite daycare facilities certainly takes upfront effort, the evidence suggests that it pays off in the long run—in both human and financial terms.

Notice that the writer mentions an important counterargument. You might want to underline this counterargument and then the reasons and details that the writer provides to address it.

ACTIVITY 26

Working from the previous paragraph, complete the following outline. (Part of it has already been filled in for you.) The outline will help you see how the writer clearly states a position, provides reasons for the position, and then gives detailed explanations for each reason. Answers may vary.

MAIN IDEA To benefit workers and improve performance, as many businesses as possible should provide onsite daycare.

REASON 1 Onsite daycare reduces absenteeism and improves productivity.

An NCSL study indicates that child care problems cause reduced workdays; onsite daycare would eliminate this problem, improving productivity.

Onsite daycare boosts morale, which in turn boosts productivity and willingness to "go the extra mile."

REASON 2 Onsite daycare helps to attract and retain workers.

A company president reports that onsite daycare has helped her business attract top talent and stand out from the competition.

Onsite daycare can reduce employee turnover.

REASON 3 Onsite daycare may actually benefit companies' financial health.

Researchers have found that daycare can be profitable, saving wage costs.

Workers may be willing to contribute to daycare costs, even if they won't use daycare.

Power Tip
Several of the professional readings in Part Three make arguments. Examples include "Be Cool to the Pizza Dude" by Sarah Adams (page 528), "The 'M-Word': Why It Matters to Me" by Andrew Sullivan (page 558), "As They Say, Drugs Kill" by Laura Rowley (page 568), and the excerpt from Morgan Spurlock's *Don't Eat This Book* (page 576).

ACTIVITY 27: Teamwork

With classmates, list reasons to support each of the following arguments. Then, select one of the topics and brainstorm for ten minutes, getting down all the details you can.

1. College students should (or should not) have an attendance requirement because . . .
2. America is (or is not) the greatest country because . . .
3. Medical marijuana use should (or should not) be legalized because . . .
4. Magazines should (or should not) discuss the private lives of celebrities because . . .
5. Non-math majors should (or should not) be required to take math classes in college because . . .

When to Use the Pattern

Many writing tasks in college and at work may require you to use argument as the main pattern of development. Assignments calling for argumentation may use words like *argue, defend, explain why, give reasons for,* or *should.*

ACTIVITY 28: Teamwork

With classmates, discuss why each of the following projects might require argument as the main pattern of development. Then, for each category (college and workplace), work together to invent a third assignment that would also use argument.

College Assignments

1. **Health:** Argue why practicing safe sex is essential.
2. **Economics:** Argue that illegal immigration is good for the U.S. economy.
3. **Women's studies:** ______________________________.

Workplace Assignments

1. In your position as president of the local parent-teacher organization, argue why music classes should be kept as part of the elementary school curriculum.
2. In your job as quality-control inspector for a chain of burger restaurants, argue why the company should offer a few "healthy choice" items on the menu.
3. In your position as president of the United States, argue ______________ ______________________________.

Appendix B

Punctuation and Capitalization

APPENDIX OVERVIEW

Using Correct Punctuation

Punctuation marks are like little traffic signals for your readers, telling them when to pause, stop, notice where your own words stop and another's start, and so on. The following sections quickly review some punctuation uses covered in earlier chapters and introduce a few new ones.

COMMAS (,)

Let's begin by reviewing some comma uses that may be familiar to you.

Commas after Introductory Words

Usually, commas come after beginning words that set up, describe, or otherwise introduce the main ideas in a sentence. Here are five types of expressions that are typically followed by commas.

1. Transitional expressions. Look at these examples:

> In the first place, athletes need to be team players.
>
> More important, the building failed to meet safety codes.
>
> Last, you should find a good financial adviser.
>
> Nevertheless, she will apply for the scholarship.

Sometimes, a transitional expression will appear after a semicolon (;). It should be followed by a comma in this case, too:

> I woke up late for my first day of work; furthermore, I forgot to iron my dress shirt.

For more information on transitional expressions, see Chapter 5, page 158, and Chapter 12, page 344.

2. Simple adverbs. Look at these examples:

> Sadly, our hamster escaped from its cage.
>
> Suddenly, the lights went out in the stadium.
>
> Reluctantly, James signed the new contract.

For more information on adverbs, see Chapter 10, page 271.

3. Prepositional phrases. Look at these examples:

> In the morning, light fills my bedroom.
>
> After the party, we will go dancing.
>
> Under her pillow, Joanne found a diamond necklace.

For more information on prepositional phrases, see Chapter 11, page 281.

4. Word groups beginning with subordinating conjunctions. Look at these examples:

> Unless we shout, they won't hear us.
>
> Because you are my friend, I told you the truth.
>
> Although I am tired, I will go to the party.

For more information on subordination, see Chapter 13.

5. Modifying phrases. Look at these examples:

> Backing down the driveway, the car ran over a tricycle.
>
> To escape from the handcuffs, the magician picked the lock.
>
> Disappointed with his salary, Jaime looked for a new job.

For more information on modifying phrases, see Chapter 15.

Teaching Tip
Recommend that students circle or highlight commas in newspaper articles or other readings in professional publications. This physical act will help build their awareness of how these important punctuation marks are used.

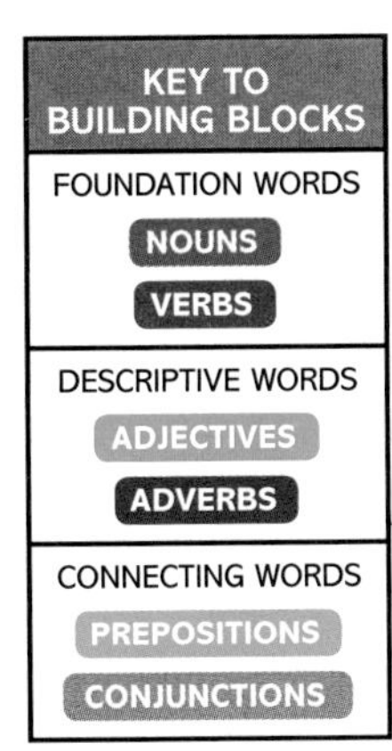

Commas in Compound Sentences

As you learned in Chapter 12, a **compound sentence** is two or more related simple sentences joined together. When simple sentences are joined with a coordinating conjunction (such as *and, but, or,* or *so*), a comma must precede this conjunction. Take a look:

SIMPLE SENTENCE 1 — SIMPLE SENTENCE 2

We walked , and they drove.

COMMA AND CONJUNCTION

However, remember that no comma is used when forming a compound subject or a compound verb:

COMPOUND SUBJECT, NO COMMA — COMPOUND VERB, NO COMMA

Liz and Ryan collect antiques and restore furniture.

For more information, see Chapter 12.

Commas Setting Off Descriptive/Modifying Word Groups

You already know that when a modifying phrase begins a sentence, it must be followed by a comma. Let's review some other rules for descriptive word groups.

Remember from Chapter 14 that if you add a descriptive clause that is *not essential* to the meaning of a sentence, you usually must set it off with commas. If the clause is in the middle of a sentence, commas come before and after the clause:

DESCRIPTIVE CLAUSE IN THE MIDDLE

Monopoly, which I hate, is my in-laws' favorite game.

If the clause is at the end of a sentence, use one comma, right before the clause:

DESCRIPTIVE CLAUSE AT THE END

My in-laws like to play Monopoly, which I hate.

Do not use commas to set off *essential* information:

ESSENTIAL INFORMATION

The Monopoly game that we purchased is missing three pieces.

Also, note these rules for modifying phrases that begin with *-ing, to,* or *-ed:*

- When the phrase is in the middle of a sentence, commas are used before and after it.
- When a modifying phrase comes at the end, commas generally are not used.

A modifying phrase in the middle:

Deirdre, listening to classical music, fell into a deep sleep.

The judge, annoyed by the attorney, called a recess.

A modifying phrase at the end:

Deirdre fell into a deep sleep listening to classical music.

My cousin visited his local recruiting office to enlist in the army.

For more information on punctuating modifying phrases, see Chapter 15, page 431.

Other Uses of Commas

Here, we will introduce four additional uses of commas.

1. To separate items in a series. When you list three or more items, separate them with commas. Take a look:

> You can select whole, skim, or 2 percent milk.
>
> Shirley bought apples, peaches, cherries, and grapes.

Note that for clarity, most instructors and other writing experts recommend putting a comma before the conjunctions *and* and *or*.

Teaching Tip
For test items on commas and other punctuation marks, see the *Testing Tool Kit* CD available with this book.

2. To set off information that renames another item. Sometimes, we follow a noun with a word group that renames that noun. Take a look at the underlined word group in this sentence:

> Andre Gomez, <u>my new boss</u>, goes to your gym.

My new boss renames *Andre Gomez*. Here's another example:

> We no longer go to Murphy's, <u>the restaurant that received three health violations</u>.

The underlined word group renames *Murphy's*.

Terminology Tip
Words that rename a noun are known as *appositives*.

3. To separate parts of an address. Look at this example:

> Danielle lives at 5 Foster Lane, Boston, MA 02130.

Notice that no comma appears before the zip code.

When the name of a city and state appear in the middle of a sentence, a comma should follow the state name:

> The brothers stayed in Dayton, Ohio, before driving on to Nebraska.

4. To separate parts of dates. When a date includes the month, day, and year, a comma must come between the day and the year:

> My daughter was born on September 15, 1998.

If a date with the month, day, and year appears in the middle of a sentence, a comma should follow the year:

> September 15, 1998, was a big day for our family.

When only a month and year are specified, no comma is needed between them:

> You must submit your application by the end of December 2009.

ACTIVITY 1

Edit the following paragraph, adding necessary commas and deleting unnecessary ones. There are twenty-six missing commas and four unnecessary commas.

(1) On June 2 2007 my husband and I got married, and started a big adventure: our honeymoon. (2) My husband Dan had always wanted to visit New England, so he rented a cabin for us in Barton Vermont. (3) On the day after our honeymoon we drove to Barton which is in a beautiful area of Vermont known as the Northeast Kingdom. (4) As we traveled country roads, we admired the green fields dotted with cows the misty lakes and the rolling hills. (5) Unfortunately that was as good as the honeymoon got. (6) Our cabin was down a muddy, rutted lane and it looked nothing like the photo of it, that we'd seen on the Internet. (7) With its peeling paint rotted porch and sagging roof, it was like something out of a horror movie. (8) Although Dan and I were somewhat shocked we decided to make the best of things. (9) We figured that we would be spending most of our time outdoors anyway. (10) We didn't realize how true that prediction would be until that first night, when a rainstorm caused part of the roof to cave in—just outside our bedroom door. (11) Deeply disturbed by this incident we decided to camp outdoors; fortunately we'd brought a tent. (12) The next morning Dan called the cabin owner about getting a refund. (13) Then he and I set off for a hike up Jay Peak. (14) As we walked up the trail at the base of the mountain, we looked forward to the dramatic views from the summit. (15) However just one mile into the hike, Dan tripped on some rocks and sprained his ankle. (16) Luckily some very kind hikers came to the rescue, and helped us back to the trailhead. (17) After Dan got his ankle bandaged at a local hospital we spent the next few days in a motel, and

watched the pouring rain from our window. (18) Finally we headed home. (19) Dan weary and disappointed apologized about the cabin but it wasn't his fault, of course. (20) Now that some time has passed, we can laugh at our honeymoon memories. (21) We plan to return to Vermont sometime soon and we're hoping that we'll have better luck.

SEMICOLONS (;)

As you learned in Chapter 12, a semicolon can be used instead of a conjunction to connect two closely related simple sentences. Here are two simple sentences joined with a comma and a coordinating conjunction:

SENTENCE 1	COMMA AND COORDINATING CONJUNCTION	SENTENCE 2
Watching basketball is fun	, but	playing it is better.

Here are the same sentences joined with a semicolon:

SENTENCE 1	SENTENCE 2
Watching basketball is fun;	playing it is better.

Remember from Chapter 12 that semicolons act as "soft" periods. Both "hard" and "soft" periods must always *follow* a complete sentence. Also, semicolons (and often periods) must also *be followed* by another complete sentence.

For more information on joining sentences with a semicolon, see Chapter 12.

Now we'll introduce a new use of the semicolon: *to separate items in a series that already contains commas.*

As you learned on page A-31, in lists of three or more items, the items are separated with commas. Now, look at these examples:

> The interview candidates will meet with Vera Canseco, director of marketing; Dennis Liu, vice president of operations; and Chris Snow, vice president of sales.
>
> The choir traveled to Detroit, Michigan; Gary, Indiana; and Madison, Wisconsin.

Without the semicolons, the groupings of items might not be immediately clear to readers. The semicolons clarify the groupings.

For online practice with the punctuation covered in this appendix, visit this book's Web site at **bedfordstmartins .com/steppingstones**.

ACTIVITY 2

Add missing semicolons to the following sentences, replacing commas if necessary. (You should use semicolons instead of periods to separate sentences.)

EXAMPLE: I want only to become class president you wish to lead the nation.

1. Chocolate alone is a treat chocolate and red wine together are divine.
2. You know that I'm older than Lisette you will discover that I'm also wiser than Lisette.
3. My European travel plans will take me to Barcelona, Spain, Lisbon, Portugal, and Paris, France.
4. Hiking up the mountain took three hours coming down took just two.
5. Robin's healthy dinner menu included spinach, which is loaded with B vitamins, lean chicken, a good source of protein, and brown rice, which is rich in fiber.

COLONS (:)

Sometimes, we follow a complete sentence with examples or explanations related to the complete sentence. In such cases, a colon may be used before the examples or explanations. Take a look:

COMPLETE SENTENCE | COLON | EXAMPLES

I am allergic to three things: shrimp, peanuts, and housework.

COMPLETE SENTENCE | COLON | EXPLANATION

Milo didn't get the job for one reason: He lied on his application.

Notice that in the second example, the word group after the colon begins with a capital *H* because it is a complete sentence.

Colons are also used in the following situations:

- Between the main titles and subtitles of books, reports, and other publications. Look at these examples:

  I read a fascinating book titled *Sellout: The Politics of Racial Betrayal.*

  The report that we were assigned, *Great Transitions: Preparing Adolescents for a New Century,* came to many surprising conclusions.

- After greetings or *to/from* directives in letters or memos. Take a look:

  Dear Ms. Landiss:

  To: The IT staff

  From: Jan Rogers

ACTIVITY 3

Write five sentences that include colons.

APOSTROPHES (')

Here, we will introduce three common uses of apostrophes.

1. To show ownership. When you want to show that a singular noun (*girl, boy, teacher*) owns something, add *-'s:*

> The girl's horse threw her.
>
> The teacher's lessons were easy to follow.
>
> Chris's dogs are cute and friendly.

When you want to show that a plural noun ending in *-s* (*girls, boys, teachers*) owns something, add only an apostrophe:

> The girls' horses slept in the barn.
>
> The teachers' offices were locked.

If a plural noun does not end in *-s* (*men, women, children*), you need to add *-'s* to form the possessive:

> The women's restroom is closed.
>
> Our library has a children's story hour.

When time expressions show ownership, apostrophes should also be used:

> Last year's holiday party was more crowded than this year's.
>
> When I resigned from my job, I gave two weeks' notice.

Power Tip
You do not need to add an apostrophe to show possession when you use a possessive pronoun.
Incorrect: This cabin is your's; our's is across the lake.
Revised: This cabin is yours; ours is across the lake.
For more on possessive pronouns, see Chapter 17, page 505.

2. To shorten words. Sometimes, especially in speech, we shorten words by omitting letters. When writing these shortened forms, known as *contractions,* we use an apostrophe to show where letters have been left out. Here are just some examples:

Long form	**Contraction**
are not	aren't
cannot	can't
did not	didn't
do not	don't
I will	I'll
I am	I'm
is not	isn't
it is, it has	it's
was not	wasn't

Be careful not to misplace apostrophes when you are writing contractions:

INCORRECT are'nt; is'nt REVISED aren't; isn't

Some instructors prefer that students avoid contractions in papers. If you are unsure of your instructors' preferences, be sure to ask.

3. To make numbers and letters plural. Occasionally, you will write plural forms of numbers and letters. Use apostrophes in these cases:

Bill writes his 2's like 7's. I got three A's and two B's last semester.

ACTIVITY 4

Edit the following paragraph, adding apostrophes where necessary and fixing any incorrectly placed apostrophes. There are nine missing apostrophes and two incorrectly placed apostrophes.

(1) During his first year of college, Mark got mostly Cs and Ds. (2) Holding down two jobs, going to school full-time, and helping take care of his girlfriends children made it difficult for him to do well. (3) Not long into Marks second year, it was clear that what he did his first year wasnt going to work. (4) With his supervisors permission, Mark cut his hours at one job, and he also cut back slightly on his course load. (5) He did'nt miss any classes, and he went to all of his teachers office hours as often as he could. (6) At night and during the childrens' nap times, he studied hard. (7) So far, Marks grades have improved, and he has started receiving his first As.

QUOTATION MARKS (" ")

When we use someone's exact words in writing, these *direct quotations* need to be enclosed in quotation marks. Take a look:

> The comedian Steven Wright once asked, "If a word in the dictionary were misspelled, how would we know?"
>
> As the suspect fled, the officer yelled, "Halt! Police!"

If we report what someone said without using his or her exact words, quotation marks are not used. Such reported speech is known as an *indirect quotation*.

> The officer told the fleeing suspect to stop.

Following are some basic guidelines for using direct quotations, most of which you learned about in Chapter 6:

- Put quotation marks at the beginning and end of the quotation.
- If the quotation is a complete sentence, capitalize the first word of it. For example: *Bill's father said, "Don't forget to take your lunch."*
- If the quotation is not a complete sentence, you do not need to capitalize it. For example: *All of us were told about the "mysterious green glow" that shone in Petrie Forest at night.*
- Use a comma to separate the quotation from the identification of the speaker. For example: *Tom said, "Go away." OR "Go away," Tom said.* Notice that in both examples, the closing quotation mark is *after the period or comma.*
- If a question mark is part of a quoted speaker's words, put it inside the quotation marks. For example: *During the fire, Rona yelled, "Where are the exits?"*
- If a question is being posed by you, the writer, not the quoted speaker, put the question mark outside of the quotation marks. For example: *Did you know what Paul meant by "dire situation"?*

Power Tip

When quoted material appears within other quoted material, put single quotation marks (' ') around the innermost quotation—for example: *Our supervisor's e-mail warned, "Do not, under any circumstances, open e-mail attachments from people you do not know, especially if the file name ends in 'exe.'"*

ACTIVITY 5

Edit the following paragraph, adding quotation marks where necessary and fixing any incorrectly used quotation marks. You may need to fix other punctuation and some capitalization as well.

You should add three pairs of missing quotation marks, remove three pairs of unnecessary quotation marks (for indirect quotations), fix four other punctuation errors, and correct two capitalization errors.

(1) My best friend told me that "she has had one bad experience" with Internet dating. (2) She said my first mistake was to go out with a guy based only on his picture; if I had read his profile, I would have realized that he was a stuck-up jerk. (3) "Her second mistake," she said, was that "she let the date go on too long." (4) The guy talked and talked about himself and wouldn't let me get a word in she painfully recalled. (5) In response to this complaint, I asked my friend "Would you go on an Internet date again"? (6) She replied, in fact, I'm going on one this Friday, but this time I read the profile.

Teaching Tip
Have students work together to write a paragraph with dialogue between two people. Then, they should check the dialogue for correct use of quotation marks and other punctuation.

OTHER PUNCTUATION MARKS

The following chart reviews some other punctuation marks, describing their functions and giving examples of each.

PUNCTUATION MARK	FUNCTION	EXAMPLES
Dashes —	Dashes set off interrupting information.	Very few people—in fact, only one—found Bob's joke funny.
	They are also used to set off the following:	
	surprising information	Michaela found a horrifying surprise on her porch—a holiday fruitcake with green cherries.
	an explanation containing commas	Three traits—alertness, physical fitness, and a respect for nature—are essential for a forest ranger.

PUNCTUATION MARK	FUNCTION	EXAMPLES
Hyphens -	Use hyphens to	
	join two or more words that form a single adjective before a noun,	This plant has heart-shaped leaves. My two-year-old son likes Cheerios. The top-earning executive was fired.
	write out fractions and spell out numbers from twenty-one to ninety-nine,	One-third of our employees are new. Thirty-five packages were delivered here today.
	break words at the end of a line. (Word-processing software will do this automatically, but if you are writing by hand, check a dictionary to see where words should be broken.)	Exotic plants grow in many jun-gle climates. Every November in Lee Falls, hunt-ing is the most popular sport.
Parentheses ( )	Use parentheses to	
	enclose extra information,	Three-fourths of the survey respon-dents (55 in all) liked the name of the cola brand.
	set off an explanation containing commas.	If you feel that you must give a gift to a co-worker, avoid personal items (such as lingerie, creams, or perfume), which may make the recipient uncomfortable.
Exclamation points !	Use exclamation points to express surprise, excitement, or fear.	To this day, I still cannot believe that I won the $30,000 prize! There is something that all of us can do to make the country a better place—vote!

In academic papers, dashes and parentheses should be used minimally because they can break up the flow of your writing. Also, exclamation points should be used infrequently because they can be perceived as shouting. If overused, they can annoy readers or cause them to doubt the seriousness of your writing.

Using Correct Capitalization

Capital letters are large letters, like the *C* at the beginning of this sentence. Aside from capitalizing the first word of every sentence, you should also capitalize

- proper nouns
- major words in titles

Power Tip

Father, mother, and other family titles are capitalized when they are used in place of the person's specific name: *Yes, Father is retired.* Otherwise, such titles should not be capitalized: *My father is retired.*

As you learned in Chapter 10, proper nouns name *specific* people, places, and things. Let's take a closer look at different types of proper nouns.

- **People.** Capitalize the names of specific people, including titles preceding those names.

  Aunt Lucia
  Father
  Maria Hernandez
  Ms. Hernandez
  Professor Grant
  Vice President Hayes

Do not capitalize titles like *president, vice president,* or *aunt* if they are used without a name.

- **Places/geographic features.** Capitalize the names of specific locations, monuments, and geographic features.

  Empire State Building
  Homer, Alaska
  Park Street
  Rome
  Yellowstone National Park
  Lincoln Memorial
  Amazon River
  Mount Rainier
  the North / the South

Do not capitalize locations like *street, park,* or *river* if you are not naming a specific street, park, river, or other location:

Our street is next to a park.

Capitalize *north, south, east,* and *west* when they name specific regions, but do not capitalize them in directions:

The South had an agricultural economy at the time of the Civil War.

Drive west for three miles, and then go south on I-71.

- **Racial and ethnic groups, nationalities, and languages**

  African American
  Asian
  Hispanic
  Latino/Latina
  French
  Guatemalan
  Spanish

- **Organizations, teams, and other specific groups or establishments.** Capitalize the names of specific groups.

  American Civil Liberties Union
  Red Sox
  Sonic Youth
  Curry College
  Fraternal Order of Police
  Sony

Do not capitalize groups or establishments if you are not naming them specifically:

Ken dropped out of his rock band and went to college.

- **Religions**

  Catholic
  Jewish
  Protestant
  Hindu
  Muslim
  Sikh

- **Months, days, and holidays**

  August
  Monday
  Hanukkah
  November
  Wednesday
  Thanksgiving

Note that *winter, spring, summer,* and *fall* are not capitalized.

- **Brand names.** Capitalize the names of specific brands.

  Johnson & Johnson
  Puma
  The North Face
  Toyota

Do not capitalize products when you are not naming a specific brand:

Jonelle put on her coat and sneakers and left the house.

- **Academic courses.** Capitalize the names of specific academic courses.

  Calculus 1
  Economics 100
  English 090
  German 101

Unless you are naming a specific course, do not capitalize a course name unless it is a specific language, nationality, or other term that you would normally capitalize:

Last semester, I took three difficult courses: math, chemistry, and German.

In addition to capitalizing proper nouns, you should also capitalize major words in the titles of publications, films, television shows, songs, and other media. You should not capitalize *a, an,* and *the,* prepositions (like *at, in, on, to,* and *with*), or conjunctions (*and, but, or,* and so on) unless they begin or end the title.

Have you read John Irving's novel *The World According to Garp?*

Today, the *Leeville Gazette* published a troubling story: "The Problem with Plastics."

Jess's favorite movie is *Romy and Michele's High School Reunion.*

Dancing with the Stars is one of the most popular television shows.

Power Tip
Notice that the titles of books, newspapers, movies, and television shows are italicized (or underlined). Titles of articles, essays, and short stories appear in quotation marks.

Teaching Tip
For test items on capitalization, see the *Testing Tool Kit* CD available with this book.

ACTIVITY 6

Correct the capitalization errors in each of the following sentences.

EXAMPLE: In august, our family will vacation at lake winnipesaukee. (A, L, W)

1. At our College, african American students have formed a scholarship fund. (c, A)
2. Next Fall, professor Sara Paradis will teach western civilization 101 and history 102. (f, P, W, C, H)
3. In the summer, aunt Barb and uncle Pete like to take boat trips along the mississippi river. (A, U, M, R)
4. During the christmas holiday, I read a hilarious book: a *confederacy of dunces*. (C, A, C, D)
5. Drive South for three miles, and then turn left at the kentucky fried chicken onto Delancey street. (s, K, F, C, S)

For online practice with capitalization, visit this book's Web site at **bedfordstmartins .com/steppingstones**.

Appendix C

Guidelines for ESL Writers

APPENDIX OVERVIEW

If English is not your first language, or if you grew up in a home where standard English was not spoken, every chapter in Part Two of this book will improve your grammar skills. Additionally, you may benefit from reviewing this appendix and completing the activities in it.

Remember, too, that the more you hear and read standard English, the faster your language skills will improve. Try to listen to news broadcasts or podcasts while driving, exercising, or preparing meals. Also, read magazine or newspaper articles as often as you can.

Note: This appendix color codes the building blocks of language according to the system used in Part Two of this book. See the nearby box for a reminder.

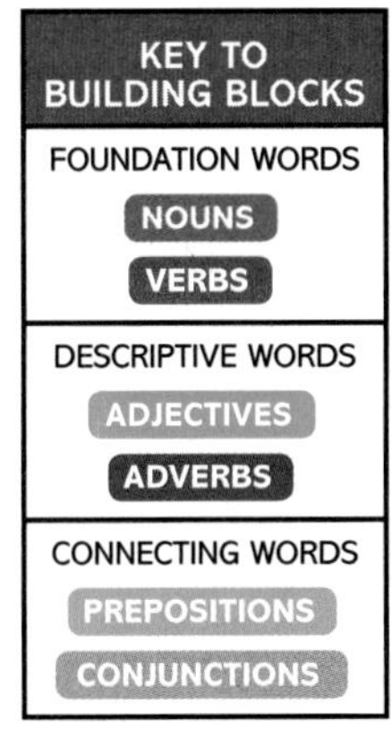

Count and Noncount Nouns and Articles

As you learned in Chapter 10, a **noun** is a word that identifies a person, place, or thing (for instance, *girl, Beatrice, city, Chicago, ball*).

Count nouns refer to people, places, or things that can be counted (for example, three *girls,* two *boys,* two *towns,* six *shoes,* seven *apples*). **Noncount nouns** refer to items, qualities, or concepts that can't be counted (for example, *flour, granite, honesty*). Here are some more examples:

COUNT NOUNS	NONCOUNT NOUNS
ball/balls	advice
boat/boats	beauty
car/cars	gold
computer/computers	health
letter/letters	information

CONTINUED >

COUNT NOUNS	NONCOUNT NOUNS
plate/plates	jewelry
shirt/shirts	knowledge
street/streets	money
tree/trees	sadness
window/windows	sand
	sugar
	wheat

Teaching Tip
Ask students to call out additional examples of count and noncount nouns.

Note that noncount nouns usually do not have plural forms; in other words, do not add *-s* or *-es* to the end of them.

INCORRECT golds, healths, sadnesses, wheats

CORRECT gold, health, sadness, wheat

ACTIVITY 1

Identify each of the following nouns as *count* or *noncount* by writing "C" or "N" in the space provided.

EXAMPLE: airplane ____C____

1. road ____C____
2. book ____C____
3. pollution ____N____
4. steel ____N____
5. peach ____C____
6. bead ____C____
7. information ____N____
8. toe ____C____
9. salt ____N____
10. stick ____C____

Articles signal that a noun is coming up. Look at the following examples, in which the articles are underlined.

The judge entered the courtroom.
A bird perched on the railing.
An apple fell from the tree.

As you use nouns in your sentences, keep the following rules for articles in mind:

1. Use *a* or *an* to signal singular count nouns whose identity is not specified.

A police officer arrived on the scene.
An eyewitness testified.

For online practice with the topics in this appendix, visit this book's Web site at **bedfordstmartins.com/steppingstones.**

In these examples, there is no information to specify the *particular* police officer who arrived or the *particular* eyewitness who testified.

Here's how to decide whether to use *a* or *an:*

- The article *a* is used before words that begin with a consonant sound: *b, c, d, f, g, j, k, l, m, n, p, q, r, s, t, v, w, x, z,* usually *h* (as in words like *hand* and *harbor*), sometimes *u* (as in words like *university* and *universe*), and usually *y*.
- The article *an* is used before words that begin with a vowel sound: *a, e, i, o,* sometimes *h* (as in words like *herb* and *hour*), and sometimes *u* (as in words like *understanding* and *unlikely*).

Teaching Tip
For test items on ESL topics, see the *Testing Tool Kit* CD available with this book.

2. Do not use *a* or *an* with noncount nouns. In standard English, the following sentence would be incorrect:

INCORRECT Eduardo borrowed a sugar from his neighbor.

You do not need the article *a* before the noncount noun *sugar*. However, if you specify a quantity of a noncount noun, you may use the article:

CORRECT Eduardo borrowed a cup of sugar from his neighbor.

3. Use *the* to signal most specific nouns—both count and noncount.

The police officer who interviewed us filed a report.

The sand on our local beach washed away.

Terminology Tip
A and *an* are known as *indefinite articles* because they signal indefinite, nonspecific nouns. *The* is known as a *definite article* because it signals definite, specific nouns.

These examples refer to *particular* nouns. Which police officer filed a report? The one who interviewed us. What sand washed away? The sand on our local beach.

4. Do not use *the* before noncount or plural nouns that mean "in general." Take a look at the following sentences:

INCORRECT The money is all Bill thinks about.

INCORRECT I buy the carrots whenever I go grocery shopping.

In the first example, the intended meaning is that Bill constantly thinks about money in general, not a specific kind of money. Therefore, the article should be dropped:

CORRECT Money is all Bill thinks about.

In the second example, the intended meaning is that I buy carrots in general whenever I shop; I do not buy a specific kind of carrot. Therefore, the article should be dropped:

CORRECT I buy carrots whenever I go grocery shopping.

5. In article + adjective + noun combinations, use the article that fits the sound of the adjective, not the sound of the noun.

INCORRECT An tasty apple is a good snack.

CORRECT A tasty apple is a good snack.

ACTIVITY 2

For each blank in the following paragraph, fill in the correct article. If no article is needed, write "N.A." in the blank.

(1) While she was in bed one night, Rosario heard ___a___ mysterious *whishing* at her window. (2) It sounded as if ___N.A.___ sand was being tossed at the glass. (3) She went to ___the___ window and saw that ___a___ violent storm was whipping sleet against her house. (4) To Rosario, ___N.A.___ storms of all kinds are interesting, so she stood there and watched the scene for several long moments. (5) She watched ___the___ trees in her yard bend from side to side. (6) The remaining leaves from last fall spun in little circles along the street. (7) On the sidewalk, ___a___ hunched-over neighbor hurried home against the wind. (8) This sight intensified ___the___ warmth and comfort of Rosario's room.

Verbs

Teaching Tip
If you have a lot of ESL students in your class, consider using *The Bedford/St. Martin's ESL Workbook*, available with this text.

As you learned in Chapter 16, mastering English verbs doesn't have to be difficult; you just need patience and practice. Also, as noted earlier, it's a good idea to read and listen to as much standard English as possible so that standard verb usage begins to sound more natural to you.

If you haven't already worked through Chapter 16, it's a good idea to do so now. Try to do as many of the activities in the chapter as you can. Also, you may want to review the coverage of helping verbs in Chapter 10 (page 270) and Chapter 11 (page 278).

This section expands on the advice in earlier chapters, covering issues that can be challenging for English-as-a-second-language (ESL) students.

VERBS WITH GERUNDS AND INFINITIVES

Gerunds are verbs that have *-ing* endings and that function as nouns. Look at these examples:

GERUND — I like running.   GERUND — Jordan enjoys sewing.

Infinitives combine *to* and a base verb (for example, *to run, to sew*). Look at these examples:

INFINITIVE — I like to run.   INFINITIVE — Jordan wants to sew a quilt.

In standard English, some verbs may be followed by a gerund or an infinitive:

GERUND: I like running.   INFINITIVE: I like to run.

Other verbs may be followed by a gerund but not by an infinitive:

CORRECT Jordan enjoys sewing. (GERUND)

INCORRECT Jordan enjoys to sew. (INFINITIVE)

Yet other verbs may be followed by an infinitive but not a gerund:

CORRECT Jordan wants to sew a quilt. (INFINITIVE)

INCORRECT Jordan wants sewing a quilt. (GERUND)

The following chart shows some of the verbs that are used with gerunds and/or infinitives.

VERBS THAT CAN BE FOLLOWED BY A GERUND OR AN INFINITIVE			
begin	hate	remember	try
continue	like	start	
forget	love	stop	
VERBS THAT CAN BE FOLLOWED BY A GERUND BUT NOT BY AN INFINITIVE			
admit	enjoy	miss	recall
avoid	finish	practice	risk
deny	imagine	quit	suggest
discuss			
VERBS THAT CAN BE FOLLOWED BY AN INFINITIVE BUT NOT BY A GERUND			
agree	decide	need	promise
ask	expect	offer	refuse
beg	hope	plan	wait
claim	manage	pretend	want

ACTIVITY 3

For each blank in the following paragraph, fill in the gerund or infinitive form of the verb in parentheses.

(1) I try to do/doing (do) my best as a parent, but I'm not perfect. (2) When I decided to have (have) children, I knew parenting would be difficult, but I figured I would know what to do most of the time. (3) When my son was born, I promised to avoid (avoid) preaching to him. (4) I knew I wouldn't have all the answers, but I expected to be (be) knowledgeable about most things he might ask me. (5) However, when he turned fifteen, he asked if he could get a tattoo. (6) I said, "No, not until you're older," and I preached to him about how the skull symbol he liked now might not look as good to him when he was thirty. (7) He agreed to accept (accept) my decision, but then he asked a tough question: "Are you tired of the shooting star on your ankle?" (8) The star was a tattoo that I got during my senior year of high school; I hid it from my own mother for years. (9) I thought for a minute. (10) Then, I managed to tell (tell) my son the truth: I didn't like the tattoo as much now as I did when I got it, but it is a reminder of who I was at seventeen. (11) For that reason, I still enjoy looking (look) at it. (12) If it were gone, I would miss seeing (see) it. (13) Finally, I said, "Ben, you get that tattoo if you really want to." (14) For now, he has decided to wait (wait).

NEGATIVE STATEMENTS AND QUESTIONS

The rules for forming negative statements and questions vary, depending on whether the original (positive) statement has a helping verb. Look at these positive statements:

Dontell likes cars.

HELPING VERB (FOLLOWED BY MAIN VERB)

Dontell has purchased a car.

As you can see, the second example has a helping verb, while the first example does not. Let's look at how to form negative statements first.

Negative Statements

To turn a sentence with a helping verb into a negative statement, put the word *not* right after the helping verb:

Dontell has not purchased a car.

Now, let's look back at the example without the helping verb:

Dontell likes cars.

To turn this type of sentence into a negative statement, put the helping verb *do* + *not* before the base form of the main verb. (The base form of *likes* is *like.*) The helping verb *do* must change to *does* to agree with *Dontell.* (For more on subject-verb agreement, see Chapter 16, page 466.)

Dontell does not like cars.

If the verb in the original positive statement is a form of *be* (*am, is, are, was,* or *were*), you do not need to add the helping verb *do* before *not* when forming a negative statement.

Positive →	**Negative**
Rita is happy.	Rita is not happy.

ACTIVITY 4

Rewrite the following positive statements as negative statements.

EXAMPLE: You have burned the toast.
You have not burned the toast.

1. Marco is happy about the game's outcome.
Marco is not happy about the game's outcome.
2. They have written angry e-mails to the congresswoman.
They have not written angry e-mails to the congresswoman.
3. The travelers are staying in an expensive hotel.
The travelers are not staying in an expensive hotel.
4. Althea vacations at the beach.
Althea does not vacation at the beach.
5. Eduardo has postponed the party at his new house.
Eduardo has not postponed the party at his new house.

Questions

Let's look back at the positive statements presented earlier:

Dontell likes cars.

HELPING VERB (FOLLOWED BY MAIN VERB)

Dontell has purchased a car.

To turn a sentence with a helping verb into a question, put the helping verb before the subject (*Dontell*) and change the period at the end of the sentence to a question mark:

Has **Dontell** purchased **a car?**

Now, let's look back at the example without the helping verb:

Dontell likes **cars.**

To turn this type of sentence into a question, put the helping verb *do* before the subject. (Note that *do* must change to *does* to agree with *Dontell.*) Then, after the subject, provide the base form of the original verb (*likes* → *like*). Finally, change the period at the end of the sentence to a question mark:

Does **Dontell** like **cars?**

Teaching Tip
Call out simple positive statements one at a time. Then, ask students to turn each statement into (1) a negative statement and (2) a question.

If the verb in the original positive statement is a form of *be* (*am, is, are, was,* or *were*), you do not need to add the helping verb *do* when forming a question. Simply move the verb to precede the subject.

Positive	→	**Question**
Rita is **happy.**		Is **Rita happy?**

ACTIVITY 5

Rewrite the following positive statements as questions.

EXAMPLE: You have burned the toast.
Have you burned the toast?

1. Marco is happy about the game's outcome.
   Is Marco happy about the game's outcome?
2. They have written angry e-mails to the congresswoman.
   Have they written angry e-mails to the congresswoman?
3. The travelers are staying in an expensive hotel.
   Are the travelers staying in an expensive hotel?
4. Althea vacations at the beach.
   Does Althea vacation at the beach?
5. Eduardo has postponed the party at his new house.
   Has Eduardo postponed the party at his new house?

Prepositions

As you learned in Chapters 10 and 11, a **preposition** connects a word to more information about the word. Take a look:

The book fell in the water.

The preposition *in* connects the verb *fell* to more information: Where did the book fall? In the water. (*In the water* is known as a prepositional phrase.)

MEANINGS OF COMMON PREPOSITIONS

Some of the most common English prepositions are *at, in,* and *on.* These prepositions may show either time or location, and you have to memorize the proper uses.

Whenever you are confused about how to use one of these prepositions, refer to the following chart.

PREPOSITION	USAGE TO SHOW TIME	USAGE TO SHOW LOCATION
at	Indicates a specific time: *The meeting began at 6:30.*	Indicates a specific place: *We arrived at the hotel early.* *Turn right at the light.* *I sat at my desk.*
in	Indicates a specific time or date: *In a week, we will leave.* *We got married in 2008.* Indicates a duration of time: *The movie will start in 15 minutes.*	Indicates someone or something being inside something else: *I stayed in my room.* *The papers were in the folder.* Indicates being in a geographic location: *I live in Boston.*
on	Indicates a specific day or date: *We were married on May 24, 2008.*	Indicates that something rests on or hangs from a surface: *Please put the book on the shelf.* *We hung the mirror on the wall.*

Teaching Tip
Ask students to go through a recent piece of writing, circling the prepositions *at, in,* and *on.* Then, they should check only these prepositions for correctness.

For a full list of prepositions, see Chapter 11, page 282.

ACTIVITY 6

For each of the following sentences, fill in the blank with the correct preposition: *at, in,* or *on.*

EXAMPLE: We arrived ___*at*___ the party early.

1. You will find Antonio ___in___ his office.
2. Josie will graduate ___on___ June 6, 2009.
3. Every weekday morning, I get up ___at___ 5:30.
4. The little yellow bird sat ___on___ the fence and groomed its feathers.
5. ___In___ a moment, we will leave for the airport.

PREPOSITIONS AFTER ADJECTIVES

As you learned in Chapter 10, **adjectives** are words that describe nouns. Some English adjectives are often followed by specific prepositions. Again, you have to memorize the correct combinations, some of which are shown in the following chart.

ADJECTIVE + PREPOSITION COMBINATION	EXAMPLE
addicted to	Charlotte is addicted to chocolate.
afraid of	Timmy is afraid of the dark.
angry about/at	I am angry about this offensive e-mail.
angry with (used for people)	I am angry with Joe for sending this offensive e-mail.
confused by	The taxpayers were confused by the new rules.
excited about	We were excited about the concert.
grateful for	They were grateful for the assistance.
happy about	The students were happy about the exam postponement.
interested in	The teacher is interested in our progress.
pleased with	The Wongs are pleased with their new landscaping.
proud of	We are proud of our children.
responsible for	Workers are responsible for setting up their own retirement accounts.
sorry about	Betsy is sorry about the mistake.
tired of	The children are tired of spaghetti.

ACTIVITY 7

For each of the following sentences, fill in the blank with the correct preposition.

EXAMPLE: All of us are responsible ___for___ our own success.

1. I am interested ___in___ all movies about aliens and outer space.
2. The students were proud ___of___ their high scores on the math test.
3. The children were excited ___about___ the new game station, but they were confused ___by___ its instructions.
4. The tourists were tired ___of___ looking for parking, so they were happy ___about___ the free parking garage by their hotel.
5. Milo is angry ___about___ the dent in his car, but he is angrier ___with___ himself for driving recklessly.

PREPOSITIONS AFTER VERBS

Some English verbs are followed by specific prepositions. Here's just one example:

> The students handed in the homework.

With some verb + preposition combinations, words can come between the verb and the preposition. Take a look:

> The students handed the homework in.

With other combinations, however, the verb and preposition cannot be separated.

CORRECT	The soldiers fought for independence.
INCORRECT	The soldiers fought independence for.

Again, you have to memorize the correct combinations and which ones can and cannot be separated. The following chart shows just some of the possible combinations.

VERB + PREPOSITION COMBINATIONS THAT CAN BE SEPARATED

Combination	Example
bring up (raise an issue)	Don't bring up that sensitive topic. / Don't bring it up.
call off (cancel)	The couple called off the wedding. / They called it off.
drop off (leave at a location)	The letter carrier dropped off a package. / She dropped it off.
fill in (add a substance until something is full / complete)	The workers filled in the old swimming pool. / They filled it in.
fill out (complete)	We must fill out these tax forms by April 15. / We must fill them out.
hand in (submit)	The customers handed in their loan applications. / The customers handed them in.
look up (find or check)	Janeece looked up the information on Google. / She looked it up on Google.
pick up (collect)	Josh picked up the children after school. / He picked them up after school.
put away (place something somewhere / remove from sight)	I put away the clean laundry. / I put it away.
put off (delay)	Don put off his dental appointment. / He put it off.
take off (remove)	Please take off your shoes before entering the house. / Please take them off.
throw away / throw out (discard)	I threw away my credit card. / I threw it away. I threw out my credit card. / I threw it out.
turn down (lower the volume of)	The party hosts turned down the stereo. / They turned it down.
turn off (shut off)	Remember to turn off the lights when you leave the room. / Remember to turn them off.
wake up (interrupt the sleep of / rise from sleep)	The barking dog woke up the baby. / He woke her up.

VERB + PREPOSITION COMBINATIONS THAT CANNOT BE SEPARATED

Combination	Example
drop in (pay a visit)	I will drop in to see you.
fight against (combat)	The researchers will fight against the deadly disease.
fight for (work on behalf of / defend)	Senator Rose will fight for the legislation.
go over (review)	Let's go over the math problems.
grow up (mature)	Some children grow up too quickly.
show up (make an appearance)	Dan showed up at the party.
stand by (stand next to)	Stand by me so that I can talk to you.

ACTIVITY 8

Read each sentence pair below and do the following:

- Determine which sentence has the correct word order and circle it.
- If *both* sentences are in the correct order, write "C" next to them.

EXAMPLE: a. Let's go the plans for our trip over.
b. Let's go over the plans for our trip.

1. **a.** I accidentally threw away my credit card.
   b. I accidentally threw my credit card away. C
2. **a.** My ex showed up at Danica's party.
   b. My ex showed at Danica's party up.
3. **a.** The car alarm woke up everyone.
   b. The car alarm woke everyone up. C
4. **a.** The neighbors in will drop over the holidays.
   b. The neighbors will drop in over the holidays.
5. **a.** The neighborhood group fought for the speed bumps.
   b. The neighborhood group fought the speed bumps for.

Order of Adjectives

Again, **adjectives** are words that describe nouns. In the following example, the adjective *ugly* describes the noun *mushrooms:*

the ugly mushrooms

If you use more than one adjective to describe a noun, the adjectives must come in a certain order, or the sentence will sound funny in standard English. To a native speaker, the first example below would sound odd, while the second one would sound "right":

AWKWARD the ear-shaped ugly little mushrooms

STANDARD the ugly little ear-shaped mushrooms

Again, as you listen to and read more standard English, you too will develop a sense of what sounds right. Until then, be aware that descriptions of more than one adjective generally follow this order:

1. Article or other word indicating number or ownership: *a, an, the, three, some, Roberto's*
2. Judgment or opinion: *pretty, ugly, honest, delicate, generous*
3. Size: *big, little, large, small*

Teaching Tip
Ask students to form small groups. Then, group members should work together to form a long string of adjectives before a noun. When the groups are finished, have volunteers read the adjective string(s). You might want to give a small reward to the group that forms the longest or most inventive adjective string.

4. Shape or length: *short, long, round, ___-shaped* (as in *ear-shaped*)
5. Age: *new, young, old*
6. Color: *red, blue, green, orange*
7. Nationality/region: *Mexican, Korean, Egyptian, western*
8. Material: *metal, glass, wooden*
9. Noun used as adjective: *gas* (as in *gas station*), *wedding* (as in *wedding cake*)
10. Noun being described: *child, shoe, mushroom, car*

ACTIVITY 9

In each of the following sentences, the adjectives are scrambled. Rewrite each sentence in the space provided, putting the words in the correct order.

EXAMPLE: Bret bought a yellow cute car.
Bret bought a cute yellow car.

1. The oval Japanese fragile platter was a wedding gift.
The fragile oval Japanese platter was a wedding gift.
2. Flavio collects new unusual metal sculptures.
Flavio collects unusual new metal sculptures.
3. We baked a train-shaped delicious birthday cake for Jordan.
We baked a delicious train-shaped birthday cake for Jordan.
4. The little pretty green parrot repeated the sailors' nasty swearwords.
The pretty little green parrot repeated the sailors' nasty swearwords.
5. The generous Italian old gentleman gave us some red delicious tomatoes.
The generous old Italian gentleman gave us some delicious red tomatoes.

Other Guidelines

This section briefly reviews some other points to be aware of if you are an ESL student or if you generally want to build your skills in standard English. Because most of these issues have been covered in more depth in earlier chapters, we provide references to those chapters.

- Remember to include subjects in all sentences:

INCORRECT	Likes movies.
REVISED	Dan likes movies.

For more details on including subjects in sentences, see Chapter 11.

Power Tip
A prepositional phrase cannot be the subject of a sentence.
Incorrect: In the trees have many leaves.
Revised: The trees have many leaves.

- Many English sentences begin with *There is*/*There are* or *It is*. Do not leave out *There* or *It* in these sentences:

INCORRECT	Are three reasons to stay in this job. Is raining today.
REVISED	There are three reasons to stay in this job. It is raining today.

- Remember to use verbs in all sentences:

INCORRECT	Rick happy about his promotion.
REVISED	Rick is happy about his promotion.

For more details on including verbs in sentences, see Chapter 11.

- Do not use pronouns to repeat subjects within a simple sentence.

As you learned in Chapter 10, **pronouns** are noun substitutes. In the following compound sentence (joining two simple sentences), the pronoun *she* substitutes for *Tara* so that you don't have to repeat Tara's name.

SENTENCE 1 SENTENCE 2
Tara speeds, and she gets a lot of tickets.
NOUN PRONOUN

Within a simple sentence, however, do not use pronouns to repeat subjects:

INCORRECT	Tara, she gets a lot of tickets.
REVISED	Tara gets a lot of tickets.

For more on simple sentences, see Chapter 11. For more on compound sentences, see Chapter 12.

Answers to Odd-Numbered Activities

Chapter 1

Activity 7: Teamwork, page 13

1. popular nonfiction; **3.** personal writing; **5.** popular fiction

Activity 8, page 16

1. journalism; **3.** personal writing; **5.** academic writing

Activity 9: Teamwork, page 17

Possible purposes: **1.** to let you know what you are doing well and what you need to improve on; also, possibly, to show that you do or do not deserve a raise; **3.** to give others an opinion of the movie to help them decide whether or not they want to see it; **5.** to inform readers about the discovery

Activity 10, page 18

General purposes: **1.** to inform; **3.** to inspire; **5.** to educate

Activity 13: Teamwork, page 22

Possible audiences: **1.** your instructor (and maybe other students); **3.** department officers who are in a position to address the problem; **5.** parents, teachers, and others attending the meeting

Activity 15: Teamwork, page 25

Possible appropriate language: **1.** formal language; moderate to difficult vocabulary; correct grammar; **3.** informal language; simple vocabulary; relaxed grammar; **5.** formal language; moderate to difficult vocabulary; correct grammar

Activity 16, page 26

Possible appropriate information: **1.** advanced, but verify with your instructor that basic information should not be included; **3.** intermediate; **5.** intermediate

Activity 17, page 27

Possible answers: **1.** definition. The paragraph defines "a good marriage." **3.** process. The paragraph explains the steps of studying for an exam. **5.** narration. The paragraph tells the story of an autism diagnosis and its outcome.

Activity 18: Teamwork, page 30

1. process; **3.** definition; **5.** description

Activity 19, page 30

Possible answers: **1. type:** personal; **general purpose:** to persuade; **specific purpose:** to explain why Hampton Beach is a good place for a family vacation; **audience:** Jameel (a friend); **pattern of development:** exemplification; **3. type:** academic writing (Journalism is also a possibility.); **general purposes:** to inform, to persuade; **specific purpose:** to describe unsanitary conditions at local restaurants and explain why stricter health measures are needed; **audience:** readers of a student academic journal or other serious publication; **patterns of development:** exemplification, description

Chapter 2

Activity 1, page 37

1. first two sentences: supporting information; **third sentence:** practical information and topic; **fourth sentence:** supporting information, or continuation of topic; **fifth sentence:** practical information; **due date:** practical information

Activity 2: Teamwork, page 38

Possible questions: **1.** What parts/features should the paper include? How much value/weight does the assignment have?

Activity 3, page 39

1. first topic: limited; **second topic:** narrow; **third topic:** broad

Activity 4: Teamwork, page 40

Possible decisions/topic identifications: **1.** The writer would have to decide which amendment to explore and think about how it is important in his/her life. This is a limited topic. **3.** The writer would have to choose which sexually transmitted diseases to write about and what to say about these diseases—for example, how they are transmitted, how they can be prevented, or what health policies are concerned with them. This is a broad topic.

Activity 5, page 41

Possible answers: **1. Narrowed for a standard essay:** Several ways to overcome boredom; **Narrowed for a short essay or paragraph:** One or two strategies to overcome boredom

Activity 10, page 52

1. broad

Chapter 3

Activity 12, page 66

1. the customers; **3.** Tom

Activity 14, page 67

1. on the sales floor; **3.** in the stockroom

Activity 16, page 69

1. two months ago; **3.** on weekends

Activity 18, page 70

1. The manager is insensitive and a bad communicator. **3.** Too many workers call in sick.

Activity 20, page 72

1. The owners are the manager's parents. **3.** admit that he is wrong

Activity 22, page 74

1. the hazardous stockroom, the dangerous floors, and the unsafe stairs; **3.** They are messy and slippery.

Chapter 4

Activity 1, page 86

1. pet, hamster, cat, dog; **3.** weather, rain, snow, thunder; **5.** OK

Activity 2: Teamwork, page 86

1. liquid, gasoline, tequila, tears; **3.** coins, nickels, dimes, quarters; **5.** war, soldier, bomb, battle

Activity 3, page 88

1. cold desserts, ice cream sundae, cherry snow cone, frozen banana; **3.** household chores, dust furniture, vacuum carpets, wash the floor; **5.** starting a new job, learning procedures, meeting co-workers, filling out forms

Activity 5, page 88

1. extreme sport, solo skydiving, bungee jumping, whitewater rafting; **3.** high-stress job, emergency room doctor, crime officer, firefighter

Activity 6: Teamwork, page 90

Possible key words: **1.** College, rewarding experience; **3.** Good communication skills, learned; **5.** Artificial sweeteners, funny taste

Activity 7, page 90

1. Skydiving was a frightening experience. Stepping out of the plane took my breath away. I was afraid my parachute would not open. Free-falling made my heart stop. **3.** Getting a college degree is beneficial. College offers social and work connections. Education improves one's self-esteem. Degree holders earn better salaries.

Activity 8, page 92

Possible answers: **1. Group 1:** non-alcoholic drinks, cola, tea, coffee; **Group 2:** alcoholic drinks, wine, beer, champagne; **3. Group 1:** hair colors, brunette, redhead, blonde; **Group 2:** hair fringes, eyelashes, mustache, bangs; **5. Group 1:** warm-blooded animals, rabbit, chipmunk, squirrel; **Group 2:** cold-blooded animals, snake, lizard, frog

Activity 10, page 94

Possible answers: **1. Group 1:** safe/comfortable places, in a comfortable home, in mother's arms, with a good friend; **Group 2:** unsafe/uncomfortable places, lost in the desert, under an avalanche, caught in a riptide; **3. Group 1:** good habits in class, sit in the front row, take good notes, ask a lot of questions; **Group 2:** good habits outside of class, do your homework, study in the library, work with a tutor; **5. Group 1:** signs of aging, wrinkles around eyes, sagging skin, weakened vision; **Group 2:** ways to address signs of aging, anti-aging cream, facelift, reading glasses

Activity 12, page 96

Possible answers: **1. Group 1:** Medical work can be demanding and stressful. Medical professionals often work long hours with few breaks. Medical work can be physically and emotionally tiring. Health workers are held responsible for the well-being of all their patients. **Group 2:** Health care can be a great field to pursue. Nurses, medical assistants, and other health professionals are in high demand. Health professionals get the satisfaction of helping others. Starting salaries for nurses can approach $40,000. **3. Group 1:** Rachel, Juan, and Robert have negative body language. Rachel sits slumped in class. Juan usually crosses his arms when he talks to others. Robert lowers his eyes when girls approach him. **Group 2:** Jessica, Michael, and Sarah have positive body language. At school, Jessica sits up straight and tall at her desk. Michael's posture and gestures show an interest in others. When meeting strangers, Sarah looks them directly in the eye.

Activity 14, page 98

Possible answers: **1.** natural disasters, tornado, hurricane, flood (word to eliminate: damage); **3.** careers, teaching, firefighting, farming (word to eliminate: danger); **5.** exercise equipment, treadmill, weights, bicycle (word to eliminate: aerobics)

Activity 16, page 99

Possible answers: **1.** electronic communication, chatting on the Internet, e-mailing on a handheld device, text messaging on a cell phone (words to eliminate: downloading songs on iTunes); **3.** coverings used with food, aluminum foil under a roast chicken, plastic wrap over steaming veggies, wax paper on a cookie sheet (words to eliminate: napkins with messy barbecue); **5.** police training, enroll in police academy, study criminal justice, train in police procedures (words to eliminate: carry a gun)

Activity 18, page 101

Possible answers: **1.** People treat illness in different ways. I drink gallons of water and sweat it out. My dad takes large doses of vitamin C. My sister goes straight to bed and rests. (Sentence to eliminate: My mom hasn't had the flu in two years.) **3.** Pollution has many bad effects. Oil from roads contaminates water supplies. Emissions from cars and factories trap heat and harm air quality. Garbage landfills leak harmful chemicals. (Sentence to eliminate: Recycling has only limited benefits.) **5.** Follow these steps to ask for a raise. Make a list of your accomplishments at work. Know what raise is reasonable based on your accomplishments. Set up a meeting to ask for the raise. (Sentence to eliminate: Show up to work early every day.)

Activity 20, page 103

Possible answers: **1. Group 1:** grooming tool, razor, toothbrush, comb; **Group 2:** personal-care product, toothpaste, deodorant, shampoo (item to eliminate: teeth); **3. Group 1:** income, salary, gift check, lottery winnings; **Group 2:** expenses, rent, food, utilities (item to eliminate: bank); **5. Group 1:** life stages, infancy, childhood, adolescence, adulthood; **Group 2:** life roles, friend, spouse, parent, worker (items to eliminate: friendship, family history)

Activity 21: Teamwork, page 105

1. Group 1: participants, minister, bride, groom, bridesmaid; **Group 2:** ceremony, vows, ring exchange, kiss, bouquet toss (item to eliminate: honeymoon)

Activity 22, page 106

1. Group 1: professional, psychologist, lawyer, accountant, dentist; **Group 2:** blue collar, plumber, electrician, carpenter, mechanic (items to eliminate: retirement, employee)

Activity 23, page 108

Possible answers: **1. Group 1:** clean house responsibly, wash dishes regularly, keep up with your laundry, throw out spoiled food, disinfect the bathroom; **Group 2:** respect your neighbors, don't play loud music, don't argue loudly, end parties at a decent hour, walk softly if you live above someone; **Group 3:** manage money well, save emergency funds, pay your bills on time, don't overspend on credit, balance your checkbook (items to eliminate: don't be alone too often, look for a roommate)

Activity 28, page 114

Key words in support point 1: be myself; **key words in support point 2:** help me, ways; **key words in support point 3:** fun together

Activity 32, page 117

Possible answers: **1. Topic:** something you hate doing; **Main idea:** I hate going to the dentist. **Support point 1/examples:** The treatments are expensive. I paid over $100 for a filling. Check-ups cost $85. A crown or bridge would bankrupt me. **Support point 2/examples:** The treatments are always painful. Cleanings hurt my gums. Novocaine injections sting. Drilling leaves my jaw sore. **Support point 3/examples:** The dentist always gives me bad news. He always finds more cavities. He says I'm grinding my teeth down. He said I may be developing gum disease.

Activity 35, page 123

Items that do not fit: **1.** cheap prices; Everyone has a favorite restaurant; managers yell at the staff

Activity 36, page 124

Items to switch: **1.** I participate in study groups *and* I have good study habits; I want to be a biology major *and* I have clear academic goals.

Activity 37, page 125

Items to replace: **1.** nurses always able to find work; media show positive images of nurses

Activity 38, page 127

Items to replace: **1.** nice (support point 1, example 3), other skills (support point 2, example 3), satisfaction (support point 3, example 2)

Activity 39, page 128

1. third example under first support point is missing; third example under second support point is unclear; second example under third support point does not fit; third example under third support point repeats another item

Chapter 5

Activity 7, page 138

Types of topic sentences: **1.** creates a contrast/identifies support points; **3.** uses creative language; **5.** adds a description

Activity 8: Teamwork, page 140

Possible answers: **1. Key words left out of topic sentence 1:** pets. Without this word, readers won't know what's good for owners' health. **Key words left out of topic sentence 2:** health. Without this word, readers won't know the exact benefit of pet ownership. **Key words left out of topic sentence 3:** their owners'. Without these words, it won't be clear exactly who benefits from pet ownership.

Activity 9: Teamwork, page 142

Possible answers: **1. Replaced words in topic sentence 1:** helped me become, mature. Meaning changed: *helped me become* is roughly similar to *teach* but being *mature* is different from being *responsible.* **Replaced words in topic sentence 2:** mother and father, demanded. Meaning changed: *mother and father* is a clear rewording of *parents,* but *demanding* is not the same thing as *teaching.* **Replaced words in topic sentence 3:** learned, parenting methods. Meaning the same: *learned* indicates that the writer was taught, and *parenting methods* has a similar meaning to *strategies.*

Activity 10: Teamwork, page 144

Possible answers: **1. New information in topic sentence 1:** probation and. This information changes the meaning because the main idea refers only to community service, not to community service *and* probation. **New information in topic sentence 2:** and enrolling in the police academy. This information changes the meaning because the main idea refers only to community service, not to community service *and* enrolling in the police academy. **New information in topic sentence 3:** especially his attitude toward women. This information is not in the main idea, but it might be fine to include it if the support points of the outline focus on changes in the cousin's attitude toward women.

Activity 11: Teamwork, page 146

Possible answers: **1. Topic sentence 1:** Changed. Key words left out and changed. **Topic sentence 2:** Changed. Key words changed. **Topic sentence 3:** Changed. Inappropriate new information added.

Activity 12: Teamwork, page 148

Possible answers: **1. Sentence 1:** Problem words: everyone has problems. "Everyone has problems" is a broader statement than "other people's problems are worse than his own." **Sentence 2:** Problem words: his own problems are not so bad. His problems may in fact be bad, even if others' problems are worse. **Sentence 3:** OK.

Activity 13: Teamwork, page 153

Possible answers: **1. Sentence 1:** Words showing first specific example: answer people's questions. Combined; **Sentence 2:** OK; **Sentence 3:** Words showing first specific example: to provide information to people who need it. Combined

Chapter 6

Activity 1, page 172

1. a. pulp fibers: precise; **b.** something strange: unclear; **3. a.** a greater distance: unclear; **b.** fifty kilometers more: precise; **5. a.** Edgar's worried expression, he is nervous about his blind date: precise; **b.** the way Edgar looks, something is wrong: unclear

Activity 2, page 173

Paragraph 1a is precise. Precise details are underlined: Carol frowned and narrowed her eyes when her husband, Leon, came home from his manager's job at McDonald's. He had promised that he would be home at 6 P.M., but it was almost 9. Carol had been slicing, dicing, chopping, and sautéing since 10 that morning. Now, the braised beef was cold and dry, the colorful vegetable medley looked faded, and the ice cream cake was a puddle on the cake plate. *Paragraph 1b is unclear. Unclear details are underlined:* Carol looked pretty angry when her husband, Leon, came home from his job. He promised that he would be home at the usual hour, but he was a few hours late again. Carol had spent so long preparing a nice dinner, and now it was ruined.

Activity 3: Teamwork, page 174

1. unclear. Possible revision: honk and scream angrily; **3.** precise; **5.** precise; **7.** unclear. Possible revision: bikers, walkers, joggers, and skaters; **9.** unclear. Possible revision: two

Activity 4, page 175

Paragraph 1 has unclear details, which are underlined: In my experience, online chat rooms are an excellent way to meet people. To begin with, people can't see you, so they are less likely to judge you. For example, I am young, but when I chat online, nobody judges me for my age. In "real" life, people sometimes discriminate against me because of my race, but nobody notices my race in a chat room. When I go online, I also appreciate that people don't judge me for my looks. Second, chat rooms are a great way to meet people with different viewpoints. I like to talk to people from faraway countries because they have such unique opinions about the world. I have had conversations with rich people and poor people. Sometimes, I chat with individuals who are in abusive situations. Finally, meeting people in chat rooms is convenient and inexpensive. When I need to talk to someone at an unusual time, I know that

I can always find a friendly person online. It's also convenient because I don't have to leave the comfort of my own place to go out and meet someone. Best of all, meeting people online is cheaper for many reasons. For all these reasons, I'm grateful for online chats and the ways in which they have broadened and enriched my world.
Paragraph 3 has insufficient details.

Activity 6, page 178

Possible imprecise or abstract wording: **1.** that guy, fairly short; **3.** a new novel, just OK; **5.** old job, factory, pretty cool, new job, construction, awesome

Activity 7: Teamwork, page 179

Concrete details in passage 1 are underlined: Being on a tight budget isn't easy, especially when your kids want (and sometimes need) expensive gadgets. Now that the holidays are approaching, Myla, my oldest, has been asking me for a MacBook computer. Myla is planning to study design in college next year, and since Macs are supposed to be the best computers for design projects, I think this investment will be wise. She will be able to practice design skills on the computer and use it in college. I feel less sure about the request of my middle child, Tarik. He already has an iPod and a cell phone, but now he wants an iPhone. I can see from all the advertising that this phone has a lot of fancy features, like Internet browsing, but does a fifteen-year-old really need all of them? When Tarik is a successful executive, he can buy a phone that communicates with Mars, but until then, I think I'll just keep paying for his guitar lessons. My youngest, Daniel, wants a Wii video game, which lets you play sports like tennis, baseball, and bowling indoors. This gadget isn't cheap, but Daniel can get hyper when he's penned up, which happens often during the cold winter months here. Therefore, the Wii might actually be a gift for Mom, if you know what I mean. As much as I can, I want to make my kids' holiday dreams come true, but I also want to be practical, because that's in *all* of our best interests.

Activity 11, page 181

Possible inexpressive verb(s): **1.** went; **3.** goes; **5.** told

Activity 12: Teamwork, page 182

Action verbs in the passage are underlined: Monday arrived and I raced to work. As I accelerated up a hill, I approached two vehicles traveling much too slowly for me. Common traffic laws were for the weak and inexperienced; I was a man and made my own rules. I darted up the left lane; the initial vehicle posed no challenge, and I passed it with ease, the first of many victories, or so I thought. My car raced beside the second vehicle. A kid no older than sixteen looked at me with pride and contempt as he sped up. I pushed the gas pedal harder; I was flying, going almost 90 mph. The other car kept pace, and I could not catch him.

Then I saw it, cresting the top of the hill: a semi truck headed straight toward me. I panicked. I looked over to my right, and there was no room to fit between the two cars I attempted to pass. Seconds flew by; I had to react as the truck barreled closer. He approached too quickly and would crush me if I tried to brake. I jerked the steering wheel to the right, now knowing what would happen. My cherished possession squeezed between the two cars—surely the sign of an expert driver. Then momentum carried me on. I veered off the road, and a telephone pole did what my brakes could not: brought me to a dead halt.

Activity 16, page 184

Possible imprecise adjectives: **1.** weird; **3.** odd; **5.** unusual

Activity 17: Teamwork, page 185

Sensory details from the paragraph are underlined: Last year, I went to a Japanese tea ceremony with my grandmother, and it was a great honor and delight. All the guests wore simple kimonos of colorful silk. My grandmother had given me a blue kimono decorated with large white flowers, and I wore it with pride, loving the feeling of the soft fabric on my skin. After we had cleansed our hands and mouths in a basin outside of the tearoom, the hostess invited us inside. We took off our shoes and entered a small, simple room with woven straw mats on the floor. Long banners with graceful Japanese writing hung from the walls, and tall ceramic vases held branches of orange blossoms. The sweet scent of the flowers perfumed the air. The room was quiet except for the low whispers of the guests admiring the decorations. As the ceremony began, we sat on the mats, feeling the cool stone of the floor beneath them. Then, we watched the hostess go through the traditional ritual of placing green tea powder in a ceramic bowl and mixing in hot water with a special whisk. When she whisked the tea, its sharp, leafy aroma filled the air. Then, carefully, the hostess passed the bowl to the first guest. The two exchanged bows, and then the guest drank from the bowl, wiped the rim, and rotated the bowl before passing it to the next guest. When it was my turn, I was a little nervous, but my grandmother had explained each step of the ritual to me. I bowed, drank the rich, bitter tea, wiped the bowl's rim, and passed the bowl to the next guest with a gentle smile. At that moment, I felt the simple beauty of the ceremony connecting me to all those present and to all of my ancestors.

Activity 22, page 188

Possible imprecise details: **1.** to do something; **3.** her gloomy prediction; **5.** something critical

Activity 23: Teamwork, page 189

Quoted details in passage 1 are underlined: "I need to end this," I said one evening to Randall, who had been my boyfriend for three years. They were the hardest words for me to express, but I'm glad I was able to get them out. In many ways, Randall is a good person, and I know he loved me. However, he always was suspicious and negative about anything that might mean that I'd spend less time with him. Whenever I made new friends, he'd say something like, "I'm not sure she sounds good enough for you." When I got a promotion at my job, he complained that I'd be working late more and wouldn't be able to make dinner for both of us. The incident that finally convinced me to end the relationship was Randall's complaining about my decision to reenter college after a break of five years. He said, "Why do you need college when you have a good job and you have me?" I tried to explain that it would be hard to advance in my profession without a degree. Also, I wanted to expand my mind and, yes, meet new people. Randall shook his head and didn't even seem to listen, and so I told him that I needed to break things off. "In time," I explained, "you might understand why I had to do it." In his next relationship, I hope Randall will learn to be more independent and less controlling. If not, he might be alone for a long time.

Activity 27, page 192

Possible imprecise details: **1.** wasn't happy; **3.** glad; **5.** normal

Activity 28: Teamwork, page 192

Emotive details in paragraph 1 are underlined: It happens too often in my neighborhood. You hear screaming and sirens, or maybe you don't, and later on, there's some kind of shrine on the street: prayer candles, red roses from the 7-Eleven, and teddy bears hugging stuffed hearts. Usually, there's a picture of the kid who got shot and taped-up signs from parents, brothers, sisters, and other kids: "We will always love you," "We miss you," "With Jesus." I've walked by shrines like these maybe four times, and each time I've felt a cold stone in my chest. The faces in the pictures are unfamiliar, and I can't make myself feel all the hurt I could feel. My attitude changed last week when I walked by a new shrine at Garden and Adams. My first thought when I saw the kid's picture was simply *I know that face.* It was like when you're on the bus and nod at someone you've seen around but don't know that well. Then, I realized it was Bo Robbins, a kid I went to grade school with. When I put this fact together with all the other things—the candles, the notes, and the flowers—it felt like someone kicked me in the stomach. I think I actually fell back a little. I had lost touch with Bo after we went on to separate schools, but I remembered him well. He got in trouble a lot for talking in class, but he was funny and made everyone laugh—even the teachers. You couldn't stay angry with him. In the picture at the shrine, he looked like he was getting ready to laugh. That's what got me. I felt the stone again, but this time it was in my throat; I couldn't swallow it down. I walked away from there fast, blinking and wiping my eyes.

Activity 32, page 196

Possible imprecise details: **1.** funny suggestion; **3.** an unusual explanation; **5.** a funny problem

Activity 33: Teamwork, page 196

Humorous details in passage 1 are underlined: One of the most memorable people in my life was my Aunt Alva, who lived in a pink house set into a steep hill in the Pennsylvania coal country. I'll never forget that house, which practically glowed on overcast days. Nor will I forget my disappointment on learning that it was pink because she and my Uncle Antonio (Tony) got a discount on the paint. I liked to think of the color as an extension of Aunt Alva's personality—fun, distinctive, and a little disruptive. As soon as my parents, my sister, and I entered her house, she offered us snacks, including my favorite: sweet-and-salty peanuts. When I think back on it, sweet and salty matched her personality perfectly. One minute, she was hugging and kissing us and saying how handsome my sister's boyfriend was. The next minute, she would snap at Uncle Tony: "Step on up and show some love, old man. They're not getting any younger." Later, Aunt Alva and I would watch reruns of *Cagney and Lacey* on her 1970 Magnavox television, which had a bright green picture. She'd put on sunglasses to cut the glare. One time, when she left the room to make lunch in the kitchen, my dad adjusted the colors so that the actors' skin looked a little less Martian-like. As soon as Aunt Alva came back, she made a face at the TV and said, "Who messed with the picture?" Then, she adjusted the knob to make the actors green again and put her sunglasses back on. I started wearing Uncle Tony's sunglasses to watch TV with her, and Dad took a picture of us slouched back in our shades. That picture has been on my refrigerator for years, and I look at it whenever I need to smile.

Activity 39: Teamwork, page 200

The main comparative details in paragraph 1 are *like being caught in the eye of a tornado, like a tin can, as if I were in an echo chamber, like giant prehistoric birds attacking their prey, like a meteorite, like an angel of mercy*

Chapter 7

Activity 1, page 209

Revisions will vary, but the topic sentence should be rewritten because it doesn't reflect the main idea of the *whole* paragraph. Also, the sentence *For starters, I work two jobs* needs to be rewritten to reflect the first support point, *I try to be a good provider.* Additionally, the sentence about annoying TV shows and reality shows should be deleted because it is unrelated to the main point, and the transition *Third,* needs to be added to introduce the third support point.

Activity 4, page 218

1. You will **lose** the bracelet if the clasp on it is **loose.** **3.** If **your** car isn't repaired by the weekend, **you're** welcome to use mine on Saturday. **5.** I can't **accept** that every child in the neighborhood **except** Martina has been invited to the party. **7.** After the children **quit** yelling, the playground was **quite quiet**. **9.** Take my **advice** and let Dan **advise** you about your home renovation.

Activity 6, page 224

Revision of paragraph 1: Although I do not make a lot of money, I have developed habits that will ensure my financial security. First of all, I carefully **monitor** how much I spend. I have figured out how much extra money I have every month after **necessary** expenses (rent, food, utilities, and so on), and I never spend more than that. **[Added period] In fact, I** make sure that I have a "cushion" of extra money in my bank account in case **an** emergency expense, like a car repair bill, arises. Second, I **avoid** luxuries unless it is a special occasion. For example, I do not eat out unless it is my birthday, a friend's birthday, or some other special event. Also, I **rent** movies instead of going to the theater and spending a lot on tickets, popcorn, and soda. In addition, I do not **buy** expensive cosmetics and face creams. **[Added period]** I make my own moisturizers with natural ingredients **like** olive oil and beeswax. Most important, I contribute regularly to my savings. I have joined **my** company's 401(k) plan, and money for this comes directly out of my pay so that I am not tempted to spend it. Also, I try to contribute money to my savings account whenever I can. I may never be rich, but because I have **accepted** personal responsibility for my finances, I am **confident** that I will never have to worry about money.

Chapter 8

Activity 1, page 231

1. the first support point; **3.** the third support point

Activity 8, page 238

1. Answers could include movies and pizza, Christmas gifts, or school supplies and uniforms; **3.** Support point 2 does not change when it becomes a topic sentence in the essay outline because it is already stated as a complete main idea.

Chapter 9

There are no answers for Chapter 9.

Chapter 10

Activity 1, page 269

1. *Water* is a concrete noun; **3.** *Chicago* is a proper noun; **5.** *Happiness* is an abstract noun; **7.** *We* is a pronoun; **9.** *Ocean* is a concrete noun.

Activity 2, page 269

Nouns and their types: **1.** *Michael:* proper, *computer:* concrete; **3.** *cousin:* concrete, *motorboat:* concrete; **5.** *We:* pronoun, *Florida:* proper

Activity 3, page 270

Action verbs: **1.** played; **3.** drove; **5.** opened

Activity 4, page 271

1. *Tastes* is a linking verb; **3.** *Were* is a linking verb; **5.** *Is* is a helping verb.

Activity 5, page 272

1. *Yellow* is an adjective; **3.** *Loud* is an adjective; **5.** *Frequently* is an adverb.

Activity 6, page 272

Possible answers: **1.** quickly (adverb); **3.** red (adjective); **5.** softly (adverb)

Activity 7, page 273

These are the prepositional phrases, and the prepositions are in bold: **1. in** a tree; **3. for** me; **5. to** Chicago

Activity 8, page 274

Conjunctions are in bold and connected items are underlined: **1.** <u>happy</u> **or** <u>sad</u>; **3.** <u>chicken</u> **or** <u>roast beef</u>; **5.** <u>talented</u> **but** <u>humble</u>

Chapter 11

Activity 1, page 277

Possible sentence completions: **A. 1.** It exploded. **3.** Bill smokes. **5.** We failed. **B. 1.** Athletes run. **3.** It stopped. **5.** Rain fell.

Activity 2, page 277

Possible sentence completions: **A. 1.** The lawnmower cuts grass. **3.** Cats love tuna. **5.** The bee stung Cathy. **B. 1.** The waiter served lunch. **3.** Bob sells boats. **5.** People filled the auditorium.

Activity 3, page 278

Possible sentence completions: **A. 1.** Adam appears upset. **3.** The crowd became restless. **5.** Ashley seems happy. **B. 1.** They look sad. **3.** I feel disgusted. **5.** The pie tastes good. **C. 1.** Maria became ill. **3.** The marchers grew tired. **5.** You seem distracted. **D. 1.** We feel satisfied. **3.** Jeremy appeared pleased. **5.** The house looks messy.

Activity 4, page 279

Possible sentence completions: **A. 1.** They might jump. **3.** The team will win. **5.** You must listen. **B. 1.** He will laugh. **3.** The judge has ruled. **5.** I might sleep. **C. 1.** Robert should go. **3.** Miguel has arrived. **5.** You could drive. **D. 1.** It has happened. **3.** Jessica must wait. **5.** We can help.

Activity 5, page 280

Possible sentence completions: **A. 1.** The old car backfires. **3.** An annoyed passenger complained. **5.** The cotton shirt wrinkles. **B. 1.** We woke up early. **3.** You play guitar beautifully. **5.** Jackson walked quickly. **C. 1.** A skillful dancer moved gracefully. **3.** Her sports car runs smoothly. **5.** The new battery charged rapidly. **D. 1.** The bank manager got upset. **3.** Rotten bananas smell bad. **5.** The little girl seems sick.

Activity 6, page 282

Possible sentence completions (prepositions are in bold): **1.** Coconuts grow **on** palm trees. **3.** The toy landed **in** the pond. **5.** We can meet **in** the parking lot.

Activity 7, page 282

Possible sentence completions: **1.** Janice lives near the park. **3.** A car at my job caught on fire. **5.** On Friday, we had a pop quiz.

Activity 8, page 283

Possible sentence completions: **1.** On the porch, you will find the paint for the shutters. **3.** The bus to New York stopped by the exit. **5.** We live near the beach so that we can swim in the ocean.

Activity 9: Teamwork, page 283

Possible sentence completions: **1.** Before dawn, the man in that house walks along the beach. **3.** In a few minutes, the winner of the music award will speak to reporters. **5.** In the evening, the jewelry store on Adams Street was damaged by high winds.

Activity 10, page 284

Possible sentence completions: **1. a.** The soldier fired the gun. **b.** The soldier fired the gun rapidly. **c.** The soldier fired the gun rapidly at the target. **3. a.** My dad lost weight. **b.** My dad lost weight quickly. **c.** My dad lost weight quickly during his diet.

Activity 11: Teamwork, page 285

Possible sentence completions: **1. a.** Sweet music played. **b.** Sweet music played softly. **c.** At the dance, sweet music played softly in the ballroom. **d.** At the dance, sweet music from another time played softly in the ballroom. **3. a.** The angry wildcat leaps. **b.** The angry wildcat leaps suddenly. **c.** In the forest, the angry wildcat leaps suddenly from a tree. **d.** In the forest, the angry wildcat with black stripes leaps suddenly from a tree.

Activity 12, page 286

Subjects: **A. 1.** Tom; **3.** mirror; **5.** You **B. 1.** Houses; **3.** It; **5.** She **C. 1.** Turkeys; **3.** She; **5.** disaster

Activity 13, page 286

Nouns (with subjects in bold): **1.** **Dogs**, bones; **3.** **Tom**, football; **5.** **babysitter**, noises

Activity 14, page 287

Nouns (with subjects in bold): **1.** **motorcycle**, ice; **3.** **snowman**, sun; **5.** **Rain**, game

Activity 15, page 287

Nouns (with subjects in bold): **1.** box, **she**, puppy; **3.** **truck**, fruit, market; **5.** **I**, money, bed

Activity 16: Teamwork, page 288

Nouns (with subjects in bold): **1.** dugout, **John**, jokes, teammates; **3.** Monday, **professor**, quiz, verbs; **5.** lunch, **we**, pie, dessert

Activity 17, page 288

A. 1. Cross out: in the cafeteria; Subject: fight; Action verb: erupted; **3.** Cross out: of snakes; Subject: fear; Linking verb: is; **5.** Cross out: on that rock; Subject: lizard; Linking verb: seems; **B. 1.** Cross out: At five o'clock, in Baltimore; Subject: train; Action verb: arrived; **3.** Cross out: under the bridge, for three days; Subject: We; Helping verb + main verb: had played; **5.** Cross out: about the war, about it; Subject: Conversations; Helping verb + main verb: should change; **C. 1.** Cross out: On New Year's Eve, of champagne, in my face; Subject: bottle; Action verb: exploded; **3.** Cross out: In the afternoon, over the ocean, from the hilltop; Subject: we; Helping verb + main verb: can see; **5.** Cross out: At the school, about the new play area, next to the parking lot; Subject: children; Linking verb: looked

Activity 18, page 289

A. 1. Cross out: quietly; Subject: motor; Action verb: ran; **3.** Cross out: difficult; Subject: exam; Linking verb: was; **5.** Cross out: guilty; Subject: suspect; Helping verb + main verb: might confess; **B. 1.** Cross out: retired, often; Subject: nurse; Action verb: volunteers; **3.** Cross out: sticky, delicious; Subject: rice; Linking verb: tastes; **5.** Cross out: popular, later; Subject: performer; Helping verb + main verb: will sing; **C. 1.** Cross out: leather, somewhat, heavy; Subject: suitcase; Linking verb: is; **3.** Cross out: Hairy, often, little; Subject: spiders; Action verb: scare; **5.** Cross out: Oddly, rich, handsome; Subject: Estelle; Action verb: dumped

Activity 19, page 290

A. 1. Cross out: After class, substitute; Subject: teacher; Action verb: cried; **3.** Cross out: On her birthday, sad; Subject: Angela; Linking verb: seemed; **5.** Cross out: Before a run, tight; Subject: you; Helping verb + main verb: should stretch; **B. 1.** Cross out: In summer, quickly; Subject: grass; Action verb: grows; **3.** Cross out: repeatedly, on his cell phone; Subject: David; Action verb: called; **5.** Cross out: in the pool, more, Subject: kids; Helping verb + main verb: might swim; **C. 1.** Cross out: At breakfast, hot, on my lap; Subject: coffee; Action verb: spilled; **3.** Cross out: After the concert, happy, with her performance; Subject: singer; Linking verb: appeared; **5.** Cross out: Before church, young, for the charity; Subject: volunteers; Helping verb + main verb: will sell; **D. 1.** Cross out: During the earthquake, frightened, quickly, under their desks; Subject: children; Action verb: crawled; **3.** Cross out: At night, nervous, on the door, twice; Subject: babysitter; Action verb: checked; **5.** Cross out: cracked, on the bridge, dangerous, to the inspector; Subject: concrete; Linking verb: appeared

Activity 20, page 293

1. Cross out: to Las Vegas; Subjects: Tyrone, friends; Verb: drove; **3.** Cross out: After the race; Subject: runners; Verbs: stretched, rested; **5.** Cross out: through the halls, of the kennel; Subjects: Barking, howling; Verbs: rang, echoed

Activity 21, page 293

1. (1) Subject: garden; Verb: is; **(3)** Subject: man; Verb: digs; **(5)** Subject: rabbit; Verb: hops; **(7)** Subject: They; Verb: chirp; **(9)** Subject: clouds; Verb: seem **2. (1)** Subject: Carlos; Verb: wants; **(3)** Subject: position; Verb: is; **(5)** Subject: It; Verbs: pays, offers; **(7)** Subject: she; Verb: emphasized; **(9)** Subject: He; Verbs: is, respects; **(11)** Subject: Carlos; Verb: has; **(13)** Subject: friends; Verb: send; **(15)** Subject: He; Verb: would be

Activity 22, page 295

1. Cross out: last, on my cell phone. Rewrite: The last call on my cell phone was from Elaine. **3.** Cross out: short, behind the curtain. Rewrite: The short man behind the curtain scared the children. **5.** Cross out: In the distance, swirling sand. Rewrite: In the distance, swirling sand danced across the desert.

Activity 23, page 296

Possible answers: **1.** Dogs were barking. **3.** I was caught. **5.** Voters are complaining.

Activity 24, page 296

Possible answers: **1.** A loud helicopter is flying over my house. **3.** My algebra teacher was shocked by my perfect exam score. **5.** A greedy executive is suing the president of the company.

Activity 25, page 297

Possible answers: **1.** Jayden ran the race. **3.** Bruno will reschedule his appointment. **5.** You may borrow money.

Activity 26, page 298

A. 1. Cross out: After school, with the soccer team. Possible sentence: After school, Natalie practices with the soccer team. **3.** Cross out: During the show, on the piano. Possible sentence: During the show, he will play two pieces on the piano. **5.** Cross out: In the parking lot, under her car. Possible sentence: In the parking lot, my sister found a diamond ring under her car. **B. 1.** Cross out: During his driver's test, near the shoe store, at the mall. Possible sentence: During his driver's test, Ezra hit the curb near the shoe store at the mall. **3.** Cross out: From a log, in the swamp, in the water. Possible sentence: From a log in the swamp, the frog watches the fish in the water. **5.** Cross out: In the yard, behind the house, for the party. Possible sentence: In the yard behind the house, my friend is hanging lights for the party.

Activity 27, page 300

Possible answers: **1.** The outfielder is jumping for the ball. **3.** I was encouraged by the teacher. **5.** Yolanda is living in Seattle.

Activity 28, page 300

Possible answers: **1.** On his sixteenth birthday, Kyle tried to pass his second driver's test. **3.** Along a dusty dirt road near the lake, we like to ride our motorcycles. **5.** Behind the convenience store, a thief was discovered with a crowbar by an angry police officer.

Activity 29, page 301

Possible edits: **1. (1)** Jack **was** going to pitch in the big game. **(3)** His pitching arm **was** looking good. **(5) He** videotaped Jack pitching the ball. **(7)** OK **(9) He** stretched to increase his flexibility. **(11)** The night of the big game, Jack **had an accident**. **(13) Jack tripped** over a stump. **(15)** As a result, **he was** unable to pitch in the game. **2. (1)** Last summer, **Maya and her mother** traveled to Canada. **(3) They** stayed in bed and breakfasts and inexpensive hotels. **(5) Maya and her mother tried** to take advantage of free attractions. **(7)** OK **(9) One store** sold postcards and lapel pins. **(11) The women were** surprised by all the fun they had for so little money. **(13)** Already, **they are** excited about taking another trip next summer! **3. (1)** OK **(3)** OK **(5)** In addition, almost no people **are** on the beach in winter time. **(7)** There **are** no tourists. **(9)** However, the sky **is** clear and blue. **(11)** Sometimes, other people **are** taking walks. **(13)** He **was** picking up smooth black rocks. **(15)** Mostly, **she** loves the sunset over the ocean. **(17) The beach** is lonely but quiet and beautiful.

Chapter 12

Activity 1, page 305

Possible sentence completions: **A. 1.** Dogs bark, and birds chirp. **3.** Terelle arrived, so I will leave. **B. 1.** The rain pours, and the sun shines. **3.** Julia disappeared, so Damien worried.

Activity 2, page 306

Possible answers (conjunctions) and relationships shown: **1.** so; result; **3.** so; result; **5.** but; contrast

Activity 3, page 306

Conjunctions and relationships shown: **1. a.** so; result; **b.** but; contrast; **c.** or; alternatives; **3. a.** so; result; **b.** but; contrast; **c.** and; combination

Activity 4, page 307

Possible sentence completions: **1. a.** The dentist found cavities, and he filled them. **b.** The dentist found cavities, so he scolded the patient. **c.** The dentist found cavities, but he didn't scold the patient. **3. a.** Tamika likes the outdoors, so she visits parks. **b.** Tamika likes the outdoors, but she hates bugs. **c.** Tamika likes the outdoors, and she loves hiking.

Activity 5, page 308

Possible responses: **1. a.** Similarity: Both people exercise. **b.** Difference: One person moves faster than the other. **3. a.** Similarity: Duane strongly dislikes both spinach and liver. **b.** Difference: Duane dislikes liver even more than spinach.

Activity 6, page 309

Possible answers: **1.** Subjects: Jennifer, Minh; Verbs: swam, played; Compound sentence: Jennifer swam laps, and Minh played tennis. **3.** Subjects: Bekka, Thomas; Verbs: enjoyed, left; Compound sentence: Bekka enjoyed the picnic, but Thomas left early.

Activity 7, page 310

Possible compound sentences: **1.** My sister told a joke, and we laughed. **3.** Marcus swerved off the road, but his car did not crash. **5.** Nina walked into the room, and the guests yelled, "Surprise!"

Activity 8, page 310

Possible compound sentences: **1.** Kristoff danced, and his wife sang. **3.** Clea told the truth, but her husband lied. **5.** The president traveled, and the vice president stayed home.

Activity 9, page 311

Compound sentences: **1.** Many people floss their teeth, but they do not realize that flossing might help prevent heart disease. **3.** Mouth bacteria can build up, and it can travel to the heart. **5.** Flossing can prevent tooth and gum disease, and it can improve one's overall health.

Activity 11, page 312

Possible sentences: **1.** Simple sentence with compound verb: Victoria buys fabric and makes quilts. Compound sentence: Victoria buys fabric, and she makes quilts. **3.** Simple sentence with compound verb: The Jacobsons volunteer and donate money. Compound sentence: The Jacobsons volunteer, and they donate money. **5.** Simple sentence with compound verb: The skier fell but did not break her leg. Compound sentence: The skier fell, but she did not break her leg.

Activity 13, page 314

Possible sentences: **1.** Compound sentence with a conjunction: Red is flattering, and I wear it often. Compound sentence with a semicolon: Red is flattering; I wear it often. **3.** Compound sentence with a conjunction: I cheated at cards, and I regret it. Compound sentence with a semicolon: I cheated at cards; I regret it.

Activity 15: Teamwork, page 316

1. Compound sentence with a conjunction: Jamie likes a lot of teams, but the Orioles are his favorite. Compound sentence with a semicolon: Jamie likes a lot of teams; the Orioles are his favorite. **3.** Compound sentence with a conjunction: Jamie's mother baked a baseball-shaped cake, and Jamie loved it. Compound sentence with a semicolon: Jamie's mother baked a baseball-shaped cake; Jamie loved it. **5.** Compound sentence with a conjunction: Jamie wanted an autographed baseball, so his parents got one from his favorite player. Compound sentence with a semicolon: Jamie wanted an autographed baseball; his parents got one from his favorite player.

Activity 16: Teamwork, page 317

Possible sentence completions: **1. a.** The car is beautiful, but the gas mileage is poor. **b.** The car is beautiful, and it is fast. **c.** The car is beautiful; I want it. **3. a.** It rained last night, but the fireworks were not canceled. **b.** It rained last night, so the golf course is soaked. **c.** It rained last night; the rain continues today.

Activity 17, page 319

Possible prepositional phrase additions: **1.** Sentence 1: Randall lost his cell phone during his lunch break. Sentence 2: He found it in the cafeteria. Combination: Randall lost his cell phone during his lunch break, but he found it in the cafeteria. **3.** Sentence 1: The pitcher threw the baseball to the batter. Sentence 2: The batter hit the ball toward the stands. Combination: The pitcher threw the baseball to the batter, and the batter hit the ball toward the stands.

Activity 18, page 320

See Activity 17 answers for possible compound sentences. With added prepositional phrases: **1.** On Tuesday, Randall lost his cell phone during his lunch break, but he found it in the cafeteria after work. **3.** In the seventh inning, the pitcher threw the baseball to the batter, and the batter hit the ball toward the stands near third base.

Activity 21, page 322

Possible compound sentences: **1.** Katie and Jessica skipped class on Thursday and claimed that they had the flu; Mrs. Fiskall listened to their excuse but didn't believe them. **3.** Katie and Jessica cut class and drove to Denver, but they arrived late and had terrible seats in the back. **5.** Mrs. Fiskall and the other students noticed and were surprised by the "Rag Dolls" stamps on Katie's and Jessica's hands, and Mrs. Fiskall smirked and asked the girls if they enjoyed the concert.

Activity 22: Teamwork, page 323

Possible sentences: **1.** Combined simple sentences: **a.** Snowboarding and skiing are great exercise. **b.** These sports can be expensive and often require travel. Compound sentence: Snowboarding and skiing are great exercise, but these sports can be expensive and often require travel. **3.** Combined simple sentences: **a.** The murder suspect and the police officer struggled on the grass. **b.** The suspect broke free and escaped in a getaway car. Compound sentence: The murder suspect and the police officer struggled on the grass, but the suspect broke free and escaped in a getaway car. **5.** Combined simple sentences: **a.** Two gorillas and one baboon escaped from the zoo and fled to a suburban neighborhood. **b.** Zoo officers and police sped to the scene and captured the animals. Compound sentence: Two gorillas and one baboon escaped from the zoo and fled to a suburban neighborhood, so zoo officers and police sped to the scene and captured the animals.

Activity 23, page 325

Possible compound sentences: **1.** Joan is a professional dancer, but her boyfriend is clumsy, so they never go dancing together. **3.** Joseph can apply for a government loan, or he can ask his family for tuition aid; his new college will not allow him to work during the semester. **5.** During the long drought, the mayor and city officials were concerned about the water supply, so they restricted the city's water use and banned citizens from watering their lawns, and they threatened fines against violators.

Activity 24, page 326

Possible sentence completions: **1.** Erika needed a gift for her boyfriend's birthday, and she had only one hour to shop, so she purchased a gift card. **3.** Randall's term paper was due on Monday, but his computer and printer were broken, so he will turn the paper in late. **5.** During the blaze at the electronics factory, firefighters brought all the workers to safety and delivered first aid to the injured, so no one perished, but several people suffered from smoke inhalation.

Activity 25: Teamwork, page 327

Possible compound sentences: **1.** Yvonne was nervous about her job interview, but the interviewer was friendly and kind, so Yvonne felt more at ease. **3.** Pamela's doctor advised her to become more active, so she began walking two miles every morning, and she also signed up for a yoga class. **5.** Mr. Cobb and Mrs. Brien argue loudly on the street every Saturday morning, so sleeping restfully is difficult; sleeping late is impossible.

Activity 27, page 329

1. Subjects: shoes, they; Verbs: feel, are; **3.** Subjects: phone, she; Verbs: rang, answered; **5.** Subjects: Gina, she; Verbs: said, kissed

Activity 28, page 329

1. Cross out: at the mall, before lunch; Subjects: Rick, he; Verbs: is, will return; **3.** Cross out: behind the counter, of the store, to the robbers, in danger; Subjects: man, life; Verbs: must give, will be; **5.** Cross out: With enthusiasm, at the front, of the line, to their seats, near the stage, of the rock stars, with their cell phones; Subjects: fans, they; Verbs: ran, snapped

Activity 29, page 330

1. Subjects: cookies, cake; carrots, apples; Verbs: are, are; **3.** Subjects: thieves, police; Verbs: entered, took; found, arrested; **5.** Subjects: Chad, Kristie; teacher, students; Verbs: whispered, laughed; became, stared

Activity 30, page 330

1. Subjects: You, you, you; Verbs: can leave, can stay, will be; **3.** Subjects: explorers, they, they; Verbs: found, were, investigated; **5.** Subjects: Violet, she, it; Verbs: discovered, opened, contained

Activity 31, page 331

1. Subjects: You, we; Verbs: won, lost; **3.** Subjects: Elena, she; Verbs: stays, likes; relaxes, enjoys; **5.** Subjects: Chelsea, sister; business, sisters; Verbs: opened, was, opened

Activity 32, page 332

1. Subjects: Marcus, friends; Verbs: ate, liked; **3.** Subjects: He, he; Verbs: has lost, is. Punctuation of this compound sentence: He has lost ten pounds since then, so he is pleased about making the change. **5.** Subject: mother; Verbs: searched, found; **7.** Subjects: mother; she, husband; Verbs: grew, decided. Punctuation of this compound sentence: After reading the article, Marcus's mother grew concerned about her family's meat-rich diet, so she and her husband decided to make a change. **9.** Subjects: parents, sister; they, he; Verbs: feel, are, is. Punctuation of this compound sentence: Marcus's parents and sister feel better, so they are grateful to Marcus for helping them to change their lifestyle, and he is happy too.

Activity 33, page 333

1. b; **3.** c; **5.** c

Activity 34: Teamwork, page 334

1. Not all romances work out, and they can turn destructive. **3.** Romances can reduce the productivity of the couple, and other employees may be less productive, too. **5.** With all the potential problems of office romances, employees should look elsewhere for romance and leave office temptations alone.

Activity 35: Teamwork, page 336

1. tries to use a comma by itself as glue; **3.** has no glue; **5.** uses some other word as glue; **7.** tries to use a comma by itself as glue

Activity 36, page 337

1. comma splice. Possible revision: No task is simple; anything can interrupt it. **3.** correct compound sentence; **5.** correct compound sentence; **7.** correct compound sentence; **9.** run-on. Possible revision: You drive home with a smile on your face and with plans for ice cream parties with your friends. Life is good, very good.

Activity 37, page 339

1. Personal pronoun: they; What pronoun refers to: Ted and Louisa. Possible rewrite: Ted and Louisa were celebrating their tenth anniversary, so they chose a special restaurant. **3.** Personal pronoun: they; What pronoun refers to: Ted and Louisa. Possible rewrite: Ted and Louisa enjoyed the food, but they will never go to the Blue Sail again. **5.** Personal pronoun: they; What pronoun refers to: Three small children. Possible rewrite: Three small children were seated with their family nearby, and they were noisy throughout the evening. **7.** Personal pronoun: she; What pronoun refers to: mother. Possible rewrite: From time to time, the mother snapped at the children, and she annoyed Ted and Louisa with her sharp voice. **9.** Personal pronoun: she; What pronoun refers to: woman. Possible rewrite: At another nearby table, a woman held her cell phone to her ear and laughed repeatedly and loudly; she did not see the cold stares from the serving staff and from other patrons in the restaurant.

Activity 38, page 341

1. Demonstrative pronoun: that; What pronoun refers to: My boss yelled at me every day. Possible rewrite: My boss yelled at me every day, but that was only one reason behind my decision to quit. **3.** Demonstrative pronoun: this; What pronoun refers to: My boyfriend buys me flowers. Possible rewrite: My boyfriend buys me flowers for every special occasion, and this always makes me happy. **5.** Demonstrative pronoun: those; What pronoun refers to: mouse-shaped chocolates. Possible rewrite: For the holidays, I will make my famous mouse-shaped chocolates; those are big hits with my friends and family.

Activity 39, page 343

1. Additive expression: then. Possible rewrite: Scott quit his job at Burger Bun, and then he went on the road. **3.** Additive expression: for example. Possible rewrite: Scott had heard about the beauty of California; for example, California is home to the Sierra Nevada mountain range. **5.** Additive expression: plus. Possible rewrite: Scott earned quite a bit of money from his yard sale; plus, he had saved money from his job. **7.** Additive expression: for example. Possible rewrite: Along the way, Scott visited some interesting attractions; for example, he stopped at the Grand Canyon in Arizona and spent one night in glittering Las Vegas.

Activity 40, page 345

1. Transitional expression: as a result. Possible rewrite: John has been called greedy; as a result, people avoid him. **3.** Transitional expression: instead. Possible rewrite: He rarely bought dinner for his former girlfriend; instead, he bought her a drink at happy-hour prices and "treated" her to the free appetizers. **5.** Transitional expression: however. Possible rewrite: For a long time, John's friends have recommended counseling to him; however, John seems unaware of his problem and would find a counselor's fees too expensive anyway.

Activity 41, page 348

Possible revisions: **1.** This world is a busy place, and it is filled with noise. This world is a busy place; moreover, it is filled with noise. **3.** In our cars, we listen to the radio, or we talk on our cell phones. In our cars, we listen to the radio; otherwise, we talk on our cell phones. **5.** At busy times, we can take a walk in a peaceful place, or we can just sit in a quiet room and close our eyes for a few minutes. At busy times, we can take a walk in a peaceful place; otherwise, we can just sit in a quiet room and close our eyes for a few minutes.

Activity 42, page 349

1. Personal pronoun: she. Possible revision: Marianna was spending too much money on gasoline, so she did research on gas mileage. **3.** Additive expression: then. Possible revision: Marianna's mechanic checked her engine's efficiency; then, he tuned up her engine in an effort to improve the gas mileage. **5.** Transitional expression: otherwise. Possible revision: She now keeps her vehicle's tires inflated to the recommended pressure; otherwise, her gas mileage will be decreased.

Activity 43, page 350

Possible edits: **1. (1)** Most of us prefer a clutter-free place for paying bills and doing other tasks, **but** many of us suffer from messy workspaces. **(3)** A filing cabinet offers valuable storage space**; furthermore,** the different drawers can

help with organizing documents. **(5)** Wire baskets are also useful for organizing materials, **and** they can be stacked to save room on a desktop. **(7)** Time management also plays a role in clutter control; **for example,** you should look at each piece of mail only once and act on it or throw it away.
2. **(1)** The Greece Athena High School basketball team was winning, **and** it was the last game of the season. **(3)** Coach Jim Johnson sent autistic student Jason McElwain onto the court; this was Jason's first and only chance to play for his team. **(5)** In spite of his size, he loved basketball and served as the team's manager; also, he was one of the team's biggest fans. **(7)** Jason's teammates wanted him to make at least one basket, **so** they kept passing him the ball. **(9)** Jason sunk one two-point basket and six three-point shots; within three minutes, he had scored twenty points for his team. **(11)** He appeared on numerous television news programs, **and** he even met President Obama. **3.** **(1)** Sarah Breedlove Walker was a successful businesswoman; moreover, she became a role model for many African American women. **(3)** After losing her parents and then her husband, Breedlove went north. In her new home, she worked as a washerwoman for little pay. **(5)** In Denver, she met advertising expert Charles J. Walker, **and** he became her second husband. **(7)** Advertising drew thousands of people to Sarah Breedlove Walker's products, **so** it was the key to her success. **(9)** In a relatively short time, Breedlove Walker became one of the largest employers of African American women, **and** this is one of her most famous achievements. **(11)** Her generosity benefited many causes; for example, she contributed to schools, orphanages, and civil-rights groups.

Chapter 13

Activity 1, page 356

Possible sentences: **1.** Compound: It was Greg's birthday, so we baked him a cake. Complex: Because it was Greg's birthday, we baked him a cake. **3.** Compound: We called Greg's friends, and we surprised him with a party. Complex: After we called Greg's friends, we surprised him with a party. **5.** Compound: Greg loved the chocolate cake, but he loved the pineapple ice cream even more. Complex: Even though Greg loved the chocolate cake, he loved the pineapple ice cream even more.

Activity 2, page 357

Possible sentences: **1.** Compound: We must leave by noon, or we will be late. Complex: If we do not leave by noon, we will be late. **3.** Compound: You should close the door, or flies will come inside. Complex: If you do not close the door, flies will come inside. **5.** Compound: We lost power on campus, so classes were canceled. Complex: Since we lost power on campus, classes were canceled.

Activity 3, page 358

Possible complex sentences: **1.** After lightning struck nearby, the house shook. **3.** Before they left on their trip, they kissed their children. **5.** When Tammy sang off key, her voice hurt our ears.

Activity 5, page 360

Possible conjunctions: **1. a.** Although; **b.** Since; **3. a.** Although; **b.** Because

Activity 6, page 360

Possible sentence completions: **1. a.** Since the Willow Creek Bridge was under construction, Marta had to take a detour. **b.** Although the Willow Creek Bridge was under construction, Marta did not have to take a detour. **3. a.** Because Steven skipped lunch, he ate too much at dinner. **b.** Although Steven skipped lunch, he ate a light dinner. **5. a.** Because this restaurant has a dress code, we must go home and change into formal clothing. **b.** Even though this restaurant has a dress code, our casual clothing is acceptable.

Activity 7, page 361

Possible sentence completions: **1. a.** If Kaylee gets the job, she will buy a new car. **b.** If Kaylee does not get the job, she cannot buy a new car. **3. a.** If it stops raining soon, our basement will not flood. **b.** If it does not stop raining soon, our basement will flood. **5. a.** If I save money this summer, I can afford a new car. **b.** If I do not save money this summer, I cannot afford a new car.

Activity 8, page 362

Possible sentence completions: **1.** If Mary is going to Brad's party, I refuse to attend. Even if Mary is going to Brad's party, I will be there. **3.** If apples are not on sale, we should buy some oranges. Even if apples are not on sale, we should buy some.

Activity 9, page 363

Possible sentence completions: **1.** Unless you earn an A on this essay, you will not pass the course. **3.** Unless Aunt Stella is out of town, we can visit her on Saturday. **5.** Unless everyone dislikes chocolate, your dessert will be a hit.

Activity 10, page 363

Possible sentence completions: **1.** Until we pay off the car, we cannot buy a new dishwasher. **3.** Until I buy more milk, I cannot eat this cereal. **5.** Until Chan arrives at the office, we cannot begin the meeting.

Activity 11: Teamwork, page 364

Possible sentence completions: **1. a.** Even if Jessica gets a better-paying job, she will not be able to buy her own home. **b.** Unless Jessica gets a better-paying job, she will not be able to buy her own home. **c.** If Jessica does not get a better-paying job, she will not be able to buy her own home. **d.** Even if Jessica does not get a better-paying job, she will be able to buy her own home. **e.** Unless Jessica does not get a better-paying job, she will be able to buy her own home. **3. a.** Even if the children finish dinner, they cannot have ice cream. **b.** Unless the children finish dinner, they cannot have ice cream. **c.** If the children do not finish dinner, they cannot have ice cream. **d.** Even if the children do not finish dinner, they can have ice cream. **e.** Unless the children do not finish dinner, they can have ice cream.

Activity 12, page 365

Possible sentence completions: **1. a.** Since it is raining outside, I cannot mow the lawn. **b.** Even if it is raining outside, I can mow the lawn. **c.** While it is raining outside, I cannot mow the lawn. **3. a.** Before you go to Germany, you have to get a passport. **b.** If you go to Germany, you should visit a major city. **c.** After you go to Germany, you will have learned some German. **5. a.** When I forgot Aaron's birthday, he was hurt. **b.** Because I forgot Aaron's birthday, he was hurt. **c.** Until I forgot Aaron's birthday, he was my good friend.

Activity 13, page 366

1. Although we had expected to have a great time, our cruise to Mexico was a disappointment. **3.** We had to wait two hours before we could enter our room. **5.** Aunt Anna fell over a railing while she was taking a yoga class. **7.** Uncle Rick disappeared after we arrived on the island of Cozumel. **9.** Aunt Anna marched into the kitchen to complain after she was served an overdone steak.

Activity 14, page 369

Possible sentence combinations: **1.** Compound—with coordinating conjunction and comma: The factory closed, and the warehouse stopped operating. Compound—with semicolon and transitional expression: The factory closed; in addition, the warehouse stopped operating. Complex—with subordinating conjunction at beginning of sentence: After the factory closed, the warehouse stopped operating. Complex—with subordinating conjunction in middle of sentence: The warehouse stopped operating after the factory closed. **3.** Compound—with coordinating conjunction and comma: Randall cooks, or we eat out. Compound—with semicolon and transitional expression: Randall cooks; otherwise, we eat out. Complex—with subordinating conjunction at beginning of sentence: If Randall cooks, we eat out. Complex—with subordinating conjunction in middle of sentence: We eat out if Randall cooks.

Activity 16, page 371

1. Subjects: baby, he; Verbs: sleeps, eats; **3.** Subjects: spider, Marco; Verbs: crawls, will scream; **5.** Subjects: Daniel, it; Verbs: drove, was snowing

Activity 17, page 371

1. Cross out: sick, in bed, for at least ten hours; Subjects: I, I; Verbs: feel, will stay; **3.** Cross out: happy, with the rosebush, in their garden; Subjects: neighbors, we; Verbs: seem, should get; **5.** Cross out: plump, from the bush, in the yard, seven, of jam, for her friends; Subjects: Iris, she; Verbs: picked, made

Activity 18, page 372

1. Subjects: you, we; Verbs: will cook, clean; **3.** Subjects: players, rain, sun; Verbs: ran, stopped, returned; **5.** Subjects: bread, rolls; chef, assistants; Verbs: bake, cool; will peel, wash

Activity 19, page 373

1. If you sleep until eleven, you will miss the beautiful sunrise. **3.** correct; **5.** Life became much more complicated and stressful for Jeremy after he won the lottery.

Activity 20, page 375

1. Fragment: Because he had a large balance on his credit card. Revision: Doug was in debt. Because he had a large balance on his credit card, he felt depressed. **3.** Fragment: Until the job was done. Revision: Bill needed help with a construction job. Doug could work for Bill until the job was done. **5.** Fragment: After Doug took the construction job. Revision: After Doug took the construction job, he put the money from this job in a separate account. He paid off the credit card from this account.

Activity 21, page 376

1. Fragment: If chipmunks become dependent on humans for food. Revision: Visitors should not feed chipmunks in the park. If chipmunks become dependent on humans for food, they can starve during a long, cold winter. Then, the population may be lower in the spring. **3.** Fragment: Even though fast food seems modern. Revision: Even though fast food seems modern, remains of fast-food restaurants have been found in ancient Roman ruins. People could sit down and eat at these restaurants or get their food "to go." **5.** Fragment: Because these workers wore through trousers quickly. Revision: In the 1800s, Levi Strauss invented denim jeans for miners in California. Because these workers wore through trousers quickly, they needed something more durable. Strauss made tough trousers from canvas and sold them to the miners.

Activity 22, page 378

1. Fragment: because the roads were icy. Revision: It was snowing heavily. We drove very slowly up the mountain because the roads were icy. **3.** Fragment: Even though we were tired; Revision: We worked in the yard until noon. Even though we were tired, we finished the mowing and the weeding. **5.** Fragment: since she has a talent for math.

Revision: Marianne handles the department budget since she has a talent for math. Lorenzo handles creative decisions.

Activity 23, page 379

Edits: **1. (1)** Fragment: Because he wanted to understand his country and himself better. Revision: In October of 1973, Peter Jenkins began a long walk across America because he wanted to understand his country and himself better. **(3)** correct; **(5)** Fragment: when he reached New Orleans. Revision: His journey began in New York and ended when he reached New Orleans. **(7)** Fragment: While Jenkins was on the road. Revision: While Jenkins was on the road, he met many kind and interesting people. **(9)** Fragment: After he completed his long journey. Revision: After he completed his long journey, he wrote a book called *A Walk across America.* **2. (1)** Fragment: Since competition for good jobs can be fierce. Revision: Since competition for good jobs can be fierce, your résumé must be correct, clear, and professional. **(3)** correct; **(5)** correct; **(7)** Fragment: Before you submit your résumé. Revision: Before you submit your résumé, proofread it very carefully for errors. **(9)** Fragment: Because an employee represents the company to others. Revision: Because an employee represents the company to others, employers look for applicants with a command of the English language. **3. (1)** Fragment: When TV personality Oprah Winfrey opened a school for disadvantaged girls near Johannesburg, South Africa. Revision: When TV personality Oprah Winfrey opened a school for disadvantaged girls near Johannesburg, South Africa, she made worldwide headlines. **(3)** Fragment: Even though this academy cost about $40 million. Revision: Even though this academy cost about $40 million, Winfrey believes that the money is well spent. **(5)** correct; **(7)** correct; **(9)** Fragment: If girls are educated. Revision: If girls are educated, they are less likely to become infected. **(11)** correct

Chapter 14

Activity 1, page 383

In the following sentences, the descriptive clauses are underlined. The rest of the sentence is the main clause. **1.** Repeated item: The vase. Complex sentence: The vase <u>that fell</u> broke. **3.** Repeated item: The monster. Complex sentence: The monster <u>that breathes fire</u> terrifies. **5.** Repeated item: A marriage. Complex sentence: A marriage <u>that is based on trust</u> succeeds.

Activity 2, page 384

In the following sentences, the descriptive clauses are underlined. **1.** The man <u>who left</u> was sick. **3.** The day <u>when I won the Megabucks</u> is now a personal holiday. **5.** The big red house <u>where we were born</u> is now a bed-and-breakfast for visitors to Mt. Monadnock.

Activity 3, page 385

Possible sentence completions: **1.** The truck that my brother owned was stolen. **3.** Within three months, the factory where Leonid works will be shut down. **5.** For me, the moment when the plane lands is the scariest part of flying.

Activity 4, page 386

Possible sentence completions: **1.** Teens who smoke endanger their health. **3.** The handsome stranger whom you kissed is my brother. **5.** The car that you hit belongs to the police commissioner.

Activity 6, page 387

Possible sentence completions: **1.** The time when you were sick was frightening. **3.** The skating rink where we met is still popular with young people. **5.** The pool where I swim was closed during the water shortage.

Activity 7: Teamwork, page 388

Possible sentences: **1.** Descriptive clause in the middle: The field where you play soccer flooded. Descriptive clause at the end: Storms flooded the field where you play soccer. **3.** Descriptive clause in the middle: The day when we went fishing was rainy. Descriptive clause at the end: It rained the day when we went fishing. **5.** Descriptive clause in the middle: The rice that we made tasted like sawdust. Descriptive clause at the end: No one will eat the rice that we made.

Activity 8: Teamwork, page 391

1. a. Descriptive clause: that we saw last night. The information is necessary; it tells us specifically which movie was seen. **b.** Descriptive clause: which starred Jack Black. The information is optional; the main point of the sentence is that the movie was a comedy set at a private school. The fact that it starred Jack Black is optional information. **3. a.** Descriptive clause: which requires much skill. The information is optional; the main point of the sentence is that chess is a good way to keep the brain sharp. The fact that the game requires much skill is optional information. **b.** Descriptive clause: that we watched on television. The information is necessary; it makes it clear that the particular chess game that was seen on television ended in a fight.

Activity 9, page 392

Possible combinations (descriptive clauses are underlined): **1.** Repeated item: Markeese's computer. Markeese's computer, <u>which was overloaded</u>, crashed. **3.** Repeated item: Pauline's vacuum cleaner. Pauline's vacuum cleaner, <u>which was cheap and unreliable</u>, chewed up her rug. **5.** Repeated item: The fireworks. The fireworks, <u>which were loud and colorful</u>, made the children cheer.

Activity 10, page 393

Possible combinations (descriptive clauses are underlined): **1.** We took the subway, which is cheaper than a taxi. **3.** We ate the pizza that was left over from the party. **5.** I like dark chocolate, which is bolder in flavor than milk chocolate.

Activity 11, page 393

Possible sentence completions: **1. a.** The dream that I had last night seemed real. **b.** The dream, which took place at my job, seemed real. **3. a.** Seashells that have unusual shapes and colors are fun to collect. **b.** Seashells, which are common on this beach, are fun to collect. **5. a.** Dance shows that feature celebrities are on television almost every night. **b.** Dance shows, which my husband hates, are on television almost every night.

Activity 12, page 394

Possible combinations (descriptive clauses are underlined): **1.** Repeated item: Yolanda. Yolanda, who was the best player on our team, quit. **3.** Repeated item: Babies. Babies who are not shown affection can grow up with emotional problems. **5.** Repeated item: Billy. Billy, who is terrified of clowns and performing animals, refuses to go to the circus.

Activity 13, page 395

Possible combinations (descriptive clauses are underlined): **1.** I will plan the party for Taki, who is my best friend. **3.** I want to pay the kid who shoveled our driveway after the snowstorm. **5.** The detective gave the crime-scene information to the officer who was in charge of investigating the murder.

Activity 14, page 396

Possible combinations (descriptive clauses are underlined): **1.** The man whom you like just walked into the room. **3.** The suspect whom prosecutors charged with the crime was found innocent. **5.** The doctor whom you recommended is my best friend's doctor.

Activity 15, page 397

Possible combinations (descriptive clauses are underlined): **1.** Nauset Beach, where my sister was married, is home to Nauset Lighthouse. **3.** On Saturdays, when many people relax, Jack works long hours. **5.** Dan plays guitar at the bar where his brother works.

Activity 16: Teamwork, page 398

Possible sentences: **1.** The warm night when we danced together on the back patio is a happy memory for me. **3.** The large yellow moon that rose over the lake dazzled us with its pale beauty. **5.** My co-worker Danice will make deliciously greasy and crunchy fish and chips, which she cooked for last year's company picnic at the state park.

Activity 17, page 399

Possible sentences: **1.** The odd-looking man who left the mysterious little package on our front porch ran into a waiting car and left the scene. **3.** The angry note that my nosy neighbor left on my car windshield in the morning made me hop up and down with fury. **5.** Detective Daniels ducked into the dark, smoke-filled club where the famous actress was last seen before she disappeared.

Activity 18, page 401

Possible sentences: **1.** Complex—with descriptive clause: Darla loves pets, which she collects. Compound—with coordinating conjunction and comma: Darla loves pets, so she collects them. Compound—with semicolon and transitional expression: Darla loves pets; therefore, she collects them. Complex—with subordinating conjunction at beginning of sentence: Because Darla loves pets, she collects them. **3.** Complex—with descriptive clause: The fan who broke into the star's apartment was arrested. Compound—with coordinating conjunction and comma: The fan broke into the star's apartment, and she was arrested. Compound—with semicolon and transitional expression: The fan broke into the star's apartment; as a result, she was arrested. Complex—with subordinating conjunction at the beginning of sentence: As the fan broke into the star's apartment, she was arrested.

Activity 20, page 403

1. Descriptive clause: that fell (circle this as subject and verb of clause); Subject of main clause: glass; Verb of main clause: broke. Two simple sentences: The glass fell. The glass broke. **3.** Descriptive clause: which fell (circle this as subject and verb of clause); Subject of main clause: stock market; Verb of main clause: rose. Two simple sentences: The stock market fell. The stock market rose again. **5.** Descriptive clause: who laughed (circle this as subject and verb of clause); Subject of main clause: boy; Verb of main clause: woke. Two simple sentences: The boy laughed. The boy woke the baby.

Activity 21, page 403

1. Descriptive clause: which were clogged with dead leaves; Subject and verb of clause: which were; Subject of main clause: gutters; Verb of main clause: overflowed. Two simple sentences: During the violent rainstorm, the gutters overflowed with brown water. The gutters were clogged with dead leaves. **3.** Descriptive clause: who works in my department; Subject and verb of clause: who works; Subject of main clause: Andre; Verb of main clause: invited. Two simple sentences: After a long day of work, my friend Andre invited me to dinner with him and some other co-workers. My friend Andre works in my department. **5.** Descriptive clause: who drives the loud and out-of-control school bus every day; Subject and verb of clause: who drives; Subject of main clause: Doreen; Verb of main clause: remains. Two simple sentences: Patient Doreen remains calm in every situation. Patient Doreen drives the loud and out-of-control school bus every day.

Activity 22, page 405

1. Descriptive clause: whom I adore; Subject and verb of clause: I adore; Subject of main clause: Jill; Verb of main clause: has arrived. Two simple sentences: Jill has arrived. I adore Jill. **3.** Descriptive clause: where Grandma lives; Subject and verb of clause: Grandma lives; Subject of main clause: house; Verb of main clause: has. Two simple sentences: The house has a barn. Grandma lives in the house. **5.** Descriptive clause: which you hate; Subject and verb of clause: you hate; Subject of main clause: Nuts; Verb of main clause: are. Two simple sentences: Nuts are healthful. You hate nuts.

Activity 23, page 405

1. Descriptive clause: where many tourists visit a 17,400-pound ball of twine; Subject and verb of clause: tourists visit; Subject of main clause: friend; Verb of main clause: lives. Two simple sentences: My best friend from high school lives in Darwin, Minnesota. Many tourists visit a 17,400-pound ball of twine in Darwin, Minnesota. **3.** Descriptive clause: that I got for my last birthday; Subject and verb of clause: I got; Subject of main clause: parrot; Verb of main clause: screeches. Two simple sentences: In the evening, the cute little parrot screeches obnoxiously. I got the cute little parrot for my last birthday. **5.** Descriptive clause: when I drove to Vermont with my ex-husband and five cats; Subject and verb of clause: I drove; Subject of main clause: summer; Verb of main clause: was. Two simple sentences: The summer was unforgettable for several unpleasant reasons. I drove to Vermont with my ex-husband and five cats that summer.

Activity 24, page 408

Possible answers: **1.** Descriptive clause: who was trapped under the boulder. Correction of fragment: The hiker who was trapped under the boulder survived. **3.** Descriptive clause: that I purchased online. Correct. **5.** Descriptive clause: when we lived in the cabin. Correction of fragment: The summer when we lived in the cabin was uncomfortable. **7.** Descriptive clause: where we worked in our youth. Correct.

Activity 25, page 409

Possible answers: **1.** Descriptive clause: which the researchers found in a narrow cave in the desert. Correction of fragment: The fragile old dinosaur skeleton, which the researchers found in a narrow cave in the desert, was fifty feet long. **3.** Descriptive clause: who caught ten pounds of fresh trout in the stream. Correction of fragment: For lunch, my aunt, who caught ten pounds of fresh trout in the stream, fried the fish in butter. **5.** Descriptive clause: where high school students used to race cars dangerously on Saturday nights. Correction of fragment: The empty riverbed, where high school students used to race cars dangerously on Saturday nights, has been filled in with cement.

Activity 26, page 410

1. Fragment: When it's warm outside. Revision: I like to swim when it's warm outside. The pool is the perfect temperature. **3.** Fragment: Which he has collected since he was a child. Revision: Dan likes stamps, which he has collected since he was a child. He gets stamps for every birthday. **5.** Fragment: Where we find many good bargains. Revision: My daughter and I shop at Marconi's, where we find many good bargains. Last week, we both bought shoes there.

Activity 27, page 412

1. Fragment: The apples that fall to the ground. Possible revision: In September, we pick apples at my uncle's farm. The apples that fall to the ground are still useful. We pick them up and save them for applesauce. **3.** Fragment: My friend Portia, who writes for our local paper. Possible revision: The media are blamed for many wrongs. My friend Portia, who writes for our local paper, gets negative comments sometimes. She is upset by people's criticism. **5.** Fragment: Exercise that gets her blood flowing. Possible revision: My mother goes jogging every morning before work. Exercise that gets her blood flowing is her favorite. She also lifts weights at the gym. **7.** Fragment: Where the stolen car was hidden. Possible revision: I saw where the stolen car was hidden. Branches had been placed on top of it. A tarp covered the side closest to the street. I called the police. **9.** Fragment: Cucumbers, which do not agree with me. Possible revision: Cucumbers do not agree with me. They hurt my stomach and make me burp. I do not put them in salads. Also, I ask waiters to leave them out of my meals.

Activity 28, page 413

Possible edits: **1. (1 / 2)** The number of Americans who have been asked to make sacrifices in the wars in Iraq and Afghanistan has been relatively small. **(3 / 4)** Soldiers and their families have carried the full burden, which many people believe to be unfair. **(5)** In other wars, however, more Americans were asked to contribute. **(6 / 7)** For example, during World War II, citizens were asked to limit their use of gasoline, sugar, certain cloth, and other materials, which helped the government supply troops and the defense industry with necessary goods. **(8 / 9)** Also, the "Victory Gardens" that many private citizens grew accounted for about 40 percent of vegetables consumed during the war. **(11)** As a result, not just thousands but millions of Americans faced the possibility of losing a loved one—or their own life. **2. (1 / 2)** People who have a positive, optimistic outlook on life are likely to be healthier than negative people, researchers report. **(3)** correct; **(4 / 5)** One study, which was done among college students, found that positive students reported having more energy and fewer minor illnesses than negative students. **(6 / 7)** When researchers looked for the reasons for the better health of positive people, they found a few possible answers. **(8 / 9)** First, positive people tend to be more connected to others, which makes it easier for them to get the help and support that they need. **(11)** correct; **(12 / 13)** Regardless of the reason for the link between optimism and health, it is a good idea to adopt a positive attitude toward even bad events that come our way. **3. (1 / 2)** Most of us know people who like to collect certain objects, like dolls, baseball cards, or stamps. **(3 / 4)** However, some people feel compelled to fill their homes with things that many others would consider worthless—even garbage. **(5)** These people are known as *hoarders*. **(7)** correct; **(8 / 9)** It may also occur when people become unusually attached to objects. **(11 / 12)** Whatever the cause, hoarding is a serious problem that can cause difficulties in the lives of sufferers and their families. **(13)** correct; **(14 / 15)** Others have even been buried under piles of boxes that were stacked dangerously high. **(17 / 18)** For example, these professionals can recommend psychotherapy, which can help hoarders explore and change their behavior. **(19)** correct

Activity 31, page 416

1. Descriptive clause: that we saw at the zoo. Revision: The lion that we saw at the zoo roared. **3.** Descriptive clause: whom you met at my wedding. Revision: Valerie, whom you met at my wedding, takes care of five horses. **5.** Descriptive clause: where we had our first date. Revision: The restaurant where we had our first date is next to a jail. **7.** Descriptive clause: who stole the jewels. Revision: The thief who stole the jewels was captured by police. **9.** Descriptive clause: which took almost ten minutes. Revision: The answer, which took almost ten minutes, disappointed the audience.

Activity 32, page 417

Possible edits: **1. (1)** The health insurance crisis in the United States is a serious problem **that has drawn more attention in recent years.** **(3)** These frightening numbers, **which are worsening every year,** have led to attempts to establish national health insurance. **(5)** Politicians and organizations have offered various plans to address the insurance crisis. **(7)** Also, the government and private insurers may have to cooperate more closely to make sure that all citizens are covered. **(9)** However, if America does not find a way to address the problem, the number of citizens **who do not have insurance** will likely grow. **2. (1)** The day **when we had my daughter Abby's birthday party** didn't go as I had planned, but Abby had fun anyway. **(3)** Then, the tent **where we were planning to hold the party** collapsed in a heap. **(5)** Finally, the actor **whom we had hired to juggle and sing for the children** called my husband to cancel. **(7)** Also, we learned that the boy **who lives next door** is training to be an acrobat. **(9)** The happiest moment was at the end of the party**, when we presented Abby with a Gibson guitar**, which she has wanted for a long time.

Chapter 15

Activity 1, page 422

Possible sentence completions: **1.** Opening the door to his apartment, Dewayne was surprised by his friends. **3.** Making lasagna for dinner, Stephen burned his hand. **5.** Chasing the neighbor's cat, my dog got covered in mud.

Activity 2, page 422

1. Verbs in simple sentences: heard, looked. Sentence combination: Hearing screeching tires, Nicole looked out her window. **3.** Verbs in simple sentences: wanted, grabbed. Sentence combination: Wanting to help, Nicole grabbed her first aid kit. **5.** Verbs in simple sentences: trembled, thanked. Sentence combination: Trembling with fear, the driver thanked Nicole for her help.

Activity 3, page 423

Possible sentences: **1.** Driving to work, Miguel listened to the radio. **3.** Investigating a burglary, the detective questioned nearby residents. **5.** Throwing a fast ball, the pitcher hurt his shoulder.

Activity 4, page 424

Possible sentence completions: **1.** To get to work on time, Frank gets up at 5 A.M. **3.** To repair the broken lamp, you will need a new switch. **5.** To learn her lines, the actress rehearsed them with her roommate.

Activity 5, page 424

1. *To* + verb combination: to remodel; Sentence combination: To remodel their home, David and Muriel took out a small loan. **3.** *To* + verb combination: to learn; Sentence combination: To learn how to lay the carpet himself, David took a free class at a building supply store. **5.** *To* + verb combination: to stay; Sentence combination: To stay out of the way, Muriel visited her sister in Lake Tahoe.

Activity 6: Teamwork, page 425

Possible sentences: **1.** To win the election, the mayor promised lower taxes. **3.** To study for exams, many students review their notes. **5.** To reduce stress, the yoga students breathe deeply.

Activity 7, page 426

Possible sentence completions: **1.** Confused by the numerous signs, the driver got lost. **3.** Excited about his new job, Isaac called his friends. **5.** Frightened by the large spider, Professor Stevens jumped onto a chair.

Activity 8, page 427

1. Complete verb: was discouraged; Sentence combination: Discouraged about his poor writing skills, Gregory talked to his instructor. **3.** Complete verb: was determined; Sentence combination: Determined to pass his writing course, Gregory made an appointment with the tutor. **5.** Complete verb: was convinced; Sentence combination: Convinced that he could pass the course, Gregory thanked the tutor and his instructor.

Activity 9: Teamwork, page 428

Possible sentences: **1.** Diagnosed with a bad sprain, the patient asked for crutches. **3.** Satisfied with the refund, the customer thanked the manager. **5.** Covered with lumps and bruises, the boxer collapsed.

Activity 10, page 428

1. Following a few tips, employees can deal with most difficult colleagues. **3.** Encouraged by such praise, a difficult co-worker may become less defensive. **5.** To avoid misunderstandings through e-mail, employees should discuss difficult situations face to face.

Activity 11, page 430

Possible sentences: **1.** Phrase at the beginning: Driving to the dinner party, Roseanne got lost. Phrase at the end: Roseanne got lost driving to the dinner party. **3.** Phrase at the beginning: To get tickets to the concert, I stood in line for five hours. Phrase at the end: I stood in line for five hours to get tickets to the concert. **5.** Phrase at the beginning: Captured as he retreated from a firefight, the enemy soldier refused to provide information on his mission. Phrase in the middle: The enemy soldier, captured as he retreated from a firefight, refused to provide information on his mission.

Activity 12, page 433

1. Ringing up purchases in a grocery store, Sarah looked longingly out the window at people who seemed happier. **3.** OK; **5.** Sarah, pleased that she took control of her life, got the job and now flies from city to city.

Activity 13, page 434

1. Modifying phrase: To keep her apartment tidy; Subject: Jennifer; Verb: spends; **3.** Modifying phrase: gliding slowly down the aisle; Subject: bride; Verb: tripped; **5.** Modifying phrase: Muttering about nosy reporters; Subject: Senator Smith; Verb; left

Activity 14, page 436

1. Question: Who or what was seated in the dentist's chair? Subject: patient; **3.** Question: Who or what was returning to the car? Subjects: Jake, I; **5.** Question: Who or what was landing the plane? Subject: pilot

Activity 15, page 437

1. Subject: Kevin; Actions: Concerned, called; **3.** Subject: you; Actions: To save, should fly; **5.** Subject: employees; Actions: To enter, must have

Activity 16, page 438

Possible sentence completions: **1.** Running backwards to catch a fly ball, the right-fielder bumped into the stands. **3.** Turning left onto Colorado Avenue, the taxi driver saw a man roller skating in a clown suit. **5.** Stung by an angry hornet, the small child cried and ran home.

Activity 17, page 438

Possible sentence completions: **1.** Frightened by the loud thunder, the dog crawled under the bed. **3.** To save money for a house, Karin took a second job. **5.** Opening up the morning newspaper, we were shocked by the photos of the huge downtown fire.

Activity 18, page 439

Possible revisions: **1.** Walking to work one morning, Salina saw a briefcase fall from a skyscraper onto the sidewalk. **3.** Seated in the back row, we found it difficult to see and hear the performers. **5.** Exhausted by the long drive, Jake found the hotel bed inviting.

Activity 19, page 440

Possible revisions: **1.** While he was fishing for salmon, Matt's fishing line became snagged on a branch. **3.** Before you bake oatmeal cookies, the pan must first be sprayed with vegetable oil. **5.** If Shelley wants to get her passport by May, the application must be submitted by March.

Activity 20, page 441

Possible revisions: **1.** First revision: Writing the last paragraph of his essay, Larry saw his cat step on the delete key. Second revision: While Larry was writing the last paragraph of his essay, his cat stepped on the delete key. **3.** First revision: To be eligible for the athletic scholarship, the athlete must be recommended by a college coach. Second revision: If the athlete is to be eligible for the athletic scholarship, a college coach must recommend the athlete.

Activity 21, page 442

Possible edits: **1. (1)** correct; **(3)** To get the best deals, **she purchases items in bulk. (5)** Driving to the store, **she snacks on** carrot sticks or peanut butter on crackers **to keep** from shopping while hungry: a major cause of over-purchasing. **(7)** correct; **(9)** correct; **(11)** To save more money, **I want to follow Marta's good example.** **2.** **(1)** Watching movies, **most of us are unaware of** the effort and history behind motion pictures. **(3)** correct; **(5) When a user spun** the device, the pictures ran together to create the illusion of real motion. **(7)** correct; **(9)** Wanting to take advantage of this new interest, **business people opened** hundreds of movie theaters **in the United States** through the early years of the twentieth century. **(11)** correct; **(13)** Experimenting with "gramophones" (record players) and film, **inventors matched** recorded sounds with motions on the screen. **(15)** correct

Activity 24, page 445

Misplaced modifiers and possible revisions: **1.** Misplaced modifier: biking down the street. First revision: Biking down the street, Melissa was thinking about Brad Pitt. Second revision: As Melissa was biking down the street, she was thinking about Brad Pitt. **3.** Misplaced modifier: using infrared cameras. First revision: Using infrared cameras, rescuers spotted the missing hikers. Second revision: Rescuers, because they used infrared cameras, spotted the missing hikers by the river. **5.** Misplaced modifier: seated at the head of the table. First revision: Grandpa, seated at the head of the table, carved the rib roast. Second revision: Grandpa carved the rib roast because he was seated at the head of the table.

Activity 25, page 447

1. Misplaced prepositional phrase: in my best work shoes. Possible revision: In my best work shoes, I chased my cat. **3.** Misplaced prepositional phrase: over the loudspeaker. Possible revision: The principal announced over the loudspeaker that students could receive free counseling. **5.** Misplaced prepositional phrase: with a rash. Possible revision: The patient with a rash sat for two hours in the doctor's waiting room.

Activity 26, page 448

1. Misplaced adverb: nearly. Revision: At the garage sale, Tiffany earned nearly $500. **3.** Misplaced adverb: even. Revision: Even my lazy roommate takes out the trash. **5.** Misplaced adverb: hardly. Revision: We had driven hardly three miles when the tire went flat.

Activity 27, page 449

Possible edits: **1.** **(1)** correct; **(3)** correct; **(5) Even cigarettes** labeled as "light" can contain enough nicotine to hook users. **(7) Compelled to get "their fix," they** smoke more and more cigarettes. **(9)** correct; **2.** **(1)** correct; **(3)** In 1840s Vienna, doctor Ignaz Semmelweis began to suspect that an "invisible agent" was causing a deadly fever **among new mothers** at his hospital. **(5) Nearly all** of the doctors failed to wash their hands between the autopsies and the deliveries. **(7)** However, he began to require that all doctors wash their hands **with a special solution** before seeing patients. **(9)** correct; **(11) Angered by the reactions to his efforts to improve sanitary conditions, he** abruptly left Vienna.

Chapter 16

Activity 1, page 456

1. walks; **3.** remains; **5.** visit

Activity 2, page 456

1. has; **3.** are; **5.** have; **7.** is; **9.** does

Activity 3, page 457

1. are; **3.** N/A; **5.** have; **7.** N/A; **9.** have; **11.** does

Activity 4, page 458

1. robbed; **3.** waited; **5.** rented; **7.** ended; **9.** arrested

Activity 6, page 467

1. Cross out: at work; Subject: coffee; Verb: tastes. The sentence is OK. **3.** Cross out: on online shopping sites; Subject: theft; Verb: are. Rewrite: Identity theft on online shopping sites **is** increasingly common. **5.** Cross out: tired after their long days of school and homework; Subject: children; Verb: collapses. Rewrite: The children, tired after their long days of school and homework, **collapse** on the couch every night.

Activity 7, page 469

1. Subject: names; Verb: is. Rewrite: What **are** your children's names? **3.** Subject: coats; Verb: are. The sentence is OK. **5.** Subject: shows; Verb: is. Rewrite: There **are** several good crime shows on television.

Activity 8, page 470

1. watch; **3.** parks; **5.** fills

Activity 9, page 471

1. likes; **3.** wants; **5.** volunteer

Activity 10, page 472

1. Do you **want to** try my recipe for lasagna? **3.** Ernest **would have** won the lottery if he had played his number this week. **5.** Nobody is **going to** believe your story; you **should have** made up a better one.

Activity 11, page 473

Corrected verbs: **1.** flooded; **3.** hit; **5.** walked

Activity 12, page 476

1. correct; **3.** She endured savage treatment, and her young son Peter **was** sold to another family who abused him. **5.** In 1843, she **changed** her name to Sojourner Truth and spread her message everywhere she went. **7.** In this speech, this genuine, plain-speaking woman **drove** home the point that women should be regarded as equals to men.

Activity 13, page 477

1. Of all NASA's space missions, one of the most familiar to Americans **is** Apollo 13 even though it never reached its destination. **3.** Official NASA records **show** that almost 56 hours into the flight, oxygen tank 2 on the spacecraft blew up. **5.** correct; **7.** correct; **9.** correct; **11.** correct

Activity 14, page 479

1. correct; **3.** correct; **5.** correct; **7.** Also, working in the trades **can** provide a lot of satisfaction and a sense of accomplishment. **9.** correct

Activity 15, page 481

1. correct; **3.** correct; **5.** If Stephen **could** have any job he wanted, he would become a partner in Pablo's studio, perhaps opening his own studio later on. **7.** correct; **9.** correct

Activity 16, page 482

1. correct; **3.** Adam and Anna's parents grilled fish and roasted lamb, and **Aunt Marie prepared** a special yogurt sauce for the lamb. **5. Other guests provided many** additional desserts. **7.** correct

Activity 17, page 483

1. (1) correct; **(3)** correct; **(5)** correct; **(7)** correct; **(9)** Gardening **provides** great exercise, and it would help many people to lose weight. **(11)** correct; **(13)** Recently, I helped to establish a garden in my own neighborhood, and I wish I would **have** done it sooner. **2. (1)** It happens every day: someone **gets** a forwarded e-mail from a friend that contains a serious-sounding warning or "news" item. **(3)** correct; **(5)** One recent "news flash" **claimed** that using a cell phone while it is charging could lead to electrocution. **(7)** Investigators **found** these items—and many others—to be false. **(9)** First, if an e-mail **shouts** "This is not a hoax!" it may very well be one. **(11)** Most important, if an e-mail **asks** for money, your credit card information, or any other personal information, do not respond, even if the sender claims to be a bank or another trustworthy-sounding organization. **(13)** Consumer-affairs offices in many states **say** that Internet fraud is mounting, and they **recommend** that people report potential scams to the authorities.

Activity 20, page 487

1. has earned; **3.** has lived; **5.** have discovered

Activity 21, page 496

1. a. "Two weeks ago": P; Verb: wrecked; **b.** "Over the past six months": D; Verb: has wrecked; **3. a.** "In 2007": P; Verb: worked; **b.** "For the past few years": D; Verb: has worked; **5. a.** "Recently": D; Verb: has collected; **b.** "During her vacation": P; Verb: collected

Activity 22, page 497

1. arrived, had disappeared; **3.** had seen, exceeded; **5.** had stolen, reached

Activity 23, page 498

1. (1) has shaped; **(3)** got; **(5)** lost; **(7)** had moved; **(9)** tried; **(11)** saves; **(13)** have heard
2. (1) have asked; **(3)** published; **(5)** do; **(7)** need; **(9)** see; **(11)** N/A; **(13)** had completed

Chapter 17

Activity 1, page 502

1. something: GT; **3.** she: SP; it: ST; something: GT; anything: GT; **5.** Everyone: GP

Activity 3, page 504

1. We: S; we: S; us: O; **3.** I: S; her: O; she: S; she: S; me: O; **5.** I: S; me: O

Activity 4, page 505

1. I; **3.** she, me; **5.** me, them, that

Activity 6, page 506

1. My, his, our; **3.** my, its; **5.** our

Activity 7, page 508

Possible edits: **1.** Late on Friday, **the phone** rang in the dark house. **3.** Then, **a voice** asked, "Is this Mark Ranco?" **5.** correct; **7.** Then, he saw **a mysterious-looking van** parked outside. **9. Mark** asked the caller, "Who are you?" **11.** correct

Activity 8, page 510

1. We have always loved Artie's Seafood Restaurant because **we** can get delicious red snapper there. **3.** As we drove over the summit of the mountain, **we** could see all the lights of Las Vegas glittering in the valley. **5.** Samantha wants to work on a cruise ship because **she** will be able to meet so many different people there.

Activity 9, page 510

1. When Annika set out to ride her bicycle across the United States, she was not prepared for the dangers and hardships that **she** would encounter. **3.** Also, Annika didn't realize how close cars would come to **her** as they passed on the highway. **5.** correct

Activity 10, page 512

Possible edits: **1.** correct; **3.** Also, applicants can prepare for **the interview** by thinking of questions to ask. **5.** correct; **7. Practicing answers to these questions** in front of a mirror will help an applicant respond confidently during the interview. **9.** For those who prepare well, **interviewing for a job** can be a life-changing experience.

Activity 11, page 514

Indefinite pronouns and possible rewrites: **1.** someone. In my history class, the A students always know the answer. **3.** anything. If we leave the house unlocked, a burglar could steal our valuables. **5.** No one. No member of this year's rival teams can beat Barry's home run record.

Activity 12, page 515

Indefinite pronouns and possible rewrites: **1.** Everyone, their. Everyone brings his or her kids to the company outing. All employees bring their kids to the company outing. **3.** Someone, their. Someone dumps his or her garbage on the street every week. Strangers dump their garbage on the street every week. **5.** Everybody, their. Everybody wants his or her children to succeed. Concerned parents want their children to succeed.

Activity 13, page 517

1. I; **3.** N/A; **5.** N/A; **7.** N/A

Activity 14, page 518

1. I; **3.** she; **5.** she

Activity 15, page 519

1. O; its; **3.** O; its; **5.** I; their

Activity 16, page 520

Possible edits: **1. (1)** My roommate, Shawn, and **I** have had several disagreements over the past few weeks. **(3)** Therefore, he claims, I should pay a higher share of the electricity bill than **he**. **(5)** correct; **(7)** correct; **(9) His lack of consideration** really bothers me. **(11)** I am going to suggest that **he** and I have a serious discussion to try to resolve our conflicts. **(13)** My family back in Texas has given me **its** decision already: absolutely not. **2. (1)** correct; **(3) Who** would help her, and **who** would stand on the sidelines? **(5)** correct; **(7) The guilt** could stem from anything—from a dishonest act at work to a fight with a friend. **(9) Seeing the concern of others** might inspire witnesses to act. **(11)** Once, my husband and **I** saw a pedestrian get bumped by a car. **(13)** correct; **(15)** The other person arrived at the scene faster than **we**, but we were all able to help. **(17)** Based on this experience and the research findings, I conclude that **all people have** the ability to help their fellow citizens.

Appendix B

Activity 1, page A-32

1. On June 2, 2007, my husband and I got married and started a big adventure: our honeymoon. **3.** On the day after our honeymoon, we drove to Barton, which is in a beautiful area of Vermont known as the Northeast Kingdom. **5.** Unfortunately**,** that was as good as the honeymoon got. **7.** With its peeling paint, rotted porch, and sagging roof, it was like something out of a horror movie. **9.** correct; **11.** Deeply disturbed by this incident**,** we decided to camp outdoors; fortunately**,** we'd brought a tent. **13.** Then**,** he and I set off for a hike up Jay Peak. **15.** However**,** just one mile into the hike, Dan tripped on some rocks and sprained his ankle. **17.** After Dan got his ankle bandaged at a local hospital**,** we spent the next few days in a motel and watched the pouring rain from our window. **19.** Dan**,** weary and disappointed**,** apologized about the cabin**,** but it wasn't his fault, of course. **21.** We plan to return to Vermont sometime soon**,** and we're hoping that we'll have better luck.

Activity 2, page A-34

1. Chocolate alone is a treat**;** chocolate and red wine together are divine. **3.** My European travel plans will take me to Barcelona, Spain**;** Lisbon, Portugal**;** and Paris, France. **5.** Robin's healthy dinner menu included spinach, which is loaded with B vitamins**;** lean chicken, a good source of protein**;** and brown rice, which is rich in fiber.

Activity 4, page A-36

1. During his first year of college, Mark got mostly C's and D's. **3.** Not long into Mark's second year, it was clear that what he did his first year wasn't going to work. **5.** He didn't miss any classes, and he went to all of his teachers' office hours as often as he could. **7.** So far, Mark's grades have improved, and he has started receiving his first A's.

Activity 5, page A-38

1. My best friend told me that she has had one bad experience with Internet dating. **3.** Her second mistake, she said, was that she let the date go on too long. **5.** In response to this complaint, I asked my friend, "Would you go on an Internet date again?"

Activity 6, page A-42

1. At our **c**ollege, African American students have formed a scholarship fund. **3.** In the summer, **A**unt Barb and **U**ncle Pete like to take boat trips along the **M**ississippi **R**iver. **5.** Drive **s**outh for three miles, and then turn left at the Kentuck**y** **F**ried **C**hicken onto Delancey Street.

Appendix C

Activity 1, page A-44

1. C; **3.** N; **5.** C; **7.** N; **9.** N

Activity 2, page A-46

1. a; **3.** the; a; **5.** the; **7.** a

Activity 3, page A-48

1. to do/doing; **3.** to avoid; **5.** No answer needed. **7.** to accept; **9.** No answer needed. **11.** looking; **13.** No answer needed.

Activity 4, page A-49

1. Marco is not happy about the game's outcome. **3.** The travelers are not staying in an expensive hotel. **5.** Eduardo has not postponed the party at his new house.

Activity 5, page A-50

1. Is Marco happy about the game's outcome? **3.** Are the travelers staying in an expensive hotel? **5.** Has Eduardo postponed the party at his new house?

Activity 6, page A-52

1. in; **3.** at; **5.** In

Activity 7, page A-53

1. in; **3.** about; by; **5.** about; with

Activity 8, page A-55

1. Both sentences are correct. **3.** Both sentences are correct. **5.** Sentence *a* is correct.

Activity 9, page A-56

1. The fragile oval Japanese platter was a wedding gift. **3.** We baked a delicious train-shaped birthday cake for Jordan. **5.** The generous old Italian gentleman gave us some delicious red tomatoes.

Acknowledgments, continued from page iv

Kathleen Stassen Berger. "What Makes Marriages Work" and "Weighing Risks and Benefits: Adolescent Decision Making." From *The Developing Person Through the Life Span*, Sixth Edition, by Kathleen Stassen Berger. Copyright © 2005 by Kathleen Stassen Berger. Reprinted by permission of W. H. Freeman Company.

José Antonio Burciaga. "My Ecumenical Father." Originally published in *Drink Cultura*. Reprinted by permission of Cecilia Burciaga.

Susan Gobin. "Nothing to Lose." From the "Readers Write" section, *The Sun* magazine, January 2007, p. 39. Reprinted by permission of the author.

Alan Gomez. "California Fire Crews Brace for Return of Santa Anas." Originally published in *USA TODAY*, October 30, 2007. Used with permission.

"Hard Times." Words and music by Joseph Simmons, Darryl McDaniels, Lawrence Smith, and William Waring. Copyright © 1983 Rabasse Music Ltd. and Rush Grove Music. All rights administrated by Warner/Chappell Music Ltd. All rights reserved. Used by permission of Alfred Publishing, Inc.

Zoë Heller. "One Friday." From *What Was She Thinking? Notes on a Scandal* by Zoë Heller. Copyright © 2003 by Zoë Heller. Reprinted by permission of Henry Holt and Company, LLC.

Pius Kamau. "A Duty to Heal." Copyright © 2006 by Pius Kamau. From the book *This I Believe*, edited by Jay Allison and Dan Gediman. Copyright © 2006 by This I Believe, Inc. Reprinted by arrangement with Henry Holt and Company, LLC.

Enrique Hank Lopez. "Why Couldn't My Father Read?" Copyright © 1979 by Plain Dealer Publishing Company. Reprinted by permission.

Robyn Marks. "Raising a Son—with Men on the Fringes." From *Newsweek*, July 19, 2004. Copyright © 2004 *Newsweek*, Inc. Used by permission and protected by the Copyright Laws of the United States. The printing, copying, redistribution, or retransmission of the Material without express written permission is prohibited.

Sharon J. Mitchler. "Writing Back." From *Teaching English in the Two-Year College*, edited by Howard Tinberg, National Council of Teachers of English, 2006.

Eboo Patel. "We Are Each Other's Business." Copyright © 2006 by Eboo Patel. From the book *This I Believe*, edited by Jay Allison and Dan Gediman. Copyright © 2006 by This I Believe, Inc. Reprinted by arrangement with Henry Holt and Company, LLC.

Brian Rickenbrode. "King of the Road." Originally appeared in the University of Akron Wayne College's Student Writing Awards publication. Used with permission.

Carl T. Rowan. "Unforgettable Miss Bessie." Originally published in the *Reader's Digest*. Copyright © 1985 by The Reader's Digest Association, Inc. Reprinted by permission from *Reader's Digest*.

Laura Rowley. "As They Say, Drugs Kill." Originally published in the February 1987 issue of *Newsweek on Campus*. Reprinted by permission of Laura Rowley, business journalist and author of several books, including *Money and Happiness* and *On Target*.

Scott Russell Sanders. "Under the Influence." Copyright © 1989 by *Harper's Magazine*. All rights reserved. Reproduced from the November issue by special permission.

Sandy Sasso. "Our Religious Diversity." Originally published in the *Indianapolis Star*, July 6, 2004. Reprinted by permission of the author, Sandy Sasso. Earlier books include *God's Paintbrush* and *God's Echo: Exploring Scripture with Midrash*.

Gary Soto. "Like Mexicans." From *The Effects of Knut Hamsun on a Fresno Boy: Recollections and Short Essays* by Gary Soto. Copyright © 1983, 2001 by Gary Soto. Reprinted by permission of Persea Books, Inc. (New York).

Morgan Spurlock. Excerpt from *Don't Eat This Book*. Copyright © 2005 by Morgan Spurlock. Reprinted by permission of G. P. Putnam's Sons, an imprint of The Penguin Group (USA) Inc.

Andrew Sullivan. "The 'M-Word': Why It Matters to Me." From *Time*, February 16, 2004. Copyright © TIME, INC. Reprinted by permission. TIME is a registered trademark of Time, Inc. All rights reserved.

Amy Tan. "Fish Cheeks." Copyright © 1987 by Amy Tan. First appeared in *Seventeen* magazine. Reprinted by permission of the author and the Sandra Dijkstra Literary Agency.

Elie Wiesel. Excerpt from *Night* by Elie Wiesel. Copyright © 1972, 1985 by Elie Wiesel. English translation copyright © 2006 by Marion Wiesel (Hill and Wang, 2006). Reprinted by permission of Farrar, Straus, and Giroux, LLC. Originally published as *La Nuit* by Les Éditions de Minuit. Copyright © 1958 by Les Éditions de Minuit. Used by permission of Georges Borchardt, Inc., for Les Éditions de Minuit.

Photograph and Illustration Credits

Pages 1 (top) and 3 (left): © Lions Gate/Courtesy of the Everett Collection.
Pages 1 (second from top) and 54: © JUPITERIMAGES/BananaStock/Alamy.
Pages 1 (third from top) and 167 (bottom): © Thomas Dobner/Alamy.
Pages 1 (bottom) and 212: Chris Juzwiak.
Page 3 (right): © Warner Brothers/Courtesy of the Everett Collection.
Page 34 (top): © Alex Griffiths/Alamy.
Page 34 (bottom): © Richard Levine/Alamy.
Pages 55, 261, 270, 285, 334, 335, 349, 350, 355, 367, 368, 382, 383, 400, 435, 455, 464, 465, 493, 494: Brian DeTagyos.
Page 59: © JUPITERIMAGES/Comstock Images/Alamy.
Page 60: © Ilene MacDonald/Alamy.
Page 61: © Images&Stories/Alamy.
Page 62 (top): © David White/Alamy.
Page 62 (bottom): © Ilan Rosen/Alamy.
Page 63: © Photodisc/Veer.
Pages 78, 79, 84 (bottom), 130 (top left and right), 267, 268, 356: Claire Seng-Niemoeller.
Page 84 (top): © Mira/Alamy.
Page 130 (bottom): © Andrew Fox/Alamy.
Page 167 (top): Beth Castrodale.
Page 180: © M. L. Pearson/Alamy.
Page 183: © Andy Lyons/Getty Images.
Page 187: © Photodisc/Veer.
Page 190: © Alloy Photography/Veer.
Page 194: © JUPITERIMAGES/Brand X/Alamy.
Page 198: © Brad Perks Lightscapes/Alamy.
Page 201: © Corbis/Veer.
Page 203 (top): © PM Images/Getty.
Page 203 (bottom): © Pictorial Press Ltd./Alamy.
Page 209: © Nordic Photo/Getty Images.
Page 222 (top): © JUPITERIMAGES/Polka Dot/Alamy.
Page 227 (top): © UpperCut Images/Alamy.
Page 227 (bottom): © RFStock/Alamy.
Page 235: © Brandon Laufenberg/istockphoto.
Page 239: © Dr. David M. Phillips/Visuals Unlimited.
Page 247: © wsr/Alamy.
Page 250: © Stockbyte/Alamy.
Page 259 (left): © MGM/Courtesy of the Everett Collection.
Page 259 (right): Library of Congress.
Page 260 (top): © Topham/The Image Works.
Page 260 (bottom): © Time & Life Pictures/Getty Images.
Page 421: © JUPITERIMAGES.
Page 458: © Joseph Jean Rolland Dubé/istockphoto.
Page A-2: © Grant Faint/Digital Vision/Getty Images.
Page A-13: © Design Pics Inc./Alamy.
Page A-20: © AP Images/Gene Herrick.
Page A-22: © Eon Images.

Index

T

Correction Symbols

Your instructor may use certain symbols to mark writing and grammar problems in your papers. Following are some common symbols and their meanings. (If your instructor uses different symbols than those shown here, write those in the spaces provided.) On the right, we've shown (in bold) chapters or sections of *Stepping Stones* that you can refer to for more help.

STANDARD SYMBOL	YOUR INSTRUCTOR'S SYMBOL	MEANING AND CHAPTER/SECTION IN THIS BOOK	
adj		Problem with adjective use	**10; Appendix C**
adv		Problem with adverb use	**10**
agr		Agreement problem between subject and verb	**16**
		Agreement problem between pronoun and what it refers back to (antecedent)	**17**
awk		Awkward wording	**7**
		Awkward sentence structure	**11–15**
cap		Capitalization error	**Appendix B**
case		Pronoun case error	**17**
cliché		Clichéd language	**7**
coh		Lack of coherence/unity in writing	**7**
combine		Combine sentences	**12–15**
coord		Coordinate sentences/coordination problem	**12**
cs		Comma splice	**12**
dev		Strengthen development of writing	**3; 5–6**
dm		Dangling modifier	**15**
frag		Fragment	**11; 13–14**
mm		Misplaced modifier	**14–15**
prep		Problem with prepositions/prepositional phrases	**10–11; Appendix C**
ref		Unclear pronoun reference	**17**
ro		Run-on	**12**
shift		Shift in tense or voice	**16**
sp		Spelling error	**7**
sub		Subordinate sentences/subordination problem	**13**
tense		Verb tense problem	**16**
trans		Transition needed	**4–5**
unity		Lack of unity/coherence in writing	**7**
vb/verb		Verb problem	**16; Appendix C**
wc		Problem with word choice	**7**
¶		Start a new paragraph	**8**
, ; ' " " : — - ( ) !		Problem with punctuation	**Appendix B**
^		Insert	
(delete mark)		Delete	
(close-space mark)		Close space	
(transpose mark)		Reverse order of letters/words	

Helpful Lists, Charts, and Visuals

Writing and Revising

Grammar